Virtual Enterprise Integration:
Technological and Organizational Perspectives

Goran Putnik
University of Minho, Portugal

Maria Manuela Cunha
Polytechnic Institute of Cávado and Ave, Portugal

D1413574

IDEA GROUP PUBLISHING
Hershey • London • Melbourne • Singapore

Acquisitions Editor:	Renée Davies
Development Editor:	Kristin Roth
Senior Managing Editor:	Amanda Appicello
Managing Editor:	Jennifer Neidig
Copy Editor:	Loni Eby
Typesetter:	Marko Primorac
Cover Design:	Lisa Tosheff
Printed at:	Integrated Book Technology

Published in the United States of America by
  Idea Group Publishing (an imprint of Idea Group Inc.)
  701 E. Chocolate Avenue, Suite 200
  Hershey PA 17033
  Tel: 717-533-8845
  Fax: 717-533-8661
  E-mail: cust@idea-group.com
  Web site: http://www.idea-group.com

and in the United Kingdom by
  Idea Group Publishing (an imprint of Idea Group Inc.)
  3 Henrietta Street
  Covent Garden
  London WC2E 8LU
  Tel: 44 20 7240 0856
  Fax: 44 20 7379 3313
  Web site: http://www.eurospan.co.uk

Library of Congress Cataloging-in-Publication Data

Virtual enterprise integration : technological and organizational perspectives / Goran Putnik and
Maria Manuela Cunha, editors.
       p. cm.
  Includes bibliographical references and index.
  ISBN 1-59140-405-3 (hc) -- ISBN 1-59140-406-1 (sc) -- ISBN 1-59140-407-X (ebook)
  1. Management information systems. I. Putnik, Goran, 1954- II. Cunha, Maria Manuela 1964-
  T58.6.V56 2005
  658.4'038--dc22
                        2004023598

British Cataloguing in Publication Data
A Cataloguing in Publication record for this book is available from the British Library.

Virtual Enterprise Integration:
Technological and Organizational Perspectives

Table of Contents

Section V: Projects and Case Studies

Preface

INTRODUCTION

For a long time, we were imagining a book like this and suddenly we received an invitation from Dr. Mehdi Khosrow-Pour to edit a book. It looked like the "push" we were waiting for.

This book addresses Virtual Enterprise Integration (VEI) — the emergent research and development issues for the virtually most advanced enterprise organizational paradigm of today — the Virtual Enterprise (VE) paradigm. VE are characterized in different ways, ranging from simple subcontracting networks to dynamic reconfigurable agile networks of independent enterprises that share all resources. This includes knowledge, market, customers, etc., in order to be permanently aligned with the highly demanding and global dynamic market. The partners in VE use heterogeneous resources, i.e., technologies, data formats, equipment, software tools, procedures, etc., that are to work effectively and efficiently together. In this context, VEI is one of the most important, if not *the* most important, requirements for making VE a real, competitive and widely implemented organizational and management concept. It is the critical success factor in creation, reconfiguration and operation of a VE. The VE models are actually of no use if there are no efforts toward the development of VEI models, strategies, solutions or tools. Or, in another words, if something is missing in the making of the VE models, a competitive reality, then it is, simply, the effective and efficient integration of VE.

However, according to many authors, the present solutions for VEI are either insufficient or inexistent. The existence of "interoperability crisis" is recognized.

In addition, we could observe that, in fact, we do not have VE implemented in compliance with a number of theoretical models developed (with the exception of supply chains, if we consider them as a VE model). A thesis is that the reason is either insufficient or inexistent VEI solutions. Consequently, the following question arises: *"Why?"*

The main reason for the situation may be the failure of "traditional" information systems and the organizations approach to deal with current turbulent markets and organizations' requirements where VEI solutions are sought. Other reasons may be: (1) the existence of different interpretations and definitions of what is, in fact, integration; (2) the existence of different interpretations and definitions of what is, in fact, VE; (3)

the higher complexity of the VE integration problem than the complexity of the "traditional" enterprise integration problem; (4) the lack of understandings about the relations between the solutions offered, the problem which is especially "hard" considering the "explosion" of the solutions in the last years; and (5) the need for a new (enterprise) integration paradigm, as the VE concept is seen as a new organizational paradigm. Therefore, it is unlikely that "traditional" integration solutions would satisfy the requirements of the new (VE) paradigm.

Considering this, the editors have conceived this book with the objective to contribute to: (1) a better understanding of the VEI phenomena; (2) an eventual framework for VEI science, engineering, development and implementations; (3) present information on cutting edge technologies for VEI and the most recent scientific and engineering development and implementation results, together with a consistent and focused discussion on the background and business requirements for VEI; and (4) provide a guidance of models and technologies for dynamic VEI development.

To respond to the above (book's) objectives, the editors define a book's "philosophy". The defined book's "philosophy" is based on two global theses concerning the VEI:

1. Effective and efficient VE integration (science and engineering) is the main VE enabler.
2. For the effective and efficient VE integration (science and engineering) it is necessary to develop a new VE integration (science and engineering) paradigm.

Responding to the first thesis (the first part of the book's philosophy), the book is focused exclusively on VEI issue as the critical VE enabler. In respect to this approach and considering the publicly available literature on VE issues, this book is probably *the first book on the market*, that:

1. focuses exclusively on the subject of VEI and
2. focuses on VEI as the critical VE success factor.

Responding to the second thesis (the second part of the book's philosophy), the book offers a view on VEI issues through "lenses" of a meta-theoretical structure (meaning a framework for a theory about the VEI theory) for relating different VEI models, concepts, theories, technologies, etc., as a necessary step toward a new VEI paradigm. Although there could exist many meta-theoretical structures (e.g., "(VE) *integration abstractions hierarchy*") the editors have applied the (VE) *Integration Semiotics*[1] as the meta-theoretical structure for the book interpretation and organization.

The book's Integration Semiotics "lenses" are the second characteristic that, in the opinion of the editors, makes this book innovative within the literature on VE.

This book contains 22 chapters authored by a group of internationally renowned and experienced professionals in the Virtual Enterprise (VE) science. Contributors also include younger authors — creating a happy "mix". The editors consider this "constellation" of authors as "value-added". Concerning the regional distribution of contributions, all chapters came from the most developed regions of the world, i.e., European Union/Western Europe, the US and Japan. Concerning the environments from which the contributions are presented, the chapters came from academia, research institutions and industry.

It is also necessary to mention that the book does not cover the whole area of VEI. The reason is simply the book's size and the VEI research state-of-the-art (meaning that it is in permanent evolution and new dimensions of the problem, and corresponded solutions, continually emerge). Although the book may not be the most comprehensive volume, it is a good representation, especially compared with other books on the issue — if they exist at all.

ORGANIZATION OF THE BOOK

The 22 chapters in this book are organized into five sections. These sections address two global perspectives of the VEI issues, i.e.:
1. VEI Organizational Perspective and
2. VEI Technological Perspective.

Organizational Perspective covers two upper levels of the integration semiotics levels, i.e., the *Social* and *Pragmatics* levels. The *Technological Perspective* covers two lower levels of the integration semiotics levels, i.e., the *Semantics* and *Syntactic* levels.

The book's organization scheme, in respect to the two perspectives addressed and in respect to the integration semiotics levels, is given in Table 1.

Section I, "Introduction – Towards a New Virtual Enterprise Integration Paradigm", introduces the issue of VEI as well as outlines approaches toward VEI solutions.

Table 1. Book organization

INTEGRATION SEMIOTICS LEVELS	BOOK ORGANIZATION		
	Perspectives	*Chapters*	
Social	Organizational Perspective	Section II – Chapters II and III	Section I – Chapter I / Section V – Chapters XX, XXI and XXII
Pragmatics		Section II – Chapters IV, V and VI **Section III** – Chapters VII, VIII, IX, X, XI, XII and XIII	
Semantics	Technological Perspective	Section IV – Chapters XIV, XV, XVI, XVII, XVIII and XIX	
Syntactic			
Empirics			
Physical World			

It contains only one chapter and presents a discussion on VEI problems. The chapter proposes two meta-theoretical structures for VEI research and development: (VE) *Integration Abstractions Hierarchy* and (VE) *Integration Semiotics*. The purposes of the meta-theoretical structures proposed are for a better understanding of the VEI phenomena as well as to provide a base for an eventual framework for VEI science, engineering, development and implementations.

Concerning "Integration Semiotic Levels", Chapter I passes over all levels, or at least the four "upper" levels (social, pragmatic, semantic and syntactic), as these levels are in fact the chapter's "objects" (i.e., Chapter I is better positioned at Level "VIII – *General VEI theories*", of the "integration abstractions hierarchy" meta-theoretical structure[2], on which (level) "the general theories about the whole framework of VEI are described".

Section II, "Societal and Organizational Requirements", contains five chapters, Chapters II through VI. Chapters II and III address societal requirements for VE while Chapters IV, V and VI present business requirements and VE organizational models as requirements for VEI. Therefore, concerning "Integration Semiotic Levels", Chapters II and III belong to the "Social" level and Chapters IV, V and VI belong to the "Pragmatics" level.

In other words, this section aims at presenting an answer to the following question: *VEI, for what?*

Chapter II, "Virtuality and the Future of Organizations", discusses how organizations are likely to develop in the context of "virtuality", i.e., following the impact of technologies relevant to the Information Society. The chapter also shows how research — in particular, research that was supported under the European Commission's R&D programs — has played a significant role in shaping these developments. It gives a better understanding of the socio-economic impact of VEs.

Chapter III, "Collaborative Networked Organizations for Eco-Consistent Supply Chains", presents a study on collaborative networked organizations for supporting the eco-consistency management of the extended artifacts. The chapter outlines, as well, trends in the economical, legal, political and social surroundings, aiming at the appropriateness of Web platform options.

Chapter IV, "Business Alignment Requirements and Dynamic Organisations", discusses the importance of networking and inter-organizational reconfiguration dynamics in the context of current business alignment requirements, face to the unpredictable turbulent changes in the market, and introduces the most relevant and pertinent concepts around the dynamic organizational models.

Chapter V, "Collaborative Network Models: Overview and Functional Requirements", introduces a classification model. This model gives an approach to classify collaborative networked organizations, especially regarding network management models. Requirements for the development of virtual organizations, inhibiting factors and critical factors in network relationships are explained.

Chapter VI, "BM_Virtual Enterprise: A Model for Dynamics and Virtuality", presents a VE model that is developed for supporting the highest level of VE reconfiguration dynamics. The formal specification and theory of the structural aspects of the BM_VE, some aspects of the BM_VE reconfiguration dynamics and some important consequences (a new definition of VE and the structure of a "traditional" enterprise virtualization process) are presented.

Section III, "Generative Integration", contains seven chapters, Chapters VII through XIII. All chapters in the section address organizational issues of VEI at the *Pragmatics* level of "Integration Semiotic Levels". Looking at VEI (and integration in general as well) through the organizational perspectives is the characteristic of approach to VEI (and integration in general) as a complex process, characterized by a (integration) life-cycle (consisting of three global phases, i.e., the phase of the integration creation, or design, or generation, or synthesis, the phase of the integration operation and finally the phase of the integration termination). This is quite a different approach than the "traditional" approach where integration is a process too, but as a more simple transaction. Due to its complexity, the integration process, in order to be effective and efficient, should be supported by appropriate tools. Besides the usually considered IT tools, organization and management (of integration processes) have emerged as a new class of necessary tools. The purpose of organization and management is to facilitate the integration process along its life-cycle, especially in the first phase — the integration generation (or design, synthesis, or creation). As this phase practically characterizes the new approach to integration, we called it (the new approach) *Generative Integration*. Following the above "view", the chapters in this section present several organizational and management solutions. Namely, Chapters VII and XI present organizations, or institutions, as a meta-structures/meta-enterprises, for VE creation, reconfiguration and operation, that serve as institutionalized organizational environments for facilitating the integration processes through lowering the "transaction" costs and assuring the VE partners' knowledge protection (through, e.g., trust assurance, intellectual property protection, security, contract enforcement, etc.). Chapters VIII, IX and X present (1) the Broker as the new integration organizational and management agent; (2) processes of contract generation (which are in fact the integration generation, or synthesis, processes); and (3) a specific architectures that support the brokering function. Finally, Chapters XII and XIII offer a view on VEI as two coupled processes of integration: integration as the "processes interaction improvement" and integration as VE design (very sophisticated design/integration techniques/algorithms are presented in both chapters). This view is extremely important as it represents a further difference from the "traditional" approach to integration — where integration is seen as decoupled from the organizational design.

Concerning "Integration Semiotic Levels", the chapters from this section clearly belong to the "Pragmatics" level. In other words, this section aims at presenting an answer to the following question: *VEI as a process, which generative processes, which "life-cycle" structure, which organization and management?*

Chapter VII, "Market of Resources as a Virtual Enterprise Integration Enabler", introduces Market of Resources (MR). MR has its process-based model, as a "meta-enterprise" or environment, for dynamic reconfiguration of VE. The chapter presents the cost functions based validation of the concept. It demonstrates that high reconfiguration dynamics are nearly impossible to implement without an MR. If this conclusion is correct (and it seems it is), then the consequences could be profound: the future development of VE is bounded by the existence and operation of MR type environments.

Chapter VIII, "Broker Performance for Agile/Virtual Enterprise Integration", discusses a Broker as an external entity whose functions and increased performance contributes to the searched agility of VE. The set of functions that the Broker can provide to the VE are, in fact, coupled functions of VE integration and design. The broker's process-based model is presented together with the cost functions based validation. Similarly to the previous chapter, the case of a Market of Resources, it is demonstrated that the high reconfiguration dynamics of VE, and especially for complex business or production processes, is not likely to be effective without a broker.

Chapter IX, "Integration in Cooperative Distributed Systems: Privacy-Based Brokering Architecture for Virtual Enterprises", discusses brokering as a capability-based aspect of coordination in cooperative distributed systems. Architecturally, the brokering service is modeled as an agent with a specific architecture and interaction protocol that are appropriate to serve various requests and ad hoc configurations. A prototype of the proposed architecture has been implemented using FIPA-complaint platform (JADE).

Chapter X, "Dynamic Contract Generation for Dynamic Business Relationships", presents a novel method for quickly generating a legal contract from the description of a business agreement — as a response to the needs of a dynamic VE to be able to create, customize and dismantle commercial relationships among partners quickly. A brief overview of the matchmaking technology that is used to determine whether a clause is relevant for a given business agreement as well as a specific detailed example of this approach are given.

Chapter XI, "Contributions to an Electronic Institution Supporting Virtual Enterprises' Life Cycle", presents the Electronic Institution as a framework that enables automatic negotiation, transactions and operation monitoring between electronic business parties, according to sets of explicit institutional norms and rules, in two most important stages of VE' life cycle: formation and operation.

Chapter XII, "Use of Situation Room Analysis to Enhance Business Integration Aspects of a Virtual Enterprise", considers the implementation of virtual organizations, seen as dynamic value constellations, multi-party collaboration and decision-making activities, based on the paradigm of a Situation Room (SR) and use of ontologies. The approach places emphasis on the notion of Web technologies and their adaptation for achieving the IT enabled shift to more efficient processes.

Chapter XIII, "Virtual Enterprise Coalition Strategy with Game Theoretic Multiagent Paradigm", focuses on the negotiation process in VE formulation as a basis for effective management in terms of partner search. Each enterprise in a VE is defined as an agent with multi-utilities and a framework of multi-agent programming with game theoretic approach is newly proposed as negotiation algorithm amongst the agents. In order to clarify the VE formulation dynamism, a simulation model is developed.

Section IV, "Technologies for Integration", contains six chapters, Chapters XIV through XIX. These chapters address some technological issues of VEI. Responding to an eventual question, which is the criteria for distinguishing the contributions in this section from the previous sections, the answer could be that in this section are presented integration solutions that could be applied as tools either for the "traditional" integration (which is so-called "transaction" based), or they could be applied for the "generative" integration (or "communication" based integration, also "pragmatic" integration). In other words, the solutions presented in this section are integration paradigm (nearly, in principle) independent. However, Chapters XIV, XVI and XVII address the integration as a complex process. This could raise the question: *Shouldn't these chapters be included in the previous section?* Nevertheless, the editors have decided to allocate these chapters to this section. This is because the conceptual base for the solutions presented is more semantic/syntactic in nature then "pure" pragmatic or organizational/managerial. In other words, the editors has decided that the "technological" perspective for these chapters is stronger than the "organizational" perspective. In a similar way, the location of Chapter XIX could be questioned. By virtually all definitions, the legal issues, e.g., issues of contracts' contents and their legal power, "norms", etc., belong to the "pragmatic" level — in this book, the "organizational" perspective. Chapter XIX presents a contract model as a standard. As standards are, conceptually, well defined concepts not subject to changes, the editors have classified the model presented in Chapter XIX as a tool, i.e., a kind of "technology", and not as a "pragmatic" issue. That would imply some negotiation processes and similar, i.e., some contract creation or synthesis process (generative integration).

Consequently, concerning "Integration Semiotic Levels", the chapters from this section belong to the "Semantic" and "Syntactic" levels. In other words, this Section aims at presenting an answer to the question: *VEI, which transaction supporting tools?*

Chapter XIV, "Semantic Distance, the Next Step?", presents some early conclusions from international workshops on a next generation strategy of how to measure imperfections in integration that will be encountered in VE. It is expected that a new class of tools and strategies will emerge. The chapter presents an outline of one proposal of a strategy.

Chapter XV, "IT Infrastructures and Standards for VE Integration Development", presents an understanding of the needs of IT in Virtual Enterprises. Technologies such as Web Services and Software Agents help Business Process Management and, thus offer the IT infrastructures to achieve VE integration.

Chapter XVI, "Interactive Models for Virtual Enterprises", presents a novel approach to the development, integration and operation of VE, based on the idea of interactive models. An interactive model is a visual model of enterprise aspects that can be viewed, traversed, analyzed, simulated, adapted and executed by the participants of the virtual enterprise. The experiences from industrial case studies are used as a basis for validation and further enhancement of the approach. A major result of the work presented is the model-driven infrastructure. It integrates and supports VE. The main innovative contributions of this infrastructure include concurrent modelling, metamodeling, management and performance of work, integrated support for ad-hoc and structured processes, and customizable model- and process-driven integration.

Chapter XVII, "Machine Learning Techniques for Web Wrapper Maintenance", describes the use of machine learning (ML) techniques that can be a base for intelligent integration mechanism in a dynamic environment. It is of the greatest importance for VE as dynamically reconfigurable networks. The structural descriptions of data extracted from Web sources are learned and these descriptions are then used to verify that the wrapper is correctly extracting data and structure, or to generate a new wrapper for that source.

Chapter XVIII, "Information Technology Infrastructure and Solutions", discusses the feasibility of the Market of Resources and its implementation using existing e-Marketplace software platforms and standards that support a wide range of features required by the Market of Resources.

Chapter XIX, "Consortium Agreement Template for Virtual Enterprises", addresses the contractual legislation problem as an integration problem within the VE context. The legislation is no more than standard procedures and guidelines to address organization's formalization within the legal system and society. An example of a consortium agreement template based on the existing Portuguese legislation is created as a real legal platform.

Section V, "Projects and Case Studies", contains three chapters, Chapters XX through XXII. The chapters from this section present two projects on VE developed in the framework of European Commission sponsored research programs, Chapters XX and XXI, and a project developed in industry, Chapter XXII. Although the projects are not explicitly defined as specific VEI projects, the VEI issues are strongly addressed. Actually, the VEI issues are coupled with the VE design issues.

In other words, this Section aims at presenting an answer to the question: *VEI, which are the applications?*

Concerning "Integration Semiotic Levels", Section V, similarly as in Section I, it is passing over all levels or at least the four "upper" levels (social, pragmatic, semantic and syntactic) as these levels are addressed by the projects presented. Section V could be positioned as well at the levels "V – *VEI methods*", "VI – *VEI process structure*" and (partially) "VII – *Theories about the internal processes of VEI users*", of the "integration abstractions hierarchy" meta-theoretical structure.

Chapter XX, "Virtual Enterprises and the Case of BIDSAVER", presents the BIDSAVER project (1999-2002) which aimed in delivering technologies and methodologies to support the creation and operation of VE. The project has run under the auspices of the European Commission Programme for Information Society Technologies (IST).

Chapter XXI, "Implementation Options for Virtual Organizations: A Peer-to-Peer (P2P) Approach", presents work within the EU-sponsored LAURA project. Its aims were to facilitate interregional zones of adaptive electronic commerce using, where applicable, the potential of the ebXML architecture. The project based on the concept of Request Based Virtual Organization (RBVO) for the typical business requirements of Small and Medium Enterprises (SME) and used the Peer-to-Peer (P2P) technology for discovering and matchmaking of business partners and services.

Finally, XXII, "Collaborative Industrial Automation: Toward the Integration of a Dynamic Reconfigurable Shop Floor into a Virtual Factory", summarizes the Chapter authors' latest results concerning the development and the industrial application of the emerging "collaborative industrial automation" technology and integration of a dynamic reconfigurable shop floor into a virtual factory. The Chapter's authors hope that understanding the underlying scientific and technological background will not only inform the academic, research and industrial world of an emerging control and automation paradigm, but also assists in the understanding of a new vision of the manufacturing systems of the 21st Century.

EXPECTATIONS

The book is expected to be read by academics (i.e., teachers, researchers and students), technology solutions developers and enterprise managers (including top level managers). It is expected to be a guide for technology solution developers, from academia, research institutions and industry, providing them with a broader perspective of VE integration requirements. It aims to increase their awareness on which types of technology and how technology can best serve the needs of an expanding and increasingly competitive organizational model. The book widens horizons for researchers interested in this emerging field. It also presents state-of-the-art background and developments.

The book is expected to raise awareness of the VE model potential that managers, who must have a proactive behavior toward new approaches to business, should be able to exploit. In other words, the book provides guidance and helps raise the awareness, pro-activeness and agility of enterprise managers. This should include top level managers, for strategic and dynamic alignment with business opportunities, on the problems of Virtual Enterprise development and implementations as well as on the evolution of their actual enterprises toward Virtual Enterprise

This work will support teachers of several graduate and postgraduate courses, from management to information technology. In particular, it will support the emerging courses on Virtual Enterprise and provide a basis for understanding content and area for further study, research and solutions development.

The editors are also expecting that the book will contribute to the diffusion of VE concept in other parts of the world, not only in the most developed countries.

In the end, the editors are grateful to the readers for any constructive criticism and indication of errors — conceptual, omissions or in typing.

The Editors,
Goran D. Putnik & Maria Manuela Cunha
Guimarães, July 2004

ENDNOTES

[1] The (VE) *Integration Semiotics* is the meta-theoretical structure on six levels: *Social, Pragmatic, Semantic, Syntactic, Empirical* and *Physical*. For more detailed discussion on Integration Semiotic Levels see Chapter I of this book.

[2] See Chapter I for the "*Integration Abstractions Hierarchy*" meta-theoretical structure.

Acknowledgments

The task of editing a book cannot be accomplished without great help and support from many sources. The editors would like to acknowledge the help of all involved in the production of this book. It is very difficult to evaluate whose help was the most valuable. Actually, the lack of help from those mentioned here would have made this project nearly impossible.

First, this book would not have been possible without the ongoing professional support of Idea Group Inc. We are most grateful to Mehdi Khosrow-Pour, Senior Acquisitions Editor, Jan Travers, Managing Director, Amanda Appicello, Senior Managing Editor, and Michele Rossi, Development Editor, for their professional and experiential guidance.

Special thanks go also to the staff at Idea Group Inc. Their contributions throughout the process of making this book available to an international audience are invaluable.

We are grateful to all of the authors, who simultaneously served as referees. We value their insights, contributions, prompt collaboration, and constructive comments. The communication and exchange of views within this truly global group of recognized individuals in the scientific domain were enriching and proved an exciting experience for us, the editors. We wish to thank all of the authors for their insights and excellent contributions to this book, which are, in fact, the *raison d'être* of the book.

A special thank you to our institutions, the University of Minho, Braga, and Polytechnic Institute of Cávado and Ave, Barcelos, in Portugal, for providing the material resources and all necessary logistics.

Warm thanks to Adamantios Koumpis, from Research Programmes Division of ALTEC, SA, Thessaloniki, Greece, for his support, encouragement, and, of course, friendship.

Thank you,

The Editors,
Goran D. Putnik & Maria Manuela Cunha
Guimarães, July 2004

Section I

Introduction –
Towards a
New Virtual Enterprise
Integration Paradigm

Chapter I

Virtual Enterprise Integration:
Challenges of a New Paradigm

Goran D. Putnik
University of Minho, Portugal

Maria Manuela Cunha
Polytechnic Institute of Cávado and Ave, Portugal

Rui Sousa
University of Minho, Portugal

Paulo Ávila
Polytechnic Institute of Porto, Portugal

ABSTRACT

Virtual enterprise integration (VEI) is virtually the most critical success factor for making virtual enterprise (VE) a real, competitive, and widely implemented organizational and management concept. However, according to many authors, the present solutions for VEI are either insufficient or inexistent. One of the reasons for the situation is the failure of the approach of "traditional" information systems and organizations to dealing with the nowadays turbulent market and organizations' requirements, where actual VEI solutions are mainly sought. This chapter presents a discussion on the VEI issue as a contribution to a better understanding of the VEI phenomenon, and it could be seen as a contribution to an eventual framework for VEI science, engineering, development, and implementation. Also, two metatheoretical structures for VEI research and development are proposed: VEI abstractions hierarchy and VEI semiotics.

INTRODUCTION

This introductory chapter presents a discussion of the virtual enterprise integration (VEI) issue as a contribution to a better understanding of the VEI phenomenon. Also, the discussion presented could be seen as a contribution to an eventual framework for VEI science, engineering, development, and implementations.

Integration of virtual enterprises (VE) is one of the most important requirements for making VE a real, competitive, and widely implemented organizational and management concept. Actually, it is virtually the most important requirement.

In the study on interoperability costs of the U.S. automotive supply chain (Brunnermeier & Martin, 1999, p. ES 5), it is estimated "that imperfect interoperability imposes at least $1 billion dollars per year on the members of the U.S. automotive supply chain. The majority of these costs are attributable to the time and resources spent correcting and recreating data files that are not usable by those receiving the files." Additionally, "these estimates are conservative because they do not include elements of cost that our industry contacts could not quantify (p. ES 5)." Consequently, "members of the auto industry generally acknowledge that imperfect interoperability is an important and expensive problem" (pp. 3-8). The study by (Jhingran et al., 2002, p. 555) reported that the "state-of-the-art" concerning information technology (IT) is such that "as enterprises buy more and more packaged applications, it is estimated that the task of combining these application 'silos' results in over 40 percent of the IT spending, even though the amount of code written for integration is significantly smaller than 40 percent," which is hardly a satisfactory situation. Consequently, "the question for software and services vendors is this: can the cost of integration be reduced to be more in line with that of packaged applications?" (Jhingran et al., 2002, p. 555).

Considering that interoperability and "information integration" are just part of the integration phenomenon, considering the supply chain as a model of VE, or at least as a transitional organizational model toward VE, with probably the least demanding requirements regarding the integration in comparison with more advanced VE models, and considering other manufacturing and business areas, it is not too difficult to imagine that the costs of ineffective and inefficient integration of VE, especially for more demanding VE models, are much higher. Further, considering that the VE concept aims to represent a new organizational paradigm for enterprises in general, and, in that way, permeate virtually the whole economy and even society [through the concept of virtual organizations (VOs)], we could talk about the social costs of ineffective and inefficient integration of VE. However, many authors recognize that the present solutions for VEI are either inexistent or insufficient. Therefore, there is a need for further effort by the community to develop satisfactory and competitive solutions, and this chapter represents part of this effort.

The presentation of the discussion is organized as follows. In the first part, the concept of the VE as a new organizational paradigm is presented. The second part presents definitions of (enterprise and system) integration. The third part presents the comparison between traditional enterprise integration versus virtual enterprise integration requirements. In the fourth part, challenges for building new approaches to the science of integration, in general, and for VEI, in particular, are presented. This fourth part outlines a metatheoretical structure for VEI that provides different views on different abstraction levels for the object-theoretical structures (VEI). The metatheoretical structures proposed are integration abstractions hierarchy and integration semiotics. Finally, the fifth part discusses a new paradigm for VEI modeling.

VIRTUAL ENTERPRISE: A NEW ORGANIZATIONAL PARADIGM

Yes, we think the VE concept is a new organizational paradigm. The concept of VE as an organizational model has emerged relatively recently, after a number of truly advanced organizational (and management) concepts[1] marked the decades from the 1970s to the 1990s. The previous concepts did not manage to successfully follow the turbulent and unpredictable market behavior of today in all required dimensions. The functional requirements for the new approach were already recognized (and published) in the 1980s (e.g., see Miles & Snow, 1984, 1986), while the most-known references appeared in the 1990s [e.g., Drucker, 1990 (cited in Staffend, 1992), and Iacocca Institute, 1991 (which defined a VE concept as part of a wider concept called agile manufacturing, or enterprise, also discussed in Nagel & Dove, 1993)]. Further developments of the idea originated in a number of proposals of new organizational models, e.g., supply chain (SC) [e.g., Stevens, 1998 (cited in Towill, 2001)], extended enterprise (EE) (Browne, 1995; IMS International, 2003), "smart" organizations[2] (SO) (Filos & Banahan, 2001; Filos, 2005). As these models did not refer explicitly to the term "virtual enterprise," we would consider them, in a way, as "transitional" models toward VE (see a selection of definitions in Box 1. Toward Virtual Enterprises).

The term, and the concept, of VE emerged in the beginning of nineties and could be seen as the further optimization and perfection of the basic ideas about dynamic networking. Conceptually, the "virtuality" is found in the fact that the networks' structural instances[3] are (1) "potentially present, i.e. 'virtual memory', (2) existing but changing, i.e., 'virtual corporation'" (Franke, 2000, p. 21, Figure 1).

However, unfortunately or not, until today, there has not been a universally accepted definition, or model, of the VE.

A selection of definitions, which explicitly use the term "virtual enterprise," is presented in Box 2. Virtual Enterprise.[4]

Many definitions in Box 2 are practically identical to the definitions of the models in Box 1, except in explicit use of the term "virtual enterprise."

Concerning the question of the VE as a new organizational paradigm, in the authors' opinion, there are three fundamental features of the VE concept that make up the fundamental difference between the VE and the traditional enterprise, and that generate a number of consequences, making that paradigm "shift." These are as follows:
1. Dynamics of network reconfiguration
2. Virtuality
3. External entities [meta- (virtual) enterprise structures] as environments for enabling, or supporting, the VE integration as well as a reconfiguration dynamics.

In Table 1, a comparison between traditional enterprises and virtual enterprises potentials, concerning the three above-mentioned features, and a number of their consequences, is presented.[5]

Box 1. Toward virtual enterprises

"companies must be able to form a **network** of reliable subcontractors, many of them large firms which have not worked together before. Some companies, therefore, have found it advantageous to focus only on the overall design, leaving the actual construction to their affiliates. …the functions of product design and development, manufacturing, and distribution, ordinarily integrated by a plan and controlled directly by managers, will instead be brought together by *brokers* and held in temporary alignment by a variety of *market mechanisms.*" (*Miles & Snow, 1984*)

"…'flotilla', consisting of modules centred either around a stage of the production process or around the number of closely related operations. Though overall command and control will still exist, each module will have its own command and control. And each, like the ships in a flotilla, will be manoeuvrable, both in terms of its position in the entire process and its relationships to other modules. This organisation will give each module the benefits of standardisation and, at the same time, give the whole process greater flexibility. Thus it will allow rapid changes in design and product, rapid response to market demands, and low-cost production of 'options' or 'specials' in fairly small batches." (*Drucker, 1990*)

Agile manufacturing system: "… a manufacturing system with extraordinary capabilities…to meet the rapidly changing needs of the marketplace (speed, flexibility, customers, competitors, suppliers, infrastructure, responsiveness). A system that shifts quickly (speed and responsiveness) among product models or between lines (flexibility), ideally in real-time response to customer demand (customer needs and wants)." (*Nagel & Dove, 1993*)

"**Extended enterprise**: core product functionalities are provided separately by different companies who come together to provide a customer defined product." (*Browne, 1995*)

Supply chain is "a system whose constituent parts include material suppliers, production facilities, distribution services and customer linked together via the feedforward flow of materials and the feedback flow of information." (*Stevens, 1998*)

"**Smart organisations** are knowledge-driven, *internet*worked, and dynamically adaptive to new organisational forms and practices, learning as well as agile in their ability to create and exploit the opportunities offered by the digital economy." (*Filos & Banahan, 2001; Filos, 2005*)

"The **extended enterprise** is an expression of the market driven requirement to embrace external resources in the enterprise without owning them. Core business focus is the route to excellence but product/service delivery requires the amalgam of multiple world class capabilities. Changing markets require a fluctuating mix of resources. The extended enterprise, which can be likened to the ultimate in customisable, reconfigurable manufacturing resource, is the goal. …
The operation of the extended enterprise requires take up of communications and database technologies, which are near to the current state of the art. However, the main challenge is organisational rather than technological." (*IMS International, 2003*)

Note: [*]: minor adaptations in the original text introduced by the authors.

The first fundamental feature of dynamics of network reconfiguration, i.e., rapidness in reconfiguration, in order to respond competitively to the turbulent and unpredictable market, the requirement *sine qua non*, is called *flexibility*, or when it is also proactive, it is called *agility*.

To what degree the network dynamics is desirable, probably the most illustrative specification is given in Kim (1990). Figuratively, the performances required for a new, "ideal" (target, future) manufacturing system or enterprise are as follows:
1.   Manufacturing one to 1,000 products simultaneously

Box 2. Virtual enterprise

"A **Virtual Enterprise** is an organization fundamentally customer-oriented which accomplish the customer needs in a particular way and which is extremely time and cost effective." (*Davidow & Malone, 1992*)

"A **virtual corporation** is a temporary network of independent companies — suppliers, customers, even rivals — linked by information technology (IT) to share skills, costs and access to one another's markets. It will have neither central office nor organization chart. It will have no hierarchy, no vertical integration" (*Byrne, 1993*)

"'**Virtual Enterprise**' with the key processes subcontracted to other suppliers." (*SME, 1993*)

"**Virtual corporates** are fluid, on-line partnerships comprised of the best practices from various companies that bring together their individual core competencies to create a new product or service during a market window of opportunity. Once the life cycle of the product or service ends, they will separate and go about their businesses." (*Hormozi, 1994*)

"The **virtual organization**, or more accurately, an organization with a virtual organizational structure, is only one of many forms that cooperation, both among companies and within a single company, can take. … A virtual organizational structure is an opportunistic alliance of core competencies distributed among a number of distinct operating entities within a single large company or among a group of independent companies. … While the virtual organization is opportunistic, its objective is to create solution products with lifetimes as long as the marketplace will allow. These products are expected to evolve, and as they do, so will the virtual organization's resource requirements. Some participants will leave to join other groups because their competencies no longer add enough value to be most profitably used in the virtual organization. For precisely the same reasons, others will join, because they can add value as the product evolves in one direction rather then another. … The virtual organization is a dynamic organizational tool for agile competitors. It is at once neither temporary nor permanent." (*Goldman et al., 1995*)

"A **Virtual Enterprise** is a temporary alliance of enterprises that come together to share skills or core competencies and resources in order to better respond to business opportunities, and whose cooperation is supported by computer networks." ESPRIT IV PRODNET. (*Camarinha-Matos et al., 1997*)

"A **virtual enterprise** is not really different from a traditional enterprise other than the fact that it can append and shed processes quickly. There are more legal and regulatory issues than technical issues when removing barriers to virtual-enterprise operations." (*Nell, 1998*)

Note: [*]: minor adaptations in the original text introduced by the authors.

2. Accommodating lot sizes from one to 1,000,000
3. Reconfiguring for a new product within *one second* (in order to satisfy 1 and 2)

A traditional enterprise is considered a "stable" organizational structure that tends to avoid organizational reconfiguration or networking because of the reconfiguration or networking costs and tends to protect its own knowledge about the organization (management and technology) from the partners, which (knowledge) provides its competitive base.[6] The reconfiguration costs, both internal and through networking, are called *transaction costs*. The transaction cost and the knowledge protection capability are the networking and network dynamics disablers. On the contrary, VE see the networking and reconfiguration as the opportunity to improve, or to keep, the efficiency. To manage this objective, VE should have the mechanisms and the specific organizational structure to minimize the dynamics and networking disablers.

Box 2. Virtual enterprise (continued)

"A **Virtual Enterprise** is a temporary partnership of independent companies and/or individuals - suppliers of specific goods and services, customers — who are linked through modern telecommunications to exploit and profit from rapidly changing business opportunities. In a Virtual Enterprise, companies can share costs, skills, knowledge and access to specialized expertise, access to regional and global markets, with each partner supplying what it can do best — whether a product or a service. ... This enterprise is called "virtual" because it is composed of partners of core competence and has neither central office nor hierarchy or vertical integration. This way of doing business in partnership is made possible by our Virtual Network Architecture (VNA). VNA will enable working groups based in different countries of the world to operate together, using multi-media (*voice, data and image*) to interact as if they shared an office. Teams will be able to work together in real time, regardless of geographical location. Partnerships will be less permanent, less formal, and based more on special opportunities. Companies will join together in strategic partnerships to seize emerging markets. They then are free to end their partnership after completion of the venture." *(VEA, 1998)*

"**Virtual Enterprises** are opportunistic aggregations of smaller units that come together and act as though they were a larger, long-lived enterprise. The *virtual* here is meant to convey that many of the advantages of a large enterprise are synthesized by its members. In most interesting cases, this synthesis is temporary, built around a specific opportunity. When the opportunity fades, the virtual enterprise vanishes into constituent parts to reassemble into other configurations. ...A VE is agile only if it is formed with the intent of dissolving, or reconfiguring, so it is possible to have a VE without having an AVE." *(Goranson, 1999)*

"A **Virtual Enterprise** (VE) is an optimised enterprise synthesised over universal set of resources with the real-time substitutable physical structure. The design (synthesis) and control of the system is performed in an abstract, or virtual, environment." *(Putnik, 2001)*

"The *virtual organization* is a multi-actor system consisting of humans and virtual actors. Human actors and virtual actors have different capabilities. Those actors communicate and cooperate based on the virtual domain." *(Gazendam, 2001)*

"**Advanced virtual enterprise** (AVE) is characterized by highly dynamic configuration, changing partners and roles, and evolving products and process well after start — also cheap, opportunistic formation, dissolving and transitions to other forms. A typical AVE might be characterized as the best configurations of smaller players quickly aggregating to address an opportunity." *(Goranson, 2003)*

"**Definition** (*Business, or product, centered*): Virtual Enterprise is a hierarchical structure, composed by elementary (hierarchical) structural patterns '*c-r-c.*'.
Definition (*Resource centered*): Virtual Enterprise is a hierarchical structure with three levels '*r-c-r*', or two levels, '*c-r*' or '*r-c*', as special cases.
Definition (*Business, or product, centered*): Virtual Enterprise is a hierarchical structure, composed by *Resource centered* VE.
(*c*: control unit, agent, client, server; *r*: resource manager, broker." *(Putnik et al., 2004)*

Note: [*]: minor adaptations in the original text introduced by the authors.

If each organizational structure instance is considered as a new enterprise, then a dynamically reconfigurable network could be described by the metaphor "'Flow' of enterprises through the product." Consequently, the number of organizational structure instances, integrated along the product/VE lifetime is very high in comparison with the traditional enterprise, where this number is much lower or one. The feature "'Flow' of enterprises through the product" means, in fact, the *inverse organizational model* in

Table 1. "Traditional" enterprise versus virtual enterprise potentials

Number	Criteria	"Traditional" Enterprise	Virtual Enterprise
1	**Number of products by enterprise**	**Multi**	**One**
1.1	"Flow" of products through the enterprise	Yes	No
2	**Organizational reconfiguration dynamics**	**None**	**Yes**
2.1	Enterprise "life" time	Long	Short
2.2	Interenterprise networking	Low	High
2.3	Organization's reconfiguration "transaction" cost (networking and dynamics disabler)	High	Low
2.4	Trust assurance and management (networking and dynamics disabler)	Low	High
2.5	Organization reconfiguration time (networking and dynamics disabler)	High	Low
2.6	"Flow" of enterprises through the product	No	Yes
2.7	Number of organizational structure instances	One/Low	Very high
2.8	Leanness	Medium	Maximum
2.9	Agility	Medium	Maximum
2.10	Operations management importance	High	Low
2.11	Organization design/integration complexity	Low	High
2.12	**Virtuality** (dynamics enabler)	No	Yes
2.13	Creativity	Medium	Medium
3	**External entities as organizational dynamics enablers**	**No**	**Yes**
3.1	"Meta-enterprise" as enterprise environment	No	Yes

comparison with the traditional one — "'Flow' of products through the enterprise." The inverse is manifested, for example, in the fact that in such an enterprise (VE), leanness can be maintained on the maximum level, and agility can be promoted at the maximum level, through permanent reconfiguration. Another example could be scheduling, which is no longer one of the most important functions for operations management but, rather, could be seen as a network design tool (entries 2.8–2.11, Table 1).

Only on the criteria "creativity" does VE not have significant differences versus traditional enterprises, as the creativity "technology" is more likely not affected by the organizational models. However, coupling the VE with the recent *Chaordic Enterprise* (CE) and related *Chaordic System Thinking* (CST) concepts (conceived to improve the creativity, see, e.g., Eijnatten & Putnik, 2004) is expected to be value added to the VE concept.

The second fundamental feature, *virtuality*, has basically two different approaches in the VE models. The first approach, widely used, interprets the virtuality as "potentially present" and "existing but changing" (Franke, 2000). This approach is criticized in Putnik (2001) as being insufficient, arguing that there is a conflict with the etymology of the term "virtual" — "virtual" means something "not physically existing as such but made by software to appear to do so" (Oxford Dictionary). But, virtuality in VE should not be confused with the virtual reality (VR) based concepts, e.g., "virtual manufacturing," which would lead us to a poor simulation. In Putnik (2001), the virtuality is implemented through two "interface" layers, hierarchically "above" and "under" the operating unit or partner, which (interface layers) are performed by brokers, hiding the "client" and/or "server." In other words, the operating unit, or partner, does not see the real structure — it sees some "virtual" structure that does not exist. In this way, the real enterprise exists, but the unit, or partner, works in a "virtual" environment without knowing who cooperates, which could be considered the second approach to the virtuality in VE. This form, VE architecture, which provides a virtual environment for the VE agent operations, is introduced in order to minimize the setup time when switching from one physical organizational structure to another. Actually, virtuality, implemented in this form of the VE architecture, is a mechanism, or a tool, for further improvement of reconfiguration dynamics capability.

One almost equivalent critical and solution approach (apparently independently conceived) is found in Gazendam:

"This discussion of the virtual organization as an organization network is unsatisfactory, because it misses the essential point of the existence of a virtual domain. We need a virtual organization concept that encompasses the virtual domain. The virtual organization is a Multi-actor system consisting of humans and virtual actors. Human actors and virtual actors have different capabilities. Those actors communicate and cooperate based on the virtual domain." *(Gazendam, 2001, p. 8)*

Finally, the third fundamental distinctive feature is the existence of "*external entities as organizational dynamics enablers*" (entry 3, Table 1). These entities are specific organizations, with the function of serving as the environment for enabling, or supporting, the VE integration, as well as the reconfiguration dynamics assuring the low (reconfiguration) transaction costs and protection of the enterprise partners' knowledge. These organizations represent, in fact, the meta-enterprises for the operating VEs (entry 3.1, Table 1). These entities (organizations) are designated, by their authors, as *Market of Resources* (Cunha et al., 2000, 2003). In Cunha (2003), it is demonstrated that the VE reconfiguration dynamics is practically impossible without Market of Resources as the environment for the VE reconfiguration dynamics, i.e., the Market of Resources (MR) is the condition *sine qua non*. One of the consequences of the Market of Resources is a different VE life-cycle model. The authors called it the "*Virtual Enterprises' Extended Lifecycle*" (Cunha, Putnik, & Ávila, 2004), and it introduces, as the main distinguished characteristic different from the usual VE life cycle, the phase of contractualization with the MR by the enterprises that want to make their resources available to integrate VE.

The needs for the existence of external entities as environments for VE reconfiguration dynamics are also recognized by other authors, although the needs are not introduced in the VE definitions (yet). Other concepts, services, and products, like the MR, include the new generation of *high value-added electronic marketplaces*, *e-alliances*, *breeding environments*, *electronic institutions*, *virtual clusters*, and *"guilds."*[7]

It is expected that these environments will be the regular environments for VE integration, reconfiguration dynamics, and operation.

INTEGRATION

The integration approach was defined in the 1970s (in traditional enterprises, of course) when the potentials of the emerging computer technology were realized.

Since then, a number of definitions of integration and enterprise integration (EI) were developed reflecting the evolution of the integration of underlying technologies, at first, the computer-based technologies and information systems, as well as the developments in organizational and management models. A literature analysis of the integration definitions offered shows the following:

1. The integration definitions are interpretative and informal, implying that there is not a formal theoretical basis. The lack of a formal theoretical basis, or at least the lack of some formalization, has generated a "dose" of confusion, even on the question about what integration is. Nevertheless, the practical results are very good, and today, many integration mechanisms became practically "standard" technology (however, these good results do not invalidate the critics in relation to ever-moving objectives, especially with VE).

2. There are two fundamentally different views on what integration is, i.e., the view on integration as the (business/manufacturing) processes interaction improvement and the view on integration as the design process.

A selection of integration definitions concerning enterprises and manufacturing systems is presented in Box 3 — Enterprise and Manufacturing Systems Integration.

Integration as Processes Interaction Improvement

Virtually, the main mechanism, or tool, for the processes interaction improvement is the computer and information technology in a variety of specific technologies and aspects (Table 2). This is explicitly referred to in a number of definitions, e.g., Veilleux (1987), Burbidge (1987), AMICE Consortium (1989), Scheer (1991), McMahon & Browne (1993), Uschold et al. (1997), Ray (2003) — see Box 3.

Along with the development of the computer and information-technology-based integration, it was recognized that there are many other possible integration mechanisms. This was the reason for the emergence of "information integration" definitions (MetaMatrix, 2001; Jhingran et al., 2002), indicating that information-based integration is only part of the integration phenomena space, while other authors intentionally avoid referring to computer and information technology, leaving the "space" for other kinds of mechanisms (e.g., Vernadat, 1996; Brunnermeier & Martin, 1999; Petrie, 1992; Barkmeyer et al.,

Box 3. Enterprise and manufacturing systems integration

> **"Computer Integrated Manufacturing system (CIM)** A system that provides computer assistance to all business functions within a manufacturing enterprise from product design and/or order entry to product shipment." (*Veilleux, 1987*)
>
> **"CIM — Computer Integrated Manufacturing system** (n) A production system based on an integrated and centralized data bank, and on the elimination of all duplication in data processing." (*Burbidge, 1987*)
>
> "Integration at the basic level includes the physical and logical connection of processes by means of data communication technology operating to specific standards. At higher levels, integration implies: (1) synchronization of functions to ensure that tasks are carried out in the correct sequence, (2) the use of common data storage, in the form of databases accesses concurrently by a number of processes, (3) operating environments common to all processes, (4) activities subject to overall business objectives and able to react rapidly to changes in business objectives." (*AMICE Consortium, 1989*)
>
> "The Five Key Integrating Actions are as follows: 1) all members of the cross-functional team are trained in Design-for-Manufacturing methods, 2) Manufacturing signs off on design reviews, 3) Novel organizational structures are used for coordination, 4) job rotation is practised in engineering functions, 5) personnel move between engineering and manufacturing — permanently." (*Ettlie, Stoll, 1990*)
>
> "Computer Integrated Manufacturing (CIM) refers to the integrated information processing requirements for the technical and operational tasks of an industrial enterprise." (*Scheer, 1991*)
>
> "'in its simplest form' **Enterprise Integration (EI)** is the task of improving the performances of complex processes by managing the interactions, as well as improving them, among interacting organisations, individuals and systems." (*Petrie, 1992*)
>
> "… integration of all manufacturing activities through the use of linked computer aids and a shared database is sometimes called **computer-integrated manufacturing**" (*McMahon & Browne, 1993*)
>
> "**Integration:** Integration means putting together heterogeneous components to form a synergistic whole. …
>
> **Enterprise Integration (EI):** Enterprise Integration is concerned with facilitating information, control and material flow across organizational boundaries by connecting all the necessary functions and heterogeneous functional entities in order to improve communication, cooperation, and coordination within this enterprise so that the enterprise behaves as an integrated whole, therefore enhancing its overall productivity, flexibility, and capacity for management of change (or reactivity). Heterogeneous enterprise functional entities to be integrated are information systems, devices, applications and people." (*Vernadat, 1996*)
>
> *Note:* [*]: minor adaptations in the original text introduced by the authors.

2003). Finally, we find definitions that explicitly refer to other integration mechanisms. For example, these are the (integrated) management and control models, organizational models, and even training (see Ettlie & Stoll, 1990; Box 3).

Thus, an interpretative, informal definition could be as follows:

The integration is the processes interaction improvement for which different kinds of mechanisms are used.

Box 3. Enterprise and manufacturing systems integration (continued)

"**Integration** must be achieved for relating information to obtain deferent views of the enterprise, for relating tasks to be performed to the tools that support them, and to establish connections between the tools themselves. ...
... perspectives of how the Enterprise Ontology was intended to be used...be summarised as follows:
• enhance human communication in organisations both inside and outside the project;
• serve as a basis for acquiring and representing enterprise models which in turn may be used:
— to ensure agreement among members in an organization — as a stable basis for specifying IT requirements
• to achieve integration of software tools, both — as part of agent communication language — as an interchange format..." (*Uschold et al., 1997*)

"**Interoperability** is the ability to communicate product data across different production activities." (*Brunnermeier & Martin, 1999*)

"Enterprise Information Integration (EII). EII provides access to information, regardless of source or storage format. EII uses existing descriptions of the physical data resources' characteristics to construct a virtual representation that hides the differences of the underlying data sources. ...How does EII accomplish this magic? Through metadata. Metadata means "data about data." ...Enterprise Information Integration depends on sophisticated technology to collect, manage, and model metadata, metamodels, and meta-metamodels, as well as query management and connection technology for available information systems." (*MetaMatrix, 2001*)

"Naively, systems integration is an engineering process for constructing systems. ...
Integration = (1) a *state* of a set of agents that enables them to *act jointly* in one or more sub-functions of a function of a larger system. The system may be pre-designed or ad hoc, and the agents may be system-specific components or reusable components. The agents must exhibit behaviors consistent with the accomplishment of the system function and *communicate* to the extent necessary to accomplish the *joint action*; (2) a systems engineering *process* — a design/ development activity that
• identifies how *joint action* of two or more independent agents enabled by particular *communications* can improve a business process,
• results in a larger *system* that can accomplish the end goal of improving the business process,
• includes assignment of *roles* in functions of the larger system to nominal *resources*, determination of the suitability of specific resources to fulfill those roles, the configuration or modification of the resources to enable them to perform those roles, and the creation or acquisition of additional resources where needed." (*Barkmeyer et al., 2003*)

"The term "manufacturing interoperability" refers to the ability to seamlessly share technical and business information throughout an extended manufacturing enterprise. This information, previously shared informally within a company, must now be passed electronically and error-free to suppliers and customers around the world. ...There are three principal avenues to achieving interoperability: developing point-to-point translators, mandating the use of proprietary tools and/or formats, or the use of neutral standards." (*Ray, 2003*)

Note: [*]: minor adaptations in the original text introduced by the authors.

Possible interpretations and developed and available mechanisms, in practice, form a complex multidimensional space. The list is large (see list in Table 2). The diversity of (mechanism) types and number of integration dimensions or aspects is also large (see list in Table 3). Also, many EI model spaces may be constructed.

Table 2. Integration mechanisms

Mechanisms	
File or document, shared database, procedure call or operation invocation, messaging, blackboard (publish and subscribe, shared memory, etc.), signals (physical signals and software events), human interface mechanisms (such as display, keyboard, mouse, etc.),	*(Barkmeyer et al., 2003)*
portals,	*(Jhingran et al., 2002)*
semantic-representation language, negotiation protocol, semantic equivalence metric, reasoning, inferencing, ontologies,	*(Ray, 2002)* *(Uschold, 1997)*
common technology for the transmission and reception of the data, common protocols for the exchange, rules for the elementary interactions,	*(Barkmeyer et al., 2003)*
common data structure and representation,	*(InterSystems, 2004)*
data adapters, enterprise application adapters, transaction systems adapters, emulation adapters, protocol adapters, technology adapters,	
standards on enterprise engineering and integration,	*(Kosanke, 2003)*
enterprise reference architectures,	*(Bernus et al., 1996)*
standard languages, standard (product) data exchange formats, standards for data share and access, datacommunication protocols, standards for system's interoperability, code mobility, information modelling,	*(Jardim-Gonçalves, Steiger-Garção, 2001)*
translator ("horizontal" integration), wrappers ("vertical" integration), distributed systems, programming languages, agents, operating systems,	
metadata, virtual meta-data, model metadata, metamodels, meta-metamodels,	*(MetaMatrix, 2001)*
query management, connection technology (for available information systems),	
direct humans communication, training, management, coordination, enterprise organization/architecture, teamwork, job rotation, deterministic translators or translation algorithms (fixed automation),	*(Ettlie, Stoll, 1990)*
soft algorithms, data mining, expert system, machine learning,	*(Barkmeyer et al., 2003)*
self-describing systems, self-integrating systems, negotiation, negotiation protocols, brokering, meta-organizations, . . .	

Unfortunately, due to the semantical and practical complexity, and due to the EI science and engineering state-of-the-art, it is not possible to avoid conflicting interpretations about the integration dimensions. For example, the integration models (based on) standard data structures, formal semantics, self-describing systems, and self-integration

Table 3. Integration dimensions

Dimensions	
Language	Legacy issues
Integration domain	Knowledge
Architectures/organization	Integration process elements
Dynamics	Aspects of integration
Automation	Integration concerns
Performance metrics	Methods and technologies
Normalization/standardization	Mechanism or tools
Management	Quality
"Intelligence location"	Legal issues
Technology	Life cycle
Task coordination	…

systems may be analyzed *diachronically*, i.e., as phases in the "evolution of systems integration approach," as it is approached in Ray (2002), or they may be analyzed *synchronically* as models of different degrees of complexity and for different domains of use.

Integration as Design

The view on integration as a design process is based on interpretations that follow the etymology of the term "integration" as well as on practices in various engineering domains. We could recall that the so-called "true engineering problems" are the problems that require integration (of functions, differential equations, etc.). For example, the definition of integration as "the composition or combination of parts or elements so as to form a whole" (Merriam-Webster Online Dictionary) is the same as the definition of one of the design process models. Moreover, in dictionaries, the synonyms and related terms for integration are explicitly "plan," "design," "plot," "scheme," and "project." This means that practice put these terms in this way.

Also, we may find that the definition of integration, "integrated …," etc., may imply the view of integration as design. For example, the enterprise reference architectures could be considered as reference models for, in fact, design of enterprise organization. The relation with the integration as processes interaction improvements is, in fact, that enterprise organization is one of the integration mechanisms by the first view on integration, e.g., "An Enterprise Reference Architecture models the whole life history of an enterprise integration project from its initial concept in the eyes of the entrepreneurs who initially developed it, through its definition, functional design or specification, detailed design, physical implementation or construction, and finally operation to obsolescence" (Bernus et al., 1996, p. 32).

Understanding and considering integration as a design process is of the greatest importance for building a new generation of integration models for VE.

TRADITIONAL ENTERPRISE INTEGRATION VS. VIRTUAL ENTERPRISE INTEGRATION

It is of the greatest interest to have effective and efficient VEI models. Unfortunately, at the state-of-the-art of VEI science and engineering, the solutions offered are still far from satisfactory, although they present significant contributions to our knowledge base for building effective and efficient integration of VE. The already referred study (Brunnermeier & Martin, 1999, pp. 3-8) said that although "a number of potential solutions have been developed over the years, including standardization on a single system for each OEM and its suppliers and sharing of files in native format, development of point-to-point translators, and development of neutral format translators, none of the solutions that have been widely used in the past have been successful at significantly reducing" (Brunnermeier & Martin, 1999)[8] the interoperability (integration) problems.

The EI and VE (integration) researchers, in the past years, have developed new and more sophisticated integration mechanisms, but we are still not satisfied. This situation could be recognized through different perspectives (one is the already referred report by Brunnermeier & Martin, 1999). For example, in the recently published "main findings" of the EU IST-2000-29478 Project *THINKcreative* (thinking network of experts on emerging smart organizations) (Camarinha-Matos & Afsarmanesh, 2004), the objective of which was "the establishment of a research agenda for emerging collaborative networks,"[9] in a way, the existence of the "interoperability crisis" was recognized:

"Efforts on general plug-and-play architecture and interoperability are also to a large extent missing. Consequently, no generally accepted reference model or interoperability base are available." (Camarinha-Matos & Afsarmanesh, 2004, p. 290)

This conclusion is surely made upon an extensive state-of-the-art analysis.
The project's further findings concerning the interoperability crisis are that...

"In the short and medium terms, the lack of interoperability of SW/HW systems represents a crucial obstacle in developing new forms of cooperation. This obstacle is however attenuated by engineering efforts. In the long term, the interoperability scenario is unclear." (Camarinha-Matos & Afsarmanesh, 2004, pp. 75-76)

Another example, by which we can claim that the solutions for VE integration are not satisfactory, is the observation that, in fact, we do not have VE implemented in compliance with a number of theoretical models developed, with the exception of supply chains (if we consider them as a VE model).

Naturally, the question that emerges is: Why we do not have satisfactory solutions for VE integration, in spite of the significant research and development effort by the research and developers community? What are the implications, analogies, and specialities of the VEI against traditional EI?

The literature on integration reports a number of influencing factors. For example, the study on information integration by Jhingran et al. (2002), reports the following:

"...three trends that have made the task of managing such data inherently more complex:

1. *The heterogeneity of data. Data are no longer just records that sit in well-defined tables (typically referred to as "structured" data). Increasingly, an enterprise has to deal with unstructured content — such as text (in e-mails, Web pages, etc.), audio (call center logs), and video (employee broadcast). In addition, data are beginning to emerge in XML format, which in some ways is the bridge between the structured and unstructured worlds, though that is an oversimplification...:*

2. *The "federation" and "distribution" of data. Data are no longer on one logical server (such as in a well-architected warehouse), but are distributed across multiple machines in different organizations (some within and some across enterprises). This is in the classic sense of distributed databases, except that the scale could be as large as billions of databases (whereas classic databases have handled distribution at the scale of around 10). In addition, federation (who owns and controls the data and access to the data) is a new problem. ... In addition, privacy and security issues need to be solved.*

3. *Using data for competitive advantage. The data need to be manipulated, aggregated, transformed, and analyzed in increasingly complex ways to produce business intelligence. And the speed of access and analysis is becoming closer to real time. ... Information integration, then, refers to the ability to analyze data across data types and over a span of control." (Jhingran et al., 2002, p. 556)*

Ray (2002) states that "the growth in the use of the Internet brings with it an increase in the number of interconnections among information systems supporting the manufacturing supply chain as well as other businesses. ...However, the sheer number of interconnections and the resulting complexity threaten to overwhelm the ability of the standards community or industry to provide the necessary specifications — a way out of this impasse must be found" (Ray, 2002, p. 65). The author proposes the self-integrating systems, wherein the systems negotiate meaningful interfaces as needed in a dynamic environment.

InterSystems (2004) said that there are differences in integration "concerns" between the "business-to-business (B2B) integration," which is also considered a domain of VEI, and the internal enterprise integration. As stated:

"Business-to-business (B2B) integration is focused on efficient interactions among enterprises and their trading partners (i.e., customers and suppliers). B2B is therefore focusing on integrating applications and data sources external to an enterprise, while application-to-application (A2A) integration is typically focused on integrating applications and data sources internal to an enterprise. While B2B and A2A share many characteristics and it is sometimes hard to differentiate between the two at a higher level, there are definite distinctions. A2A integration solutions do not necessarily provide the appropriate capabilities needed for B2B, and vice versa. Among the key differences that organizations should examine are security standards, support for industry standards (such as Rosettanet), and support for B2B-specific capabilities such as trading standards and catalog information sharing." (InterSystems, 2004, p. 7)

Finally, Gazendam (2001) provides us with an analysis referring to the cognitive, dynamical, and organizational issues, the issues of the future research by the VEI community, i.e.:

"Traditional information system methods and theories fail to give a clear account of three connected phenomena we see nowadays: virtuality and virtual organizations, horizontalized (network-based) organization structures and governance forms, and multiple active representations. Firstly, information systems are part of a virtual world and of virtual organizations. Information systems are no longer well understood when using the idea of passive representation, because information systems do not only represent something in the nonvirtual world, but also act upon that nonvirtual world, and create a virtual domain. Secondly, virtual organizations and information systems do no longer have a structure and governance form that can be understood well using theories of centralized decision making and top-down design. Structures and governance forms are horizontalized now, and have a network character. Thirdly, the use of symbol structures by (semi) intelligent beings can no longer be understood as the central processing of well-structured data. It has to be seen as a collection of processes of self-organization of multiple active representations." (Gazendam, 2001, p. 4)

We would add the following factors:
1.   The existence of different interpretations and definitions of what is, in fact, integration.
2.   The existence of different interpretations and definitions of what is, in fact, VE.

Table 4. A comparison of traditional and VE integration

		Traditional Enterprise	Virtual Enterprise
1	Location of the integration focus	Intraenterprise	Interenterprise
2	Organizational structure (design) versus integration (design)	Decoupled	Coupled
3	Structural complexity (of organization)	Low	High
4	Volume of integration relations	Low	High
5	Dynamics of establishment of integration relations	Low	High
6	Dynamics of integration processes	Low	High
7	Dynamics of needs for new integration mechanism	Low	High
8	Generative integration[*]	No	Yes
9	Life cycle	No	Yes
10	Language complexity	Low	High
11	Integration base	Transaction	Communication
12	Needs for multidimensional/multilevel approach	Low	High

Note: [*]Includes "self-integration" as a model.

Box 4. Virtual enterprise integration

> "Information integration requires a shared reference model. ...Experience shows that
> to be effective, such a model should be developed from *de facto* best practices rather
> than imposed *de jure*... The model should explicitly support business practices with
> special attention to processes across distributed systems. The resulting formal
> architecture should describe the components, capabilities, and processes of AVE's,
> and must provide for such functions as human/machine integration, security, access,
> accounting, monitoring, recovery and emergency handling, and contingency
> operations. The model should also specify methods for easy implementation of
> systems based on it.
> ...The *information infrastructure* must include a consensus AVE reference model,
> building on and collaborating closely with other government and industry modeling
> activities in the US and abroad. ...Such a reference model provides a common
> vocabulary across the different technical domains that need to collaborate in
> developing the infrastructure, and maps out the various interfaces for which standards
> need to be developed." (*Parunak, 1997*)
>
> *Note:* [*]: minor adaptations in the original text introduced by the authors.

3. The higher complexity of the VE integration problem than the complexity of the traditional EI problem.
4. Lack of understanding about the relations between the solutions offered, the problem which is especially "hard" considering the "explosion" of the solutions in last years.
5. The need for a new (enterprise) integration paradigm, as the VE concept is seen as a new organizational paradigm, and, therefore, it is unlikely that the traditional integration solutions would satisfy the requirements of the new (VE) paradigm.

A comparison of traditional and VE integration, by the selected criteria and underlining the elements for the new paradigm of VEI, is given in Table 4.

Concerning VEI definitions in literature, it is difficult to find them, if possible at all. An example is in Parunak (1997) — Box 4. Virtual Enterprise Integration. The definition refers to the need for a shared and consensus AVE reference model as well as that the reference model "should be developed from *de facto* best practices rather than imposed *de jure*" (Parunak, 1997. p. 3).

Thesis About VE Integration

Resuming, we could formulate two main global thesis concerning VE integration:
1. The effective and efficient VE integration (science and engineering) is the main VE enabler.
2. For effective and efficient VE integration (science and engineering), it is necessary to develop a new VE integration (science and engineering) paradigm.

CHALLENGES FOR THE SCIENCE
OF VIRTUAL INTEGRATION:
METATHEORETICAL APPROACHES

To respond to the challenges concerning the VEI, which implies dealing with VEI complexity, to control a number of influencing factors (a very important one is a better understanding about the relations between the solutions offered), etc., the authors think that an external view on the VEI discipline would be useful.

Speaking in engineering terms, a framework for VEI research and development would be useful, if not absolutely needed. The functions of such a framework are to improve the effectiveness and efficiency in development and implementation of VEI solutions, including, validation of the solutions proposed. Or, speaking in theoretical terms, we would need a theory about the VEI theory. The theory about the theory is designated as the metatheory, and a theory treated by the metatheory is designated by the object-theory.

"A meta-theoretical perspective, ...(is) a critical framework for analysis, and create a structure that enables elements of different theories and concepts to be located relative to each other."[10] (Love, 2000, p. 304)

Analyzing the literature on EI, VE, and VEI, as well as the above text of this chapter, the metatheoretical approaches to the VEI issues are only implicit and on an ad-hoc basis.

As a contribution to an explicit metatheory on VEI, in response to the VEI challenges, we propose here two possible approaches for a metatheoretical structure for VE integration:

1.   VEI abstractions hierarchy
2.   VEI semiotics

Integration Abstractions Hierarchy

The proposal for the metatheoretical approach based on the VEI abstractions hierarchy follows the work by Love (2000). "It offers a means of classification that is hierarchical and relatively independent of the domain-based meanings associated with each theoretical element. This method provides a straightforward means of clarifying and externalising many of the hidden dependencies between abstractions in" VEI[11] theory. The abstractions classification is "focused not on the *content* of the abstractions or theories. This is a taxonomy of abstractions and theories in terms of their theoretical *behaviour*" (Love, 2000, p. 305).

The hierarchical levels of VEI abstractions, in which VEI might be researched, are as follows (following and paraphrasing Love, 2000, pp. 305-306)[12]:

I.   **Direct perception of realities:** At this level, we observe the daily work-life interactions.
II.   **Description of objects:** At this level, we describe VEI objects, processes, and systems.
III. **Behaviour of elements:** At this level, the behavior of VEI elements that may be incorporated in objects, systems, and processes is described.

IV.   **VEI mechanisms of choice:** At this level, we describe the way choices are made between different objects, processes, or systems, and how solutions are evaluated.

V.   **VEI methods:** At this level, the theories about the underlying structure of the VEI process are described.

VI.   **VEI process structure:** At this level, the theories of the underlying VEI processes are described.

VII.   **Theories about the internal processes of VEI users:** At this level, theories about the reasoning and cognitions of individuals and collectives using VEI are described.

VIII.   **General VEI theories:** At this level, the general theories about the whole framework of VEI are described.

IX.   **Epistemology of VEI:** This level contains the critical study of the nature, grounds, limits, and criteria or validity of VEI knowledge.

X.   **Ontology of VEI:** This level contains the philosophical study of the ontological basis for VEI, such as assumptions, ethics, and human and social values.

"Looking at this list, we conclude that the development of a complexity paradigm in" VEI "has only just begun. There is much work to engage in" (Putnik & Eijnatten, 2004, p. 493).[13]

Integration Semiotics

The proposal for the metatheoretical approach based on VE integration semiotics follows the emerging areas of organizational semiotics and research of the fundamentals of information systems based on the semiotic framework (organizational semiotics, semiotic framework) that have emerged in response to the failure of the traditional "technocentric" approach to today's information systems (IS) and organizations (ORG) requirements as well as to the "software development crisis." The software development crisis is manifested by the approximately 50% failure rate of the software projects (e.g., see Liu, 2000, for the "shameful numbers"). According to R. Stamper ["A Dissenting Position" in *FRISCO*[14] *Report* (Falkenberg et al., 1998)], the traditional approach fails "not for technical reasons - most delivered software performs efficiently to specification - but for organisational reasons - they do not relate correctly to the world of business reality. The sad facts that, in general technical people do not understand business problems and business-oriented people do not understand the need for detailed, formal precision contribute to the problem." In the *FRISCO Report* (Falkenberg et al., 1998), it is identified that "there are at least three major sources of problems: (a) the large variety of interest groups, (b) conflicting philosophical positions, and (c) the lack of understanding communication." Also, it was realized that "the social, cultural and organizational aspects play more decisive roles then technology itself" (Liu, 2000, p. 3). "Organization is achieved not by doing things but by talking and writing about them," said Stamper. Thus, a better understanding of IS should be based on a broader sociotechnical view and should "encompasses human beings, organizations, business processes, standards and tools" (Hesse & Verrijn-Stuart, 2000, p. 1; see also Table 6). According to Moor and Weigand, information systems should be approached "much more as the communication systems than computation systems" (Moor & Weigand, 2002; see also Table 5). To deal with the communication systems, the "move away from the traditional information flow paradigm, in which positivistic modeling of symbol manipulating functions aimed at

Table 5. From information to communication systems (Moor & Weigand, 2002)

	Information Systems	Communication Systems
Focus:	Information	Communication
Supports:	Transaction processes	Communication processes
Design objects:	Clear specifications	"Fuzzy" process definitions
Development process:	Single project	Continuous process
Developers	Elite development team	Many stakeholders

Table 6. From information flow to information field (Moor & Weigand, 2002)

	Information Flow	IS Information Field
Change:	Static	Dynamic
Responsibility:	Anonymous	Individual responsibilities
Design process:	Representation	Interpretation
Objective:	Control	Perceive, understand, value, act
Control logic:	Rules	Norms

producing automated solutions is central, …, (towards) an information field paradigm is needed (Stamper, 2000). … The information systems built on the information field paradigm do not produce sterile data, but aim to generate and communicate information that can lead to true knowledge that helps people to perceive, understand, value, and act in the world" (Moor & Weigand, 2002; see also Table 6).

Concerning virtual organizations, according to Gazendam, "to deal with these phenomena, a shift (1) from technology to virtuality based on multiple ideas, (2) from central planning and control to negotiated social patterns based on multiple actors and (3) from central processing of data to self-organization of multiple active representations" (Gazendam, 2001, pp. 4-5) is needed. "The self-organization of these representation types is based on resolution, narration, and abstraction, respectively. Together, these representation types are involved in the mechanisms of induction, abduction, and deduction that generate new knowledge" (Gazendam, 2001, p. 6). Interactions are characterized by cooperation, coordination, problem solving, and learning, focusing on "their own way of understanding of what happens in the interaction" (Gazendam, 2001, p. 6). Understandings, methods, and tools come from "different disciplines and theories: semiotics, organization theory and economics, and cognitive psychology" (Gazendam, 2001, p. 6)

According to Stamper (1996; cited in the *FRISCO Report*, Falkenberg et al., 1998, p. 13), semiotics offers the explanation of the new approach on six semiotic levels (called the "semiotic ladder") (Figure 1).

In Table 7 are given characterizations of the organizations and information systems through the semantic level "lenses" from Moor and Weigand (2002), Filipe (2004), and

Figure 1. The "semiotic ladder"

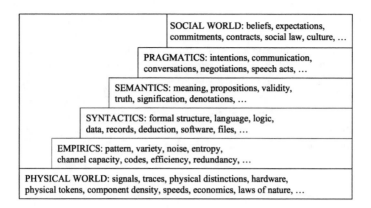

Table 7. Organizations and information systems characterizations through the semiotic level "lenses"

Semiotic Levels	(*Moor & Weigand, 2002*)	(*Filipe, 2004*)	(*Gazendam, 2001*)	
Social	Communication (organization)	Human interaction functions	Virtual Organization architecture	Basic idea or the basic *requirements*
Pragmatic	Communication (objective)			Desired *behaviour* of human actors and virtual actors (information systems) — norms, protocols, or other interaction patterns
Semantic	Information (semantics)			*World model* of human actors or virtual actors (information systems) has to be defined based on multiple active representations
Syntactic	Information (syntax)	IT platform		*Component architecture*
Empirical	Media (dynamic aspects)			
Physical	Media (structural aspects)			*Technical infrastructure*

Gazendam (2001). Concerning VO, according to Gazendam, "VO has to do with the top three levels (social, pragmatic and semantic)" (Gazendam, 2001, p. 5). Also, according to Nell, "There are more legal and regulatory issues than technical issues when removing barriers to virtual-enterprise operations" (Nell, 1998).

Now, we can look at the VE integration. It is obvious that the VEI interoperability crisis is just a case of the information systems and organizations traditional approach crisis. Actually, the transaction-based integration is, in many cases, effective only within limited well-organized domains and on the lower levels of communication. Even for the traditional enterprise domains [e.g., intraenterprise domains such as enterprise resource planning (ERP)] the traditional approaches failed to provide effective and efficient solutions. For example, theoretically, the integration open-system architecture, based on standards by the rule, is more flexible than integration-federated architecture. However, the practise refutes this idea. In practise, an integration-federated architecture that uses 250 prebuilt adaptors "is capable of immediately connecting to virtually any information system, rapidly integrating more data sources on more platforms and across more network protocols than any other integration solution" (InterSystems, 2004, p. 7). Development of those 250 adaptors is probably less time and energy consuming than the development of standards for the same application domain (for problems on standards and ontologies development, see, e.g., Libes et al., 2004, and Nell, 1998). This is the pure example of solutions on the pragmatic level (while standards are the solutions on the syntactic and semantic levels).

The problems of the VEI are even more difficult, see Table 4. Actually, VEI implies dynamic establishments and management of the interactions among potential partners. It is not realistic to expect that every perspective partner is in possession of the standard-based solutions, the state-of-the-art technology, and even the "ideal" knowledge. It means that in such imperfect solutions, which are part of the real world, the partners must have the ability to create or to synthesize the integration solution. Moreover, the partners must have the ability to implement integration process management, as VE integration is a complex process and not only a data transaction. For that reason, we coined the term **"generative integration"**.

Generative integration is, thus, characterized by the integration life cycle (Figure 2). It consists of three global phases: synthesis (or design), operation, and termination.

In the phase "integration synthesis" (or design, or generation), representing a communication-based integration process, integration generation tools are used, which, might be, negotiations, brokering, cooperation and coordination, integration management, sophisticated VE design algorithms, learning and machine learning, law mechanisms, contracting processes, cost management, specialized agencies, or meta-enterprises as the environments for integration facilitating, common human communication, etc. How does the particular VE architecture affect the integration process? How do the social requirements, as culture, (international) law, ecology, energy, etc., affect the

Figure 2. Integration process life cycle basic model

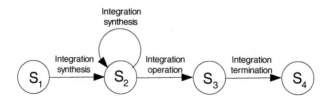

particular integration solutions? All of these tools are the tools of integration practice. Obviously, these issues, including the so-called generative integration, are the objects of higher-level communication and organization, which we will call the *organizational perspective of the VE integration.*

The issues of data formats, shared databases, standards, ontologies, deterministic algorithms, wrappers, contracts (as fixed documents), etc., which are tools of the integration life-cycle phase of operation, represent a transaction-based integration process that we will call *technological perspective of the VE integration.*

The termination phase of the integration process life cycle, for any of the situations referred to before, might correspond to a simple disconnection of the two elements (in the transaction-based integration), or it may require subprocesses in the communication-based integration.

Both perspectives, organizational and technological, together with the creative approach to their interrelation, are indispensable for developing, implementing, and practicing effective and efficient VE integration.

To conclude this section, in Tables 8 and 9, a view on VE integration through the semiotics lenses is presented.

Table 8. VE integration life-cycle semiotics

Virtual Enterprise Integration				
Semiotic Levels	**Integration Life Cycle**			**Perspectives**
	Type	**Processes**	**Tools**	
Social	Generative integration (*communication-based integration*)	1) VE/VEI synthesis (coupled design and integration); 2) operation (transactions); 3) termination	Social and cultural requirements identification, meta-enterprise environments, VE architectures, VE/VEI synthesis, negotiation, brokering, cooperation, coordination, trust, integration management, VE design algorithms, learning, law, regulations, cost management, etc.	**Organization**
Pragmatic				
Semantic	Transaction-based integration (*information-based integration*)	Transactions	Data-file transfer, shared databases, procedure call, standards, ontologies, metadata, etc.	**Technology**
Syntactic				
Empirical		Transfers	Hardware and physical processes	
Physical				

Table 9. VE integration system semiotics

Virtual Enterprise Integration processes		
Semiotic Levels	**Aspect**	**Characterization**
Social		social requirements, culture
Pragmatic	*Focus*	communication,
	Support	communication process,
	Design objects	"fuzzy" process-definitions
	Devt. Process	continuous,
	Developers	many stakeholders
	Change	dynamic
	Responsibility	individual
	Design process	interpretation
	Objective	perceive, understand, value, act
	Control logic	norms
Semantic	*Focus*	information,
	Support	transaction process,
	Design objects	clear specifications
	Devt. Process	single project,
	Developers	elite development team
	Change	static
Syntactic	*Responsibility*	anonymous
	Design process	representation
	Objective	control
	Control logic	rules
Empirical		component architecture, technical
Physical		infrastructure

CONCLUSIONS: TOWARD THE NEW PARADIGM OF THE INTEGRATION MODELING, OR SCIENCE

This chapter was about the challenges of a new paradigm, i.e., of the VE paradigm to the VEI issues. There are presented concerns and proposals for the new approach. Basically, the new approach proposed is based on organizational and technological perspectives, using the metatheoretical structures that we called "integration abstractions" and "integration semiotics." The new approach proposed has, in fact, the characteristics of the new integration paradigm. The questions that emerge are as follows:

Do we need a new VE integration paradigm?

Does the approach to the VE integration based on the above metatheoretical structures justify calling it a new paradigm?

We think the answer to both questions is yes. Actually, we are facing two new phenomena. The first is that the VE concept has real potential to become a new enterprise organizational paradigm. Expecting that the traditional approach to EI could be simply extended (adding a couple of new functions and tools) is quite optimistic. Actually, how is it possible to expect it when it is already clear that the traditional approach to information systems and organization fails (the second phenomena)? But, on the other hand, what are the criteria to proclaim a new approach as a new paradigm?

Based on the discussion by Kuhn (1996), resuming for the purpose of this chapter, in order to recognize if some proposed model is a new paradigm or not, or in which degree it is, we would say that a new paradigm is characterized by the following:

- A new paradigm emerges when the actual one is in "crisis," i.e., when there are new facts and observations that do not fit the accepted paradigm.
- When the accepted paradigm enters the crisis, a number of candidates emerge to establish a new paradigm.
- In its initial stage, it is a promising concept, rather than a proved concept.
- It attracts a group of researchers who commit themselves to the new paradigm.
- It is either a radical qualitative change and the old paradigm is not comparable or measurable, or it is simply a higher-level theory or one that links a whole group of lower-level theories without substantially changing any.

The new VEI paradigm could be characterized by the following:

- Redefinition of the integration and VE integration in a way that integrates the concept of design, therefore, speaking about the VEI would mean that we speak about the VE design too, and vice versa (i.e., coupled integration and design).
- The base for the VEI model would be a new VE reference model that clearly shows the difference from the traditional enterprise models. This requirement would discard some organizational models called "virtual enterprises," but they would become "extensions" of the "traditional" enterprises (e.g., model by SME, 1993).
- The VEI is the social, communication, pragmatic, and dynamic process where the IT might be used. The VEI process is characterized by its life cycle.
- The number of VEI dimensions and process parameters is of high complexity, or hypercomplexity, horizontally and vertically and over the hyper-plane defined by "abstraction levels" × "semiotic levels". This is the quantitative criteria.

REFERENCES

AMICE Consortium. (1989). *Open systems architecture for CIM*. New York: Springer-Verlag.

Barkmeyer, E. J., Feeney, A. B., Denno, P., Flater, D. W., Libes, D. E., Steves, M. P., & Wallace, E. K. (2003). *Concepts for automating systems integration*. National Institute of Standards and Technology, NISTIR 6928.

Bernus, P., Nemes, L., & Williams, T. J. (1996). *Architectures for enterprise integration*. London: Chapman & Hall.

Browne, J. (1995). The extended enterprise - Manufacturing and the value chain. In L. M. Camarinha-Matos & H. Afsarmanesh (Eds.), *Balanced automated systems - Architectures and design methods*. London: Chapman & Hall.

Brunnermeier, S. B., & Martin, S. A. (1999). *Interoperability cost analysis of the U.S. automotive supply chain*. NC: Research Triangle Institute, Research Triangle Park.

Burbidge, J. L. (1987). *IFIP glossary of terms used in production control*. Amsterdam: IFIP, Elsevier Science.

Byrne, J. (1993, February 8). The virtual corporation: The company of the future will be the ultimate in adaptability, *Business Week*, 37-41.

Camarinha-Matos, L. M., & Afsarmanesh, H. (Eds.). (2004). *Collaborative networked organizations*. Dordrecht: Kluwer.

Camarinha-Matos, L. M., Afsarmanesh, H., Garita, C., & Lima, C. (1997). Towards an architecture for virtual enterprises, *Journal of Intelligent Manufacturing*, 9(2).

Cunha, M. (2003). *Organization of a market of resources for agile and virtual enterprise integration*. PhD Thesis, University of Minho, Braga.

Cunha, M. M., Putnik, G. D., & Ávila, P. (2000). Towards focused markets of resources for agile/virtual enterprise integration. In L. M. Camarinha-Matos et al. (Eds.), *Advances in network enterprises - Virtual organizations, balanced automation and systems integration* (pp. 15-24). Dordrecht: Kluwer.

Cunha, M. M., Putnik, G. D., & Ávila, P. (2004). Virtual enterprises' extended lifecycle. In *Proceedings of the 9th International Symposium SYMORG 2004*, Zlatibor, Serbia, and Montenegro.

Davidow, W. H., & Malone, M. S. (1992). *The virtual corporation: Structuring and revitalizing the corporation for the 21st century*. New York: HarperCollins.

Drucker, P. (1990). The emerging theory of manufacturing. *Harvard Business Review*, (May/June), 94.

Eijnatten, F. M. van, & Putnik, G. D. (2004). Chaos, complexity, learning, and the learning organization: Towards a chaordic enterprise. *The Learning Organization — An International Journal*, 11(6).

Ettlie, J. E., & Stoll, H. W. (1990). *Managing the design-manufacturing processes*. New York: McGraw-Hill.

Falkenberg, E. D. et al. (1998). *A framework of information system concepts — The FRISCO Report* (Web edition), FRISCO, IFIP. Available online *ftp:// ftp.leidenuniv.nl/pub/rul/fri-full.zip*

Filipe, J. (2004). The organizational semiotics normative paradigm. In L. M. Camarinha-Matos & H. Afsarmanesh (Eds.), *Collaborative networked organizations*. Dordrecht: Kluwer.

Filos, E. (2005). Virtuality and the future of organisations. In G. Putnik & M. M. Cunha (Eds.), *Virtual enterprise integration: Technological and organizational perspectives*. Hershey, PA: Idea Group Publishing.

Filos, E., & Banahan, E. (2001). Towards the smart organization: An emerging organizational paradigm and the contribution of the European RTD Programmes. *Journal of Intelligent Manufacturing*, 12(2), 101-119.

Franke, U. (2000). The knowledge-based view (KBV) of the virtual Web, the virtual corporation and the net-vroker. In Y. Malhotra (Ed.), *Knowledge management and virtual orgaizations* (pp. 20-42). Hershey, PA: Idea Group Publishing.

Gazendam, H. W. M. (2001). Semiotics, virtual organizations, and information systems. In K. Liu, R. J. Clarke, P. B. Andersen, & R. K. Stamper (Eds.), *Information, organisation and technology: Studies in organisational semiotics.* Dordrecht: Kluwer.

Goldman, S. L., Nagel, R. N., & Preiss, K. (1995). *Agile competitors and virtual organizations.* New York: Van Nostrand Reinhold.

Goranson, T. (1999). *The agile virtual enterprises — Cases, metrics, tools.* Westport: Quorum Books.

Goranson, T. (2003). Architectural support for the advanced virtual enterprise. *Computers in Industry,* 51, 113-125.

Hesse, W., & Verrijn-Stuart, A. (2000). Towards a theory of information systems: The FRISCO approach. In *Proceedings of the 10th European–Japanese Conference on Information Modelling and Knowledge Bases* (pp. 81-91), Saariselkä, Finland. Presentation of the paper available online *http://www.mathematik.uni-marburg.de/~hesse/papers/FRISCO.pdf*

Hormozi, A. M. (1994). Agile manufacturing. In *Proceedings of the 37th International Conference,* American Production and Inventory Control Society, San Diego.

IMS International. (2003). Intelligent Manufacturing Systems (IMS) program. Available at *http://www.ims.org/index_tor.html*

InterSystems. (2004). Ensemble, InterSystems Corporation. Available online *http://www.intersystems.com /index.html*

InterSystems (2004). *Evaluating integration brokers: Applying 13 technical selection criteria to ensemble universal integration platform.* Available online *www.intersystems.com/ensemble/technology/evaluating-integration-btrokers.pdf*

Jardim-Gonçalves, R., & Steiger-Garção, A. (2001). Putting the pieces together using standards. In A. Gunasekaran (Ed.), *Agile manufacturing: 21st century manufacturing strategy* (pp. 735-757). Amsterdam; New York: Elsevier.

Jhingran, A. D., Mattos, N., & Pirahesh, H. (2002). Information integration: A research agenda. *IBM Systems Journal,* 41(4).

Kim, S. H. (1990). *Designing intelligence.* Oxford: Oxford University Press.

Kosanke, K. (2003). Standardisation in enterprise inter- and intra-organizational integration. In R. Jardim-Gonçalves, J. Cha, & A. Steiger-Garção (Eds.), *Concurrent engineering: Enhanced interoperable systems.* Rotterdam: A.A. Balkema/Exton, PA: Abington.

Kuhn, T. S. (1996). *The structure of scientific revolutions* (3rd ed.). (1st ed., 1962). Chicago: The University of Chicago Press.

Libes, D., Flater, D., Wallace, E., Steves, M., Feeney, A. B., & Barkmeyer, E. (2004). The challenges of automated methods for integrating systems. *SE 2004 — IASTED International Conference on Software Engineering.* Available online *http://www.mel.nist.gov/msidlibrary/doc/challenge.pdf*

Liu, K. (2000). *Semiotics in information systems engineering.* London; New York: Cambridge University Press.

Love, T. (2000, May). Philosophy of design: A meta-theoretical structure for design theory. *Design Studies,* 21(3), 293-313.

McMahon, C., & Browne, J. (1993). *CADCAM — From principles to practise.* Reading, MA: Addison-Wesley.

MetaMatrix. (2001). *Enterprise information integration*, White Paper, MetaMatrix, Inc. Available online *www.metamatrix.com/whitepapers.html*

Miles, R. E., & Snow, C. C. (1984). Fit, failure and the Hall of Fame. *California Management Review*, XXVI(3), 10-28.

Miles, R. E., & Snow, C. C. (1986). Organizations: New concepts for new forms. *California Management Review*, XXVIII(3), 62-73.

Moor, A., & Weigand, H. (2002). Towards a semiotic communications quality model. In K. Liu, R. J. Clarke, P. B. Andersen, R. K. Stamper, & E. -S. Abou-Zeid (Eds.), *Organizational semiotics: Evolving a science of information systems* (pp. 275-285). Dordrecht: Kluwer.

Nagel, R., & Dove, R. (1993). *21st century manufacturing enterprise strategy*. Bethlehem, PA: Iacocca Institute, Lehigh University.

Nell, J. G. (1998). Enterprise representation: An analysis of standards issues. Available online *http://www.mel.nist.gov/msidlibrary/doc/jimnell95.pdf*

Parunak, H. Van D. (1997). Technologies for virtual enterprises. Available online *http://www.erim.org/~vparunak/agilejnl,.pdf*

Petrie, C. (Ed.). (1992). *Enterprise integration modeling*. Cambridge, MA: MIT Press.

Putnik, G. D. (2001). BM virtual enterprise architecture reference model. In A. Gunasekaran (Ed.), *Agile manufacturing: 21st century manufacturing strategy* (pp. 73-93). Amsterdam; New York: Elsevier.

Putnik, G. D., & van Eijnatten, F. M. (2004). Chaordic systems thinking for learning organization: Reflections and some suggestions for use. *The Learning Organization — An International Journal*, 11(6).

Putnik, G. D., Cunha, M. M., Sousa, R., & Avila, P. (2005). BM virtual enterprise — A model for dynamics and virtuality. In G. Putnik & M. M. Cunha (Eds.), *Virtual enterprise integration: Technological and organizational perspectives*. Hershey, PA: Idea Group Publishing.

Ray, S. R. (2002). Interoperability standards in the Semantic Web. *Journal of Computing and Information Science in Engineering*, 2(March).

Ray, S. R. (2003). Manufacturing Interoperability. In *Proceedings of the 13th Annual International Symposium — INCOSE 2003*.

Scheer, A. -W. (1991). *CIM: Towards the factory of the future*. Heidelberg: Springer-Verlag.

SME. (1993). *The new manufacturing enterprise wheel*. Dearborn, MI: Society of Manufacturing Engineers.

Staffend, G. S. (1992). Making the virtual factory a reality. In *Proceedings of AUTOFACT '92 Conference*, Detroit.

Stamper, R. (2000). New directions for systems analysis and design. In J. Filipe (Ed.), *Enterprise information systems* (pp. 14-39). Dordrecht: Kluwer.

Stamper, R. K. (1996). Signs, information, norms and systems. In B. Holmqvist et al. (Eds.), *Signs at work*. Berlin: De Gruyter.

Stevens, J. (1998). Integrating the supply chain. *Int. J. Phy. Dist. Mat. Man.*, 13(1), 37-56.

Towill, D. R. (2001). Engineering the agile supply chain. In A. Gunasekaran (Ed.), *Agile manufacturing: 21st century manufacturing strategy* (pp. 377-396). Amsterdam; New York: Elsevier.

Uschold, M., King, M., Moralee, S., & Zorgios, Y. (1997). *The enterprise ontology.* Edinburgh: AIAI, The University of Edinburgh.

VEA. (1998). The virtual enterprise concept. The Virtual Enterprises Association. Available online *http://www.vea.org*

Veilleux, R. (1987). *Dictionary of manufacturing terms.* Dearborn, MI: Society of Manufacturing Engineers.

Vernadat, F. (1996). *Enterprise modeling and integration.* London; New York: Chapman & Hall.

ENDNOTES

1   For example, computer integrated manufacturing (CIM), intelligent manufacturing system (IMS), one-of-a-kind-production (OKP), matrix organization, concurrent engineering (CE) based organization, holonic enterprise, bionic enterprise, fractal enterprise, lean enterprise, focused enterprise, agile enterprise, etc.

2   Regarding smart organizations (SO), the concept draws much from the general idea of networked and virtual organizations, although the precedence of SO versus VE is not clear. Anyway, SOs were an action line, together with dynamic networked organisations and dynamic value constellations of the Key Action II (New Methods of Work and Electronic Commerce) of IST - EU programme with "a strong focus on the 'virtual organisation'" (Filos, 2005).

3   "Dynamic network" refers the dynamics of the network's organizational structure, i.e., along the time the network's structure changes.

4   Other definitions could be found as well, e.g., "an organization distributed geographically and whose work is coordinated through electronic communication," using Internet, EDI (electronic data interchange), e-mail, and, frequently related to electronic commerce (e-commerce, e-business, etc.) and other Internet-based services.

5   When we compare "the potentials of VE," in fact, we refer to the features of an "ideal" VE model. Naturally, in practice, the real VE models will be somewhere in between.

6   For the enterprise's knowledge protection, various mechanisms could be used, e.g., trust assurance and management, legal framework, etc.

7   "Guilds" is the MR-like concept identified as a possible scenario for the virtual organizations by the MIT 21st Century Manifesto Working Group in their discussion paper, "What we really want? A manifesto for the organizations of the 21st Century," within the "MIT Initiative on Inventing the Organizations of the 21st Century."

8   Minor modifications of the original text were made by the authors of this chapter, in order to adapt it to this text's context.

9   Collaborative networks are considered a model of VE as well.

10   Minor adaptations of the original text were made by the authors of this chapter.

11   The original text refers to "abstractions in Design Theory." The "...abstractions in VEI theory" were introduced by the authors of this chapter.

[12]   The same abstraction levels are proposed for research of CST for Learning Organization (Putnik & Eijnatten, 2004). The last paragraph "Looking at the list..." is from Putnik and Eijnatten (2004) and was paraphrased for VEI.

[13]   Paraphrased from Putnik and Eijnatten (2004). The original text refers to "a complexity paradigm in CST."

[14]   "FRISCO = FRamework of Information System Concepts, IFIP WG8.1 Task Group, established 1988 because of concern about harmful confusion due to (or manifesting itself in) fuzzy terminology and absence of a consistent conceptual reference."

Section II

Societal and Organizational Requirements

Chapter II

Virtuality and the Future of Organizations

Erastos Filos

European Commission, Information Society Directorate-General, Belgium

ABSTRACT

This chapter aims at drawing a picture of how organizations are likely to develop in the context of "virtuality," i.e., following the impact of technologies relevant to the information society. Organizations will expand their traditional boundaries to form new organizational patterns that will allow them to adapt to the changing environment of the information society as well as to exploit the opportunities of a digital economy. The chapter, therefore, shows how research, in particular research that was supported under the European Commission's R&D programs, has played a significant role in shaping these developments. The research aimed at developing the underpinning information and communication technologies as well as at understanding the business processes and the socioeconomic impact of virtual organizations. Although many of the features of this new organizational paradigm are still not fully understood, there is hope that organizations in the future will be smart in various respects and will develop in a way that maximizes the leveraging of knowledge and innovation.

INTRODUCTION

During the industrial revolution, enterprises changed dramatically from close-knit rural communities to a core of structured and independent urban organizations. In the 1980s and 1990s these became more global and collaborative, a transition encouraged by fiercer competition, the introduction of information and communication technologies (ICTs), and the rapid emergence of the electronic business paradigm. The enterprise in the digital age is *internet*worked (Kalakota, 1998), i.e., virtual and interlinked and networked on various levels. At the information infrastructure level, the interlinking happens via the Internet, which enables "boundarylessness" and the formation of virtual organizations. At the organizational level, hierarchies are supplemented or replaced by networked teams. At the competencies level, intellectual capital is shared or traded via knowledge networking and associated tools (Filos & Banahan, 2001a).

The trend toward virtual collaborative scenarios has given rise to a blurring of organizational boundaries. For many business organizations, strategic partnerships have become central to competitive success in fast-changing global environments. Because many of the skills and resources essential to an organization's capabilities lie outside its boundaries, and as such, outside management's direct control, collaborations are no longer considered an option, but are a necessity (Doz & Hamel, 1998). Organizations, profit and nonprofit, will more than ever rely on an increased ability to conceive, shape, and sustain a wide variety of virtual collaborations.

Furthermore, the uncertain and fast-changing environments of the digital economy require new organizational abilities and competencies. Competitive advantage will be derived from organizational flexibility, rapidity, and adaptability, which go beyond mere efficiency objectives. Thus, the impact of virtuality on an organization's behavior and management is far reaching.

The traditional concept of the organization as a hierarchical structure of collocated personnel managed by a set of deterministic rules is disappearing. Because organizations are becoming more dependent on technology, and as technology moves toward invisibility by becoming user-intuitive and ubiquitous, will organizations be deemed to follow?

EUROPEAN R&D PROGRAMMES' CONTRIBUTION TO THE DEVELOPMENT OF THE VIRTUAL ORGANIZATION

The European R&D Programmes have played a substantial role in supporting the development of technologies and applications relevant to digital business. Key to this were R&D efforts in electronic commerce and digital business on the basis of virtual organization concepts. In the early 1990s, R&D focused on concurrent engineering (Fan & Filos, 1999), computer-supported collaborative work (CSCW), and product and process data modelling technologies as key activities. The Advanced Communication Technologies and Services programme (ACTS, 1999) and the Telematics Applications programme (TAP, 1999) were successful in setting up strong CSCW pilots. These and other activities provided the first steps toward remote working and distributed collaborative engineering (Filos & Ouzounis, 2003).

In parallel to these European activities, the United States supported research for the virtual organization under defence projects funded by DARPA and through NIST and NSF projects (Goranson, 1999).

Activities Under the IT Programme (Esprit)

Supporting the development of electronic commerce technologies and, in particular, technologies that enable distributed (electronic) business, has been a priority of the Commission's R&D programmes over the last decade. The 1997 work programme of Esprit (ESPRIT, 1997) contained explicit support for R&D relevant to the virtual enterprise, under "networked multi-site applications" in the domain of High-performance Computing and Networking, under "innovation for business pilots" in the Technologies for Business Processes domain, and under an action "management tools for the agile enterprise" in the Integration in Manufacturing domain. Under the European Commission's Fourth Framework Programme for research, between 1994 and 1998, more than 50 industry-led projects were set up-shared cost funding with 50% industrial contribution — with funding support of 100 million euro. In addition to regular consultations with industry, a number of user group reference projects were established that brought together major industrial users of IT and the vendor community. The common aim of these projects was to set long-term targets for, and give direction to, the research efforts of the IT industry in order to meet a well-formulated industrial need. The AIT user group reference project dealt with the automotive and aerospace industries (AIT, 2001). The initiative comprised 22 R&D projects that also had major impact on standardization developments. The projects were operating concurrently within a harmonization framework (Garas & Naccari, 2001). Forty percent of organizations participating in Esprit collaborations were user industry enterprises. In total, 65% of participants in Esprit were industrial companies. Until 1999, R&D support for the "virtual enterprise" in Europe was mainly through Esprit and its international cooperation branch under the Intelligent Manufacturing Systems initiative (IMS, 2004).

Activities Under the Information Society Technologies (IST) Programme

In 1999, the Information Society Technologies programme (IST, 1999) emerged as an integrated programme from the previous Esprit, ACTS, and Telematics programmes. In the IST work programme (1999), the perspective had changed from the virtual enterprise to any type of virtual organization. The Key Action II (New Methods of Work and Electronic Commerce) of IST, with its action lines "Dynamic Networked Organizations," "Smart Organizations," and "Dynamic Value Constellations" now had a strong focus on the "virtual organization." The R&D programme "Competitive and Sustainable Growth" followed suit. In its 2000 work programme (GROWTH, 2000), a dedicated "Targeted Research Action 1.7" focused on the extended manufacturing enterprise.

Between 1999 and 2002, under IST, more than 200 R&D projects targeting organization, e-business, and e-work research were launched, with a total budget of about 450 million euro (Zobel & Filos, 2002). These fall into three subareas: ICT aspects; work, business, and organizational issues; and the socioeconomic perspective.

ICT Aspects of Virtual Organizations

The part of this project portfolio dealing with (virtual) organizational platforms, i.e., activities related to the design and development of generic infrastructures to support collaborative business in a networked environment, involved issues such as safe communications, interoperability and tools integration, information and knowledge sharing, repositories, coordination mechanisms, and collaborative environments. Several projects addressed aspects of basic virtual organization infrastructure. These projects provided a critical mass for a Europe-wide understanding of the problem, and efforts aimed at pulling together these activities toward the emergence of a general "plug-and-do-business" architecture for interoperability (Bacquet & Naccari, 2002; Doumeingts & Chen, 2003). The issues involved are complex. For example, participants in a virtual organization will aim to preserve a company's right to make local choices and solutions and to protect proprietary information (especially the part of information that should not be shared). A company may provide access to information only to those partners with whom agreements have been established. Project GLOBEMEN aimed at creating an IT infrastructure to support globally distributed and dynamically networked operations in one-of-a-kind industries (Karvonen et al., 2003). COMMA and BUSINESS ARCHITECT made extensive use of modelling and knowledge sharing to support virtual enterprise process integration. Those projects contributed to the understanding of the different levels of interoperability in a virtual enterprise.

As far as the characteristics and requirements regarding interoperability and information exchange are concerned, innovative approaches are required. Interoperability should become a "design principle," while aiming to preserve the diversity, autonomy, and heterogeneity of components and environments. For example, project ECOLNET sought to validate different business strategies for independent small and medium-sized enterprises (SMEs), focusing on their national market. E-COLLEG investigated an infrastructure to establish a backbone for collaborative engineering (Witczynski & Pawlak, 2002), CO-OPERATE focused on coordination of manufacturing planning and control activities in supply chain management, and WHALES developed a planning and management infrastructure for distributed organizations working as networks on large-scale engineering projects.

The projects portfolio was strong in demonstrating the feasibility of operating the virtual organization. The technologies used involved the Java framework, CORBA, XML, Web services, multiagents, and modelling tools based on UML. In general, the aim was to use standards whenever possible. This aspect is particularly clear with respect to de facto standards being proposed by industry groups such as OMG, WfMC, W3C, and ebXML.

The significance of virtual organization modelling and interoperability of applications arose from the need to model the virtual organization as a means to properly understand and manage it. A problem with existing business process modelers lies in how to translate one model based on one proprietary modelling technique into an equivalent model represented by another. One strategy pursued in Europe was in agreeing on a basic language that makes such transformations possible. Consensus was reached, and the Unified Enterprise Modelling Language was defined (UEML, 2004).

Some projects dealt with ontologies, e.g., conceptual information models that describe things that exist in a domain and that have a purpose:

- To support human understanding and organizational communication
- To be machine-processable and, thus, facilitate content-based access, communication, and integration across different information systems.

A decade of international research has led to the creation of ontology languages, editors, reasoning techniques, and development guidelines. Various languages for ontology specification and implementation are now available. These languages have built-in reasoning techniques, and they also allow for the development of special-purpose reasoning services.

An area of impact is the Semantic Web, in which computers "find the meaning" of data in automated Web services, such as functional agents. DAML and OIL, developed by the World Wide Web Consortium and the European OIL community (W3C, 2004), provide a rich set of constructs with which to create ontologies and to mark up information so that it becomes machine readable. A significant number of European projects addressed knowledge technologies in the context of the virtual organization and business collaboration (Filos, 2002).

Work, Business, and Organizational Issues

This subarea involved reference models and architectures, e.g., the specification of logical reference architectures for new/emerging cooperative organizations by identifying the main functional blocks, interactions, actors and their roles, resources, and value systems, as well as the definition and the characterization of collaborative business models, the forms of cooperation in networked environments, and means to assess the effectiveness of virtual organizations. This work involved virtual organization reference models, collaborative business models (and related case studies), cooperation methodologies, and performance measurement. The projects addressed centralized support services as well as services that are distributed across the virtual organization (Hartel et al., 2002; Kazi et al., 2002; Katzy & Sung, 2003).

Some projects addressed business functions of the various parts of the life cycle of a virtual organization. Research activities included partner registration and search, marketplace management, e-procurement and negotiation, distributed business process planning and management, etc., with a particular focus on domain-independent services covering the various phases of the life cycle of a virtual organization. They also comprised supervision and monitoring, as well as specialized services, such as contract modelling and negotiation, a support infrastructure to help virtual enterprises address the legal issues involved, as well as a Web-based infrastructure for alternative online dispute resolution for SMEs (Gouimenou, 2001).

The Socioeconomic Perspective

Between 1999 and 2002, socioeconomic research within an IST was a significant nontechnological research activity that aimed at complementing the R&D activities. It was implemented through a series of calls for proposals. The primary scope of this research domain was research in methods and tools and the new phenomena brought about by ICT-induced change. As such, the main recipients of results were the Programme's research community, industry, and policy makers (Hayfa & Filos, 2003). More than 40 projects addressed socio-organizational or socioeconomic issues, i.e., industrial and organizational aspects of the digital economy (e-business, e-work), as well as societal aspects; e-business models and intangible assets; impact assessment, mainly at the microlevel; corporate social responsibility; and statistical indicators. Half of these projects concerned the major challenges industry and economy face because of the new digital technologies and applications.

A number of key legal and regulatory issues emerged as a result of this research work. Some were explicitly addressed, for example, legal aspects of virtual enterprises, contract law (intra-/interorganizational or that of individuals), alternative dispute resolution, digital rights management, intellectual property rights, consumer protection, and legal aspects (Merz et al., 2001; Hassan et al., 2001; van Schoubroeck et al., 2001; Carter, 2002).

All of these activities are likely to contribute to the definition of a facilitating framework for virtual organizations (Camarinha-Matos et al., 2004).

THE CHANGING ORGANIZATIONAL PARADIGM

The virtual organization is not just an object of academic endeavour. Many large industrial companies, e.g., aeronautical and car manufacturers, maintain remote (or "virtual") business links with their suppliers and customers. These links facilitate collaboration and the extension of business processes and activities beyond the companies' borders. However, the degree of virtual collaboration and the maturity of ICTs used are often not adequate. Many business processes are still far from automated, with productivity gains yet to be exploited.

Typical examples of virtual enterprises today include value-adding service providers. For example, a travel agency that provides flight ticket reservations, hotel reservations, conference booking services, as well as a full vacation holidays package should be considered as a virtual enterprise, in a sense that parts of these services are provided by other specialized companies, e.g., airlines, hotels, etc.

Various attempts have been made to define the "virtual enterprise." Goranson (1999), for example, classified the virtual enterprise according to four types of "opportunistic aggregation": opportunity-driven, capability-driven, supplier-chain, and bidding consortia. Other researchers (Camarinha-Matos & Afsarmanesh, 1999) aim at classifying the different types of virtual enterprises according to their characteristics and requirements with respect to ICTs, organizations, and work practices. These include duration, topology, coordination, and visibility scope. Their ultimate aim is to establish a virtual enterprise taxonomy.

Organizational Teaming

With the broad advent of virtual enterprises and the emergence of new electronic business paradigms, terminology is becoming confusing, and expressions such as the "extended enterprise," the "virtual organization," the "networked organization," the "value net" — often used interchangeably — require clarification:

- **Extended enterprise vs. virtual enterprise:** The concept of the extended enterprise is the closest "rival" term to the virtual enterprise. It is better applied to an organizational aggregation in which a dominant enterprise "extends" its boundaries to some of its suppliers. On the other hand, a virtual enterprise can be seen as a more "democratic" structure, in which the cooperation with other enterprises is peer-to-peer. Also, while the extended enterprise concept may also be applied to a more long-term collaboration, the virtual enterprise is understood as an "organizational project," with an aim to dissolve at the end of its lifetime. Similarly, the *organizational network* is a pool of enterprises with the capability to cooperate virtually and be potential partners in a virtual enterprise. These enterprises are "registered" in a directory, where their core competencies are "known" or "declared." Based on this information, a virtual enterprise integrator can select partners to form a new virtual enterprise.

- **Virtual organization:** This is a generalization of the concept of the virtual enterprise, comprising a network of organizations that share resources and skills to achieve a mission/goal, but this network is not necessarily limited to business enterprises. An example of a virtual organization could be a "virtual municipality," a virtual (faster and more efficient) collaboration between the city hall, municipal water distribution services, internal revenue services, public leisure facilities, cadastre services, etc.

- **Value net (or e-business community):** This is a business environment ("ecosystem") in which clusters of *internetworked* organizations collaborate around a particular technology and make use of a common architecture to deliver independent elements of value. This environment grows with the number of participating organizations (Kalakota, 1998).

Organizational "Smartness"

The digital economy resembles an ecology of organisms, interlinked and coevolving, constantly in flux, deeply tangled, and ever expanding at its edges. Because it is characterized by uncertainty and unpredictability, organizations will have to cope with this new environment. Ultimately, this will change the ways organizations relate, to each other and to the individuals who provide their core competencies and to their environment. What will this "smartness" involve?

First, organizations, like complex organisms, need to develop a "nervous system" that will enable them to thrive on chaos and to guide them through turbulent times. This organizational nervous system will provide functions such as sensing and learning, communications (internal and external), coordination, and memory. In fast-moving, unpredictable environments, "nervous system" functions are essential to provide the organization with anticipatory, filtering, empathic, learning, and adaptive capabilities in real time (Por, 2000).

Second, economic activity seems to follow a fractal pattern. It shows a similar structure and obeys similar rules for creating value at the level of the economy, at the organizational level, and at the individual level. Organizations that are adaptive to their economic environment are open, with permeable boundaries, operating at the edge of chaos (Davis & Meyer, 1998).

Third, the fittest will survive. Sustainable innovation is the result of a persistent disequilibrium between chaos and order. Organizations become fit through the variety and diversity of concepts and ideas that breed innovation. Cross-functional, multidisciplinary teams are capable of developing the creativity that is an essential element to this. Combined with openness, by developing or taking up ideas from the market or from interorganizational exchanges, organizational fitness grows.

Fourth, be big and small at the same time. The essence of an ecosystem is the balance between big and small organisms dependent on one another. Likewise, organizations must be big to be capable of large-scale investments, and they must be small, nimble, unified around a purpose, and capable of paying attention to the details of important relationships (e.g., "value nets" in Figures 1 and 2).

The implications of the above trends for organizations have led to a proliferation of adjectives applied primarily to enterprises: among others, the agile enterprise, networked organization, virtual company, extended enterprise, ascendant organization (Wickens, 1998), knowledge enterprise (Nonaka & Takeuchi, 1995), learning organization (Senge, 1990), and ambidextrous organization (O'Reilly & Tushman, 2004). The definitions all have their nuances, deriving from the emphasis on one or another combination of the aspects above. Ultimately, however, they all point to the need to respond to the changing landscape of the digital economy in dynamic and innovative ways.

Figure 1. Networked organizations and associated types of collaboration (Filos & Banahan, 2001b)

Organisational form	Organisational structure	Type of collaboration
corporate, co-located	functional units + cross-functional co-located teams	intra-organisational
extended enterprise	functional units + virtual teams	supply-chain integration
virtual enterprise	organisational 'project': virtual teams	strategic alliance, co-operation agreement, joint venture
value network/ e-business community	organisational network of competencies: virtual teams	economic web

Figure 2. From tightly and vertically integrated organizations to the "value nets" of smart organizations

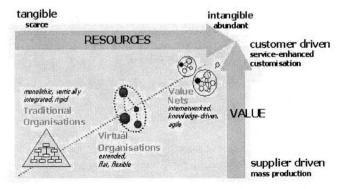

Within the European Commission's IST programme, the term "smart organization" was coined for organizations that are knowledge-driven, *internet*worked, and dynamically adaptive to new organizational forms and practices, learning as well as being agile in their ability to create and exploit the opportunities offered by the digital economy. Smart organizations involve more than the capability of setting up and exploiting a digital infrastructure and the ability to enter into a virtual collaboration with other partner organizations (Filos & Banahan, 2001b).

Virtuality, thus, provides the essential precondition for organizations to become smart in a digital economy.

Intangible Resources

In a digital economy, value becomes increasingly dependent on intangible resources. Whereas industrial-age organizations derive value from investment in tangible assets, such as plant and machinery, smart organizations rely on "smart" resources, such as information, knowledge, brands, relationships, and the capability to innovate.

Brands are a source of value, not unlike capital. For the owner organization, they represent accumulated surplus value turned into client loyalty, which translates into lower marketing costs, higher prices, or larger market share (Davis & Meyer, 1998). In digital markets, brands are an invaluable source of trust and orientation to consumers who are looking for quality and security. Many organizations invest heavily in building a reputation that is conveyed by an associated brand image. Some have even outsourced almost all other activities and keep a focus on managing the brand as their core competence.

To leverage the power of knowledge, one must know where to find it, and once found, know what to do with it. According to Nonaka and Takeuchi (1995), a basic precondition for organizational knowledge to grow is the "hyperlinking" of the organization. In their view, a value-creating company is made up of three interconnected layers: the (bureaucratic) business system, flexible project teams, and a (corporate) knowledge base. The bureaucratic structure efficiently implements, exploits, and accumulates new knowledge. Project teams generate conceptual and synthesized knowledge. The efficiency and stability of the bureaucracy is combined in this model with the effectiveness and dynamism of the project team. Moreover, the knowledge base serves as a "clearinghouse" for the new knowledge generated in the context of the business system and that of the project teams. This way, the hyperlinked organization has the capability to convert knowledge from inside the organization by being an open system that also features continuous and dynamic knowledge interaction with outside partners.

Another key success factor for value creation in the digital economy that is facilitated by connectivity is the ability to foster relationships. In a networked economy, hyperlinks do more than link information sources over the Internet. They link people (Levine et al., 2000) and organizations (Damaskopoulos, 2003; Mentzas, 2003).

Fuzzy Management

Relationships between more than two people can be structured either as hierarchies or as networks. In the absence of plentiful information (e.g., on the battlefield), the most intelligent way to construct and manage a complex organization is via a hierarchy. However, when information is plentiful, rank is replaced by peer competence. Organizations looking to the future are coming to recognize the synergies inherent in multifaceted relationships with customers and collaborators.

Industrial-age organizations were highly mechanistic systems. They evolved to cope with an environment that was, generally speaking, stable and predictable. The metaphor of "organization as machine" clearly has limited relevance to organizations in the digital age, where the economic environment is constantly shifting.

A more appropriate metaphor, perhaps, would be to view organizations as organic systems, constantly evolving to cope with the demands of their environments. While this view of organizations as living organisms seems more appropriate, it fails to illustrate the fact that in a networked economy, the roles of "superior" and "subordinate" are becoming somewhat blurred, and management becomes fuzzy, i.e., laid-back, trust-based, less controlling.

Organizations are communities, not properties (Handy, 1997): They are communities of partners, colleagues, or associates who share a vested interest and common purpose. A community is a set of relationships, a shared asset, created through the investment of its members. They depend on human interaction, individuals who share information and experiences, something that is only possible where there is a high level of trust. Trust is a key issue in determining the success of relationships in the digital economy. The value of the partner's contribution is recognized and used for the good of the community.

Digital-age organizations, unlike those of the industrial age, will, therefore, not seek to control their environments, recognizing that any such attempt would, at best, fail, and at worst, stifle the creativity and imagination necessary to support innovation. In a digital economy, markets are global, and participants are free to focus and refocus their commitment as they see fit. With this in mind, management style is evolving from one that placed emphasis on planning, organizing, and controlling, to one that emphasizes providing vision, motivation, and inspiration.

Or, as Wigand put it:

"Organizations do not achieve and maintain effectiveness by technology alone. Studies have shown that the effectiveness of an organization is contingent upon the degree of fit it achieves between the technology and its structural design. Since organizations are not things, but people, it is ultimately people who will be changed by the impact of information technologies. As organizational structures change, the distribution of power will change as well." (Wigand, 1985, p. 256)

THE DISAPPEARING ORGANIZATION

The digital economy challenges the organization in many ways. First, ICTs and globalization lead to a blurring of organizational boundaries. Second, uncertain and fast-changing environments require smart organizational abilities, such as flexibility, speed, adaptability, and techniques to deal with complexity. Third, value creation becomes more dependent on intangible assets, such as knowledge, relationships, and brands.

Digital-age organizations are becoming increasingly dependent on technology. As technology becomes prevalent and ubiquitous, it moves toward invisibility. Is the changing organizational paradigm, as discussed above, driving organizations to follow suit?

Beyond Physics

A rule similar to the Heisenberg Uncertainty Principle could be assumed to apply to organizations. The Heisenberg principle says that in the quantum world, it is impossible to have precise simultaneous knowledge of a particle's momentum and its location. In other words, the principle says, if it is possible to determine (somehow) exactly the location of the particle, then the uncertainty about its momentum must be very high, and vice versa.

The corresponding variables in the organizational context are "impact" and "locality." Organizational impact here means innovation momentum and operational efficiency. Organizational locality implies stability and structural rigidity (as opposed to "boundarylessness," i.e., fuzziness at the organization's borderline).

Following the analogy of the Heisenberg Uncertainty Principle, a great uncertainty — a large delta ("Δ") — in an organization's impact should be directly related to a rigidly structured, closed organization (corresponding to a very small delta in organizational locality). The tighter an organization's structure, e.g., the more it shuts itself off against outside ideas and knowledge, the more uncertain its dynamism and innovative capabilities are likely to be.

On the other hand, the larger the organization's nonlocality ("boundarylessness"), the more ideas and knowledge can be leveraged. Organizational impact becomes almost certain.

Or, mathematically:

$$\Delta(\text{org. locality}) \times \Delta(\text{org. impact}) = \text{constant}$$

Does the Disappearance of Technology Lead to a Disappearance of the Organization?

One of the trends in the evolution of technology is that the more pervasive, ubiquitous, and commonplace it becomes, the more it tends to disappear. This disappearance can be explained only partly as the result of the lack of attention it gets by moving from the centre to the periphery of people's attention. Disappearance also means that it becomes truly invisible (miniaturized) and embedded in everyday objects. Examples for this are the ubiquity of the electricity grid, the ubiquity of electrical motors, the embeddedness of computer chips, the ubiquity of software and communications in almost all objects.

As ICTs are becoming commonplace in today's business environment, leading to organizational boundarylessness and virtuality, the business organization could disappear, too. It may ultimately be that organizations develop into "markets" of competent individuals, or what Deal and Kennedy (1982) called the "atomized organization." Whichever form a business organization may take in the future, organizational competence will have to rely on the collective knowledge of empowered individuals and the organization's ability to leverage it.

CONCLUSIONS

This chapter aimed at drawing a picture of the changing organizational paradigm based on technologies for the information society ("virtuality"). The European R&D Programmes have played a significant part in these developments. The research efforts aimed at understanding and modelling virtual organizations and digital business processes. Still, many of the features of the new organizational paradigm are not understood, but there is hope that organizations in the future will become smart in various respects. The unprecedented opportunities offered by the information society for individuals to relate with one another, to work, and to do business in a digital environment will change the way organizations relate to each other and to the individuals that provide their core competencies, the basis of their new "raison d'être."

And, as technology is moving into invisibility, by becoming user-intuitive, though indispensable, a similar evolution may be expected for organizations. They will undoubtedly be there, but they will become invisible, though smart and ubiquitous, but more focused on the individual and his well-being.

ACKNOWLEDGMENTS

The views expressed in this chapter are those of the author and do not necessarily reflect the views of the European Commission.

REFERENCES

ACTS (1999). Advanced Communications Technologies and Services programme, European Commission, Brussels. Available online *http://www.cordis.lu/acts/home.html*

AIT (2001). Advanced information technology programme (see Garas & Naccari, 2001). Similar projects involving the process industries (PRIMA), and the construction or large-scale engineering industries ELSEWISE (see Mitrovic et al., 1999; MacAffer & Garas, 1999); of similar impact on the furniture industry was the project FUNSTEP (see Jardim-Gonçalves et al., 1999).

Bacquet, J., & Naccari, F. N. (2002). "Plug and do business" and the European R&D Programmes. In L. Camarinha-Matos (Ed.), *Collaborative business ecosystems and virtual enterprises* (pp. 283-292). IFIP TC5/WG5.5 Third Working Conference on Infrastructures for Virtual Enterprises (PRO-VE'02), May 1-3, Sesimbra, Portugal. Boston: Kluwer.

Camarinha-Matos, L.M., & Afsarmanesh, H. (1999). The virtual enterprise concept. In L. M. Camarinha-Matos & H. Afsarmanesh (Eds.), *Infrastructures for virtual enter-prises: Networking industrial enterprises* (pp. 3-30). Boston: Kluwer Academic Publishers.

Camarinha-Matos, L. M. et al. (2004). A strategic roadmap for advanced virtual organizations. In L. M. Camarinha-Matos & H. Afsarmanesh (Eds.), *Collaborative networked organizations: A research agenda for emerging business models* (pp. 289-312). Norwell, MA: Kluwer Academic Publishers.

Carter, C. (2002). The impact of contractual support for ICTs on working practices. In Stanford-Smith et al. (Eds.) (pp. 1291-1298).

Cunningham, P. et al. (Eds.). (2003). *Building the knowledge economy: Issues, applications, case studies.* Amsterdam: IOS Press.

Damaskopoulos, P. (2003). Toward a network topology of the knowledge economy: Organizational passages from knowledge to innovation. In Cunningham et al. (Eds.) (pp. 866-873).

Davis, S., & Meyer, C. (1998). *Blurr: The speed of change in the connected economy.* Oxford: Capstone.

Deal, T. E., & Kennedy, A. A. (1982). *Corporate cultures.* Reading, MA: Addison-Wesley.

Doumeingts, G., & Chen, D. (2003). Interoperability development for enterprise applications and software. In Cunningham et al. (pp. 207-214).

Doz, Y. L., & Hamel, G. (1998). *Alliance advantage:. The art of creating value through partnering.* Boston: Harvard Business School Press.

ESPRIT. (1997). European Strategic Programme for Research in Information Technologies (Esprit), Building the Information Society, Work Programme 1997, European Commission, Directorate-General III--Industry, Brussels. Available online *http://www.cordis.lu/esprit/*

Fan, I. -S., & Filos, E. (1999). Concurrent engineering: Esprit-supported R&D projects in a world-wide context. In Wognum et al. (Eds.) (pp. 177-189).

Filos, E. (2002). European collaborative R&D projects related to the "smart organization." A first evaluation of activities and implications for construction. In Z. Turk & R. Scherer (Eds.), *eWork and eBusiness in architecture, engineering and construction* (pp. 27-32). Lisse: Swets and Zeitlinger.

Filos, E., & Banahan, E. (2001a). Will the organization disappear? The challenges of the new economy and future perspectives. In L. M. Camarinha-Matos, H. Afsharmanesh, & R. J. Rabelo (Eds.), *E-business and virtual enterprises: Managing business-to-business cooperation* (pp. 3-20). Dordrecht: Kluwer.

Filos, E., & Banahan, E. (2001b). Towards the smart organization: An emerging organizational paradigm and the contribution of the European RTD Programmes. *Journal of Intelligent Manufacturing, 12*(2), 101-119.

Filos, E., & Ouzounis, V. K. (2003). Virtual organizations: Technologies, trends, standards and the contribution of the European R&D programs. *International Journal of Computer Applications in Technology, 18*(1-4), 6-26.

Garas, F. K., & Naccari, F. N. (2001). Assessment of the AIT initiative, report to the European Commission, Brussels. Available online *http://www.cordis.lu/ist/ka2/rptspolicyconf.htm*

Goranson, T. H. (1999). *The agile virtual enterprise: Cases, metrics, tools.* Westport; London: Quorum.

Gouimenou, J. (2001). E-Arbitration-T: An alternative dispute resolution for SMEs. In Stanford-Smith & Chiozza (Eds.) (pp. 526-531).

GROWTH (2000). Competitive and sustainable growth programme, Work Programme 2000, European Commission, Directorate-General Research, Brussels. Available online *http://www.cordis.lu/growth/*

Handy, C. (1997). *The hungry spirit.* London: Hutchinson.

Hartel, I. et al. (2002). The information roadmap of virtual enterprises. In Stanford-Smith et al. (Eds.) (pp. 1380-1387).

Hassan, T. et al. (2001). e-LEGAL: Dismantling the legal barriers to ICT up-take in virtual enterprises. In Stanford-Smith & Chiozza (Eds.) (pp. 602-608).

Hayfa, T., & Filos, E. (2003). How ICTs impact policy-making, Thirteen IST project examples, European Commission, Directorate-General Information Society, Brussels. Available online *ftp://ftp.cordis.lu/pub/ist/docs/dir_c/rd_report_en.pdf*

IMS (2004). Intelligent manufacturing systems initiative. Available online *http://www.ims.org*

IST (1999). Information Society Technologies, Work Programme 1999, European Commission, Directorate-General Information Society, Brussels. Available online *http://www.cordis.lu/ist/ist-fp5.html*

Jardim-Gonçalves, R., Sousa, P. C., Pimentão, J. P., & Steiger-Garcão, A. (1999). Furniture commerce electronically assisted by way of a standard-based integrated environment. In Wognum et al. (Eds.) (pp. 129-136).

Kalakota, R. (1998). Joined at the bit. The emergence of the e-business community. In D. Tapscott, A. Lowy, & D. Ticoll (Eds.), *Blueprint to the digital economy: Creating wealth in the era of e-business.* New York: McGraw-Hill.

Karvonen, I. et al. (Eds.). (2003). Global Engineering and Manufacturing in Enterprise Networks. GLOBEMEN. VTT Symposium, Helsinki, December 9-10, 2002. Available online *http://www.vtt.fi/inf/pdf/symposiums/2003/S224.pdf*

Katzy, B. R., & Sung, G. (2003). State-of-the-art virtual organization modeling. In Cunningham et al. (Eds.) (pp. 959–966).

Kazi, A. S., Hannus, M., & Ollus, M. (2002). Layered architecture for inter-enterprise collaboration. In Stanford-Smith et al. (Eds.) (pp. 1373-1379).

Levine, R. et al. (2000). *The Cluetrain Manifesto: The end of business as usual.* Cambridge, MA: Perseus.

McCaffer, R., & Garas, F. (Eds.). (1999). eLSEwise: European large scale engineering wide integration support effort. *Engineering Construction and Architectural Management [Special Issue], 6*(1).

Mentzas, G. (2003). Inter-organizational knowledge sharing and trading. In Cunningham et al. (Eds.) (pp. 923-930).

Merz, M. et al. (2001). Electronic contracting in the construction industry. In Stanford-Smith & Chiozza (Eds.) (pp. 595-601).

Mitrovic, D., Hunter, I., & Male, S. (1999). Characteristics of networked enterprise in global construction. In Wognum et al. (Eds.) (pp. 447-454). [See also McAffer & Garas, 1999.]

Nonaka, I., & Takeuchi, H. (1995). *The knowledge-creating company: How Japanese companies create the dynamics of innovation.* Oxford: Oxford University Press.

O'Reilly, C. A., & Tushman, M. L. (2004). The ambidextrous organization. *Harvard Business Review,* April, 74-81.

Por, G. (2000). Knowledge, intelligence, wisdom: The new economic value chain and its enabling technologies. In *Future organizations and knowledge management,* Programme Consultation Meeting, European Commission, Directorate-General Information Society, Brussels.

Senge, P. M. (1990). *The fifth discipline: The art and practice of the learning organization.* New York: Random House.

Stanford-Smith, B., & Chiozza, E. (Eds.). (2001). *E-work and e-commerce: Novel solutions and practices for a global networked economy*. Amsterdam: IOS Press.

Stanford-Smith, B. et al. (Eds.). (2002). *Challenges and achievements in e-business and e-work*. Amsterdam: IOS Press.

TAP (1999). Telematics Applications Programme, European Commission, Brussels. Available online *http://www.cordis.lu/telematics/*

UEML (2004). Available online *http://www.cimosa.de/Modelling/UEML02.html* and *http://www.rtd.computas.com/websolution/Default.asp?WebID=239*

Van Schoubroeck, C. et al. (2001). Virtual enterprise legal issue taxonomy. In Stanford-Smith & Chiozza (Eds.) (pp. 609-615).

W3C (2004). Web ontology working group. Available online *http://www.w3.org/2001/sw/WebOnt/* and *http://www.ontoknowledge.org/oil/misc.shtml#ackn*

Wickens, P. D. (1998). *The ascendant organization* (revised and updated edition). New York; London: Macmillan.

Wigand, R. T. (1985). Integrated communications and work efficiency: Impacts on organizational structure and power. *Information Services and Use, 5*, 241-258.

Witczynski, M., & Pawlak, A. (2002). Virtual organizations enabling Net-based engineering. In Stanford-Smith et al. (Eds.) (pp. 908-915).

Wognum, N., Thoben, K. -D., and Pawar, K. S. (1999). *Proceedings of ICE'99, International Conference on Concurrent Enterprising*, The Hague, The Netherlands, March 15-17, 1999. Nottingham: University of Nottingham.

Zobel, R., & Filos, E. (2002). Work and business in the e-economy. Technology and Policy Issues, Third European e-Business and e-Work Conference, Prague, October 16-18. In B. Stanford-Smith et al. (Eds.) (pp. 52-66).

Chapter III

Collaborative Networked Organizations for Eco-Consistent Supply Chains

Rinaldo C. Michelini
Università di Genova, Italy

Roberto P. Razzoli
Università di Genova, Italy

ABSTRACT

The present study aims at exploring how to turn information and communication technology (ICT) networked tools to supply cooperative added-value duties and ecocompatibility certifying activities, as competitiveness is the permanent goal, but ecosystem preservation is a nonremovable asset. The chapter is organized into four sections. The first introduces the basic sustainability paradigm shifts, to switch from the affluent to the thrifty communities, showing that the knowledge society critically affects this transition. The following section deals with the information framework requested to characterize the extended artefact (or product-service) on the life-cycle span, dismissal included. The subsequent section considers the collaborative networked organizations needed to support the ecoconsistency management of the extended artifacts by means of net concerns, under the direct oversight of independent certification bodies. The last section outlines trends in the economical, legal, political, and social surroundings, aiming at the appropriateness of Web platform options.

KNOWLEDGE PARADIGMS
FOR ECOCONSERVATIVENESS

Sustainability is a demanding precept, and to sidestep, keep off, or delay its urgent incumbents shall only worsen future situations. The epochal changes asserted by the ICT and the opportunities prospected by the knowledge society propose technological and organizational betterments, inconceivable up to a few years ago. Certainly, technology-driven improvements deserve suspicious reception, and the knowledge aids to ecoconservativeness need harmonizing and integrative socioeconomical supports, and must match and comply with political-legal rules. Thus, in the analysis, these aspects need proper attention.

The knowledge society shows a potential discontinuity in the value chain buildup of the traded goods. For the welfare growth, industrialized countries, until now, profited from the haphazard consumption of tangibles, thus widening the manufacture market. The affluent community prizes trading new offers in order to outdate the previous ones; wealth generation stresses quantities, as factories return increases by selling huge amounts of wares, with the struggle built on the *scale* economy, to supply items at prices that greater numbers of buyers can afford. Market saturation and technology options, recently, became rivals of the *scope* economy, to supply items to satisfy clients, exploiting the plants' flexibility to manufacture a market-driven variety of items. The change is consistent with simultaneous engineering, which leads to the merging of design and fabrication into *intelligent* organizations, as compared to earlier *scientific* ones, ruled by their division, with strictly off-process design.

The shift toward the scope economy brings in life-cycle properties and, specifically, extensions to grant operation conformance at the point-of-service, out of the point-of-sale. The welfare growth of the industrial countries, thereafter, aims at the *service* market, by supply chains, jointly embedding *commodity* and *utility* provision. A divide establishes, with alternative staples in mercantile fields: *consumables* or *intangibles*. The extended artifact[1] (product-service) blends commodity and utility, by information-intensive delivery, to grant specified functions, by life-cycle indenture. This is the first ICT outcome, helping to focus on the utility, rather than on the commodity side when pricing a delivered instrumental item, as the purchaser directly perceives the fit-to-purpose effectiveness and considers the ownership attribution, mainly, as formal practice.

The explicit attention on the information content in the value chain of an artefact brings in the covert suggestion on how to deal with sustainability. Actually, the scope economy pursuit and the related quality engineering schedules contribute to fix the set of properties marketed as inherent attributes of the artefact. A further step, this time, is to distinguish two sets of properties: customer satisfaction and ecoconsistency: sustainable quality is achieved, whether or not this second attribute is granted. The supposition leads to the careful weighing of consumables vs. intangibles in the supply chain. *Consumables* (raw materials and grown or manufactured commodities), have prevailing birth from nonrenewable sources and, as the earth is a closed system, development sustainability shall asymptotically cause wealth downgrading, unless the staple turns to yield value chains prevailingly based on delivery of *intangibles* (knowledge, know-how, technology, etc., with embedded utilities, services, functions, etc.).

The guess mainly resorts to information technologies, believed capable of strengthening and unfolding the paradigm shift to scope economy, with changes in habits enhancing the knowledge K- vs. the tangibles T-marketing and leading to ecoconsistent progress, without lowering welfare, by proper balance of the K and T factors. On these premises, this section addresses three points:

- The conventional growth, entangled with the manufacture market, is referred to a more elaborate model to provide a general description of the industrial delivery, with explicit dependence on the recalled factors: K, proprietary knowledge, and T, booked tangibles.
- The measurement of resources depletion due to life-cycle exploitation of the marketed artifacts by means of objective standards (the TYPUS metrics), to provide quantitative assessment of direct and indirect impacts, and, thereafter, to establish coherent reward taxations.
- The exploration of information-driven mechanisms capable of supporting value chains maximizing intangibles content, stressing utilities (marketing functions) that replace commodities (marketing artefacts).

The ICTs, it should be said, are instrumental aids, directly and indirectly affecting sustainability by pervasive provisions. To switch from affluent communities (with staple in consumables) to thrifty communities (with staple in intangibles), however, the technical — scientific patterns merely represent the necessary support; legal — political and socioeconomical patterns will be further established, so that technicalities reach appropriateness by method innovation.

KILT Model of the Manufacture Activity

The traditional description of the manufacture activity links the actual delivery Q to only two factors: C, capital, and L, labor. Then, the industrial countries, to highly remunerate both factors, followed aggressive strategies, taking up the market of less-developed regions. Subsequent analyses looked at a trim balance, to include human capital H further to the financial capital F and, sometimes, material resources M plus labor resources L. The two entries show the offsetting capabilities contributed by internal know-how and skill and expertise, especially relevant because of the emerging ICT aids; and by raw provisions effectiveness, by now, nonnegligible, once required to assess ecoconservativeness. Recent studies (Michelini, 2002) moved to slightly update the four independent factors, to explicitly deal with the (abstract) knowledge K (rather than the human capital) and the actual net consumed tangibles T (rather than the original raw material provision). For more information, see the KILT model (Figure 1).

Purposely established assessments show the relevant role of the quantity K, knowledge, know-how, technology, expertise, etc., leading to value chain increases up to 40% to 50% or more (slightly retrenched after the ICT bubble flattened out), asserting the increasing role of the information content when society progresses.[2] At the turn of the millennium, ecology-concerned people required that the (quasi) free access to nonrenewable resources be stopped, purporting profit for manufacturers and purchasers and damage for present and future populations. The basic claim is to perceive a tax, to refund the humans for the tangibles T decay diverted along the supply chain. Thus, manufacture delivery Q follows the KILT model (Figure 1) and assumes that:

Figure 1. KILT model of the industrial manufacture delivery

$$Q = a_0 \, K \, I \, L \, T - a_K \, K - a_I \, I - a_L \, L - a_T \, T$$

where   *K*, proprietary knowledge and technology

       I, invested financial capital

       L, directly engaged labour

       T, actually consumed tangibles

- The four (scaled) factors have similar effects, and a balanced setting exists that optimizes the manufacture delivery, for the chosen (scaled) configuration.
- The introduction of slight unbalances has similar negative effects, and the total disregard of any factors leads to negative built-in overall delivery.

The dependence on each of the four factors also characterizes the clustered companies that could resort to nonproprietary technologies, to venture capitals, to outsourcing or to leased provisions, in order to keep the business profitable, by merging facilities, liabilities, utilities, and commodities to achieve balanced settings. Four productivity figures (Figure 1), accordingly, appear as for the *K*, *I*, *L*, and *T* factors; thereafter, the fair competition needs equal opportunity players, compelled:

- To bring out the explicit dependence on material resources consumption when pricing artefacts.
- To refer to third-party certification for ruling the ecolabelling by means of objective metrics.

TYPUS Metrics for Tangibles Depletion Assessment

The explicit inclusion of natural resources spoilage in pricing the life-cycle artefacts operation should be based on worldwide accepted metrological standards. The exacted amounts will become public income, with a twofold goal (Michelini, 2004, pp. 83-98):

- To remunerate the people not involved by specific transactions.
- To spur thrifty choices or to hinder squandering.

With this taxation, there is no intention to hamper or stop the progress, rather to modify the staple in consumables, by enhanced focus on renewable (natural) stuffs and on recycled commodities. The selective nature of the charging rules will give account of specificity and intensity in consuming fixed quantities of raw materials, to obtain given amounts of actually enabled functional delivery.

The approach requires worldwide withdrawals for tangibles decay, by equivalent tax burden, objectively linked to the life cycle of every traded artefact, including on-duty provisions and dismissal recoveries. On these ideas, several metrics can be proposed, with figures stated according to acknowledged legal metrology precepts, on the condition that full visibility will be provided for the artefact life-cycle data and proper control on the actual operation will fall off. The definition of measurement standards is preliminary fulfillment. A coherent answer looks after defining a collaborative networked organization, involving the consumer's side (supplier and user) and the controller's side (certifying body, with governmental accreditation), which accounts for all material-and-energy flows activated along the considered artefact life-cycle and assumes that the net depletion is assessed at the life-cycle end, including side-effects to remove negative impacts and positive contributions due to recycling and recovery.

The approach splits, as shown, into a two-step accomplishment:

- Specification of standards by means of legal metrology rules.
- Establishment of a third-party monitoring and assessment organization.

Coherently, thereafter, the first step leads, for instance, to the *TYPUS* (tangibles yield per unit of service) metrics (Figure 2). The framework is built on the assumption that most buyers are primarily interested in the functions delivered by the instrumental artefacts they purchase (independently from their actual legal ownership), and thus, a scale based on the unit of service is especially relevant to turn users to conservative behavior, as prizing the *tangibles yield*, more than abstract quality figures, shows that actual needs are favored (while fancy whims shall be properly paid).

The second step is typical ICT contribution. The collaborative network, presumed by the TYPUS metrics, is a challenging development that only highly structured Web environments afford. A set of services, tools, provisions, etc., exploiting federated organization recurrent management, will interlace with the main supply chain, giving birth to a breeding adaptive environment by collaborative (vs. antagonistic) data interchange. Broadband Internet plus mobile communication makes possible life-cycle recording, to extract the pertinent figures and to separate, into protected files, all information that could conflict with manufacturers' secrecy and with users' privacy.

Figure 2. The TYPUS metrics to assess net resources depletion

TYPUS *(tangibles yield per unit of service)*

The metrics is used as follows:

- To define a scale for measuring the life-cycle *function* supplied by the artefact

- To record the material and energy provisions during the *manufacture* phase

- To record the material and energy provisions during the *operation* service

- To evaluate the material and energy recovery at *dismissal* and recycling

Value Chain Balance and Infrastructures Management

The drastic rise in prices for the charges on resources consumption could obtain social acceptance, if alternatives are provided:

- To market *equivalent* functions/services supplies, assuring demand satisfaction and ecoconsistency.
- To support additional (based on intangibles) sources of wealth, to keep steady the overall welfare.[3]

Besides the technology-based innovation, the trends require properly established legal frames (Figure 3).

At this point, the technical side of value chains maximizing intangibles content is exemplified with resorting to ICT provisions, the social and legal aspects being deferred to the last section of the chapter. Product development of high-tech or new technology delivery is a challenging area. It involves multiple disciplines, endless series of trade-offs, dilemmas, and dead ends. The ICT offers interesting areas for learning about emerging high-technology product and service development, whether for purposes of understanding, working, managing, or studying it.

Net infrastructures are a turbulent framework to work with. Clients, end-user service dealers, mobile communication makers, core network operators, and access providers are all participating players. The main objective of this study is to place a birds-eye view on these processes and to trace state-of-the-art issues and basic attributes (Figure 4), while keeping course on sustainability.

Figure 3. Breakthrough of sustainability legal frames

The following are needed by the bylaw frames:

- To be stated on objective (legal metrology patterns) assessments with worldwide coverage
- To act on the consumer's side, to foster **thrifty** communities instead of **affluent** communities
- To re-orient the supplier side, to offer *functions*, instead of *artefacts*, for satisfying instrumental needs, when they, eventually, arise
- To support the infrastructures of the *service* **economy** and to discourage any process with intensive tangibles spoilage
- To stimulate jobs for the reuse of tangibles (the **backward cycle**: to collect, disassemble, recover, classify, sell, etc., the recycled materials)
- To establish positive actions (not series of vetos that simply give rise to hidden bargains) in order to empower, according to *fair* trade rules, the *service* economy to be respectful of the ecological side of human welfare

Figure 4. Basic issues about ICT sustainability actions

- Totally new artefacts and provisions, typically belonging to (mostly intangible) ICT-based developments

- Knowledge-based team facilitators, anticipating engineers' needs, to improve traditional manufacture

- Net concern's infrastructures and methods in operation and servicing, to support artefacts life cycle

- Clients- and suppliers-selective interlinks, underlying trade-offs to adapt functions and items provision

- Multiparty supply-chain managers, with monitoring and routing options for certifying bodies

- Information aids, stressing utilities (functions trade) that replace commodities (artefacts trade)

- Intelligent tracking and tracing in logistics (emergency, surveillance, etc.) for sustainability recording

- Knowledge management for the ecosystems business and the emerging collaboration forms

- Organisational know-how for the reprocessing of used and obsolete artefacts into valuable resources

- Frames for constitution and operation of dynamic networked supports to services/functions delivery

- Intelligent consulting systems to supply backward-cycle (reverse logistics) economical return

- Any other practice grounded on the factual exploitation of knowledge as conditioning aid.

These example hints show how intangibles contributions in the value chain can drastically cooperate in the build up of wealth. Moreover, the new opportunities help modify the way that consumers confront themselves with artefacts: the knowledge dependence becomes a competitive feature, qualifying the embedded functions.

INFORMATION DESIGN AIDS
FOR EXTENDED ARTEFACTS

In the earlier practice of industrial engineers', computer aids followed two tracks: along the *design* or the *manufacture* information surroundings:
- To enhance the ideation and development ability and efficiency by *CAD* tools.
- To enable the factory flexible automation effectiveness by the *CIME* tools.

The merging of the two, by simultaneous engineering, is a noteworthy achievement, to optimize the benefits of the enterprise (Michelini, 1992) according to intelligence integration within the individual company frame and leading to client satisfaction by the scope economy.

Then, the information aids expand out of the enterprise surroundings to deal with the artefact life cycle. The economy of scope starts to include customer-oriented quality as a competitive feature, and looks after point-of-service performance as a further benchmark. This leads to supporting extended artefacts, conceived since ideation to possess a set of operation attributes and to grant a set of on-duty functions. At the development steps, the life-cycle extension is investigated and assessed by using a proper computer aid, the *product life-cycle manager* (PLM) that enables a factual evaluation structure based on the virtual testing of digital mock-ups.

The integrated design, thus, is effective support for analyzing the technological sustainability, leading to the definition of the instruction guide for safe running, proper maintenance, and consistent dismissal of the traded goods, in keeping with the out-of-all balance of the induced impacts.

The Life-Cycle Conformance Assessment

In the past, integrated design developed as a response to the market saturation of mass products. To aim at customized offers, diversified developments are established, and, for return on investment, the factual resort to scope economy targets is enabled. The central role is played by the extended artefact or product–service, i.e., instrumental (tangible and intangible) delivery to a client, granting the enjoyment of specified functions, by a life-cycle indenture. The extension obliges the supplier to the user for conformance assessment at the point of service, both being bound by enacted (safety, environment, etc.) protection rules. A traded extended artefact is characterized because:

- The market-driven quality aims to reach customer satisfaction by using a mix of lifelong operation properties.
- The sustainable quality becomes a monitored attribute, under transparently acknowledged schemes.

Figure 5. The deployment of green-engineering patterns

Sustainability is satisfied by integrated design accomplishments, showing how ecology concern is dealt with by the *extended* artefact, as for materials choice, energy saving, waste avoidance, etc.:

- Along the manufacture process, by conservative inner-enterprise organisation
- During the forward-cycle operation, upkeeping, refurbishing, etc., by teaching the users

   with the duty and maintenance guide and by presetting effective ecocertifying

   collaborative networks

- At dismissal, recycling, or discharge of warn-out/damaged items and scraps, by detailing

   environmentally safe incumbents, according to transparent overseeing of control

The knowledge-intensive frames of the integrated design complement the *extended* enterprise organisation, assuring instrumental fulfillment to sustainability.

Green-engineering develops, fostering product and service innovation, spurred by market-driven targets (to win new buyers, facing worldwide competition) and by governmental bylaws (to satisfy the enacted operation and dismantling rules).

The legal frame of extended artefacts delivery, accordingly, modifies:
- From (mainly bilateral) supplier to customer responsiveness.
- To (jointly liable) consumer responsibility (against ecoconsistency).

The on-duty properties of extended artefacts come up to affect the third-parties sphere and safeguard, according to the emerging patterns of green-engineering (Figure 5). The management of the conformance assessment incumbents becomes a relevant business, covering the supply chain, with the joint liability of purveyors and users for the protection of the ecosystem, according to the enacted rules.

Design for the Forward-Cycle Ecoeffectiveness

The ecoconsistency is, formally, direct addition of targets in the integrated design by modulating the economy of scope requirements. Simple ecodesign hints lead to conservative actions, such as:
- To prefer renewable resources, less energy-expensive or recycled materials, etc.
- To favor high-effectiveness, low-energy work cycles, materials recovery, etc.
- To select recycled packaging, efficient dispatching, self-sufficient setting, etc.
- To foster highly effective setting and operation conditions, proactive maintenance, etc.
- To forecast extended life span, conservative refurbishing, low energy consumption, etc.
- To preset quality management, easy dismantling, materials backutilization, etc.

Basically, all of these actions lead to design practices that improve the artefacts life cycle, orient the resource choice, and preset efficient recycling. The know-how accumulated in the companies represents an intellectual asset and will be systematically upgraded as an ecodesign practice.

The current situation concerning ecodesign is that, in general, the methods are informally practised and weakly supported by inclusive techniques. Regarding resource choice and reuse options, little is done inside, and there is practically no way to exchange data outside companies. To establish a means for systematic reuse, the design flows need be formalized, into a glossary and a taxonomy in order to provide unified views for the transparent data and know-how exchange between organizations and for various kinds of extended artefacts. In fact, sustainability is consistent with formal design and development goals, provided that the ability of ecoefficiency assessment (by TYPUS or other metrics) and the attention on the function and duty visibility for third-party oversight (Figure 6) are granted, so that the access directly applies to every physical component and supplied function. Generic modularity is addressed as the typical means for enhancing reuse.

The design for the forward-cycle effectiveness, thereafter, is assumed to deal with previous knowledge only, and it aims at forecast sustainability. Following the prospective lines, the cost of consumed tangibles shall entirely be transferred into wealth created by the associated information content, thus, mainly, by crafty contrivances and techniques (Figure 7) that keep or restore conformance to specification, through low-impact procedures. The monitoring maintenance practice is especially relevant and presumes

Figure 6. Ecodesign criteria based on generic modularity

For function and duty visibility, the integrated construction will exploit *generic modularity* with the following:

• Digital mock-ups, to assign the structural and functional modules, with their impact analysis

• Artefacts architectures based on items conceived to split into reusable fractions

• Limited series of provisions, based on clear mutual combinableness fractions

• Operation specialisation, to separate functionally coherent subassembles

• Duty analyses, to define regulation and upkeep plans for assigned work conditions

• Duty analyses, to define antipollution and reclamation deeds, for sustainability targets

• Distinct subassemblies, with groupings of dangerous or polluting materials

• Easily accessible disjoining or cutting boundaries, to avoid complex parting

• Part identification, to make refurbishing, dismantling, and recycling easy

• Simple division and handling, with parts recognition codes or signatures

• Properly established outlets, bleeding or spurge discharges and protections

The *generic modularity* combines physical and operation modularity, in order to specialise the (material) parts and the (intangible) functions. The technique block-scheme analysis has detailed specification of the command/information flows and of the energy/material flows that assure extended artefact operations.

the availability of on-process diagnostics to monitor the running conditions and to detect deviations (*proactive* mode) or failure states (*reactive* mode), so that the extended artefact applies to built-in fixtures and procedures to recover the nominal operation conditions.

Design for Backward-Cycle Effectiveness

The *backward* cycle strictly deals with parts and materials processing after (partial or total) dismissal of the handled commodity. Nevertheless, as we are concerned with extended artefacts, the information contents are not neutral, and two restricting patterns are established:

- Feedback of *forward*-cycle features, to recognize the appropriate *design-for-x* specifications.
- Forecast of *backward*-cycle features, to include suitable *design-for-recycling* specifications.

Figure 7. Crafty techniques to improve the ecoconservativeness

Expansion of the artefacts' on-duty availability by *monitoring* maintenance options through the following:

• *Reactive mode*: at diagnosis of the failure, the process is self-stopping and upkeep and repairing deeds are directly started.

• *Proactive mode*: at deviation from nominal conditions, the procedures for the process regulation and duty fixing are accomplished.

Protraction of the artefacts' operation life, after renovation or revision deeds is as follows:

• *Revamping*: recovery of consistent functional state, by proper renovation and updating of every critical module, according to enacted bylaws.

• *Reintegrating*: restoration to the original state, by full revision and (possible) replacement of every defective module.

The former, typically, requesting larger designer responsiveness with further data, obtained from on-process monitoring; the latter, considering the tangibles flows after the artefact dismissal.

The practice of *design-for-restoring, -for-maintenance, -for-dismantle, -for-recycling*, etc., is forward-cycle duty to improve conservativeness. This leads to shrewd features, such as self-tuning ability, when disturbances offset the running requirement; proactive maintenance based on monitored indices; schemes for tangibles call-back or final withdrawal, linked to actually assessed work conditions and the like, showing that *feedback* is an inherent commitment, as designers' responsibility needs to cover the all-duty cycle.

Based on these premises, the *backward* cycle is a further option, with targets to be weighed against others, when ecodesign becomes the main purpose (Figure 8) so that the trend will steadily drift to coherent artefact layouts, according to the generic modularity criteria (Figure 6) to grant *backward* cycle efficiency through structured, general-purpose approaches.

As the concern on the opportunities offered by the backward cycle increases, new special-purpose design choices appear (Figure 8), and reconditioning or remanufacturing are relevant means to modify the tangibles yield after artefacts dismissal. However, the integrated design steps are not sufficient, by themselves, to grant economical return to the thrifty community surroundings; they, actually, establish when the artefact's true

Figure 8. Example targets to improve the backward chain

The backward-cycle effectiveness is improved by generic design settings, such as the following:

• Planning for quality protection of the used items, easy disassembly, material reuse, etc.

• Designing for long-life availability, rare maintenance, low energy consumption, etc.

• Preferring self-tuned rigs, high yield applications, reused packaging, improved logistics, etc.

• Setting optimal on-duty effectiveness, proactive upkeep, etc., *extended* artefacts

• Choosing high throughput, material saving, energy recovery, etc., operation processes

• Making extensive use of recycled, less energy-intensive, renewable, etc., materials

Backward-cycle effectiveness is improved by special-purpose design choices aimed at the following:

• Reconditioning, to back-establish the original conformance to specification, by combined industrial processes applied at the life end of artefacts; reconditioning is limited, if resetting is partial

• Remanufacturing, to recover parts and material matching original properties, by combined industrial processes applied to dismissed artefacts, and to candidate them to new duty cycles; the issue is limited, if the processed parts do not recover the original characteristics

price will include the overall cost for materials and energy depletion suffered by the ecosystem. Thereafter, only the worldwide use of the TYPUS metrics, or equivalent taxing reference, will be the enabling procedure for looking after combined backward cycles, at the different ranges of the forward cycle, in order to devise efficient layouts, as compared to the overall ecoconservativeness.

COLLABORATIVE NETWORKS
FOR CERTIFYING BODIES

The ICT aids are playing a fundamental role in the development of extended artefacts. Moving to current lifelong concern, the knowledge society appears as necessary surroundings, to make possible the assessment of item impact and natural resources decay. The TYPUS metrics proposal, as pointed out, can actually become a current development means, on condition to arrange suitable *collaborative* networks that manage the life-cycle (operation fall-offs and dismissal included) data, by transparent and scrupulous recording. Mainly, the arrangement requires three facts (Figure 9):

- Marketing of extended artefacts, with proper collaborative networks to support client requests.
- Involvement of extended enterprises, assuring point-of-service conformance guarantees.
- Overseeing of third-party certifying bodies to record tangibles yield per unit service.

Figure 9. Collaborative networks for life-cycle visibility

The networked organisation, granting the information service for customers, is required to do the following:

- Provide collaborative forms and behaviours for product life-cycle management
- Rule conformance assessment and restoration within networked responsible bodies

The *extended* enterprise profits of a networked organisation to expand buyers' satisfaction are as follows:

- Cooperative design and shared knowledge make multitechnology *extended* artefacts possible.
- Life-cycle data pricing becomes relevant, and *new* competition is featured between companies.

The sustainability assures *fair* trade conditions, provided that networks are available, in order to do the following:

- Employ objective, worldwide-referenced, metrological standards (e.g., TYPUS metrics)
- Record the artefact life-cycle behaviour controlled by independent certifying bodies

The network bears direct links with conventional extended enterprise implementations, and it is a critical enabling tool to foster and to control sustainability, the two actions being connected with managing the artefact life-cycle visibility. The information nested infrastructures are basic aids, on these conditions: to set the requested transparency and to rule the selective data communication between the involved parties. From a merely technical viewpoint, if suppliers have the contract obligation to support the fit-for-purpose life span of every sold item, the trading price will include the ecoconsistency charges for use, maintenance, refurbishing, and replacement, and the collaborative networked organizations will supply a threefold link for users, manufacturers, and controllers, according to well-established patterns (Figure 9): to safeguard users, to rule competition, and to protect the ecosystem.

These collaborative networks face three types of topologies:

- Inner cluster, to link the partners of the extended enterprise, for any extended artefact delivery.
- Specialized bounds to support the point-of-service communication with individual buyers.

Figure 10. Information setup of the collaborative networks

Collaborative links to certify the resource yield (artefact tax collection level):

- Technical documentation standardisation for internal/external use, to simplify equipment conformance assessment
- Standardisation of monitoring, data storing, and restitution, to rationalise estimations and to minimise errors
- Extension of formalised methods, in order to manage forward- and backward-cycle data with respect to *unit service* delivery
- Expansion of controlled procedures in the buildup and the controlled access of the tangibles decay data vaults
- Preparation of the reference data for the taxing accomplishments and the charges fulfilment acknowledgement

Collaborative links to reach the ecocompatibility (artefact sustainability level):

- Choosing low-impact materials (to avoid regulated/restricted items, to segregate poisonous components, etc.)
- Developing modular architectures with reusable platforms/blocks and with recycled materials/parts
- Automatically generating the low-impact manufacturing/packaging/installation processes, removing/minimising pollution
- Automatically generating operation/maintenance guides and presetting frameworks for life-cycle recording
- Preparation of the *product–service* support, according to (enacted/forecast) technical sustainability bylaws

Figure 10. Information setup of the collaborative networks (continued)

<u>**Collaborative links to grant point-of-service visibility**</u> (artefact life-cycle level):

• Aiming, during the integrated design, at life-cycle reliability consistent with acknowledged

   performance figures

• Developing products' *extensions* to cover current usage, service support, monitoring abilities,

   operation records, etc.

• Looking after intelligence, for tangibles *extended* products, use friendliness, function-embedded

   options, etc.

• Stressing knowledge-intensive deliveries: for intangibles, *extended* products, stressing on knowledge-

   intensive deliveries, and providing engineering functions

• Assuring, for trade fairness, life-cycle operation transparency, protecting against artefacts' abuse or

   misuse

<u>**Collaborative links to exploit the self-consistency**</u> (artefact construction level):

• Automatic management of change consistency (by parameter fitting, etc.), anticipating checks at

   decision setting

• Automatic propagation of local changes, by file updating and revision, showing effects by virtual

   testing

• Access to technical specifications files, with real-time involvement of purchasing and manufacturing

   functions

• Incorporation of CAM and CAP files under the CAD frames, to optimise work-cycles, assembly

   plans, etc.;

• Standardisation of CAT files, for company-wide quality-control, zero-defects and trend monitoring

   maintenance

<u>**Collaborative links to compress the incumbents**</u> (artefact ideation level):

• Reduction (by 30% or more) of lead time, from ideation to delivery of new products, by standard

   design methods

• Paralleling development activities, by exploiting data, as soon as made available, through digital

   mock-up checks

• Resort to value-chain models, support design to cost methods, and monitor the "added" value of

   competing alternatives

• Automatic supervision on standard componentry, with inclusion of specifications without any

   attendance duplication

• Generation (with artefact customisation) of technical specifications files, operation and maintenance

   guides, etc.

- Selective data channels, to give access to the certifying bodies under proper security protocols.

The common, varying topology information setup (Figure 10) is the unifying context, sliced into layers, with:
- The lowest levels (artefact ideation and construction) within the extended enterprise inner cluster.
- The intermediate level (artefact life cycle), for the data management at the clients' satisfaction.
- The highest levels (artefact sustainability and tangibles charges) ruled by the certifying bodies.

The listed duties (Figure 10) provide example hints to develop the databases involved by an advanced PLM, once the prospected sustainability context is enabled.

The Web-Driven Extended Enterprise

The extended enterprise (Figure 11) is the main actor in the extended artefact life cycle (Figure 13). Compared to habits currently in use, operational surroundings and legal frameworks, through the given definition, modify from (internal) regulation contracts undersigned by the clustered partners to enacted precepts ruling (varying entry) collaborative networks (open to the certifying bodies).

The *net-infrastructure*, associated with the defined *extended* enterprise, requires sets of attributes, today, only partially supported by current ICT tools. Several collaborative setups are available, built on provider-ruled links, with the inherent risks on data protection and transaction security of the Web-based facilities. New and safe collabo-

Figure 11. The extended enterprise: definition and features

The *extended* enterprise, or *net concern*, is a factual alliance of partners,

merging, into a shared infrastructure, skills, know-how and resources, to enable

codesigning, comanufacturing, comarketing, comaintaining, coservicing,

corecycling, etc., efforts, to offer *extended* artefacts at purchaser's benefit *and*

environment safety.

The *extensions* (of artefacts *and* enterprises) grant visibility on the delivered

products–services operation-life to support:

• The resources consumption and surroundings impact recording

• The third-party conformance assessment and ecofigures certification

rative protocols and conducts are, actually, sought by larger factories, resorting to special-purpose facilities; a number of inhibitors exist, however (Figure 12), when factual alliances of complementary partners try to merge into clusters, simultaneously dealing with designers, manufacturers, users, and controllers, to achieve the outlined organization (Figure 11).

The short analysis helps us to realize that the existing technical frames are, in this case, relevant domains for application-driven developments that need the incorporation of a lot of ingenuity to match sustainability requests, after exploring three lines, for nested enterprises integration:

Figure 12. Barriers for collaborative networks interoperability

The interconnected concerns suffer drawbacks when selective sophistication is needed, due to the following:

• Want of properly established common reference models, to be shared as *type*-facility

• Ineffectiveness of reliable-interoperability mechanisms and multiple-control approaches

• Complex development incumbents in front of the many-offered and quick-changing

  technologies

• Shortage of efficient eligible protocols and frames, free from nonowned (and conflicting)

  details

• Deficiencies in the supporting frameworks, with detailed characterisation and steady

  properties

• Heavy design and engineering efforts to make proprietary technologies cooperate

• Rapid software and hardware obsolescence, frustrating advance issues, and provisional

  goals

• Actual obstacles in the transfer of locally tested instruments due to short life-cycle tools

• Lack of viable leadership, proposing low-cost linking environments with safe operability

The listed inhibitors need theoretical research and formal models capturing concepts,

behaviours, and operations, and breeding environments and brokerage to build effective

collaborative networks.

- The dependence on engineering design to conceive ecoconsistent extended artefacts by detailed life-cycle specifications, with inherent operation, maintenance, and dismissal guides.
- The dependence on information infrastructures to provide life-cycle visibility, by monitoring environmental impact of the *full* supply chain (recycling included).
- The dependence on fixed standards (TYPUS metrics) to foster conservative behavior (method innovation) by charging the net tangible resources consumption.

To summarize, the Web-driven extended enterprise concept (Figure 11) is the starting point from which to develop the information environment of thrifty communities. The theoretical and technological prerequisites are well acknowledged, with core processes: strategy formulation and deployment, *extended* artefact innovation, *extended* enterprise setting, supply-chain transparency, tangibles decay assessment and certification, etc. The resulting main issue aims at a global engineering network (Figure 13) for multiusers' trading and granting support for manufacturing, logistics, sales, operations, monitoring, recycling, etc.

Then, the study should address the paradigm shifts, keeping sight on the prospects, with extended artefacts and extended enterprises in the background, to show the main business arrangements (backward cycle factories, conformance assessment bodies, etc.) that will arise, and the related fall-offs in the industrial economy. Of course, in

Figure 13. The extended enterprise information setup

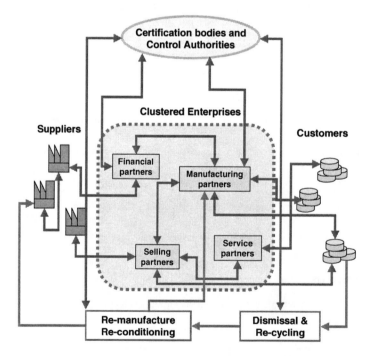

the foreground, the existing engineers' surrounding provides reference starting points; continuity, indeed, suggests guesses in the mercantile fields: *intangibles* will never completely replace *consumables*, as grown or manufactured *commodity* did not fully override natural-stuffs and farm produce. The pursuance of surroundings leads us to consider *extensions* on the basis of already detected trends, even if we are aware that, by shifting, original means and meanings become *new* contexts.

The Certifying Bodies Arrangement

To open the collaborative networked organization to the certifying bodies access, the management of the resource allocation and related information framework and of the tangibles decay assessments deserves a three-party ruling (Figure 13), where the

Figure 14. The collaborative networks for sustainability

The collaborative infrastructure requires the interlinked participation of the following:

• **Purveyors**, covering the entire *supply chain*: materials provision, item manufacture, life-cycle upkeep, and backward recovery; the ecological responsibility is dealt with by clustering several firms within a factual alliance of cooperating multisectional-interest businesses

• **Users**, purchasing *extended* artefacts (*products–services*), to profit from the delivered *functions* with reliability figures close to one; the payments will include conformance certification at the point of service, after tax collection against tangibles depletion

• **Supervisors**, assuring *third-party* incumbents for (today and tomorrow) environmental and societal protection; the certifying bodies report to governmental authorities and use objective standards, having access to the *extended* artefacts life-cycle databases

The transparency of the environmental impact is achieved by continuous monitoring and recording of the actual running conditions, both of the *forward* and the *backward* cycles.

The governmental agencies collect the charges for the net consumed tangibles, following assessments of the authorised certifying bodies.

---

consumers lump together purveyors and users, both subject to the monitoring by independent (and duly accredited) supervisors. This is but a realistic scheme; alternatives are possible, once extended artefacts are supplied by extended enterprises and third-party certification bodies oversee the life-cycle incumbents (Figure 14). The three-party ruling, however, seems to be a good compromise to enhance competition and to balance responsibilities, under real *fair-trade* conditions.

The picture is coherent with a controlled collaborative network, directly linking an extended enterprise to individual clients, so that the supply chain of each delivered extended artefact is transparently available to an accredited certifying body, for conformance assessment purposes. The commodity and utility mix, in fact, could show the following with alternative prospects:

- A single supplier keeps in charge all incumbents along the *product–service* life-cycle, dismissal included.
- A team of dealers grants *special provisions*, due to oriented qualification and infrastructure-based setups.

Figure 15. The third-party certifying service

The third-party certifying body operates as follows:

- Interacts with the *collaborative* network support, established by the *extended* enterprise to manage the *extended* artefact administration, with full visibility on the life-cycle data and proper security restrictions

- Verifies the monitoring and control network integrity, and provides conformance assessment records by progression statements, as partial estimates for T-factor *refunds*, based on the TYPUS metrics

- Oversees the *extended* enterprise accomplishments in terms of ecocharge payments, accounting progress balances, based on the unified responsibility established by the two *consumer* parties indentation

- Guarantees data vault and privacy protection, with proper specifications in case the certifying duty is transferred to a different body and/or the joint consumer parties modify the binding contracts

- Operates within an accreditation scheme, notified to national (governmental) authorities and international organisations, having worldwide acknowledgement

The involvement of third-party certifying bodies needs, of course, proper regulations, enacted by the national authorities, but suitably harmonised to assure worldwide equivalence.

In both cases, as for sustainability, the seller-to-buyer indenture specifies a further relationship, as these two parties together (*consumers*) oppose all other people (*ecoresource inherent holders*) (Figure 14). Beyond, the governmental regulations and the international agreements establish protection rules, according to political or legal deputation and shared consent.

The service paradigms aim at well-defined duties (Figure 15) typically supported by the knowledge society. This is a realistic prospect, showing that the certifying bodies compete in a free market, being, possibly at any time, replaced, exactly as the partners of an extended enterprise could be modified or the agreements about the extended artefact responsibility might be updated. These changes do not interrupt the supply-chain monitoring; they simply request that the new entries would be accepted by proper data transfer, and the new duties would be assigned.

The Privacy and Data Protection Rules

The entitlement of local authorities faces non-fully-defined duties (specification of charges and fees; time horizon for resources cost balance; sharing out of perceived taxes; etc.), as they refer to limited numbers of citizens, without concern about other nations and future generations. At the same time, the pervasive control of local authorities infringes upon privacy rights (the Orwell's forecast comes true), as they sum up the many data directly concerning habits and whims of individuals. The true worldwide concern is for a higher-level entrustment, so that taxes are managed by international treaties, through clearing and compensation agreements between national entities. On such grounds, third-party certification builds up as a competition-driven service:

• The joint consumers' side lets out (on contract) the overseeing incumbents and the related conformance assessments, but can, at any time, change the certifying body.
• The authorities are entitled to rule the legal frames but without any direct involvement in data keeping and recording, accomplished under proper secrecy by parcelled-out services.

The threefold relationship (Figure 14) reduces to a twofold ruling: consumers, on one side, and certifying bodies and accreditation agencies on the other side. The ecoeffectiveness is the joint business of the former, e.g., to raise tangibles productivity: during life cycle, condition upkeep, and proactive maintenance are clever contrivances; at life end, recovering and recycling are relevant benefits. The ecoconservativeness is a standard controller duty; transparency of environmental impact is achieved by continuously monitoring and recording the actual running conditions of the forward and the backward cycles.

The collaborative network complexity appears highly tangled, as several firms are involved, through competing offers, to manage equivalent product–service settings. Thus, the interlaced net-infrastructures will exist within almost worldwide contexts and need grant the protected (through hierarchical priorities) access to the extended artefacts life-cycle databases, to the overseeing certification bodies.

The network technicalities of the certifying service, as previously exemplified, still suffer several barriers (Figure 12), but in the removal of them, one does not face insurmountable hurdles. Instead, better positioning of research and development ef-

Figure 16. Short- and long-term knowledge assets

Turns in consumer conditioning information to deal with sustainability:

• The habits change to deal with nonrenewable resources, explore the KILT

model to work out sustainable quality features (TYPUS metrics) and

coherent support (*net-concerns* and *collaborative* networks), needed to fulfil

the paradigm shift to ecoconsistency (*method* innovation)

• The longer-term analysis considers the technicalities for *thrifty*

achievements through *extended* artefacts, once the TYPUS metrics charges

consumers for resources decay: *backward*-cycle factories, *third-party*

certifying bodies, and *product–service* business are main fall-offs

The collaborative network technicalities need to evolve at the pace the people

accept to deal with sustainability charges.

forts, once the ecoconservativeness, through tangibles decay taxing, becomes accepted practice. The prospected evolution might distinguish short-term from longer-term outcomes (Figure 16) for the knowledge assets or for the needed ICT tools.

The approach makes possible an incremental establishment of thrifty achievements, turn by turn adding new fulfillments. The trend is followed by the EU regulation when, for instance, the differentiated waste disposal, etc., are entitled to the local responsiveness (municipalities); the sellers of the replacing items are given charge of the collection of exhausted domestic appliances, etc., even if further operators can be involved, being delegated by the in-charge entities. The personal data protection, however, cannot fully come out with mandatory restrictions; the ecoconsistency will not avoid addressing, with proper cautions, individual responsibilities, and availability of coherent metrics and data collaborative hierarchic networks will come out as the coherent issue of today's virtual concerns.

METHOD INNOVATION AND SUSTAINABILITY APPROPRIATENESS

With focus on the extended artefacts (products-services), a critical opportunity is to enable the practice of technological sustainability, by moving wealth generation from a typically manufacturing market, to a mainly function market. Fundamental steps are established along the track: design, fabrication, and servicing, with the basic role played by infrastructures; design needs are structured according to the economy of scope approach, including ecoconservativeness among the sought requirements; fabrication will exploit intelligent automation to incorporate customized quality aiming at knowledge-driven value; servicing will expand, as truly new business, to encompass the backward cycle (Michelini, 2004, pp. 415–428). After the background topics of the knowledge paradigms for ecoconservativeness (KILT model, TYPUS metrics), the information flows of integrated design (targeted to client satisfaction and sustainable quality) and the collaborative networks, open to certifying bodies (decay assessment for

Figure 17. The method innovation *fundamental assets*

Political–legal actions and governmental regulation of ecocompatibility, in order to do the following:

• Charge resources decay, so that the artefact *true* price includes *ecorefunds*

• Stimulate thriftiness in consumers' habits, through conservativeness detaxing

• Forbid (or heavily discourage) trading/using highly penalising tangibles

Socioeconomical promotion of the appropriateness of ecoconsistent behaviours, by implementing the following:

• Education programmes, to explain *affluent* community effects and *thrifty* community requirements

• Specialised boost on *utility*-, rather than *commodity*-driven surroundings

• International agreements, to harmonise ecoprotection acts and to grant *fair* trade

Technical–scientific support of innovation by targeted R&D projects, with concern of the following:

• Acknowledged metrics and certifying controllers, for T productivity transparency

• *Extended* artefacts, enhancing tangibles ecoefficiency or moving them off by *equivalent* intangibles

• *Extended* enterprises, assuring the multiple-task *collaborative* network for life-cycle visibility

---

charges collection), the study somehow leaves out technicalities, and does not point to the socioeconomical and political-legal contributions that will affect the setup of *thrifty* communities, according to a complex of changes referred to as *method* innovation (Figure 17).

Indeed, the knowledge society is viewed as a winning path to the thrifty community, providing technical aids, directly, by mixed utility-commodity ICT provisions, and indirectly, by supplying extended artefacts delivery and functions market. However, the technology-driven issues, needed to make thriftiness possible, are not sufficient to generate sustainability. Today:

- The purchasing decisions that favor a product–service, with lower impacts in resource provision, in life-cycle use, etc., with properties that facilitate reuse or recycling, etc., are qualitative spurs.
- The resource productivity (TYPUS, tangibles yield per unit service) is an hypothesis: no established standard is available; no testing and overseeing body exists.
- The prospective new deal requires advances in technologies, possibly, as a third instance (Figure 17), while the legal and the social aspects (Michelini, 2004, pp. 83-98) play necessary roles.

Social and Political Conditioning Surroundings

The area of social and political goals is full of contrasting propositions: many years ago, several actors got concerned with ecology bounds and pointed out the need for restrictions on resources consumption.

Then, being hard to foretell the arrangements of *method* innovation for the *thrifty* community, the shifts, capable to address the humanity toward stable setups, could be addressed, combining three backdrops:

Figure 18. Typical social and political goals for ecoconsistency

Public spirit orientation and civic-mindedness focusing on the following:

- Education with incremental concern about resource protection, based on feasible steps
- Ecology consciousness, grounded on scientifically consistent theories and forecasts
- Promotion of new trends, e.g., the *function* market to replace the *manufacture* market
- Marketing strategies to foster clients' habits about the artefacts *use* and *upkeep*
- Advertising based on teaching and promoting environmentally and socially safer habits
- Any actions improving, through public spirit orientation, ecoconservative behaviour

Figure 19. Typical ecoreturns of extended artifacts

> *Supply chains with knowledge-based consistent balance*:
> • users' special requests shall be incorporated pre-emptively, designing solutions for them;
> • the artefacts characteristics must be attuned to the existing level (modular design helps);
> • integration shall bind all actors of supply life-cycle (e.g., for clear incentives transmission);
> • schemes for tangibles call-back or final withdrawal should exploit efficient reverse logistic;
> • alternative abilities of artefacts use could be foreseen, with included users' data sheets;
> • point-of-service and point-of-sale overlay shall ensure *smart* (eco-consistent) usage;
> • any attribute improving, through information effectiveness, eco-conservative results.

Figure 20. Typical ecoprovisions of the collaborative networks

> *Finalised communication patterns for knowledge management and filtering*:
>
> • Networks interoperability by integration and sharing of *federated* information
>
> • Management of distributed activities, based on decentralised *self-acting* clusters
>
> • Supply-chain transparency provided by *ecoconsistency* assessment *records*
>
> • *Goal-oriented* cooperative knowledge buildup and problem-solving capabilities
>
> • *Sectional-bounded* and case-driven trust-building processes with secrecy
>
>   preservation
>
> • Consent-selective and operation-safe access for the overseeing certifying bodies
>
> • Any options improving, by communication effectiveness, ecocharges collection

1. Goals in the social and political frameworks that are consistent with shared people agreements (Figure 18).
2. Advantages of knowledge-intensive supply chains, directly perceived by purchasers (Figure 19).
3. Tailored provisions of the ecocharges, managed through collaborative networks (Figure 20).

The three backdrops lead to a blend of behavioral suggestions, where the betterments are supported by ICT instruments, and correspond to focus, for the extended artefact deliveries, on specializing the Web links of the extended enterprises to individual resources utilization requirements (Michelini, 1976). Even in front of defective cross-link occurrences, decisiveness helps establish along finalized patterns, assist in the surfacing of the pertinent filtered knowledge (whether the series of consents are verified for the selected tracks), leading to the set of tailored provisions (Figure 20) by proper ecoreturn on the *extended* artefact (Figure 19), under the public spirit awareness of the achieved goals. The social and political frames bring in only smooth changes (Figure 18) consistent with little improvement (this is better than regression). The joint backdrops contribute to the *knowledge* society coherence, at least, what we, today, conceive, as being grounded on existing ICT tools.

Partial changes could be deceitful; on the supply-chain side, the evolution leads to jointly embedded utility and commodity delivering, so that the value of intangibles becomes prevalent, as compared to the one of consumables (if nonrenewable resources are concerned; Figure 19). The setting is, possibly, not new, as the boasted merit of industrial society was the marketing of low-price artefacts, as compared with people wealth, based on the wide resort to natural raw materials. After a while, this becomes a misleading virtue: for growth, alternative provisions need to be explored for the value chain of artefacts, based on squandering earth treasures. Of course, it is difficult to grant that alternative raw materials always exist, unless the extensive resort to intangibles is explored, giving rise to the knowledge society.

Legal and Economical Spurs to Development Conservativeness

The backdrops based on social and political conditioning show tiny adaptation, and this, only when in the average, people consent follows a steady line. Actually, in past years, social communities and political movements did not impress coherent suggestions, especially, when dealing with the life quality of the generic citizen. Sustainability, nevertheless, is an urgent demand, and effective solutions need to be found. The breakpoint is here presumed to happen with the knowledge society deployment, when the function/service market will largely overtake the (grown and manufactured) commodities market.

The change will not happen by itself. It can develop on the availability of technologies, on condition of the compulsory shove of bylaws. The thrifty community buildup, then, could settle after wide alteration of trade acts and civil codes, including leasing-like indentures for durables (cars, house appliances, etc.); shared hold replacing ownership; restriction on consumables, to rule end-of-life dismissal (cotton clothes, e.g., today contain toxic by-products, and recycling requires more energy than manufacturing). Restricting the analysis to the utmost trivial prerequisites, the continuity is sought by referring to trading extended artefacts, with the support of extended enterprises. Both entities will not be specified by univocal prospects (as for artefact ownership, etc., as for corporation boundary, etc.), then the backdrop setting might even be updated in the meanwhile. On these premises, the industrial systems could follow coherent trends to sustainability, along the five dimensions (Figure 21):
1. Artefact pricing with the KILT model setup.
2. Life-cycle conformance-to-specification scheme.
3. Collaborative network joining consumers side.

Figure 21. Prerequisites for sustainability-driven fair trade

> *The five dimensions of ecoconsistent* collaborative *networks* are as
> follows:
>
> • Pricing based on business productivity, involving *resource*
>   effectiveness, besides *investment, labour,* and *technology* effectiveness
>   (KILT model)
>
> • Product–service offers, by all-inclusive indentures, with visibility of the
>   sustainability prescriptions (assured by the appropriate artefact
>   *extension*)
>
> • Information infrastructures, with access on supporting know-how and
>   transparency of artefacts life-cycle performance (enterprise *extension*)
>
> • Ecological responsibility up to the *points-of-service,* with
>   ecomonitoring, further to clients' satisfaction at the points-of-sale
>   (TYPUS metrics)
>
> • Accredited *ecoconsistency*-driven quality systems, by *third-party*
>   oversight and control of the supplied *product–service,* through
>   interoperated nets

4. Tangibles net decay assessed by the TYPUS metrics.
5. Ecocharges management by third-party certifying bodies.

The five dimensions bear logical continuity, once the frameworks offered by the ICT tools are addressed assuming that stable solutions are actually achieved by the knowledge society. Today, many ecological acts are puzzling. Most of the environmental impact results from law provisions. These fixed consumption patterns and social habits cover infrastructures (facilities, equipment, logistics, technologies, etc.), human needs (individuals and their well-being, with outcomes in learning, training, etc.), and social layouts (cultures, manners, traditions, and orienting decision-making), and little is done for thriftiness. On the contrary, empowerment is moved to the supply side through economical incentives.

Information Market and the Growth Sustainability

The method innovation concept (Figure 17) is brought in so as to mention the criticality of the appropriateness of technological and organizational issues. The above analysis aims at providing:

- Further elements of the hypotheses, linking the knowledge society and the sustainability demand.
- Guidance for social and political alignments, along (plausible) civic-mindedness agreements trends.
- Outlines for legal and economic updating, consistent with (actual) sustainable business prospects.

The hypotheses assume that the affluent community (ceaseless replacement of artefacts, built through low-cost artificial energy) should give rise to the thrifty community (predominant services/functions provision, supported by pervasive artificial intelligence).

The underlying technical paradigm shifts are ideally recognized, as well as is the factual issue leading to the knowledge society, grounded on trading information and assuring high revenue based on intangibles. The final outcomes can only be imagined. Human activity will go through deep restructuring, and a different glossary might be established (following shifts such as the one undergone by the term "industry"[4]). The coming market, in fact, bears quite unusual peculiarities, some of which are mentioned below:

- Trading *information* will never dispossess the dealer of the original know-how.
- Sharing *information* is based on individual commitment and does not follow from paying for it.
- Developing *information* is a typically nonlinear process, grounded on synergic accumulation.
- Augmenting *information* could be costless, whether built on teamwork with additive specialization or not.
- Managing *information* leads to employee empowerment, delegation, communication, participation, etc.

The establishment of fair trade rules, on these facts, might appear to be difficult and conflicting, even with earlier concepts of *enterprise* that fight to remain competitive, due to know-how secrecy, in the demanding global market. Similarly, the concept of *patented artefact*, while meaning an item due to a given man's art and craft, starts assuming fuzzy ridges in distributed organizations (due to interaction between individuals and teams), in collaborative settings (due to knowledge management and integration), in reconfigurable dynamics (due to brokerage and breeding environments), and in the many other situations where complex interoperability and fast adaptability to surroundings do not allow for the one-to-one mapping of the knowledge origin, due to boundary fuzziness. These facts make the *information* market something different than that to which we get accustomed; still, a few guesses are possible. The analysis has already referred to acknowledged entities (extended artefacts and enterprises) supplied by advances in ICT, assuring the capability of permanent and rapid business alignment by scope economy by an integrated information setup (Figure 13). A further insight shows that similar paradigm shifts are the basic prerequisites for the sustainability of growth. Then, why not fulfil the course? The extended artefact supply chain represents a challenging bet, and the fall-offs on the manufacture market could bring to the thrifty community, with the many facets this study has tried to sketch, notably, the emerging collaboration duties, entrusted to the ecocompatibility certifying business.

CONCLUSIONS

The chapter proposes insights linking the collaborative nested concerns to the sustainability demands. The business alignment to ICT tools brings to extended enterprises and dynamic supply chains, with typical delivery, the extended artefacts, and the characterizing feature, the Web, based on selective and hierarchic setup transparency, when the case arises, to certifying bodies. The study moves from the recently acknowledged KILT model (Michelini, 2004, pp. 83–98), which links manufacture delivery Q, to four independent factors: K, proprietary knowledge; I, invested capital; L, directly involved labor; and T, net worn out tangibles. The implied assumption aims to exploit additional K productivity to balance the charges set aside to pay the T net decay. For sustainability, the affluent community, supported by ceaselessly replacing artefacts, needs evolve to the thrifty community, based on carefully controlling the decay process and by sparing the natural resources. The sustainability of growth, indeed, shall first address broadband ecocompatibility goals, assuming that transition to the thrifty community requires changes in habits, strictly connected to method innovation. The final buildup of the knowledge society represents a turn in the human history, with characteristics that, today, we can only figure out as trends in technologies.

Does this provide effective sustainability? Yes, on condition that the enabling aids, referred to as method innovation, are fulfilled. On the technical–scientific sides, powerful tools are provided by the ICT, and these options are worth careful consideration from the area experts. The discussion, thereafter, needs to expand out of narrow strictly oriented targets, at least, to establish reference goals, also in the economic, legal, political, and social surroundings. Before attempting to consider these topics, the basic technicalities of the underlying paradigm shifts need to be reviewed for extended artefact design and for collaborative network deployment, in terms of ecoconservativeness achievements. These ideas, already present in the EU V FP, emerge in the VI FP (CORDIS database, NEST prospected lines within the PATHFINDER scheme, etc.), and the urgency of the topics deserves wide attention, including backdrop actions toward enhanced *product–service* delivery.

Based on technological issues, everyday life can be arranged differently. This will lead to deep concerns of natural resources spoiling, with drastic changes, also, of the industrial organizations, supporting the new business of the *backward* cycle (from dismissed scraps, to recovered materials). The existing wealth, on these ideas, rather than decrease, could widen, recovering by the K-growth, the taxes paid for the T-decay.

The buildup of bylaws, rather than neutrality, will be a spur toward sustainability, giving transparency of the performance between competing solutions. The ecoqualified company, with extended artefacts, increases its market share, based on information extended infrastructures, advertising the ecoconsistency by connected frames, binding, at the points-of-service, suppliers and users with accredited certifying bodies, under worldwide regulation acts. The innovation aspects connect with legal ones, within net concerns (e.g., ownership and responsibility attribution, data visibility, and privacy protection) and for the worldwide fair trade ruling (e.g., sell-in vs. sell-out strategies, provisions volatility *vs.* manufacture stability), when resources downgrading and on-progress decay are measured to fix growth limitations.

REFERENCES

Michelini, R. C. (1976). Foreword to the XIV BIAS: Automation and resources utilisation. In *Proceedings of the XIV Intl. Conf. Automation and Instrumentation, FAST*, November 23–24 (pp. 5-12), Milano.

Michelini, R. C. (1992). Decision anthropocentric manifold for flexible-specialisation manufacturing. In *Proceedings of the Fourth ASME-ISCIE Intl. Symposium on Flexible Automation*, San Francisco, American Society of Mechanical Engineers, July 12–15, (Vol. 1, pp. 467–474).

Michelini, R. C., & Kovacs, G. L. (2001) Integrated design for sustainability: intelligence for eco-consistent extended-artefacts. *Invited Lecture, Intl. IFP Conference PROLAMAT: Digital Enterprise, New Challanges: Life Cycle Approach to Management and Production*, November 7-9, Budapest.

Michelini, R. C., & Kovacs, G. L. (2002). Integrated design for sustainability: Intelligence for eco-consistent products-and-services. *EBS Review: Innovation, Knowledge, Marketing and Ethics, ISSN-1406-0264, Winter, Tallin,* (15), 81–95.

Michelini, R. C., & Razzoli, R. P. (2004). Product-service eco-design: Knowledge-based infrastructures. *Journal of Cleaner Production, 12*(4), 415–428.

Michelini, R. C., & Razzoli, R. P. (2004). Product-service for environmental safeguard: A metrics to sustainability. *Journal of Resources, Conservation and Recycling, 42*(1, August), 83–98.

ENDNOTES

[1]   Artifact: any object made by man, esp. with a view of subsequent use; something made with skill.
      Extended artefact (or product-service): any supply joining manufactured commodities and enabling utilities.

[2]   See, e.g., Z. Grilliches: "The discovery of residuals", J. of Economic Lit., vol. 34, 1994, pp. 256-283.

[3]   The welfare economics is addressed, the branch of economics concerned with improving human welfare and social conditions *chiefly through the optimum distribution of wealth.*

[4]   Say, the shift of the term *industry*, from *assiduous and diligent activity*, to *aggregate of manufacturing businesses*.

Chapter IV

Business Alignment Requirements and Dynamic Organizations

Maria Manuela Cunha
Polytechnic Institute of Cávado and Ave, Portugal

Goran D. Putnik
University of Minho, Portugal

ABSTRACT

The business environment of today's demands organizations to be permanently aligned with the market. As knowledge and physical resources associated to the development and production of most of today's products often exceed what a single firm is able to accomplish, this business alignment requirement suggests that a successful company must acquire the capability to achieve and explore the competitive advantage in synergy, i.e., using the best available resources, corresponding to a shift from "self-centered close-enterprises" to networked structures. Complementarily, permanent business alignment also implies a high dynamics of the networked structure reconfigurability, so that the structure is able of fast adaptability face to the unpredictable changes in the market, to be closely aligned with it, corresponding to the concept of dynamic organizations. The chapter discusses the importance of networking and inter-organizational reconfiguration dynamics in the context of the actual business alignment requirements and introduces the most relevant and pertinent concepts around the dynamic organizational models.

INTRODUCTION

In today's competitive business environment, some trends are already determining the adoption of new organizational concepts, with extremely high performances, strongly time-oriented while highly focused on cost and quality and permanently aligned with business opportunities.

The combination of the shorter life span of new products, increasing product diversity over time, rapid technological developments, increased technological complexity, market globalization, frequent changes in demand, uncertainty, strong competition, are the main trends of the actual worldwide economic context. Unlike the past, where manufacturers were the drivers (pushers) of supply chain management activities, today customers are themselves the drivers (pullers) of the supply process. Manufacturing takes place in a global context where local markets are subject of global standards and where customers are more demanding. State-of-the-art information technology and communication technology is enabling cross-boundary business activities, and a number of best practice approaches are being considered for new organizational structures.

"Competition is at the core of the success or failure of firms" (Porter, 1985, p.1). Competition determines the appropriateness of a firm's activities that can contribute to its performance.

A successful company must acquire the capability to achieve and explore the competitive advantage in synergy (Yusuf, Sarhadi, & Gunasekaran, 1999), i.e., using the best resources available to an organization (Cunha, Putnik, & Ávila, 2000), which requires a shift from "self-centered close-enterprises" (Browne & Zhang, 1999) to dynamically reconfigurable collaborative networked structures, corresponding to the recent approaches of the Extended Enterprise (Browne, Sacket, & Wortmann, 1995), the Virtual Enterprise (Byrne, 1993; Drucker, 1990; Goldman, Nagel, & Preiss, 1995), the Agile Enterprise (Nagel & Dove, 1992), the Virtual Value Chains (Benjamin & Wigand, 1995), the Agile/Virtual Enterprise (Cunha et al., 2000; Cunha, Putnik, & Gunasekaran, 2002; Putnik, 2000a), the Intelligent Enterprise (Quinn, 1990), the Smart Organization (Filos & Banahan, 2001), the OPIM model (One Product Integrated Manufacturing) (Putnik, 1997; Putnik & Silva, 1995) and other models, each with its characterizing nuances. In the text these models are generally addressed as Virtual Enterprise (VE) models.

Several factors appear as supreme factors of competitiveness, namely: (1) the organizations' *capability to achieve and explore competitive advantages in synergy*, by using or integrating the optimal available resources for the functions that the organization undertakes, (2) the capability of *fast adaptability to the market*, together with (3) the capability of *managing all business processes independently of distance*. The recent Virtual Enterprise (VE) organizational models traduce these factors (Cunha & Putnik, 2002).

In summary, the goals of this chapter are to providing a better understanding for the evolution of these inter-organizational relationships and arrangements and to stress the importance of networking and inter-organizational reconfiguration dynamics in the context of the emerging organizational models and modern business alignment requirements.

The chapter discusses the main trends of the actual economic environment that dictate the concept of inter-organizational reconfigurability dynamics as a main functional requirement, and introduces the most relevant and pertinent concepts around the emerging virtual enterprise organizational models, in particular the dynamic organizations, which address this new business requirement.

TOWARD BUSINESS ALIGNMENT

During the 1970s and 1980s we have assisted to changes in the world economic scene, particularly the failure of large corporations to adequately respond to new competition from Asia. Until the beginning of the eighties, price was the dominant factor that determined customers' preferences, while quality and speed were not of considerable significance as consumers were passively accepting the products pushed by the *offer side*. This resulted in extensive mass production of goods at lower prices, until a moment with the industry pushing goods to a market that wanted to require, to pulling. To Boyer (1987), the problems posed by the contemporary society are the result of reaching the limits of *taylorism*, the extension of the labor organization has become anti-productive, mass production was directed to global dimensioned markets, and consume has deviated from the model of standardized production.

Global competition throughout the last two decades has strengthened the significance of a company's ability to introduce new products, while responding to increasingly dynamic markets with customers rapidly changing needs, demanding for shorten the time required to design, develop and manufacture, as well as for cost reduction and increased quality.

In the past a product could exist without great changes (adaptations, redesigns); face to the challenges of today's, besides the shorter duration of a product, it suffers several redesigns in order to be competitive, i.e., aligned with the market demands.

As mentioned in the Iacocca Institute report *"21st Century Manufacturing Enterprise Strategy"* (Nagel & Dove, 1992), the main trends of the actual economical context are: (1) to meet the rapidly changing needs of the marketplace; (2) to shift quickly between product models or between product lines, in order (3) to respond in real-time to the customer demands.

Today, the number of worldwide products and services is increasingly growing, together with the growing number of global enterprises and global brands (this happens also for the services sector). Major global manufacturers and suppliers internationalize, in order to give fast response at the best price, to the products required by the market. Most of current products integrate components coming from different parts in the world, while manufacturers (Original Equipment Manufacturers – OEM) get specialized in designing, assembly and marketing, and manage a network of suppliers.

The driving force of business is to fully satisfy customers each time more demanding, each time more global, with products each time more customized to their individual needs, at the right time, at the right price and with the required quality. At the same time, although the constant stream of innovations in the goods and services allows manufacturers and service providers to offer higher quality products, it increases customers' expectations, and thus requires higher levels of competition. Thus, business alignment is a main requisite for competitiveness.

By business alignment we mean the actions to be undertaken to gain synergy between business, that is, a market opportunity, and the provision of the required product, with the required specifications, at the required time, with the lowest cost and with the best possible return (financial or other).

BUSINESS ALIGNMENT INDUCERS

In the context of knowledge economy, competitiveness is not only dependable on manufacturing technology, automation, etc. Several competitiveness priorities emerged in the first half of the nineties, which include responsiveness to the market, fast product introduction, flexibility and agility, and high standards of quality.

According to several authors, firms wish a flexible organizational structure, able to adjust rapidly to the changes in the environment, sufficiently lean to win the prices, innovative enough to assure the highest pattern of technological performance, and sufficiently devoted to assure the maximum satisfaction of its customers demands. Firms are supposed to be lean, agile, flexible, proactive, competitive, innovative, efficient, customer oriented and... profitable!

Proactivity, which is strongly dependent upon the integration and coordination, offers strategic advantages (Yusuf et al., 1999), is also proposed in the literature as a main competitiveness criteria. Networking or inter-organizational collaboration is indispensable to efficiently meet the market demands. Agility and reconfigurability dynamics appear as intrinsic characteristics of networking to assure permanent business alignment. Information technology also appears as a main enabler of the dynamics.

In this section we review some of the most relevant drivers of competitiveness, or, in other words, the main business alignment inducers.

Flexibility and Agility

For almost two decades, authors converge on the idea that the solution to the trends in the global competitive environment of today's relies in flexibility, the most important organizational innovation that the future deserves to enterprises, as Donovan & Wonder (1993) describe it.

Flexibility that, for example, to Miles and Snow (1984) or to T. Ohno (1988) could be found on a networked organization, Womack expressed through the conceptualization of lean systems (Womack & Jones, 1994; Womack, Roos, and Jones, 1990), corresponds to agile distributed systems to Nagel and Dove (1993), Staffend (1992) associates to virtual factories, Verpsalainen (1991) associates to the supply of teleservices, Warnecke (1995) associates to the Fractal Factory, can be found in the model of a learning organization of Peter Senge (1990), to the IMS (Intelligent Manufacturing Systems) Programme is found in a Holonic Manufacturing System (IMS, 1995), according to Lehner (1991) is found in an anthropocentric production system, can be given by a Virtual Enterprise (Byrne, 1993) or an Agile/Virtual Enterprise (Cunha & Putnik, 2004; Putnik, 2000a), etc., just to mention some representative and comprising approaches over the last few years.

Another related concept is the agility one. A very complete and comprehensive definition of agility is the one suggested by Yusuf, Sarhadi and Gunasekaran (1999): "Agility is the successful exploration of competitive bases (speed, flexibility, innovation, proactivity, quality and profitability) through the integration of reconfigurable resources and best practices in a knowledge-rich environment to provide customer-driven products and services in a fast changing market environment."

According to Putnik (2000a), within the concept of FMS (Flexible Manufacturing Systems), *flexibility* is conceptually defined as a capability of the (manufacturing) system to adapt to the new tasks (i.e. to reconfigure or to reprogram itself in order to satisfy the demand in an optimal way), without interruption of the production (manufacturing) process. Adaptation must be so fast that the production process will not be affected.

Functionally, i.e., abstracted from an application or application domain, Putnik (2000b) defends that *flexibility* and *agility* correspond to each other. Flexibility is a concept defined for the manufacturing workshop environment, while agility is a concept defined for the enterprise, business environment.

However, flexibility is a reactive concept, it is a fast and efficient answer to change, after its detection, while agility is a proactive concept, almost implying the ability to predict change. As such, by introducing the proactiveness characteristic of the agility concept, we agree to consider flexibility to be part of agility (flexibility $\subseteq$ agility).

In any case, the reconfigurability, as part of agility or flexibility, implies the search of new resources, to be allocated to the task to be performed. If the enterprise searches for resources within its boundaries, we are talking about *intra-company agility*, otherwise, we are talking about *inter-company agility*.

Networking

One of the most widely discussed area in recent business literature is that of organizational network structures, as the basic principle to achieve flexibility, adaptability to the market and quick response in a highly complex environment, as proposed for example by Miles & Snow (1986).

Outsourcing or sub-contracting has become an important strategy for many firms, as recognized during the late eighties and nineties, partly due to an increased pressure towards downsizing and a growing recognition of possible advantages of cooperative inter-firm relations, as defended by many researchers, just to mention, Miles & Snow (1984; 1986), Naisbitt (1982), Naisbitt & Aburdene (1985), Toffler (1985), Jarrilo (1988), Davidow & Malone (1992), Bradley, Hausman, & Nolan (1993), Byrne (1993), Kidd (1994; 1995), Handy (1995), Browne & Zhang (1999).

If traditionally the goal of the enterprise was to fulfil the customer requirements using its internal limited set of resources, the knowledge and physical resources associated to the development and production of most of today's products often exceed what a single firm is able to accomplish. To solve the problem of the lack of resources that could bring to the company a competitive advantage, the company searches for cooperation with other companies, under several formats, ranging from the well-known solutions of subcontracting other companies or creating strategic partnerships or joint-venture associations, until some emerging networked and knowledge-based organizational models.

According to Cullen (2000), the Kauffman's (1995) metaphor of a "knowledge landscape" suggests that firms can improve their fitness within that landscape by sharing knowledge between firms and by extending the sum of the whole beyond its individual components.

The new enterprise is viewed as a network that shares experience, knowledge and capabilities.

The Core Competence Theory (Prahalad & Hamel, 1990) outlines that success and failure of an organization are necessarily based on its unique or specific potentials, assets or resources. Core competencies are a competitive advantage and should provide access to a wide range of markets, should substantially contribute to the benefit of the product and should be visible for the client and also hard to copy and out of competitors reach. In a network-based structure, partners contribute with its best practices and core competencies to achieve the highest competitiveness of the structure as a whole.

Let us use Figure 1 to illustrate the importance of networking. Multi product companies i.e., those which organizational model consists on the production of various products, present different performance levels for the different products, as represented in Figure 1 (a), as a consequence of the different performances of its resources in the execution of the different operations of a given product, as in (c). In general, the operations performed with larger efficiency correspond to the core competencies of the company. Contrarily, under the concept of a network organization, it is possible to conceive a new physical structure of the production system for each new product (in Figure 1 (b), one network created for each product), where all the processes to produce a product are decomposed in operations performed by partners of the network. For each

Figure 1. Performance analysis of: multi-product company (a) and (c); network structure (b) and (d)

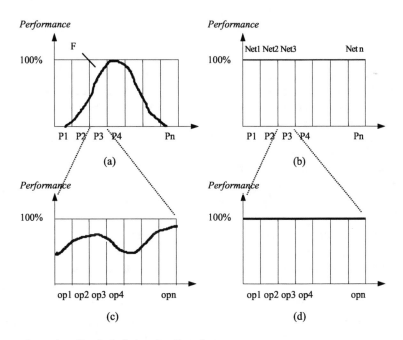

Legend: F = single factory for all products
           Pi = Product i
           opi = operation i
           Net i = Network for product Pi (a different structure for each Pi)

operation is selected the partner presenting the highest possible performance, so that the overall performance of the network is optimized (ideally 100%), as in Figure 1 (d).

Reconfigurability Dynamics

In the last years new factors have emerged that brought a different view on the enterprise organization. A new requisite for extremely high dynamics of the company reconfigurability, i.e. in search for new resources, through companies' association creation, cooperation, networking etc., has been introduced.

Face to the need of business alignment that the competition environment is demanding, enterprises are expected to present at least the following characteristics:

- Fast reconfigurability or adaptability: the ability of fast change face to the unpredictable changes in the environment/market, implying the substitution of resources (i.e., the network structure can have as many instantiations as required either by product changes or as a requirement of quality and competitiveness improvement), and the
- Evolutionary capability: the ability to learn with history.

These requirements imply the ability of (1) flexible and almost instantaneous access to the optimal *resources* to integrate in the enterprise; (2) design, negotiation, business management and manufacturing management functions independently from the physical barrier of space; and (3) minimization of the reconfiguration or integration time.

Business and product life cycles tend to shorten, time to market also, and firms are implementing a wide variety of different techniques, management processes and development strategies in their quest for shorter development cycles.

Reconfiguration, meaning substitution of resources providers, generating a new instantiation of the network, can happen mainly from three reasons:

1. Reconfiguration during the network company life cycle is a consequence of the product redesign in the product life cycle, to keep the network aligned with the market requirements.
2. Reconfiguration as a consequence of the nature of the particular product life cycle phase (evolutionary phases).
3. Reconfiguration can happen also as a consequence of the evaluation of the resources performance during one instantiation of the network, or voluntarily by rescission of participating resources, wiling to disentail from the network.

As Webster (Merriam-Webster) defines it, dynamics consists on "a pattern or process of change, growth, or activity". In our context dynamics means precisely the intensity of change a network structure is subject of, the intensity of reconfiguration.

Information Technology

"The introduction of reliable low-cost electronic computers into the economy was the most revolutionary technical innovation of the twentieth century" (Freeman & Soete, 1997, p. 158). "The fact that a new technology has many potential applications does not mean that all of these will occur simultaneously, or even over a short period. On the contrary, the assimilation of a major new technology into the economic and social system is a matter of decades, not years, and is related to the phenomenon of long cycles in the economy" (Freeman & Soete, 1997, p. 184). Schumpeter already suggested it in 1939 (Schumpeter, 1939).

The focus of information technology within organizations has shifted over the last thirty years, from improving the efficiency of business processes within organizations, to improving the effectiveness of the whole value chain. The last decade has seen the use of information and communication technologies to create electronic networks within and between organizations.

Information and communication systems and technologies are the support of concepts as distributed systems, computer supported cooperative work, telework, electronic commerce, electronic marketplaces, teleoperation, virtual prototyping, concurrent engineering, which more deeply or less deeply are connected with the implementation of the networked information-based organizational models.

ON THE DYNAMICS OF NETWORK RECONFIGURABILITY

This section introduces the main concepts related with network reconfigurability and discusses the requirements of dynamic organizations.

Basic Concepts

Let us start with the definition of some introductory concepts, such as the definition of *basic* and *complex resources*, *selection complexity* and *solution space dimension*.

Basic and Complex Resources

A resource represents an entity that can contribute or add value, providing either a product (component, assembly), a service or an operation. A resource is (a view of) an enterprise object, which is used to realize, or to support the execution of, one or more processes and it is the subject of control (or management) (Putnik, 2000a). It is important to notice that resource is a recursive construct.

Resources can be classified into *Basic Resources* and *Complex Resources*, as represented in Figure 2.

Basic Resources are task specific and, when outsourced, do not require detailed contracts or specifications, are usually of fixed and short duration, and support lower-level organizational tasks. Examples include: payroll services, word processing, CAD drawing services, testing/measuring services, cleaning services, maintenance services.

Complex Resources require detailed and complex contracts, detailed specifications, are usually of long duration (except if anything goes wrong), involve high costs and risks. Its search or qualification is time consuming and costly, as well as negotiation, selection, integration in the partnership, performance monitoring and contract enforcement. Examples include: product development, software development and turnkey manufacturing services.

As *Complex Resources* outsourcing is complex, time consuming and risky, it is expected that complex resources do not change much, that is, the partnership at higher levels of the process tree are expected to be lasting or stable (less dynamic). Concerning

Figure 2. Product processes and corresponding Basic and Complex Resources (Cunha & Putnik, 2002)

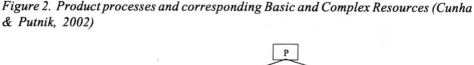
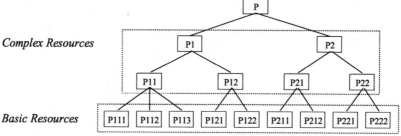

the provision of *Basic Resources* there exists a larger pool of potential providers and links within partnerships are weaker. Reconfiguration dynamics for *basic resources* is higher than for *complex resources*, as we will discuss.

A possible instantiation of a network structure (or of a VE) to produce a product P could involve outsourcing of parts P1 and P2 to resources providers R1 and R2 (*complex resources outsourcing*), as represented in Figure 3 or could involve outsourcing primitive parts (*basic resources outsourcing*), to resources providers also able to supply *complex resources*, as represented in Figure 3 for resource P11, or able to supply only *basic resources* as represented in Figure 4.

Figure 3. Outsourcing basic and complex resources (Cunha & Putnik, 2002)

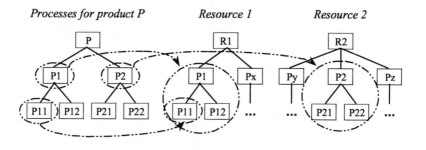

Figure 4. Outsourcing basic resources (Cunha & Putnik, 2002)

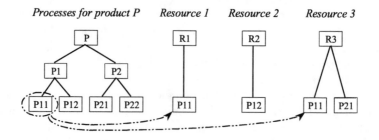

Selection Complexity and Solution Space Dimension

The complexity of resources selection is a function of the solution space dimension and the selection algorithm. The solution space dimension is, in turn, a function of the selection model used in the evaluation of the eligible resources to integrate in a network/partnership/VE instance. Considering the need to integrate k resources in a partnership, the evaluation of the eligible resources providers can be performed using two approaches (designated selection models):

- Independently, i.e., analyzing the n eligible resources providers one by one, independent of the other resources that they are able to provide
- Dependently, considering all the possible combinations of the k required resources being provided by all the possible combinations of the n eligible resources providers

Selection of Resources to Perform One Task

If we are evaluating the performance of n resources providers to perform one task, the *solution space dimension* is n, both for *dependent* and *independent* selection models.

Selection of Resources to Perform k Tasks

Assuming that the number of tasks to perform is k, we can identify several situations concerning the ability of the eligible resources providers to provide more than one task, up to the ability of a provider to provide all the k tasks under analysis, and including the application of a dependent or independent selection model.

If each of the n resources is able to provide only one task, we have only the possibility to apply an independent selection model, and we face the lower limit of the solution space dimension. Our solution space would be n, the number of resources able to provide each of the k tasks.

We then face the upper limit of the *solution space dimension*, when all the n resources are able to provide all the k tasks, i.e., the k tasks can be performed by any combination of resources providers. In this situation, according to the *selection model*, we have the following:

- A solution space dimension of $n.k$ if the n resources able to provide the k tasks are selected under an independent selection model. The selection complexity is ($O(n.k)$).
- A solution space dimension of n^k if the n resources able to provide the k tasks are selected under a dependent selection model. The associated selection complexity is very high, ($O(n^k)$).

In practice, not all the resources are able to provide all the tasks under analysis, so the solution space dimension is situated within the intervals:

$$n \leq \text{solution space dimension}_{\text{independent selection}} \leq n.k$$

$$n \leq \text{solution space dimension}_{\text{dependent selection}} \leq n^k$$

Solution Space Dimension for Basic and Complex Resources

We focus now on the several levels of the process plan of the product to be produced by an instantiation of a dynamic organization.

Concerning *complex resources*, the general situation is that usually the number of required resources (k) is low, and depending on the product, the selection method can be a *dependent* or *independent* one. However, the number of *complex resources* to be subcontracted at once (k), especially for high process levels, is usually small ($k = 1, 2,$ or 3, for example), and n is small, so even if we reach n^k complexity, the problem is tractable. Also, at higher product process levels, resources selection corresponds in general to an *independent selection*, so complexity is $O(n.k)$ as represented in Figure 5.

Performing the same reasoning for *basic resources* where reconfigurability dynamics is very high, the number of possible providers is high and it is possible sometimes a *dependent* selection, but most of the eligible suppliers are of small size and much specialized, so the selection is, in general, *independent*, conducting to a $O(n.k)$ complexity (see Figure 5).

At the intermediate level of the product process plan (in the middle of the curve of Figure 5), the possibility of performing a *dependent* evaluation increases, and it is likely to find an $O(n^k)$ complexity with a large k and n.

Independent of the selection algorithm, in Cunha (2003), we demonstrate that the complexity associated with the selection of resources to integrate/reconfigure a dynamic organization depends on the *solution space dimension*, which is represented in Figure 5, in function of the level of the product process plan.

Dynamics Parameters

We identify two main parameters of *reconfigurability dynamics*: the number of requested reconfigurations per unit of time and the time to reconfigure. Reconfigurability dynamics is directly proportional to the number of requests and inversely proportional to the time to make operational the reconfiguration (selection, negotiation, and integration). Reconfigurability dynamics can be measured by a ratio between the frequency of reconfiguration requests and the reconfiguration time.

Figure 5. Representation of the solution space dimension in function of the process level

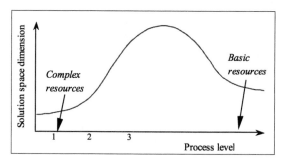

Reconfiguration Request Frequency

Alignment between a dynamic networked organization and the market implies the permanent evaluation of opportunities of reconfiguring the partnership.

By the definition of *basic* and *complex resources*, we are expecting to have a lower *reconfiguration request frequency* for *complex resources* and higher frequency for *basic resources*. The reason is not only the duration of contracts or the nature of the resources integrated in an instantiation, but also the number of subcontracts at each level of the product process plan, which makes *reconfiguration request frequency* grow exponentially with the level of the process, i.e., to grow from level 1 (or higher/top level) to the primitive level (corresponding to the *basic resources*).

Reconfiguration Time

Selection complexity also depends on the *selection algorithm* to be used, which should be dependent of the level of the function to be integrated. The *solution space dimension* implies search complexity (computational complexity), which can be dealt with automatically, but at high levels, it is not a computational complexity.

Selection (regarding further integration) involves the identification of potential candidate resources providers, followed by processes of evaluation and negotiation. Thus, *selection time* can be decomposed on:

$$t_{Selection} = t_{Search} + t_{Negotiation}$$

Search time corresponds to the time required to identify potential resources providers, which grows from the top level of the product process plan to *basic resources*.

Time to create/reconfigure (reconfiguration time) an instantiation includes, besides the selection time, the contracting time, and integration time, and reflects the importance of the function to be integrated (this importance can be stated in terms of contract value, dependability of other functions on that one, etc.). Complex resources usually corresponds to increased contracting time, which decreases for lower product process levels:

$$t_{Reconguration} = t_{Selection} + t_{Contracting} + t_{Integration}$$

Time to reconfigure a structure at high-level processes highly surpasses the time required to identify potential resources, which is essentially a computational effort. Stability (low reconfigurability dynamics) at higher levels is a consequence of the high reconfiguration time required.

Selection time and contracting time have behaviors inversely proportional to the function of the level of the searched function in the product process level.

Reconfigurability Dynamics

Focusing on the definitions of basic and complex resources, contract duration decreases along with the process level, as well as selection time, contracting time, and integration time. Basic resources are usually contracted for well-defined periods, usually short, and reconfiguration time is reduced. The opposite situation is verified for complex resources.

Figure 6. Representation of the reconfiguration dynamics and contract duration as functions of the product process level

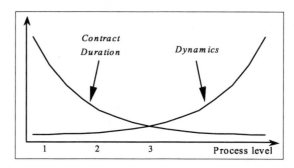

At the level of complex resources, dynamics is low, according to the two parameters of dynamics: a low reconfiguration requests frequency and a high reconfiguration time, while dynamics increases along with the product process level, with growing reconfiguration requests frequency and decreasing reconfiguration time.

If the utilisation of a low-level function is very high, the function could be internalized, otherwise, it is outsourced.

In Figure 6, we present *reconfiguration dynamics* and *contract duration* as functions of the product process level. *Reconfiguration requests frequency* has the same behavior as *dynamics*, and thus has been omitted from the figure.

Figure 6. Representation of the *reconfiguration dynamics* and *contract duration* as functions of the product process level.

Dynamic Organizations

A dynamic organization is a reconfigurable network to assure permanent business alignment, in transition between states or instantiations (configurations) along time, as represented in Figure 7. Dynamics means the intensity of change a network enterprise is subject to. Networking dynamics considers a succession of network's states along the time, i.e., the network reconfigurability dynamics. (Do not confuse reconfigurability dynamics with operational dynamics.)

The main factor against reconfigurability dynamics, i.e., the main factor disabling reconfiguration frequency, is reconfiguration of cost and time, reducing dynamics by increasing the duration of stable configurations.

The implementation of dynamic organizations requires adequate tools and environments that, by reducing reconfiguration costs and reconfiguration time, can support a higher reconfiguration dynamics.

An Example of Potential Reconfigurability Dynamics

We will use a study from a U.S. automotive industry supply chain (a most relevant industrial sector) to highlight the potential of an *organizations' reconfigurability dynamics*.

According to the Research Triangle Institute study (Brunnermeier & Martin, 1999), an original equipment manufacturer (OEM) estimates that as many as 453,000 exchanges

Figure 7. Networking dynamics considers a succession of network's states along the time line

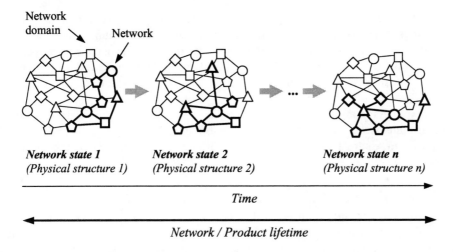

Network state 1   *Network state 2*   *Network state n*
(Physical structure 1) *(Physical structure 2)*   *(Physical structure n)*

Time

Network / Product lifetime

of product data occur each year within the company and between the company and its suppliers. This figure could lead to the possibility of 453,000 different instantiations of the networks of subcontractors created around the OEM. If the network of subcontractors is considered as a VE, then 453,000 different instantiations of the hypothetical VE are possible, or at least there is a possibility of having 453,000 evaluations of the VE performance, in order to determine the need for reconfiguration. These 453,000 annual instantiations would mean an interval of 50 seconds between reconfiguration requests in a continuous-operating industry (24 hours per day, 260 days per year), or an interval of 17 seconds between reconfiguration requests in a single-turn-operating industry (eight hours per day).

The above-mentioned data only regard product changes, without considering additional requirements (such as production process improvements, cost reductions, market conditions, etc.). We should also consider the possible reconfigurations originated by the substitution of resources providers, voluntary disentail of a partner, etc. In general, and considering those multitude of requirements, it is more than likely to expect that the typical time interval between reconfiguration requests will be dramatically reduced from hours, to minutes, to even seconds or less.

DYNAMICS DISABLERs

The main critical aspects associated with the recent concept of dynamically reconfigurable global networked structures, i.e., the main factors against networking and reconfigurability dynamics, are the transaction costs and the leakage of private information.

In an ideal business environment, a firm makes an informed assessment of the relevant costs, benefits, and risks of outsourcing versus internal procurement. If there exists a profitable opportunity to outsource a service or operation, the client and the suppliers enter into a contract with full knowledge of the nature of the work, signing a complete and explicit written agreement covering all aspects of the outsourced service and payments, eventually including contingency plans. But in most contractual relationships, things do not happen this way, processes are much more complex than idealized.

The costs of outsourcing are composed of both the explicit cost of carrying out the transaction as well as hidden costs due to coordination difficulties and contractual risks. The major costs associated with outsourcing include the transaction costs and the leakage of private information.

The implementation of the dynamic organizations requires the existence of tools and environments that overcome these two disabling factors, allowing dynamics as high as required to assure business alignment, without the constraints of the disabling factors.

Leakage of Private Information

A firm's private information is information that no one else knows, and it gives a firm an advantage in the market. Most of the time, this private information is held as a core competitive advantage that distinguishes a firm from its competitors. It may concern production know-how, product design, or consumer information.

Networking or partitioning tasks between resources providers increases the risk of losing control of such types of information, which only through complete contractual agreements could be safeguarded, and furthermore, through an environment assuring trust and accomplishment of the duty of seal. The implementation of the networked structures requires tools to enable the preservation of the firm's knowledge. When considering dynamically reconfigurable networks, the risk of leakage of private information increases.

Transaction Costs

Firms can carry out their transactions wholly within the firm (internally), outside the firm (completely externalized), or in the grey area between the firm and the marketplace (Oster, 1994). Every organization has a set of strategic decisions that involves the decision of which transactions are to be made internally (performed within its organizational boundaries) and of which transactions will be made using the market (use of external market agents for carrying out activities). This set of decisions on how deeply to vertically integrate, i.e., how to structure its transactions (internally and externally), is known as the "make-or-buy" decisions.

The principles governing these decisions were first articulated in 1937 by Ronald Coase (1937), the father of transaction costs economics, in his pioneering work, "The Nature of the Firm." Coase's central argument was that, by vertically integrating, a firm opts to make its resource decisions internally using whatever management mechanisms are available (centralized direction), as opposed to using market transactions. Several recent schools of thought developed other institutional modes of economic governance, for example, Collins (1990, 1997) and Powell (1991), but this is beyond the scope of our work.

Transaction costs include the time and expense of negotiating, writing, and enforcing contracts. They include the adverse consequences of opportunistic behavior, as well as the costs of trying to prevent it. Coase (1937) and Williamson (1975) distinguished four types of transaction costs: search costs, contracting costs, monitoring costs, and enforcement costs.

In dynamic organizations, transaction costs are the firm reconfiguration costs, associated with partner search, selection, negotiation, and integration, as well as permanent monitoring and evaluation of partnership performance (Cunha & Putnik, 2003).

If externalizing functions can involve high transaction costs, networking relies intensively on extending the enterprise boundaries and partnering functions. Dynamic organizations, in general, are extremely dependent not only on networking but also on dynamically reconfiguring.

A REVIEW OF DYNAMIC ORGANIZATIONAL MODELS

During the 1980s, a plethora of acronyms and advanced manufacturing concepts were introduced, such as CIM (computer-integrated manufacturing), FMS (flexible manufacturing systems), JIT (just-in-time), TQM (total quality management), OPT (Optimized Production Technology), Concurrent Engineering, etc., that required management or manufacturing to be information intensive.

During the first half of the 1990s, several criteria for competitiveness emerged, including quick response (responsiveness), high flexibility and quality, etc. Supply-chain management, networked organizations, holonic manufacturing systems, lean production, agile manufacturing, fractal factory, and anthropocentric production systems, are examples of organizational models or of production systems, with flexibility as the main characteristic, and all of them represent attempts to answer these requirements of increased competitiveness and efficiency.

Other recent organizational models rely on networks/partnerships more or less strong (dependency), more or less collaborative, more or less dynamic, more or less information-based, and more or less supported by ICT, but all require the support of advanced interorganizational information technology, some of which can be classified as the dynamic organizational models.

Several models have been proposed, since the "Virtual Factory" suggested in 1990 by Peter Drucker (1990), in opposition to the rigid and hierarchical inflexible structures.

According to several definitions (for example, Browne & Zhang, 1999; Byrne, 1993; Camarinha-Matos & Afsarmanesh, 1999; Cunha & Putnik, 2005; Cunha et al., 2000; Davidow & Malone, 1992; Preiss, Goldman, & Nagel, 1996; Putnik, 2000a; Skyrme, 1996), VEs are defined as enterprises with integration and reconfiguration capability in useful time, integrated from independent enterprises, primitive or complex, with the aim of taking profit from a specific market opportunity. After the conclusion of that opportunity, the VE dissolves, and a new VE is integrated, or it reconfigures itself in order to achieve the necessary competitiveness to respond to another market opportunity (Cunha & Putnik, 2005). Even during the operation phase of the VE, the configuration can change, as the need for readjustment or reconfiguration due to unexpected situations arises, raising the importance of the reconfigurability dynamics, as recognized in the Agile/Virtual Enterprise (A/VE) model (Cunha & Putnik, 2002, 2005; Cunha et al., 2000).

We can distinguish between several different forms of dynamically reconfigurable collaborative networked structures classified as VEs in a broad sense: the *extended enterprise*, the *VE* in *stricto sensum*, the *Agile/VE* and the *OPIM* (one product integrated manufacturing) model, for instance, to mention the most relevant developments. The literature offers several other collaborative models, such as Value Nets or the Concurrent Enterprise, but we do not consider them as representative as the previous.

All have in common information and communication technology as a prerequisite and facilitator, or even the core. However, there is so far no unified definition of these concepts, and a variety of definitions exist in the literature (Camarinha-Matos et al., 1997). There exists a broad terminology for this range of concepts, sharing similarities and sometimes overlapping, and yet few of them have been rigorously systematized.

The objectives for enterprises participating in a VE are to increase its market share and benefits. According to Martinez et al. (2001) strategic objectives addressed by the VE models are as follows:

- Maximize flexibility and adaptability to market requirements
- Develop a pool of competencies
- Control the enterprise dimension
- Optimize the global supply chain

The VE differs from existing interorganizational models by the degree of shared information and of responsibility of the participants and the structure by which companies contribute their competencies or integrate the VE processes (Reid et al., 1996). It is recognized that a major issue in the formation of the VE is the rapid integration of the business processes of the participating companies. While the integration of computer and communication technologies are no doubt critical issues, the successful attainment of the business goals of the VE often depends on the ability to align the business processes and practices of partner enterprises (Presley & Rogers, 1996).

According to Browne and Zhang (1999), individual companies work together to form interenterprise networks across the product value chain. The extended enterprise and the VE can be seen in the context of enterprise partnerships, designed to facilitate cooperation and integration across the value chain, the first more concerned about long-term relationships and the second on more dynamic configuration.

The extended enterprise extends beyond traditional organizational boundaries to include the relationships that an enterprise has with its customers, suppliers, business partners, even former competitors, and so on (Browne et al., 1995). The extended enterprise is responsible for the whole product life cycle, from material procurement to component production and manufacturing, to final assembly, further to distribution and customer service, and in an increasing number of cases, to the dispositioning and, where possible, recycling of end-of-life products (Browne & Zhang, 1999). The extended enterprise can be regarded as represented by all those enterprises, customers, suppliers, and subcontractors, engaged collaboratively in designing, developing, manufacturing, and delivering a product to its end user (Browne, Harhen, & Shivnan, 1996).

The IMS project (IMS, 1996) defined the VE as the next generation of manufacturing enterprise, which consists of a globally distributed assembly of autonomous work units linked primarily by the goal of profitably, serving specific customers and operating in an environment of abrupt and often unanticipated change.

In Goldman et al. (1995), the VE concept is seen as a special case, or an implementation of the agile enterprise (or manufacturing) concept. "A virtual organization structure is an opportunistic alliance of core competencies distributed among a number of distinct operating entities within a single large company or among a group of independent companies" (Goldman et al., p. 87). "While the virtual organization is opportunistic, its objective is to create solution products with lifetimes as long as the marketplace will allow. These products are expected to evolve, and as they do, so will the virtual organization's resource requirements. Some participants will leave to join other groups, because their competencies no longer add enough value to be most profitably used in the virtual organization. For precisely the same reasons, others will join, because they can add value as the product evolves in one direction rather than another.... The virtual organization is a dynamic organizational tool for agile competitors. It is at once neither temporary nor permanent" (Goldman et al., 1995, p. 89).

The fundamental idea of the virtual corporation, for Franke (2001), is that it is a partnership created when it is needed.

A VE is "virtual" to Parunak and VanderBok (1998), because it relaxes the conventional restrictions that an enterprise be a single legal entity, headquartered in a single place, with close synchronization among its various functions.

Forbairt (1996) defended the VE as a response to the speed and globalization of the digital age. It is an enterprise that may have no physical head office, very few full-time workers, and exists as a combination of specific skills from individuals or enterprises.

The NIIIP (National Industrial Information Infrastructure Protocols) reference architecture (NIIIP, 1996) defines a VE as a temporary consortium or alliance of companies that comes together to exploit some fast-changing market opportunity. Within the VE, companies share costs and skills and access global markets with each participant contributing with its core competence.

Similarly, Byrne (1993) stressed that the VE is a temporary network of independent companies — suppliers, customers, even rivals — linked by information and communication technology to share skills and costs and access to one another's markets. Each partner company contributes only what it regards as its core competencies. Once the market opportunity is met, the VE will disband. According to the author, the VE will have neither central office nor organization chart, nor hierarchy, nor vertical integration.

Finally, Putnik (2000a) highlighted a very important characteristic of the VE concept that many authors do not point out. The virtual organization model expresses the need of agile competitors to create or assemble new productive resources *very quickly* and *frequently and concurrently* because of decreasing profitable lifetimes of individual products and services.

"Through the combination of the core competencies of member enterprises, the VE may become a best-of-everything enterprise" (Hongmei et al., 2003, p. 333).

An A/VE (BM_A/VE) is a dynamically reconfigurable global networked organization, networked enterprise, or network of enterprises, sharing information and knowledge, skills, core competencies, market and other resources, and processes, configured (or constituted) as a temporary alliance (or network) to meet a (fast-changing) market window of opportunity, presenting as main characteristics, agility, virtuality, distributivity, and integrability (see Chapter VI). It is a VE in a total or partial conformance with the BM_VE Architecture Reference Model (Putnik, 2000a).

96 Cunha & Putnik

OPIM is a recent organizational concept for manufacturing systems of a specific product (Putnik, 1997; Putnik & Silva, 1995). According to its authors, manufacturing systems conceived to produce several products are technically less efficient when compared with dedicated systems, and this level of efficiency or of performance reaches its maximum when manufacturing systems are dedicated to one single product, which corresponds to the existence of a productive structure for each new product. This way, this concept corresponds to a distributed manufacturing system at the highest level and to a highly dynamic structure. The best structure for the OPIM enterprise is constituted from primitive entities, i.e., the system is integrated by primitive resources (for example, a "single person," an individual machine/operation) and for single-product manufacturing. The integrated primitive resources are specialized in a *type of service* (conception, planning, management, and production) or in a *type of operation*, or in a *type of component*. It is a special case of A/VE (or a BM_VE) (Putnik et al., 2005).

Market and product characteristics and product processes dictate the adequate partnership characteristics of the VEs (in broad sense) in terms of product characteristics (standardization level, kind of production series, and product complexity), kind of resources provided by the integrated partners (basic *versus* complex resources), partnership stability (durability), degree of dependability between partners, and reconfiguration dynamics (see Table 1).

Table 1. Comparison of virtual enterprise models

	Extended Enterprise	Virtual Enterprise	BM_A/VE	OPIM
Product characteristics				
	−Traditional to semistandardised −Long and medium series −Simple and complex products	−Semistandardised to customised −Small and medium series	−Highly customised products −Small series −Simple and complex products	−Highly customised products −Small series and one-of-a-kind −Simple and complex products
Kind of resource providers				
	−Complex (usually first tier, in the automotive industry)	−Basic and complex	−Basic and complex	−Basic resources
Partnership stability (durability)				
	−High	−Low	−Very low	−Very low
Dependency between partners				
	−Very high	−Low	−Very low	−Very low
Reconfigurability dynamics				
	−Low	−High	−Very high	−Very high

Dynamic Organisational Models

Increased degree of dynamics →

Copyright © 2005, Idea Group Inc. Copying or distributing in print or electronic forms without written permission of Idea Group Inc. is prohibited.

Dynamic organizational models represent solutions for highly customized products, small series, in highly competitive and changing environments where permanent business alignment is crucial. Partnership stability is low (sometimes very low), dependency between partners is very weak, and reconfiguration dynamics should be as high as possible, given the permanent monitoring of the structure to traduce the most competitive solution at every moment of the product life cycle.

CONCLUSIONS

We have discussed the main trends of today that dictate the concept of interorganizational reconfigurability dynamics as a main functional requirement, and have introduced some emerging virtual enterprise organizational models, classified as dynamic organizations. But at the same time, two disabling factors of networking and dynamics were identified that restrict the implementation of these organizational models. Virtually, one of the most important objectives of the future organizational developments is the development of tools or mechanisms for enabling reconfigurability dynamics. Several contributions can be found in literature (for example, in Putnik, 2000a), some of them in this same book (see Ávila, Putnik, & Cunha, 2005; Cunha et al., 2005; Putnik et al., 2005).

REFERENCES

Ávila, P., Putnik, G. D., & Cunha, M. M. (2005). Broker performance for agile/virtual enterprise integration. In G. D. Putnik & M. M. Cunha (Eds.), *Virtual enterprise integration: Technological and organizational perspectives*. Hershey, PA: Idea Group Publishing.

Benjamin, R., & Wigand, R. (1995). Electronic markets and virtual value chain on the information super highway. *Sloan Management Review, 36*, 62–72.

Boyer, R. (1987). *La flexibilité du travail en Europe*. Paris: La Découverte.

Bradley, S. P., Hausman, J. A., & Nolan, R. L. (1993). Global competition and technology. In S.P. Bradley, J.A. Hausman, & R.L. Nolan (Eds.), *Globalisation technology and competition: The fusion of computers and telecommunications in the 1990s* (pp. 3–31). Boston: Harvard Business School Press.

Browne, J., & Zhang, J. (1999). Extended and virtual enterprises: Similarities and differences. *International Journal of Agile Management Systems, 1/1*, 30–36.

Browne, J., Harhen, J., & Shivnan, J. (1996). *Production management systems—An integrated perspective* (2nd ed.). Reading, MA: Addison-Wesley.

Browne, J., Sacket, P. J., & Wortmann, J. C. (1995). Future manufacturing systems— Towards the extended enterprise. *Computers in Industry, 25*, 235–254.

Brunnermeier, S., & Martin, S. A. (1999). *Interoperability and cost analysis of the U.S. automotive supply chain* (RTI Project Number 7007-03 Final Report). NC: Research Triangle Institute.

Byrne, J. A. (1993, February 8). The virtual corporation: The company of the future will be the ultimate in adaptability. *Business Week*, 98-103.

Camarinha-Matos, L. M., & Afsarmanesh, H. (1999). The virtual enterprise concept. In L. M. Camarinha-Matos & H. Afsarmanesh (Eds.), *Infrastructures for virtual enterprises* (pp. 3–14). Porto, Portugal: Kluwer Academic Publishers.

Camarinha-Matos, L. M., Afsarmanesh, H., Garita, C., & Lima, C. (1997). Towards an architecture for virtual enterprises. *Journal of Intelligent Manufacturing, 9*(2), 189–199.

Coase, R. (1937). The nature of the firm. *Economica, 4*, 386–405.

Collins, H. (1990). Ascription of Legal Responsibility to Groups of Complex Patterns of Economic Integration. *Modern Law Review, 53*, 731–744.

Collins, H. (1997). Quality assurance and contractual practice. In S. Deakin & J. Michie (Eds.), *Contracts, co-operation and competition: Studies in economics, management and law*. Oxford: Oxford University Press.

Cullen, P. -A. (2000). Contracting, co-operative relations and extended enterprises. *Technovation, 20*, 363–372.

Cunha, M. M. (2003). *Organisation of a market of resources for agile and virtual enterprises integration*. Doctoral Thesis, University of Minho, Guimarães, Portugal.

Cunha, M. M., & Putnik, G. D. (2002). Discussion on requirements for agile/virtual enterprises reconfigurability dynamics: The example of the automotive industry. In L. M. Camarinha-Matos (Ed.), *Collaborative business ecosystems and virtual enterprises* (pp. 527–534). Boston: Kluwer Academic Publishers.

Cunha, M. M., & Putnik, G. D. (2003). Market of resources versus e-based traditional virtual enterprise integration—Part I: A cost model definition. In A. Gunasekaran & G. D. Putnik (Eds.), *Proceedings of the First International Conference on Performance Measures, Benchmarking and Best Practices in New Economy*. Guimarães, Portugal.

Cunha, M. M., & Putnik, G. D. (2004). Trends and solutions in virtual enterprise integration. *Tekhné - Review of Politechnical Studies, 1*(1).

Cunha, M. M., & Putnik, G. D. (2005). Business alignment in agile/virtual enterprise integration. In M. Khosrow-Pour (Ed.), *Advanced topics in information resources management* (Vol. IV). Hershey, PA: Idea Group Publishing (forthcoming).

Cunha, M. M., Putnik, G. D., & Ávila, P. (2000). Towards focused markets of resources for agile/virtual enterprise integration. In L. M. Camarinha-Matos, H. Afsarmanesh, & H. Erbe (Eds.), *Advances in networked enterprises: Virtual organisations, balanced automation, and systems integration* (pp. 15–24). Berlin: Kluwer Academic Publishers.

Cunha, M. M., Putnik, G. D., & Gunasekaran, A. (2002). Market of resources as an environment for agile/virtual enterprise dynamic integration and for business alignment. In O. Khalil & A. Gunasekaran (Eds.), *Knowledge and information technology management in the 21st century organisations: Human and social perspectives* (pp. 169–190). London: Idea Group Publishing.

Cunha, M. M., Putnik, G. D., Gunasekaran, A., & Ávila, P. (2005). Market of resources as a virtual enterprise integration enabler. In G. D. Putnik & M. M. Cunha (Eds.), *Virtual enterprise integration: Technological and organizational perspectives*. Hershey, PA: Idea Group Publishing.

Davidow, W. H., & Malone, M. S. (1992). *The virtual corporation—Structuring and revitalising the corporation for the 21st Century*. New York: HarperCollins.

Donovan, P., & Wonder, J. (1993). *The flexibility factor.* Montreal, Canada: Les Éditions de l'Homme.

Drucker, P. F. (1990, May/June). The emerging theory of manufacturing. *Harvard Business Review,* 94–102.

Filos, E., & Banahan, E. (2001). Towards the smart organization: An emerging organizational paradigm and the contribution of the European RTD Programmes. *Journal of Intelligent Manufacturing, 12*(2), 101–119.

Forbairt. (1996). *Virtual corporation defined* (Sumary Section for Forbairt Internet Report). Ireland: Forbairt.

Franke, U. (2001). The concept of virtual Web organisations and its implications on changing market conditions. *Electronic Journal of Organizational Virtualness— EJOV, 3*(4), 43–64.

Freeman, C., & Soete, L. (1997). *The economics of industrial innovation* (3rd ed.). London: Pinter.

Goldman, S., Nagel, R., & Preiss, K. (1995). *Agile competitors and virtual organizations: Strategies for enriching the customer.* New York: van Nostrand Reinhold.

Handy, C. (1995). Trust and virtual organization. *Harvard Business Review, 73*(3), 40–50.

Hongmei, G., Huang, B., Wenhuang, L., & Xiu, L. (2003). A framework for virtual enterprise operation management. *Computers in Industry, 50,* 333–352.

IMS. (1995). *Holonic concepts.* Holonic Manufacturing Systems, Intelligent Manufacturing Systems. Retrieved 1999 online *http://www.ims.org*

IMS. (1996). *IMS Project.* Intelligent Manufacturing Systems. Retrieved 2000 online *http://www.ims.org*

Jarillo, J. C. (1988). On strategic networks. *Strategic Management Journal, 9*(31), 31–41.

Kauffman, S. (1995). Technology and evolution: Escaping the red queen effect. *The McKinsey Quartely, 1.*

Kidd, P. (1994). *Agile manufacturing: Forging new frontiers.* Reading, MA: Addison-Wesley.

Kidd, P. (1995). *Agile corporations: Business enterprises in the 21st century—An executive guide.* Cheshire: Henbury.

Lehner, F. (1991). *Anthropocentric production systems—The European response to advanced manufacturing and globalisation.* Brussels: FAST—Forecasting and Assessment in Science and Technology, European Commission.

Martinez, M. T., Fouletier, P., Park, K. H., & Favrel, J. (2001). Virtual enterprise— Organisation, evolution and control. *International Journal of Production Economics, 74,* 225–238.

Merriam-Webster. *Merriam-Webster Online.* Retrieved November 2001 online *http://www.m-w.com/dictionary.htm*

Miles, R. E., & Snow, C. C. (1984). Fit, failure and the Hall of Fame. *California Management Review, 26,* 10–28.

Miles, R. E., & Snow, C. C. (1986). Organizations: New concepts for new forms. *California Management Review, 28,* 62–73.

Nagel, R., & Dove, R. (1992). *21st century manufacturing enterprise strategy.* Bethlehem, PA: Iacocca Institute, Lehigh University.

Nagel, R., & Dove, R. (1993). *21st century manufacturing enterprise strategy.* Bethlehem, PA: Iacocca Institute, Lehigh University.

Naisbitt, J. (1982). *Megatrends: Ten new directions transforming our lives*. New York: Warner Books.

Naisbitt, J., & Aburdene, P. (1985). *Re-inventing corporation*. New York: Warner Books.

NIIIP. (1996). *The NIIIP Reference Architecture*. National Industrial Information Infrastructure Protocols. Retrieved online *http://www.niiip.org*

Ohno, T. (1988). *Just-in-time for today and tomorrow*. Cambridge, MA: Productivity Press.

Oster, S. M. (1994). *Modern competitive analysis* (2nd ed.). New York: Oxford University Press.

Parunak, R., & VanderBok, R. (1998). *Modelling the extended supply network* (Working paper). Ann Arbor, MI: Industrial Technology Institute.

Porter, M. E. (1985). *Competitive advantage: Creating and sustaining superior performance*. New York: The Free Press.

Powell, W. (1991). Neither market nor hierarchy: Networks forms of organisation. In G. Thomson (Ed.), *Markets, hierarchy and networks: The co-ordination of social life* (pp. 265–276). London: Sage.

Prahalad, C. K., & Hamel, G. (1990, May/June). The core competence of the corporation. *Harvard Business Review, 68,* 79–91.

Preiss, K., Goldman, S., & Nagel, R. (1996). *Cooperate to compete: Building agile business relationships*. New York: van Nostrand Reinhold.

Presley, A., & Rogers, K. J. (1996, August). *Process modelling to support integration of business practices and processes in virtual enterprises*. Paper presented at the International Engineering Management Conference, Vancouver.

Putnik, G. D. (1997). Towards OPIM system. In M. A. Younis & S. Eid (Eds.), *Proceedings of the 22nd International Conference on Computers and Industrial Engineering* (pp. 675–678). Cairo.

Putnik, G. D. (2000a). BM virtual enterprise architecture reference model. In A. Gunasekaran (Ed.), *Agile manufacturing: 21st century manufacturing strategy* (pp. 73–93). UK: Elsevier Science.

Putnik, G. D. (2000b). *BM virtual enterprise architecture reference model* (Technical Report RT-CESP-GIS-2000-<GP-01>). Portugal: University of Minho.

Putnik, G. D., & Silva, S. C. (1995). One-product-integrated-manufacturing. In L. M. Camarinha-Matos & H. Afsarmanesk (Eds.), *Balanced automation systems—Architectures and design methods* (pp. 45–52). London; New York: Chapman & Hall.

Putnik, G. D., Cunha, M. M., Sousa, R., & Ávila, P. (2005). BM virtual enterprise—A model for dynamics and virtuality. In G. D. Putnik & M. M. Cunha (Eds.), *Virtual enterprise integration: Technological and organizational perspectives*. Hershey, PA: Idea Group Publishing.

Quinn, J. B. (1990). *The intelligent enterprise*. New York: The Free Press.

Reid, L., Liles, D., Rogers, K., & Johnson (1996). *A methodology for engineering the virtual enterprise*. Paper presented at the Agility Forum Conference, Boston.

Schumpeter, J. A. (1939). *Business cycles*. New York: McGraw-Hill.

Senge, P. M. (1990). *The fifth discipline: The art and practice of the learning organization*. London: Century.

Skyrme, D. (1996). *Networking for a better future*. Management Insights. Retrieved 1999 online *http://www.skyrme.com/insights/*

Staffend, G. S. (1992). *Making the virtual factory a reality*. Paper presented at the Autofact '92, Michigan.

Toffler, A. (1985). *The adaptative corporation*. New York: McGraw-Hill.

Verpsalainen, A. (1991). Systems that turn manufacturing into service. In E. Eloranta (Ed.), *Advances in production management systems, IFIP 1991*. North-Holland: Elsevier Science Publishers.

Warnecke, H. J. (1995). *The fractal company*. Berlin: Springer-Verlag.

Williamson, O. (1975). *Markets and hierarchies: Analysis and antitrust implications*. New York: Free Press.

Womack, J. P., & Jones, D. T. (1994). From lean production to the lean enterprise. *Harvard Business Review, 2*.

Womack, J. P., Roos, D., & Jones, D. T. (1990). *The machine that changed the world*. New York: Rawson Associates.

Yusuf, Y. Y., Sarhadi, M., & Gunasekaran, A. (1999). Agile manufacturing: The drivers, concepts and attributes. *International Journal of Production Economics, 62*, 33–43.

Chapter V

Collaborative Network Models:
Overview and Functional Requirements

Sonja Ellmann
Universität Bremen, Germany

Jens Eschenbaecher
Universität Bremen, Germany

ABSTRACT

This chapter introduces a classification model that provides an approach to classify collaborative networked organizations. Many models with different names and organizational backgrounds can be found in today's network literature. From a time perspective, traditional and innovative models provide two classification groups for collaborative networked organizations. In the process of this chapter, models with different names and organizational backgrounds will be introduced. Special attention will be given to the virtual organization. A classification model shows that collaborative networked organizations can be separated by using the body of knowledge and literature currently available. Requirements for the development of virtual organizations and inhibiting factors will be explained, and an organizational environment that supports the development of trust is subject to closer examination. The authors provide an overview regarding network management models. The reader should develop an understanding for critical factors in network relationships and understand essential requirements of networked organizations.

INTRODUCTION

Caused through an increased networking tendency, virtual integration of organizations has become more important in the last years and turned into a key success factor for the European industry as such. This becomes especially important, because the so-called next economy (Horx, 2003) drives new ways of doing business forward. Values such as collaboration, trust, confidence, and culture within and between enterprises become important success factors. Those values are essential for virtually networked and globally distributed organizations and their competitiveness. Innovative answers to solve evolving and new problems out of the increasing "virtualization" are key for remaining competitive.

In this respect, collaborative networks had a considerable development in the last couple of years. As a consequence of many different opinions represented by various authors, the evolving landscape of innovative collaborative network models has become confusing, and people are irritated because of non-standardized terminology. The term "collaborative networks" (Camarinha-Matos, 2004, p. 4) is in what follows used to summarize various kinds of enterprise networks.

In the first part of this chapter, the most relevant models that represent collaborative networks are discussed. The second part provides a classification model for differentiating collaborative networks. The dimensions have been developed after analyzing the collaborative networks in the first part with respect to criteria that characterize them. The dimensions of collaboration, virtuality, and organizational learning/knowledge have been selected, because they play a highly relevant role in every model. Those dimensions can be used to classify the organizational models and help to identify functional requirements for collaborative networks. Furthermore, all models require a different set of functional requirements for their evolution, existence, and development.

This chapter focuses on trust as the most important requirement. Yet, further requirements have been identified in a Delphi study and in a thesis on that topic (Smyth, 2003; Ellmann, 2003). Consequently, the following section discusses trust building as the main functional requirement for the evolution of collaborative networks. It presents a model that turns decentralized collaborative networks into mutually trusting environments.

The chapter answers the following research questions:

- What are the main concepts of collaborative networks with a special focus on the virtual organization?
- Can a classification model contribute to a better differentiation of collaborative networks? What would such a model look like?
- Does the model solve the classification need for network modelling?
- What are main barriers for collaborative networks?
- What main functional requirements can be deduced from these barriers for collaborative networks?
- The chapter provides a specific example for a barrier and a functional solution to overcome this barrier: What can a trust-building environment be like when focussing on virtual organizations?

PARADIGM OF
COLLABORATIVE NETWORKS

Collaborative networks summarize a number of terms and terminologies. They are used as a superordinated term to summarize the collaborative organizational forms referred to in this chapter. This section provides an overview of approaches frequently found in literature.

Background

An important hypothesis is that all networks considered have a major interest in collaboration. Some authors postulate that in 10 years from now, most enterprises will be part of some sustainable pool that will act as breeding environments for the formation of dynamic virtual organizations in response to fast-changing market conditions (Camarinha-Matos & Afsarmanesh, 2003). Due to continued development of new organizational forms, such as virtual organizations or smart organizations in the last years, many new terms that describe this evolving landscape of organizational models have been developed. Consequently, the research community faces an intensive discussion about the most appropriate terminology to describe and differentiate those models. The authors have developed three dimensions to categorize organizational models and a supplementing classification mechanism.

Collaborative Network Models

Recent developments are characterized through high degrees of ICT and virtuality involved; more complicated and complex relationships between partners and, with respect to the final product, higher complexity, more service, and a higher degree of customization. The underlying principles and operational issues that are prevalent in a supply chain and in virtual communities are also prevalent in more sophisticated collaborative network models (Jagdev & Thoben, 2001). The theoretical foundation of collaborative networks has been discussed by Eschenbaecher and Ellmann (2003) and will not be subject to closer examination in this chapter. Models that try to handle and even take advantage of complexity that arises from network relationships have been discussed intensively during the past years. In what follows, the most important facts regarding the emergence of these complex collaborative networks are discussed. The most important collaborative models are differentiated.

Table 1 shows an author's selection of approaches mentioned frequently in the available literature. The approaches are explained in more detail in the remainder of the text.

It is beyond the scope of this chapter to elaborate on all existing organizational models in detail. The following section elaborates on approaches for collaborative networks. The interested reader is asked to consult the recommended literature (e.g., Camarinha-Matos & Afsarmanesh, 2004; Ellmann, 2003; Eschenbaecher & Ellmann, 2003) for information on other models.

The innovative models are explained in more detail in what follows:

Table 1. Examined and classified organizational models (Source: Ellmann, 2003)

Model	Authors	Main arguments
Traditional approaches are characterized by point-to-point relationships between the partners		
Supply Chain Management	Kotzab (2000), Mentzer (2001)	In traditional supply chain management theory, customer demand is satisfied with an inflexible product range. The whole chain functions in a linear way.
Professional Virtual Community	Burn et al. (2002)	Professional Virtual Community is a collective term for types of cooperation that emerge from Internet-enabled societies. Clusters of Internet-enabled organizations collaborate around a particular technology and make use of a common architecture to deliver independent elements of value that grow with the number of participating organizations.
Virtual Supply Network	Rayport, Sviokla (1996)	Virtual supply networks have an increased number of electronic connections compared to regular supply chains. Digitized delivery and further simplified processes allows for shrinking and speeding up of the supply chain.
Innovative models are characterized by multi-point connections and intense use of ICT		
Value Nets	Martha, Bovet (2000)	Value nets are the logical extension of supply chains. The traditional supply chain manufactures products and pushes them through the distribution channels. A value net starts with the customer, allows him to self-design products and afterwards builds to satisfy actual demand.
Network Enterprise in Concurrent Engineering Context	Stevens et al. (2002)	In this model, concurrent engineering techniques are used for one-of-a-kind product deployment. The deployment is realized by actors that belong to a distributed, temporary alliance of independent, cooperating companies.
Virtual Organization	Byrne (1993), Camarinha-Matos, Afsarmanesh (2003)	A virtual organization is a set of cooperating (legally) independent organizations. The set changes with time; it is a dynamic configuration depending on the function and service to be provided at a particular point in time.
Concurrent Enterprise	Weber, Thoben (1997), Tönshoff et al. (2002)	Concurrent enterprises consist of independent manufacturers with a different background, language and organizational structure. CEs are temporary alliances that use systematic approaches, methods and advanced technologies for increasing efficiency in the design and manufacturing of complex products.
Extended Enterprise	Jagdev, Browne (1998)	Extended enterprise describes a partnership among enterprises that is characterized through close collaboration between manufacturers, customers and suppliers. External resources and services are thus embraced without owning them and competitive advantages are achieved through formal linkages between partners in the network.
Future models, multi-point connections, strong organizational learning		
Smart Organization	Filos, Banahan, (2000), Filos (2002)	A smart organization is an organization that comprises best practice of various forms of organization. It is thus a network excellence model.

Value Nets

A value net is a business design that uses advanced supply-chain concepts to achieve both superior customer satisfaction and company profitability (Figure 1). In the traditional supply chain, products are manufactured and pushed through distribution channels. It is intrinsically expected that someone will buy the products. A value net, contrarily, begins with customers, allows them to self-design products, and then builds

Figure 1. Value net (Source: Bovet & Martha, 2000)

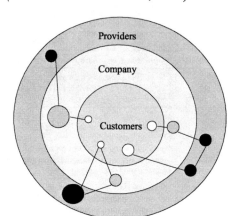

to satisfy actual demand. Value nets take into consideration important elements of supply-chain management, virtual supply chains, and professional virtual communities. They are the logical extension of supply chains and minimize their weaknesses (Bovet & Martha, 2000).

Catalyst for this shift is the choiceboard; an interactive interface that allows customers to design their own products by choosing from a set of components and service options. Customer's choices send signals to the supplier. These signals accordingly set in motion the wheels of sourcing, assembly, and delivery. Value nets integrate the essential front-end understanding of customer needs with the crucial back-end that precisely delivers on the front-end promise. "Value nets are digital, collaborative, agile powerhouses that unlock hidden profits for shareholders," (Slywotzky, 2000). Digital information is used to move products rapidly and to bypass costly distribution layers. Providers that work in concert are connected to deliver tailored solutions. Operational design is elevated to the strategic level.

Value nets are built around the customer. The starting point in a value net is to capture what is important to different customers and work back to physical production and distribution processes enabled by unifying information flow design. The customer is in the center, so that real demand can be determined in real time and passed on in digital form to other members of the network. The relationship between customer and supplying company/service providers is symbiotic, interactive, and value increasing.

Network Enterprise Model in Concurrent Engineering Context

Concurrent engineering techniques are used for one-of-a-kind product deployment realized by actors that belong to a distributed, temporary alliance of independent, cooperating companies (Stevens et al., 2002). Typical scenarios include industrial equipment, shipbuilding, and aerospace. One-of-a-kind production usually comprises the process design, manufacturing, and erecting (Stevens et al., 2002). All processes are accompanied by integrated project management, which reduces rework and ensures a smooth course of events. Processes and project management are divided among different enterprises and employees. The major goal is to shorten the product life cycle, which is very valuable for complex and time-consuming one-of-a-kind production. The only way to reach this goal in the end is to adapt an organizational strategy that is based on networking, thus creating a network enterprise. As mentioned before, concurrent engineering is just the technique to accomplish the business purpose.

This technique has to be implemented into an organizational environment in order to provide a complete business model. Stevens et al. (2002) use the notion network enterprise in this context for an integrated organizational form (more integrated than extended enterprises) that relies on formal agreements. From a technological perspective, this includes the existence of collective data visibility and integrated information systems. This workspace is, therefore, truly shared and collaborative; sensitive information is being disclosed, and tasks and activities are synchronized. Physical nodes are identified that correspond to autonomous organizational units, and links are defined that allow integration of data and cooperation between the nodes. The choice of nodes depends upon specialization and capabilities and resources they can provide. Stevens et al. call this underlying structure the work network structure; the bottom layer of the organizational model.

The second level is referred to as the work accountability structure. On this level, grouping and linking of nodes takes place. In this way, a project-oriented structure can be built up and maintained. This also ensures a smooth working multisite and multicompany infrastructure created to carry out one or more projects at the same time. The work breakdown structure as the highest layer represents a network-wise enhancement of work-breakdown and is supported by traditional project planning tools. The whole work breakdown structure describes network objectives and achievements. Participating enterprises are registered in a directory, where their core competencies are declared (Filos & Ouzounis, 2000, p. 4).

This is similar to the concept of the virtual organization, which will be explained later.

Figure 2. Network enterprise in CE context (Source: Ellmann, 2003, following Kazi, 2003)

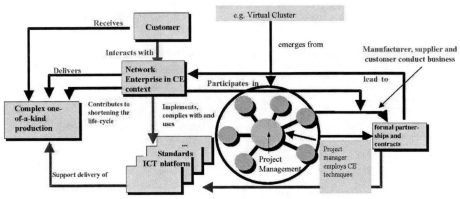

This model is based on a high degree of trust between partners that can only be guaranteed through formal agreements and a common history. Furthermore, the complete integration and data sharing causes high costs.

All in all, this model has a broker. The project manager can be seen as a broker, because he or she provides global coordination among actors, defines roles, and sets up the network.

The model requires formal agreements and trust among partners.

The major goal is to provide a profound network for efficient state-of-the art production with a long-term planning horizon. Every participant is connected to every other participant to ensure ongoing data exchange and collaboration. The model is more integrated than the extended enterprise (EE) or the virtual organization (next subchapters). The integration degree on a scale from one (relatively high) to three (very high) is three. Partners collaborate closely, and data sharing takes place on all levels (Figure 2).

Virtual Organizations

A virtual organization (VO) is a set of cooperating (legally) independent organizations. The set can change with time; it is a dynamic configuration depending on the function and service to be provided at a particular point in time (Camarinha-Matos & Afsarmanesh, 2003). A VO (Figure 3) represents a temporary network of companies. Potential partners come together to quickly exploit fast-changing opportunities (Byrne, 1993). A VO acts and can be managed as if it was a single organization (Nottingham, 1998). VOs originate from breeding environments. Breeding environments provide a pool of potential partners for the composition of a VO. Collaboration cannot happen out of the blue, and that is why these environments are crucial for the setup of VOs. The customer does not realize the virtuality of the organization or of the preceding value chain. Related to the specific order, a broker puts together suitable partners from a breeding environ-

Figure 3. Virtual organization (Source: Ellmann, 2003, following Kazi, 2003)

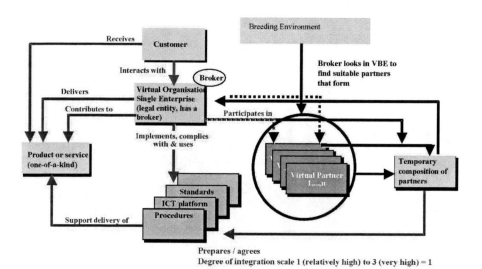

ment. The result is a VO that will collaborate for the duration of the order and return to the breeding environment afterwards to wait for the next order, which might be processed in a totally different constellation of partners. The customer always receives a product out of one hand, but can expect lower prices, more choice, and increasing service and quality. VOs are able to pool expertise on a temporary basis as an order-specific reaction (Mertens & Faisst, 1995) and are, therefore, highly efficient organizations.

They are applicable for small and medium series and one-of-a-kind production and for complex products and turnkey systems (Jagdev & Thoben, 2001).

All in all, the configuration of enterprises in a VO changes in time, as the whole network is very dynamic. The degree of integration and standardization is a critical issue: On the one hand, a high degree is necessary in order to ensure close collaboration; on the other hand, systemic integration is always a high cost factor, and because of the relatively short term- and project-oriented character of a VO, integration cannot be as far going as in case of EE or network enterprise in concurrent engineering context (in the following called Network Enterprise).

A broker ensures the right constellation of individuals for specific tasks. Integration has an estimated degree of one (thus lower than in the cases of network enterprise and extended enterprise).

Extended Enterprise

The extended enterprise (EE) model describes a partnership among enterprises, characterized through close collaboration between the manufacturer, customers, and suppliers (Figure 4). It usually evolves from enterprises that have known each other and conducted business for some time. The whole concept of EE arises partly from the attempts of manufacturers that are situated at geographically dispersed locations to build formal partnerships in order to gain a competitive advantage. The logic is to embrace external resources and services without owning them. Its goal is to achieve competitive

Figure 4. Extended enterprise (Source: Ellmann,2003, following Kazi, 2003)

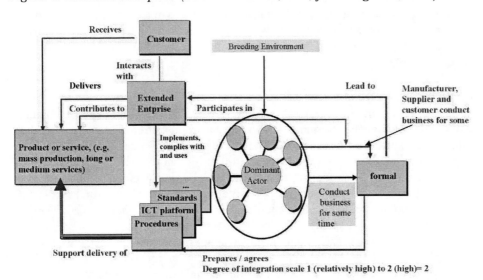

advantages by forming formal linkages (contracts) and maintaining distributed cooperation throughout the network.

Coordination of the respective manufacturing schedules including production,
dispatch, transport and delivery, and receipt notification is performed through modern
ICT (Jagdev & Browne, 1998, pp. 216-230). Every enterprise focuses on activities that
require special competencies and skills. EEs are organizations in which a dominant
enterprise, a hub (usually the manufacturer), extends its boundaries to all or some of its
suppliers and customers. The automobile industry provides a good example for EEs. EEs
rely on the extensive use of technical standards, advanced computer communication
facilities, and data interchange techniques and tools. EEs allow full-scale integration of
information systems (Stevens et al., 2002). The main difference in comparison to the VO
is the fact that the degree of integration between partners is higher (but less than in case
of the network enterprise). EEs have a longer life span (long-term orientation) compared
to VOs. They do not only form in response to a given market opportunity. ICT is not only
an integrator, as it is in a VO, but it is also a facilitator. The business purpose persists
for a relatively long time and does not dissolve after a comparably short period, as is the
case for (and also part of the purpose of) VOs.

The example of automotive manufacturing is suitable: The business purpose—
manufacturing a car — remains the same for many periods. Therefore, it is not supportive
to have a dynamic pool of changing partnerships. It is rather advisable to strengthen and
improve relationships that are provably working. These should be ICT enhanced,
integrated, and standardized with a maximum of available technology. This strong
integration would not make sense in case of a VO, because partnerships resolve after a
while. Therefore, it would not pay off to invest too much into large-scale technology
integration. EEs are advantageous in case of mass production and production of long
and medium series and for simple to complex products (Jagdev & Thoben, 2001). They
are static.

All in all, the role of the broker is taken over by a dominant enterprise.

Formal linkages and agreements ensure enduring collaboration. Coordination is
distributed. Not all interfaces are connected to all other interfaces. Sharing of information
that is relevant to carry out the manufacturing process takes place. The collaboration has
a long-term character and is not very dynamic. EEs are less integrated than network
enterprises but more integrated than virtual organizations and have an estimated degree
of integration of two.

Concurrent Enterprise

A concurrent enterprise (CE) is an enterprise that consists of independent manufacturers with different backgrounds, languages, and organizational structures. It is thus
an important feature of a CE to support different views on a common pool of information.
Tönshoff et al. call these views ontologies, meaning "an explicit specification of a
conceptualization" (Tönshoff et al., 2002). Furthermore, products and components may
be of high complexity and have to match in order to form a successful final product. A
CE is only a temporary alliance. One challenge is to implement concurrent engineering
processes in the one-of-a-kind product deployment realized by actors who belong to a
distributed, temporary alliance of independent, cooperating companies. CE is an amalgam that brings together the paradigms of concurrent engineering and EE or VO: It
describes a distributed, temporary alliance of independent, cooperating manufacturers

with different backgrounds, languages, and organizational structures (compare also *http://www.ice2003.org*). Customers and suppliers use systematic approaches, methods, and advanced technologies for increasing efficiency in the design and manufacturing of complex products and services by means of parallelism, integration, standardization, and teamwork for achieving common goals in global markets (Tönshoff et al., 2002). CE is thus a combination of intraorganizational features of concurrent engineering and interorganizational features of EE and VO.

Smart Organization

"The term 'smart organization' is used for organizations that are knowledge-driven, internet-worked, dynamically adaptive to new organizational forms and practices, learning as well as agile in their ability to create and exploit the opportunities offered by the e-economy" (Filos, 2002). Ultimately, all these terms point to the need to respond to the changing landscape of the digital economy in dynamic and innovative ways. Therefore, adaptability is a crucial feature of the smart organization. The concept of smart organization is currently seen as the peak in organizational development that started with forms of organization with only one organization involved, hierarchically organized. This development had its first turning point with increased networking structures followed by the innovative concepts described before. Three characteristics of the smart organization make it unique:

- First, it is committed to building collaborative partnerships that encourage and promote the clash of ideas. Customer focus and meeting (or even surpassing) customer expectations is recognized as a key success factor.
- Second, the smart organization survives and prospers in the new economy, because it can respond positively and adequately to change and uncertainty.
- Third, the smart organization identifies and exploits new opportunities by leveraging the power of so-called smart resources, i.e., information, knowledge, relationships, brands, and innovative and collaborative intelligence (Filos & Banahan, 2000).

It is, therefore, a best practice organization. The shift from supplier-driven mass production to customer-driven mass customizing becomes visible, as does the important notion of extended products that incorporate more intangible assets, such as provision of services.

Synthesis

The preceding section provides an attempt to describe concepts for collaborative networks. Nevertheless, efforts to classify and distinguish popular concepts of collaborative networks are necessary in order to derive trends to indicate where the development of networking organizations goes and what features are necessary in order to remain competitive in the future.

The Internet and other innovations in information technology are reshaping the concept of organization, product, and market. The organization of the future needs to be more agile, products need to be packed with additional services (so-called "extended products," see Thoben et al., 2001), and markets will depend on trust, partnerships, and collaboration. This trend was basically started under the heading of e-business (Kalakota & Whinston, 2002). Innovative and intelligent solutions that integrate the customer into the process of service creation and simplify the collaboration with business partners and customers are in the center of attention regarding this new trend. The idea of a stronger interlinkage of enterprises through ICT originated mainly from supply-chain management. Applications like CRM, e-procurement, CAD, ECR, or continuous replenishment are typical applications that support supply-chain optimization. These solutions can be further leveraged through Internet technology. The ideas have been picked up, adapted, and developed further in the process of finding solutions for far-reaching enterprise collaboration. ICT is, therefore, a major criterion for all new models.

Moreover, the next-generation Internet is about much more than high-speed networks — "the real issue is not what the technology can do, but what we can do with it" (Ladid, 2000). This quotation underlines the fact that recent technological developments have to be accompanied by new organizational models and theories. Along with these developments, one network-centric application occupies experts' minds: collaborative commerce (c-commerce) (Zwegers & Eschenbaecher, 2002). A working definition by Gartner Group clarifies what c-commerce is: "C-Commerce is the set of electronically-enabled collaborative interactions between an enterprise, its suppliers, trading partners, customers and employees" (Rayner, 2001). The next section presents an approach to classify all collaborative models presented previously in a three dimensional model.

CLASSIFICATION MODEL
FOR COLLABORATIVE NETWORKS

Study of the literature that led to the aggregated descriptions of networks models in the last chapter proved that differences between various authors' understanding on the particular models exist. The discussion in research and academia is dominated by a rather vague usage of terms and terminologies. For this reason, the authors tried to develop classification criteria to differentiate the main conceptual ideas. Two basic research questions are answered in what follows:

1.   How can *organizational models be classified* and differentiated from each other?
2.   What are *functional requirements for collaborative network* models?

The next section presents the outcome of a one-year literature study (compare Ellmann, 2003; Ellmann & Eschenbaecher, 2003) in combination with a workshop at the last ICE-conference in Helsinki in 2003. As a result, three dimensions have been developed that will be explained in more detail in the next section of the chapter. The classification of the concepts is further used for deriving functional requirements for collaborative networks.

Classification Criteria

Virtuality

Many authors have viewed virtuality as a key success factor for successful companies in the 21st Century. The main objective of virtuality is an increase in flexibility, which means the adaptation of a company towards permanently changing market conditions, 24-hour engineering and across geographical borders. Furthermore, this

Figure 5. Virtuality (Source: Griese & Sieber, 1996)

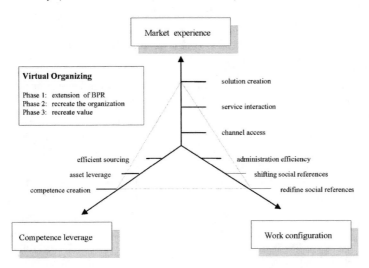

concept can be viewed as company strategy. Figure 5 gives an overview about virtuality, showing a triangle including market experience, work configuration, and competence leverage (Griese & Sieber, 1996).

The concept of virtuality depends on the use of ICT. As already stated, the Internet enables completely new business processes that change the organizational environment. This is an optimal enabler for virtuality.

Collaboration

Collaboration is the ultimate requirement for any network or virtual organization (Ellmann & Eschenbaecher, 2003). Every organizational model shown before has stressed the crucial importance of this dimension. This dimension is in the three dimensional model used to differentiate the intensity of the collaboration between partners.

In literarture, collaboration and cooperation are often separated from each other (e.g., Scheer, Angeli & Herrmann, 2003): Cooperation describes a close, regular exchange between partners while collaboration is not that intense and regulated. In this chapter, only collaboration is used while collaboration is used as classification dimension. However, different levels of collaboration indicate the closeness/regularity and the intensity of the relationship.

Altogether, it classifies the degree of dependence of one company upon another company in order to reach a specific business goal and characterizes the complexity of those relationships.

Organizational Learning/Knowledge

The final dimension refers to *organizational learning and knowledge*. Collaborative networks act in a highly dynamic environment, which clearly makes organizational learning and knowledge an absolute necessity for the survival and information transfer of such networks. Indeed, the ability of a collaborative organization to implement learning processes is a strong characteristic for competitiveness.

Classification of Collaborative Networks in Three-Dimensional Space

Classifying collaborative networks in three-dimensional space depicts the closeness of different business models and their relation in terms of typical characteristics. The three-dimensional model does not have the claim to be mathematically correct; it is more a visualization of important findings. The attempt is to give academics and professionals a tool at hand that allows them to get a good understanding and overview about different business models.

The traditional supply chain describes a collaborative environment that cannot achieve high degrees of product customization. Point-to-point connections are evidence for little collaboration and low degrees of organizational learning. Virtuality involved is relatively low compared to the other models in the cube. However, supply-chain management is an initiating and foundational power for further developments regarding enterprise networking. The degree of the three dimensions increases in case of virtual supply networks. Virtual supply networks have a higher degree of collaboration between the partners due to the inherent network character. Furthermore, the degree of virtuality and, thus, ICT involved is higher, and learning effects increase through higher collaboration. Professional virtual communities have a slightly higher degree of collaboration, because a bigger audience is addressed.

Value nets are characterized as logical extensions of supply chains, and thus, the three dimensions have the same composition in the three-dimensional space but on a higher level. CEs are placed between VOs, EEs, and network enterprises in three-dimensional space. By definition, they unify features of VO, EE, and the concurrent engineering paradigm that is crucial for networked enterprises. Networked enterprises have a slightly higher degree of organizational learning/knowledge and virtuality involved than CE and are placed between EEs, VOs, and CEs.

The main distinction between VOs and EEs in this diagram can be made on the level of organizational learning and virtuality: The more long-term oriented an alignment is, the higher is the degree of organizational learning, for a simple reason — learning is likely to be high when collaboration is formally agreed upon and has a long-term orientation, because those preconditions will also increase the level of trust and the willingness to reveal important and secret information. Also, it is more likely that knowledge management systems are established. Therefore, EE have a higher degree of organizational learning than VO's. VOs have a higher degree of virtuality. The degree of collaboration is higher for the VO, because collaboration is very dynamic, compositions change, new partners enter the scene, and the complexity of relationships is thus high. The network organization has approximately the same learning effects as the EE, but the degree of employed ICT is even higher, because complete integration of information systems is one of the most important requirements of the network organization accompanied by concurrent engineering framework. Finally, the smart organization covers all dimensions in an outstanding fashion and has the highest values in all three dimensions in this diagram.

Figure 6. Three-dimensional model of the findings (Source: Ellmann, 2003; Ellmann & Eschenbaecher, 2003)

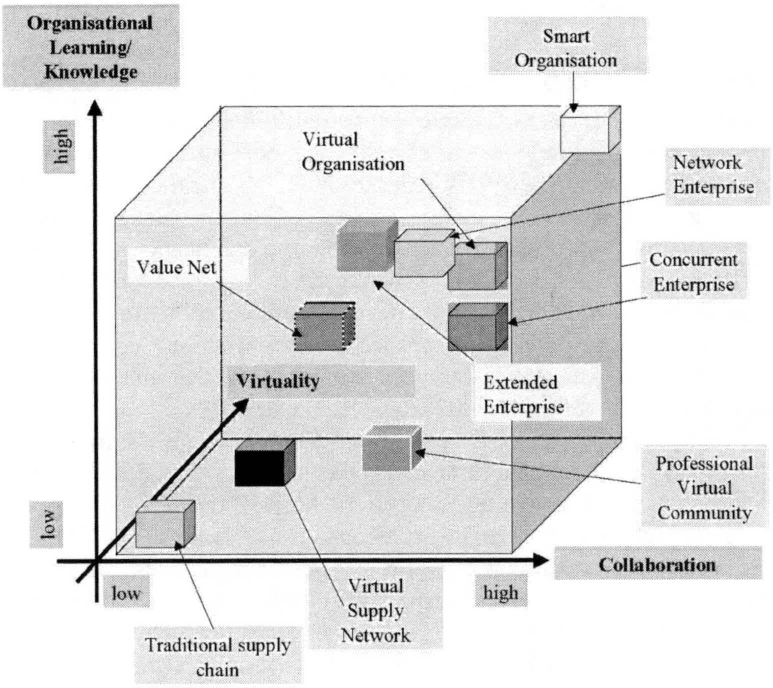

Gain Through the Model

The three-dimensional model helps to analyze forms of collaborative networks and gives users a tool at hand to compare forms of collaboration with respect to the three dimensions and define the specific model without contradiction. Most of the models located in the upper right-hand corner can still be viewed as exceptions with respect to their functioning in reality. This is the case, because inhibiting factors prevent organizations from adapting perfectly to their environment. Consequently, the following section discusses such inhibiting factors and the evolving functional requirements to overcome those factors.

IDENTIFICATION OF FUNCTIONAL REQUIREMENTS FOR THE EXAMPLE OF A VIRTUAL ORGANIZATION

Virtual organizations were identified as a topic of high interest in the 1980s. At that time, many authors claimed a tremendous development of this organizational form. Indeed, this has not taken place to that extent so far, mainly because of factors that inhibit the evolution of virtual organizations. This section presents results from two studies that have analyzed inhibiting factors. Results come from a European Delphi study on collaboration in expanding value-creating international networks (*www.companion-roadmap.org*) and from a thesis on collaboration in networks (Ellmann, 2003). Functional requirements have been derived from these results.

Barriers for Collaboration in Networks

Collaboration is still an evolving phenomenon. Since its first appearance in the supply-chain management field almost 20 years ago, collaboration has evolved from a one-to-one strategic arrangement between individual organizations into a value-chain requirement for success (Smyth, 2003). The use of the Internet has supported this process by extending supply networks across geographical distances. This requires the use of collaboration tools and collaborative business process applications to enable virtual partners to stay in contact. At the heart of collaboration, however, remain the issues of trust, security, flexibility, and profit sharing among partners. Trust was determined to be the main inhibiting factor for collaborative environments in both studies mentioned above (compare Smyth, 2002, 2003; Ellmann, 2003).

Trust, transparency, the inability to setup equal win–win relationships and the inability to see payback in the near future are key cultural barriers. Problems of adapting different systems involve technological barriers. Most of these "blocs" are expressed negatively. However, there are also positive reasons that block the development, such as waiting for the tools to mature, waiting for the right opportunities, and waiting for the market to pick up. It is not necessarily true that collaboration means "sharing profits". Table 2 summarizes ranking results from the Delphi study sector by sector. Ranking is organized into four groups: University/ Research, Technology providers, Consulting, Industry end user.

Figure 7 provides an overall ranking of the inhibiting factors. Many barriers have been identified by experts.

Table 2. Potential barriers to collaboration — ranking sector by sector (Source: Smyth, 2002, 2003)

Potential Barrier	University/Research Institute Rank	Technology Provider Rank	Consulting Rank	Industry End-User Rank
Lack of trust	1		1	1
Competitive nature	2	2		
Unwillingness to share				
Profit	3	1		
Lack of agreement on				
common goals		2	2	3
Inability to define				
"win–win"		2	3	
Financial constraints				2

Figure 7. Ranking of inhibiting factors (Source: Smyth, 2002, 2003; Ellmann, 2003)

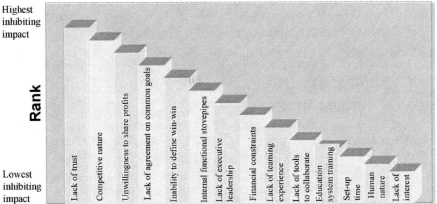

Traditional forms of organization have been affected substantially by the aspects mentioned in Table 2 and Figure 7. Trust is viewed as the number one inhibiting factor by end users, universities and institutes, and technology providers. This illustrates the importance of establishing trust between partners once networking is envisaged.

Functional Requirements for Collaborative Networks

The findings of the Delphi study are supported and enhanced through findings from a thesis (Ellmann, 2003). The functional requirements for collaborative networks vary when looking at the respective forms of collaborative networks described before. With respect to these barriers, the following functional requirements can be derived for networks:

- Creating of trust-building environments
- Focusing on cooperation rather than competition
- Creating a profit-sharing mechanism
- Defining a methodology for common goal and strategy definition
- Defining win–win scenarios
- Developing mechanisms to overcome internal stovepipes
- Using clear leadership mechanisms
- Developing solutions for financial constraints
- Creating better collaboration environment tools
- Improving education and training
- Improving teamwork abilities of the employees
- Shortening the setup time of collaborative networks
- Increasing collaboration interest within the organization
- Preparing humans to collaborate

The functional requirements listed above create many questions for research and academia that are beyond the scope of this chapter. Consequently, the authors focus on the main barrier and, at the same time, functional requirement for virtual enterprise integration: creation of trust in collaborative networks. Trust has been clearly defined as the major inhibiting factor for the further evolution of collaborative networks. For this reason, trust-building environments can be viewed as the major functional requirement for the evolution of virtual organizations. The development of a virtual organization thus provides the example for the next section.

Trust Building Environments that Support Collaborative Network Integration

It is crucial to understand that trust is an essential and critical requirement for the development and smooth working of collaborative networks. The examined virtual organizations are usually built on network relationships. Uncertainty about strategic partners and fear for opportunistic behavior are high, and the existences of environments that reduce this kind of fear are important preconditions for modern networks (Ellmann, 2003).

Another important requirement includes technical standards to ensure smooth working. Almost every business-process-oriented publication stresses interoperability and interface problems (Eschenbaecher & Zwegers, 2002). Network coordination is also an aspect one has to be aware of. Disembedding from historically developed arrangements of social institutions took place, and players (companies) have to look for new supporting structures and security in this undersocialized institutional disequilibrium (Elsner, 2003, p. 4).

Early proposals on innovative network models, such as virtual organizations, for example, have been too technology-driven and have so far underestimated difficulties in the creation process. However, soft factors, such as trust, might lead to a complete avoidance of collaborative networks. Many authors neglected that technology is already available and that the main limits result from lack of trust, motivation, and doubt about the benefit of a collaborative situation. "The motivation and self-interest of the collaborating enterprise and their ability to handle the complex logistics involved only restrict it. Communication technology is already available to develop complex inter-enterprise networks" (Jagdev and Browne, 1998).

Camarinha-Matos and Afsarmanesh adds that "trusting your partner" is a gradual and long process (Camarinha-Matos & Afsarmanesh, 2004). The creation of clusters of industry or service enterprises is one attempt to overcome the restrictions and obstacles mentioned above. The following part elaborates on environments that enable the development of innovative network relationships.

Example: Breeding Environment for Virtual Enterprise Integration

A breeding environment (Camarinha-Matos & Afsarmanesh, 2003) is an environment with the special purpose of allowing trust-building processes in scenarios characterized through agility and dynamism. This is an extremely difficult task. Cooperation between dynamic organizations without former collaboration experience is usually limited to very simple market transactions.

However, the development of more efficient ICT infrastructures allows for the emergence of a new form of environment that enables "pooling" of expertise from different and geographically dispersed companies. Based on an interdisciplinary pool of selected enterprises that perform best practice in their area, products and services are produced in build-to-order networks.

Motivating factors (in addition to the available infrastructure) to form such associations that represent the virtual breeding environments (VBEs) can be cultural ties or even particular human relationships.

VBE are, by definition, environments for the dynamic formation of virtual organizations. For each business opportunity found by the VBE-broker, a subset of the VBE enterprises is chosen to form a VO for that specific business opportunity. Therefore, a fast configuration of the most adequate set of partners for each opportunity is necessary. Breeding environments, therefore, support the emergence of cooperation that does not necessarily have a long-term orientation. Geographical closeness is an advantage, but due to deployment of ICT, it is not a necessity. New members can gradually join the environment, but they have to accept the operating principles of the association. Enterprises involved in the VBE are registered in a directory with their core competencies declared. Therefore, the whole VBE provides a long-term framework, even though the business purpose of the single projects that are conducted by the specific VO constellation are short or medium term (Camarinha-Matos & Afsarmanesh, 2003).

Figure 8 shows the process of creating a VO both with (path 1a + 1b) and without (path 2) a breeding environment (Camarinha-Matos & Afsarmanesh, 2003). The figure demonstrates the efficiency gain achieved through the existence of a breeding environ-

Figure 8. Breeding environment (Source: Camarinha-Matos & Afsarmanesh, 2003)

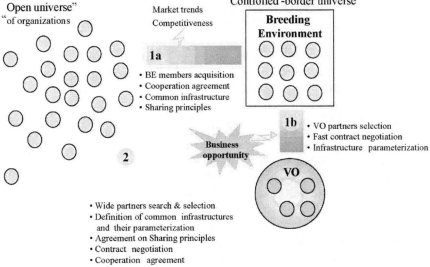

ment that serves as a platform for the creation of trust between partners and that simplifies partnership-building processes a lot.

Additionally, worldwide known regions such as the Silicon Valley in California or Route 128 show a good example for a breeding environment. Virtual organization partner integration can be supported effectively by breeding environments. Besides trust building, also the following points can be addressed by VBEs:

- Focus on coopetition rather then competition
- Create a profit-sharing mechanism
- Define a methodology for common goal and strategy definition
- Improve education and training
- Shorten the setup time of collaborative networks

This shows that some of the factors named as major inhibiting factors can be solved by the existence of a virtual breeding environment.

Practical Aspects

The concepts presented in this chapter have a theoretical background. Nevertheless, some examples can be summarized to demonstrate the practical value of organizational models for virtual organizations:

- The Star Alliance coordinated by Lufthansa represents a virtual organization that collaborates smoothly to the benefit of the customer (Hess, 2003).
- Virtuelle Fabrik Euregio at Bodensse (Germany) has created a network of around 50 companies collaborating with each other. Their organizational model is based on resource and competence bundling (Mertens & Faisst, 1995).
- The U.S. toy maker LewisGaloob toys has about 100 employees and sells goods worth more than $50 million. Ideas for products are bought from engineers, and the development process is done through independent engineering offices. Production is conducted through subcontracting in Hong Kong, and the products are delivered by carriers to the United States and distributed by independent distributors. Even factoring and accounting is outsourced, and Galoob is thus the strategic leader of this virtual network (Arnold et al., 1995).

These examples underline that innovative organizational models have become reality. It is, therefore, necessary to classify them and find a standardized scheme for their description. This chapter has provided a pragmatic approach to address this problem.

CONCLUSIONS

The introduction indicated that collaborative networks can be seen as future paradigm for innovative organizations.

It has been discussed that currently, many different terms for collaborative networks prevent a clear discussion in research and academia. Consequently, the authors claim that a classification model supports a clear differentiation of the various approaches. Indeed, the different dimensions show very clearly that every organizational form incorporates different characteristics leading to differences in functional requirements.

Furthermore, functional requirements have major impact on virtual enterprise integration. Similarities, such as the fact that all models depend on trust between partners, and differences, such as the time horizon of collaboration, are visualized. It has become obvious that organizations in the age of global spreading can no longer rely on being able to form regional or even local clusters with their suppliers. They have to enlarge their view and look at international collaborative networks. Nevertheless, barriers and inhibiting factors prevent these innovative organizational forms from fast and easy development.

The Aberdeen Group defines Collaborative Commerce as a class of software that uses internet technology to permit individuals to collaboratively share intellectual data, improving the development, manufacture, and management of products throughout the entire life-cycle.

Obviously, that will not become reality in the near future, because major functional requirements for virtual enterprise integration need to be solved first.

Functional requirements are of major importance for the evolution of collaborative networks. The authors consider trust to be the major requirement for any kind of collaboration in networks. Breeding environments address these aspects. Functional requirements, which are not covered in this chapter, are subject to further research.

The existence of trust-building and -maintaining environments proves that, currently, research and practice are strongly taking the various functional requirements into account and try to achieve improvements. Nevertheless, it can be stated that such environments are still exceptions in the real world.

The smart organization concept includes most of the functional requirements.

Implication for Further Studies

The authors have spent a considerable amount of time classifying organizational models for VO. The three dimensional model provides a helpful instrument for further analysis of collaborative networks. Nevertheless, the conclusions presented here are not final. New organizational models will appear, and others will probably cease to exist. The authors have provided a "living model" and it should be treated as such. New perceptions of theory and practice will change the model. Therefore, the ideas provided in this chapter should be part of further studies in this research area.

REFERENCES

Arnold, O., Faisst, W., Härtling, M., & Sieber, P. (1995). Virtuelle Unternehmen als Unternehmenstyp der Zukunft? *Handbuch der modernen Datenverarbeitung 32*, 185, 8–23.

Bovet, D., & Martha, J. (2000). *Value nets breaking the supply chain to unlock hidden profits*. New York: John Wiley & Sons.

Byrne, J. (1993). The virtual corporation. *Business Week*, 8, 37–41.

Camarinha-Matos, L. M. (2004). New collaborative organizations and their research needs. In *Processes and Foundations for Virtual Organizations* (pp. 3-12). Boston; Dordrecht; London: Kluwer Academic Publishers.

Camarinha-Matos, L. M., & Afsamanesh, H. (2004). *Collaborative networked organisations: A research agenda for emerging business models.* Boston; Dordrecht; London: Kluwer Academic Publishers.

Camarinha-Matos, L. M., & Afsarmanesh, H. (2003). Elements of a base VE infrastructure. *Computers in Industry,* 51(2), 139–163.

Camarinha-Matos, L. M., & Afsarmanesh, H. (2004). A roadmap for strategic research on virtual organisations. In *Processes and Foundations for Virtual Organisations.* Boston/ Dordrecht/London: Kluwer Academic Publishers.

Carrol, M. (2001). Collaborative commerce - The next big thing in global manufacturing. *eAI Journal,* July, 20-24.

Ellmann, S. (2003). *Collaboration in enterprise networks—Theory, technological background, network management and roadmap.* Bremen: Diplomarbeit Universität Bremen.

Ellmann, S., & Eschenbaecher, J. (2003). Popular concepts of the smart, dDynamic enterprise—An evaluation approach. *Proceedings of the Ninth Conference on Concurrent Enterprising: Enterprise Engineering in the Networked Economy,* Espoo, Finland, 16–18 June, (pp. 317–325).

Elsner, W. (2004). The "new" economy and a hybrid governance approach. *International Journal of Social Economics,* 31(11/12), 1029- 1049.

Eschenbaecher, J., & Ellmann, S. (2003). Foundation for networking: A theoretical view on the virtual organisation. In L. Camarinha-Matos & H. Afsarmadesh (Eds.), *Processes and foundations for virtual organisations* (pp. 163–171). Kluwer Academic Publishers.

Eschenbaecher, J., & Zwegers, A. (2002). A research agenda for collaborative commerce. In B. Standford-Smith, E. Chiozza & M. Edin (Eds.), *Challenges and achievements in e-business and e-work* (pp. 607–614). Kluwer Academic Publishers.

Filos, E. (2002). European collaborative R&D projects related to the "smart organisation." A first evaluation of activities and implications for construction. *ECPPM papers,* No. 356.

Filos, E., & Banahan, E. (2000). Towards the smart organisation: An emerging organisational paradigm and the contribution of the European RTD Programmes. *Journal of Intelligent Manufacturing,* 2, 101–119.

Filos, E., & Ouzounis, V. (2000). Virtual organisations: Technologies, trends, standards and the contribution of the European RTD program. *International Journal of Computer Applications in Technology,* Special Issue: "Applications in Industry of Product and Process Modeling Using Standards" Virtualorganisation.net, "Newsletter," 1(3–4).

Gartner. (2002). Collaborative commerce: An overview of the new c-commerce equation. Retrieved March 26, 2004 online *www.gartner.com/2_events/conferences_briefings/conferences/spc5_qa.pdf*

Griese, J., & Sieber, P. (1996). Die Virtuelle Fabrik - ein Überblick. *Industrie Management,* (12), 15–17.

Horx, M. (2003). *Accent on the Future: die Zukunftsstudie von Accenture und Matthias Horx.* Wien: Accenture.

Jagdev, H. S., & Browne, J. (1998). The extended enterprise—A context for manufacturing. *Production, Planning & Control,* 9(3), 216–229.

Jagdev, H. S., & Thoben, K. -D. (2001). Anatomy of enterprise collaborations: Typological issues in enterprise networks. *Production Planning Control*, 12(5), 437–451.

Jagdev, H. S., & Thoben, K. -D. (2001). Typological issues in enterprise networks. *Production Planning Control*, 12(5), 421–436.

Kalakota, R., & Whinston, A. B. (2002). *Electronic commerce: A manager's guide*. Boston: Addison-Wesley Longman.

Kazi, S. A. (2003). *Distributed Innovation Management*. Presentation, VTT, Finland.

Mertens, P., & Faisst, W. (1995). Virtuelle Unternehmen—eine Strukturvariante für das nächste Jahrtausend? In K.A. Schachtschneider (Ed.), *Wirtschaft, Gesellschaft und Staat im Umbruch*, Duncker und Humbolt, Berlin (pp. 150-167).

Nottingham, A. (1998). *The virtual organisation as a community built on trust*. The Fourth EATA Conference on Networking Entities, Leeds, West Yorkshire, UK.

Rayner, N. (2001). The c-Commerce transformation of the enterprise—Pushing beyond four walls. Gartner Symposium, *c-Commerce: The new enterprise in the Internet age*, Amsterdam, May.

Rayport, J. F., & Sviokla, J. J. (1996). Exploiting the virtual value chain. *Harvard Business Review*, (11), 75–85.

Rycroft, R. W., & Kash, D. E. (1999). *The complexity challenge: Technological innovation in the 21st century*. London; New York: Pinter.

Scheer, A.W., Angeli, R., & Hermann, K. (2003). Moderne Informations – und Kommunikationstechnolgien – Treiber neuer Kooperations – und Koordinationsformen. In J. Zentes, B. Swoboda, & D. Morschett (Eds.), *Kooperationen, Allianzen und Netzwerke* (pp. 359–384).

Smyth, M. (2002). COMPANION Delphi Interim Report—Summary of Delphi 1 Responses that Support Companion Delphi 2 Questionaire.

Smyth, M. (2003). Companion—Collaborative commerce in expanding value creating international betworks, *IST–2001-37493, Report on the Delphy Study for Companion*, Version 1.0.

Stevens, R., Felice, M. Gazzotti, D., Paganelli, P., & Pepe, A. (2002). Supporting collaborative product and project life-cycle management in network enterprises. ICE 2002. In K.S. Pawar, F. Weber, & K.D. Thoben (Eds.), *Proceedings of the Eighth International Conference on Concurrent Enterprising*, Rome, 17–19 June (pp. 235–244).

Thoben, K. -D., & Weber, F. (1997). Information and communication structures for product development in the concurrent enterprise: Requirements and concepts. In P.P. Grumpous & B.E. Hirsch (Eds.), *ASI 97: Life cycle approaches to production system management, control, supervision*, Budapest, 14–18 July, University of Patras, Rion, (pp. 460–467).

Thoben, K. -D., Jagdev, H., & Eschenbaecher, J. (2001). Extended products: Evolving traditional product concepts. In K.S. Pawar, F. Weber, & K.D. Thoben (Eds.), *Proceedings of the Seventh International Conference on Concurrent Enterprising: Engineering the Knowledge Economy through Co-operation*, Bremen, Germany, 27–29 June (pp. 429–439).

Tönshoff, H. K., Apitz, R., Lattner, A. D., & Schäffer, Ch. (2002). Support for different view on information in concurrent enterprises. ICE 2002. In K.S. Pawar, F. Weber, & K.D. Thoben (Eds.), *Proceedings of the Eighth International Conference on Concurrent Enterprising*, Rome, 17–19 June (pp. 143–150).

Chapter VI

BM_Virtual Enterprise:
A Model for Dynamics and Virtuality

Goran D. Putnik
University of Minho, Portugal

Maria Manuela Cunha
Polytechnic Institute of Cávado and Ave, Portugal

Rui Sousa
University of Minho, Portugal

Paulo Ávila
Polytechnic Institute of Porto, Portugal

ABSTRACT

BM_virtual enterprise (BM_VE) is a virtual enterprise (VE) in a total or partial conformance with the BM_virtual enterprise architecture reference model (BM_VEARM). BM_VE is a kind of VE characterized as a dynamically reconfigurable network integrated over the global domain, satisfying the requirements for integrability, distributivity, agility, and virtuality as competitiveness factors. BM_VE uses three main mechanisms, or tools: market of resources, broker, and virtuality. This chapter presents the three fundamental mechanisms for the VE reconfiguration dynamics and virtuality; introduces the basic concept of the BM_VEARM, which serves as the conceptual and formal base for building BM_VE instances; shows the formal specification and theory of the structural aspects of the BM_VE as well as some aspects of the BM_VE reconfiguration dynamics; presents the BM_VE as an agile/virtual enterprise (A/VE); and finally, describes some important consequences of virtuality in BM_VE, i.e., that the BM_VE structure is hierarchical, a new definition of the VE (in which the network as the VE characteristic is irrelevant from the operational unit's point of view), and the process of a "traditional" enterprise virtualization.

INTRODUCTION

BM_virtual enterprise (BM_VE) is a virtual enterprise (VE) in a total or partial conformance with the BM_virtual enterprise architecture reference model (BM_VEARM) developed in the literature (Putnik, 2001). BM_VE is the VE as a dynamically reconfigurable network integrated over the global domain, satisfying the requirements for integrability, distributivity, agility, and virtuality as the competitiveness factors. BM_VE uses three main mechanisms, or tools: market of resources, broker, and virtuality. Virtuality as a tool is a specific organizational structure pattern that contributes to further improvement of agility/reconfiguration dynamics.

The objective of this chapter, in the context of this volume, is to present a VE model for which the requirements for integration organization and technology solutions are very demanding [due to the inherent high (organizational) reconfiguration dynamics, virtuality (as its implementation is conceived), and other related semantic, pragmatic, and societal problems-for more detailed discussion on the integration problems for VE, see Putnik et al., this volume], for which the integration science and engineering should provide a new generation of solutions. In this text, as the representative of the highly demanded VE models, the BM_VE model is presented.

Thus, in spite of some proposals by the authors toward the VE integration solutions, e.g., the *normalized virtual enterprise (NVE) model* (NVE model investigation is at an initial stage and deals only with a part of the VE integration problem "space"), this presentation of the BM_VE model should be seen, first, in the context of this volume, as the presentation of the functional requirements for the VE integration solutions to be proposed and to be considered.

The chapter is organized as follows. The first part presents briefly the three fundamental mechanisms, or tools, for the VE reconfiguration dynamics and VE virtuality. The second part introduces the basic concept of the BM_VEARM, which serves as the conceptual and formal base for building BM_VE instances. The third part shows the formal specification and formal theory of the structural aspects of the BM_VE as well as some aspects of the BM_VE reconfiguration dynamics. The fourth part presents the BM_VE as an A/VE. In the fifth part, some important consequences of virtuality in BM_VE are described, i.e., that the BM_VE structure is hierarchical, a VE new definition (in which the network as a VE characteristic is irrelevant from the operational unit's point of view), and the process of a "traditional" enterprise virtualization. Finally, the chapter finishes with the sixth part-Conclusions and References.

THREE TOOLS FOR DYNAMICS AND VIRTUALITY

Market of resources (MR), the first mechanism, or tool, that BM_VE uses, is an institution, or enterprise, that serves as a meta-enterprise of the operating VE. In other words, MR is an environment to support the VE dynamic integration, operation, and reconfiguration, as well as "boost" the networking (VE) dynamics, providing a way to overcome (i.e., minimizing) the two fundamental networking disablers: "transaction," i.e., reconfigurability and cost, and the VE partners' knowledge and rights protection. On the first view, MR looks like a common marketplace that offers marketplace functionalities, like searching partners for integration in the VE, or searching goods, filtering information, or helping negotiation, that might use simple tools as well as advanced tools as electronic brokerage and intelligent agent technology. However, the MR does not rely only on the basic information and communication infrastructure. This is absolutely necessary, but the added value comes from the higher-level functions necessary for supporting the VE dynamic reconfiguration (networking), i.e., (1) to *shorten the transaction time* (search time, contracting time, monitoring time, and enforcement time), as well as to *lower transaction costs* (search costs, contracting costs, monitoring costs, and enforcement costs), in the process of resources integration, i.e., in the process of networking; (2) to *build the trust*, knowledge/technology transfer protection, as well as *the legal framework*, between the partners in the network through the trust assurance mechanisms, intellectual property protection, security between partners, and against third parties, etc.; (3) to provide specialized services for *decision-making support*; (4) to provide the *data/knowledge base on resources and transactions*; (5) to *mediate offer and demand of resources* to dynamically integrate in an A/VE and "brokers"; and (6) to *manage the environment for* networking.[1]

The second mechanism, or tool, that BM_VE uses is the broker. The broker is an external entity, or agent, that has two fundamental roles. The first is to be the agent of agility and organization reconfiguration dynamics. The broker is functionally an *"organisation configuration manager,"* also called the *resource manager*. The *resource manager* or *broker* performs different particular tasks within the global task of the "organisation configuration management," e.g., *resource selection, resource integration, resource integration scheduling, resource (dynamic) reconfiguration, resource monitoring and reliability analysis, resource control*, etc. Organizationally, or structurally, the broker is used as the middle, or the second level between a "client" and a "server" partner in the VE (BM_VE). This is known in organizational theory as the *"three-layer hierarchy"* organisational model or, in other words, *"principal/supervisor/ agent"* or *"manager/foreman/worker"* hierarchy.[2] The motivation for the application of the second layer, the "supervisor" or "foreman," is that "the principal *lacks either the time or the knowledge required to supervise the agent."* In our case, the case of BM_VE, the motivation for the application of the broker as an external entity for VE reconfiguration management, or as the third entity besides the main "actors"-the client and the server--and between them, is that the broker is supposed to have an expert knowledge, more effective and more efficient than the client's knowledge on search and integration of the VE partners (servers) and the VE reconfiguration management, which is absolutely necessary to achieve the highest levels of the reconfiguration dynamics.[3]

The second fundamental role of the broker is to be the agent of virtuality. In this role, the broker provides the intermediation services "online," with the operations of the client and the server and in a way that the operating agents, the client and the server, are not aware of each other. The client and server are hidden from each other. The *rigorous hierarchy* of the model implies that client and server communicate through the broker. During the operation, the client does not have direct contact with the server, who provides the service (or production). The structure proposed allows for enterprise reconfigurability during the (single) operation, i.e., the organisational structure may change during the operation, *at the runtime*. The resource manager, or broker, can reconsider the organisational structure during the operation, at the runtime, as well as between two operations, and act with the objective to adapt it (to reconfigure it). The model could be described as a model by the *operation online reconfigurability* of the enterprise. As a consequence of the operation online reconfigurability model, the underlying physical structure of the enterprise is hidden to the client. The broker must provide the transition from one physical structure to another in a way that the client is not affected by the system reconfiguration, in which case, the operation would be interrupted and split in two, implying immediately some time loss (the lost time can have two components: by interruption of the operation (e.g., setup time for restarting the operation), and the principal's adaptation time to the new specific organisational structure). In other words, the broker, i.e., the resources management level, together with the integration mechanism levels (see the next section), e.g., the translators, *emulate* the underlying organisational (hardware) structure in a format that is understandable by the client. The client does not see the real structure, he sees some "virtual" structure that does not exist.[4] By this structure, a VE, in this case the BM_VE, could be seen as a homomorphism of distributed (software) system architecture (e.g., common object request broker architecture, CORBA). CORBA is "the object bus" architecture that "lets objects transparently make requests to, and receive responses from, other objects located locally or remotely. The client is not aware of the mechanisms used to commu-nicate with, activate, or store the server object. ... (it) lets objects discover each other at run time and invoke each other's services" (Orfali et al., 1997, p. 7). The distributed system concept is of the greatest importance for the VE concept, and we would say that it is *a model of the VE*. Virtually, the homomorphic relation between these two concepts is primarily on an abstract level, as there are, of course, differences in the implementation and application levels. In this way, the online operation of the broker, i.e., the online reconfiguration of the VE, together with the *specific organizational structural pattern*, that is, the three-layer hierarchy of client/broker/server, makes virtuality the third mechanism, or tool, that BM_VE uses in order to achieve the highest reconfiguration dynamics. The ideal goal to be achieved, in terms of time, is the capability of the VE "reconfiguration within 1 second." The BM_VE structural specification shows clearly the position of the broker in the BM_VE overall structure as well as the structural patterns conceived for agility, i.e., for reconfiguration dynamics, and virtuality. However, the market of resources is not embraced by the specification presented, although it is one of the fundamental mechanisms for the BM_VE functioning. But, it should be assumed that the market of resources is the environment for BM_VE operation and reconfiguration.[5]

BM_VE REFERENCE MODEL

Elementary Structure

The BM_VEARM (Putnik, 2001) is a reference model to design and control virtual enterprises/production systems ensuring four fundamental characteristics: integration, distribution, agility, and virtuality. According to BM_VEARM, a VE is "... an optimized enterprise, synthesized over a universal set of resources, with a real-time replaceable physical structure. The synthesis and control are performed in an abstract or virtual environment" (Putnik, 2001, p. 86).

The VE integration capability is fundamental to deal with the available resources in the market and is ensured by integration mechanisms (Figure 1a). The VE (geographical) physical distribution capability is supported by wide area networks and correspondent protocols, e.g., the Internet (Figure 1b). Agility and virtuality are guaranteed within BM_VEARM VEs by the resource manager, or broker, element (Figure 1c).

The BM_VEARM elementary structure, or structural pattern, which is a hierarchical structure, is represented in Figure 2 and is used as a building block during the VE structure synthesis process.

Some instances of BM_VEARM VE structures are represented in Figure 3.

An integration mechanism (Figure 4a) acts as an interface between adjacent levels, and from the implementation viewpoint, it is usually included within those levels (Figure 4b).

Thus, to unburden representation diagrams, integration mechanisms can be omitted (Figure 4b). Further developments on this issue can be found in Putnik et al. (2002).

Figure 1. Elementary structures with (a) integration, (b) distribution, and (c) agility and virtuality (Source: Putnik, 2001)

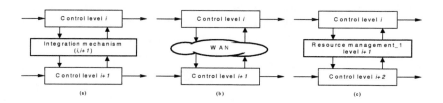

Figure 2. BM_VEARM elementary structure, or structural pattern (Source: Putnik, 2001)

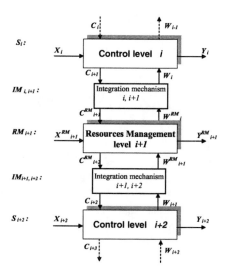

Figure 3. BM_VEARM hierarchical structures instances

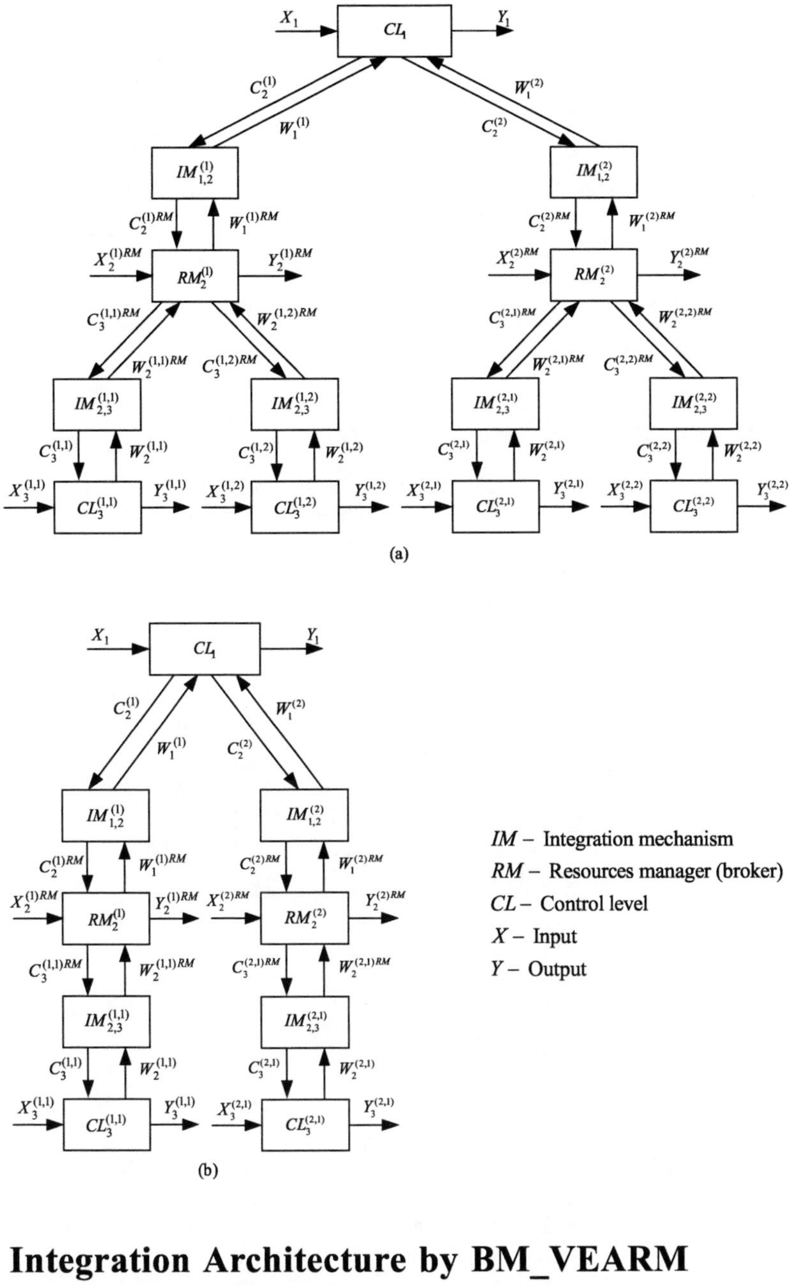

(a)

(b)

IM – Integration mechanism
RM – Resources manager (broker)
CL – Control level
X – Input
Y – Output

VE Integration Architecture by BM_VEARM

The VE, and BM_VE, integration architecture by BM_VEARM is the NVE model (under development), conceived to provide the environment and knowledge base semantics translation, to serve as an unification and a global model to which links any other particular model, integrating international standards already developed or to be developed in the future (Figure 5). BM_VEARM is characterized by the following

Figure 4. Integration mechanism (a) logical structure and (b) typical implementation (Source: Putnik, 2001)

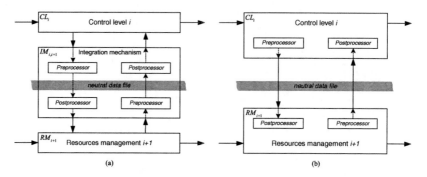

(a)   (b)

Figure 5. BM_VEARM and the correspondent NVE model

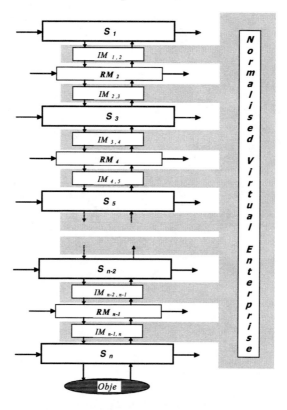

attribute values from an enterprise integration model space: (1) semantics oriented (through the *NVE data model*); (2) global and unifying (through the *NVE model*-all other models should translate to it); (3) translator based; (4) dynamic — supporting the highest VE reconfiguration dynamics ("within 1 second") for any type of production (provided by the three-level hierarchical organisation model introducing the broker as an agent of agility and virtuality), and (6) interenterprise-supporting the interenterprise integration and operation.

Open questions concern pragmatic and societal levels of the VE integration meta-theoretical framework (see Putnik et al., this volume).

BM_VE:
FORMAL SPECIFICATION AND THEORY

At the present, BM_VE is rigorously formalized for the structural aspect. Structural aspect is one of the most important aspects of system modelling in general. In our case, the structural aspect is related to the BM_VE organizational structure as well as to the BM_VE process and control structures. This is possible as the formalization is based on the general system theory, with a relatively high level of abstraction, which provides a capability for interpretations for different aspects of BM_VE functions and characteristics.

Canonical Structure

For the formalization of the BM_VE structural aspects, an attributed context-free formal grammar, denoted as G_{BM} (Definition 1), was developed in Sousa (2003). As integration mechanisms can be omitted from the representation of the BM_VE structure (Figure 4b), G_{BM} deals with only two types of building blocks: control level block (represented by the terminal symbol c_i) and resource management block, or *broker*, (represented by the terminal symbol r_j) (Figure 6).

Definition 1: $G_{BM} = (V_T, V_N, S, R)$ is an attributed context-free formal grammar dedicated to the structural project of VE/production systems compliant to BM_VEARM referential architecture, where:

$$V_T = \left\{ c_1, \ldots, c_{n_c}, r_1, \ldots, r_{n_r}, s_{eq}, \equiv, \downarrow\uparrow,), (\right\}$$

$$V_N = \{S, A, B\}$$

Figure 6. Building blocks used by G_{BM}: (a) control level and (b) resources management

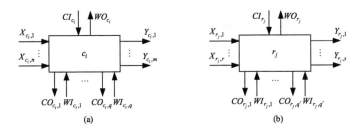

(a)   (b)

---

132 Putnik, Cunha, Sousa & Ávila

Table 1. Productions and application conditions for G_{BM} grammar

Production	Application condition
$S \rightarrow c_i\left(\downarrow\uparrow A\right) \equiv s_{eq}$	$1 \le i \le n_c \wedge o_{c_i} = 0$
$A \rightarrow r_i\left(\downarrow\uparrow B\right)$	$1 \le i \le n_r \wedge o_{r_i} = 0$
$A \rightarrow AA$	—
$B \rightarrow c_i\left(\downarrow\uparrow A\right)$	$1 \le i \le n_c \wedge o_{c_i} = 0$
$B \rightarrow BB$	—
$B \rightarrow c_i$	$1 \le i \le n_c \wedge o_{c_i} = 0$

Figure 7. BM_VE system canonical instances generated by G_{BM} grammar

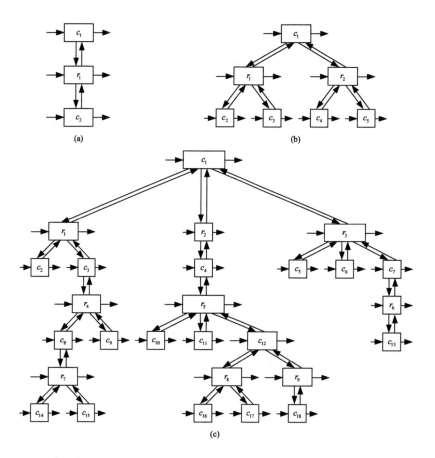

Figure 8. Possible internal composition of a virtual enterprise instance

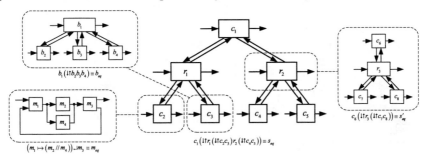

R contains productions and application conditions of Table 1 and attributes and assertions listed in Sousa (2003).

Some examples of BM_VE structures synthesized by G_{BM} are represented in Figure 7. These system structure instances are BM_VE canonical structures, because they are fully compliant with the BM_VEARM architecture. The semantic part of G_{BM} allows for the previous definition of some requisites for the intended system, guarantying, thus, that G_{BM} only generates system structures satisfying those requisites. The language generated by G_{BM} is denoted by L_{BM}.

Definition 2: $L_{BM} = L(G_{BM})$ is a formal language dedicated to the structural project of VE/ production systems compliant to BM_VEARM referential architecture, generated by G_{BM} grammar (Definition 1).

The components of a BM_VE may obviously have their own internal compositions (Figure 8).

The G_{BM} grammar is a representational class of a formal theory of BM_VE structures (Sousa, 2003), i.e., the grammar G_{BM} describes, or represents, a formal theory of BM_VE canonical structures.

Noncanonical Structure

Some structures can be BM_VE noncanonical structures. An example of a potential BM_VE noncanonical system instance is represented in Figure 9. For example, the control blocks c_1 and c_4, c_3 and c_8, etc., are directly connected, i.e., there is no broker between them, as the BM_VE canonical structure requires.

It is possible to transform the structure in Figure 9 into a BM_VE canonical structure assuming the aggregations represented in Figure 10.

Thus, the structure in Figure 9 is, in fact, a BM_VE noncanonical structure, and its corresponding BM_VE canonical structure is represented in Figure 11. Consequently, we can state that any noncanonical BM_VE structure can be transformed into a BM_VE canonical structure. It is thus possible to determine if a given enterprise is or is not a BM_VE.

Figure 9. Potential BM_VE noncanonical structure instance

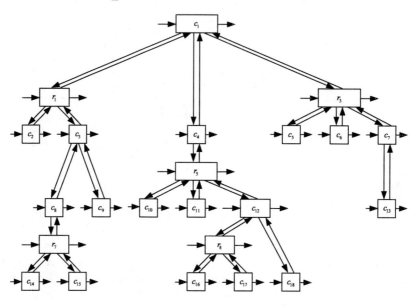

Figure 10. Transformation into BM_VE canonical structure

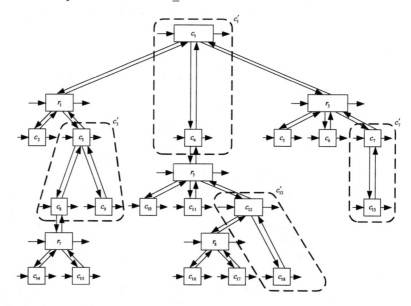

Figure 11. BM_VE equivalent canonical structure

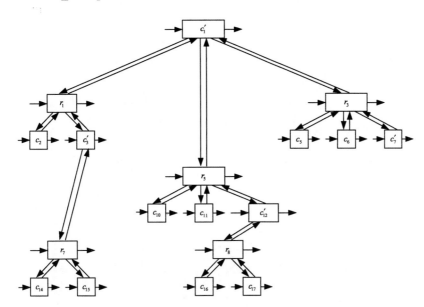

Structural Dynamics or Reconfigurability

As an example of a possible formalization of the BM_VE system dynamics, a trivial regular grammar denoted by G_1 was developed (Sousa, 2003). Despite being trivial, this grammar $G_1 = (V_T, V_N, S, R)$ where $V_T = \{a\}$, $V_N = \{S\}$, and $R = \{S \rightarrow a, S \rightarrow aS\}$, allows for the description of a sequence of BM_VE operations (each operation is denoted by one instance of the terminal symbol a). As an example, consider three operations *aaa* performed by different BM_VE configurations, each one determined by the brokerage function as the most adequate for that moment (Figure 12).

Figure 12. BM_VE reconfigurability dynamics

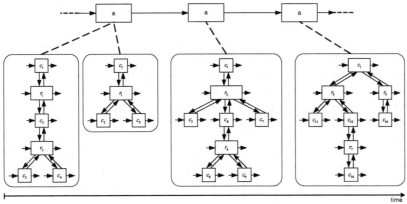

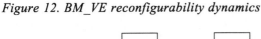

Figure 13. BM_VE reconfigurability dynamics (Source: Putnik, 2001)

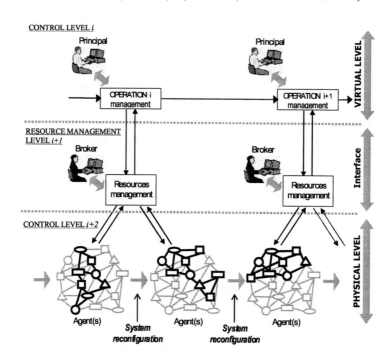

Figure 13 represents an operational informal diagram of a BM_VE.

As seen before, BM_VE reconfiguration can occur not only between operations but also during an operation, without knowledge of the upper hierarchical level.

BM_VE AS A/VE

Relaxing the conditions of BM_VEARM, we could permit VE to operate in a different way. During the production operations (represented by the symbol *a*, Figure 14), the VE operates as a traditional (networked) enterprise, without virtuality. But, during the configuration/reconfiguration process, or operation (represented by the symbol *d*, Figure 14), the business "owner" employs a broker, and at that moment, the enterprise operates with virtuality, as a BM_VE instance. It means that we have alternations of the "traditional" structures (without virtuality/brokers) and BM_VE structures. The first structure should necessarily be a BM_VE structure, as it is the moment of initial configuration of the enterprise. Enterprises that operate in this way we will call agile enterprise[6] (AE) or agile/virtual enterprise (A/VE).

To formalize the description of AEs or A/VEs operation, a regular grammar denoted by G_2 was developed (Sousa, 2003). This grammar $G_2 = (V_T, V_N, S, R)$, where $V_T = \{a,d\}$, $V_N = \{S\}$, and $R = \{S \rightarrow da, S \rightarrow daS\}$ uses two terminal symbols, *a* and *d*, to represent normal operation and brokerage operation. Examples of words generated by G_2 are *da*,

Figure 14. AE or A/VE operation

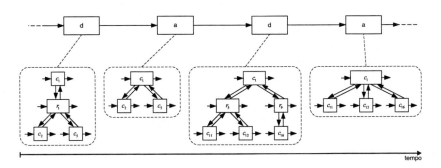

dada, dadada, etc., showing that there is always a brokerage operation before a normal operation (Figure 14).

This means that the resources used by the agile enterprise owner c_1 to execute a given normal operation are previously selected by a brokerage operation performed by one or more brokers. Although extremely simple, the grammars G_1 and G_2 show that BM_VE reconfiguration may occur between operations or even during an operation (Figure 12), while in agile enterprises, reconfiguration occurs only for each new normal operation (Figure 14). Furthermore, in the BM_VE, the enterprise owner has no knowledge about the resources used (due to virtuality introduced by the broker), while in the agile enterprise, the owner has direct contact with those resources.

Figure 15. Operational informal diagram of an AE or A/VE (Source: Putnik, 2001)

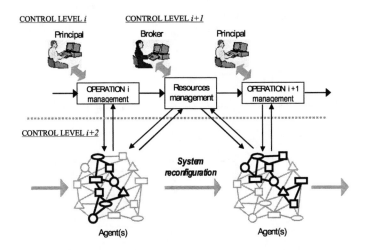

CONSEQUENCES OF VIRTUALITY IN BM_VE

The virtuality inherent to the BM_VEARM reference model has some important consequences.

Consequence 1

In any BM_VE, hierarchy is always present. Table 2 reflects the correspondence between typical interprocess relations inside traditional enterprises and BM_VEs.

Consequence 2

As mentioned before, the agent does not see the structures above and below. Actually, for the agent, the enterprise finishes with the broker above and below. From the agent's point of view, the enterprise, that is, the VE, is bounded by the brokers. The consequence for VE definition is radical. Now, we can say that the VE is a structure "r-c-r" (Figure 16), or its special cases, structures "c-r" and "r-c" (Figure 17b and c). The general VE structure "r-c-r" means that the agent ("c") receives the task/job from the broker (in which case, the agent acts as a server) and can ask the broker hierarchically below for some other resources that can do part of the job received (assumed), in which case, the agent acts as a client. The special case "c-r" is the case when the agent acts only as a client. This is, actually, the case when the agent is the VE initiator or entrepreneur. The special case "r-c" is the case when the agent acts only as a server and does by himself the whole task he received. From this viewpoint, a BM_VE instance can be seen as a structure composed by "r-c-r" patterns and its special cases (Figure 18).

The above-described consequence of virtuality has another implication: we can now define the VE in two ways. The first one, which is in conformity with the first part

Table 2. Interprocess relations substitutions

Figure 16. The "r-c-r" pattern within a BM_VE

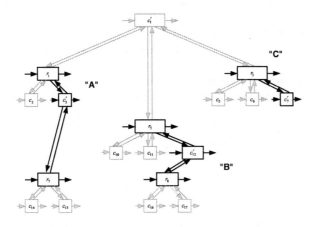

Figure 17. The "r-c-r" pattern and its special cases

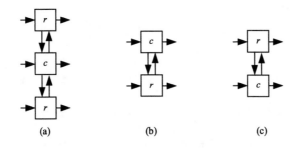

Figure 18. A BM_VE from the "r-c-r" pattern viewpoint

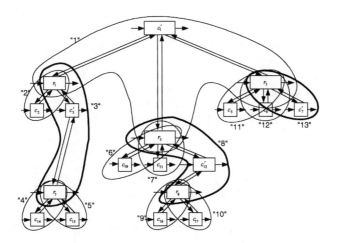

of this text, will be designated as a business-, or product-, centered definition. This definition considers the whole structure, as it is described in the section "BM_VE: Formal Specification and Theory," which is formally defined by the grammar G_{BM}. Looking at the whole structure, we can easily notice that it is composed regularly (canonically) from the patterns "c-r-c," which ("c-r-c") is, in fact, the minimal BM_VE structure (Figure 7a).

Definition 3 (business-, or product-centered): VE is a hierarchical structure composed of elementary (hierarchical) structural patterns "c-r-c."

As mentioned before, the second definition arises from the second consequence of virtuality and will be designated as resource-centered definition.

Definition 4 (resource-centered): VE is a hierarchical structure with three levels "r-c-r," or two levels, "c-r" or "r-c," as special cases.

Furthermore, the first VE definition — business- or product-centered — can be expressed in terms of the second VE definition-resource-centered-as in Definition 5.

Definition 5 (business- or product-centered): VE is a hierarchical structure composed by *resource-centered* VE.

Consequence 3

The third consequence is a better understanding of the virtualization process, i.e., the transition process of traditional enterprises to VEs. The virtualization of a traditional enterprise c can be achieved by two ways:
1. Enterprise includes two external brokers, keeping its internal organization (Table 3).
2. Enterprise decomposes itself in a number of independent enterprises and connects them using brokers, in order to continue its business. (Some examples of virtualizations are represented in Figure 19.)

Table 3. Virtualization of a traditional enterprise c employing external brokers

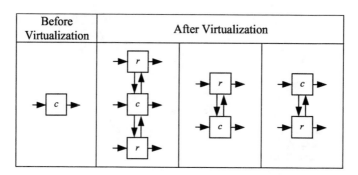

Figure 19. Virtualization of a traditional enterprise c decomposing its own structure

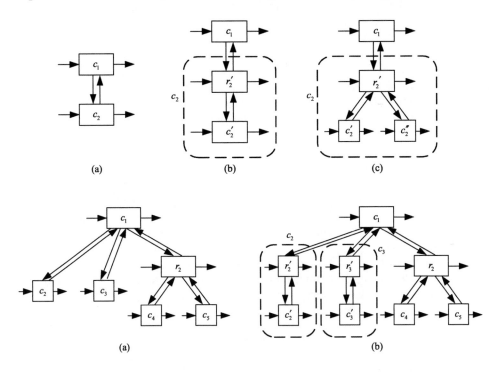

CONCLUSIONS

BM_VE as a model represents a synthesis over functional requirements for integrability, distributivity, agility, and virtuality as the competitiveness factors. At this stage of development, the model is characterized by four particularities:

1. The model has resulted in three main tools, or mechanisms, providing the maximum capability for the structural reconfiguration dynamics ("*reconfiguration within 1 second*"), but at the same time, these tools, assure the minimization of the main structural organization dynamics disablers, which are the *transaction costs* and the *preservation of the enterprise's knowledge*. These tools are the market of resources, broker, and virtuality.

2. The specific organization structural pattern provides the virtuality in the sense of virtual environment for the VE partners as well as the conditions for the VE structure reconfiguration online. This structural pattern is specific for the BM_VE and BM_VEARM.

3. The rigorous formalization is based on formal grammars and automata as the representation class, which are, in fact, the formal theory model for the BM_VE structures. The formal theory provides the capability to generate regular and consistent structure, in full compliance with the reference model (BM_VEARM). These structures are called BM_VE *canonical structures*. Additionally, dynamic aspects of the structure reconfiguration are formalized too.

4.   The emergence of new definitions of the VE and a specification of processes of virtualization, are consequences of the model of virtuality conceived. Virtualization of an enterprise is of the greatest importance for transition from a "traditional" enterprise into a VE.

BM_VE is a ubiquitous enterprise too. The issue of VE integration is the key success factor for the BM_VE. The needs for the integration are present between any two control blocks, and additionally, the integration is subjected to the dynamic creation of new interactions, due to the supposed high reconfigurability dynamics of the BM_VE structure.

There is a lot of work to be done in the future. For example, improvement of definitions, especially the one that unifies the model integration and design, and also the market of resources; specification of the normalized VE model as the integrating structure; homogeneous specification of the structural and dynamical aspects as well as the (BM_VE) VE extended life cycle; other views of the VE (information systems, hardware, etc.); system validation-analytical and within real-life environment; development tools; etc.

At the end, we would say that the project of BM_VE is carried on the University of Minho since 1995, and it will continue for the next several years. During the past period, several PhD and MSc theses were finished, and at the moment, several are on course.

REFERENCES

Avila, P. (2004). *Rigorous resources system selection model for the project of agile/ virtual enterprises for complex products.* PhD Thesis, University of Minho, Braga, Portugal.

Avila, P., Putnik, G. D., & Cunha, M. M. (2005). Broker performance for agile/virtual enterprise integration, *(this volume).*

Cunha, M. (2003). *Organization of a market of resources for agile and virtual enterprises integration.* PhD Thesis, University of Minho, Braga, Portugal.

Cunha, M. M., Putnik, G. D., Gunasekaran, A., & Avila, P. (2005). Market of resources as a virtual enterprise enabler, *(this volume).*

Orfali, R., Harkey, D., & Edwards, J. (1997). *Instant CORBA.* New York: John Wiley & Sons.

Putnik, G. D. (2001). BM_Virtual enterprise architecture reference model. In A. Gunasekaran (Ed.), *Agile manufacturing: 21st century manufacturing strategy* (pp. 73–93). Amsterdam; New York: Elsevier Science.

Putnik, G. D., Cunha, M. M., Sousa, R., & Avila, P. (2005). Virtual enterprise integration: Challenges of a new paradigm, *(this volume).*

Putnik, G. D., Spasic, Z. A., Sousa, R. M., & Naldinho, J. (2002). Systems theory application for manufacturing systems or enterprise integration modeling. In Erden et al. (Eds.), *Proceedings of the Sixth International Conference on Mechatronic Design and Modelling,* Cappadocia, Turkey, (pp. 31-46).

Sousa, R. (2003). *Contribuição para uma Teoria Formal de Sistemas de Produção.* Tese de Doutoramento, Universidade do Minho, Braga, Portugal.

ENDNOTES

[1]   For a more detailed discussion, see Cunha (2003) and Cunha et al. (this volume).

[2]   The broker is never on the "top" of the hierarchy, as in that case, he would be the entrepreneur and not the broker; he would be the owner of the VE network and not the broker. Thus, broker is always an external entity or agent that always acts by the order or on behalf of the "principal" or "client," otherwise he will not be a "broker."

[3]   For a more detailed discussion, see Avila (2004) and Avila et al. (this volume).

[4]   There is an important critique of the concept of virtuality as it is conceived in our work. It is the lack of direct relation, or contact, between the human operators. Another critic could be that if the principal does not know the underlying physical structure, then he cannot take the advantage from the specifities of the particular resource. But we think that this argument is relative, because it imples that the principal should know the specifities of all resources that will hypotheticaly participate in the enterprise, at one or another moment, which is impossible.

[5]   An integrated formal specification of the market of resources together with the operating BM_VE is the issue of future work.

[6]   Rigorously, an enterprise could be agile with a broker too but when a broker's operation does not provide virtuality.

Section III

Generative Integration

Chapter VII

Market of Resources as a Virtual Enterprise Integration Enabler

Maria Manuela Cunha
Polytechnic Institute of Cávado and Ave, Portugal

Goran D. Putnik
University of Minho, Portugal

Angappa Gunasekaran
University of Massachusetts - Dartmouth, USA

Paulo Ávila
Polytechnic Institute of Porto, Portugal

ABSTRACT

The search for increased competitiveness and efficiency during the last decade resulted in several organizational approaches that presented flexibility as a main characteristic. Some of these approaches rely on dynamically reconfigurable partnerships in permanent alignment with the market and strongly supported by information and communication technology, with the agile/virtual enterprise *(A/VE) organizational model as a leading example. Several technologies and valuable applications have been developed to support some of these emerging models, however, the full potential of the A/VE model requires an* environment *coping with its requirements, and the Market of Resources concept is defended as a solution for virtual enterprise (VE) integration. The chapter discusses the requirements for the A/VE model and introduces the global structure and functionalities of the Market of Resources.*

INTRODUCTION

The combination of the shorter life span of new products, increasing product diversity over time, rapid technological developments, increased technological complexity, market globalization, frequent changes in demand, uncertainty, and strong competition, are challenges of the actual worldwide economic context. Competitiveness is a main requisite of enterprises, whose satisfaction requires the definition of new organizational concepts, with extremely high performance, being strongly time-oriented while highly focused on cost and quality and permanently aligned with business opportunities.

One of the most widely discussed area in recent business literature is that of organizational networked structures as the basic principle to achieve flexibility and quick response in a highly complex and competitive environment (Bradley, Hausman, & Nolan, 1993; Byrne, 1993; Davidow & Malone, 1992; Handy, 1995; Miles & Snow, 1986; Naisbitt, 1982; Naisbitt & Aburdene, 1985; Toffler, 1985). Several models have been proposed since the "Virtual Factory" concepts suggested in 1990 by Peter Drucker (1990), which include the concepts of virtual organizations, virtual enterprises, extended enterprises, knowledge networks, agile enterprises, agile manufacturing, and other developments gaining increasing interest.

The need to keep a close alignment with the market environment in permanent change implies the high dynamics of the organizations' structure reconfigurability, introducing a new concept of *dynamically reconfigurable global networked structures*, traduced by the A/VE organizational model. In its BM_virtual enterprise architecture reference model (BM_VEARM), Putnik (Putnik, 2000a; Putnik, Cunha, Ávila, & Sousa, 2004) presented "fast adaptability" or "fast reconfigurability" as the main enabler of business alignment and the main requirement for competitiveness.

Two critical factors against this concept of dynamically reconfigurable global networked structures, i.e., against reconfigurability dynamics and networking, can be identified:

- The *transaction costs*, i.e., the firm reconfiguration cost, associated with the partners' search, selection, negotiation, and integration as well as permanent monitoring and the evaluation of the partnership performance
- The *preservation of firm's knowledge* on organizational and management processes, as it is the firm's competitive factor

The efficient implementation of the A/VE model requires tools to overcome the networking and dynamics disabling factors.

The main tools suggested in the BM_VEARM (Putnik, 2000a) for managing, controlling, and enabling networking and dynamics, overcoming the two critical factors against networking, are as follows:

- The *Market of Resources* is the environment for enabling and management of efficient configuration, and assuring virtuality, at low transaction costs and reduced risk of knowledge leakage.
- The *broker* or organization configuration manager is the main agent of agility and virtuality, acting either between two operations of the A/VE (off-line reconfigurability, providing agility only) or online with the operation (online reconfigurability, providing virtuality and a higher level of agility).

- *Virtuality* makes possible the transition from one physical structure (instance) to another in a way that the enterprise or process owner is not affected by the system reconfiguration and is not aware of the reconfiguration — the underlying service structure and reconfiguration process are hidden.

In this chapter, we discuss the A/VE model requirements and present the Market of Resources as a tool for managing, controlling, and enabling networking and dynamics. We also discuss some results of the demonstration of the ability of the Market of Resources to cope with the A/VE requirements, in comparison with the traditional Web-based applications.

RECONFIGURABILITY DYNAMICS AND BUSINESS ALIGNMENT AS REQUIREMENTS FOR THE A/VE MODEL

In order to achieve its maximum competitiveness, i.e., to be competitive in delivery time, quality, and cost, and to yield satisfactory profit margins, the implementation of the A/VE model requires a supporting environment assuring two main interrelated aspects (designated A/VE requirements): (1) reconfigurability dynamics (assuring fast transition between A/VE instantiations) and (2) business alignment (aligning the A/VE with the market). This section introduces and discusses these two A/VE requirements.

We will designate by *resource* any function, service, or product provided by the independent enterprises (*resources providers*), candidates to integrate an A/VE.

Reconfigurability Dynamics in A/VE Integration

If traditionally the goal of the enterprise was to fulfil the customer requirements using the limited set of resources available within the walls of the organization, today, and according to Yusuf, Sarhadi, and Gunasekaran (1999), a successful company must acquire the capability to achieve and explore the competitive advantage in synergy, i.e., using the best resources available to an organization (Cunha, Putnik, & Ávila, 2000), which requires a shift from "self-centered close-enterprises" (Browne & Zhang, 1999) to dynamically reconfigurable global networked structures, corresponding to the recent approaches of the extended enterprise (Browne, Sacket, & Wortmann, 1995; Browne & Zhang, 1999), the VE (Byrne, 1993; Drucker, 1990; Goldman, Nagel, & Preiss, 1995), the agile enterprise (Nagel & Dove, 1993), the A/VE (Cunha et al., 2000; Putnik, 2000a), the intelligent enterprise (Quinn, 1990), the smart organization (Filos & Banahan, 2001) and the one-product integrated manufacturing (OPIM; Putnik & Silva, 1995) models, each with its characterizing nuances. In the text, these models are generally addressed as VE models. However, the VE model proposed by the authors — the A/VE model — reinforces a requirement for high reconfigurability dynamics.

Several factors appear as supreme factors of competitiveness: (1) the organizations' *capability to achieve and explore competitive advantages in synergy*, by using or integrating the optimal available resources for the functions that the organization undertakes; (2) the capability of *fast adaptability to the market*; together with (3) the capability of *managing all business processes independently of distance*. The A/VE organizational model achieves these factors.

Fast reconfigurability or adaptability means the ability to change fast to face the unpredictable changes in the environment and market, implying substitution of resources (transition to a new A/VE instantiation).

Responsiveness to the market demands requires shorter product life cycles and shorter time to market, as well as it forces the product life cycle to suffer frequent redesigns, which implies the requirement for increased dynamics to the A/VE model. Even A/VEs tend to last for shorter times, while simultaneously addressing a highly dynamic reconfiguration; an A/VE can have as many instantiations as required either by product changes or as a requirement of quality and competitiveness improvement, to assure a permanent alignment with such market demands. By alignment, in this context, we mean the actions to be undertaken to gain synergy between business, that is, between a market opportunity, and the provision of the required product, with the required specifications, at the required time, with the lowest cost and with the best possible return.

The implementation of the A/VE model implies the ability of (1) flexible and almost instantaneous access to the optimal *resources* to integrate in the enterprise; (2) design, negotiation, business management, and manufacturing management functions independent from the physical barrier of space; (3) minimization of the reconfiguration or integration time; and (4) evolutionary capability, or the ability to learn with history.

Enterprise integration, or intraenterprise integration consists of the establishment of effective and efficient interactions, as well as interaction improvement, among the enterprise's elements, or organizational units and functions, and provides an easy enterprise reconfiguration (without significant conversion/reconfiguration costs). In the case of an A/VE, integration means the establishment of effective and efficient interactions among the partners of the A/VE network and one of the enablers of the A/VE dynamic reconfiguration, i.e., *interenterprise integration*. A/VE integration (and reconfiguration) activity involves the search and selection of potential resources providers for integration, negotiation among them, selection of the optimal combination of resources providers, establishment and implementation of integration procedures, and contractualization between the resources providers and the A/VE owner.

A/VE reconfigurations can happen mainly for three reasons:

1.   Reconfiguration during an A/VE life cycle as a consequence of the product redesign (a new instantiation of the A/VE is to be considered) in the business/ product life cycle, to keep the A/VE aligned with the market requirements.
2.   Reconfiguration as a consequence of the nature of the particular product life cycle phase (evolutionary phases).
3.   Reconfiguration can also happen as a consequence of the evaluation of the performance of the resources providers during one instantiation of the A/VE, or voluntarily, by the participating resources providers, generating another instantiation, due to the substitution of resources.

Partners (resources providers) search, negotiation, selection of optimal solutions, establishment of contracts, and integration of the A/VE, enforcement of contracts, etc., are complex and risky activities required by this model.

The organizational challenge of partitioning tasks among partners in the distributed manufacturing environment so that they fit and take advantage of the different competencies in A/VE, integration of the same, coordination, and reconfigurability in order to keep alignment with the market requirements, is of main concern, and can determine the success or failure of a project.

Business Alignment in A/VE Integration

Business alignment in A/VE integration is complex and challenging, as alignment has to incorporate immaterial components in the relationships within the integration of resources providers. It is not just an internal strategy but a set of integrated and interrelated integration strategies that must be verified so that the integrated A/VE is able to meet the objective giving rise to the A/VE itself, that is, to meet the market requirements (or customer requirements).

Strategic alignment between business and A/VE integration involves a mix of dependencies between *market* requirements, *resources* requirements (product/service/ operation) and *resources providers* requirements.

We will designate by *client* the entity looking for resources to create or reconfigure an A/VE. The *client* wants to answer to a market opportunity, by capturing the corresponding market requirements, and asks the Market of Resources for optimal A/VE design, selection, and integration, traducing the market requirements into resources providers requirements, process requirements, and resources requirements.

The client needs to assure the alignment between the market and the resources providers to be selected and integrated in the A/VE. It must also be assured that the client has correctly captured the market requirements. This way, the process must align the client with the market (business), and then align the resources providers (by the search, selection, and integration processes) with the client and with business.

Integrating an A/VE corresponds to aligning the entities *client*, *A/VE*, *resources providers*, and *resources* with business. The BM_VEARM proposes tools to guide the client in aligning the A/VE with the market (customer) opportunity.

CRITICAL ASPECTS OF A/VE INTEGRATION AND RECONFIGURABILITY DYNAMICS

The main critical aspects associated with the recent concept of dynamically reconfigurable global networked structures, corresponding to the A/VE model — precisely based on networking and reconfigurability dynamics — are the transaction costs and the leakage of private information.

In an ideal business environment, a firm makes an informed assessment of the relevant costs, benefits, and risks of outsourcing *versus* internal procurement. If there exists a profitable opportunity to outsource a service or operation, the client and the suppliers enter into a contract with full knowledge of the nature of the work, signing a complete and explicit written agreement covering all aspects of the outsourced service and payments, eventually including contingency plans. But in most contractual relationships, things do not happen this way, as processes are much more complex than idealised.

In reality, when integrating an A/VE rather than outsourcing a service or a set of simple products or operations, difficulties arise. Selection, negotiation, contractualization, and enforcement can be too complex and too delicate. There is a vast spectrum of available resources providers, each with different characteristics, leading to difficult selection and integration decisions.

The costs of outsourcing are composed of both the explicit cost of carrying out the transaction as well as hidden costs due to coordination difficulties and contractual risks. The major costs associated with outsourcing include (1) the transaction costs and (2) the leakage of private information.

MARKET OF RESOURCES: A TOOL FOR MANAGING, CONTROLLING, AND ENABLING NETWORKING AND DYNAMICS

BM_VEARM is a VE reference model conceived for enabling the highest organizational/structural/reconfiguration and operational *interenterprise* dynamics of an A/VE, employing three main mechanisms for A/VE dynamic creation, reconfiguration, and operation: (1) *Market of Resources*, (2) *broker*, and (3) *virtuality*. Additionally, BM_VEARM implies the highest level of integration and (geographic) distribution of A/VE elements (resources providers) (Putnik, 2000b).

This section introduces the Market of Resources as an environment for A/VE dynamic integration and business alignment, according to the BM_VEARM.

Global Structure of the Market of Resources

Offer and demand are usually matched under several different circumstances, from unregulated search to oriented search, from simple intermediation mechanisms to the market mechanism, all of them with the possibility of being either manually performed or automated (Cunha, Putnik, & Gunasekaran, 2002). A marketplace of resource providers will provide the matching between firms looking for potential partners for integration and firms offering their resources, facilitating A/VE integration, and offering to participants a larger number of business opportunities.

Information technology (Internet and WWW technologies, agent technology, e-marketplaces, etc.) supports or automates purchasing activities, helping from procurement processes until the search of partners for a partnership, including electronic automated negotiation, electronic contracting, and market brokerage services. Although the basic information technology infrastructures and tools are absolutely necessary as support, the added value comes from the higher-level functions, to support search, selection, and integration of resources under the format of an A/VE, coping with the high reconfigurability dynamics requirements (overcoming the disabling factors) intrinsic to the A/VE model (Cunha, Putnik, Carvalho, & Ávila, 2002).

The general model of electronic commerce, if concerning business-to-business relations, suggests that the Internet provides more information, more choice opportunities either to consumers or to establish networks, lowering the cost of information and, as classified as the "democracy of the Internet," reducing information asymmetries. However, the new models of A/VE, or the new forms of value creation, where market information concerns information about resources (complex and primitive) to integrate, although reinforced by the ability to use more globally distributed resources and by lower transaction costs provided by information and communication technology and Internet usage, claims for a wider support environment, assuring better quality and better response at lower time. This corresponds to the *Market of Resources* concept.

Several supporting infrastructures and applications must exist before we can take advantage of the A/VE organizational model (Carvalho, Putnik, & Cunha, 2002), such as: electronic markets of resources providers, legal platforms, brokerage services, efficient and reliable global information systems, electronic contractualization and electronic negotiation systems, and software tools (selection algorithms, etc.) (Cunha, Putnik, & Carvalho, 2002).

The Market of Resources appears as an alternative to existing applications that were developed to support isolated activities, such as procurement and partners search and selection, negotiation, enterprise collaboration, within supply chains, but without the purpose of responding to the A/VE requirements. It is an alternative to the dispersedly developed Internet-based solutions (*traditional e-based solutions*), to support search and selection of partners to integrate a supply chain (Cunha, Putnik, Carvalho et al., 2002).

Market of Resources is an institutionalized organizational framework and service assuring the accomplishment of the competitiveness requirements for A/VE dynamic integration and business alignment. The operational aspect of the Market of Resources consists of an Internet-based intermediation service, mediating offer, and demand of resources to dynamically integrate in an A/VE, assuring low transaction costs (demonstrated in Cunha & Putnik, 2003b, 2003c) and the partners' knowledge preservation. Brokers act within the Market of Resources as intermediation agents for agility and virtuality.

In this virtual environment, *offer* corresponds to resources providers (individuals, enterprises) that make their resources (products, components, operations) available, as potential partners for A/VE integration, and *demand* corresponds to client or A/VE owner, the entity looking for resources to create/integrate/reconfigure an A/VE to satisfy a given *customer*. *Customer* is the entity giving rise to a business opportunity and is considered outside the Market of Resources, as the *client* entity is the bridge between the Market of Resources and the *customer* (Cunha et al., 2000).

The service provided by the Market of Resources is supported by (1) a knowledge base of resources and history of previous performance results, (2) a normalized representation of information, (3) computer-aided tools and algorithms, (4) brokers, and (5) a regulation, i.e., management of negotiation and integration processes, as well as contract enforcement mechanisms. It is able to offer (1) knowledge for resources search and selection and its integration in an A/VE, (2) specific functions of A/VE operation management, and (3) contracts and formalizing procedures to assure the accomplishment of commitments, responsibility, trust, and deontological aspects, envisaging the accomplishment of the A/VE objectives.

The Market of Resources is subscribed to by independent resources providers. To this subscription corresponds the formal description of the resources using a resources representation language and its integration in a knowledge base. The organizational aspect of the Market of Resources consists of an electronically delivered intermediation service, between the resources providers, integrating the knowledge base and clients, which are organizations looking for resources to integrate in an A/VE, to answer to a market opportunity.

If the resources selection domain, to satisfy the tasks of the enterprise, within the same enterprise, represents the *lower limit* of the resources selection domain space, then the global resources selection domain, to satisfy the tasks of the enterprise, implying subcontracting other enterprises, represents the *upper limit* of the resources selection domain space. The global domain provides virtually, and from a practical point of view, an almost infinite resources selection domain size for the optimal organization structure synthesis providing the highest level of competitiveness; however, the search in the global domain is prohibitive because of the infinite effort required.

The overall functioning of the Market of Resources (Figure 1) consists of the creation and management of the market as the environment (Process A.1.) to support the design and integration of the A/VE (Process A.2.) and the A/VE operation (Process A.3.) offering technical and procedural support for the activities of identifying potential partners, qualifying partners, and integrating the A/VE, as well as coordination and performance evaluation mechanisms.

- *Process A.1. Market of Resources creation and operation:* This process corresponds to the creation and operation (management and maintenance) of the environment proposed, from the technological aspects, such as the creation of databases and development of software tools, implementation of communication systems, etc., to the definition and permanent adaptation and updating of the managerial aspects, such as regulation and rules, criteria for selection, management and brokerage procedures, organization of the market, commitments definition, evaluation, etc., including the performance of the market in order to improve the market of resources organization. It also includes the organization of the resources providers into meaningful combinations of resources, to increase efficiency of the selection process and to reduce search time. This process of decomposition takes place off-line, and its results are designated as "focused markets" (Cunha et al., 2000).

- *Process A.2. A/VE design and integration:* The process consists of two activities: resources selection and A/VE integration. Resources selection involves the design of the A/VE that matches the requirements to produce the desired product and the search for the "best" combination of resources that will be integrated in the A/VE. Selection is performed on a specific domain consisting of combinations of focused markets. The redesign or reconfiguration of an A/VE, implying the substitution or integration of new resources, is also considered in this process, as well as is the dissolution of the A/VE. Integration consists of formalizing the A/VE (contractualization) and of establishing procedures regarding the integration of the participants and the implementation of management and evaluation techniques.

- *Process A.3. A/VE operation:* The service provided by the market controls the operation of the integrated A/VE, tracking the performance of each resource, and restructuring the A/VE design whenever necessary (dynamical adjustment) to make possible the achievement of the results. The operation results are of interest to keep actual historical information concerning the performance of the resources, to be taken into consideration in future selection processes, and to adjust the management procedures.

Figure 1. IDEF0 representation of the global process for the Market of Resources and for A/VE design, integration, and operation (Source: Cunha, Putnik, & Gunasekaran, 2002)

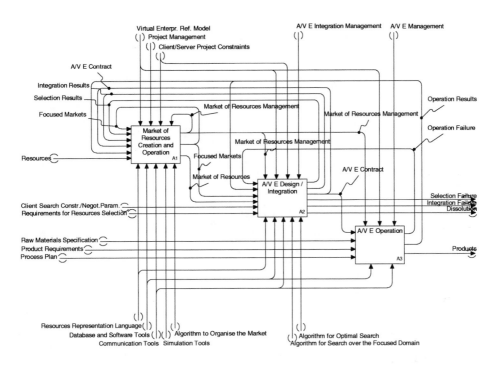

A/VE Design and Integration in the Market of Resources

The process of A/VE design and integration (Process A.2.) consists of traducing the customer or the market requirements for a certain business opportunity into an A/VE project (Process A.2.1), selecting the best combination of resources providers capable of assuring the alignment between that business opportunity and the A/VE (Process A.2.2.), and effectively integrating (Process A.2.3.). Process A.2. is detailed in Figure 2.

To keep the dynamics of the A/VE model, the optimal search of resources to integrate should be obtained almost in real time. The complexity of the resources selection in general means that a compromised domain size (as a base for the solution space construction) should be used for each resource search. This concept, proposed in Cunha (2003) and Cunha et al. (2000) is designated by *focused Market of Resources*, and is defined as a subset of the *Market of Resources*, where a given search for an independent resource is to take place. The proposal of a *focused market* approach, complemented by automatic search over the knowledge base, makes it possible to solve the problem, if possible, almost in real time. *Focused markets'* identification takes place *off-line*.

Figure 2. IDEF0 representation of Process A.2 — A/VE design and integration (Source: Cunha and Putnik, 2004)

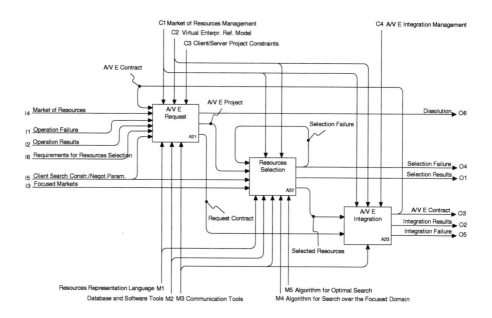

For each search, the *Market of Resources* proposes a *focused domain* (composed by *focused markets*), reasonably dimensioned, to allow a good match in a limited time (Process A.2.2.1. in Figure 3).

The first step of the design and integration process is the design of the A/VE, i.e., the A/VE project (Process A.2.1. in Figure 2), which means (1) translating the specification parameters provided by the client and traducing the market requirements (input flow "Requirements for Resources Selection") into "Normalized Resources Requirements," and (2) translating specific search constraints defined by the client under the format of "Negotiation Parameters" (input flow "Client Search Constraints/Negotiation Parameters") into "Normalized Negotiation Parameters."

The resources selection (Process A.2.2.) corresponds to visiting all the elements proposed by the focused domain, in order to identify negotiation parameters (availability, time to respond to the demand, or time to offer the resource, and costs) and perform an optimal search algorithm considering the client's negotiation parameters and subject to the client project constraints (time to complete the product, cost, etc.). The dimension and the quality of the focused domain proposed for this process are critical, as the dynamics of the A/VE model demands the selection to take place almost at real time. This process takes place online.

The A/VE integration (Process A.2.3.) consists of the formalization of the partnership: establishing procedures, normalizing processes, interoperability, responsibilities, and commitments.

Figure 3. IDEF0 representation of Process A.2.2 — resources selection

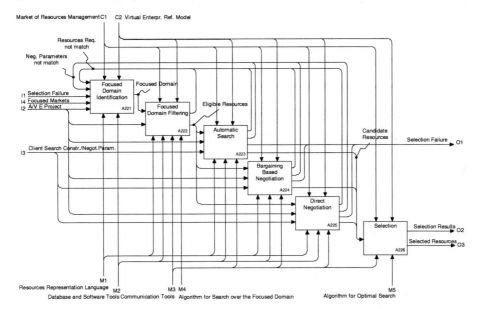

While selection means to check availability and to find the best resources that meet the requirements, integration means effective allocation and formalization of the partnership.

The resources selection process (A.2.2.) takes place in three phases: (1) eligible resources identification, (2) negotiation (identification of candidate resources), and (3) final selection (identification of selected resources), and it is formally presented in the IDEF of Figure 3.

The dimension and the quality of the focused domain proposed for this process are critical. The dynamics of the A/VE model demands the selection to take place almost at real time. To increase efficiency, Process A.2.2. (Figure 3) starts with the proposal of the domain where selection takes place, the focused domain identification (Process A.2.2.1.), to be filtered into the set of eligible resources, according to the A/VE project, which already resulted from the translation of the A/VE requirements, in Process A.2.1.

The process of focused domain filtering (Process A.2.2.2.) corresponds to a search performed on the subset of the market database designated as the focused domain, in order to identify the resources characteristics and perform a first match considering the resources requirements The result is the set of resources providers able to provide the required resources, with which the second phase will take place. If the resulting set of eligible resources does not present a satisfying dimension face to the client search constraints and negotiation parameters defined by the client, i.e., not allowing a "good" search, the focused domain must be redefined.

The set of eligible resources is then submitted to a second phase, corresponding to negotiation with the resources providers. Different resources can be reached according to different negotiation methods or as a combination of them: automatic search

(Process A.2.2.3.), auction-based negotiation (Process A.2.2.4.), and direct negotiation (Process A.2.2.5.). Negotiation results in the set of candidate resources, consisting of the resource providers in condition of providing the required resources, i.e., in condition to integrate the A/VE. However, as different selection models can be used, and some processes can be combinatorial, all the combinations of resources must be analyzed to find the best. "Candidate resources" are the resources providers that meet all the requirements and constraints.

The selection of resources within an enterprise is a function of (1) cost, (2) resources availability and timing, and (3) schedule. The process of resources selection must consider essentially the techniques of activity-based costing, artificial intelligence, and simulation-based scheduling techniques. In the case of configuration of an A/VE, the algorithm for the selection of resources shall include strategic and qualitative factors besides the three mentioned. The third phase is the final selection (Process A.2.2.6.), which is supported by an algorithm and controlled by the broker, and this produces a combination of resources providers considered to be the best possible within the solution space. The output of the selection process (the output flow "selected resources") corresponds to one of the various possible instantiations of the A/VE project.

If the concept of A/VE is revolutionary, the new concept of Market of Resources has the potential to radically alter most of the economical activities and the surrounding social environment, claiming new frameworks for conducting business. As an intermediate service, it will provide mechanisms for efficiently putting in contact and agreement buyers of services (those looking for resources and operations to integrate) and sellers (resources providers to be integrated), conciliating opportunities, negotiation parameters, limitations, managing, controlling, and evaluating the process. The function of management provided by the Market of Resources is crucial. In the manufacturing sector, for instance, the network/partnership is mostly integrated from resources provided by the SMEs, having no definite relations among them. This situation leads to complex management of the value chain, as well as complex coordination of the logistics.

PERFORMANCE OF THE MARKET OF RESOURCES

There is already tradition in the use of information technology systems to support or even automate purchasing activities. The Internet and World Wide Web technologies are raising hopes of helping from procurement processes until the search of partners for a partnership, including negotiation and contractualization, in terms of quality, flexibility, speed, and cost efficiency (Cunha & Putnik, 2003a). However, if these systems do not cover the full process, they could hardly support the A/VE model.

This section summarizes some of the results of the validation of the Market of Resources using a demonstrator specifically developed to simulate the Market of Resources performance, and its comparison with the utilization of traditional Internet-based techniques (WWW search engines, WWW directories, and e-mail) to support search, negotiation, and selection of a set of resources providers to integrate or reconfigure an A/VE. These simulations were based on cost and effort models, respectively, for the Market of Resources and for the traditional techniques.

Basic Concepts

The analysis and comprehension of the complexity inherent to the problem of searching and selecting resources to integrate or reconfigure an A/VE are essential in the project of A/VE systems (Ávila, Cunha, & Putnik, 2003; Ávila, Putnik, & Cunha, 2000, 2002). The complexity of the problem of resources selection is a function of the solution space dimension and of the selection algorithm. The solution space dimension is, in turn, a function of the selection model used in the evaluation of the eligible resources to integrate in an A/VE instance. Considering the need to integrate k resources in an A/VE instance, the evaluation of the eligible resources providers can be performed under two approaches:

- *Independently*, i.e., analyzing the n eligible resources providers (for the provision of a certain resource) one by one, and independently of the other resources that they are able to provide

- *Dependently*, considering all the possible combinations of the k required resources being provided by all the possible combinations of the n eligible resources providers, i.e., considering different negotiation processes to the provision of more than one resource by each resources provider

Effort Models for Performance Analysis

The models developed for the performance analysis differ considerably according to the selection model used (independent or dependent selection model). We have developed effort models that can be easily traduced in cost models, as effort (user effort and also broker effort in the Market of Resources) is the source of cost.

The main entity responsible for cost that we are going to consider is human resources time, i.e., (1) the user time required for searching the WWW, visiting and negotiating with the eligible providers, and decision-making time for selection when under the Internet-based traditional way (or simply *traditional*); and (2) *user time* and *broker time* when using the Market of Resources. From now on, we will designate as *cost* the sum of *search costs* with *contracting costs*.

The model we developed is based on several variables, represented by the abbreviations listed in Table 1 (the index T and M in the variables distinguishes between *traditional* and Market of Resources). Table 2 represents the effort model used when considering an independent selection model, and Table 3 represents the effort model when considering a dependent selection.

Performance Analysis

In this section, we present some simulation results for the search and selection efforts, using independent and dependent selection methods, for different dimensions of search and focused domains and different values of K.

Considering independent selection, Figure 4 represents the efforts of search and selection of one, two, and five resources (K), using the traditional technologies and using the Market of Resource.

For $K = 1$, it is possible to have a more reduced search time using the e-traditional way only for a search domain (SD) *of less than 16 records*, meaning a visit domain of three eligible resources providers (20% × 16) and a focused domain with three records.

Table 1. List of variables

Abbreviations	Meaning
K	Number of required resources
SD	Search domain in traditional method (directory): the dimension of the result of the first step of the search in the WWW
FD	Focused domain in the market (we will assume that $FD = 20\% * SD$)
VD	Visit domain in traditional method: number of resources to be visited in order to evaluate its eligibility; we will assume that $VD = 20\% * SD$
ND_T and ND_M	Negotiation domain, or set of eligible resources: the number of resources providers with whom to undertake a negotiation process: $ND_T = VD_T * R1_T = 20\% * SD_T * R1$; $ND_M = FD_M * R1_M$
CD_T and CD_M	Candidate resources providers, resultant from negotiation process: $CD_T = ND_T * R2_T$; $CD_M = ND_M * R2_M$
SS_T and SS_M	Solution space, possible combinations of candidate resources providers in order to perform the final selection process; in dependent selection, $SS \approx CD$.
C_{xT}	Setup time (constant) to perform operation x using the e-based traditional way: $x = C_{RfBT}$ (auction-based negotiation), C_{DnT} (direct negotiation), C_{ST} (selection, per required resource)
C_{xM}	Setup time (fixed time/constant) to perform operation x using the market; $x = C_R$ (request negotiation), C_D (design), C_V (validation), C_{FD} (focused domain identification), C_{Aut} (automatic search), C'_{RfB} (global fixed time for auction-based negotiation), C_{RfBM} (setup time per auction), C_{DnM} (direct negotiation), C_{SM} (selection), C_C (contractualisation)
t_{xT}	Time to perform operation x using the e-traditional way: $x = t_{DT}$ (first step of the search), t_A (analysis of each of the results contained in SD), t_E (resource provider visit, to determine its eligibility), t_{RfBT} (contact and request for bid), t_{DnT} (contact and direct negotiation), t_{ST} (analysis and evaluation of negotiation results), t_{CT} (contract with selected resource)
t_{xM}	Time to perform operation x using the Market of Resources: $x = t_{DM}$ (specification of the resource requirements per required resource), t_V (validation of resources requirements per required resource), t_{FD} (per record analysis), t_{Aut} (automatic search operation within ND), t_{RfBM} (contact and request for bid), t_{DnM} (contact and direct negotiation), t_{SM} (analysis per candidate resource, for evaluation of negotiation results), t_{CM} (contract with selected resource)
$R1_T$	Ratio between the identified eligible resources (ND_T) and the number of visited resources (VD_T): $R1_T = ND_T/VD_T$
$R1_M$	Ratio between the eligible resources and the focused domain (FD): $R1_M = ND_M/FD_M$
$R2_T$	Ratio between the candidate resources and the eligible resources: $R2_T = CD_T/ND_T$
$R2_M$	Ratio between the candidate resources and the eligible resources: $R2_M = CD_M/ND_M$

Considering 50% of them as eligible for negotiation (let us consider two), the negotiation (auction-based, in our example) within this set of two leads to one candidate resource (by application of the defined ratios of Table 1) for the selection of the best solution to provide the required resource. For a larger search domain of a larger K, the Market of Resources is always more attractive.

Table 2. Search, selection, and integration of K resources, considering the independent selection model

Activity	Traditional	Market of Resources
A/VE request		
- *Request negotiation*		C_R
- *A/VE design*	$\leq K * t_{DT}$	$C_D + K * t_{DM} + C_V + K * t_V$
Resources selection	It will be considered that $R1_T = R1_M$, and $R2_T = R2_M$ to allow for comparative analysis in the validation	
- *Eligible resources identification*	$\leq [\sum_{i=1}^{K} (t_A * SD_i) + \sum_{i=1}^{K} (t_E * VD_i)]$	$K * C_{FD} + \sum_{i=1}^{K} (t_{FD} * FD_i)$
- *Negotiation*		
. Automatic		$K * C_{Aut} + \sum_{i=1}^{K} (t_{Aut} * ND_{Mi})$
. Auction	$K * C_{RfBT} + \sum_{i=1}^{K} (t_{RfBT} * ND_{Ti})$	$C'_{RfB} + K * C_{RfBM} + \sum_{i=1}^{K} (t_{RfBM} * ND_{Mi})$
. Direct negotiation	$K * C_{DnT} + \sum_{i=1}^{K} (t_{DnT} * ND_{Ti})$	$K * C_{DnM} + \sum_{i=1}^{K} (t_{DnM} * ND_{Mi})$
- *Selection*	$K * C_{ST} + \sum_{i=1}^{K} (t_{ST} * CD_{Ti})$	$K * C_{SM} + \sum_{i=1}^{K} (t_{SM} * CD_{Mi})$
VE Integration		
- *Contractualisation*	$K * t_{CT}$	$C_C + K * t_{CM}$

Considering dependent selection, Figure 5 represents the relation of effort between using the traditional way and the market in the search and selection of two, three, and five resources ($K = 2$, $K = 3$, and $K = 5$), in function of the search domain size (SD).

When the SD is reduced and for a small K, the Market of Resources contributes to the possibility of reconfiguring an A/VE within a few hours, which is not possible in the traditional way. If dealing with simple projects, broker intervention could be reduced, and reconfiguration is faster.

Table 3. Search, selection, and integration of K resources, considering the dependent selection model

Activity	Traditional	Market of Resources
A/VE Request		
- *Request negotiation*		C_R
- *A/VE design*	$\leq K * t_{DT}$	$C_D + K * t_{DM} + C_V + K * t_V$
Resources selection	It will be considered that $R1_T = R1_M$ and $R2_T = R2_M$ to allow for comparative analysis	
- *Eligible resources identification*	$\leq [\ \sum_{i=1}^{K} (t_A * SD_i) + \sum_{i=1}^{K} (t_E * VD_i)\ ]$	$K * C_{FD} + \sum_{i=1}^{K} (t_{FD} * FD_i)$
- *Negotiation*	$ND \leq \sum_{i=1}^{K} (R1 * VD_i)$	
. Automatic		$\leq [\ K * C_{Aut} + ND_M * \sum_{i=1}^{k} C_k^i * t_{Aut}]$
. Auction (request for bids/inverse auction)	$\leq [\ K * C_{RfBT} + ND_T * \sum_{i=1}^{k} C_k^i * t_{RfBT}]$	$\leq [\ C'_{RfB} + K * C_{RfBM} + ND_M * \sum_{i=1}^{k} C_k^i * t_{RfBM}]$
. Direct negotiation	$\leq [\ K * C_{DnT} + ND_T * \sum_{i=1}^{k} C_k^i * t_{DnT})]$	$\leq [\ K * C_{DnM} + ND_M * \sum_{i=1}^{k} C_k^i * t_{DnM}]$
- *Selection*	$\leq [K * C_{ST} + CD_T^K * t_{ST}]$	$\leq [K * C_{SM} + CD_M^K * t_{SM}]$
VE integration		
- *Contractualisation*	$K * t_{CT}$	$C_C + K * t_{CM}$

According to the validation results obtained for the Market of Resources demonstrator, it is possible to search, negotiate, and contractualize an A/VE creation or reconfiguration, for example, for five independent resources and an average focused domain of size 50 (which corresponds to a SD of 250), in around 7.5 hours, using reverse auction-based negotiation and the Market of Resources. Using the traditional technologies (search engines and e-mail), the time required for the same purposes is around 52 hours.

Figure 4. Traditional method vs. Market of Resources using independent selection method: search and selection time for K = 1, K = 2, and K = 5, in function of search domain size

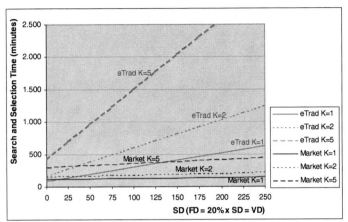

Figure 5. Traditional method vs. Market of Resources using dependent selection method: search and selection time for K = 2, K = 3, and K = 5, in function of search domain size

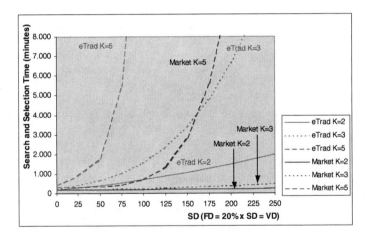

For three dependent resources and a focused domain of around 50, the time using the market and reverse auction-based negotiation is around 8.5 hours, and for five dependent resources, the time can rise to 600 hours (36,000 minutes). Using the traditional technologies, the corresponding times are, respectively, 180 and 25,000 hours, this last an unbearable effort.

With dependent selection, Figure 6 represents the opportunity domain, where the Market of Resources has been revealed to be more efficient than the utilization of traditional Internet-based techniques, corresponding to the area above the line. The line

Figure 6. Breakeven points based on search and selection efforts in the function of the number of required resources (K), considering dependent selection

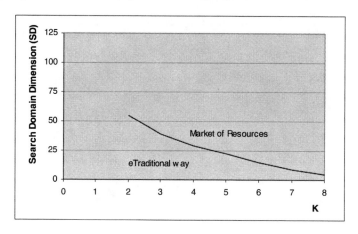

represents the breakeven points between the market and the traditional techniques; for each value of *K*, the graphic represents the search domain dimension where the search, selection, and integration effort using the traditional Internet-based techniques equals the effort using the Market of Resources.

CONCLUSIONS

The A/VE model is of increasing relevance in the organizational panorama, due to its intrinsic agility, dynamic adaptability, and efficiency. The authors introduce the Market of Resources as an environment and enabler that, overtaking the disabling factors of networking and dynamics, is able to cope with the A/VE requirements of reconfigurability dynamics and business alignment, a conclusion supported by a validation experiment summarized in the chapter.

The Market of Resources is part of an umbrella of research projects under development at the University of Minho addressing VE theory, design, and control tools and technologies, and the corresponding environment. In particular, the practical objective of the underlying reference model (BM_VEARM) is to serve as a framework for cooperation and coordination of this group of research projects.

We are proposing that the Market of Resources is capable of supporting the A/VE model, but if we consider a supply chain where reconfigurability dynamics is an important parameter, the Market of Resources model is able to cope with it more efficiently than the traditional way, in the conditions identified in the chapter.

Other, similar Market of Resources concepts, services, and products include the new generation of high value-added electronic marketplaces, e-alliances, and virtual clusters, however, they have not been developed to address the A/VE model requirements.

REFERENCES

Ávila, P., Cunha, M. M., & Putnik, G. D. (2003). A contribution for the classification of resources selection algorithms for agile/virtual enterprises integration brokerage. In A. Gunasekaran & G. D. Putnik (Eds.), *Proceedings of the First International Conference on Performance Measures, Benchmarking and Best Practices in New Economy*. Guimarães, Portugal.

Ávila, P., Putnik, G. D., & Cunha, M. M. (2000). *Análise da Complexidade do Problema de Selecção de Sistemas de Recursos para o Projecto de Empresas Ágeis/Virtuais*. Paper presented at the 2° Encontro Nacional do Colégio de Engenharia Mecânica, Coimbra, Portugal.

Ávila, P., Putnik, G. D., & Cunha, M. M. (2002a). Brokerage function in agile/virtual enterprise integration—A literature review. In L. M. Camarinha-Matos (Ed.), *Collaborative business ecosystems and virtual enterprises* (pp. 65–72). Boston: Kluwer Academic.

Ávila, P., Putnik, G. D., & Cunha, M. M. (2002b). A contribution for the classification of resources selection algorithms for agile/virtual enterprises integration. In L. M. Camarinha-Matos (Ed.), *Balancing knowledge and technology in product and service life cycle*. Boston: Kluwer Academic.

Bradley, S. P., Hausman, J. A., & Nolan, R. L. (1993). Global competition and technology. In *Globalisation technology and competition: The fusion of computers and telecommunications in the 1990s* (pp. 3–31). Boston: Harvard Business School Press.

Browne, J., & Zhang, J. (1999). Extended and virtual enterprises: Similarities and differences. *International Journal of Agile Management Systems, 1*(1), 30–36.

Browne, J., Sacket, P. J., & Wortmann, J. C. (1995). Future manufacturing systems—Towards the extended enterprise. *Computers in Industry, 25*, 235–254.

Byrne, J. A. (1993, February 8). The virtual corporation: The Ccompany of the future will be the ultimate in adaptability. *Business Week*, 98–103.

Carvalho, J. D. A., Putnik, G. D., & Cunha, M. M. (2002). Infrastructures for virtual enterprises. In A. Baykasoglu & T. Dereli (Eds.), *Proceedings of the Second International Conference on Responsive Manufacturing* (pp. 483–487). Gaziantep, Turkey.

Cunha, M. M. (2003). *Organisation of a market of resources for agile and virtual enterprises integration*. Doctoral Thesis, University of Minho, Guimarães, Portugal.

Cunha, M. M., & Putnik, G. D. (2003a). Agile/virtual enterprise enablers: A comparative analysis. In D.A. Sormaz & G. A. Süer (Eds.), *Proceedings of Group Technology/ Cellular Manufacturing—World Symposium 2003*. Colombus, Ohio University.

Cunha, M. M., & Putnik, G. D. (2003b). Market of resources versus e-based traditional virtual enterprise integration—Part I: A cost model definition. In A. Gunasekaran & G. D. Putnik (Eds.), *Proceedings of the First International Conference on Performance Measures, Benchmarking and Best Practices in New Economy* (pp. 667-675). Guimarães, Portugal.

Cunha, M. M., & Putnik, G. D. (2003c). Market of resources versus e-based traditional virtual enterprise integration—Part II: A comparative cost analysis. In A. Gunasekaran & G. D. Putnik (Eds.), *Proceedings of the First International Con-*

ference on Performance Measures, Benchmarking and Best Practices in New Economy (pp. 667-675). Guimarães, Portugal.

Cunha, M. M., & Putnik, G. D. (2004). Trends and solutions in virtual enterprise integration. *Tekhné— Review of Politechnical Studies, 1*(1).

Cunha, M. M., Putnik, G. D., & Ávila, P. (2000). Towards focused markets of resources for agile/virtual enterprise integration. In L. M. Camarinha-Matos, H. Afsarmanesh, & H. Erbe (Eds.), *Advances in networked enterprises: Virtual organisations, balanced automation, and systems integration* (pp. 15–24). Berlin: Kluwer Academic.

Cunha, M. M., Putnik, G. D., & Carvalho, J. D. (2002). Infrastructures to support virtual enterprise integration. In R. Hackney (Ed.), *Proceedings of 12th Annual BIT Conference—Business Information Technology Management: Semantic Futures*. Manchester, UK: The Manchester Metropolitan University (CD-ROM).

Cunha, M. M., Putnik, G. D., & Gunasekaran, A. (2002). Market of resources as an environment for agile/virtual enterprise dynamic integration and for business alignment. In O. Khalil & A. Gunasekaran (Eds.), *Knowledge and information technology management in the 21st century organisations: Human and social perspectives* (pp. 169–190). Hershey, PA: Idea Group Publishing.

Cunha, M. M., Putnik, G. D., Carvalho, J. D., & Ávila, P. (2002). A review on environments supporting virtual enterprise integration. In M. Vladimír, L. M. Camarinha-Matos, & H. Afsarmanesh (Eds.), *Balancing knowledge and technology in product and service life cycle* (pp. 133–140). Dordrecht: Kluwer.

Davidow, W. H., & Malone, M. S. (1992). *The virtual corporation—Structuring and revitalising the corporation for the 21st century.* New York: HarperCollins.

Drucker, P. F. (1990, May/June). The emerging theory of manufacturing. *Harvard Business Review,* 94–102.

Filos, E., & Banahan, E. (2001). Towards the smart organization: An emerging organizational paradigm and the contribution of the European RTD Programmes. *Journal of Intelligent Manufacturing, 12*(2), 101–119.

Goldman, S., Nagel, R., & Preiss, K. (1995). *Agile competitors and virtual organizations: Strategies for enriching the customer.* New York: van Nostrand Reinhold.

Handy, C. (1995). Trust and virtual organization. *Harvard Business Review, 73*(3), 40–50.

Miles, R. E., & Snow, C. C. (1986). Organizations: New concepts for new forms. *California Management Review, 28,* 62–73.

Nagel, R., & Dove, R. (1993). *21st century manufacturing enterprise strategy.* Bethlehem, PA: Iacocca Institute, Lehigh University.

Naisbitt, J. (1982). *Megatrends: Ten new directions transforming our lives.* New York: Warner Books.

Naisbitt, J., & Aburdene, P. (1985). *Re-inventing corporation.* New York: Warner Books.

Oster, S. M. (1994). *Modern competitive analysis* (2nd ed.). New York: Oxford University Press.

Putnik, G. D. (2000a). BM_Virtual enterprise architecture reference model. In A. Gunasekaran (Ed.), *Agile manufacturing: 21st century manufacturing strategy* (pp. 73–93). Amsterdam; New York: Elsevier Science.

Putnik, G. D. (2000b). *BM_Virtual enterprise architecture reference model* (Technical Report RT-CESP-GIS-2000-<GP-01>). Portugal: University of Minho.

Putnik, G. D., & Silva, S. C. (1995). One-product-integrated-manufacturing. In L. M. Camarinha-Matos & H. Afsarmanesk (Eds.), *Balanced automation systems— Architectures and design methods* (pp. 45–52). London; New York: Chapman & Hall.

Putnik, G. D., Cunha, M. M., Ávila, P., & Sousa, R. (2004). BM_Virtual enterprise. In G. D. Putnik & M. M. Cunha (Eds.), *Virtual enterprise integration: Technological and organisational perspectives* (this book). Hershey, PA: Idea Group Publishing

Quinn, J. B. (1990). *The intelligent enterprise.* New York: The Free Press.

Toffler, A. (1985). *The adaptative corporation.* New York: McGraw Hill.

Yusuf, Y. Y., Sarhadi, M., & Gunasekaran, A. (1999). Agile manufacturing: The drivers, concepts and attributes. *International Journal of Production Economics, 62*, 33–43.

Chapter VIII

Broker Performance for Agile/Virtual Enterprise Integration

Paulo Ávila
Polytechnic Institute of Porto, Portugal

Goran D. Putnik
University of Minho, Portugal

Maria Manuela Cunha
Polytechnic Institute of Cávado and Ave, Portugal

ABSTRACT

The implementation of the virtual enterprise (VE) model requires an agent, called a broker, who undertakes several functions and whose increased performance contributes to the searched agility of this organisational model. From the set of functions that the broker can provide to the VE, there are some that may explicitly contribute to the process of VE integration. One of the processes that contributes to VE integration, either in the project phase, during the resources system configuration, or in the operation phase, when the system reconfiguration is required, is the resources system selection process. We will approach, in this work, the importance of the broker in the resources system selection through the comparison of his performance in that process to the performance expected of the VE itself, if the person for whom it is responsible (or principal) performs the same process. This comparison is made based on the simulation results obtained from a numeric demonstrator specifically constructed to quantify the time and cost of the selection process for both the selectors (the broker and the principal). We demonstrate that the domain of advantage for the broker, i.e., where the broker's performance exceeds the principal's, grows with the dimension of the tasks plan and with the number of preselected resources, and also with the complexity of the selection method.

INTRODUCTION

Virtual enterprises, that concept related to the distribution of competencies (services) by different resources, that are integrated with the aim of developing a business, have appeared in the literature as organisational models capable of satisfying the new market requisites and, principally, the requisite of rapid adaptation, i.e., flexibility if the system answer is reactive or agility if the answer is proactive. We believe in that, but they need means and resources that perform tasks of project (configuration and resources system reconfiguration, i.e., integration) and of operation with high effectiveness and efficiency.

We all have the perception that VE can bring better performance, in some domains, than the conventional production systems, that is why there exist indicators that the enterprises tend to find new forms of intercollaboration. According to the VOmap project, "in 2015 most enterprises shall be part of some sustainable collaborative networks that will act as breeding environments for the formation of dynamic virtual organizations in response to fast changing market conditions" (Camarinha-Matos & Afsarmanesh, 2003, refereed in Camarinha Matos & Abreu, 2003).

There are studies, some more optimistic than others, but according to the works that we have analyzed, to refer to some (Gebauer, 1996; Agrawal & Graves, 1999; Ávila, 1998; Leimeister, J. et al., 2001; Putnik & Ávila, 2002), nobody denies that there exists room for that organizational model. However, the success of each production system (PS) does not depend only on the organizational model that is adopted in each time. This is why it will be expected that different cases of VE present different performances like in the conventional models. Our perspective is that the VE models that incorporate the broker's services have higher potential to build more agile VE, or if we prefer, agile/virtual enterprises (A/VE).

In this work, we will present the broker as one of the elements that can contribute to improving the performance of VE integration process, namely, through his better ability to select the resources that will integrate the VE. First, we will make an analysis to the brokers' models that are proposed in the literature in order to justify his necessity in the process of integration and operation of VE, but especially in the selection process. After, we propose a resources selection model for the broker, and over that, we introduce a demonstrator that was developed. With this demonstrator, numeric, resorting to simulations, we will show that as the system to integrate is more complex, i.e., how larger the dimension of task plan is, the larger is the number of preselected resources; and how complex the selection method is, the higher is the broker's importance in undertaking the selection process.

BROKER'S INDISPENSABILITY IN THE VE MODEL

Several authors justified that the broker can improve the performance of virtual enterprises, but the main justifications have appeared to the electronic markets, and that can be seen as a particular case of VE.

In Resnick et al. (1994), the broker's value is justified by costs reduction, privacy improvement both for the consumer and for the supplier, larger and better information available to the consumer (namely, about quality product/service and market satisfaction), a decrease in nonaccomplishment risks by the involved parties, and by the improvement of prices through the creation of mechanisms that induce only the adequate sales.

According to Sarkar et al. (1995), with the elimination of barriers between client and supplier brought by the electronic markets, it should be predicted that the elimination of the traditional intermediaries, like the wholesalers and the retailers, enables costs reduction that in certain cases could achieve the 60% mark. However, the same author in his work reiterates that the new information infrastructures creates room for the growing of a new kind of intermediaries. Sarkar justified this affirmation, not only describing some intermediary functions that are not easily performed by the producers and the clients but also, through calculus, made them founded in transaction costs theory.

In Caughey et al. (1998), the authors argue that the electronic market in the future will yield a larger number and variety of brokers. The authors justify this by pointing out reasons on how the broker may add value to the services that they will supply, such as, aggregating the services of different suppliers and presenting them in a more consistent format; inquiring or searching for a set of services that match the client requisites; monitoring a set of services and informing the clients of something of interest for them; combining and integrating information from different suppliers (e.g., combining bus timetables with airplane ones); and supplying, the broker himself, other services based on the information he acquires and what he knows about the suppliers.

For Hands et al. (2000), the necessity of the electronic broker is justified with the answer to these kinds of questions: how does the client locate the supplier; how is the purchase effectuated; how do we find the products and services that meet needs with a just market price; and how is it known which supplier the client can trust or vice versa. In his opinion, the mediation between suppliers and clients introduced by the broker is the ideal solution to overstep those problems.

Putnik (Putnik, 2000a, 2000b) still says that the high agility (dynamic, real-time A/VE structure reconfiguration — the ideal goal is reconfiguration within one second), intended to A/VE, will be achieved with broker introduction only. The broker contributes decisively for the high performance of the A/VE agile design (project) and operation. Still according to the same author, A/VE is virtuality related to the fact that the physical structure of the enterprise could be hidden to the project manager, that in fact, it is only obtained with the broker intermediation between two control levels from the A/VE structure. In this sense, the broker serves like an agent of virtuality, or the broker supplies the mechanism of virtuality. In Figure 1, we see the broker actuation according to the BM_virtual enterprise architecture reference model (BM_VEARM) in the resources management for the system reconfiguration (Putnik, 2000b).

In summary, we can organize the justifications for the necessity and importance of the broker by different authors in three groups:

- The high agility portended to the A/VE can only be achieved with the broker introduction; at the beginning, he will have better performance in the functions that he performs.
- The broker can be an element of trust between the partners, e.g., through the creation of mechanisms that support the transaction risks and positioning as neutral element in the supply chain.

Figure 1. Broker as the principal agent of agility in the selection and reconfiguration of the A/VE (Source: Putnik, 2000a)

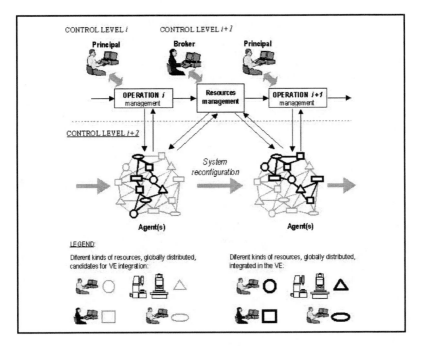

• The broker intermediation between two control levels of the A/VE serves like an agent of the virtuality.

From the exposed justifications, we will explore in this work the first group. We will approach the performance of some broker's functions in an integrated process of resources system selection, not function by function.

Several authors express whose functions should be assumed by the broker inside the A/VE. In Ávila, Putnik, and Cunha (2002), we introduced a broker's functions taxonomy distributed into two possible groups, one involving the functions directly available to the client (A/VE), which we have designated by *explicit functions*, and the other involving support functions to the first group, designated by *implicit functions* (see Table 1).

After we have made a classification of several broker's models retired from the literature (in a total of nine) according to the defined functions, we verify that in spite of the absence of uniformity in functions attributed to the broker in the A/VE models in which he participates,[1] the resources selection function is unique in that it is considered explicitly by all the analyzed models.

Nevertheless, the resources selection process that could be multifunctional and of exponential complexity is one of the critical processes of VE integration that hardly could be done by his manager (or principal) with good performance. For this suspicion, we will compare the broker and principal performance according to a selection model that we introduce now.

Table 1. Broker's functions taxonomy (Source: Ávila, Putnik, & Cunha, 2002)

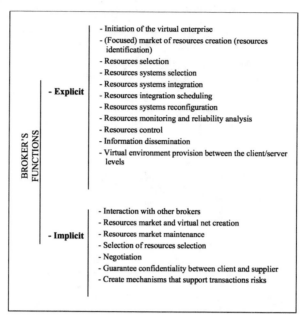

THE SELECTION MODEL DEFINED

The selection model was defined considering its activities and the corresponding expressions of time and cost. This model was designed taking into account the limitations of other selection models in the scope of the VE. We observed from the literature that the models were rigid, i.e., conceived only for particular cases; were not defined in a structured form; did not present performance quantifiers; and did not refer or justify that responsible for the resources selection.

Model of Activities

We defend that the resources selection should be performed with the broker; consequently, this process should be seen as *the broker model of resources selection*. However, this does not mean that the principal could not apply the model, as we will see later. Then, the proposed model should be sufficiently flexible to adjust for any A/VE selection requisites. The resources selection process is divided into two main phases (see Figure 2): (1) the resources preselection (Process A21), and (2) the resources system selection (process A22). The performance of these two phases is critical for the project and the reconfiguration of the A/VE. However, the performance of the second process is influenced by the results of the first, namely, by the "quality" of the preselected resources and by the quantity (dimension) of preselected resources per task. The latter affects the complexity of the resources system selection, which is exponential if the selection model is integral[2] (Ávila, Putnik, & Cunha, 2000).

Figure 2. IDEF0 representation of the process A12 — resources selection

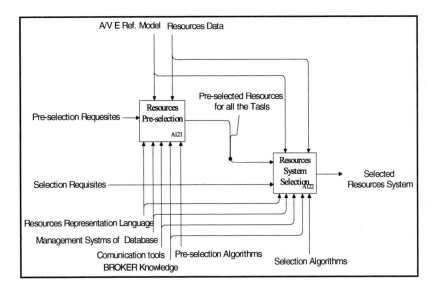

The resources preselection process, shown in Figure 3, has two main phases: the resources search (process A1211) and the identification of preselected resources (processes A1212, A1213, and A1214).

In the resources system selection, we consider three processes (see Figure 4): space solutions evaluation (process A1221), selection and integration of selection algorithms (process A1222), and final selection of the resources system (process A1223).

The model presented above, with activities that are described in Ávila, Punik, and Cunha (2003), shows two activities that have never been approached by other authors: the *space solutions evaluation* and the *selection and integration of selection algorithms*.

The first is related to the determination of the rude performance of the resources system (the best possible that can be achieved), and to the determination of the solution space dimension, with results that are important in analyzing the complexity of the selection problem. The rude performance of the resources system is the quantification of the selection system's limits that the resources system may tend, and it can be calculated considering independent selection.[3] [It is the limit of fractionated selection (Ávila, Putnik, & Cunha, 2000) for the resources system.] These limits can function in the decision if the A/VE project is feasible, and we can then proceed with the selection or compare these limits with the results of the final selection process.

The second is the selection of the most adequate selection algorithms for each task plan requested by the A/VE. This activity is justified, because the problem of resources system selection is a combinatorial problem, and with the increase in the number of tasks and the number of preselected resources to perform each task, the problem becomes more complex. Our reference is plural, because a single algorithm cannot be sufficient to satisfy the requisites of selection. More than one algorithm can be applied if we take into account fractionated selection, or if we can apply different algorithms to each selection requisite, or if it is first necessary to consider time compatibility.

Figure 3. IDEF0 representation of the process A121 — resources preselection

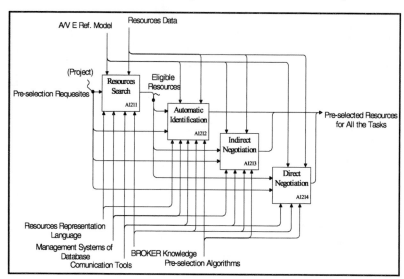

Figure 4. IDEF0 representation of the process A122 — resources system selection

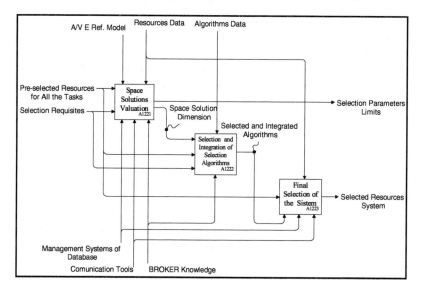

Time and Costs Models Associated with the Selection Model for Each Selection Method

For each of the activities defined in the model, we will identify an expression that translates with variables the time and cost spent in processing them, regardless of the tools used and the agent responsible for selection (broker or principal).

As to the expressions obtained for the costs, only two types of direct costs are considered without considering indirect costs, which are normally an important share of the costs of any economic activity, but, for the moment, are not significant to our analysis. In processing activities, we consider labor costs proportional to time and costs related to the tools used. We have ignored other types of direct costs, like, for example, raw materials or consumables, because they seem irrelevant when considering the others.

In order to specify the expressions of the times and costs of the different activities that constitute the selection model, we will first define a set of variables and constants, with abbreviations and meanings that can be found in Table 2.

According to the nomenclature presented, we arrive at the different formulas of the total time and cost associated with each activity in our selection model, and these expressions are shown in Table 3.

To conclude the time and costs model, the expression of their totals must be defined. However, these depend on the selection method that has been defined in the selection requisites to unchain the selection process. We will consider the following three selection methods, placed in increasing order of complexity:

- Independent selection method (ISM)
- Dependent selection method without preselection of transport resources (DSMWO)
- Dependent selection method with preselection of transport resources (DSMW)

Table 2. List of variables applied in the cost model associated with our selection model

Abbreviation	Designation
D_O	Domain of observed resources
X_O	Number of resources observed per task
D_E	Domain of eligible resources
X_E	Number of eligible resources per task
D_P	Domain of preselected resources
X	Number of preselected resources per task
n	Number of tasks
T_J	Total time of activity J
C_J	Total cost of activity J
A_J	Preparation time, setup related to activity J
t_J	Time to process an elementary part of activity J
c_i	Percentage coefficient
K_J	Total number of iterations/repetitions in a process
P_J	Time period dedicated to task J
Ch_J	Cost per time unit in human resources for activity J
Cf_J	Cost per time unit in tools for activity J

Table 3. Formulas to calculate the time spent on and the cost of each activity in the selection process for tasks plan with n *processing tasks*

Activity	Time and Cost Expression	Explanation
	Preselection of Resources	
	During the search for resources, resources are observed that we call domain of observed resources, D_O. If we break this domain down by task, and if we consider it of equal value for all the tasks, we then designate the number of observed resources per task as X_o.	
Search for Resources	$$T_P = n * \sum_{i=1}^{j} (A_{Pi} + t_{Pi} * X_O)$$ $$C_P = n * \sum_{i=1}^{j} [(Ch_P + Cf_{Pi}) * (A_{Pi} + t_{Pi} * X_O)]$$	A_P: preparation time for the tool used, e.g., updating or inserting the search requisite (subset of the preselection requisites) t_P: search time of the tool and selector $i = 1 \dots j$: number of search tools used
	From this search, the domain of eligible resources is obtained, D_E. If we break this domain down by task, and if we consider it of equal value for all the tasks, we then designate the number of eligible resources per task as X_E. $$X_E = r_1 * X_O$$ r_1: *percentage of X_O that becomes eligible and that we will consider 30% in the simulations[1]*	
Automatic Identification	$$T_{IA} = c_1 * n * \sum_{i=1}^{j} (A_{Iai} + t_{Iai} * X_E)$$ $$C_{IA} = c_1 * n * \sum_{i=1}^{j} [(Ch_{IA} + Cf_{Iai}) * (A_{Iai} + t_{Iai} * X_E)]$$	A_{IA}: time to update and insert a set of preselection requisites t_{IA}: search time of the tool $I = 1 \dots j$: number of automatic identification tools used, which at most will be equal to the number of search tools c_1: coefficient relative to the percentage of tasks where automatic identification can be achieved ($0 \leq c_1 \leq 1$)

Independent Selection Method

First, not all the functions presented above are necessary to proceed with selection, seen as in this method, the simplest of them all, the selection independently analyzes task by task the best resource to execute. This means that each resource is selected for each task without considering its allocation in the rest of the resources system, e.g., in time and transportation costs. Thus, the necessary activities are search for resources, automatic identification, indirect negotiation, direct negotiation, and final system selection.

Table 3. Formulas to calculate the time spent on and the cost of each activity in the selection process for tasks plan with n *processing tasks (continued)*

Indirect Negotiation	$T_{NI} = c_2 * n * [K_{NI} * (A_{NI} + t_{NI} * X_E) + P_{NI}]$ $C_{NI} = (Ch_{NI} + Cf_{NI}) * c_2 * n * [K_{NI} * (A_{NI} + t_{NI} * X_E) + P_{NI}]$	A_{NI}: preparation time of task offer t_{NI}: time to send a resource's task offer and subsequent revision of the resource's proposal X_E: number of eligible resources per task P_{NI}: predefined time period for reception of proposals K_{NI}: number of indirect negotiation iterations or repetitions (it will most probably be $K_{NT} = 1$) c_2: coefficient relative to the percentage of tasks where indirect negotiation can be achieved ($0 \le c_2 \le 1$)
Direct Negotiation	$T_{ND} = c3 * n * [K_{ND} (A_{ND} + t_{ND} * X_E) + P_{ND}]$ $C_{ND} = Ch_{ND} * c3 * n * [K_{ND} (A_{ND} + t_{ND} * X_E) + P_{ND}]$	A_{ND}: preparation time of task offer t_{ND}: time of the selector's direct contact with a resource during each iteration in the negotiation process X_E: number of eligible resources per task P_{ND}: predefined time period for direct negotiation K_{ND}: number of direct negotiation iterations and repetitions Note: $c_1 + c_2 + c_3 = 1$

After identifying the preselected resources, we are left with D_P. *If we break this domain down by task, and if we consider it of equal value for all the tasks, we then designate the number of preselected resources per task as* X.
$$X = r_2 * X_E$$
r_2: *percentage of* X_E *that becomes preselected and that we will consider 30% in the simulations[1]*

The total time spent by this selection method is not, nor should it be, equal to the sum of the times spent by the different activities, because some activities can take place simultaneously or with small differences in their beginning times. Broadly speaking, if we assume that the duration of any of the activities is equal to a constant value, Figure 5 presents a diagram that could qualitatively define the duration of the selection process. To define the total duration (*TT*) of the selection process in this method, we have the following expression:

$$TT \le Máx\{T_{IA}, T_P\} + Máx\{T_{NI}, T_{ND}\} + T_{SF}$$

As to costs, their total value (*CT*) is independent of how the selection activities are related among themselves, and consequently, we obtain:

Table 3. Formulas to calculate the time spent on and the cost of each activity in the selection process for tasks plan with n *processing tasks (continued)*

Selection of the Resources System		
Space Solutions Evaluation	$T_{AS} = A_{AS1} + A_{AS2} + n *$ $* t_{AS} * X$ $C_{AS} = (Ch_{AS} + Cf_{AS}) * (A_{AS1}$ $+ A_{AS2} + n * t_{AS} * X)$	A_{AS1}: time to calculate the determination of the solutions space dimension; the calculation can be simple, if not more than one proposal per preselected resource is considered A_{AS2}: preparation time of the objective function t_{AS}: time to calculate the objective function with the data obtained from the resource and the comparison of the best calculated so far Note: both functionalities of this activity are considered, as well as the evaluation of solutions space and the quantification of the resources system's performance limits
Selection and Integration of Selection Algorithms	$T_{SI} = t_S + A_I * K_I$ $C_{SI} = (Ch_{SI} + Cf_{SI}) * (t_S + A_I * K_I)$	t_S: time of algorithm selection; if the selector possesses a database of several algorithms classified according to validation criteria and with a selection procedure, we can then consider this time constant A_I: time for each integration and adjustment that must be made to the algorithm K_I: number of integrations and adjustments
Final System Selection	$T_{SF} = \sum_{i=1}^{j} (A_{SFi} + t_{SFi} * CSi)$ $C_{SF} = \sum_{i=1}^{j} (Ch_{SF} * A_{SFi} + Cf_{SF}$ $* t_{SFi} * CSi)$	A_{SF}: preparation time of the final selection, analysis of the algorithm's results, and choice of the resources system t_{SF}: time spent in each iteration of the algorithm CS: complexity of the selection that depends on the type of algorithm and the selection method $I = 1 ... j$: number of tools (algorithms that are "run")

Figure 5. Qualitative model of times in the independent selection method

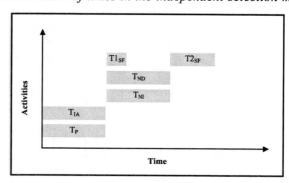

Figure 6. Qualitative model of times in the dependent selection method without preselection of transport resources

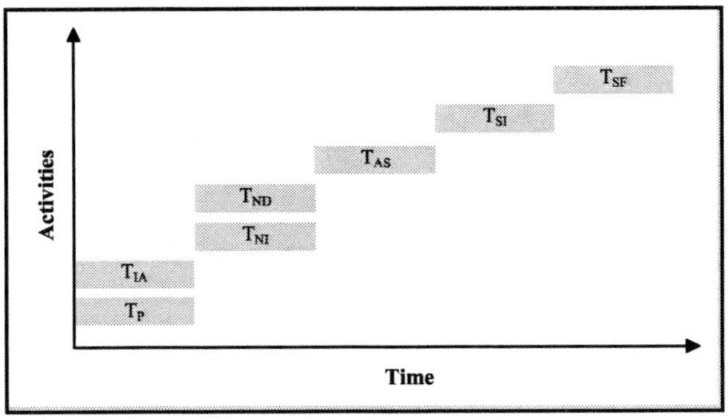

$$CT = C_P + C_{IA} + C_{NI} + C_{ND} + C_{SF}$$

Dependent Selection Method without Preselection of Transport Resources

In this selection method, all the functions of the model presented are necessary, because here the problem of selection is a question of combinatorial analysis, despite the fact that the preselection of transport resources is not used, although the values are still necessary for the estimated transports of any process.

The total time spent by this selection method is, similar to the previous method, different from the sum of the times spent by the different activities, where we can verify that the graphic representation of the activities included in the preselection phase is identical, a situation that does not occur in the others. Broadly speaking, if we also assume that the duration of any of the activities is equal to a constant value, Figure 6 presents a diagram that could qualitatively define the duration of the selection process.

Total time (*TT*) and total cost (*CT*) are given by:

$$TT = Máx\{T_P, T_{IA}\} + Máx\{T_{NI}, T_{ND}\} + T_{AS} + T_{SI} + T_{SF}$$

$$CT = C_P + C_{IA} + C_{NI} + C_{ND} + C_{AS} + C_{SI} + C_{SF}$$

Dependent Selection Method with Preselection of Transport Resources

In this selection process, the most complex of the three,[6] apart from using all the functions of the model presented, the preselection functions are doubly executed, the first time to unchain the preselection of the processing resources, and the second time, which can only function once the first one is concluded, in the preselection of transport resources.

Using the same type of assumptions applied to the two previous methods and now bearing in mind the doubling of preselection activities, Figure 7 presents a possible diagram in qualitatively defining the duration of the selection process. In this diagram, the inscriptions *rp* and *rt* next to the designation of each activity identify whether it is relative to processing resources or to transport resources, respectively.

Figure 7. Qualitative model of times in the dependent selection method with preselection of transport resources

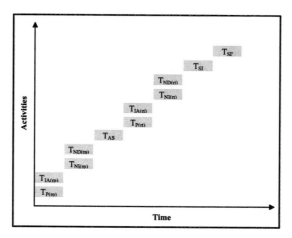

We have the following:

$$TT = \text{Máx}\{T_{IA(rp)}, T_{P(rp)}\} + \text{Máx}\{T_{NI(rp)}, T_{ND(rp)}\} + T_{AS} + \text{Máx}\{T_{IA(rt)}, T_{P(rt)}\} + \text{Máx}\{T_{NI(rt)}, T_{ND(rt)}\} + T_{SI} + T_{SF}$$

$$CT = C_{P(rp)} + C_{IA(rp)} + C_{NI(rp)} + C_{ND(rp)} + C_{AS} + C_{P(rt)} + C_{IA(rt)} + C_{NI(rt)} + C_{ND(rt)} + C_{SI} + C_{SF}$$

VALIDATION OF THE BROKER AND PRINCIPAL IN THE SELECTION PROCESS

In order to validate the broker in the selection process, it must be compared with the A/VE, represented by its principal, in accomplishing this process. A demonstrator was defined to support the simulation plans for the three selection methods (ISM, DSMWO, and DSMW) and for the different values of X and n.

Construction of the Demonstrator

Certain conditions were assumed for the demonstrator, which is of a numerical type [belonging to the class of mathematical models (Law & Kelton, 1991)], and the time and cost expressions defined in the previous chapter were adjusted to the case of the selection being processed by the principal or by the broker, according to the tools each has available.

The assumptions on which our validation are based and on which we will make a few comments are related with the following aspects:

1.   Relation of the principal and the broker with the selection model
2.   Requisites and specificities of the A/VE associated with the task plan

Table 4. Time and cost expressions for the principal and the broker according to the tools used

Activities	Time and Cost Expressions	
	Principal	**Broker with "tool 4"**
Resources search	$T_{P(P,2)} = (A_{P(P,2)} + t_{P(P,2)} * X_O) * n$ $C_{P(P,2)} = Ch * (A_{P(P,2)} + t_{P(P,2)} * X_O) * n$ (2 – browsers as tools)	$T_{P(B,2,4)} = (1 - a) * (A_{P(B,2)} + t_{P(B,2)} * X_O) * n + a * (A_{P(B,4)} + t_{P(B,4)} * X_O) * n$ $C_{P(B,2,4)} = Ch * (1 - a) * (A_{P(B,2)} + t_{P(B,2)} * X_O) * n + (Ch + Cf_{P(B,4)}) * a * (A_{P(B,4)} + t_{P(B,4)} * X_O) * n$ (4 – broker's specific tool)
Automatic identification	Does not have	$T_{IA(B,4)} = c_1 * (A_{IA(4)} + t_{IA(B,4)} * X_E) * n$ $C_{IA(B,4)} = c_1 * (Ch + Cf_{IA(4)}) * (A_{IA(4)} + t_{IA(B,4)} * X_E) * n$
Indirect negotiation	$T_{NI(P,5)} = n * (A_{NI(P,5)} + t_{NI(P,5)} * X_E) + P_{NI(P,5)}$ $C_{NI(P,5)} = Ch * n * (A_{NI(P,5)} + t_{NI(P,5)} * X_E)$ (5 – e-mail or other tools, like fax and manual or semiautomatic proposals treatment)	$T_{NI(B,4)} = (1 - c_1) * n * (A_{NI(B,4)} + t_{NI(B,4)} * X_E) + P_{NI(B,4)}$ $C_{NI(B,4)} = (Ch + Cf_{NI(B,4)}) * (1 - c_1) * n * (A_{NI(B,4)} + t_{NI(B,4)} * X_E) + Cf_{NI(B,4)} * (1 - c_1) * P_{NI(B,4)}$
Space solutions evaluation	$T_{AS(P,6)} = A_{AS1(P,6)} + A_{AS2(P,6)} + n * t_{AS(P,6)} * X$ $C_{AS(P,6)} = Ch * (A_{AS1(P,6)} + A_{AS2(P,6)} + n * t_{AS(P,6)} * X)$ (6 – manual or semiautomatic calculus, e.g., calculus sheet database, management system as tools)	$T_{AS(B,4)} = A_{AS1(B,4)} + A_{AS2(B,4)} + n * t_{AS(B,4)} * X$ $C_{AS(B,4)} = (Ch + Cf_{(B,4)}) * (A_{AS1(B,4)} + A_{AS2(B,4)} + n * t_{AS(B,4)} * X)$
Selection and integration of selection algorithms	$T_{SI(P,6)} = A_{I(P,6)} * K_{I(P,6)}$ $C_{SI(P,6)} = Ch * (A_{I(P,6)} * K_{I(P,6)})$ (6 – the principal may develop a complete enumeration algorithm or prepare any calculus tool, e.g., Excel, Matlab)	$T_{SI(B,4)} = t_{S(B,4)} + A_{I(B,4)} * K_{I(B,4)}$ $C_{SI(B,4)} = (Ch + Cf_{SI(B,4)}) * (t_{S(B,4)} + A_{I(B,4)} * K_{I(B,4)})$
Final system selection	$T_{SF(P,8)} = A_{SF(P,8)} + t_{SF(P,8)} * CS_{(P,8)}$ $C_{SF(P,8)} = Ch * A_{SF(P,8)}$ (8 – developed algorithm as a tool)	$T_{SF(B,4)} = A_{SF(B,4)} + t_{SF(B,4)} * CS_{(B,4)}$ $C_{SF(B,4)} = Ch * A_{SF(B,4)} + Cf_{SF(B,4)} * t_{SF(B,4)} * CS_{(B,4)}$

3.   Relation of the principal's knowledge in comparison with the broker's in relation to the selection process

4.   Relation of the selection agents with the mechanisms/tools available to unchain each activity

In relation to point (1), we are going to consider that both agents, principal and broker, will follow the same selection model[7] proposed, in terms of the activities to be performed. However, the principal will have difficulty in performing at least two of those activities, as we will see next, i.e., Automatic Identification and Algorithms Selection.

As to point (2), we assume that the complexity of all the tasks is the same as for any tasks plan, and, as we want to analyze the time and cost of selection, not only in terms of the selection method and the number of preselected resources per task X, but also in terms of the number of tasks n, we are not going to define a specific task plan for a certain product, but rather consider different task plans, where only the total number of tasks differs.

Figure 8. Validation of the performance of the principal and the broker in the ISM

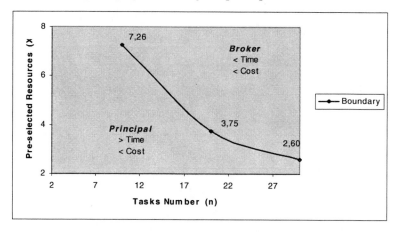

Figure 9. Validation of the performance of the principal and the broker in the DSMWO

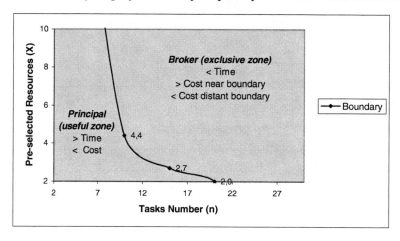

Figure 10. Validation of the performance of the principal and the broker in the DSMW

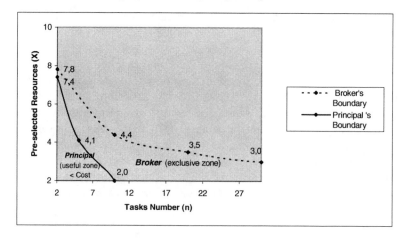

With regards to point (3), we are not going to quantify the difference in greater knowledge that the broker may and should have in relation to the principal.

As to point (4), the principal will apply or develop tools to unchain the selection process according to its needs, in a manner similar to other models analyzed in the literature (Ávila, 2004). In the case of the broker, we will admit that it has direct access to the same tools as the principal as well as to its own software tool (identified as "tool 4" in Table 4), which here we assume possesses all the functionalities of the selection model.

Once the tools the principal and the broker have available or which they can use, or have to develop to unchain the activities of the selection model, have been analyzed, in Avila (2004), the time and cost expressions are adjusted to some of them, to obtain the expressions presented in Table 4.[8] Furthermore, the parameters of the expressions we have assumed to be constant are determined, making the expressions dependent only on X and n.

Results Obtained

Simulations of times and costs were carried out for the principal and broker in the three selection models, independent, dependent without preselection of transport resources, and dependent with preselection of transport resources. For each method, several dimensions of the task plans ($n = 10, 20$, and 30) were considered, and for each task plan, different values for the preselected resources ($X = 2, 4, 6$, and 8) were considered.

As expected, the three selection methods considered, the ISM, DSMWO, and DSMW, which are in this order successively more precise, showed that they are, by reason of their very order, progressively more difficult to apply in the selection of resources for the A/VE, regardless of whether it is the principal or the broker who is responsible for the selection. This difficulty is felt because of the progressive increase in the selection times and costs verified in the simulations accomplished. However, this increase is not felt in the same way by the two participants or for the same reasons.

After processing the results of the simulations for the three methods, graphs were constructed for each one (Figures 8, 9, and 10), where it is possible to identify performance zones for the broker and the principal, according to the number of tasks and the number of preselected resources.

In the three models, we found a boundary line that delimits the principal's validations. This line, which in the ISM is associated with costs, and in the other two methods results from a limitation on the principal's domain, due to the fact that selection times exceeded the useful time considered (50.000 min), shifted toward the lower values of n and X. We can make the following comments on the zones that this boundary delimits:

- Below the boundary, the principal has its only possibility of competing with the broker, because it presents lower costs.
- Above the boundary, the broker dominates the performance of the selection process, because it presents lower costs and lower times in the case of the ISM, and also because the principal cannot carry out selection in useful time in this zone, for DSMWO and DSMW.
- In the case of the DSMW, a mobile boundary appears above the principal's boundary, which causes the broker to encounter difficulties in carrying out selection in the useful time above it.

Figure 11. The principal's and broker's validation

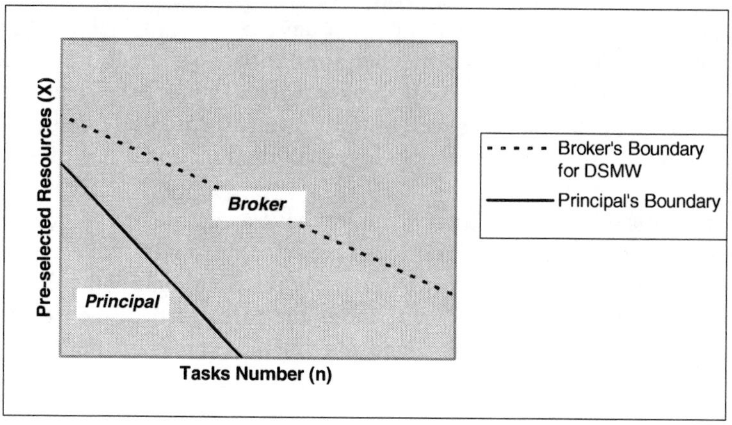

From the three points made above, which are directly related to three validation zones, the only one that raises no doubts is point (2), as here the selection is validated by the broker.

With regards to point (1), below the principal's boundary, there are factors that we believe provide the principal with certain advantages. Notwithstanding the fact that the principal presents lower costs, and bearing in mind that we have not included the broker's profits and taxes, which would make this difference even more significant, we could not disregard the principal's times and costs in transacting with the broker. That is, when confronted with the decision to make the selection himself or to resort to the broker to do so, the principal has to take into account, apart from the broker's time and cost, the time and cost associated with transactions with the broker. These costs, according to Besanko et al. (1996) can be broken down into coordination costs between levels in the logistic chain, costs with private information loss, and transaction costs.

From this set of costs, the first two are difficult to quantify, whereas transaction costs are quantifiable. The concept of transaction costs, associated with the transaction cost theory, was first described by Coase (1937) and developed by Williamson (1975). According to the latter (Williamson, 1985), transaction costs can be broken down into four separate costs: search costs, contracting costs, monitoring costs, and costs in fulfilling the established contract. This said, we consider that the principal gains the advantage in the selection process performance below his own boundary.

However, point (3) indicates that the broker may also have selection difficulties in the DSMW, which are essentially caused by activities related to the preselection of transport resources. We believe the resource market project defined in Cunha (2003) can provide the broker with a tool that he can use to improve the performance of these activities.

To illustrate what has been said so far, Figure 11 presents the principal's and broker's qualitative validations for the three selection methods.

In the zone near the principal's boundary line, the decision as to who is responsible for the selection process is more complex. In this zone, we feel that the available economic models of decision support for subcontracting, which are, according to Dekkers (2000), whom we quote: "the transaction cost theory of Coase and Williamson; the political model of Pfeffer; the central competence paradigm of Quinn; the subcontracting model for the Loof information system, and the objective fund model of Hoogeveen," can make an important contribution to the A/VE decision-making process.

CONCLUSIONS

Given all that has been said above, there can be no doubts as to the fact that the broker is a necessary agent in the selection process of the resources system for the A/VEs. We can go further by stating that, in the reconfiguration process of a resources system, in which there are data at the outset on the preselected resources in the system's first configuration (meaning that the preselection phase has been, if not totally, at least partially, concluded), the broker is a key agent in the agility expected in reconfiguring the A/VE, because it is able to select the algorithm and proceed in useful time to the final selection. The need for the broker in the selection process is higher, the higher the number of tasks, the number of preselected resources, and the more complex the selection method.

REFERENCES

Agrawal., A., & Graves, R. (1999). A distributed systems model for estimation of print circuit board fabrication Costs. *Production Planning & Control, 10*, 7, 650–658.

Ávila, P. (1998). *A contribution for processing resources selection for VE/OPIM system design*. MSc Thesis, University of Minho, Braga.

Ávila, P. (2004). *Rigorous resources system selection model for the project of agile/ virtual enterprises for complex products*. PhD Thesis, University of Minho, Braga.

Ávila, P., Putnik, G., & Cunha, M. (2000). Analysis of the problem of resources selection complexity to agile/virtual enterprise design. In *Proceedings of the 2° National Encounter of the Mechanical Engineer College*, Coimbra, Portugal.

Ávila, P., Putnik, G., & Cunha, M. (2002). Brokerage function in agile/virtual enterprise integration—A literature review. In L. M. Camarinha-Matos et al. (Eds.), *Collaborative business ecosystems and virtual enterprises* (pp. 65–72). Dordrecht: Kluwer.

Ávila, P., Putnik, G., & Cunha, M. (2003). Activity-based model for the resources systems selection for agile/virtual enterprises integration. In *Proceedings of Group Technology/Cellular Manufacturing Symposium*, Columbus, Ohio, (pp. 1-6).

Besanko, D., Dranove, D., & Shanley, M. (1996). *Economics of strategy*. New York: John Wiley & Sons.

Camarinha-Matos, L., & Abreu, A. (2003). Towards a foundation for virtual organizations. In *Proceedings of Business Excellence '03—First International Conference on Performance Measures, Benchmarking and Best Practices in New Economy*, Guimarães, Portugal (pp. 647-652).

Camarinha-Matos, L. M., & Afarmanesh, H. (2003). Draft research roadmap for virtual organizations, *Vomap report D5*.

Caughey, S., Ingham, D., & Watson, P. (1998). *Metabroker: A generic broker for electronic commerce* (Report 635). New Castle upon Tyne: Department of Computing Science, University of New Castle upon Tyne.

Coase, R. (1937). The nature of the firm. *Economica, 4*, 386–405.

Cunha, M. (2003). *Organization of a market of resources for agile and virtual enterprises integration*. PhD Thesis, University of Minho, Braga, Portugal.

Dekkers, R. (2000). Decision models for outsourcing and core competencies in manufacturing. *International Journal of Production Research, 38*, 17, 4085–4096.

Gebauer, J. (1996). Virtual organizations from an economic perspective. In J. Coelho, T. Jelassi, W. Konig, H. Kremar, R. O'Callaghan & M. Saaksjarvi (Eds.), *Proceedings of the Fourth European Conference on Information Systems*, Lisbon, Portugal.

Hands, J., Bessonov, M., Blinov, M., Patel, A., & Smith, R. (2000). An inclusive and extensible architecture for electronic brokerage. *Decision Support Systems, 29*, 305–321.

Law, A., & Kelton, W. (1991). *Simulation modeling & analysis*. New York: McGraw-Hill.

Leimeister, J. et al. (2001). Efficiency of virtual organizations: The case of AGI. *Electronic Journal of Organizational Virtualness—EJOV, 3*, 3, 12–43.

Putnik, G. D. (2000a). BM_Virtual enterprise architecture reference model. In A. Gunasekaran (Ed.), *Agile manufacturing: 21st century manufacturing strategy* (pp. 73–93). Amsterdam; New York: Elsevier Science.

Putnik, G. D. (2000b). *BM_Virtual enterprise architecture reference model*. Technical Report RT-CESP-GIS-2000-<GP-01>. Universidade do Minho, Portugal.

Putnik, G., & Ávila, P. (2002). Part II: Towards OPIM system—Results of the OPIM system design simulation and an applicability analysis. *International Journal of Networking and Virtual Organisations, 1*, 2, 151–169.

Resnick, P., & Avery, R. (1994). Online *http://ccs.mit.edu/papers/ccswp179.html*

Sarkar, M., Butler, B., & Steinfield, C. (1995). Intermediaries and cybermediaries: A continuing role for mediating players in the electronic marketplace. *Journal of Computer Mediated Communication, 1*, 3. Available online *http://www.ascusc.org/jcmc/vol1/issue3/vol1no3.html*

Williamson, O. (1975). *Markets and hierarchies: Analysis and antitrust implications*. New York: Free Press.

Williamson, O. (1985). *The economic organizations of capitalism*. New York: Free Press.

ENDNOTES

[1]   There are A/VE models that do not refer to broker functions and are supported mainly by intelligent agents technology.

[2]   The integral selection method is the selection method that defines the resources systems for the A/VE in the function of its performance for the execution of the tasks plan considering parameters that reflect the distributiveness of the resources (e.g., transport time and cost).

[3]   This means that each resource is selected for each task without considering its allocation in the rest of the resources system, e.g., in time and transportation costs.

[4]   Value obtained based on a search with the Google tool.

[5]   Admitted value.

[6]   It is perhaps for this reason that it has never been introduced in other selection models.

7   To follow exactly the same model would mean that, apart from the activities, the mechanisms/tools available and used by both the principal and the broker would be the same, which, in fact, does not happen.

8   The numbering used for each of the activities is exclusively aimed at identifying the different tools and not to establishing any specific order of application or priority.

Chapter IX

Integration in Cooperative Distributed Systems:
Privacy-Based Brokering Architecture for Virtual Enterprises

Abdulmutalib Masaud-Wahaishi
University of Western Ontario, Canada

Hamada Ghenniwa
Univeristy of Western Ontario, Canada

Weiming Shen
University of Western Ontario and
National Research Council Canada, Canada

ABSTRACT

A cooperative distributed systems approach is a promising design paradigm for many application environments, such as virtual enterprises, distributed manufacturing, e-business, and tele-learning. However, coordination is a major challenge in developing cooperative distributed systems in open environments. This chapter discusses in detail, brokering as a capability-based aspect of coordination in cooperative distributed systems. Architecturally, the brokering is viewed as a layer of services where a brokering service is modeled as an agent with a specific architecture and interaction protocol that are appropriate to serve various requests. The architecture of the proposed brokering layer supports ad hoc configurations among distributed, possibly autonomous and heterogeneous entities with various degrees of privacy requirements in terms of three attributes: entity's identity, capability, and preferences. A prototype of the proposed architecture has been implemented to support and provide information-

gathering capabilities in healthcare environments using a FIPA-complaint platform (JADE).

INTRODUCTION

A cooperative distributed systems (CDSs) approach is a promising design paradigm that is suitable for many application domains, such as virtual enterprises, distributed manufacturing, e-business, telecommunication, and tele-learning. A virtual enterprise (VE) is an organization that consists of multiple cooperating autonomous entities (enterprises) that jointly act in a specified limited domain to fulfill a common enterprise mission (Amin, 2002). VEs are supported by geographical distribution and heterogeneous entities with no central control. Therefore, building VEs involves dealing with challenges that go beyond traditional integration approaches and design paradigms. The future success of building systems in terms of more sophisticated components, often entire systems, and integrating them requires an engineering and scientific basis that supports a high-level of abstraction for connection and interaction in VEs.

VE integration, as opposed to vertical integration, requires the right information and services at the right time. This, in turn, requires explicit knowledge of the dynamically changing information and functionalities of the different activities in the VE operation (Hammer, 2000). Also, it highly depends on the degree of cooperation in sharing the participants' activities and their supporting systems to support new or composed legislations, new customer demands, and new technology or paradigm.

Fundamentally, we view integration as an abstraction level at which a distributed system environment can be viewed collectively as a coherent universe. Within this context, we model VE as a cooperative distributed system in which the entities are able to exercise some degree of authority in sharing their capabilities. In a cooperative distributed system, entities usually need to work together to accomplish individual or social tasks. However, in open environments, this becomes a challenge where it is no longer feasible to expect designers or users to hardcode, to determine or to keep track of the entities and their capabilities.

Brokering is a coordination and cooperation activity among heterogeneous entities in a cooperative distributed systems environment that can be used effectively to support integration in VEs. From the user perspective, the unification and integration of the ubiquitous diverse heterogeneous services means that a user can access these services from anywhere and at any time, but unfortunately, dealing with integration in such environments is rarely easy. The main integration challenge is to hide the distribution nature and provide a virtual homogenous environment.

With the rapidly growing development of applications in open VE environments, such as e-business, privacy is becoming a critical issue. Consequently, distributed systems architects, developers, and administrators are faced with the challenge of securing the requester's privacy as well as the provider's. In general, requesters and service providers are concerned about their privacy from different perspectives. For example, they may wish to protect their identities from being used, or decide by whom it will be revealed, and for what purposes, or retain the choice about whether or not to reveal their personal interests or capabilities.

Tremendous efforts have been devoted to privacy and security issues in distributed systems for the last few decades, however, the objective of the work presented here focuses on privacy from the perspective of protecting the identity of the requester and provider, the preferences of the requesters, and capabilities of the providers.

This chapter reviews integration approaches of CDSs, discusses in detail our view of brokering services and the role of software agents in facilitating integration in VEs, and then describes an agent-based architecture for privacy-based brokering services. Brokering is a coordination activity that involves locating and associating requests, capabilities, and entities in an open environment. In this context, we model a brokering service as an agent with a specific architecture and interaction protocol that is appropriate to serve requests while maintaining the required degree of privacy.

RELATED WORK

Over the years, several approaches were proposed to support coordination in distributed systems, ranging from data sharing to advanced systems supporting a multitude of services. In particular, several integration solutions in cooperative distributed systems were proposed in various application domains. In the context of database systems, the focus was on issues related to the distribution, heterogeneity, and autonomy of information in the perspective of providing integrated access to databases. Global and federated approaches have been proposed for cooperation between distributed databases based on the overall system architecture. In the former, all the local schemata may be integrated into a single global schema that represents all databases in the entire distributed system (Sheth & Larson, 1999).

Other approaches (InfoTech, 1998) focus on agent-based integration solutions that employ the concept of mediator (Wiederhold, 1992). The mediator-based approaches provide dynamic solutions for integration of information, and the architecture focuses on software modules that perform value-added activities but keep the information model hidden. Examples include TSIMMIS (Garcia-Molina et al., 1995) and OBSERVER (Gruber, 1993). The focus of TSIMMIS was on developing a mediator-based tool for automatic generation of translators and mediators to access and combine information from heterogeneous data sources. The OBSERVER project focuses on information integration using intensional descriptions of preexisting ontologies expressed in description logics characterizing information of different domains.

Others have utilized the concept of "broker," in which all the communication between paired agents has to go through the broker. Examples of broker-based systems include MACRON (Decker et al., 1995) and NZDIS (Purvis et al., 2000). In MACRON, the brokering services are supported through an agent-based architecture for cooperative information gathering. User queries [in hypertext markup language (HTML) format] are translated into information gathering plans, which, in turn, are executed by different agents. In NZDIS, collaborating agents and CORBA objects form a basic structure for providing brokering services. Information sources are encapsulated as data source agents that accept messages in an agent communication language (FIPA ACL).

In the matchmaker-based approaches, an intermediary entity identifies the relevant provider(s) for the requester, which then choose and contact the appropriate provider directly. Examples of matchmaker-based systems include InfoSleuth (Bayardo et al.,

1996), RETSINA (Sycara et al., 2001), IMPACT (Arisha et al., 1998), and COINS (Kuokka & Harrada, 1995). InfoSleuth is an agent-based infrastructure for integrating information sources in which a set of various agents perform syntactic and semantic matchmaking for the information sources that are described in a domain ontology consisting of terminology descriptions and other domain-specific information. RETSINA introduced a multiagent infrastructure at the architecture level to support reusable agent type, namely, interface, task, and information agents. Interface agents interact with users to receive queries and deliver back results of the queries. The task agent formulates the queries and generates problem-solving goals and, hence, executes them. The main function of the information agent is to provide information retrieval to the received queries. In IMPACT, the system supports multiagent interactions and agent interoperability. The focus was on providing matchmaking services among requesters and providers agents based on a weighted verb and noun hierarchy maintained in a hierarchal ontology of standard data types and concepts.

The facilitator-based approaches extend the functionality of the mediator architecture with automatic resources identification and data conversion. This level of automation depends on the supporting ontologies to describe the resources. Facilitators are responsible for using meta-information in converting, translating, or routing data and information. The Infomaster (Genesereth et al., 1997) is an information integration system that utilizes this architecture.

The FIPA agent software integration specification defines how software resources can be described, shared, and dynamically controlled in an agent community (FIPA, 2001). The specification enables builders to develop brokering services by building: (1) wrappers for software services, which are to be utilized and controlled by a community of agents (public services); and (2) agent resource broker (ARB) services.

Several architectural approaches for building VEs have been proposed, especially for the e-commerce domain (Grover & Teng, 2001). Kashyap and Sheth proposed an architecture consisting of information providers, information brokers, and information consumers (Kashyap & Sheth, 1994). Another approach proposes information brokering architecture by modeling the information exchange and the collaborating activities for manufacturing (D'Atri & Motro, 2002).

Modeling VEs as independent entities that collaborate on manufacturing products has been proposed in the literature, with the main focus on organizational issues, communication processes, and information systems support (Monge & DeSanctis, 1999).

Some approaches propose software-specific platforms and methodologies that support VEs, with the main focus on integrating various business processes of enterprise entities (Suter, 1998; Georgakopoulos et al., 1999).

The BCKOA (business-centric knowledge-oriented architecture) framework has proposed integration architecture for CDS (Ghenniwa & Huhns, 2003). The BCKOA specifications provide the abstraction to support the domain entities and applications independent of any specific technology. BCKOA coordination and cooperation services support ad hoc and automated configurations. This includes locating and discovering applications and services that are potentially relevant to a domain or specific service. The work presented here deals with the brokering services as part of the coordination and cooperation family. Cooperation among different teams in a VE requires that participating entities access and share data and services of each other. Certainly, this cooperation raises a great concern to enterprises to protect their privacy. Several solutions dealing with the privacy issue have been proposed (Wulf & Hartman, 1994). Korba and Song surveyed and reviewed the different approaches and solutions that have been proposed and implemented for network privacy and have also analyzed these approaches based upon the threats from different types of attacks (Korba & Song, 2001). Privacy-enhancing technologies (PETs), such as encryption, anonymity, and pseudonymity, applied to the Internet environment are based on eliminating or reducing personal data by preventing unnecessary and undesired processing (and storage) of personal information, all without losing the functionality of the system (Goldberg et al., 1997). The work in Kenny and Borking (2001) introduced the concept of privacy engineering, in which it is defined as a systematic effort to embed privacy-relevant legal primitives into technical and governance design. The approach introduced a framework that utilizes and extends the digital rights management (DRM) technology (Feigenbaum, 2001). DRM was proposed for protecting user privacy in an open environment, such as the Internet, by restricting the use and access of digital files in order to protect the interests of copyright holders. The goal is to manage the distribution of digital content in a manner that protects the rights of all parties involved, including copyright owners, distributors, and users.

The privacy incorporate software agent (PISA) targets the creation of privacy-enhancing technologies for next-generation electronic business applications (PISA, 2002). The platform for privacy preferences (P3P) is an industry standard that enables Web sites to express their privacy polices in a standardized format that can be automatically retrieved and interpreted by user agents (Cranor, 2002). With P3P, users need not read the privacy policies at every site they visit; instead, key information about what data is collected by a Web site can be automatically conveyed to a user, and discrepancies between a site's practices and the user's preferences could be automatically flagged.

Other approaches adopted an agent-based integration with different roles of middle agents based on the initial status of the preferences and capabilities of the participants (Decker et al., 1997).

However, none of the above-mentioned approaches have treated privacy as an architectural element within the integration services. The objective of the work presented here is to develop brokering services that deal with various degrees of privacy as related to the identities and capabilities of the participant entities (requesters and providers) of a cooperative VE. Unlike traditional approaches, in this work, the brokering role is further classified into several subroles based on the privacy attributes of the provider and the requester. Architecturally, the brokering service is viewed as a layer of services, where a brokering service is modeled as an agent with a specific architecture and interaction protocol that are appropriate for serving various requests while preserving the desired privacy degree.

AGENT-BASED BROKERING ARCHITECTURE FOR COOPERATIVE DISTRIBUTED VE

Integration in cooperative distributed systems that compose VE usually involves complex and nondeterministic interactions between different participating entities. In addition, the dynamic nature of these systems requires that the components of the system be able to change configurations to participate in different roles. Those requirements could not be accomplished using traditional ways of manually configuring software.

We strongly believe that agent orientation is an appropriate design paradigm for integration in these environments. Indeed, such a paradigm is essential to modeling open, distributed, and heterogeneous environments in which an agent should be able to operate as a part of a community of cooperative distributed systems environments, including human users. A key aspect of agent orientation is the ability to design artifacts that are able to perceive, reason, interact, and act in a coordinated fashion. Here we view agent orientation as a metaphorical conceptualization tool at a high level of abstraction (knowledge level) that captures, supports, and implements features that are useful for distributed computation in open environments. These features include cooperation, coordination, interaction, as well as intelligence, adaptability, and economic and logical rationality. We define an agent as an individual collection of primitive components that provide a focused and cohesive set of capabilities. Agents are designed and implemented based on the coordinated intelligent rational agent (CIR-agent) (Ghenniwa & Kamel, 2000).

Based on a layered architecture shown in Figure 1, specialized entities (brokering agents) are responsible for handling interactions between different requesters and providers. These interaction processes are categorized by the privacy concern of both requesters and providers. Within the brokering layer, requesters and providers are recognized as agents' roles: a requester is an agent with goals beyond its capability, while a provider is an agent that is able to provide some specific services in the domain.

Brokering agents with core behaviors provide the main functionalities of the system that vary from one brokering agent to another according to the level of privacy desired by any entity within the environment. The functionalities include accepting providers' advertisements; receiving requests and engaging in various interaction protocols with providers to fulfill requester's demand; and monitoring the addition or removal of any information source at runtime.

Figure 1. Layered brokering system's architecture

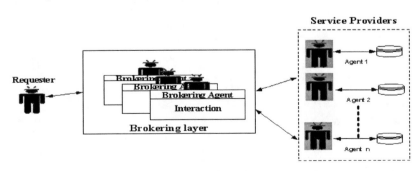

PRIVACY-BASED MODEL

Unlike traditional approaches, the proposed brokering role is further classified into subroles based on the privacy attributes; identities (I), goals (g), and capabilities (C) of both the provider agents and the requester agents. Examples include "advertiser," "mediator," and "broadcaster." Architecturally, the brokering service is viewed as a layer of services in which each brokering service is modeled as an agent with a specific architecture and interaction protocol that are appropriate for a required privacy degree. Table 1 summarizes the different roles that might be played by the brokering layer categorized by the privacy concern of the requester (RA) and provider (PA) agents. A detailed description for each role and the associated interaction protocol is presented hereafter.

The Broker

The broker agent protects the privacy of both requesters and providers. It understands the preferences and capabilities, routes requests, and replies appropriately. Neither the requester nor a provider ever knows about the other in any particular transaction. However, agents wanting to benefit from the services supported by the broker agent are required to reveal their identities, goals, and capabilities to the broker. The interaction pattern of the broker agent with both the requester and provider agent is shown in Figure 2. When a service provider agent registers itself with the broking layer,

Table 1. Brokering layer roles categorized by the privacy concern of the requesters and providers agents

Brokering Agent Name	Brokering Layer's Knowledge				The Brokering Layer Interaction Protocol	
	g(RA)	I(RA)	I(PA)	C(PA)	With Requesters	With Providers
Broker	Known	Known	Known	Known	Receive request Deliver result	Search for relevant agents Negotiate Obtain result
Advertiser	Known	Known	Known	Not known	Receive request Deliver result	Advertise request to known PA
Anonymizer	Known	Known	Known	Not known	Receive request Deliver result	PA check for requests PA to reply back with results
Mediator	Known	Not known	The identities and capabilities of the provider agents can be either one of the statuses shown in cases (1,2, or 3)		Receive request RA retrieve result	The brokering layer's interaction protocols with providers agents will follow the same interaction protocol depicted in any selected case shown in (1,2, or 3)
Broadcaster	Not known	Known			Advertise services to known RA	
Bulletin board	Not known	Not known			RA to check for services	

Figure 2. The interaction pattern for broker agent

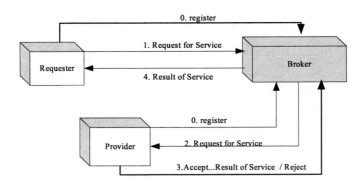

along with the description of its capabilities specified in a common description language, it is stored as an advertisement in the layer. Thus, when an agent inputs a request for services, the broker's functionality will be typically as follows: (1) formulates the request; (2) contacts (a set of) the relevant providers, forwards, and controls appropriate transaction to achieve a better deal that fulfills the requester's goal; and (3) returns the result of the services to the requester agent.

Assigning requests to providers can be based on either broadcasting or focusing, however, the interaction of the broker with other agents is neither restricted to specific service providers nor committed to a fixed number of requesters. This ability is particularly useful, because the broker acts in a dynamic environment in which entities may continually enter and leave the agent society.

The broker (acts as the manager) receives a requester's goal and then issues a call-for-proposals (CFP) to those relevant provider agents (potential contractors), informing them of the problem specifications. Each potential contractor (provider) determines the evaluation parameters (such as goal quality, goal expiration time, and cost) and accordingly submits a bid to the brokering agent, or might reject the proposal. After receiving the bids, the brokering agent selects the most appropriate bid that satisfies the request's parameters. This will involve invoking the local scheduler to determine the possible schedule time for that particular request. Note that in case of rejecting the request, a proper rejection message is sent back to the requester agent.

The Advertiser

The advertiser provides brokering services for providers that do not wish to reveal their own capabilities. After receiving a request, the advertiser interaction protocol with providers will be classically the same as in the case of the broker agent. In contrast to the broker, the advertiser formulates the requests and then forms them out to every registered provider that its capability is unknown. It is noteworthy that, for every advertised request, the provider agent has to determine whether the request is within its capabilities and is of interest, which implies that a considerable elapsed time will be spent

Figure 3. The interaction pattern for advertiser agent

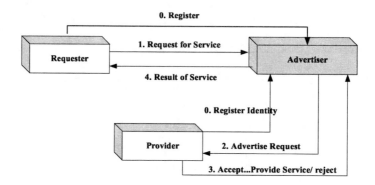

on evaluating every request. Therefore (under the assumption of an open environment), providers would be deluged by a variety of service requests, which significantly impacts performance and efficiency. Figure 3 shows the interaction pattern for the advertiser agent with provider and requester agents.

Note that the advertiser is responsible for evaluating any submitted *bids* (for example, utilizing contracting-based approaches) and evaluates them to determine the best deal that satisfies the requester agent's preferences based on the heuristics described before.

The interaction pattern of the advertiser agent is similar to the broker's case. The only difference is that the problem-solver component of the advertiser agent searches the brokering layer's knowledge component and determines any available registered agent, which will be listed as a potential contractor. This is in contrast with the broker agent, in which the searching process relies on performing a *matching search* for agents with registered capabilities that fulfil the required request.

The Anonymizer

The anonymizer agent is an agent that protects both the identity and the capability of any provider within the environment. The brokering layer's functionality is mainly seen as a directory service, in which the anonymizer maintains a repository of service's requests along with any required preferences. Providers will have the ability to browse this repository and then determine the relevant requests that might be of interest and within their capabilities.

As shown in Figure 4, the provider agent responds with the service's result (a result location within the layer has to be identified to the provider upon registration within the brokering layer). Note that providers with this degree of privacy have to take in consideration linking the result of the service to the request.

Agents who wish to request services through the anonymizer might have the ability to check for the availability of the services' result themselves; the challenge is that they should be able to identify the result of the request and, hence, retrieve it.

Additionally, a performance trade-off will be highly considered, as there might be

Figure 4. The interaction pattern for anonymizer agent

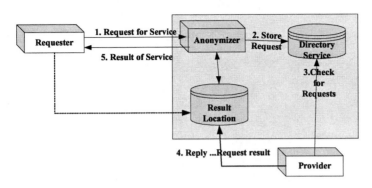

possibilities where there are no capable or interested providers existing in the environment when requesting specific service, and consequently, the time spent waiting at a provider who is willing to fulfil the request will exceed the desired satisfying time.

The anonymizer's problem solver stores requests from various domain agents and allows providers to browse these requests (*directory service*). Note that the anonymizer is responsible for checking the availability of the service's result and thus delivering back to the requester agent.

The Mediator

The mediator agent protects the identity of a requester, dynamically identifies service providers, and acts on behalf of the requesters to achieve a better deal that fulfills their goal(s). Requesters may not wish to reveal their identities; they can only request a specific service by revealing their goal(s) to the mediator. As shown in Figure 5, requesters will be responsible for checking the availability of the service's result, which implies that requesters should be aware of the result location.

Note that in this degree of privacy, the interaction pattern between the mediator agent and the provider is typically governed by the providers' privacy concern. For example, the architecture of the mediator will follow the same interaction pattern depicted in the broker situation in case of existing registered providers with known capabilities in the environment, or the architecture imposes the same interaction processes described in the advertiser agent's interaction protocol with providers of unknown capabilities. Moreover, the mediator's architecture will vary successively to include the directory service functionality, as explained previously in case of the anonymizer agent, if there are providers hiding both the identities and capabilities.

The interaction patterns by which a mediator assigns a request to providers, however, will have a significant effect on the performance and efficiency. System performance is clearly dependent on a number of parameters, including the number of providers willing to carry out the request, and the time needed by each provider to fulfill that request. It is noteworthy that the interaction protocol of the mediator is equivalent to the broker's case. The only difference is that the domain agent's problem solver is responsible for retrieving the available result.

Figure 5. The interaction pattern for mediator agent

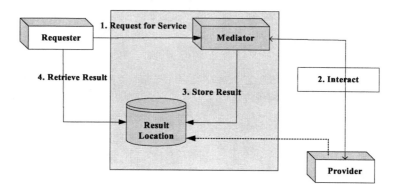

The Broadcaster

A broadcaster agent controls a set of stored services from various providers. Requesters that prefer to hide their goals from the environment could do so by registering with the broadcaster agent. The broadcaster functionality is basically similar to the advertiser: the broadcaster forwards every advertised service out to every registered requester with unknown preferences or interests. The broadcasting parameters include service description, service constraints (such time and cost), and the corresponding link to these services (within the service repository).

In an open environment where the number of different services providers continually increases and where there is a competitive manner to *sell* their services, requesters would be flooded by a variety of service advertisements and notifications.

Requesters have to determine whether the service advertised to them is of an interest or not. Clearly, this process implies that a significant time is required to assess

Figure 6. The interaction pattern for broadcaster agent

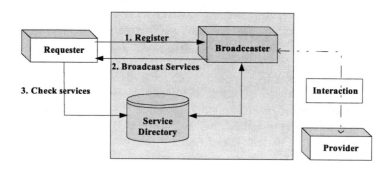

each service notification. The mediator sends the notifications along with any related parameters required for providing the service (such as name of the service, cost, location, and so on).

As shown in Figure 6, the requesters will accordingly check the service's repository for further information or browse other services that have been previously posted (by providers interested in hiding their identities or capabilities). Additionally, the broadcaster's architecture will vary significantly to include the interaction pattern with providers of different degrees of privacy as previously mentioned. Note that the requester agent has to determine the appropriate advertisement that might be of interest. Additionally, requesters might check the services repository for further information related to a particular advertisement.

The Bulletin Board

A bulletin board agent's functionality is similar to that of the anonymizer but with requester and provider behaviors reversed. Requesters may wish to hide their identities and goals from the entire environment, as shown in Figure 7. They have the possibility of either posting their want ads to the bulletin board's service repository directly, or they might check for any services that would be of interest.

For this degree of privacy, it is the requester's responsibility to check for the availability of the service's result and, hence, retrieve it; this implies that the requester should be aware of linking the result to its own request in addition to the knowledge of both the service repository and the result location. Additionally, the requester is responsible for checking the availability of the service's result and, hence, retrieving it; this implies that the requester should be aware of linking the result to its relevant request in addition to being aware of both the service repository and the result locations.

It is to be noted that a requester with this degree of privacy will have no further dynamic notification in case the service directory becomes unavailable. The broadcaster's interaction pattern with provider agents governs the overall architecture of the bulletin board agent. For any degree of privacy required by providers, the architecture will vary significantly.

Figure 7. The interaction pattern for bulletin board agent

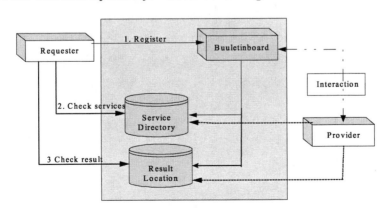

SYSTEM DESIGN

Cooperative distributed systems provide an integrated solution in dealing with several design issues, such as autonomy, heterogeneity, and transparency, and present more efficient solutions for many technical problems such as brokering. The following sections focus on the important design aspects of the proposed model. In agent-based cooperative distributed systems, models should give a formal description of the observable characteristics, like agents' actions, roles, behaviors, and interactions. As shown in Figure 8, the functionalities (services) of the brokering layer can be described as a standard UML (unified modeling language) use case model (UML, 2003). Each use case describes an intended functionality within the proposed system, which includes the following:

- Register: To enable different participants (requesters or providers) to register within the layer; the layer will update a basic knowledge of the overall community.
- Deregister: To enable participants to deregister from the layer (disjoin the environment).
- SelectBrokerAgent: To allow the brokering layer agent to determine the appropriate brokering service that is suitable for a particular request.
- UpdateKnowledge: To allow the layer to have updated knowledge about the whole environment.
- BrokeringServices: A set of all types of brokering agents, which will be discussed later.

Figure 8. The brokering layer's services depicted in a use case diagram

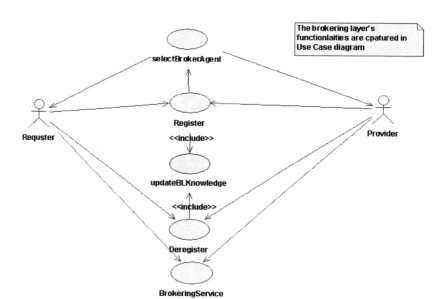

Figure 9. The broker agent components modeled as nested packages

Figure 10. The broker's capability component

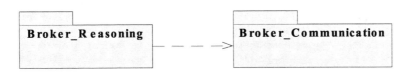

As previously mentioned, we view an agent as an entity that possesses knowledge and capability; the agent's components in the proposed system are modeled as UML packages that are possibly nested. Each package contains an interface that is realized by its set of public classes. An agent (for example, the broker) is composed of two packages, namely, the *knowledge* and *capability*, shown in Figure 9. The agent's knowledge contains the information that it has in its memory about the environment as well as the expected world. This knowledge includes the agent self-model, other agents' models, goals that need to be achieved or satisfied, possible solutions generated for achieving a goal, and the local history of the world that consists of all possible local views for an agent at any given time. It also includes the agent's *desire, commitments*, and *intentions*.

The *capability* package includes communication, reasoning, and domain action components as shown in Figure 10. The communication capability allows the agents to exchange messages with the other elements of the environment, including users, agents, and objects. The communication component of the agents is equipped with an incoming message inbox, and message polling can be both blocking and nonblocking, with an optional timeout.

The *reasoning* component is further decomposed into the *problem-solver* component and *coordination* component as shown in Figure 11. The *problem-solver* component maps the agent's goal into a solution. For example, the broker's problem solver evaluates all the received proposals and makes its choice of the accepted offer, taking into consideration the parameters set out in the agent's request. This involves aggregating bids and evaluating them against certain criteria. The *coordination* component includes several interaction devices that deal with various interdependency problems, such as capability dependency (Ghenniwa & Kamel, 2000). The architecture of each individual agent is based on the CIR-agent. It provides a generic agent model for cooperative distributed systems that is appropriate for designing the privacy-based

Figure 11. The broker's problem-solver and interaction components

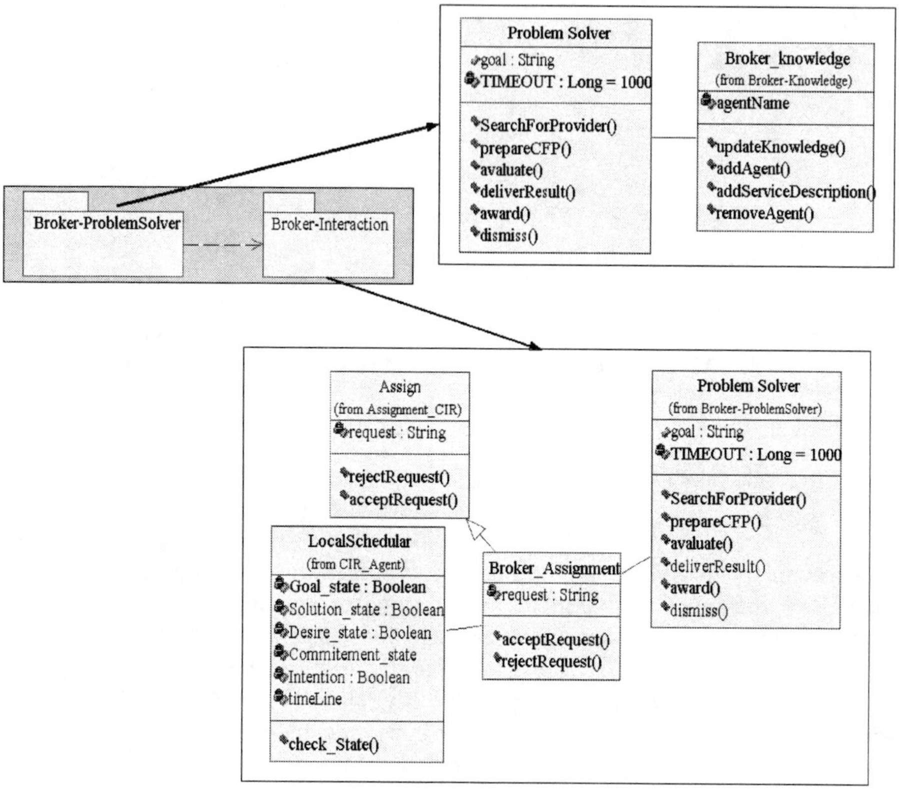

brokering services. The domain agent is a domain-specific agent that might play the role of a service provider as well as the role of a requester.

The Agent's Architecture

Figure 12 depicts the knowledge and the capabilities possessed by the agents, where the domain agent's knowledge includes self-model, models of brokering agents, and the domain specification. The brokering agent architecture is similar to the domain agent architecture but differs in a way that their knowledge includes self-model, models of the existing domain agents in terms of their roles (requester/provider), and capabilities. A brokering agent might also have models of other brokering agents to assist in achieving some goals or to avoid redundant effort.

Figure 12. The agent architecture

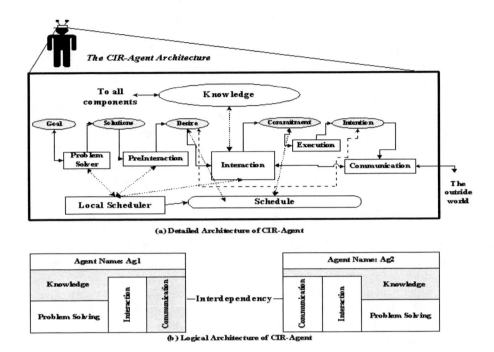

(a) Detailed Architecture of CIR-Agent

(b) Logical Architecture of CIR-Agent

Registration with Brokering Layer

In order to benefit from the services provided by the brokering layer, agents are required to register their presence with a special registration agent known as a brokering layer agent. The parameters specification for the registration might include goal-name, identity, capability, and the required degree of privacy. A request for registration can be formally represented as:

$$Req_j \underline{\underline{def}} \langle id_j, g_j, cap_j, staus_j \rangle, \text{ where}$$

$$status_j \in \{hide_{(id,g,cap)}, reveal\}.$$

The *status* parameter of the registration request indicates the desired degree of privacy required by the requesting agent. Upon acceptance of the request, the name of the matching brokering agent relevant to the required parameters is sent back to the registered agent.

IMPLEMENTATION

A prototype of the proposed model has been implemented to support and provide information-gathering capabilities in healthcare environments where the accessibility of private information is a desirable feature to various categories of healthcare administrators, professionals, and patients. Healthcare services can be modeled and implemented as VEs. Virtual healthcare enterprise (VHE) is a collection of autonomous units that can act independently and cooperate in providing services and synergize medical data according to mutual interests. The infrastructure of the participants of VHE can handle only the internal administrative and clinical processes. The proposed model enables the integration capability among the participants of VHE transparently with desired privacy requirements. The model provides querying ability and coordination activities that enhance the overall connectivity of distributed, autonomous, and possibly heterogeneous information sources (databases) of different healthcare providers and hospitals. The proposed architecture has been implemented using a CIR-agent model for distributed healthcare information using JADE, a FIPA-complaint platform (Jade, 2003).

As shown in Figure 13, three relational databases were designed and implemented using mySql (mySql, 2003). The databases contain information about various patients in a hospital, doctors' records, and a pharmacy, respectively, and each are managed by a dedicated agent (provider agent). An interface agent acts on behalf of the user to achieve a better goal that satisfies the user's request. A set of CIR-agents represent the different brokering layer's agents and are available to healthcare domain agents. Any domain agent needing to have access to the services provided by the brokering layer may do so by registering its presence with the layer as shown in Figure 14b. As shown in Figure 14a, the user will have the choice of defining the degree of privacy needed, and accordingly, the relevant brokering agent (the *broker* in this example) is sent back to the interface agent.

Figure 13. A prototype of a healthcare privacy-based brokering architecture

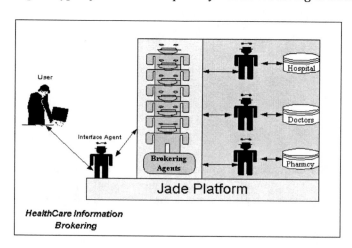

Figure 14. Healthcare information brokering implementation

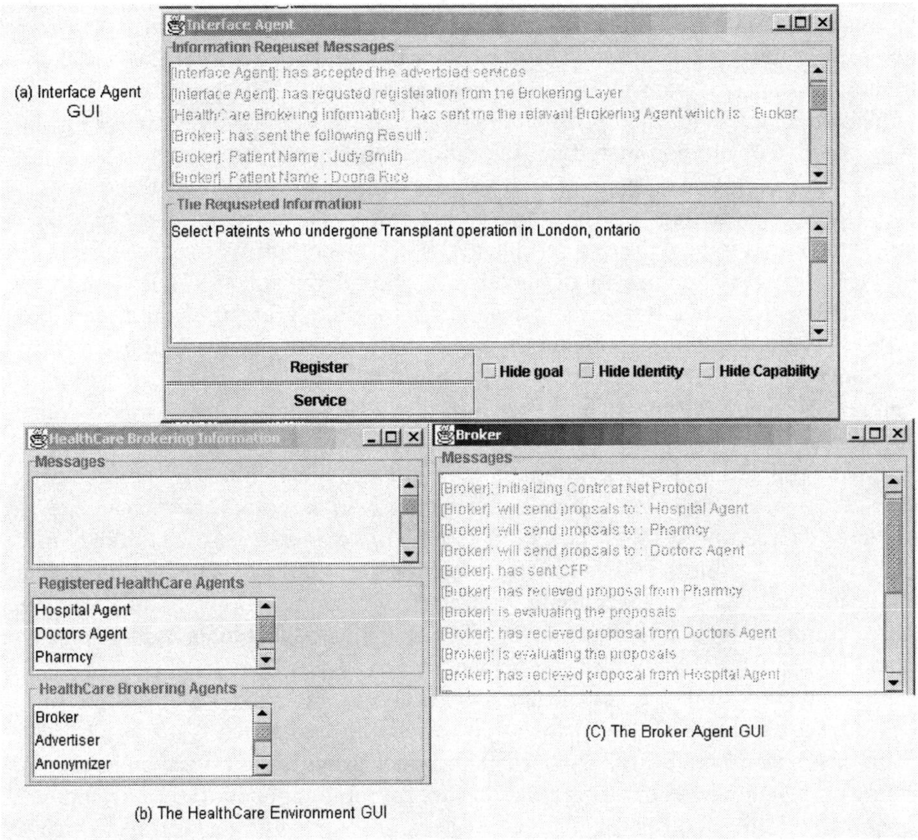

(a) Interface Agent GUI

(b) The HealthCare Environment GUI

(C) The Broker Agent GUI

Upon registration, the interface agent interacts with the *broker* and solicits assistance for the required goal (e.g., finding names of patients who have undergone transplant operation in London, Ontario); the former receives the request, formulates it, determines the appropriate online provider agents, and forwards the request to each one by sending a call for proposal (CFP) message that specifies the request's parameters.

After receiving all the proposals, the broker makes its choice of the accepted offer based on the heuristics mentioned previously as shown in Figure 14c. As a result of the evaluation, a proper message (acceptance or rejection) will be sent to the potential information providers and a result of the request is delivered back to the requester (interface agent) and displayed, as shown in Figure 14a.

DISCUSSION AND CONCLUSIONS

The main goal of the work presented here is to develop a multiagent system architecture for integration in cooperative distributed systems with a special focus on coordination and cooperation services that support ad hoc and automated system configurations. The architecture provides privacy-based brokering services to VEs, various entities that are modeled as cooperative distributed systems. Based on a layered architecture, the brokering role is further classified into several subroles based on the privacy attributes of both the provider and the requester. The proposed approach is innovative, in the sense that it treats the privacy as a design issue for brokering, and it supports ad hoc and automated configurations among distributed, possibly autonomous and heterogeneous, entities with various degrees of privacy requirements.

The work presented by Decker and Sycara preserves the privacy of the participants only at the initial state of the system, and considers the possibility for one agent to learn the capabilities and the identity of the other (Decker & Sycara, 1997). By contrast, the proposed architecture allows agents to solicit help without revealing their identities or goals to any entity within the community, including brokering agents assigned to provide such help. In another approach (Kuokka & Harad, 1995), agents' capabilities and preferences come to be known by all participants in the society, which leads to a chaotic environment where agents might violate any privacy requirements.

The proposed multilayer architecture minimizes the architecture complexity encountered in *direct-interaction* architectures (where interactions between agents often take more complex processes for encompassing series of message exchange and forming a single point of failure), and makes it less vulnerable to failures. The proposed layered architecture provides an appropriate separation of responsibilities, letting developers and programmers focus on solving their particular application's problems in a manner and semantics most suitable to the local perspective.

Software agents are very promising technology to model and design VEs. It provides high degrees of decentralization of capabilities, which is the key to system scalability and extensibility. A CIR-agent model provides software engineers with features at a higher level of abstraction that are useful for cooperative environments. It supports flexibility at different levels of the design: system architecture, agent architecture, and agent component architecture. These degrees of flexibility allow entities of VE to adapt to changes with minimum requirements for redesign. Different application domains can benefit from the proposed model, such as healthcare, intelligent cooperative information systems, and agent-based electronic business. In a cooperative information system, the proposed brokering services can help users to locate and retrieve information from distributed resources in an open environment.

The privacy model is desirable in different healthcare sectors, where it can efficiently govern different types of health data, such as genetic, HIV, mental health, and pharmacy records from not being distributed or abused. Based on the level and the amount of information that can be released, users can securely translate their privacy policies to an applicable related privacy case in the proposed model. One of the important directions for future work is to expand the proposed system to include the capability of semantic brokering, by introducing new functionality in the layer to resolve common types of structural and semantic heterogeneity. We believe that it will be necessary to support multiple, independently created and managed ontologies that capture the terminologies of different and sometimes overlapping domains.

REFERENCES

Amin, T., & Keng, P. H. (2002). Inter-organizational workflow management system for virtual healthcare enterprise. Presented at the *Third IFIP Working Conference on Infrastructures for Virtual Enterprises PRO-VE'02*, Portugal, May 1–3.

Arisha, K., et al. (1998). IMPACT: The interactive Maryland platform for agents collaborating together. *IEEE Intelligent Systems,* 14, 64-72.

Bayardo, R., et al. (1996). *Infosleuth: Agent-based semantic integration of information in open and dynamic environments.* MCC Technical Report MCC-INSL-0088-96, October.

Cranor, L., et al. (2002). The platform for privacy preferences 1.0 (P3P1.0) specification. W3C Recommendations. Accessed April 2002 online *www.w3.org/TR/P3P/*

D'Atri, A., & Motro, A. (2002). *Virtue: Virtual enterprises for information market.* Presented at the ECIS, June 6–8, Poland.

Decker, K., et al. (1995). MACRON: An architecture for multi-agent cooperative information gathering. *Proceedings of the CIKM '95 Workshop on Intelligent Information Agents.* Baltimore.

Decker, K., Sycara, K., & Williamson, M. (n.d.).Middle-agents for the Internet. In *IJCAI'97 International Joint Conference on Artificial Intelligence*, Nagoya, Japan (Vol. 1, pp. 578-583).

Feigenbaum, J., Freedman, J., Sander, T., & Shaostack, A. (2001). Privacy engineering for digital rights management systems. Presented at the *ACM Workshop on Security and Privacy in Digital Rights Management.*

FIPA Agent Software Integration Specification. Available online *http://ww.fipa.org/specs/fipa00079/XC00079B.htm*

Garcia-Molina, H., Hammer, J., Ireland, K., Papakonstantinou, Y., Ullman, J., & Widom (1995). Integrating and accessing heterogeneous information sources in TSIMMIS. In *Proceedings of the AAAI Symposium on Information Gathering,* Stanford, California, (pp. 61–64).

Genesereth, M., et al. (1997). Infomaster: An information integration system. In J. Pecikhamn (Ed.), *Proceedings of 1997 ACM SIGMOD Conference,* Tuscon, Arizona (pp. 539-542).

Geotgakopoulos, D., et al. (1999). Managing process and service fusion in virtual enterprises. *Information Systems: Special Issue on Information Systems Support for Electronic Commerce,* 24(6), 429–456.

Ghenniwa, H., & Huhns, M. (2004). Intelligent enterprise integration: eMarketplace model. To appear in J. Gupta, & S. Sharma (Eds.), *Creating knowledge based organizations* (pp. 46–79). Hershey, PA: Idea Group Publishing.

Global InfoTech, Inc. (1998). *A report on the applicability of mediation in ALP.* A Technical Report.

Goldberg, I., Wagner, D., & Brewer, E. (1997). Privacy-enhancing technologies for the Internet. In B. Werner (Ed.), *Proceedings of IEEE COMPCON '97,* California (pp. 103–109).

Grover, V., & Teng, T. (2001). E-commerce and the information market. *CACM,* 44(4), 79–86.

Gruber, T. (1993). A translation approach to portable ontology specifications. *Knowledge Acquisition,* 5, 2, 199–220.

Hammer, M. (2000). Out of the box: The rise of the virtual enterprise. *Information Week Online,* March 20, 2000. Available online *http://www.informationweek.com*

JADE (n.d.). Java Agent Development Environment. Available online *http://sharon.cselt.it*

Kashyap, V., & Sheth, A. (1994). Semantics-based information brokering. In N. Adam (Ed.), *Proceedings of the Third International Conference on Information and Knowledge Management,* Maryland (pp. 363–370).

Kenny, S., & Borking, J. (n.d.). The value of privacy engineering. Available online *http://elj.warwick.ac.uk/jilt/02-1/kenny.html*

Korba, L., & Song, R. (2001). *Investigating of network-based approaches for privacy.* NRC Report: ERB-1091, NRC No.: 44900, November.

Kuokka, D., & Harrada, L. (1995). On using KQML for natchmaking. In V. Lesser (Ed.), *CIKM-95 Third Conference on Information and Knowledge Management* (pp. 239-245). Cambridge, MA: AAAI/MIT Press.

Monge, P., & Desanctic, G. (Eds.). (1999). Special issue on virtual organizations. *Organization Science, 10*(6).

MySql. (n.d.). Available online *http://www.mysql.com*

PISA—The Privacy Incorporated Software Agent. (n.d.). Available online *http://www.cbpweb.nl/bis/top-1-1-9.html*

Purvis, M., et al. (2000). The NZDIS project: An agent-based distributed information systems architecture. Jr. Sprague (Ed.), *CDROM Proceedings of the Hawaii International Conference on Systems Sciences (HICSS-33).* IEEE Computer Society Press.

Sheth, A., & Larson, J. (1990). Federated database systems for managing distributed, heterogeneous, and autonomous databases. *ACM Computing Surveys, 22,* 3, 183–235.

Suter, B. (1998). A cooperation platform for virtual enterprises. In P. Sieber & J. Griese (Eds.), *Proceedings of VoNet, Workshop on Organizational Virtualness* (pp. 155–164). Bern: Simowa-Verlag.

Sycara, K., et al. (2001). The RETSINA MAS Infrastructure. Technical Report CMU-RI-TR-01-05, Robotics Institute, Carnegie Mellon University, March. [Online]. Available online *http://www.ri.cmu.edu/pubs/pub_3509.html*

UML: Unified Modeling Language. (n.d.). Available online *http://www.omg.org/uml*

Wiederhold, G. (1992). Mediators in the architecture of future information systems. *IEEE Computer, 25,* 3, 38–49.

Wulf, V., & Hartmann, A. (1994). The ambivalence of network visibility in an organizational context. In A. Clement, P. Kolm, & I. Wagner (Eds.), *Networking: Connecting workers in and between organizations,* A-38. Amsterdam: North-Holland.

Chapter X

Dynamic Contract Generation for Dynamic Business Relationships

Simon Field
Matching Systems, UK

Yigal Hoffner
IBM Research Laboratory GmbH, Switzerland

ABSTRACT

A dynamic virtual enterprise needs to be able to create, customize, and dismantle commercial relationships among partners quickly. The need to establish legal contracts before enactment begins can undermine the benefits gained by using advanced technology to form dynamic virtual enterprises, if it cannot be done quickly when needed, efficiently, in an up-to-date manner and result in a correct contract. There is, therefore, a need for the dynamic creation of contracts to reflect these constraints. An electronic representation of the contract can be constructed rapidly and brings the added advantage of being available to other software components. The chapter presents a novel method for generating a legal contract from the description of a business agreement. This is done by breaking up the constituent parts of the contract into clauses and using matchmaking technology to determine whether a clause is relevant for a given business agreement or not. A brief overview of the matchmaking technology that is used to do the transformations of a business agreement into a contract is given. We then show one specific detailed example of this approach — the translation of a business projection agreement into the relevant agreement in the legal projection, namely, a contract.

THE IMPORTANCE OF CONTRACTS

A dynamic virtual enterprise needs to be able to create, customize, and dismantle commercial relationships among partners quickly. The need to establish legal contracts before enactment begins can undermine the benefits gained by using advanced technology to form dynamic virtual enterprises, if it cannot be done quickly when needed, efficiently, in an up-to-date manner and result in a correct contract. There is, therefore, a need for the dynamic creation of contracts to reflect these constraints. An electronic representation of the contract can be constructed rapidly and brings the added advantage of being available to other software components.

The chapter presents a novel method for generating a legal contract from the description of a business agreement. This is done by breaking up the constituent parts of the contract into clauses and using matchmaking technology to determine whether a clause is relevant for a given business agreement or not. A brief overview of the matchmaking technology (Facciorusso, Field, Hauser, Hoffner, Humbel, Pawlitzek, Rjaibi, & Siminitz, 2003; Field & Dazler, 2004; Field & Hoffner, 2002) that is used to do the transformations of a business agreement into a contract is given. We then show one specific detailed example of this approach—the translation of a business projection agreement into the relevant agreement in the legal projection, namely, a contract.

The manner in which the terms agreement and contract are used in the e-business-related literature is presented and discussed. A number of conclusions drawn from this discussion lead us to look for a new information model for describing relationships between organisations. This, together with the process of transforming the agreement into a contract, leads us to develop a new model that consists of a typed domain with projections that describe the entire relationship between two organisations, each from a different perspective. The typed domain describes all the possible relationships that can be established within the domain between two organisations. Each potential relationship in a typed domain is fully described by the four projections, ensuring that the principle of "no surprise" can be enforced within the domain.

The idea of agreement transformation shown earlier is then generalized and exploited in showing how agreement and other information in one projection can be translated into their counterparts in other projections. For example, the business description can be used to generate a blueprint for the configuration and instantiation of the client and service-side infrastructure and components that are needed to enact the agreement between them.

The chapter draws upon the experience gained in a number of activities conducted in the e-business group at the IBM Zurich Research Laboratory (ZRL):

- *The CrossFlow project* (2000)—dealt with business processes crossing organizational boundaries (Grefen, Aberer, Hoffner, & Ludwig, 2000; Hoffner, Ludwig, Grefen, & Aberer, 2001b), was led by ZRL, and included seven university, research, and industrial organisations.
- *The ViMP, WME, and WSME projects*—covered extensive work on advanced forms of matchmaking (Field & Hoffner, 2002; Hoffner, Field, Grefen, & Ludwig, 2001a).
- *The SilkRoad project*—focused on e-Negotiations (Ströbel, 2002).

Agreements and Contracts in the Computer World

The words "agreement" and "contract" are frequently encountered in e-business-related literature but appear to mean different things to different people and communities (Angelov & Grefen, 2003). All the different uses of the term "contract" appear to carry the notion of an agreement between usually two (but possibly more) parties with regards to some issue or a set of issues. The main difference between the uses of the terms appears to concern the extent of the agreement between the parties. The following is an exposition of the different ways in which the terms "agreement" and "contract" are used.

The CORBA standard refers to an interface definition written in IDL (Interface Definition Language; Object Management Group [OMG], 1996) as a contract. In this limited client–service relationship, agreement to adhere to the interface definition when invoking and when replying to an invocation is assumed. The interface definition is often seen as a statement made by the provider as to the kind of service interface it will provide; there is no mention of the obligation of the client to respect the same specification — it is implicitly assumed to be the case. The IDL and WSDL (Web services description language) definitions serve as a point of reference for the developers of the client and service-side programs and stubs/gateways. The notion of the interface definition as a contract is extended to encompass the protocols by which the invocation is made. In the context of Web services, WSDL (2001) and port-types cover similar ground as CORBA IDL and interoperable object references (IOR) (OMG, 2003).

An interesting extension to the somewhat static definition of the client–service relationship in terms of the service interface is to specify how a sequence of operations can be conducted. This is borne out of the realization that Web services are likely to be complex and long-lived entities requiring extended series of interactions. The suggested definition of the choreography of interactions [e.g., using BPEL (business process execution language for Web services), 2002] can be seen as an extension of the interface contract. Weigand and van den Heuvel (2002) proposed the use of a specification document (created with the XLBC language) to coordinate the behavior of workflows in both parties to an agreement.

Although some references are made to this level of specifying behavior, it is only a limited effort, because, like the interface descriptions, no specification of the effect of the interactions is given. To include behavioral information, IDL, WSDL, and BPEL specifications will have to at least be annotated by preconditions and posteffects.

The advantage of being able to specify interface and protocol definitions in a computer-readable form, is that it is possible to use them to generate components that can be employed by the two parties at runtime. For example, IDL or WSDL definitions can be used by stub-compilers to generate the stubs that serialize the invocation and reply parameters to and from an agreed-on-the-wire format. Such technology helps overcome (language) differences in the environments of the client and service sides. The advantage of specifying other service and client aspects including quality of service (QoS) ones (as mentioned), is that the configuration of components and the allocation of resources at the point of instantiation can be driven by these specifications.

The notion of an interface specification as a contract is further developed into the concept of design by contract (Meyer, 2000). Here a contract is expected to provide more than the mere structural information in IDL, instead, it provides a combination of:

- The class invariant, describing global constraints
- The operation precondition, describing constraints on calling the operation
- The operation effect or postcondition, describing expected properties of the result

The term "contract" is also encountered when adding QoS attributes and statements to the technical description of a service. The QoS attributes are often referred to as nonfunctional attributes and are seen as an attempt to bridge the gap between the technology and the business aspects of service provision–consumption.

Milosevic and Dromey (2002) acknowledged the use of the term "contract" as specifically applied to "part of the collective behavior of a set of objects." It proposes the use of *deontic policy language* with which to specify a set of policies that will govern this behavior and its use combined with genetic software engineering to find incompleteness and inconsistencies within a proposed contract. In "The WSLA Framework: Specifying and Monitoring Service Level Agreements for Web Services" (Keller & Ludwig, 2002), a solution more specific to services delivered via Web services is proposed, combining a language for specifying Web service-level agreements (WSLAs) with a compliance monitoring tool that can independently monitor compliance to the agreement. SLAs also include some references to penalties for nondelivery of the service and therefore also refer indirectly to notions of costing and billing. SLAs cover a mixture of the service as well as some of the business aspects of a relationship.

The advantage of being able to specify such statements in a computer-readable form is that it is possible to create monitoring facilities that will supervise the enactment of the agreement and notify the concerned party or parties when the required and promised QoS guarantees are not met. Further use of such statements could be corrective actions that are initiated either on the consumer or service side.

Another use of the term contract that is similar to an extended SLA can be found in the CrossFlow project (CrossFlow, 2000; Grefen et al., 2000; Hoffner et al., 2001a, 2001b). The contract contained a specification of the parties, the common view of the service (described and implemented as a workflow) that was to be provided and consumed. The COSMOS project had a similar approach to contracts (Griffel, Boger, Weinreich, Lamersdorf, & Merz, 1998; Wienberg & Merz, 2000).

The word "contract" is also used when referring to the business relationship between the service consumer and provider, not just the rather asymmetric view of the client–service relationship. This use of the term "contract" usually entails a high-level description of the relationship between two organisations and also involves the notion of consideration — of something given in return for the service delivered (Weigand & van den Heuvel, 1998). This is, therefore, likely to define the involvement of auxiliary services such as measuring, costing, billing, payment, and receipt handling. This type of contract also includes a reference to what happens if things go wrong, if promises are not kept or are not deemed to have been kept, and what can be done in case any disputes arise. Another important issue when discussing the relationship from a business point of view, is that of penalties for failure to deliver the promises made concerning the service. The business aspect also entails a specification of the termination of the relationship: what defines a satisfactory enactment of the contract, how is the termination agreement conveyed to the other party, and ultimately, what is the termination procedure (Hoffner, 2003).

In "Identifying Requirements for Business Contract Language: A Monitoring Perspective," Neal, Cole, Linnington, Milosevic, Gibson, and Kulkarni (2003) proposed an extensible markup language (XML)-based business contract language (BCL) with which the monitoring requirements of a business service can be specified. The proposed scope goes beyond monitoring the delivery of the service and includes consideration of auxiliary services, such as billing and payment. An example specifying quality of service guarantees is given, illustrating how the language can form part of an overall agreement that can subsequently be used by service monitoring tools.

Although we know of no such commercial use at the moment, the advantage of being able to specify the use of auxiliary services in a computer-readable form is that their inclusion and integration may be automated in a similar manner to the automation of stub generation and component configuration and instantiation.

The term "contract" is also used in the more traditional sense — as a legal document and agreement (Angelov & Grefen, 2003; Milosevic, Berry, Bond, & Raymond, 2003). A legal contract requires several things: agreement — offer and acceptance, certainty — what exactly is on offer, consideration—something of value to be given in return for a service or goods delivered, and an intention to enter into a legally binding relationship (Boundy, 1998; Smith, 1989). Legal contracts are likely to include or at least refer to the common understanding or standards that exist in a specific domain. This may also include any exclusions that are commonly agreed.

Summary: Agreements and Contracts

The differences between the uses of the term appear to concern the extent of the agreement between the parties, going from the implied low-level technical and static description of interfaces, to the more dynamic aspects of the sequencing of interactions, QoS issues, and business-level description of the exchanges. The common distinction made between the different types of agreements/contracts is of "levels," implying a hierarchy of layers or of containment as shown in Figure 1. We believe that such models are flawed and will therefore introduce our own model later.

The use of the terms "agreement" and "contract" often conveys an asymmetric view of the relationship: the service provider makes promises to the service consumer. Legally binding contracts usually define a complete and a two-way relationship — both parties make explicit promises and have explicit expectations. No matter how much of the business relationship is going to be carried out within or between computer systems, the business and legal aspects of any serious relationship have to be well defined and present. The technical and service relationship must be anchored in a wider context of a comprehensive agreement that also entails the two-way nature of the relationship.

While many people use the words "contract" and "agreement" loosely and often interchangeably, for the purpose of this chapter, we will use the term "contract" to mean a "legal agreement," i.e., a contract is one specific type of agreement. By agreement, we usually refer to an understanding covering issues other than legal ones.

Typed Domain and Its Projections

Our alternative model consists of a typed domain with four projections that describe the relationship between two organisations, each from a different perspective. The

Figure 1. Classic representations of the different agreements/contracts surrounding a (client-service based) business relationship — both the containment and the layered models provide a wrong sense of a "higher" and "lower" level of description

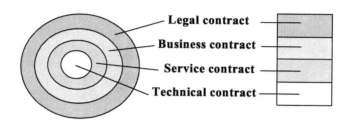

projections are interrelated and interdependent but do not necessarily relate to each other in a layered or containment fashion:

- *Technical projection*: This projection provides a detailed engineering specification of the point of contact between the client and service sides, the interfaces, the interactions, the data carried, the protocols, and the destinations.
- *Service projection*: This projection provides a functional description of the relationship and a behavioral description of services in terms of invariant attributes, global constraints, operation preconditions, effects, or postcondition.
- *Business projection*: This projection describes what each side provides and consumes from a commercial point of view. This usually involves the notion of consideration, which is usually defined in monetary terms.
- *Legal projection*: This projection outlines the promises made by the two parties in a legal framework, specifying what recourse to the law the parties have in case of disputes. It deals with legal issues such as scoping of the relationship, exclusions, legal notices in case of problems, penalties, and arbitration.

The typed domain consists of the information, protocols, template agreements, and other documents for establishing, enacting, and terminating business relationships within the domain. The domain provides the context for the projections and the relations among them. The typed domain is a full description of all possible relationships in such a manner that safe relationships can be built within its boundaries.

Due to space limitations, a fuller description of the typed domain and the projections is outside the scope of this chapter.

TRANSFORMING AGREEMENTS TO CONTRACTS

In the commercial world, it is often the case that a relationship is formed by first negotiating and specifying it from a business point of view. Furthermore, the establishment of the relationship is often made within a known application domain and is, therefore, based on familiarity and assumptions of common knowledge and understanding. However, at some stage in the establishment of a relationship, people and organisations require a document that specifies the relationship from a legal point of view. At that stage, the business agreement has to be transformed, and the implicit understanding that is part of the application domain has to be made explicit.

An example of this approach, the translation of a business agreement into the relevant legal agreement, namely, a contract, is shown in Figure 2.

The process looks at the description of the business agreement, analyses it, and then determines on the basis of the analysis what the contract should look like. When transforming an agreement to a contract, there may be a need for additional information from one or both of the parties. The process will differ largely depending on the constituent parts or building blocks of the contract assembly defined in the domain.

There is a spectrum of options:

- *Monolithic* contract templates: complete contract templates that require no assembling from smaller granularity clauses, but require filling in the relevant information from the business agreement
- *Compositional* contracts: instead of complete contract templates, the domain consists of contract clause templates that have to be assembled into complete contracts and filled with the relevant information from the business agreement; in such a case, there is a need to define:
  - Building blocks: template contract clauses of finer granularity than the monolithic templates
  - Composition rules: clause selection and exclusion rules that will use the information from the business agreement to determine which clauses should be included or excluded
  - Ordering, consistency checks, and restrictions: postcontract clause selection processing to see if the assembled contract is valid in the domain
- *Hybrid contracts*: using a combination of a small number of monolithic templates together with a number of contract clause templates that can be assembled in different ways

Figure 2. Transformation of a business agreement into a legal agreement (contract)

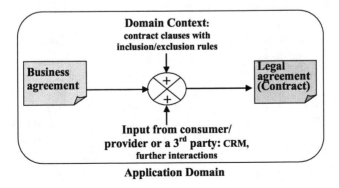

Depending on which of the above approaches is chosen, there are a number of different ways in which the process of transformation shown in Figure 2 can proceed:

1.   Filling the (only) monolithic contract template with relevant information from the business projection agreement data
2.   Selecting one monolithic contract template from multiple ones available and filling the selected one with relevant information from the business projection agreement data
3.   Composing a contract from finer granularity building blocks (clauses) by:
     •   Selecting the appropriate clauses based on the information from the business projection agreement data
     •   Filling the relevant information from the business projection agreement data
     •   Ordering and checking for consistency of the resulting composition
     •   Integrating the result into a coherent contract
4.   Using a hybrid solution of templates and contract clauses or, in other words, finer and coarser granularity of building blocks

One way of implementing the above transformation is to use matchmaking technology. This technology is ideal for selecting the monolithic contract templates or the contract clauses, suitable for a given service agreement. In order to achieve this, the available clauses and their inclusion and exclusion rules have to be translated into the appropriate matchmaking concepts. But before we describe how this is done in detail, we present the process of matchmaking and the characteristics that it must support in order to make this process of dynamic contract generation feasible.

USING MATCHMAKING FOR AGREEMENT TRANSFORMATIONS

This section provides an introduction to the concepts behind matchmaking and matchmaking engines (MMEs). It has its origins in distributed systems (ANSAWare (1993) Trader, CORBA/ODP Trading Service [open distributed processing (ODP) reference model, 1995; OMG, 1996], and has been further refined to manage the complexity of finding and configuring a wide range of services that might be offered or delivered via the Internet [ViMP (Hoffner, Facciorusso, Field, & Schade, 2000), WSME (Facciorusso et al., 2003; Feller, 2002)]. The concepts and features are therefore described here in the context of service consumers seeking suitable services from service providers.

Symmetry of Information Exchange and Selection

The process of finding the right service for a given service consumer is not necessarily a one-way process of having the consumer state their requirements and select a winner from the matching services. Service providers may wish to receive information from the consumer before deciding to make a particular service available to that consumer. The input to the matchmaking process (Figure 3), therefore, needs to take account of the demands of both service consumers and providers, relating these demands to information provided by both parties, and resulting in a symmetric exchange by service consumers and providers of both information and demands.

Figure 3. Two-way exchange of information and demands in the symmetric matchmaking process

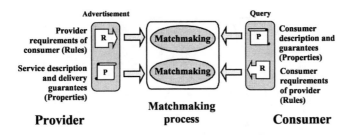

Each advertisement and query provides properties and may also provide rules for the selection of the other party.

Powerful Description and Requirement Language

Powerful languages are needed to describe complex services, and similarly, powerful languages are needed to describe complex compatibility criteria, i.e., requirements relating to the description of the other party. The matchmaking language has to be sufficiently powerful to express the types of properties that organisations are looking for when selecting a partner. The descriptions created with this language should be capable of using complex data structures to express complex attributes, such as delivery dates with price tags attached and associated QoS parameters, etc. Similarly, there is a need to be able to access these complex data structures and extract the relevant information from them.

Dynamic Service Configuration

Matchmaking should allow a provider to describe its offer as a skeleton or a generating function that can be used to offer different service configurations. This can be done in the form of a reference to an external system as shown in Figure 4 or, alternatively, by supplying a script that the MME can evaluate locally.

Thus, the MME can generate the specific service offer dynamically at the time of searching. Input to the process that provides the specific value can contain information from the potential consumer, and each service configuration can be tailored to the circumstances of the specific consumer. This is needed for several reasons:

- It facilitates an up-to-date description of the service where service properties such as the cost, availability, or quality of service may be subject to variations. Such variations can, for example, be due to load, maintenance, etc.
- It provides a way to specify a range of services without having to enumerate all the options associated with them in the MME, as this may overload the MME.
- It provides a way to configure the service and the consumer application according to the needs and properties of both parties. This facilitates personalization of the service.

Figure 4. Dynamic properties can be updated when needed during the matchmaking process either by the script provided to the MME or by calling a back-end system on the provider side

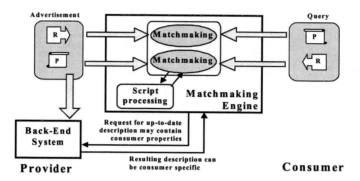

- It provides a way to integrate existing applications that reside on back-end systems.

Pre- and Postmatchmaking Processing

Prematchmaking processing of queries and postmatchmaking processing of matching offers is shown in Figure 5. Prematchmaking processing of queries allows credit ratings, party evaluation, and personal or commercially sensitive information to be brought into the matchmaking process. Furthermore, special agreements that already exist between the parties can also be brought in and taken into account.

Figure 5. Prematchmaking processing of queries and postmatchmaking processing of matching offers

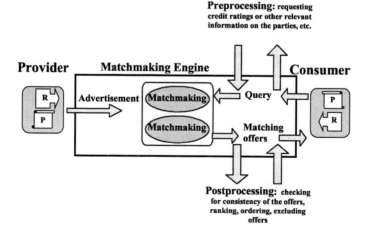

Postmatchmaking processing of matching offers provides an opportunity to check for consistency of the selected offers to see if any conflicting clauses have been selected. It is also the place where the selected clauses can be ordered before being presented or aggregated into a single contract.

Example Matchmaking Engines

A number of matchmaking engines that satisfy the above requirements have been implemented and deployed in production systems environments. Among them are the Web Services Matchmaking Engine (Facciorusso et al., 2003), developed as a prototype system at IBM's ZRL, and the Matching Systems Engine, a commercially available software product developed by Matching Systems Limited.

The Web Services Matchmaking Engine (WSME) features a Data Dictionary component, using XML schema, that explicitly declares the typed information model for different advertisement and query types. This allows advertisement and query submissions to be checked for compliance with the information model specification. By contrast, the Matching Systems Engine tolerates heterogeneous advertisements or queries of a given type name, but will log runtime errors if information expected by an advertisement is not found in a query. The typed information model needed to make the matchmaking process meaningful is part of our notion of a typed domain, which will be explained later. A typed domain is, therefore, a prerequisite for both implementations but is explicit with WSME and implicit with the Matching Systems Engine.

WSME supports a fully symmetric model, with both the information exchange and specification of requirements (rules) taking place in both advertisements and queries. The Matching Systems Engine supports a symmetric information exchange, with queries and advertisements containing named properties, but only advertisements may contain requirement specifications (rules).

Both engines are implemented in Java and provide Web services interfaces for their main functionality, though the Matching Systems Engine may also be embedded directly within existing Java applications. More information about the two systems can be found at *www.zurich.ibm.com/csc/ebizz/ebod.html* and *www.matchingsystems.com*, respectively.

Using Rules to Configure and Select Contract Clauses

Many of the features and concepts explored in the previous sections in the context of service matching can be applied equally to the dynamic selection and configuration of contract clauses, with the clauses taking the place of configurable services:

- A contract clause requires information describing the proposed agreement and contains structured information representing the content of the clause — a symmetric exchange of information.
- Not all clauses are required in every agreement — a requirement language is needed with which to specify the circumstances in which each clause should be included.
- The content of clauses will vary according to the individual circumstances of each agreement — clauses must, therefore, be capable of dynamic configuration.

• The set of clauses needs to be sorted and brought together to form a complete document — there is a requirement for postmatchmaking processing of the selected and configured clauses.

The matchmaking engines described previously, therefore, have the necessary features for an application to generate a contract dynamically to suit a given business agreement. This is achieved by breaking down a contract to a set of configurable clauses that are advertised in the matchmaking engine, and that can be selected and configured by the engine via rules.

The matchmaking process, as it relates to the dynamic construction of contracts, is shown in Figure 6:

1. Following the "no surprises" principle, it is essential that the contract clauses relate to a well-defined and typed domain. This is because information in clause advertisements will refer to information in the query, and vice versa. For some matchmaking engines, such as IBM's WSME, the domain's information model is explicitly declared in a Data Dictionary. For others, such as the Matching Systems Engine, it is implicit in the XML documents presented as advertisements and queries.

2. Advertisements that include the dynamic parts of clauses, together with the rules that determine the circumstances in which each clause is relevant to the contract, are submitted to the matchmaking engine. At the same time, the static "template" content of each clause is stored in a database or file system.

3. A business description of the agreement is submitted in the form of a query to the matchmaking engine. Like the clause advertisements, this contains named properties and may also contain rules.

Figure 6. Symmetric matchmaking process used to generate a contract from a business agreement description

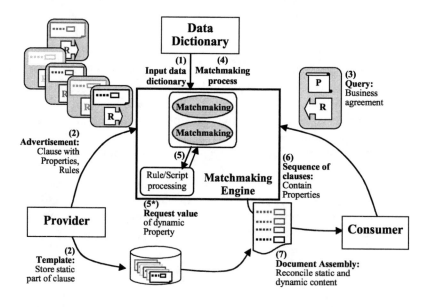

4.   The matchmaking process is triggered by the arrival of the query. Each contract clause advertisement is evaluated, its rules determining whether the clause should form part of the contract or not.

5.   During the process or rule evaluation, dynamic properties belonging to advertisements containing scripts may be evaluated in order to determine suitable values for those properties. This may involve reference to the properties supplied as part of the query, or even reference to external information systems or databases.

6.   The result is a set of offers, each representing the dynamic content of a clause that has been selected for inclusion in the contract. Each offer contains a set of properties with values that have been resolved for this particular query during the matchmaking process.

The contract is assembled by reconciling the dynamic content of the selected clauses with the static content that was stored separately as a set of templates. The completed clauses are sorted and "stitched together" to form a single document — the completed contract that has been created to suit the circumstances described in the query.

CREATING A CONTRACT TO FIT THE BUSINESS AGREEMENT WITH MATCHMAKING

This section shows how the concepts described in the previous section can be applied in the real-world example of derivatives trading confirmation contracts.

Systems that create contracts by filling out monolithic templates are quite common, and provided all or most required contracts conform to a common template, this approach mainly involves filling out a form that contains the variable content, and then populating the template with this [New Jersey Law Revision Commission (NJLRC), 1998]. However, this approach does not cope well when there is a wide variety of contract possibilities. As the number of different contracts grows, each demanding its own template, the reusability of the templates reduces, and the number of exceptions that need individual attention grows.

The management of extensions and change can quickly get out of hand if a new monolithic template is required with each small extension to existing ones. Where the monolithic templates have a considerable number of common parts, this would rapidly come to a point where it is expedient to break the monolithic templates into finer granularity clauses and devise rules for their assembly.

Use of a matchmaking engine that satisfies the requirements described above allows contract matchmaking to be achieved at a lower level of granularity. Individual contract clauses are advertised into the matchmaking engine. Each advertisement contains business rules describing the circumstances in which that particular clause should be included in the contract. Some clauses do not have variable content — they are just static text that is either included or excluded depending on the particular case. Other clauses have variable content that has to be configured on a case-by-case basis, i.e., they are dependent on the information from the query. The rules to compose that variable content are also included with the advertisement, together with a reference to the file that contains the static text of the clause.

This approach allows clauses to vary in size and complexity, and the whole approach of dynamically assembling and configuring the contract could be likened to having dynamic clause templates, where the template is constructed and filled to suit individual cases. The result is a system that can create individually tailored contracts with many variations, provided, of course, that those variations and possibilities have been foreseen and catered for with appropriate clause advertisements.

This example is drawn from a prototype system developed with the Matching Systems Engine.

Derivatives Confirmations

There is a requirement for banks and other players in derivatives markets to confirm trades with a legal confirmation contract within a statutory period. This is frequently not achieved, and therefore, confirmations are sometimes agreed on up to a year after the trade commenced. Simple "vanilla trades" can often be handled with straightforward templates, but all other trades are typically dealt with by a legal department that drafts a confirmation based on a trade description.

The use of a matchmaking engine in this context can enable a bank to obtain automatically an immediate draft confirmation without the involvement of the legal department. The flexibility of the matchmaking system also ensures that subtle variations will be correctly handled (e.g., a particular client expecting a particular way of setting out the trade description). This will further reduce costs, as agreement with the trading party will be achieved more easily, and the approval process will be streamlined.

In this example application, an economic description of the trade is submitted to the matchmaking engine in the form of an XML document. The proposed trade is described using the Financial Products Mark-up Language (FpML™, 2003), an emerging standard developed for the purpose of describing financial trades. Additional information, such as client details and client credit ratings, is brought in from a data file, simulating the incorporation of additional information from a client database and external systems.

The matchmaking engine contains advertised clauses and dynamically determines which ones are appropriate, and returns the content for those clauses that is deal-specific. In a postmatchmaking phase, the Matching Systems Engine fetches the clause template data for the matching clauses [stored as simple hypertext markup language (HTML) files], and inserts the dynamically derived content into each clause template. The contract is then assembled by sorting and merging the completed templates, resulting in a single HTML file representing the draft contract. This is returned by the Matching Systems Engine, allowing the user to view or amend the document using a word-processing application, such as Microsoft Word.

The following sections look at the process of creating this matchmaking space in more detail, beginning with the definition of the clause templates.

The Clause Template

Figure 7 shows an extract from a contract confirming an equity derivatives trade.

It is a relatively simple task to identify those elements of the contract that will not vary according to the details of the trade (static content) and those that will (dynamic

Figure 7. An extract from a contract confirming an equity derivatives trade

Dear Fred Smith

The purpose of this letter (this "Confirmation") is to confirm the terms and conditions of the Transaction entered into between us on the Trade Date specified below (the "Transaction"). This Confirmation constitutes a "Confirmation" as referred to in the ISDA Master Agreement specified below.

The definitions and provisions contained in the 2002 ISDA Equity Derivatives Definitions (the "Equity Definitions"), as published by the International Swaps and Derivatives Association, Inc., are incorporated into this Confirmation. In the event of any inconsistency between the Equity Definitions and this Confirmation, this Confirmation will govern.

1. This Confirmation supplements, forms part of, and is subject to, the ISDA Master Agreement dated as of 28 May 2001, as amended and supplemented from time to time (the "Agreement"), between ABC Bank plc ("Party A") and XYZ Bank Inc. ("Party B"). All provisions contained in the Agreement govern this Confirmation except as expressly modified below.

2. The terms of the particular Transaction to which this Confirmation relates are as follows:

General Terms:

Trade Date:	13 July 2001
Option Style:	American
Option Type:	Call
Seller:	Party A
Buyer:	Party B
Shares:	STMicroelectronics N.V. ordinary shares
Number of Options:	150000
Strike Price:	32

Procedures for Exercise:

Commencement Date:	13 July 2001
Latest Exercise Time:	17:15:00 (local time in GBLO)
Expiration Date:	27 September 2001
Multiple Exercise:	Applicable
Minimum Number of Options:	1
Maximum Number of Options:	150000
Integral Multiple:	1
Automatic Exercise:	Applicable

content). We have highlighted the dynamic content in the above example. Populating the dynamic content programmatically would result in a reusable contract template that could be applied to similar trades that might involve different trading parties, dates, numbers of options, and the like.

However, such a template has severe limitations on its reusability. For example, if the third paragraph is always to be present, then this monolithic contract template can only be applied to trades between parties who have in place an ISDA Master Agreement. A different template would be required for trades between parties where no master agreement exists. Furthermore, different option styles have different procedures for exercise, so again, each possible option style would require a different monolithic template, and if multiple exercise were not applicable, the three lines immediately following should be omitted. Adopting this monolithic contract template approach would result in a proliferation of templates to suit the many-varied trading situations that can occur.

Figure 8. The resulting contract shown as an aggregation of several clauses, each with its information derived from the trade description

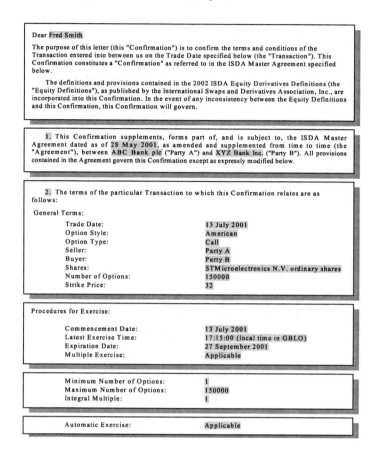

What is required is a more finely grained approach, whereby individual sections or clauses of the contract, which are templates containing both static and dynamic content, can be included in the overall contract according to the application of business rules. Figure 8 shows the same extract, divided into clauses. The granularity of our contract building block has changed so that each advertisement is now a clause template.

Notice that even the section numbers are now dynamic, because the total quantity and position of clauses will be variable. Notice also that there is a spectrum here in the granularity of the clause, from a single line to several paragraphs.

The Clause Advertisements

The dynamic parts of each of these contract clauses can be advertised in the Matching Systems Engine, while the static "template" parts can be stored in separate HTML files. For example, the advertisement of the fourth clause, "Procedures for Exercise" will contain string properties called "CommencementDate,"

"LatestExerciseTime," "LatestBusinessCentre," "ExpirationDate," and "MultipleExercise." In addition, it will contain a string property indicating the name of the file containing the static clause template, and numeric properties indicating the position of this clause relative to others in the overall contract. Finally, it will also contain a rule ensuring that the clause is only included in American option trades.

In this example, the properties submitted with the query represent the business agreement concerning the trade. Fortunately an XML standard already exists for describing derivatives trades, the FpML. The query properties presented to the matching engine can therefore be an FpML document describing the desired trade, and where advertisement properties or rules need to access query property values, these can be obtained with the use of xpath expressions.

The "Procedures for Exercise" clause advertisement is given below:

Property Name	Type	Value
Rule	Rule	return xpath("equityAmericanExercise[1]") != null;
Section	Long	2
Position	Long	6
File	String	"C:\Contracts\Clause\G6.htm"
CommencementDate	Dynamic String	xpath("//commencementDate/adjustableDate/unadjustedDate")
LatestExerciseTime	Dynamic String	xpath("//latestExerciseTimeType")
LatestBusinessCentre	Dynamic String	xpath("//latestExerciseTime/businessCenter")
ExpirationDate	Dynamic String	xpath("//expirationDate/adjustableDate/unadjustedDate")

MultipleExercise	Dynamic String	if (xpath("//equityMultipleExercise") == null)
		
		   return "Not Applicable";
		
		else
		
		   return "Applicable";

The rule will ensure that this clause is only selected if this trade is an American Equity trade, by returning *true* if the query properties contain an *equityAmericanExercise* section, and *false* if it does not.

The *Section* and *Position* properties enable the Matching Systems Engine to insert the clause in the right part of the document, if it is selected for inclusion in the final contract. The *File* property points to the file that contains the static "template" content of the clause, so that the Matching Systems Engine can reconcile the static and dynamic parts of the clause. The remaining properties represent the dynamic parts of the clause and obtain their values from the FpML (FpML, 2003) structure of the incoming query properties.

This example has been taken from a working prototype application, developed with the Matching Systems Engine. Once all possible clauses have been similarly described and advertised, the submission of an FpML query to the Matching Systems Engine triggers the matching process, and the rules of all clauses are evaluated. For those clause advertisements with rules that evaluate to *true*, the dynamic property expressions are evaluated, resulting in a set of matching clauses with resolved values for all of their descriptive properties.

Finally, a Java plug-in retrieves the static content from an HTML file and inserts the relevant dynamic content for each matching clause and assembles the contract by sorting the clauses according to their *Section* and *Position* properties. The resulting HTML document represents a complete contract, tailored to reflect the requirements of the deal described in the original FpML query.

MODEL OF THE TYPED DOMAIN AND ITS PROJECTIONS

This section shows how the generalization of the agreement transformation process can be used extensively when specifying a full relationship between organisations. In order to achieve this, we first develop a model of a domain and its information.

Managing Multiple Agreements

The relationship between two enterprises partnered in a virtual enterprise will involve more than one agreement over the course of the relationship life cycle (Hoffner, 2003; Dignum, 2001; Vetter, 2001). While below, we will illustrate the dynamic construction of a specific type of legal agreement between two banks, the method and technology described can be applied to a wide range of agreements and documents that form a partnership relationship, including the following:
- Agreements establishing a business relationship between partners
- Service agreements specifying services to be delivered, quality guarantees, costs, and payment terms
- Technical agreements specifying the ways in which the systems of the two enterprises will communicate with each other
- Legal agreements (i.e., legally enforceable contracts)

These different agreements that together describe the virtual enterprise relationship are related to each other. Each will have its own typed domain as described in the previous section, but those from different agreement types, they will inevitably share common data elements. The restricted typed domains of each agreement type can thus be combined to form a larger typed domain representing the information model for the spectrum of agreements that will be required to manage the relationship between the two partnering enterprises. Thus, each "subdomain" of a specific agreement type can be considered to be a projection of the larger relationship domain, and the relationship between the projections can be exploited to assist in the generation of agreements and documents.

Using Agreements to Generate Agreements

In a typed domain, the mapping among the projections is fully specified—every relationship specified in the domain will have its description in each of the projections, and these descriptions will be related to each other. Selecting a type of relationship in one projection and fixing some of its details is likely to reduce the options in the related projections that will fit the entire relationship. It is, therefore, possible to generalize from the example given previously of a business to legal agreement (contract) transformation, and conclude that other agreement transformation both within and between the projections is possible (Figure 9).

On occasions, it is easier to isolate those views and treat them (as much as is possible) separately. This often simplifies the negotiation process; thus, the business details may be discussed in isolation of the exact technical details, or the service may be discussed without referring to the business aspects. Similarly, business agreements are often done without explicit or direct reference to legal issues. The assumption is that those can be sorted out at another point. The assumption behind the separation is that there is a common model (of the domain of discourse) that allows assumptions to be made and provides the assurance that in spite of the separation, the entire relationship will work.

In the establishment stage of the life cycle, there are two general approaches for fully specifying a relationship in all projections:

1. Carry out the negotiation process (with matchmaking responsible for different degrees of it) with respect to all the projections at the same time.
2. Carry out the negotiation process with respect to a single or a mixture of some of the projections, then use the agreement reached to prune the options in the other projections and generate the agreement in the other projections.

This second approach has the advantage that having determined the type and details of the relationship in one projection, it is clear that there is at least one counterpart in each of the other projections that may satisfy the requirements of the other party and vice versa. Fixing the type and details of an agreement or document in one projection greatly reduces the number of options and therefore exchange of information and decisions that both sides have to make concerning the agreements and documents in other projections. A likely scenario is to negotiate the business agreement and then transform it into the other agreements. With each transformation, the degrees of freedom will be reduced, leaving less options and decisions to be made.

Figure 9. The generic process of transformation of an agreement in one projection into agreement in another projection

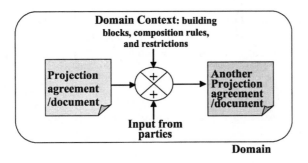

OPEN ISSUES AND AVENUES
FOR FURTHER RESEARCH

Underlying our information model of relationships is the belief that there is no single agreement between two organisations entering a complex service consumer–provider relationship. In fact, there are multiple agreements, among them a legal agreement — the contract. The different agreements and related information can be structured in a number of projections that help deal with the complexity of the relationships. A compelling reason for separating the different projections is that they are typically dealt with by different people in the organisations, for example, business managers, legal departments, IT departments, and operational departments. Yet another reason for the separation is that if appropriately structured within a well-defined context, the agreements and accompanying information can be transformed from one projection into another, reducing the complexity of many of the activities needed during the establishment, deployment, operation, and termination of a relationship between two organisations.

There is a need to accumulate experience with this model by looking at application domains where existing standards and conventions exist. Initially, domains based on monolithic templates should be investigated. Subsequently, it will be important to look for domains where the building blocks are of smaller granularity than the monolithic templates. Interestingly, once modularity is introduced as a means to create greater variety, it has to be reflected throughout the relationship life cycle, starting with components from which it is possible to build different services, as well as finer contract building blocks, such as contract clauses, from which it is possible to construct a variety of complete contracts. The equivalent modules mirroring the granularity of the service and contract building blocks must then also be created for other phases of the life cycle. Building blocks, rules, and mechanisms for composition must then be specified, and ways of checking the validity of these compositions must be developed.

REFERENCES

Angelov, S., & Grefen, P. (2003). *An analysis of the B2B e-contracting domain: Paradigms and required technology.* Beta Technical Report WP102. Eindhoven University of Technology, The Netherlands.

The ANSAware 4.1 Reference Manual. (1993). Castle Park, Cambridge, UK: Architecture Projects Management (APM). Available online *http://www.ansa.co.uk/*

Boundy, A. (1998). *A concise business guide to contract law.* Aldershot,UK: Gower Publishing.

Business Process Execution Language for Web Services. (2002). Version 1.0. Retrieved July 31, 2002 online *http://www-106.ibm.com/developerworks/library/ws-bpel/*

CrossFlow. (2000). Cross-organizational workflow support in virtual enterprises. ESPRIT Project 28635. Available online *http://www.crossflow.org/*

Dignum, F. (1991). Agents, markets, institutions and protocols. In F. Dignum & C. Sierra (Eds.), *Lecture notes in artificial intelligence: Vol. 1991. Agent Mediated Electronic Commerce, the European Agentlink Perspective* (pp. 98–114). Heidelberg: Springer-Verlag.

Facciorusso, C., Field, S., Hauser, R., Hoffner, Y., Humbel, R., Pawlitzek, R., Rjaibi. W., & Siminitz, C. (2003). A Web services matchmaking engine for Web services. In K. Bauknecht, A. Min Tjoa, & G. Quirchmayr (Eds.), *Lecture notes in computer science: Vol. 2738. E-commerce and Web technologies: Fourth International Conference, EC-Web, Prague, Czech Republic, September 2–5* (pp. 37–49). Heidelberg: Springer-Verlag.

Feller, J. (2002). IBM Web Services ToolKit—A Showcase for Emerging Web Services Technologies. Retrieved online *http://www-3.ibm.com/software/solutions/webservices/wstk-info.html*

Field, S., & Dazler, G. (2004). DESTION—A dynamic link between employers and their employee benefit providers. In L. M. Camarinha-Matos & H. Afsarmanesh (Eds.), *Processes and foundations for virtual organizations* (pp. 519–526). Dordrecht: Kluwer.

Field, S., & Hoffner, Y. (2002). In search of the right partner. In L.M. Camarinha-Matos (Ed.), *Collaborative business ecosystems and virtual enterprises* (pp. 56–62). Dordrecht: Kluwer.

FpML™. (2003). The XML standard for saps, derivatives and structured products. Retrieved online *http://www.fpml.org/*

Grefen, P., Aberer, K., Hoffner, Y., & Ludwig, H. (2000). CrossFlow: Cross-organizational workflow management in dynamic virtual enterprises. *International Computer Systems Science & Engineering, 15*, 277–290.

Griffel, F., Boger, M., Weinreich, H., Lamersdorf, W., & Merz, M. (1998). Electronic contracting with cosmos—How to establish, negotiate and execute electronic contracts on the Internet. In *Proceedings Second International Enterprise Distributed Object Computing Workshop (EDOC '98)*, La Jolla, CA.

Hoffner, Y. (2003). The e-Business on demand life cycle. In L.M. Camarinha-Matos & H. Afsarmanesh (Eds.), *Processes and foundations for virtual organizations*. Dordrecht: Kluwer.

Hoffner, Y., Facciorusso, C., Field, S., & Schade, A. (2000). Distribution issues in the design and implementation of a virtual market place. *Computer Networks, 32*, 717–730.

Hoffner, Y., Field, S., Grefen, P., & Ludwig, H. (2001a). Contract-driven creation and operation of virtual enterprises. *Computer Networks, 37*, 111–136.

Hoffner, Y., Ludwig, H., Grefen, P., & Aberer, K. (2001b). CrossFlow: Integrated workflow management and electronic commerce. ACM: Special Interest Group on Electronic Commerce, Vol. 2.1, Winter. Available online *http://www.acm.org/sigecom/exchanges*

Keller, A., & Ludwig, H. (2002). *The WSLA framework: Specifying and monitoring service level agreements for Web services*. IBM Research Report RC22456. IBM Research, T.J. Watson Research Center, Yorktown Heights, NY. Available online *http://domino.watson.ibm.com/library/CyberDig.nsf/home*

Meyer, B. (2000). Contracts for components. *Software Development Magazine*, July. Retrieved online *http://www.sdmagazine.com/articles/2000/0007/*

Milosevic, Z., & Dromey, R. G. (2002). On expressing and monitoring behaviour in contracts. In *Proceedings Sixth International Enterprise Distributed Object Computing Workshop (Edoc 02), Lausanne, Switzerland* (pp. 3–14). Los Alamitos, CA: IEEE Computer Society.

Milosevic, Z., Berry, A., Bond, A., & Raymond, K. (1995). An architecture for supporting business contracts in open distributed systems. In *Proceedings of the Second International Workshop on Services in Open Distributed Processing (SDNE95), Whistler, Canada*. Retrieved online *http://staff.dstc.edu.au/zoran/papers/SNDE95.ps*

Neal, S., Cole, J., Linnington, P., Milosevic, Z., Gibson, S., & Kulkarni, S. (2003). Identifying requirements for business contract language: A monitoring perspective. In *Proceedings Seventh International Enterprise Distributed Object Computing Workshop (EDOC 03), Brisbane, Queensland, Australia* (pp. 50–61). Los Alamitos, CA: IEEE Computer Society.

New Jersey Law Revision Commission (NJLRC). (1998). Final report relating to "Standard Form Contracts." John M. Cannel, Executive Director, New Jersey Law Revision Commission, Newark, NJ. Retrieved online *http://www.lawrev.state.nj.us/rpts/contract.pdf*

ODP. (1995). Open Distributed Processing Reference Model. ISO/IEC 10476, ITU-T Recommendation X.900, Parts 1–3.

OMG. (1996). Object Management Group and X/Open Standard: CORBA Trading Object Service. Document orbos/96-05-6.

OMG, (2003). Object Management Group, CORBA 3.0: Common Object Request Broker Specification. Retrieved online *http://www.omg.org/technology/documents/formal/corba_2.htm*.

Smith, J. C. (1989). *The law of contract*. London: Sweet & Maxwell Ltd.

Ströbel, M. (2002). *Engineering electronic negotiations*. New York: Kluwer.

Vetter, M., & Pitsch, S. (2001). Towards a flexible trading process over the Internet. In F. Dignum & C. Sierra (Eds.), *Agent Mediated electronic commerce, The European Agentlink Perspective. Lecture Notes in Artificial Intelligence* (Vol. 1991, pp. 148–162). Heidelberg: Springer-Verlag.

Weigand, H., & van den Heuvel, W. J. (1998). Meta-patterns for electronic commerce transactions based on FLBC. In *Proceedings of the 31st Annual Hawaii International Conference on System Sciences, Vol. 4. Formal Aspects of Electronic Commerce Track* (pp. 0261ff). Los Alamitos, CA: IEEE Computer Society Press. Retrieved online *http://infolab.kub.nl/people/wjheuvel/hicss.ps*

Weigand, H., & van den Heuvel, W. J. (2002). Cross-organizational workflows integration using contracts (extended version of the OOPSLA2000 paper). *Decision Support Systems*, July.

WSDL. (2001). Web Services Description Language (WSDL) 1.1. W3C Note. 15 March. Retrieved online *http://www.w3.org/TR/wsdl*

Wienberg, F., & Merz, M. (2000). *The COSMOS Project*. Retrieved online.

Chapter XI

Contributions to an Electronic Institution Supporting Virtual Enterprises' Life Cycle

Ana Paula Rocha
University of Porto, Portugal

Henrique Lopes Cardoso
University of Porto, Portugal

Eugénio Oliveira
University of Porto, Portugal

ABSTRACT

Electronic commerce competitiveness, due to market openness and dynamics, enabled the arising of new organizational structures, as it is the case with virtual enterprises. The virtual enterprise (VE) concept can effectively answer to new demanding market requirements, as it combines the core competencies of independent and heterogeneous enterprises that collaborate in a temporary and loosely linked network, thereby presenting high flexibility and agility. However, institutional and social laws must be introduced here to enforce and regulate individual enterprises' behavior. An electronic institution is a framework that enables through a communication network automatic transactions between electronic business parties, according to sets of explicit institutional norms and rules. This chapter presents and discusses tools for automatic negotiation and operation monitoring that make an electronic institution a suitable framework for helping in the two most important stages of a VE's life cycle: formation and operation. Moreover, the electronic contract concept is defined and discussed.

INTRODUCTION

The growth of information and communication technology has changed the way traditional commerce has been done by eliminating time and space restrictions. A new way of commerce, based on network communications, encompasses two fields: the business-to-consumer (B2C) and the business-to-business (B2B) electronic commerce. In the B2C electronic commerce, business participants are individual buyers and sellers that announce and negotiate over a final product or service. In the B2B electronic commerce, contrary to what happens in B2C, the goal of the business transaction is not a final product, and generally, business participants are enterprises that need to include in their own processes products that are outside of their expertise domain or resources they do not own. The work reported here is related to the last-mentioned type of electronic commerce, that is, the B2B electronic commerce.

The electronic commerce has increased the business competitiveness, due both to the market openness and dynamics. Enterprises try to answer these new market requirements by engaging themselves in temporary corporations, thereby presenting a flexible structure that changes dynamically according to current market situations. This new agile organizational structure is called VE. All those enterprises collaborate for a global goal with their competencies, knowledge, and resources. Agility is possible, because individual enterprises that belong to the VE are loosely coupled in this networked structure, and, although working for the VE global goal, enterprises maintain their autonomy.

A computing platform named *ForEV* (acronym for *Virtual Enterprises Formation* equivalent in Portuguese) was developed for supporting the VE formation stage. The VE formation stage has as its primary objective the creation of an organization able to compete as well as respond to the demanding requirements coming from an open market, by including in that organization those enterprises that have either the higher competence or present the best transaction conditions for that business opportunity. Our approach includes an iterative, adaptive, multiattribute negotiation protocol using qualitative argumentation (the "Q-negotiation" algorithm).

The negotiation that takes place during the VE formation stage leads to the agreement of an electronic contract that should be signed by all individual enterprises selected as partners in the VE. The VE operation stage uses this electronic contract to monitor the VE activity. The electronic contract describes the rights and duties of all VE partners, as well as penalties to apply to those that do not satisfy the agreement.

The rationale of this chapter includes the understanding of the VE concept, a definition of a generic model of an electronic institution, our proposal of tools enabling the electronic institution's role in helping in the VE formation stage, the exploitation of electronic-contracting services within an electronic institution that helps in the VE operation stage, and conclusions and directions for future work.

VIRTUAL ENTERPRISE

The VE is generally associated with the concept of a network of enterprises. However, a network of enterprises is not, necessarily, a VE. Figure 1 summarizes and clarifies several networked organizations categories according to two dimensions:

uncertainty and mutual dependency (Camarinha & Afsarmanesh, 1999; Jagers, Jasen, & Steenbakkers, 1998). The uncertainty level measures the uncertainty found by one enterprise when initiating a business relationship with other enterprises in the network. The mutual dependency level measures the enterprise's autonomy.

An *extended enterprise* can be seen as a network of enterprises where one is dominant, and thereby subcontracts other (dominated) enterprises by outsourcing the products it needs.

In a *strategic alliance*, all enterprises have interest in each others' success, because their activities are mutually dependent.

The organizational structure named *VE* presents a more democratic structure than the extended enterprise, where all its members are equally important. The main difference between a *stable VE* and a *dynamic VE* (or simply VE) is that in the first case, members are chosen from a closed set of already known enterprises, while in the second case, enterprises are in an open network and are not known in advance.

A *virtual organization* differs from the VE, because its members can be any kind of organization (with or without profit means), and not necessarily enterprises.

The *networked organization* encompasses all organizational structures where participants are entities linked with a computational network.

The subject of our study is the VE structure, that is, a set of independent networked enterprises that cooperate to a global goal. Following this general VE definition, different visions can even be formulated according to different authors. These are summarized in the following three topics:

- A temporary enterprise network (Fischer, Muller, Heimig, & Scheer, 1996; Peterson & Gruninger, 2000)
- A permanent network of enterprises (Camarinha & Lima, 1998)
- Virtual images of an enterprise structure and available data (Shmeil & Oliveira, 1997)

Figure 1. Networked organisational structures

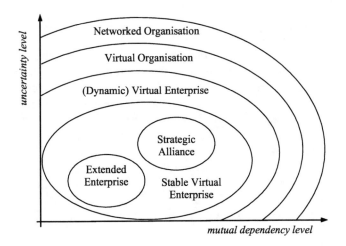

Our perspective on a VE is related to the first of these views, and a complete definition can be formulated as follows (Rocha & Oliveira, 2002): "A Virtual Enterprise is a temporary aggregation of autonomous and independent enterprises connected through a network and brought together to deliver a product or service in response to a customer need (Rocha & Oliveira, 2002, p. 232)."

In an electronic market, because of its openness, transactions complexity is increased due both to the huge amount of available information and the environment dynamics. The presence of a large number of business participants also originates higher market competition and increases the customers' demands. The response to these market requirements implies a new organization's concept that needs to have a (virtual) very large size needed for satisfying all the required skills. However, this type of organization, contrary to what happens with large traditional organizations, has to be flexible enough in order to deal with the dynamics of the market. VEs can satisfy these new challenges, as they combine the core competencies of several autonomous and heterogeneous enterprises aggregated in a temporary network, thereby presenting high flexibility and agility.

The VE life cycle is decomposed in four stages (Fischer et al., 1996), as follows:

- *Identification of needs*: Appropriate description of the product or service to be delivered by the VE, which guides the conceptual design of the VE
- *Formation (Partners Selection)*: Automatic selection of the individual organizations (partners), which based in its specific knowledge, skills, resources, costs, and availability, will integrate the VE
- *Operation*: Controlling and monitoring the partners' activities, including resolution of potential conflicts, and possible VE reconfiguration due to partial failures
- *Dissolution*: Breaking up the VE, distributing the obtained profits, and storing relevant information for future use for the electronic institution

Electronic tools for helping on the automatic VE life cycle imply the need of a framework for secure and reliable agents' encounters. The next section describes the electronic institution, which provides the means for helping on several stages of the VE life cycle.

ELECTRONIC INSTITUTION

An electronic institution (EI) is a framework that enables, through a communication network, automatic transactions between parties, according to sets of explicit institutional norms and rules. Thereby, the EI ensures the trust and confidence needed in any electronic transaction. However, each EI will be dependent on the specific application domain for which it has been designed. Here, we need to introduce the notion of a meta-institution, which is a shell for generating specific electronic institutions for particular application domains. The meta-institution includes general modules related to social and institutional behavior norms and rules, ontology services, as well as links to other institutions (financial, legal, etc.). The main goal of a meta-institution is to generate specific electronic institutions through the instantiation of some of these modules that are domain dependent according to the current application domain.

Figure 2. General architecture of an electronic institution

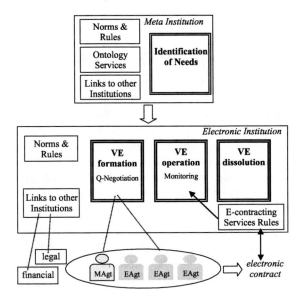

In this chapter, the electronic institution framework is analyzed in the VE scenario, and it can effectively help in making automatic several aspects of the VE's life cycle. It helps in both providing tools and services for supervising the intended relationships between parties. Figure 2 presents the general architecture of an electronic institution used in the VE scenario.

The meta-institution, as said previously, generates specific electronic institutions through the instantiation of some of these modules that are domain dependent. So, it can help in the first VE life cycle stage (the Identification of Needs), where a particular customer/market need is identified, that will be the goal of the future VE. The VE Identification of Needs stage will not be detailed here, we only note that the result of this stage is the instantiation of an electronic institution for a particular application domain.

In the next section, we discuss the electronic institution services to help in the second VE life cycle stage, that is, the VE formation process. The VE formation stage has as its primary objective the creation of an organization composed of several independent and possibly heterogeneous enterprises, which have higher competence for that business opportunity. Our approach includes an iterative, adaptive, multiattribute negotiation protocol using qualitative argumentation (the "Q-negotiation" algorithm).

In electronic transactions, in general, and in the VE formation, in particular, an important issue is to preserve the enterprise's private information during the negotiation process. An entity participating in a business transaction, and an enterprise in particular, tries to hide from the market its own private evaluation of the goods under negotiation. Adaptation is another important characteristic to be included in any entity present in an electronic market. Moreover, simultaneous partial interdependent negotiations may arise during the VE formation stage. The following sections detail the Q-negotiation algorithm, highlighting these advanced negotiation issues.

THE NEGOTIATION PROCESS

In the VE formation process, participants in the negotiation can be either market or enterprise agents. The market agent plays the role of organizer, meaning that it is the agent that starts and guides all the negotiation process. The enterprise agents play the role of respondents, meaning that they are those who are willing to belong to the future VE, and therefore, they have to submit proposals during the negotiation phase. We consider that the VE goal is decomposed in a set of components, and for each of these components, an independent negotiation process takes place. Multiple negotiations are done simultaneously during the VE formation process.

The Negotiation Protocol

In order to agree in a VE structure, agents (market and several enterprises) naturally engage themselves in a sequential negotiation process composed of multiple rounds of proposals (sent by enterprises to market) and counterproposals that are actually comments to past proposals (sent by market to enterprises). This is what really happens in traditional commerce, where humans exchange proposals and counterproposals trying to convince each other to modify the issues' values that they evaluate the most. A negotiation protocol should then be defined in order to select the participants that, based on capabilities and availability, will be able to make the optimal deal according to its own goals.

Our proposed Q-negotiation algorithm introduces new and important advanced features in electronic markets' negotiation: *multiple-attribute negotiation*, *learning in negotiation*, *distributed dependencies resolution*. These features are detailed in the next sections.

Multiattribute Bid Evaluation

Negotiation implies, for most of the economic transactions, that not only one, but multiple, attributes for defining the goods under discussion be taken into consideration. For instance, although the price of any good is an important (perhaps the most important) attribute, delivery time and quality can also be, and generally are, complementary issues to include in the decision about to buy or sell or not a specific good.

Attaching utility values to different attributes under negotiation solves the problem of multiattribute evaluation. Generally, an evaluation formula is a linear combination of the attributes' values weighted by their corresponding utility values. In this way, a multiattribute negotiation is simply converted in a single attribute negotiation, where the result of the evaluation function can be seen as this single issue (Vulkan & Jennings, 1998).

However, in some cases, it could be difficult to specify absolute numeric values to quantify the attributes' utility. A more natural and realistic way is to simply impose a preference order over attributes. The multiattribute function presented in formula (1) encodes the attributes' and attributes values' preferences in a qualitative way and, at the same time, accommodates intradependencies of the attributes.

$$Ev \;=\; \frac{1}{Deviation}, \quad Deviation \;=\; \frac{1}{n} * \sum_{i=1}^{n} \frac{i}{n} * dif(\text{PrefV}_i, \text{V}_i) \qquad (1)$$

where n = number of attributes that defines a specific component,

$$V_x = f(V_1, .., V_n), \quad x \notin \{1, ..., n\}, \text{ and}$$

$$dif(\text{PrefV}_i, V_i) \;=\; \begin{cases} \dfrac{V_i - \text{PrefV}_i}{\max_i - \min_i} & , \;\; \textit{if continuous domain} \\[2mm] \dfrac{Pos(V_i) - Pos(\text{PrefV}_i)}{nvalues} & , \;\; \textit{if discrete domain} \end{cases}$$

A proposal's evaluation value is calculated by the market agent, as the inverse of the weighted sum of the differences between the optimal ($PrefV_i$) and the real (V_i) value of each of the attributes. In the formula, each parcel should be presented in increasing order of preference, that is, attributes identified by lower indexes are least important than attributes identified with higher indexes. The proposal with the highest evaluation value so far is the winner, because it is the one that contains the attributes' values more closely related to the optimal ones from the market agent point of view.

The negotiation process is realized as a set of rounds (see Figure 3) where enterprise agents concede, from round to round, a little bit more, trying to approach the market agent preferences, in order to be selected as partners of the VE. The market agent helps enterprise agents in their task of formulating new proposals by giving them some hints about the directions they should follow in their negotiation space. These hints are given, by the market agent, as comments about attributes' values included in current proposals.

Figure 3. Negotiation protocol

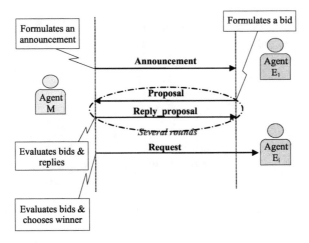

Qualitative Feedback Formulation

The response to proposed bids is formulated by the market agent as qualitative feedback, which reflects the distance between the values indicated in a specific proposal and the optimal one received so far. The reason why the market agent compares a particular proposal with, not its optimal, but the best one received so far, can be explained by the fact that it is more convincing to say to an enterprise agent that there is a better proposal on the market than saying that its proposal is not the optimal one.

A qualitative feedback is then formulated by the market agent as a qualitative comment on each of the proposal's attributes values, which can be classified in one of three categories: sufficient, bad, or very bad.

Enterprise agents will use this feedback information to its past proposals, in order to formulate, in the next negotiation rounds, new proposals trying to follow the hints included in the feedback comments.

Learning in Bid Formulation

The Q-negotiation algorithm uses a reinforcement learning strategy based on Q-learning for the formulation of new proposals. The Q-learning algorithm (Watkins & Dayan, 1992) is a well-known reinforcement learning algorithm that maps evaluation values (Q-values) to paired state/action.

The selection of a reinforcement learning algorithm seems to be appropriate in the negotiation process that acts as a conduit to VE formation, because organization agents evolve in an, at least, partially unknown environment. And, in particular, Q-learning enables online learning that is an important capability in our specific scenario where agents will learn in a continuous way during the negotiation process, with information extracted from each one of the negotiation rounds, and not only in the end with the negotiation result.

Q-learning is based on the idea of rewarding actions that produce good results, and punishing those that produce bad results, as indicated by parameter r in the correspondent formula [see Equation (2)].

$$Q(s,a) \;=\; Q(s,a) + \alpha \left(r + \gamma \max_b Q(s',b) - Q(s,a) \right) \tag{2}$$

In the Q-negotiation process, we assume that:
- A state is defined by a set of attributes' values, thus representing a proposal.

$$s = \langle v_1, v_2, \ldots, v_n \rangle \quad \begin{array}{l} , n = number\ of\ attributes \\[4pt] , v_x : value\ of\ attribute\ x \end{array}$$

- An action is a relationship that is a modification of the attributes' values through the application of one of the functions: increase, decrease, or maintain.

$$a = \langle f_1, f_2, ..., f_n \rangle \quad \begin{array}{l} , n = number\ of\ attributes \\ \\ , f_x \in \{increase, decrease, ma\ \text{int}\ ain\} \end{array}$$

The adaptation of the Q-learning algorithm to our specific scenario, the formulation of new proposals in the negotiation to become VE partners, leads to the inclusion of two important features: how to calculate the reward value and what part of the exploration space to consider.

The reward value for a particular state is calculated according to the qualitative feedback received from the market agent, in response to the proposal derived from this state [see formula (3)].

$$r = \begin{cases} n & , \quad if\ winner \\ \dfrac{n}{2} - \sum_i penalty_i & , \quad if\ not\ winner \quad (0 \le penalty_i \le 1) \end{cases} \qquad (3)$$

The exploration space, which can became very large and thus implies a long time to learn, is reduced in order to include only those actions that can be considered as promising actions. A promising action is an action that can be applied to a previous state proposed to the market agent hints included in the feedback formulated by this agent.

Distributed Dependencies Resolution

One of the requirements for the negotiation protocol we are here proposing, besides dealing with intradependencies of attributes, is the capability to deal with attributes' interdependencies. This is an important requirement to be considered in our scenario, because in the VE formation process, interdependent negotiations take place simultaneously, and proposals received from different organization agents may have incompatible dependent attributes' values. Therefore, agents should negotiate in order to agree between them on mutual admissible values, what can be seen as a distributed dependencies satisfaction problem.

The distributed dependencies satisfaction problem has been the subject of attention of other researchers, addressing the study of both single (Yokoo, Durfee, Ishida, & Kuwabara, 1992) and multiple dependent variables (Armstrong & Durfee, 1997; Parunak, Ward, & Sauter, 1999). In the VE formation process, dependencies may occur between multiple variables, making the latter approaches more relevant to our research. The first mentioned paper (Armstrong & Durfee, 1997) describes algorithms to reach one possible solution, not the optimal one. The second paper (Parunak et al., 1999) introduces an algorithm that, although reaching the optimal solution, imposes that all agents involved in the mutual dependencies resolution process have to know all agents' private utility functions.

Different from all these proposals, our distributed dependencies satisfaction algorithm, besides reaching the optimal solution, keeps agents' information as much as possible private.

Each agent involved in the distributed dependent problem resolution should know its space of states, that is, all possible values for its own dependent attributes. Agents will then exchange between them alternative values for the dependent attributes, in order to approach an agreement. As in any iterative negotiation process, agents start the negotiation by proposing its optimal (from a local point of view) solution and, in the next rounds, start conceding trying to reach a consensus.

In order to properly understand the way the algorithm works, first we should introduce the concept of "decrement of the maximum utility" of an alternative state. State transitions are due to relaxation of one or more state variables. The decrement of the maximum utility of a particular alternative proposal can be calculated as the difference between the evaluation values of this alternative proposal and the optimal one. We will abbreviate "decrement of the maximum utility" to "decrement of the utility," meaning that the successive amount of utility agents has to concede compared to the (local) optimal bid. Formula (4) represents the decrement of utility for agent i, corresponding to the particular state s^k, where s^* is the agent's optimal state (proposal).

$$ du_i^k = Ev(s^*) - Ev(s^k) \qquad (4) $$

At each negotiation step, the agent selects as a new proposal the one that has the lowest decrement of the utility of those not yet proposed. During the negotiation process, agents do not reveal their own state's utility, but only the state's decrement utility, which enables keeping important information private.

This process ends when all agents cannot select a next state better than one already proposed. In this way, agents, although remaining self-interested, will converge for a solution that is the best possible for all of them together, because it represents the minimum joint of decrement of the utility. The joint decrement of the utility is calculated according to formula (5):

$$ jdu^k = \sum_{dag} du_{dag}^k \quad , dag = \{1...n\} \, set \, of \, mutual \, dependent \, agents \qquad (5) $$

After agreement in a global solution, agents involved in the dependencies resolution process generally get different local decrement of utility values, and, therefore, some agents become more penalized than others. In order to guarantee that all agents involved in the distributed dependencies resolution get the same real decrement of utility (rdu), the joint decrement of the utility will be distributed between them according to formula (6):

$$ rdu = \frac{jdu^m}{n}, \quad n = number \, of \, agents \qquad (6) $$

As a consequence, some agents have to pay or get a compensation value to others. Once agent i has previously calculated dui^m as its local decrement of utility, the compensation value is calculated according to formula (7):

$$cValue_i \;=\; rdu - du_i^m \tag{7}$$

If the agent's real decrement of the utility is greater than its local decrement of the utility, it will pay a compensation value to others, that is calculated as the difference of these two values. If not, the agent will get a compensation value.

Through all the steps mentioned before (multiattribute bid evaluation, learning in negotiation, and distributed dependencies resolution), the VE formation stage is accomplished. In the next sections, we will discuss how to formalize through an e-contract all the commitments that have been made.

E-CONTRACTING

The result of the negotiation process leading to the VE formation should be "compiled" in an electronic contract that establishes rights and duties, as well as associated penalties, for all the individual enterprises included in the final agreement. This electronic contract can be used in the VE operation stage, for the sake of monitoring all the VE activities.

In B2B electronic commerce, more attention has been given recently to contract formation and fulfillment. In fact, this issue is part of the so-called B2B life cycle model, as presented in He, Jennings, and Leung (2003). Approaches to B2B contract handling (e.g., Goodchild, Herring, & Milosevic, 2000) identify the need to specify and represent contracts, and further to monitor and enforce them.

Figure 4 shows some of the services that may be available within an electronic institution. When considering contracts as the result of a business negotiation process, we can identify certain typified relations that can be assisted through the use of contract templates. After the negotiation phase, the obtained contract must be checked for compliance to existing business norms; it is then registered with a notary. The business relation is then carried out, and services like contract monitoring and enforcement may be provided, ensuring coherent behavior between the parties and registering the fulfillment of transactions. In the following subsections, we develop these issues.

Figure 4. E-contracting services

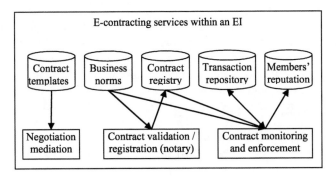

E-Contracts and Norms

Contracts are formalizations of the behavior of a group of agents that jointly agree on a specific business activity. Contracts are used as a means of securing transactions between the involved parties, forming a normative structure that explicitly expresses their behavior interdependencies. *Electronic contracts* are virtual representations of such contracts. The aim of e-contracting is to improve the efficiency of contracting processes, supporting an increasing automation of both e-contract construction (using automated tools) and execution (integrating with business processes).

The components of a contract include the identification of the participants, the specification of the products and/or services included, and a discrimination of the actions to be performed by each of the participants. These actions are normally accompanied with time and precedence constraints. Typified business relations can recurrently use preformatted contracts. In this case, contracts usually have a set of identified *roles* to be fulfilled by the parties involved in the relation.

The core of a contract is composed of contract clauses. These clauses can specify different types of behavior *norms* that will guide the interaction between the parties. This normative conception of contracts is generally adopted (e.g., Dignum & Dignum, 2001; Kollingbaum & Norman, 2002; Sallé, 2002). Broadly speaking, three types of norms can exist within a contract structure:

*   *Obligation*: an agent has an obligation to another agent to bring about a certain state of affairs (by executing some action), before a certain deadline
*   *Permission*: an agent is allowed to execute some action, within a given window of opportunity (specified either by a deadline or more generally by a state of affairs)
*   *Prohibition*: an agent is forbidden to bring about a certain state of affairs (some action is interdicted)

A formal approach to model such norms is *deontic logic* (von Wright, 1950; Meyer, 1988), which is also known as the logic of normative concepts, a branch of modal logic. The normative concepts obligation, permission, and prohibition are analogous to the modal concepts of necessity, possibility, and impossibility, respectively.

When representing contracts, another fundamental concept is typically added to the norms above: the *sanction*. Any obligation must be accompanied by at least one sanction, as obligations without sanctions are ineffective (Kollingbaum & Norman, 2002). Thus, obligations are not absolute but are relative to their associated sanctions in case of nonperformance (Sallé, 2002). Prohibitions can be addressed in an analogous way. A prohibition is sometimes handled as a negated obligation, that is, a duty for not performing some action (see, for instance, Kollingbaum & Norman, 2002).

Approaches to the automation of contractual relationships necessarily include this sanction component. Particularly when that automation is based on the autonomous agent paradigm, norms cannot be taken as constraints on the behavior of each contractual party. Each agent is able to deliberatively reason about its goals and the norms to which it has committed; hence, the notion, in Castelfranchi, Dignum, Jonker, and Treur (2000), of *deliberative normative agents*. An agent can violate a norm in order to accomplish a private goal that it considers to be more important. When doing so, the agent is aware of the sanction to which it will be subject. Some researchers address the advantages of anticipating sanctions (also called decommitment penalties) in multiagent contracting, introducing the concept of a *levelled commitment contract* (Sandholm & Lesser, 2001), and study reasoning decision processes that consider strategic breaches (Sandholm & Lesser, 2001; Excelente-Toledo, Bourne, & Jennings, 2001).

Norms and Electronic Institutions

Contracting is normally subject to contract law. This law is enforced by the court and can be seen as a normative system that contracts must respect. Furthermore, we can conceptualize norms at different levels of abstraction. For instance, we can consider those that are applied to contracts in general (thus being inherited in all established contracts), those that refer to particular contractual domains, and those that are created when a specific business relation is formalized.

Electronic institutions, while regulating the interactions that can take place between agents, can represent normative systems that limit the behavior of participants and describe the penalties incurred when norms are violated (Dignum, 2001). Contractual relations created inside the institution must abide to the imposed norms, specifying the details of a particular business relation. This two-level conception of normative agent interactions is proposed by some researchers. In Dignum and Dignum (2001), the authors model a society of agents distinguishing between an institutional level (where social norms and rules are specified) and an operational level (dependent on the goals of each agent).

E-Contracting Life Cycle

Any contractual relationship can be said to evolve through a number of steps. These can be resumed to the following three stages:
* *Information discovery*: Clients find potential suppliers.
* *Contract negotiation*: The parties negotiate the contract terms — the result of this stage is a legally binding contract, reflecting the agreement made.
* *Execution*: The contract terms are fulfilled by the parties, namely involving product delivery or service rendering, and the corresponding payments.

The first stage thus comprises the brokering phase of B2B electronic commerce. One can also conceptualize it as a *precontractual phase* involving a definition of the products or services sought/sold by clients/suppliers, and the utilization of yellow-pages services allowing potential partners to contact each other.

The second stage is devoted to the negotiation of the terms of an agreement — it is the *contractual phase*, because a contract is being constructed. That agreement will express a number of steps to be performed by the contractual parties. Hence, the parties negotiate not only attributes of products/services (as explained in the ForEV platform) but also details of how those products/services will be delivered/rendered and paid. The document that represents the agreement reached is a legally binding contract, signed by those involved. Typically, it will also specify how to handle exception conditions, such as those related to nonfulfillment of duties (e.g., late delivery or nonpayment).

The third stage is the *postcontractual phase*, that is, after the contract is established, it is time to proceed as agreed. It is also referred to as the fulfillment phase. In more complex and integrated interactions, the parties involved will eventually engage their business processes, forming an interenterprise workflow.

Representing E-Contracts

A normative conception of contracts is normally used for contract representation. Hence, languages for representing norms in contracts have been proposed.

Normative statements, based on the operators of deontic logic, can be formally represented as follows (Sallé, 2002):

$$ns: \varphi \rightarrow \theta_{s,b}\,(\alpha < \psi)$$

where *ns* is a label; φ is an activation condition; θ is a deontic operator (obligation, permission, or prohibition); *s* is the subject of *q*; *b* is the beneficiary of *q*; α is the action to perform or the state of affairs to bring about; and ψ is a deadline.

In this approach, obligations are not absolute but are relative to their associated sanctions. That is, deviation from prescribed behavior is admitted and properly addressed through sanctions. These are defined just like the other normative statements, but by specifying as the activation condition the nonfulfillment of a given obligation. Sanctions may give rise to other obligations or prohibitions: either the beneficiary of the violated norm is granted a right (the subject has a new obligation toward the beneficiary) or the subject of the violated norm is refused a right (he is forbidden to do something).

A number of standards for contract representation are also emerging, mostly founded on rule-based markup languages (see Angelov & Grefen, 2001, for a survey). Developing on these standards, Grosof and Poon (2002) described the SweetDeal system as a rule-based approach to the representation of business contracts. Emerging Semantic Web standards for knowledge representation of rules (RuleML) are combined with ontology representation languages (DAML+OIL).

E-Contract Negotiation

When the outcome of the negotiation phase is to be formally represented and (eventually) automatically executed, it is beneficial to consider this formal representation in the negotiation phase.

The need for a starting ground in contracting is acknowledged by several researchers (see, for instance, Kollingbaum & Norman, 2002; Sallé, 2002). In fact, starting a negotiation where nothing is fixed represents a problem that is too ill-structured to consider automating. The importance of a *contract template* resides on its ability to provide a structure on which negotiation can be based.

Certain kinds of business relations are formally typified (for instance, sales and purchases). In this sense, instead of beginning from scratch a new contractual relation, two (or more) agents can use an electronic contract template, which is a contract outline containing domain-independent interaction schemata and variable elements (such as price, quantity, deadlines, and so on) to be filled in with domain-specific data resulting from a negotiation (Kollingbaum & Norman, 2002). If all goes well, the result of the negotiation will be an actual contract, instantiated from the template, that will be signed by the parties. Templates thus provide a structure that allows negotiation, as a process of cooperative construction of a business relation, to be focused on those elements that, when instantiated, will distinguish the agreement obtained from other contractual relationships. Meanwhile, the common elements in relations of the same type will be preserved. These common elements might include, for example, outlined commitments of the involved parties, which when instantiated through negotiation will detail their concrete objects (eventually including technical properties) and temporal references.

As already described within the *ForEV* framework, negotiation mediation services are important mechanisms that allow business agreements to be obtained in a regulated fashion. Preestablished protocols can be used, taking advantage of template structures and ensuring that resulting contracts are in accordance with business norms.

Electronic institutions can provide means of validating contracts, by checking them against existing institutional norms. Valid (and signed) contracts are then stored using notary services, in order to ensure their legal existence.

E-Contract Execution

The execution of an e-contract consists of the parties following the norms they committed to when signing the contract. If any deviations from the prescribed behavior should occur, sanctions can be applied as specified in the contract or in its normative system of reference. However, the parties involved will typically not voluntarily submit themselves to such penalties. Therefore, appropriate mechanisms are needed to monitor and enforce norm execution. Within the framework of electronic institutions, monitoring and enforcement services can be rendered by the institution. Only a trusted third party can enable the necessary level of confidence between the parties involved in a business relation.

In Kollingbaum and Norman (2002), a supervised interaction framework is proposed, where a trusted third party is included as part of any automated business transaction. Agents are organized in three-party relationships between two contracting individuals (a client and a supplier) and an authority that monitors the execution of contracts, verifying that errant behavior is either prevented or sanctioned. This authority enables the marketplace to evaluate participants, keeping reputation records on the basis of past business transactions.

In Sallé (2002), a *contract fulfillment protocol (CFP)* is proposed, a collaborative protocol based on the normative statements' life cycle. The idea is that as contractual relationships are distributed, there is a need to synchronize the different views each agent has about the fulfillment of each contractual commitment. Each norm has a set of states it might go through. For instance, an obligation is first *agreed* (when the contract is signed), it then becomes *pending*, and later on might be *refused* (triggering appropriate sanctions) or *accepted*. In the latter case, it will become *in progress* and afterwards *executed*. When executed, it might be *rejected* (again requiring correction measures) or considered as *fulfilled*. Agents use this life cycle to communicate their intentions on fulfilling contractual norms, allowing their contractual partners to know what to expect from them. This ability is referred to as *dynamic forecasting of partners' behavior*, and it permits a fluent and prompt execution of contracts, as agents do not have to wait for the fulfillment of their partners' obligations to start executing their own (hence the collaborative nature).

The real-world application of agents in automated contract fulfillment is challenged by the presence of complex legal issues and subjective judgments of agent compliance (He et al., 2003). Some work on these matters has been made, for instance, in Daskalopulu, Dimitrakos, and Maibaum (2001), where an e-market controller agent (a third party) is

244 Rocha, Cardoso & Oliveira

suggested to resolve disputes arising from subjective views on contract compliance, thereby playing the role of a judge. This agent holds a representation of the contract, and when a conflict occurs, it collects evidence from the involved parties and obtains information from independent advisors, such as certification authorities, regulators, or controllers of other associated markets.

FUTURE TRENDS AND CONCLUSIONS

ForEV is an agent-based tool we have developed aiming at facilitating automatic partners selection in the context of VEs.

Appropriate negotiation protocols, for multiattribute evaluation, keeping information private as much as possible, and solving mutual constraints between attributes, are efficient tools to be used by agents as delegates of enterprises in finding the best temporary consortium to respond to an opportunity of business.

The VE formation stage has been tested in a simplified textile example using the *ForEV* framework, and a coherent consortium was established.

However, we soon realize that these facilities need to be made available in the context of a larger framework representing some secure, trustful institution, responsible for supervising the entire VE life cycle.

An electronic institution, as we are proposing here, encompasses all the facilities needed to help in the VE formation and operation processes, making it possible to follow these steps and enforcing agents to comply with norms and rules according to their specific roles in the VE.

Our next move will be the inclusion of a real, flexible although compliant electronic contract, as a result of the negotiation process between all the parties, so as to be explored during the VE operation phase. The electronic contract will be the guarantee that what was previewed and agreed upon is being accomplished and that the right measures will be taken whenever agent misbehavior occurs. Also, learning facilities to derive new rules of behavior from past events and situations have to be included in the electronic institution, enabling both an evolution along time and some specialization of the general rules for specific scenarios.

We see, thus, *ForEV* as a seed for a more complex tool helping VEs along their life cycles.

REFERENCES

Angelov, S., & Grefen, P. (2001). *B2B eContract handling—A survey of projects, papers and standards*. University of Twente: CTIT Technical Reports.

Armstrong, A., & Durfee, E. (1997). Dynamic prioritization of complex agents in distributed constraint satisfaction problems. In M. Pollack (Ed.), *Proceedings of the 15th International Joint Conference on Artificial Intelligence* (pp. 620-625). Nagoya, Japan: Morgan Kaufmann Publishers.

Camarinha-Matos, L., & Lima, C. (1998). A framework for cooperation in virtual enterprises. In J. Mills & F. Kimura (Eds.), *Information infrastructure systems for manufacturing* (pp. 305–321). Dordrecht: Kluwer.

Castelfranchi, C., Dignum, F., Jonker, C., & Treur, J. (2000). Deliberative normative agents: Principles and architectures. In N. Jennings & Y. Lesperance (Eds.), *Intelligent agents VI: Agent theories, architectures, and languages* (pp. 364–378). Heidelberg: Springer.

Daskalopulu, A., Dimitrakos, T., & Maibaum, T. (2001). E-contract fulfilment and Agents' attitudes. Presented at *Proceedings of the ERCIM WG E-Commerce Workshop on the Role of Trust in e-Business*, Zurich, Switzerland.

Dignum, F. (2001). Agents, markets, institutions and protocols. In F. Dignum & C. Sierra (Eds.), *Agent mediated electronic commerce: The European Agentlink perspective* (pp. 98–114). Heidelberg: Springer.

Dignum, V., & Dignum, F. (2001). Modelling agent societies: Co-ordination frameworks and institutions. In P. Brazdil & A. Jorge (Eds.), *Progress in artificial intelligence: Knowledge extraction, multi-agent systems, logic programming, and constraint solving* (pp. 191–204). Heidelberg: Springer.

Excelente-Toledo, C. B., Bourne, R. A., & Jennings, N. R. (2001). Reasoning about commitments and penalties for coordination between autonomous agents. In E. André, S. Sen, C. Frasson, & J. P. Müller (Eds.), *Proceedings of the Fifth International Conference on Autonomous Agents* (pp. 131–138). New York: ACM Press.

Fischer, K., Muller, J., Heimig, I., & Scheer, A. (1996). Intelligent agents in virtual enterprises. In B. Crabtree & N. Jennings (Eds.), *Proceedings of the 1st International Conference on the Practical Application of Intelligent Agents and Multi-Agent Technology* (pp. 205-223). London: The Practical Application Company Ltd.

Goodchild, A., Herring, C., & Milosevic, Z. (2000). Business contracts for B2B. In H. Ludwig, Y. Hoffner, C. Bussler, & M. Bichler (Eds.), *Proceedings of the CAISE'00 Workshop on Infrastructure for Dynamic Business-to-Business Service Outsourcing (ISDO'00)* (pp. 63–74). CEUR Workshop Proceedings.

Grosof, B., & Poon, T. C. (2002). Representing agent contracts with exceptions using XML rules, ontologies, and process descriptions. In *Proceedings of the International Workshop on Rule Markup Languages for Business Rules on the Semantic Web, First International Semantic Web Conference*. Sardinia, Italy.

He, M., Jennings, N. R., & Leung, H. (2003). On agent-mediated electronic commerce. *IEEE Transactions on Knowledge and Data Engineering, 15*(4), 985–1003.

Jagers, H., Jansen, W., & Steenbakkers, G. (1998). *Characteristics of virtual organisations*. Working Paper 98-02. Department of Information Management, University of Amsterdam, The Netherlands.

Kollingbaum, M. J., & Norman, T. J. (2002). Supervised interaction—Creating a Web of trust for contracting agents in electronic environments. In C. Castelfranchi & W. Johnson (Eds.), *Proceedings of the First International Joint Conference on Autonomous Agents and Multiagent Systems: Part 1* (pp. 272–279). New York: ACM Press.

Meyer, J.-J. C. (1988). A different approach to deontic logic: Deontic logic viewed as a variant of dynamic logic. *Notre Dame Journal of Formal Logic, 29*(1), 109–136.

Parunak, H., Ward, A., & Sauter, J. (1999). The MarCon algorithm: A systematic market approach to distributed constraint problems. *Artificial Intelligence for Engineering Design Analysis and Manufacturing Journal, 13*, 217–234.

Peterson, S., & Gruninger, M. (2000). An agent-based model to support the formation of virtual enterprises. In *Proceedings of the International ICSC Symposium on Mobile Agents and Multi-Agents in Virtual Organisations and E-Commerce.* Woolongong, Australia: ICSC Academic Press.

Rocha, A., & Oliveira, E. (2001). Electronic institutions as a framework for agents' negotiation and mutual commitment. In P. Brazdil & A. Jorge (Eds.), *Progress in artificial intelligence: Knowledg extraction, multi-agent systems, logic programming, and constraint solving* (pp. 232-245). Springer.

Sallé, M. (2002). Electronic contract framework for contractual agents. In R. Cohen & B. Spencer (Eds.), *Advances in Artificial Intelligence: 15th Conference of the Canadian Society for Computational Studies of Intelligence* (pp. 349-353). Springer.

Sandholm, T. W., & Lesser, V. R. (2001). Leveled commitment Ccontracts and strategic breach. *Games and Economic Behavior, 35,* 212–270.

Shmeil, M., & Oliveira, E. (1997). The establishment of partnerships to create virtual organisations: A multi-agent approach. In L. Camarinha-Matos (Eds.), *Re-engineering for sustainable industrial production* (pp. 284–294). London; New York: Chapman & Hall.

Vulkan, N., & Jennings, N. (1998). Efficient mechanisms for the supply of services in multi-agent environments. In *Proceedings of the First International Conference on Information and Computing Economics* (pp. 1-10). Charleston, SC: ACM Press.

Watkins, C., & Dayan, P. (1992). Q-learning. *Machine Learning,* 8(3/4), 279–292.

Wright, G. von (1950). Deontic logic. *Mind, 60,* 1–15.

Yokoo, M., Durfee, E., Ishida, T., & Kuwabara, K. (1992). Distributed constraint satisfaction for formalizing distributed problem solving. In *Proceedings of the 12th International Conference on Distributed Computing Systems* (pp. 614-621). Yokohama, Japan: IEEE Computer Society.

Chapter XII

Use of Situation Room Analysis to Enhance Business Integration Aspects of a Virtual Enterprise

Bob Roberts
Kingston University, UK

Adamantios Koumpis
ALTEC S.A., Greece

ABSTRACT

In this chapter, we present recent results of a wider research work in defining a methodological framework for situation room analysis (SRA) and its deployment for complex (business enterprise) systems study. Within this remit, we also consider virtual organizations as dynamic value constellations with certain challenges involved for realizing both business efficiency and technology integration. In our approach, we propose the use of ontologies as a powerful means to support the implementation of multiparty collaboration and decision-making activities that build on the paradigm of a situation room (SR). The approach described places heavy emphasis on the notion of Web technologies and their adaptation for achieving the IT enabled shift to this more efficient process orientation.

INTRODUCTION: SETTING THE STAGE

In the world of business, changes in the working environment of enterprises are now driven by the needs of industry to respond in an agile manner to market forces, such as customer demands, increased competition, and shifting patterns of global trade, etc. This also requires a clear identification and redeployment of traditional business functions.

A major challenge for virtual enterprises (VEs) in that respect is the integration of their various heterogeneous organizational structures, information and communication infrastructures, and personnel. There also remains a need for greater understanding of how such virtual enterprises will operate in a "shared data/information/knowledge environment," through distributed working approaches and based on the paradigm of using the SR metaphor as the core paradigm for carrying out joint operations.

According to Putnik (2000), there is not a universally accepted definition of the VE concept and he suggests at least two (main) approaches in VE concept definition, or specification:

"In the first approach the most important characteristic of the virtual enterprise concept is dynamic networking of enterprises [...]. The second approach emphasizes the 'virtuality' of the system [...] The VE is reduced to the simulation program."

In the following pages we shall present achievements of wider research work in defining a methodological framework for situation room analysis (SRA) and its deployment for complex (business enterprise) systems study. Within this remit we also consider virtual organisations as dynamic value constellations with certain challenges involved for realizing both business efficiency and technology integration.

Furthermore, in our approach we propose the use of ontologies as a powerful means to support the implementation of multi-party collaboration and decision-making activities that build on the paradigm of a situation room (SR). The approach is complementary to others in the area of business planning and is characterized as top-down in that the SR paradigm is conceptualized through three related models: the situation room model (SRM), the information management model (IMM), and the situation analysis model (SAM). The ontology-based approach includes the semantic features of the exchanged decision-making information, thus offering the integration of the SRA framework with existing corporate decision-making grids.

As a means for facilitating formation and life cycle management of VEs, we made use of concepts from two key information research areas. These deal with information flow management and with the shift from a function orientation of enterprises toward a more efficient process orientation.

The approach described places heavy emphasis on the notion of Web and object technologies and their adaptation for achieving the IT-enabled shift to this more efficient process orientation. It covers specification, design, and conceptual realization of how information supply chains and routes can be organized and navigated across VE activities within the context of a branch independent model (i.e., independent of any particular domain specializations governed by respective domain-specific rules).

The harmonized combination of the concepts formulated in the SRA theoretical framework and their IT realization can be employed within the context of real-world applications and in direct linkage with an industrial ERP system such as ALTEC's ATLANTIS® ERP.

SR ESSENTIALS

As mentioned in the first section, the, work presented forms part of a wider research in defining a methodological framework for SRA, and its deployment for complex (business enterprise) systems study. In our approach, we propose the use of ontologies as a powerful means to support the implementation of multiparty collaboration and decision-making activities that build on the paradigm of a SR. The latter term is broadly used in the context of military operations and has specific semantical connotations. These connotations are deliberately exploited in order to propose an analytical scheme based on it, which aims to assist planning initiatives and decision making in a particular application domain.

Like all systems of notation and semantics, SRA can never be anything but a model; it is a map to a territory, with validity that may be evaluated by reference to that underlying reality in the "real world."

Historically speaking, a SR is considered as the intelligence analysis centre used to stay abreast of the latest intelligence reports and updates. Such intelligence allow an army's or an army unit's senior officers to make informed command decisions and stay current on news throughout the federation of other units and beyond. Within this aim, i.e., the multiparty collaboration and decision-making activities from within the SRA framework, it is easy to see that the latter should be data driven. In this respect, we can consider the case of, for example, a company planning to create a virtual market response SR to improve how it collects and assesses information regarding its own and competitors' products. Such an approach would enable stakeholders to obtain important data in a more timely and effective manner.

For strategic decisions, senior management need information about markets, customers, and technology development in their industry as well as changing economic circumstances, among others. Bovet and Martha (2000), for example, argue that decision support systems have a critical role to play in supporting longer-term, strategic decisions across highly interdependent "value networks." However, such information systems have rarely satisfied this information requirement, and Ward and Peppard (2002) suggest that the main reasons for this include the paucity of external information included in the systems, the rawness of the data, and its lack of context. This latter point, in particular, underlines the requirement for knowledge as opposed to just information (Huplic, 2002; Skyrme, 1999).

The SRA framework proposed by Koumpis and Roberts (2003) emphasizes the idiosyncratic characteristics of the ICT sector, such as innovation, technological change, transfer of technology, and technology diffusion. These require the development of a design space where different scenarios will be subject to *in vitro* assessment and evaluation. The employment of the framework may take place during any phase of the life cycle of an ICT service or product, i.e., from the early design phases up to the phase of its launching into the market.

We regard our approach as complementary to others in the areas of business planning; (Mandal et al., 2003, p. 132), for example, suggest that managers should "conduct a pre-alliance planning exercise to assess the compatibility of business goals of partners, determine a method for implementation, and indicate the key informational as well as cultural challenges that may arise throughout the alliance's duration." In their work, they report on a set of key concepts related to the formation of an alliance that may prove critical for its successful execution, which include the "efficient and effective decision making." They argue that actions to build and sustain a strategic alliance include, among others, performance indicators concerned with benchmarking, knowledge management in the team environment, and decision making involved with technology management.

Collaborative business decision-making software, and all forms of business software, may be viewed as a representation or a set of symbols for some underlying reality. An analogy may be drawn with classic double-entry accounting systems that may be seen as providing both a methodology and metadata framework capable of representing different kinds of business transaction and financial state change that can exist in the business problem space. Similarly, there is a need for systems to describe corporate decision-making activities that build on (elementary) information management transactions. However, such a system also needs to represent subtle relationships and hierarchies, and it is at that point that the need to exploit the expressive power of ontologies comes to the foreground.

Furthermore, it seems that the central challenge faced by a VE will be the implementation of flexible, time-variant cooperation models. As a result, our work on dynamic change in the structure of information supply chains is of direct utility; it is essential nowadays for the created structures to be able to dynamically modify their formation (i.e., to evolve continuously) as time goes by and as various patterns fade in or out. A specific example of this is when supply-chain partners modify their behavior that in turn has knock-on effects on the related management systems of the VE's partners (e.g., purchasing, orders, design, production, control, resources, personnel, materials, quality, etc.).

Modelling Aspects of the SR

This section includes some additional information on the models pertaining to the SR concept. Our goal is to support high-level corporate operations, such as planning and project programming, by means of defining the SRA as a powerful vehicle to support this need. The main entities for defining the basics of SRA are related to:

- The concept of the SR per se
- The managed information within the SR
- The main items of the conducted analysis, which in our case, focus on products and services in the IT market

In regard to all three of them, three corresponding models are defined. Figure 1 illustrates these submodels, namely:

- The Situation Room Model (SRM)
- The Information Management Model (IMM)
- The Situation Analysis Model (SAM)

Figure 1. Three submodels of the SRA modelling space

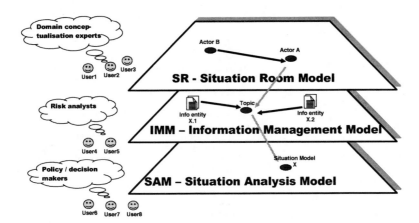

They all concern descriptive conceptualizations of entities and activities, annotated with the interactions and possible relationships among them, which results in a supermodel, namely, the SRA. Furthermore, we elaborate on this by providing the specifications for setting up the implementation of this to an IT framework using emerging technologies (XML, software agent, Semantic Web, and ontology technologies) and established system design approaches (UML). In both modeling and interpreting the impact of information in the context of the virtual network, the research is also informed by game theory and transaction cost theory (Friedman, 1991; Casson, 1991).

In Table 1, we provide a description of the supported actions on a given information entity, as this is realized within the information management model of the SRA framework.

As can be seen from Table 1, the central notion for an information entity within the information management model is linking it to other entities. Another important notion is that of *placeholders*, in which a specific entity will be input. These may either be predefined if we expect specific entities to populate them, or released *ad hoc*. Such ad hoc creation of a placeholder often takes place under time and resource pressure, and therefore, its results are usually suboptimal. For this reason, it is essential that placeholders be reconsidered on a periodic schedule and, if needed, can be adapted, renamed, or consolidated with others.

In regard to the placeholders, the same actions hold as for the information entity. There is, however, an exception, and this is for the creation of a new placeholder. The reason for this is that while a piece of information has arrived and we recognize its existence, a placeholder is an artificial artifact for which we are solely responsible for its construction. However, this is not always the case. There is frequently information creation, based on synthesis of other (previously existing) information or even "out of nothing." (This is a case of making some hypothesis, because we simply want to make it or need to make it.) It has been considered as out of the scope of our research to further investigate this aspect.

Table 1. Potential supported actions on an information entity

Number	Identifier	Action Type	Description
1	RM	Remove	It is destroyed as if it never came under consideration within a set structure under use in the SR. This is not a usual or recommended practice but may simplify procedures in several situations. A more recommended practice is to justify reasons for its irrelevance and ignore it (see below). However, as long as logging of events is taking place, tracing back to this state is possible.
2	IGN	Ignore	It exists but is not used for any current inferences made within a set structure under use in the SR. This is the case of trying to simplify a problem by ignoring (temporarily or permanently) a set of information regarding specific aspects of the subject under consideration.
3	LN	Link	With some other piece of information within a set structure under use in the SR. How? By means of choosing one of the enabled link types as described below [(a) through (f)].
3a	LN_TO	As above	Link as **related to** with a unidirectional link *to* the other information entity
3b	LN_FROM	As above	Link as **related to** with a unidirectional link *from* the other information entity
3c	LN_BOTH	As above	Link as **related to** with a unidirectional link *for both* information entities
3d	LN_ONL	As above	Link "only" to the other information entity without any further predefined relationship between them
3e	CUST_LN	As above	This type enables user-defined link types to be created by means of enabling users of the system to develop their own link categories, which may be domain- or user-specific and which may vary among each of the users or usage types.
3f	LN_LN	As above	This forms an important type of linkage as it provides the means to link one link with another link.
4	ADD	Add it	It concerns the insertion of a particular information entity to a set structure under use in the SR.
5	CRT	Create	Creation of a new placeholder

A further important aspect of the information management model relates to the ability to represent all actions performed or attributed to particular information entities. In this respect, what is actually needed is a "device" that guards some conditions and performs some actions when the conditions are true. This idea is not new in computer science theory and practice, as it is expressed by well-known metaphors like demons in artificial intelligence and triggers in databases, and it has been widely used in several modelling languages and development environments (see, for instance, Widom & Ceri, 1996). Our notion of a *linker element* (in brief: *linker*) realizes this idea in a slightly different fashion. While, normally, the condition is defined by a universal predicate, which means that the guard needs to observe the whole or a large part of a database to find any place where the condition is true, our linker works locally, as it guards only its own operands.

According to our approach, the linker is the only way:

- To express relationships among information entities, be they passive or active relationships: Thus, we use the same notion for describing both static information entities and actions to them. The uniformity allows actions to be treated in the same way as static links, i.e., we can add and delete actions in the same way as we add and delete static relationships during a database transaction.
- To define actions on information entities. In this respect, any action that takes place within the SR to enrich or explain an information entity is simply linked to the previous state of the entity, providing also the last inherently proprietary characteristic of that last action.

USE OF ONTOLOGIES

According to Hahn (2003), Semantic Web technologies and management tools can be used to link the model entities of a distributed model. More specifically, two integration concepts have been used:

- File-based, where the information is stored in an XML representation enriched with meta-information expressed in RDF (resource description framework)
- Online, where tools can provide the information online with an interface implemented as a Web service

A promising approach that we propose exploits semantic indexing techniques. The latter, though not new, is a sophisticated indexing schema that allows us to support the kinds of operations necessary in an efficient way.

The employed indexing scheme is based on ontologies: taxonomic information with additional links that represent associated properties. While some ontologies represent very general knowledge, others specifically target a particular domain (Ankolekar et al., 2001). We first need to define a mapping between the attributes used in the SR data warehouse and the terminology represented in the ontology. Users (are expected to) employ terms defined in the ontology when generating SR data warehouse queries. Ontologies can also provide a way to group records of a database in a semantically meaningful way. This type of semantic grouping can be used to optimize query performance. We anticipate that SR participants will frequently access data using groupings defined in a particular ontology; this ontology can be used to create indices that will allow SR participants to retrieve data grouped by ontological concepts. Similar to b-trees that permit the retrieval of a range of data, we are able to retrieve a set of records that are semantically associated with a concept in an ontology. Such optimizations make it practical to develop a tool for formulating complex queries such as those envisaged by the implementation of the SR framework.

In order to use ontologies for indexing, we have to establish links between the data in the SR data warehouse and the concepts in the ontology. All pairs of attributes and values in the database are mapped to concepts in the ontology. (Throughout this paper, the simplifying assumption is made that data are stored in a universal relation. This is not a necessary condition, but it simplifies the discussion of the basic ideas.) This mapping requires the use of a data dictionary to translate database attribute value pairs to

Figure 2. Use of ontologies for indexing data/information entities used for SRA

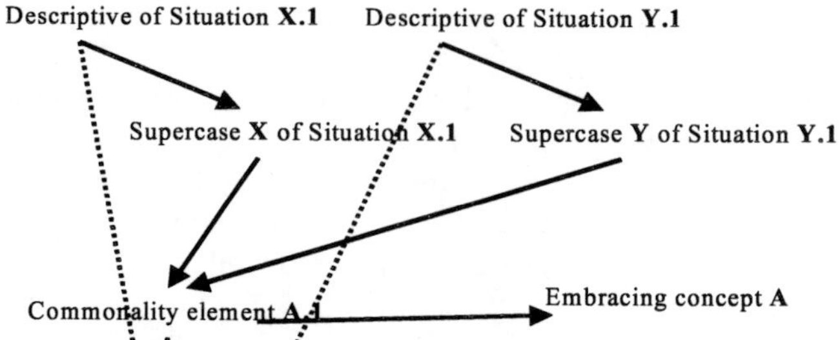

Descriptive of Situation **X.1**   Descriptive of Situation **Y.1**

Supercase **X** of Situation **X.1**   Supercase **Y** of Situation **Y.1**

Commonality element **A.1**   Embracing concept **A**

#	Entity Title	Entity type descriptor	Location
1	Relevant situation actors	HTML file	http://sr/today/actors.htm
2	Case description	Word file	http://sr/today/situation.htm
3	Resources consumed till now	Excel file	http://sr/today/res-till-now.xls
4	Briefing notes	Audio file	http://sr/today/morning_briefing_comments.wav
112			
113	Relevant situation actors	HTML file	http://sr/history/march99/actors.htm
114			

ontology concepts. An example is given in Figure 2. The solid links are ontological links, and the dashed links are indexing links.

The aim is to provide support for the following type of queries: Which actions are effective against 80% of situations sharing commonality element A.1 with the situation we are facing today?

The integration of ontologies into the VE corporate legacy information and database systems is of growing interest, as they can increase the efficiencies of the way a VE uses existing information (re)sources. For instance, in the case of a VE that uses the widespread paradigm for breaking down its "composing parties" into different cost or profit or value centres, each centre is related to different tasks, and the aims it is expected to fulfil relate to different elements of the VE corporate objectives (see Figure 3). To address this, each "department" or "business unit" of the VE uses a particular ontology that provides the communication means for assisting coordination of the VE core business.

Such a local ontology may heavily vary from centre to centre. One obvious way to cope with the assignment of centres to the different parts of the VE is to allocate them to each of the composing parties. This, of course, is of no added value; however, it simplifies many integration perspectives. Another one, also of a simple nature, is to integrate similar or adjacent parts; in this case, the financial unit of each party involved in the VE participates in the same centre. For example, the introduction of a new product

Figure 3. Organization and mapping of semantics for the different cost/profit/value centres of a VE with ontologies

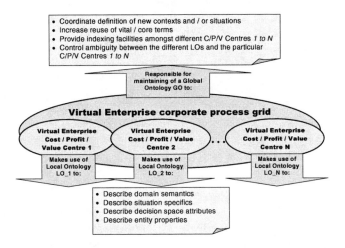

relates to profitability aspects for the finance department and invokes the possibility of stopping any further production and selling of older products that have reached their maturity in the market. It also raises questions related to campaigning, competitors' attitudes, etc., for the marketing department, as well as minimization of production costs and waste for the production department.

From Figure 3, it is clear that there is need for a treatment of the semantics for each different notion as this appears at the local ontology level; this is the role that can be assigned to the global ontology, which affects the entire corporate process grid.

The problem with this the way it is often currently done by companies is that it is not an integral part of a wider development process. It is rather more of a predevelopment process, where a model of how the business works is produced independently of the developers. From the developers' perspective, such a model has no relevance as a development artifact. The challenge is to produce modelling artifacts that are an integral part of the development process and that automatically generate the supporting applications, as well as the respective application protocols.

Before going into a deeper level of analysis for the use of ontologies in our framework, we provide some background information on modelling aspects of the SRA framework. We also consider some basic services it is expected to provide to SR participants, and for which the use of ontologies is considered as a contributing factor to overall efficiency.

Implemention of Ontologies within the SRA Framework

Our approach builds on the adoption of a service-oriented architecture that encompasses the simplicity and scalability of the Web services model (see Figure 4). Besides the simplicity of implementation, the advantage of modularity also enables the "repackaging" of any existing SRA services into new, composite services. This increases

Figure 4. Adoption of the Web services model for the provision of basic SRA services

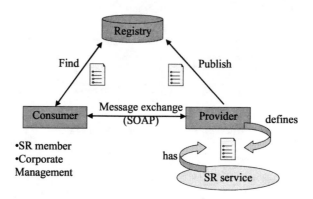

the added value of the framework and should encourage companies to invest in its usage and population with new situation data. Preliminary developments that we have been experimenting with took place across a network of workstations emulating the conditions of a realistic SR.

As a result of this, we identify the need for introducing semantics in our approach as:

- Synonyms of situations in various corporate contexts
- Equivalent situation types in various corporate contexts

  but also for

- Synonyms of situations in the same corporate context
- Equivalent situation types in the same corporate context

It is in this respect that there is a need to support semantic-level processing for the collaborative SRA services to be delivered through the underlying application. For this, the technical goal is to provide a transparent system architecture. This system architecture will act as a broker between cross-cost/profit/value centres, will automatically handle the inconsistencies among the different situations, and will also coordinate inter-cost/profit/value centre process management.

Based on this, it became clear that we need declarative forms of scripting complex Web services, which would also enable composition of scenarios that represent real-world coordination among the different members of the SR, also taking into account temporal and synchronization aspects.

Ankolekar et al. (2001) described DAML-S, a DAML+OIL ontology, designed by the DARPA Agent Markup Language (DAML) Services Coalition, to specify the capabilities of Web services. DAML+OIL provide a semantic and further expressive power to the XML and the RDF. Furthermore, DAML-S provides service descriptions in three conceptual areas:

- The profile, which describes what the service does
- The process model, which depicts how the service works
- The grounding, which states how the particular service is used

Below, we describe three basic services that are provided by the framework and that have been implemented using the approach outlined above.

Representative SRA Services

We used our services by means of building and adapting three of the essential products of the C4ISR Architecture Framework (C4ISR, 1997) that are indicative of the expressive power of the SRA model, thus providing the means of application domain and context-specific customization of it.

Situation Synopsis

The situation synopsis facility addresses essential aspects of a situation considered by means of providing answers to questions related to *Who? What? When? Where? How?* of a particular situation under consideration. In this respect, it may facilitate the initial phases of planning. It is easy to recognize the need for it to be provided in a consistent form that will allow quick reference and comparison among other situations, thus disabling error proneness with respect to linkings with the "wrong" situations. It is upon the situation synopsis that indexing and retrieval operations will be based. It is time-dependent, i.e., as time goes by, it may change — after the completion of a situation, it is still important that this has been appropriately documented in the situation synopsis.

Integrated Situation Dictionary (ISD)

There is considerable textual information in the form of definitions and metadata (i.e., data about an item) associated with the various situations encountered. The Integrated Situation Dictionary (ISD) provides a central source for all these definitions and metadata, including those that may be provided for convenience within another architectural component as well. At a minimum, the ISD is a glossary with definitions of terms used in a given situation description. The ISD makes the set of components capable of standing alone and allows a set of situation-related documents to be read and understood without reference to other documents.

Each labeled item (e.g., terms, phrase, or acronym) in the situation literature should have a corresponding entry in the ISD. For instance, when we speak about a *Sales downsizing*, the ISD provides a unique explanation for this. The same also applies when speaking about a *Sales downscaling*, whatever this may mean too. By using specific terminology, actions and reactions can be standardized, and this saves time and decreases error rates.

The type of metadata included in the ISD for each type of item will depend on the type of component from which the particular service item is "taken." For example, the metadata about a labeled input/output connector from an activity model will include a textual description of the type of input/output information designated by the label.

The contents for the ISD entries for each component type should be regarded as evolving, as is the case for any dictionary of a natural language. SR participants should use standard terms where possible (i.e., terms from existing, approved situation dictionaries). However, in some cases, new terms and modified definitions of existing terms may be needed. This can happen when new concepts are devised. In those cases, the new terms contained in a given architecture's ISD should be submitted to the maintainers of the SR for approval. All definitions that originate in existing dictionaries should provide a reference to show the source, which may be the first situation in which a particular term was used. Furthermore, indicative references to a term may be used for helping in the comprehension of the particular term(s). In this respect, the terms *Sales downsizing* and *Sales downscaling* might have been used for the first time in situations ABC and XYZ, respectively, while the "best" example for conceiving their notion may be situations abc and xyz, respectively. Indexes and thesauri that provide support for synonyms, or other types of processing of the particular semantics of a term are not considered part of the ISD.

Situation Concept

The situation concept is the most general of the architecture-description service components and the most flexible in format. Its main utility is as a facilitator of human communication, and it is intended for presentation to SR participants and decision makers. This kind of service can also be used as a means of orienting and focusing detailed discussions. A possible template may show generic icons that can be tailored as needed and used to represent various classes of actors in a particular situation under consideration. The icons could also be used to represent missions or tasks. The lines connecting the icons can be used to show simple connectivity or can be annotated to show what information is exchanged.

How the template is tailored depends on the scope and intent of the implementation, but in general, a situation concept should be capable of communicating to interested parties some basic information regarding causality and time dependencies, as well as interactions among the various actors involved.

APPLYING CONCEPTS OF SR IN A VE INTEGRATION PROJECT

For demonstrating the steps needed to be taken for applying basic concepts of SRA in a real-world environment, we considered the case of applying it in order to facilitate decision-making tasks related to competition watch for new products. This business environment was the export division of a VE scheme responsible for manufacturing and distributing kitchen sinks.

In the following paragraphs, we illustrate that the VE integration approach in project design by means of SRA results in significant quality enhancement and achieves cost effectiveness in the adopted VE scheme responsible for manufacturing and distributing kitchen sinks. As shown in Figure 5, a VE case study using SRA was applied at two different design stages of the VE integration project using the function approach and following the VE job plan.

The procedural model of SRA implementation within the participating organisations is not that of a "conventional" combined consultancy and IT project. By optimally combining both a results-oriented project and that of a process-oriented initiative, the SRA implementation aimed to accomplish a maximum impact to ensure postproject VE sustainability.

In manufacturing projects, normally a VE study is conducted once on the project. In the context of our validation of the applicability of the SRA framework as part of VE

Figure 5. Application of SRA during the VE integration process

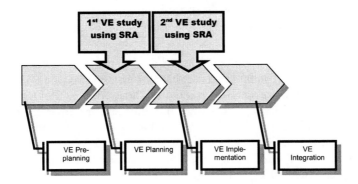

integration activities (both planning and implementation), we addressed a case study in which one VE workshop was conducted at two different design stages. The aim was to bring VE participants together to promote (research) interaction and a cross-fertilization of ideas and techniques that are not easily shared in a traditional ME ("monolithic" or "mono"-enterprise) organization.

At the schematic stage, the first VE study reduced the project cost from 3.7 million Euro to 3.0 million Euro, approximately. During the design development, the project exceeded the fixed limit of initially planned cost. Therefore, the second VE study was conducted at the design development stage to further enhance project quality and reduce total project cost to meet the fixed limit cost of 2.78 million Euro without sacrificing any essential function of the project.

Objective of the VE Studies

The main objectives of these two VE studies using the SRA framework can be summarized as follows:

- Illustrate that significant quality enhancement and cost-effectiveness could be achieved by using the SRA approach of conducting multiple VE integration studies on a commercial project at two different design stages
- Reduce initial costs of the VE integration project to meet the overall limited time and budget availabilities
- Minimize operation and maintenance costs
- Optimize resources layout and cost-effectiveness
- Identify and resolve issues of value prior to implementation

The Employed VE Models

The VE modeling approach has been employed during these studies. The following VE models have been introduced and enhanced to assist the VE team to achieve the main objectives:

- *Quality Model*: The quality model serves as the basis of the VE design process and generating criteria that follow. Attitudes and expectations once defined serve as the sensitive measure by which the VE team evaluates various design alternatives.

Each of the participating companies representatives and design team at the workshop independently voted for the most significant and the least significant elements in the design of this project. Those elements with the most votes had been image and visibility of the project, operational effectiveness, and cost-effectiveness.

- *Functional Cost Worth Model*: The cost information was used for both VE integration studies. The function cost model was prepared using historical information, and then costs were distributed by functions based on cost systems as indicated by the operating breakdown into the various corporate cost centres in all VE participants. This helped identify high-cost areas that could lead to potential VE savings. Due to the time limitation, the VE team followed Pareto's Law by concentrating on the high-cost items that could be 20% of the project components but that contained 80% of the project costs.

SRA Application Results

The implemented savings for this project (total 7.44 million Euro) was the result of applying the multiple SRA approach and applying it to the VE integration process. From the multiple VE integration studies that we applied at different design stages, the following results were observed:

- Applying SRA as a means for the VE integration at multiple design stages of the project does not adversely affect the design completion schedule.
- Each of the two VE integration studies using SRA contributed to reducing the project costs to meet the fixed limit of cost.
- Both VE integration studies improved cost efficiency by increasing the net-to-gross ratio.
- The savings that resulted from the schematic VE integration study were substantially more than those from the design development study. Therefore, the earlier the project stage at which SRA is applied, the higher the potential savings that is to be expected.
- The number of VE integration proposals produced by each VE team remained about the same, whether at schematic or design development stage. However, the emphasis of the second VE integration study was focused on quality enhancement features rather than on cost-saving items.
- Multiple VE integration studies result in improving cost-effectiveness and enhancing project quality throughout all project stages.
- As an added benefit, the involvement of the company owner, the users, the design groups, and the VE integration team in positive decision making resulted in solving a variety of issues in the real-time SRA setting.

CONCLUSIONS

In the world of business, changes in the working environment of enterprises are now driven by the needs of industry to respond in an agile manner to market forces, such as customer demands, increased competition, and shifting patterns of global trade, etc. This also requires a clear identification and redeployment of traditional business functions.

Copyright © 2005, Idea Group Inc. Copying or distributing in print or electronic forms without written permission of Idea Group Inc. is prohibited.

A major challenge for virtual organisations in that respect is the integration of their various heterogeneous organizational structures, information and communication infrastructures, and personnel. There also remains a need for greater understanding of how such VEs will operate in a shared data/information/knowledge environment, through distributed working approaches and based on the paradigm of using the SR metaphor as the core paradigm for carrying out joint operations.

The fast growth of innovations in the last 20 years (coming mainly from the service and engineering disciplines) exposes companies and their shareholders to varied risks and different types of risk that may be difficult to quantify. Though extended report-centric infrastructures have been established (with companies investing several thousands of euros on them on an annual basis, many of which are simply wasted and misspent), these often result in extensive, yet largely meaningless statements, enumerating every possible risk yet still exhibiting insufficient specific risk disclosures.

The concept of SRA is proposed as a means of achieving the expected level of integration, thus closing the gap between the (envisaged) functionality and the (supporting) semantics of any particular VE integration process and especially the one related to intangible goods such as information and knowledge. Activities related to both the preparatory actions needed for establishing a session within the SR as well as for organizing information management and processing within it, can make apparent the fact that there are plenty of infinite regress problems, and that we need to disaggregate the concept of information before we can get a better understanding of the arguments. Furthermore, it seems that the central challenge faced by a VE is the implementation of flexible, time-variant cooperation models. As a result, our work on dynamic change in the structure of information supply chains is of direct utility; it is essential nowadays for the created structures to be able to dynamically modify their formation (i.e., to evolve continuously) and to have the necessary knowledge to do so appropriately in relation to the actions of others.

REFERENCES

Ankolekar, A., Burstein, M., Hobbs, J. R., Lassila, O., Martin, D. L., McIlraith, S. A., Narayanan, S., Paolucci, M., Payne, T., Sycara, K., & Zeng, H. (2001). DAML-S semantic markup for Web Services. In *Proceedings of the First Semantic Web Working Symposium (SWWS '01)*, Stanford, The SAML Services Coalition.

Bovet, D., & Martha, J. (2000). *Value Nets: Breaking the supply chain to unlock hidden profits.* New York: Wiley.

C4ISR Command, Control, Communications, Computer, Intelligence, Surveillance and Reconnisance. (1997). *Architecture Framework Version 2.0.* 18 December, Architecture Working Group.

Casson, M. (1991). *The economics of business culture: Game theory, transaction costs and economic performance.* Oxford: Clarendon Press.

Friedman, J. W. (1991). *Game theory with applications to economics.* Oxford: Oxford University Press.

Hahn, A. (2003). Integration and knowledge management platform for concurrent engineering. In *Ninth International Conference of Concurrent Enterprising (ICE2003)*, Espoo, Finland, 16–18 June.

Huplic, V. (2002). *Knowledge and business process management.* Hershey, PA: Idea Group Publishing.

Koumpis, A., & Roberts, B. (2003). A framework for situation room analysis and exploration of its application potential in the IT sector. In *First International Conference on Performance Measures, Benchmarking and Best Practices in New Economy—Business Excellence '03*, University of Minho, Guimaraes, Portugal, 10–13 June.

Mandal, P., Love, P. E. D., & Irani, Z. (2003). Pre-alliance planning: Development of an information system infrastructure to support strategic alliance activities. *Management Decision, 41*, 2.

Putnik, G. D. (2000). BM_Virtual enterprise architecture reference model. In A. Gunasekaran (Ed.), *Agile manufacturing: The 21st century competitive strategy.* Amsterdam; New York: Elsevier.

Skyrme, D. (1999). *Knowledge networking: Creating the collaborative enterprise.* Oxford: Butterworth-Heinemann.

Ward, J., & Peppard, J. (2002). *Strategic planning for information systems* (3rd ed.). New York: Wiley.

Widom, J., & Ceri, S. (1996). *Active database systems: Triggers and rules for advanced database processing.* San Francisco: Morgan Kaufmann.

Chapter XIII

Virtual Enterprise Coalition Strategy with Game Theoretic Multiagent Paradigm

Toshiya Kaihara
Kobe University, Japan

Susumu Fujii
Kobe University, Japan

ABSTRACT

Nowadays, virtual enterprise (VE) is a crucial paradigm of business management in an agile environment. VE exists in both service and manufacturing organizations, although the complexity of each enterprise in a VE may vary greatly from industry to industry. Obviously, there is a need for a mechanism through which these different functions can be integrated together transparently. In this contribution, we focus on the negotiation process in VE formulation as a basic research to clarify its effective management in terms of partner search. Each enterprise in VE is defined as an agent with multiutilities, and a framework of multiagent programming with game theoretic approach is newly proposed as a negotiation algorithm among the agents. Each unit is defined as an agent in our VE model, and their decision making is formulated as a game theoretic methodology. We develop a computer simulation model to form VEs through multiple negotiations among several potential members in the negotiation domain, and finally clarify the formulation dynamism with the negotiation process.

INTRODUCTION

Nowadays, VE is a crucial paradigm of business management in an agile environment. VE exists in both service and manufacturing organizations, although the complexity of each enterprise in VE may vary greatly from industry to industry. Realistic VE handles multiple end products with shared components, facilities, and capacities (Camarinha-Matos, 1999). Because the flow of materials in VE is not always along an arborescent network, various modes of transportation may be considered, and the bill of materials for the end items may be both deep and large (Ganeshan, 2004).

Traditionally, marketing, distribution, planning, manufacturing, and the purchasing organizations operated independently. These organizations have their own objectives, and these are often conflicting. Marketing's objectives of high customer service and maximum sales conflict with manufacturing and distribution goals. Many manufacturing operations are designed to maximize throughput and lower costs with little consideration for the impact on inventory levels and distribution capabilities. Purchasing contracts are often negotiated with very little information beyond historical buying patterns. The result of these factors is that there is not a single, integrated plan for the organization — there were as many plans as businesses. Clearly, there is a need for a mechanism through which these different functions can be integrated. Although cooperation is the fundamental characteristic of the VE concept, due to its distributed environment and the autonomous and heterogeneous nature of the VE members, cooperation can only succeed if a proper management of dependencies between activities is in place, just like supply-chain management (Fisher, 1994; Goldratt, 1983).

We focus on the negotiation process in VE formulation as a basic research to clarify its effective management. Each enterprise in VE is defined as an agent with multiutilities, and a framework of multiagent programming with game theoretic approach (Von Neumann, 1947) is newly proposed as a negotiation algorithm among the agents. Although there are several researches about multiagent-based VE systems, most are mainly related to IT systems architecture rather than to negotiation algorithm (Rabelo, 2000; Dignum, 2002; Shen, 1999). Our approach is dedicated to the VE negotiation mechanism so as to facilitate effective VE partnering with rationality. Each unit is defined as agent in our VE model, and their decisions are formulated as a game theoretic methodology. We adopt the contract net protocol (CNP; Smith, 1980; Durfee, 1987) as the coordination and negotiation mechanism among the units. CNP models transfer control in a distributed system with the metaphor of negotiation among autonomous intelligent beings. CNP consists of a set of nodes that negotiate with one another through a set of messages (Kaihara, 2002a, 2002b, 2002c). Nodes generally represent the distributed computing resources to be managed, corresponding to "enterprises" in this chapter.

Additionally, we introduce an adaptive behavior (i.e., learning effects) into our VE model, by adopting a reinforcement learning algorithm (Sutton, 1998) into the node so as to attain the dynamic evaluations with time domain. We develop a computer simulation model to form VE through multiple negotiations among several potential members in the negotiation domain, and finally clarify the macro VE formulation dynamism with the micronegotiation process.

ENTERPRISE AGENT

VE Model

VEs are defined as "agile" enterprises, i.e., as enterprises with integration and reconfiguration capability in useful time, integrated from independent enterprises, primitive or complex, with the aim of taking profit from a specific market opportunity. After the conclusion of that opportunity, the VE dissolves, and a new VE is integrated, or it reconfigures itself in order to achieve the necessary competitiveness to respond to another market opportunity. The general definition of VE is as follows (Camarinha-Matos, 1999):

A virtual enterprise is a temporary alliance of enterprises that come together to share skills or core competencies and resources in order to better respond to business opportunities and whose cooperation is supported by computer networks.

For the independent, primitive, or complex enterprises, or companies, candidates to integrate a VE, we will use the designation "resource," the sense that from the point of view of the VE, these enterprises represent the potential "resources" for integration. It is important to notice that the resource is a recursive construct; resources can be primitive or complex.

The knowledge and physical resources associated with the development and production of most of today's products often exceed what a single firm is able to accomplish. The new production enterprise is a network that shares experience, knowledge, and capabilities — it is critical in this new environment for a manufacturing company to be able to efficiently tap these knowledge and information networks.

The organizational challenge of partitioning tasks among partners in the distributed manufacturing environment so that they fit and take advantage of the different competencies in VE, integration of the same, coordination, and reconfigurability in order to keep alignment with the market requirements, is of main concern and can determine the success or failure of a project.

Facing the requirements of competitiveness that the competitive environment is demanding, enterprises are expected to present at least the following characteristics:
1. Fast reconfigurability or adaptability: the ability to quickly change in order to face the unpredictable changes in the environment and market, implying substitution of resources [transition to a new agile/virtual enterprise (A/VE) instantiation]
2. Evolutionary capability: the ability to learn with history

A large number of diversified networked organisations of enterprises fall under the general definition of VE. We assumed our VE model in the simplest possible definition as a basic research, as follows:
1. Duration: Single business — An alliance of the enterprises is established toward a single business opportunity and is dissolved at the end of such a process.
2. Topology: Fixed structure — There exist established supply chains with almost fixed structures.

3. Participation: Single alliance — All the enterprises are participating in only a single alliance at the same time.
4. Coordination: Democratic alliance — A different organization can be found in some supply chains without a dominant company. All the enterprises cooperate on an equal basis, preserving their autonomy.
5. Visibility scope: Single level — All the enterprises in VEs communicate only to its direct neighbors in its architecture (Figure 1). That is the case observed in most supply chains.

Needless to say, it is a very important and difficult activity in forming a VE to select appropriate business partners, i.e., partnering, because each enterprise considers not only pursuing its profit but also sharing the risk to join the VE. The partnering is described as coordination activity among the enterprises, and some sophisticated coordination mechanism is required to realize efficient interactions.

The development of a coordination mechanism in computer science can be found in the area of workflow management systems, computer-supported cooperative work (CSCW), and multiagent systems.

The area of multiagent systems, especially when involving intelligent autonomous agents, has been discussing coordination issues and supporting mechanisms (Kaihara, 2002a). The interaction capability, both among agents and between agents and their environments, is one of the basic characteristics of an agent.

We focus on the CNP, which is one of the mechanisms from the early works on multiagent systems (Smith, 1980), as the coordination and negotiation mechanism among business units in VE.

Figure 1 shows the assumed VE model in this paper. We call an enterprise a unit, and there exist m layers, which have m_n units in the VE model. $Unit_{ij}$ means the jth unit in layer i. All the units in one layer belong to the same business segment, such as retailer, manufacturer, supplier, and so on. The lowest level corresponds to consumers who can create original task requests to the VE. As the layer number, m, increases, we describe it as "lower," based on the product flow order in this chapter.

Figure 1. VE model

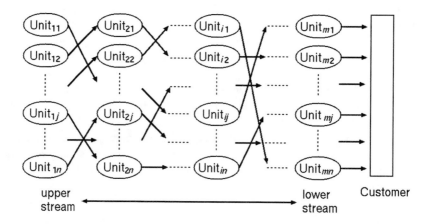

At first, the customer dispatches a new order to all the units in layer m, and then several units, which are satisfied with the order, respond and circulate the order toward upper units in the VE model. Finally, a VE with a single supply chain will be established for the order as a consequence of their negotiations through all the layers.

Unit Structure

Each unit is defined as an agent in our VE model, and its structure is described in Figure 2. We adopt CNP as the coordination and negotiation mechanism among the units. CNP models transfer control in a distributed system with the metaphor of negotiation among autonomous intelligent beings. CNP consists of a set of nodes that negotiate with one another through a set of messages. Nodes generally represent the distributed computing resources to be managed, corresponding to "units" in this paper.

An agent (= unit) can act both as a manager and a contractor of delivery sets. When a unit receives a new order (= task announcement) i, it creates a contractor/manager set (Manager i / Contractor i) for the task inside. Manager i creates a new order toward the lower units to secure the contract with the upper layer.

Basic Assumption

There exist several situations in partnering among enterprise agents. In this paper, it is assumed that the product demand is predictable in the negotiation under multipurpose criterion. That means that order patterns are previously given, and the negotiations start after the order reaches each enterprise agent. They should prepare robust solutions with maximum utilities against the order. We propose agent behaviors based on the game theoretic approach according to this assumption.

Negotiation Algorithm

The time line of the proposed negotiation mechanism in this paper is shown in Figure 3. Negotiation steps according to agent roles are described as follows.

Figure 2. Unit structure

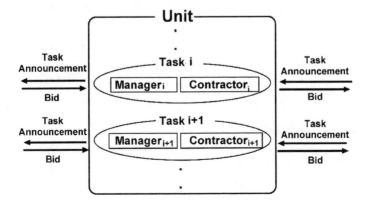

Figure 3. Negotiation flow

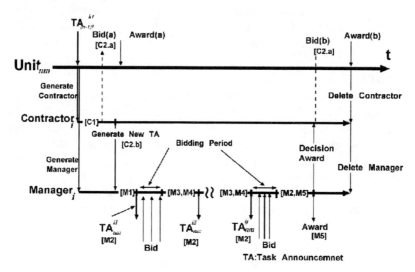

Manager

Step M1: Create a new task based on the received bid information.

Step M2: Task announcement (TA) to the lower units.

Step M3: After the bidding period expired, check all the acquired bids according to its standard. If there is no bid to select, go to M4. Otherwise, go to M5.

Step M4: Modify the task and go to M2.

Step M5: Select the task and send reward (Reward) to the corresponding unit.

Contractor

Step C1: Create an estimated bid.

Step C2: Send the bid.

Step C3: Request task announcement to the manager.

Agent Formulation

In this model, all the orders are clearly given before the negotiations. Agent behaviors are described in each negotiation step.

Bidding (Step C2)

Each contractor (U_{ij}) has three attributes, such as cost, lead time, and quality, in their bid for order k, defined as follows:

$$Cost_{ij}^k = E_{ij}^k + D_{ij}^k + P_{ij}^k \tag{1}$$

$$Leadtime_{ij}^k = \lambda_{ij}^k / E_{ij}^k \tag{2}$$

$$Quality_{ij}^k = \mu_{ij}^k D_{ij}^k (1 - \exp^{-v_{ij}^k P_{ij}^k}) \tag{3}$$

where

$Cost_{ij}^k$: total cost for U_{ij} to process order k

$Leadtime_{ij}^k$: lead time for U_{ij} to process order k

$Quality_{ij}^k$: product quality for U_{ij} to process order k

$E_{ij}^k, D_{ij}^k, P_{ij}^k$: equipment/development/personnel cost

$\lambda_{ij}^k, \mu_{ij}^k, v_{ij}^k$: constant values

Cost vs. lead time, and cost vs. quality are in trade-off relationships in those equations with reality.

Reward (Step M5)

After the bidding by contractors, managers compute the following payoff matrix according to their utilities against all the bids. The matrix based on game theory is used in the partner selection:

$$
\begin{array}{c}
\\
Unit_{i1} \\
Unit_{i2} \\
\cdots \\
Unit_{ij} \\
\cdots \\
Unit_{in}
\end{array}
\begin{array}{ccc}
C & L & Q \\
\begin{bmatrix}
C_{i1}^k & L_{i1}^k & Q_{i1}^k \\
C_{i2}^k & L_{i2}^k & Q_{i2}^k \\
\cdots & \cdots & \cdots \\
C_{ij}^k & L_{ij}^k & Q_{ij}^k \\
\cdots & \cdots & \cdots \\
C_{in}^k & L_{im}^k & Q_{im}^k
\end{bmatrix}
\end{array}
\qquad (4)
$$

where

$$C_{ij}^k = (\overline{c_i^k} - Cost_{ij}^k)/s_{c_i^k} \qquad (5)$$

$$L_{ij}^k = (\overline{l_i^k} - Leadtime_{ij}^k)/s_{l_i^k} \qquad (6)$$

$$Q_{ij}^k = (Quality_{ij}^k - \overline{q_i^k})/s_{q_i^k} \qquad (7)$$

and, where

C_{ij}^k : utility on cost for U_{ij} to process order k

L_{ij}^k : utility on lead time for U_{ij} to process order k

Q_{ij}^k : utility on quality for U_{ij} to process order k

$\overline{c_i^k}, \overline{l_i^k}, \overline{q_i^k}$: average utility of all the bids on cost, lead time, quality

$s_{c_i^k}, s_{l_i^k}, s_{q_i^k}$: standard deviation of all the bids on cost, lead time, quality

Five strategies are defined as selection mechanisms using the payoff matrix in Equation (4).

Method 1: Cost minimization strategy:
$$\max_{j=1,2,\ldots,n} = C_{ij}^k \tag{8}$$
Method 2: Lead time minimization strategy:
$$\max_{j=1,2,\ldots,n} = L_{ij}^k \tag{9}$$
Method 3: Quality maximization strategy:
$$\max_{j=1,2,\ldots,n} = Q_{ij}^k \tag{10}$$
Method 4: Total utility maximization strategy:
$$\max_{j=1,2,\ldots,n} = C_{ij}^k + L_{ij}^k + Q_{ij}^k \tag{11}$$
Method 5: Max–min strategy:
$$\max_{j=1,2,\ldots,n} \min\{C_{ij}^k, L_{ij}^k, Q_{ij}^k\} \tag{12}$$

Method 5 is the so-called "max–min strategy" in game theory, which has been proven to conduct Nash equilibrium solution by min–max theorem, if the game is in a zero-sum situation like our formulation shown in Equation (4).

Adaptive Behavior (Reinforcement Learning)

In nonsequential tasks, a unit must learn a mapping of situations to actions that maximizes the expected immediate payoff in general. Put in a better context, units have their actions-to-reward manual by their side. Sequential tasks are more difficult, because actions selected by units may influence its future situations and thus its future payoffs. In this case, the unit interacts with the environment over an extended period of time, and it needs to evaluate its actions on the basis of their long-term consequences. This involves a credit assignment problem, i.e., a whole sequence of actions takes place before long-term consequences are known. This would be difficult, because actions in a sequence may have different values with respect to the consequences.

Reinforcement learning dates back to the early days of cybernetics and work in statistics, psychology, neuroscience, and computer science. In the last five to 10 years, it has attracted rapidly increasing interest in the machine learning and artificial intelligence communities. Its promise is beguiling — a way of programming agents by reward and punishment without needing to specify *how* the task is to be achieved. But there are formidable computational obstacles to fulfilling the promise.

Reinforcement learning is the problem faced by an agent that must learn behavior through trial-and-error interactions with a dynamic environment. The learning mechanism consists of three devices, named recognition, learning, and selection of actions, as shown in Figure 4. There are two main strategies used by reinforcement learning for solving problems. The first is to search in the space of behaviors in order to find one that performs well in the environment. This approach has been taken by work in genetic algorithms and genetic programming, as well as in some more novel search techniques (Sutton, 1998). The second is to use statistical techniques and dynamic programming methods to estimate the utility of taking actions in states of the world.

Q-learning is a recent form of reinforcement learning algorithm that does not need a model of its environment and can be used online. Therefore, it is suited for repeated games against an unknown opponent. The Q-learning algorithm works by estimating the values of state–action pairs. The value $Q(s,a)$ is defined to be the expected discounted sum of future payoffs obtained by taking action a from state s and following an optimal policy thereafter. Once these values have been learned, the optimal action from any state is the one with the highest Q-value. After being initialized to arbitrary numbers, Q-values are estimated on the basis of experience as explained next.

From the current state s, select an action a. This will cause a receipt of an immediate payoff r, and arrival at the next state s'.

We update $Q(s,a)$ based upon this experience as follows:

$$Q(s,a) = (1-\alpha)Q(s,a) + \alpha(r + \gamma \max Q(s',b)) \tag{13}$$

Where α is the learning rate, and $0 < \gamma < 1$ is the discount factor.

This algorithm is guaranteed to converge to the correct Q-values with the probability one if the environment is stationary and depends on the current state and the action taken in it; called Markovian, a look-up table is used to store the Q-values, every state–action pair continues to be visited, and the learning rate is decreased appropriately over time. This exploration strategy does not specify the action to select at each step.

Figure 4. A concept of learning mechanism

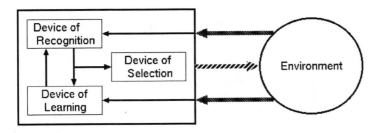

Experiments with a Q-learning agent have been done in the past with favorable results. It is natural to assume that enterprise units have an adaptive behavior in terms of the negotiation process. We especially focus on the bid creation mechanism in step C1 and introduce the reinforcement learning algorithm into it. Contractor's behavior in each enterprise unit is improved by its experience so as to dispatch a better offer to attain the rewards from managers. The state and the action for Q-learning are defined in the VE model as follows:

State: State is defined by three kinds of attributes, equipment cost (E_{ij}^k), development

cost (D_{ij}^k), and personnel cost (P_{ij}^k). So, state domain is divided by N^3 space, and a unit recognizes its state in the state domain map shown in Figure 5.

Action: Seven types of actions are prepared to respond adaptively to the state as follows:
Action 1: Cost: fix ^ Lead time: reduce
Action 2: Cost: fix ^ Quality: increase
Action 3: Lead time: fix ^ Cost: reduce
Action 4: Lead time: fix ^ Quality: increase
Action 5: Quality: fix ^ Cost: reduce
Action 6: Quality: fix ^ Lead time: reduce
Action 7: No changes

Rewards: A manager unit gives the improved value of each attribute as a reward to the negotiating contractor unit.

Figure 5. An example of state space

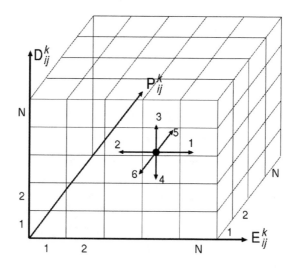

EXPERIMENTAL RESULTS

Simulation Parameters

A three-layered VE model for computer simulation was developed to clarify VE formulation dynamism with the proposed negotiation mechanism. Each layer consists of five enterprises in this simulation model described in Figure 1.

Simulation parameters are shown in Table 1. All the results are the average of 500 trials in each simulation scenario.

Simulation Results

(1) Cost Parameter Effects (E, D, P)

First, we try to clarify cost parameter effects on VE formulation. So, the parameters except E, D, P, are fixed in this experiment, such as λ: 300, μ: 5, ν: 0.1, for clear explanations of the simulation analysis.

Table 1. Simulation parameters followed by uniform random distribution*

m	n	N	E	D	P	λ	μ	ν
3	5	5	5–15*	5–15*	5–15*	150–450*	2.5–7.5*	0.05–0.15*

Table 2. Simulation results in cost effects (negotiation attributes)

	Method 1		Method 2		Method 3	
	Ave.	St. Dev.	Ave.	St. Dev.	Ave.	St. Dev.
Cost	72.87	5.08	99.89	7.47	104.17	6.61
LTime	119.53	18.47	68.32	4.84	90.21	18.06
Quality	65.10	10.58	92.59	18.05	132.34	12.44

Method 4		Method 5	
Ave.	St. Dev.	Ave.	St. Dev.
98.96	8.79	91.19	5.54
80.72	11.04	91.04	12.24
106.84	20.22	93.23	12.97

Table 3. Simulation results in cost effects (utilities)

	Method 1	Method 2	Method 3	Method 4	Method 5
E_{ij}^{k}	8.13	13.35	9.96	11.68	10.38
D_{ij}^{k}	8.13	10.11	12.84	11.47	10.61
P_{ij}^{k}	8.03	9.84	11.92	9.83	9.41

Figure 6. Method comparison

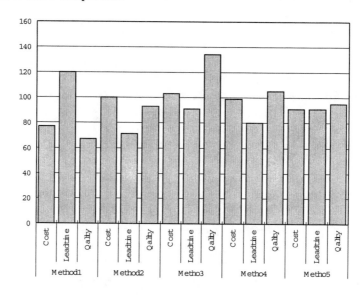

Simulation results in terms of negotiation attributes and utilities are shown in Tables 2 and 3, respectively. All the results are shown in the average (AVE.) and the standard distribution (St. Dev.) in Table 2. Figure 6 also illustrates the average of each negotiation attribute to compare the proposed methods.

We summarize the characteristics of each method as follows:

Method 1: Cost Minimization

Because the negotiation among enterprises is cost-oriented in this method, cost parameter is the best of all the methods in Ave. Additionally, Cost and Quality are better in St. Dev., because they are correlated to $E_{ij}^{k}, D_{ij}^{k}, P_{ij}^{k}$ shown in Equations (1) and (3). It has been observed that all the utilities are small to minimize total cost in this method at Table 3.

Method 2: Lead-Time Minimization

The lead-time-oriented method naturally conducts the minimal LeadTime in Ave., and the St. Dev. Cost parameter is not good, because Leadtime and E_{ij}^k is in a trade-off relation in Equation (2), and that leads to higher cost.

Method 3: Quality Maximization

It is obvious that the quality maximization strategy caused the worst result in Cost, and this fits well to our general sense. In this method, enterprises do not pay any attention to LeadTime shown in Equation (2).

Method 4: Total Utility Maximization

Generally, the result is moderate in balance among the three parameters because of the attempt to maximize total utility. In Figure 6, it has been observed that they are relatively better in its LeadTime and Quality but worse in its Cost. That is because the general relationship among $E_{ij}^k, D_{ij}^k, P_{ij}^k$, in Equations (1), (2), and (3) means that enterprise agents sacrifice LeadTime to increase Cost and Quality.

Method 5: Max–Min Strategy

Acquired result is completely well-balanced in Ave. It has also been confirmed that this strategy conducts minimally in St. Dev., and their negotiation is stable and robust enough to deal with agile trading situations. That is because each agent tried to minimize the risk based on the min–max theory.

(2) Utility parameter effects (λ, μ, ν)

Then, we try to clarify agent utility parameter effects on VE formulation.

Table 4 shows simulation parameters in this scenario, and we decrease the probability range of cost parameters to eliminate the cost influence. We define the following equations to define the relationship among utility parameters as a constraint to keep balance on productivity among all the units. The weight parameter t is set to 0.5 in this experiment.

$$\frac{\lambda_{ij}^k}{\bar{\lambda}} = (1-t)\frac{\mu_{ij}^k}{\bar{\mu}} + t\frac{\nu_{ij}^k}{\bar{\nu}} \quad 0 \tag{14}$$

where $0 \le t \le 1$ (t: weight parameter) and $\bar{*}$ means average value of parameter *.

Table 4. Simulation parameters in utility effects followed by uniformed random distribution

m	n	N	E	D	P	λ	μ	ν
3	5	1	9– 11*	9– 11*	9– 11*	150– 450*	2.5– 7.5*	0.05– 0.15*

Table 5. Simulation results in utility effects (negotiation attributes)

	Method 1		Method 2		Method 3	
	Ave.	St. Dev.	Ave.	St. Dev.	Ave.	St. Dev.
Cost	86.47	1.07	90.48	1.76	90.61	1.77
LTime	94.00	10.65	68.31	6.31	110.84	7.58
Quality	86.89	16.47	59.86	9.70	132.60	12.50

Method 4		Method 5	
Ave.	St. Dev.	Ave.	St. Dev.
86.91	1.26	89.31	1.31
91.98	11.66	90.74	6.87
88.24	18.22	92.66	11.61

Simulation results in terms of negotiation attributes and utilities are shown in Tables 5 and 6, respectively. All the results are shown in the average (AVE.) and the standard distribution (St. Dev.) in Table 5, as shown in Table 2.

Method 1: Cost Minimization

Because the negotiation among enterprises is cost-oriented in this method, cost parameter is the best of all the methods in Ave. Additionally, three attributes are relatively well-balanced, as shown in Table 5, because each utility parameter is converged into a theoretical average value (Table 6). Utility parameters are not included in Equation (1), so the cost-oriented method has little influence on them. That also leads to relatively large St. Dev. in this simulation scenario.

Method 2: Lead-Time Minimization

The lead-time-oriented method naturally conducts the minimal LeadTime in Ave. and St. Dev. in this scenario. The cost parameter is not good, because the unit with smaller l is selected to reduce Leadtime, and that causes decreases in m and n defined by Equation (14).

Method 3: Quality Maximization

It is obvious that the quality maximization strategy caused the worst in all items in Table 5. This method selects the unit with larger m and n, and that leads the unit to increase by Equation (14), shown in Table 6. Thus, all items, such as Cost, LTime, and Quality, are converged to a higher value.

Table 6. Simulation results in utility effects (utilities)

	Method 1	Method 2	Method 3	Method 4	Method 5
Unit11	485	379	750	535	323
Unit12	101	175	64	131	166
Unit13	139	149	71	108	177
Unit14	131	145	52	123	172
Unit15	144	152	63	103	162

Method 4: Total Utility Maximization

This method computes moderate solutions in balance among three parameters by trying to maximize total utility. It also tends to have bigger value in St. Dev. compared with Method 5.

Method 5: Max–Min Strategy

Acquired result is also completely well-balanced in Ave. It has also been confirmed that this strategy conducts minimally in St. Dev., and their negotiation is stable and robust enough to deal with agile trading situations. That is because each agent tried to minimize the risk based on max–min strategy. It has been confirmed that this strategy is robust and keeps stable in various simulation cases.

We summarize the characteristics of each method based on this simulation results as follows.

Adaptive Behavior Effects

Simulation parameters in the Q-learning algorithm are as follows:

γ: 0.2
N : 5
the number of simulation trials for initial learning : 1000

Learning rate $\pm$ decreases as follows:

$$a = 1 - (\text{Current trial} / \text{Total trial}) \qquad (15)$$

All the simulation data are equivalent to those in Table 1. Two types of scenarios are simulated to investigate adaptive behavior effects on VE formulation. It is assumed that the units in the first row (i.e., Unit $_{*1}$) in Figure 1 only attain adaptive behavior by Q-learning in the first scenario (Scenario 1). On the other hand, all the units, regardless of their locations, attain adaptive behavior in another scenario (Scenario 2).

(1) Scenario 1

We compared all the methods in the adaptive conditions. Table 7 shows the total number of rewards during 1000 simulation trials in unit layer 1, after 1000 initial trials for

Figure 7. Reward of unit

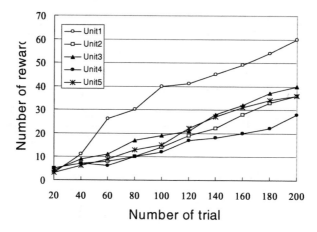

Figure 8. Cost fluctuation

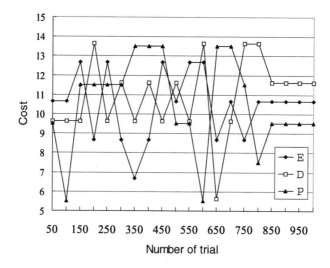

agent learning. Figures 7 and 8 illustrate transitional changes of the number of awards at each unit and each cost parameter, respectively.

First, Unit11 successfully took advantage of its adaptive behavior to accept more rewards compared with the other units, shown in Table 7 and Figure 7. It has been clarified that the adaptive behavior based on the Q-learning mechanism is efficient to develop sophisticated strategies in VE negotiations. It is shown that the cost parameters are finally converged as $P < E < D$, in Figure 8. This order is equivalent to the order of max–min strategy in Table 3, and that means the acquired behavior is sufficiently rational in this scenario. By the comparison of methods in Table 7, it is obvious that Method 3 has the highest number in Unit11. This is because quality is defined by parameters D and P shown in Equation (3) and that causes only the units with large values in both D and P

Table 7. Number of reward (Layer 1)

	Method 1	Method 2	Method 3	Method 4	Method 5
Unit11	485	379	750	535	323
Unit12	101	175	64	131	166
Unit13	139	149	71	108	177
Unit14	131	145	52	123	172
Unit15	144	152	63	103	162

to be selected. Consequently, it is difficult for other units to get rewards, because they decide *D* and *P* randomly.

(2) Scenario 2

Simulation results in terms of negotiation attributes and utilities are shown in Table 8. All the results are also shown in the average (AVE.) and the standard distribution (St. Dev.) in this table. The results in the conventional method correspond to Method 5, and these values are equivalent to those in Table 2.

It is obvious that the standard deviation is smaller in Q-learning-based negotiation compared with the conventional negotiations, although there is not so much difference in the average.

A manager in a unit has to select one contractor among several bids, at least by relative evaluations in our negotiation mechanism. Therefore, it is natural that the randomness of the attributes in bid causes large standard deviation in their compromised trade. On the other hand, the contractor's bidding strategy based on the Q-learning algorithm produces more acceptable attributes in their bid, and that concludes little randomness with small standard deviation. It is obvious that Q-learning-based bidding strategy leads to stable trading between VE units.

Table 8. Q-learning effects

	Conventional		Q-Learning	
	Ave.	St. Dev.	Ave.	St. Dev.
Cost	91.19	5.54	90.94	3.82
Lead time	91.04	12.24	89.21	7.49
Quality	93.23	12.97	92.15	6.71

CONCLUSIONS

In this paper, we focused on the negotiation process in VE formulation as our basic research. Each enterprise in VE was defined as an agent in our VE model, and their decision-making strategies were formulated as game theoretic methodology with adaptive behavior, i.e., the Q-learning algorithm. Although our investigations have clearly not been exhaustive, it is already apparent that the agent (i.e., unit) behaviors have great influence on autonomously formulated VE structure as a basic study. Simulation results have proved that the proposed game theoretic formulation on agent decision mechanism with multiagent paradigm is reasonable to facilitate rational negotiation processes among enterprises.

ACKNOWLEDGMENTS

This research was supported by the International Research program IMS (Intelligent Manufacturing System) of IMS centre Japan, under contract No.0219 (HUTOP project).

REFERENCES

Camarinha-Matos, L. M. et al. (1999). *The virtual enterprise concept, infrastructures for virtual enterprise*s (pp. 3–14). Dordrecht: Kluwer.

Dignum, V. et al. (2002). *Towards an agent-based infrastructure to support virtual organisations, collaborative business ecosystems and virtual enterprises* (pp. 363–370). Dordrecht: Kluwer.

Durfee, E. et al. (1987). Coherent cooperation among communication problem solvers. *IEEE Transaction on Computers*, 36, 1275–1291.

Fisher, M. L. (1994). Making supply meet demand in uncertain world. *Harvard Business Review*, May/June.

Ganeshan, R. et al. (2004). An introduction to SCM. Available online *http://lcm.csa.iisc.ernet.in/scm*

Goldratt, E. M. (1983). *The GOAL*. North River Press.

Kaihara, T., & Fujii, S. (2002a). A study on virtual enterprise coalition with multi-agent technology in agile manufacturing environment. *International Journal of Advanced Manufacturing Systems, 1*, 2, 125–139.

Kaihara, T., & Fujii, S. (2002b). IT based virtual enterprise coalition strategy for agile manufacturing environment. In *Proceedings of the 35th CIRP International Seminar on Manufacturing Systems* (pp. 32–37).

Kaihara, T., & Fujii, S. (2002c). *A proposal on negotiation methodolvances in networked enterprises* (pp. 81–90). Dordrecht: Kluwer.

Shen, W. et al. (1999). *Implementing Internet enabled virtual enterprises using collaborative agents, infrastructures for virtual enterprise* (pp. 343–352). Dordrecht: Kluwer.

Smith, R. (1980). The contract net protocol. *IEEE Transaction on Computers, C-29*, 1104–1113.

Sutton R. S., & Barto, A. G. (1998). *Reinforcement learning: An introduction.* Cambridge, MA: MIT Press.

Von Neumann, J. et al. (1947). *Theory of games and economic behavior.* Princeton, NJ: Princeton University Press.

Section IV

Technologies for Integration

Chapter XIV

Semantic Distance, the Next Step?

Ted Goranson

Sirius-Beta and Old Dominion University, USA

ABSTRACT

Enterprise integration has, in the past, focused on strategies for complete harmonization of various dimensions using collected technologies and techniques. The virtual enterprise case presents us, almost by definition, with cases where preharmonized infrastructure is neither feasible nor desirable. Through international workshops, the community has identified a next-generation strategy for how to measure the imperfections in integration that will be encountered. Presumably, a new class of tools and strategies will emerge. The idea is still very early in its life. This chapter presents a snapshot of early conclusions. One proposal of a strategy is outlined.

INTRODUCTION

Work toward enterprise integration is easily justified as the core science of the engineering discipline that drives world economies by empowering infrastructure. Basics of collaboration and the resulting work in industry depend on the ability to convey meaning in a trustworthy manner. In 1990, the major research sponsors in the United States and European Union formed a partnership to define a research agenda for this important science of enterprise integration. That collaborative exercise has been repeated every five years since, as the International Conference on Enterprise Integration Technology.

In 1992, the international workshops and associated book codified the discipline of enterprise integration and was directly responsible for so-called unified approaches.

These were vendor-specific and function-centered as in enterprise resource planning. The 1997 exercise was a landmark in recognizing the economic advantages of opportunistic integration in the form of virtual enterprises. A conclusion was that prior integration strategies based on centralization and homogeneity were hampering business flexibility. The science behind enterprise integration shifted from "standards" to ontologies.

The 2002 activity noted the reality of many competing ontologies with the costs and difficulties of harmonizing them. An idea emerged to consider context. Often, integration is measured as a matter of exhaustive possibility: two diverse methods or representations are said to be integratable if every possible condition and context permits complete semantic conveyance. But the real virtual enterprise situation is that partners need to integrate in a specific context consisting of processes that will present only a few of all the possible conditions.

In such cases, it may be possible that the integration as a whole is imperfect, but is "close enough;" either it is perfect in a limited context, or it is imperfect but easily repairable, or it is imperfect but the consequences are tolerable. The notion of "semantic distance" was developed to cover the notion of "how close is close enough."

The U.S. National Institute of Standards and Technology had independently identified this need in the course of developing support of ontology standards. In November of 2003, they — with the aid of several European projects — hosted a several-day international workshop on the topic to determine best approaches. A variety of disciplines and viewpoints were represented, with the workshop identifying a number of challenges. The concept of semantic distance is likely to play a major role in some way in the future of virtual enterprise integration and, incidentally, the semantic Web (and other applications), but it is too early to guess in exactly what form, as there are all sorts of political and economic forces at work.

This chapter represents one proposal for addressing the need for a measure of semantic distance. As it happens, the term "virtual enterprise" has by many been significantly watered down from its original usage. Today, people use it for uninteresting cases: distributed but stable aggregations of firms (even supply chains!), or firms that band together for coordinated marketing of their everyday services. We use the original

Figure 1. ICEIMT results

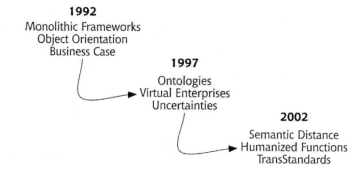

Figure 2. Features of advanced virtual enterprises

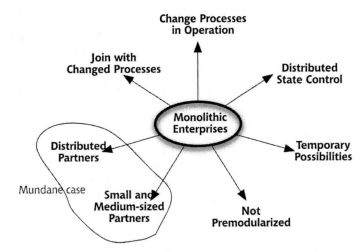

intent: opportunistic, often temporary aggregations of mostly small and medium-sized firms that come together to address or create an opportunity. A key part of the notion is that the integration is sufficiently tight that partners may radically adapt their processes as a result of requirements of the system. They may even have been identified as partners, because they are judged to be capable of doing something that they currently do not do, and may never have thought of. The virtual enterprise is dynamic in the sense that it forms and dissolves but also in the more interesting behavior that it evolves when operating.

ONTOLOGICAL PARSING OF THE ENTERPRISE

The science behind enterprises suffers from a wide variety of theories and philosophies employed with the purpose of design and management. This fact affects the root problem (we have ontological mismatches within the enterprise) and also complicates the problem of shaping a solution (we have many differing theories of just what constitutes and operates an enterprise and, particularly, a virtual enterprise). Under Advanced Research Project Agency (ARPA) tasking and the guidance of the Defense Manufacturing Board, we developed a parsing of the enterprise intended to:

- Highlight the ontological domains (which correspond in some respect to different functions within the enterprise)
- Provide for an easy mapping of tools and philosophies from other breakdowns that played significant roles in the marketplace and academy
- Provide a basis for a rigorous study of metrics within and about the virtual enterprise

That decomposition divides the problem space first into "infrastructure" and then "metrics":

- "Infrastructure" describes the "medium" in which an enterprise operates. This includes the various types of rules and constraints that apply to it as well as its kinds and sources of energy. This is all of the stuff of the environment, including the underlying laws and "physics," plus the material of which the enterprise is made. Some of the infrastructure is man-made (like telephones), but other elements are "natural" (like the laws of physics). This parsing of the environment is independent of its representations and can be equated to differences in high-level ontologies (world views).
- "Metrics" concerns the basic stuff of the language used when an enterprise and its components reason and communicate about themselves. We use the term in a richer, broader sense than mere quantitative measures, intending instead to focus on the notions of "value" and "effect" that motivate activity and advise decision making.

Business Enterprise Infrastructures

Enterprise infrastructure is divided according to fundamental differences in how their worlds operate. Some worlds operate like the "real" world and are tied to physics and the impression of absolute truth. Other worlds are man-made, for instance, the legal world. There, for instance, something is true if it can be shown to be "true" by artificial principles of submissability, even if it is not so in the physical world.

Because these infrastructures are something that we can perceive and reason about, the degree to which they can formally and unambiguously be defined is another discriminator. Therefore, we have three large families of infrastructures:

- Those that can be explicitly described and also conform to the laws of natural physics
- Those that can be explicitly described but do not conform to natural physics
- Those that have neither quality — that is, they neither conform to physics nor can be explicitly modeled

Each has further breakdowns of discrete ontologies as listed shortly below. The integration problem in an enterprise is of two orders: integrating across infrastructures that are in the same domain but use different terms (like the shipping departments of two companies), and between infrastructures that live in different worlds (like the goals of a legal department and the operations on a manufacturing floor).

The reason we spend so much time on these divisions is to provide an ontological framework for the distance metrics. Similar parsings have been performed for other enterprises related to homeland defense.

Physically-Based and Explicable Infrastructures

- Physical Laws: These are the basic properties of containment, gravity, motion, and so on.
- Physical Activities: These are the fundamental actions associated with physical operations of manufacturing, conversion of material, and assembly. This is differentiated from the above by adding human intent.

Figure 3. Key (ontological) enterprise infrastructures

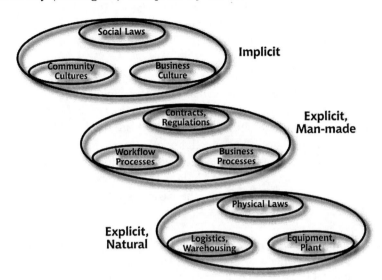

- Logistics: This includes principles associated with presence, location, and movement. This differs from the above two: it captures intent, but the basic ontology is driven by the environment rather than the action.

Most process modeling (especially that associated with enterprise resource planning) only addresses the above infrastructures with some annotations from business rules.

Nonphysically Based but Explicable Infrastructures

- Business Rules: These are the actions that define and drive how the organization operates as a business. Included here are responsibility and control dependencies and most processes associated with trust.
- Financial Rules: This is the world defined by the reward structure, denominated in value metrics and associated currency. In some cases, this infrastructure splits into two siblings: the financial models associated with internal operations and the accounting rules associated with the reporting for the financial infrastructure that finances the enterprise from the financial ecology that surrounds it.
- Legal Systems: This is the ontology concerned with contracts, liabilities and responsibilities, and societal constraints that are codified. This is the least "logical" of the three. In countries with a British colonial heritage, this ontology has unusual ontological properties as a result of dynamic "case law." The rest of the civilized world uses more explicit "code," and some regions have individual, capricious ontologies as result of despotism.

Copyright © 2005, Idea Group Inc. Copying or distributing in print or electronic forms without written permission of Idea Group Inc. is prohibited.

Because the above group consists entirely of man-made "rules," one can say that every element is modeled in some way by the "maker" of the process. Both this and the previous group have formal standard ontology efforts underway in each of the discrete areas, at various levels of maturity and formalism.

Not Fully Explicable Infrastructures

- Enterprise Culture: What is often called "corporate culture," this is the unique collection of rules and practices concerned with influence and status within the enterprise and discrete from the communities that surround it.
- Community Cultures: This is the collection of ethnic, religious, and civil rules and practices that people identify themselves with as individuals "outside" of the enterprise. This includes engineered "brand" and political values.
- Laws of Group Dynamics: These are the basic underlying "physics" of group behavior, independent of culture or enterprise.

This last group is "soft" science and may not be logically modeled. In any case, these behaviors are rarely modeled and poorly, so far as computable predictability. (Tools for stock market prediction are the most advanced in this domain.) On the other hand, historically, most business catastrophes come from some lack of insight here.

Brief Observations

Clearly, some ontologies are more closely linked, or dependent, than others: for instance, business culture and business rules obviously have a dependency, as do financial and legal infrastructures. These have been discovered under the ARPA enterprise ontology project by observation and interview. The ontological dependencies are an essential tool in formalizing discrete ontologies that minimize problems between infrastructure and between simulations and reality.

There is much to say about this ARPA effort. The original impetus was to guide ontological research to aid in metrics for integration. (The approach is outlined in the next section.) Since then, ontologies have become a focus for several large communities: as the basis of the "semantic Web" and as a key component in engineering intelligent agents, software engineering, and simulation of complex systems. Ontologies continue to be the center of the newly revived (and huge) discipline of enterprise engineering for business enterprises and particularly advanced virtual enterprises.

One result is worth mentioning: one would guess that successful enterprises would be those that do well in all of these infrastructures and that lack of excellence in any one would drag the whole system down. Extensive case studies (Goranson, 1999) have discovered the unintuitive result that this is not so. There does appear to be a threshold of incompetence in each infrastructure, but once beyond that, simple competence in most is adequate so long as one or two of the others have special strengths. For instance, if your corporate culture is particularly strong, you can bridge problems in poor management of business rules and legal issues.

We should note that this breakdown of infrastructures is for the ontology level only and is not intended to replace any paradigm used in the actual representation of models or formalisms: the ontological issues are independent of modeling paradigms, such as

Figure 4. Infrastructure linkages

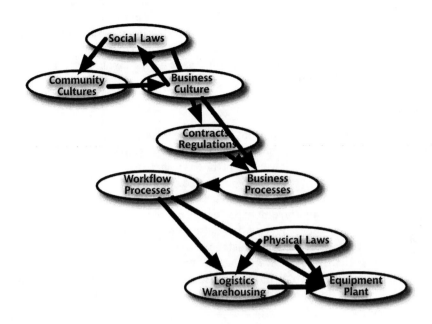

actors; actions; events; relations; dependencies; constraints, behaviors, interactions; or what have you.

METRICS AND SEMANTIC DISTANCE

Ontological foundations are an essential part of the solution to a large general class of problems, but researchers now understand that some better tools are needed concerning the semantics of the communications within and between the ontological domains we identified above as "infrastructures." Two results are notable: a focus on metrics and the previously mentioned research agenda in "semantic distance."

Metrics

All sorts of messages are conveyed within an enterprise. Fortunately, all of these are unlike communications in the open world in that they have a generally explicable purpose. Any reasonable approach to the semantics of collaboration needs to focus on the core semantics of the enterprise. For historical reasons, we call that subset of the semantics the "metrics" subset, but we intend it in a larger sense than a scalar measure like dollars or quality.

The reasoning behind this is simple: we want to reason about the effectiveness of communication within a situation that includes ontological context. The semantics of effectiveness reside in those metrics. Indeed, they constitute a meta-semantics of sorts, information that one can employ when evaluating information. Moreover, the metrics are often embedded in the communications themselves, or motivate them.

Instead of a number, we propose that metrics are semantic entities and that a combination of several metrics in a given context can be characterized algebraically or geometrically in some manner that conveys "fittedness" or "closeness." Moreover, whatever the form of the information, an enterprise will certainly have a (presumably local) algorithm for deriving a cost-benefit scalar from it.

Semantic Distance

The second fundamental element of the approach is brand new. In the past, we crudely assumed that the infrastructure had only two states of effectiveness: either communication was perfect or it was not. In the case where it was not, fatal problems could occur so the infrastructure was not to be trusted.

We now know otherwise. After all, in the real world, communication among all the various ontological domains is seldom perfect. People negotiate to clarify meaning until it is decided that they understand well enough to do what they need to do.

We need a notion of "semantic distance" (or "fittedness"). If we were reasoning about semantics effectively, we would be able to tell things like the following (given a communication between two different representation systems in a specific context):

(1)   This is perfect (the information sent is precisely as understood).
(2)   This is not perfect, but it is good enough for the use intended.
(3)   This is not good enough, but it is "close" and worth the trouble of clarifying this one time.
(4)   This is not good enough, but it is "close" and it is reasonable to change things permanently.
(5)   This is not good enough, and it is "close," and things will or could go wrong, but the consequences are manageable or recoverable and probably tolerable.
(6)   This is not good enough, and it is "close," and things will or could go wrong, and the consequences are potentially catastrophic.
(7)   This is too far apart to be easily fixed, regardless of the extent of consequences.

Figure 5. Four levels of "metrics"

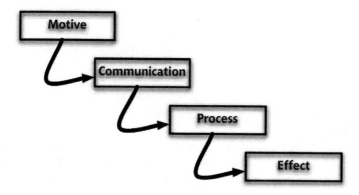

The key elements of the problem appear to be as follows:
- A method of "zooming" from very inexpensive high-level abstraction to elementary details. The high-level perspectives will allow identification of potential mismatches in semantics.
- Formalisms to characterize context, application, and consequences without requiring a complete or certain model of the immediate world.
- Expressions to usefully report and reason about "fittedness."
- Leading approaches to these challenges are (respectively) situation theory (Devlin, 1991), some techniques in reasoning under uncertainty, and a synthesis of group and graph theories (Leyton, 1992).

The notion of distance is better suited to a normal form of "fittedness," perhaps geometric (as in graph patterns) or topological. But there likely needs to be a facility at some point to use local methods with accounting practices to reduce the "geometric distance" to a cost-derived scalar. In that way, managers can "see" the cost to adapt or the cost of consequence. Nevertheless, this number would be a derived, flattened result.

Two Problem Spaces

The workshop identified two scenarios that likely would produce different tools:
- The "lab test bed" scenario, where a tool is tested and certified against a number of peer tools in a wide set of characterized contexts
- The "field environment" scenario, where an operating or newly formed virtual enterprise encounters a single, limited context and wishes to know how well it collaborates

In the lab case, you have the luxury of time. You have the ability to test and discover failure by cheap observation. You almost certainly will have a well-characterized set of scenarios (aka "a test suite") against which the effectiveness of semantic conveyance

Figure 6. Notion of "distances"

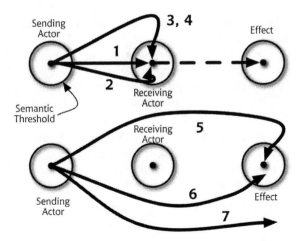

is tested. The distance characterizations are likely to consist of a spectrum of effectiveness against this collection of contexts.

The metric in this case is likely to include information such as:

- Which of the infrastructure categories listed above the tested configuration falls in (There will be a finer breakdown of ontology characterizations of course.)
- A characterization of the situations or contexts in which the condition holds

Additional information might be included. Two types have been identified:

- In case (3) above, where the semantic fit is within shooting distance of being acceptable, there is a characterization indicating the effort required to bridge the inadequacy. This may even be a cost metric and is the only result expected to naturally be a scalar.

In the first two cases, the "semantic robustness characterization" is for the current state of the sending and receiving process, together with a set of contexts.

In the real world, processes rarely remain the same. Any change, however small, could have significant effect on the semantic interoperability, even if the semantics proper do not change. Obviously, that is because the contexts in which the semantics are "safe" might change. The semantic robustness characterization presumably already contains a description of what contexts are "safe" with the current semantics. It would be nice to also have a characterization of contexts in which certain semantic "growth" would be tolerated. Such a "negative distance" would report: "this set of processes not only has these measures of effective conveyance and additionally there are other contexts in which the conveyance can be expected to be effective, and those additional contexts look like this."

The lab test bed scenario is useful for vendors and integrators who want to certify products or increase the trustworthiness of integration frameworks. But there are a large number of instances of virtual enterprise users being confronted with process-to-process collaboration scenarios that have not been precharacterized as described above.

These users will need the ability to determine semantic robustness on the fly, and may need additional tools to help correct an identified problem. In this case, many of the conveniences of the lab will be gone. Time is likely to be an issue. Probably, the most useful implementations would be iterative in that a very inexpensive process would be applied to identify a problem with successively more expensive and detailed iterations that drill into the semantics and context.

This use has been identified in other forums as the "self-organizing (or self-annealing or self-integrating) enterprise" (Kosanke & Nell, 1997).

The projected set of tools includes those of the test bed but adds some additional mechanisms to conduct conversations and support the layered zooming. Anticipated services might be as follows:

- A means of identifying when a mismatch has occurred or is likely to. This could simply be a gross characterization that one or more of the processes involved have not been evaluated in a test bed mode (or, obviously, semantically harmonized). In this case, all semantic interactions are suspect.
- A lightweight language to support dialogue about the semantics involved. This might be called a "semantic interoperability language."

- A technique for quickly guessing contexts and semantic "anchor points" for a first, cheap evaluation to advise on whether further drilling is required.

- A process for guided drilling. The test bed has the luxury of potentially exhaustive examinations of every pocket in every context. The field situation will instead only examine the instant context and the relevant subset of semantics. Identifying these may be nontrivial; it may be easier to follow and certify. However, there is a suspicion that guided anticipatory drilling is possible.

- A concurrent metric of cost of the process for incremental examining and certifying (or not). This might be tied to a "semantic benefit" metric.

- Remaining tools and metrics as inherited from the "simpler" use scenario.

HOW THIS MIGHT WORK

Already, this topic has attracted attention, and there are many suggested directions for solutions and research topics. We feel that the approach that characterizes ontology types by infrastructure and separately employs internal metrics (trust, effectiveness) as the basis for semantics of the external metric (semantic distance) is the way to go. It will require research in three areas to enhance the applicable formal tools.

A Semantic Interoperability Language

We need a semantics to reason about semantics; it needs to include a logic to support formal reasoning over contexts and semantics. Ideally, it should support some sort of "zooming" from high-level, cheap abstraction to thorny details. Fortunately, we have such a thing in situation theory, a system of logic originally developed by linguist mathematicians to formally manage the information from context (Barwise, 1989). Incidentally, it is suited for reasoning about semantics in general and has been used in "zooming" applications in the enterprise context (Rosenberg, 1996).

The focus for activity in situation theory is the Center for the Study of Language and Information at Stanford University.

The first order of business is to extend the Situation Logic and Process Specification Language (PSL) to be friendlier. PSL is a sufficiently formal framework for process-aware ontology dialog.

A Method of Characterizing Unknown Contexts

This speaks only to the operational field environment; the test bed will have well-formed models of the test contexts and associated environments. The field environment is blessed with a simpler case in one regard; it has only one context. But that context is likely to be poorly understood and almost certainly unmodeled in important respects. One must reason over unknowns and uncertains, rather than force the enterprise to go through the extraordinarily expensive process of discovering and modeling their environment. Even many of the facts that will be known by someone may be too expensive to harvest.

We will require a grab bag of techniques for reasoning over uncertainty. The NIST workshop revealed that there is certainly no clear winner here, and that a variety of theories will likely come to bear. Just what techniques are appropriate for which situations is a research topic, one of which our group has not yet investigated.

Note that this supposes that modeling the environment can be orthogonally separated from models of the processes. This is routinely done in the business enterprise but is to be examined for other contexts. For instance, we have studied the combat enterprise (Goranson, 2004) and determined that the uncertainties span both worlds. Almost certainly, this will require further sponsorship in early exploration.

A Robust Means for Modeling and Operating on the "Distance"

Preference and tradition seem to converge on a graph or lattice expression for the actual form of the characterization we have been calling the "fitness metric." We believe it likely that such a thing can have a user-friendly graphical expression using a structured, hyperlinked narrative. Toward that end, we are exploring tools such as Tinderbox (Bernstein, 2004) and have established an expertise in outliner interfaces (Goranson, 2004).

But we need a theory and algebra to manage the representations apart from the logic — the semantic interoperability language — that generates them. This would, in effect, be a metamodeling method, geared toward two levels:

- One level that maps to whatever the native semantics of the metric are. These are abstracted from the models and process codes involved and are one step removed from them. (As mentioned, it is a matter of practice and philosophy as to whether those models and process codes represent an abstraction from reality or constitute a part of the enterprise reality.) This level must have some correspondence between expression and content (between syntax and semantics if you will) to be able to support both the less abstract intuitive graphical user display (based on shape) and the higher level described below.

- A second level that supports an algebra over distance models so that history (context) is captured and also so that a higher level of abstraction for semantic clustering by representation topology is supported. By this clever means (infrastructure categories to distance shape-based groups via "core metrics" semantics), we can work with the clean and flexible mechanics of group theory. It is our belief that if we intend to have an ultimate algebra of semantics, this is the level one must seek.

We favor the work of Michael Leyton for this. He has developed a rudimentary but workable system in the product model domain that has the links to intuitive shape perception, enterprise-sensitive models (albeit not process models), and higher-level group-driven bundles for both simple calculations and meta-reasoning.

We intend to bring his tools from the product model side to the process semantics side, something that "follows the tide" in enterprise integration studies already.

A Collection of Accessible Meta-Metaphors

No metric will survive in the business domain unless it is intuitively accessible to managers. We already noted the requirement to map the complex representation of fittedness into a cost scalar using context-specific mappings. But a semantic distance characterization is a meta-metric, a metric of metrics. That is because we based our reduction of the system semantics to those elements that have effect, in other words, those that affect basic metrics.

Managers will require an accessible metaphor for such "folding." Elsewhere, we describe our proposal for such a metaphor, drawn from popular film (Goranson, 2000c). As it happens, a great many popular movies employ sophisticated folding metaphors that are readily understandable to an ordinary viewer. The notion may seem a little strange, but no more than using sports or war metaphors.

These four areas are being tracked by our group at Old Dominion University. Further international workshops are planned, and an online collaboration infrastructure has been established by NIST.

CONCLUSIONS

The discipline of enterprise integration is maturing beyond the "one-religion" model and dealing with the real-world situation faced by advanced virtual enterprises. We will have to deal with ontological mismatches that are imperfect but sufficiently effective. Some hard research topics are in front of us but with enormous potential.

We are already committed to catalyzing the community and serving as a forum for firming up the research agenda, which at this point is wide open.

However, we have embarked on what we think may be the most promising directions, as described. Probably other approaches will be useful earlier but it appears to us that the community should be aiming high. All productivity gains since World War II can be attributed to improvements in the science underlying infrastructure. We can and must create revolutions for the next era.

In a related activity, the ICEIMT gathering has been taken over by the community as a more regular conference on advancing the science of enterprise integration and could serve to advance the agenda.

REFERENCES

Barwise, J. (1989). *The situation in logic*. Palo Alto: CSLI Press.

Barwise, J. (1990). Constraints, channels and the flow of information. In P. Aczel, D. Isreal, Y. Katagiri, & S. Peters (Eds.), *Situation theory and its applications*. Palo Alto: Stanford University.

Barwise, J., & Seligman, J. (1997). *Information flow, the logic of distributed systems*. Cambridge: Cambridge University Press.

Bernstein, M. (2004). Tinderbox. Available online *http://www.eastgate.com/Tinderbox*

Devlin, K. (1991). *Logic and information*. Cambridge: Cambridge University Press.

Devlin, K., & Rosenberg, D. (1996). *Language at work*. Palo Alto: CSLI Press.

Dove, R. (Ed.). (1995). *Agile practice reference base*. Bethlehem, PA: Lehigh University.

Goranson, H. T. (1999). *The agile virtual enterprise*. Westport: Quorum.

Goranson, H. T. (2003). *Metaphoric concepts for scopable enterprise modeling*. Norfolk: AERO/J9 Report.

Goranson, H. T. (2004). *Counterterrorism infrastructure modeling*. Norfolk: AERO/J9 Report.

Goranson, H. T. (2004). *Semantic distance collaboration group*. Available online *http://interop.cim3.net/*

Kosanke, K., & Nell, J. G. (Ed.). (1997). *Enterprise engineering and integration*. New York: Springer-Verlag.

Kosanke, K., & Nell, J. G., Jochem, R., & Ortega Bas, A. (Ed.). (2003). *Enterprise inter and intra organizational integration*. Dordrecht: Kluwer.

Leyton, M. (1992). *Symmetry, causality, mind*. Cambridge, MA: MIT Press.

Petrie, C. J. (Ed.). (1992). *Enterprise integration modeling*. Cambridge, MA: MIT Press.

Chapter XV

IT Infrastructures and Standards for VE Integration Development

Nicolaos Protogeros
University of Macedonia, Greece

ABSTRACT

In recent years, the new notion of virtual enterprises has sparkled, concentrating efforts to adapt existing technologies and realize this new paradigm. This chapter attempts to understand the needs of information technology (IT) in the virtual enterprises, and to research existing technologies that can help tackle the problem. Technologies such as Web services and software agents are examined that help business process management and thus offer the IT infrastructures to achieve integration. Also, the efforts toward standardization are considered along with the current situation in this area.

INTRODUCTION

The development of technologies that can efficiently handle information complexity, such as software agents, combined with the development of Internet technologies for business process integration and automation, such as Web Services, will experience considerable impact on the way economic actors implement their roles in the worldwide marketplace. This technological evolution will lead to the development of a new value-creating economic paradigm, where the concept of the "virtual enterprise" shall have a central position, and where sets of economic actors are combining their strengths (and where possible, minimizing the impact or consequences of their weaknesses) to provide a specific service traditionally provided by a single enterprise. Such a possibility will offer, in the long term, deep influence on the economy and enterprise development strategies.

Historically speaking, small and medium-sized enterprises (SMEs) have been establishing their competitiveness on statically established cooperations, which have again been based on personal relationships and on the proximity of the involved companies' locations. Groups of SMEs have exhibited in several regions of Europe and the United States the ability to successfully exploit a business opportunity that none of its members has the financial and technological possibility to realize individually.

This approach, even though effective in the past years scenario, is showing its limits in the capability of facing the requirements of the global market, where the search for competitiveness cannot be limited by geographical and personal constraints.

Yet if we could find a way to exploit the tremendous advancement of ICT and the promises of the border-less electronic market in order to harvest the cultural attitude toward cooperation of SMEs and transpose it from its local environment to the worldwide market, we would unleash a tremendous competitive potential in the global market.

Furthermore, within both the overall industrial policy and the enterprise policy, there is a clear imperative to support initiatives that will facilitate and enhance the current way of SMEs "daily" and "routine" working activities. Particularly, the European Commission White Paper on Growth, Competitiveness and Employment proposed a synergetic strategy to ensure economic operators mobilization to support the development of 17 million European SMEs.

The purpose of this discussion is to show how today's technologies can help virtual enterprise integration development and modify the way work can be organized and conducted. It starts by presenting the requirements and technological patterns of virtuality. Next, the challenges issuing from the transition from traditional to virtual are explained, and finally, an overview of the most appropriate technologies that unify work and the conditions required for these technologies to be applied efficiently is presented.

REQUIREMENTS OF VIRTUALITY

The availability on the Internet of standardized SME information, relevant for participating to virtual enterprises, will dramatically multiply the number of business opportunities transformed into successful business ventures.

Cooperation between remote companies and interoperability of relevant business processes is enabled through the integration of the product, process, and organizational data.

The proposed ICT environment must allow for the constitution of optimized, dynamic organization and for the management of complex business operations.

The ICT environment will have to accommodate online consultation of the project status by any of the participating actors, thus supporting decision process through the continuous monitoring of project and product evolution.

Visibility Across the Virtual Enterprise

Thanks to the new ICT tools and methodologies, which aim at the improvement of SMEs' virtual enterprises management, the overall visibility on the entire life cycle of the product, starting from its development to its launch into the market is made possible. Such a visibility must also be permitted to all the SMEs' personnel involved in the virtual enterprise operation and, in particular, to the project managers that often, in the traditional supply chain, cannot adequately follow the development of important sub-systems, which are supplied by a subcontractor.

Consistent and Uniform Business Model

A uniform business model is very important for the viability of the virtual enterprise. It should support the evolution of the product, process, and organizations according to the increasing detail of the attributes representing the same concept (such as the status of an order, categorization of the order, customer contact information, customer account representation, etc.) in a consistent manner.
This model should support, specifically:

- A uniform look of the virtual enterprise to the stakeholder and the customer. A solution could be a portal where the stakeholder can search, view, and potentially update the information on the customer.
- A uniform management of interfaces at product level and at organizational level.
- A concurrent definition of the virtual enterprise organization, based on integrated product design, for the establishment of optimized business ventures.

Consistent Cooperative Process and Data Model

The data model of the companies can capture various behavioral semantics of the business entities. Thus, it is not sufficient to have just a consistent conceptual business model of the business entities for smooth operation (Setrag, 2002). Data semantics and operational behavior must also be represented and applied consistently.

The most important implication of data model consistency for IT is perhaps in the transactional dimension. Transactions need to be atomic, consistent, isolated, and durable — the so-called ACID test for transactions. This means that updates on distributed business entities should be guaranteed by the framework so as to propagate consistently (ACID properties).

Uniform Organizational Model

The organizational view of enterprises captures information about departments, roles, employees, partners, and entire organizations. The organizational model of the virtual enterprise should encompass ownership, privileges, and responsibility of messages, documents, and activities that are involved in the processes of the virtual enterprise. It also has to involve extensive security as well as personalization requirements.

Virtual enterprises can be thought of as an aggregation of processes. Thus, these processes use information, operations, roles, and sequencing of tasks to carry out specific objectives in the virtual enterprise.

TECHNOLOGICAL PATTERNS
OF VIRTUALITY

There are huge gaps in the business scope and different working standards between the large enterprises and the SMEs. SMEs significantly contribute to the value chain by supplying required equipment and subsystems to the large enterprises. In Europe, for example, the need to harmonize the large and SMEs business approaches and practises has been pointed out several times at a European Community level.

These differences reflect on the IT applications used and, thus, on the integration process. Technologies should support the three main phases of a virtual enterprise life cycle (BIDSAVER), which are as follows:

- The search for partners in a business opportunity that will form the virtual enterprise
- The construction of the management frame for a business opportunity (constitution of the virtual enterprise)
- The operation phase of the virtual enterprise

Virtual Enterprise Formation — Search for Partners

The initial phase of the virtual enterprise life cycle addresses the search for partners; such a search requires the capability of:

- Understanding specific market characteristics
- Specifying the structure of product and of associated development and production activities
- Specifying the requirements for the execution of development and production activities
- Searching potential partners over the Internet and evaluating their suitability to enter the virtual enterprise

Information capturing agents can be developed to be in charge of searching, collecting, storing, and evaluating information on potential partners for the virtual enterprise, to verify their suitability.

Constitution of the Virtual Enterprise

The constitution phase of the virtual enterprise entails the establishment of the cooperative frame and of the support environment.
Major steps of this phase consist of the following:

- Establishing the actual list of partners and related roles and responsibilities
- Defining operational procedures and management mechanisms
- Entering the legal agreement for the operation of the virtual enterprise
- Implementing the upgrades to individual partners' work environments, whenever required for full operation of the virtual enterprise

Elements that have to be developed in support of this phase are as follows:

- The cooperation model, specifying the virtual enterprise in its subdivision of roles and responsibilities
- The virtual enterprise model, specific to individual business opportunities, specifying the sequencing of tasks and related relationships
- The legal frame, supporting the virtual enterprise's partners to enter binding agreements
- The business information integration module that is in charge of translating virtual enterprise models into specific data structures

Virtual Enterprise Operation

The operation phase of the virtual enterprise covers the product development and production phases and ends with the formal closure of the virtual enterprise.

Activities that are addressed during this phase include the typical industrial operation tasks, like accounting, material management, design, engineering, production, marketing, and so on.

Elements that have to be developed in support of this phase are as follows:

- The operational model, supporting the organizational evolution of the virtual enterprise
- The information retrieval systems, supporting the automated collection of operational information
- The business information integration tools, supporting the operational tasks through the interfacing to existing tools of the members
- The legal frame, regulating the relationships among partners and the evolution of virtual enterprises, until closure of the cooperation

Virtuality and Physical Presence

Physical presence is not necessary to the virtual enterprise. Instead, the technology permits the virtual presence of the participants. This means that the organizations and its employees are available, they participate and carry out their work as their roles in the virtual enterprise prescribe, without physically being there. Internet technology permits the creation of virtual offices where the individuals, the roles, the organizational structures, and the various applications appear to be virtually present.

Virtuality and Resource Aggregation

Resource aggregation is the most important issue to tackle when forming a virtual enterprise. The key concept of a virtual enterprise is that organizational structure, business practices, roles, and applications appear to be well aggregated and integrated. We will expand more in the subsequent sections on this concept, as it appears to be the key success factor.

Virtuality and Dynamics

Cooperation among SMEs in a virtual enterprise is performed only according to business opportunities and purely competitiveness-oriented criteria. This allows for the constitution of virtual enterprises with a strong dynamic connotation, characterized by the possibility of selecting an optimized partners' set.

The main objective of a virtual enterprise is the catch of an appeared business opportunity that none of each members alone would be able to exploit. Therefore, the notion of dynamics is inherent to the virtual enterprise. Partners enter and leave the virtual enterprise as it evolves over time. The underlying IT must be able to support both the search of new partners and the operation phase of existing partner sets. The selection of potential partners to join the virtual enterprise could depend on product or service specifications, price, availability, time schedules, etc. The corresponding processes should be invoked, involving different organizations, roles, and other resources to execute specific transactions. Interfaces could also change. Whether they are based on simple document exchange to describe the various process elements or follow more strict exchange choreographies, such as the partner interchange process (PIP), following the RosettaNet standard, they are subject to constant evolution and change over time. The core of virtuality is the ability to dynamically adapt to these constant changes.

Virtuality and Integration

In the constitution and operation of a virtual enterprise, a business-centric approach must be adopted: the virtual enterprise is the equivalent of a set of projects, managed through the continuous search for the best skills and capabilities, where selection and management of resources is performed both at the level of individual SMEs and at the aggregation level of virtual enterprise.

Due to this nature of the virtual enterprise, the heterogeneity characterizes the variety of applications, business practices, and production methods within the partners of a virtual enterprise. Thus, integration appears to be the dominant challenge, spanning all the different dimensions of virtuality. Integration is possible in the business process layer (Sriganesh, 2003).

Business processes can be divided into two distinct but converging domains:

- Public processes are those that an enterprise shares with its customers, suppliers, or other partners. This is the business-to-business integration (B2Bi) domain.
- Private processes are those that are internal to the enterprise. This is the enterprise application integration (EAI) domain.

These two domains have similarities in many of their characteristics. For example, both the EAI and B2B domains use extended markup language (XML) document exchange between applications for loosely coupled integration of applications. Additionally, public and private business processes interoperate to perform the overall operations of the business.

Among the differences between the domains, we can note the stricter legal and security requirement that applies to public processes and the finest execution details of the private process models that are not present in public process models.

There has been great experience gained in the IT community from integration projects in the past, which has shown that integration is a difficult task to achieve. Whether it concerns back-end and legacy applications or databases and information from multiple sources, integration has to pass through various types of repositories, databases, file formats, and applications that very often manage the same type of information (e.g., customers) with very different semantics.

In the heart of integration of virtual enterprises is the process. Its internal processes and procedures characterize the virtual enterprise, much like in a traditional organization. If integration is to be achieved, it is much easier done in the process model that includes the business policies, the roles, and the relationships between the participants along with the business logic of the interactions and exchanges between the partners.

Some researchers and analysts have proposed (BIDSAVER) that the integration concept of virtual enterprises should be based on three separate integration tasks: the integration of product breakdown structure (bill of materials), work breakdown structure and organizational breakdown structure. This could allow for cross-mapping of the following:

- Product physical/functional items
- Tasks and associated resources, risks, and timing
- Responsible entities and organizations and associated contractual elements

FROM TRADITIONAL TO VIRTUAL

In the industrial scenario, the larger involvement of SMEs is especially related to the supply of design and production of intermediate products or, in the best cases, of subsystems to large enterprises.

The cultural background of the majority of the European SMEs, for example, is mainly related to the specific industrial sector they have been operating since the beginning of their operations. Although SMEs accumulate a deep knowledge relevant to the specific industrial sector, they hardly succeed in redeploying their skills and capacities in industrial sectors different from the original one because of the lack of general view on the market opportunities and, above all, the excessive specialization of their business processes.

A major problem of SMEs is the absence of explicit, documented, and standardized private and public processes. There is a need for them to streamline their processes, with the aim to facilitate the redeployment of their skills and capacities in different industrial sectors. In order to participate in a virtual enterprise and exchange information on activities, roles, processes, and procedures, they will have to adapt to a standard. This is feasible if we separate the business processes operations (Setrag, 2002) or process logic within the organization from the applications.

Cope with Traditional Applications

Applications usually contain a number of processes that carry out manual (need user intervention) or automatic tasks in a specific order and at a specific time. The process logic that consists of steps involved within the call sequence of the procedures or functions of the application's API or message exchange is something different from the application's logic (or business logic). However, the business logic and the application logic are, at worst, intertwined.

Virtual enterprise seamless integration will be possible as this separation becomes prevalent. With the emergence of a separate layer with consistent semantics and

Figure 1. Business process stack

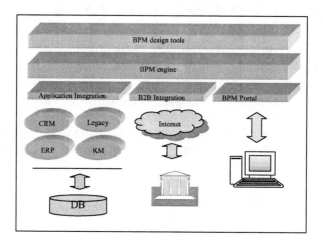

predictable execution models of processes, various systems with different semantics will make integrating through this commonplace system possible. According to many analysts, in the near future, different systems will state what standards compliant business process management systems (BPMSs) they support, much like today, applications state what type of operating system or database they support.

In the separation of the business process layer, a stack is formed where BPMS is the upper layer and traditional applications such as enterprise resource planning (ERP), accounting and knowledge management systems form the lower layers (Figure 1). The BPM engine is the environment where process execution takes place. Typically, the process engine activates each process template. Upon activation, various tasks are assigned to roles. If the task involves an application, the BPM engine will invoke that application or send a message to it. The BPM engine also maintains the audit trail of all the executed processes. BPM engines are typically state transition machines. Examples of process or activity states include running, suspended, resumed, or completed. In the following chapters, we will examine the most common standards.

A couple of BPM systems are commercialized today. They are usually based on Java and follow the Java2 Enterprise Edition (J2EE) specifications. They can be integrated with most ERP, EAI, and B2Bi systems. Examples include BEA's Process Integrator, SAP's Business Workflow, Software AG's EntireX, etc. Oracle, IBM, Microsoft, webMethods, Vitria, and others also provide BPM solutions. In the following, we will examine technologies such as EAI, B2Bi, knowledge management, and workflow and their relationship with BPM.

Enterprise Application Integration

EAI is the set of tools and technologies developed to integrate various dissimilar applications within the organization. Mostly, they consist of flowcharts or maps for invoking applications or sending and receiving messages in specific orders. Often, several of these applications need to be involved in system transactions.

EAI has many common features as BPM, but there are differences between the two, and some of these are discussed below.

EAI contains tools and technologies that tie preexisting packaged applications together. Many EAI products have tools that enable a business to automate business processes by superimposing them across existing applications. BPMS (Jenz , 2001) is a mechanism which rapidly develops and evolves custom business automation solutions by directly integrating with legacy and packaged systems as an implementation detail. In a way, BPM compliments EAI by creating new processes and services that EAI tools are designed to integrate.

Workflow Management

Work management technologies are a collection of tools designed to assist production of work. They are sometimes categorized as production, administrative, and ad-hoc workflows. Historically, workflow systems have their roots in document imaging. Paper-intensive and manual processes were replaced with automated workflow systems. They included such tools as e-mail, meeting scheduling, forums, collaboration tools, groupware, and various other activities like human processing through annotations, data entry, filing and archiving on optical media, etc.

As workflow systems evolved, they started to be used with many applications, such as the following:

- Document management, which stores large quantities of documents in an organized way, and maintain versions, renditions, indexes and so on
- Human resource management applications (such as hiring processes)
- Financial accounting applications (such as purchase approval), and much more

In particular, the more recent workflow systems started to invoke applications (system participants), not just humans. So, work was carried out either by a human participant or a back-end system. These systems could be:

- Packaged applications
- Custom applications
- Legacy systems
- Other workflow systems that supports business processes for their whole lifetime

At first glance, BPM and workflow systems look similar. However, there are some differences that state that BPM is not the same as workflow.

Workflow is a technology that facilitates the flow of activities mainly in the form of documents that are carried out by human participants. Of course, systems can also be involved, but the core model is assigning tasks to individuals. Usually, it handles document flow models, decision authorities, roles, and workers, while BPM systems encompass workflow along with pure automation and pure decision making. BPM addresses how automation is organized at a refined level of detail and can represent intelligent self-acting business concepts, which is more than workflow systems do with passive documents in handling rules. Finally, BPM can describe workflows, which can complete manual steps in business processes.

Knowledge Management

Knowledge management (KM) technologies are a collection of tools designed to store and retrieve knowledge. They include such tools as:

- Document management to store and retrieve documents
- Data warehouses and data mining tools to store and analyze data coming from accounting-based applications
- Full text indexing and search agents, basis of search engines as known today on the Internet, to search documents based upon their content
- Thesaurus to enable intelligent search on full text indexes by storing terms hierarchies, relationships, and similarities
- Linguistic tools to support natural language queries
- Semantic networks to store meaning of documents as a network of actions on objects and enable powerful searches on a document based on network patterns matching (e.g., all documents speaking about exportation regulations)
- Intelligent document retrieval tools with "learning capabilities" of both the user interest, and the target systems delivering capabilities

These tools are used for understanding the marketplace, and the possibilities that are offered in various areas, in order to make better decisions, orient product definitions, and better organize (Ader, 2001).

Business-to-Business Systems

B2B commerce is about extending the business processes outside the organization, to be shared with its partners, suppliers, and customers. Organizations involved in supply or value chains develop specific message and information exchange choreographies with specific policies. The exchange is bound by specific structure of the various messages that get exchanged, by specific business rules, timing constraints, security requirements, and process flow logic.

B2B integration can be regarded as BPM, because flow maps also get executed in EAI engines or B2Bi exchanges. In fact, organizations such as ebXML (ebXML, 2001, 2003) and Rosetta Net recognize the exchange choreographies between trading partners as processes. Rosetta Net defines many PIPs that involve the activities, messages, and partner role interactions between two partners in the supply chain. They can all be categorized as business processes that span the entire spectrum of the organization.

TECHNOLOGIES THAT UNIFY

As we mentioned above, the key concept for unification under a virtual enterprise is integration. Integration is difficult, and many complex integration projects have failed. However, that is something that is starting to change with Web services. With Web services, integration is seamless. The technologies that Web services use, such as HTTP and SOAP/XML at the wire level and XML standards for registries and payload, are robust and readily available. And if we combine the tremendous flexibility and complete independence from programming language and operating system of Web services with the efficiency and autonomy of software agents, then we can get a robust framework for real unification.

In the following, we will emphasize the following technologies:

- *Web Services* (WS) technologies that provide the means for real BMP in the private as well as in the public processes layers
- *Software Agent* (SA) technologies that provide a very efficient way to manage complex information environments, by dividing them into smaller autonomous manageable pieces.

Web Services

Web services are software components that use standard Internet technologies and are able to interact with one another dynamically (Figure 2). Web services offer a robust and flexible environment to develop such systems today. Most of these systems are based on this technology. Web services technology is a collection of XML-based standards that provide a means for passing information among applications using XML documents. The ability of Web services to reach beyond the firewall, the loose coupling between applications encouraged by Web service interfaces, and the wide support for core Web service standards by major enterprise software vendors are the key reasons why Web services technology promises to make integration of applications both within the enterprise and among different enterprises significantly easier and cheaper than before.

Virtual enterprise formation and operation can be based on Web services, because loose coupling means that not only can applications be implemented on different platforms and operating systems, but also that the implementations can readily be changed without affecting the interfaces, a necessary element for supporting virtual enterprise dynamics.

A business process standard that provides comprehensive support for both public and private processes should consider the features discussed below (Apshankar, 2002).

Figure 2. Web Services fundamental operations

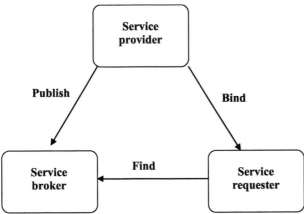

Collaboration-Based Process Models

In collaboration-based process models, processes are described as a set of collaborations between various participants, including organizations, applications, employees, and other business processes. Usually, participants can be abstracted in model descriptions using roles. Collaboration-based process models are usually based on UML.

Workflow

The workflow defines how the participants in a process work together to execute a process from start to finish, which is also called choreography or orchestration. Most workflow standards support subprocesses, which allow activities within a workflow to be implemented as another workflow. Workflow descriptions can be generated from collaboration models or specified independently.

Transaction Management

Transactions are vital building blocks of business process. Business process standard must provide a means for specifying how transactions are managed. There are two kind of transactions: ACID (coordinated) and long-running transactions that may take hours or weeks to complete. Time constraints for receiving responses or acknowledgments may also be required.

Exception Handling

The BPMS should allow associating actions with exceptions. If an exception is raised during the course of a business process, then the associated recovery actions are taken.

Service Interfaces

Those are the interfaces that provide the basis for passing messages between participants in collaboration-based processes. Some recently proposed business process standards such as Business Process Execution Language for Web Services (BPEL4WS) use Web services description language (WSDL) interfaces to describe the loosely coupled services exposed by participants.

Message Security and Reliability

For mission-critical processes, reliable and secure message delivery is required. Additionally, B2B messages may need to be digitally signed and authenticated. These quality-of-service semantics may vary for different transactions.

Audit Trail

It is generally very important for legal purposes (such as nonrepudiation) that an audit trail of certain business transactions be kept in B2B processes. Audit trail requirements may also include digitally signed receipt acknowledgments of messages.

Agreements

An agreement represents a contract between two or more partners that carry out specific functions (identified by roles) in a public business process. Agreements are specifically used in B2B processes.

Execution

In order to be able to fully automate the execution of the business process within an organization, the complete information flow within that organization as well as across its firewalls must be specified. This requires the process models to fully describe the private as well as the public activities of the organization.

TODAY'S EFFORT TOWARD
BPM STANDARDS STACK

In order to understand the efforts to develop standards related to the above features and how it maps to specific architectures from prominent organizations or companies, we will examine in the following the most important architectures. The next section examines some of the business process specifications in more detail.

In Figure 3, we have a generic architecture of the BPM stack showing the relations between the various proposed standards. In this architecture, we have the layers as discussed below.

Agreements

This layer describes the parts of the protocol that permits the collaboration among trading partners to execute shared business processes.

Orchestration

This layer describes how services interact in business processes by means of a language for the description of Web services compositions, using workflow descriptions. This layer is also sometimes referred to as the choreography layer.

Figure 3. Simplified representation of today's BPM stack

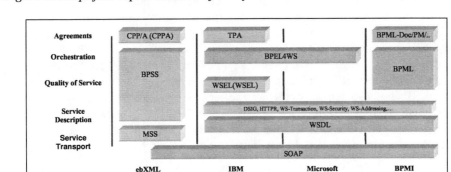

Quality of Service

This layer describes reliability and security and other nonoperational characteristics of services.

Service Description

This layer describes the Web services interface. It is a way to describe services and how they should be bound to specific network addresses.

Service Transport

This layer provides the envelope for sending Web services messages reliably and securely over the Internet or the intranet.

For brevity's sake, we will now examine in more detail only the specifications that address the orchestration layer that describes business process semantics, because it is the most important. These are BPSS, BPEL4WS, and BPML. Each supports some subset of the aforementioned features, depending largely on the domain they are addressing.

BPSS

Business process specification schema (BPSS) is a standard framework by which business systems may be configured to support execution of business collaborations consisting of business transactions. It is part of the comprehensive ebXML (ebXML, 2001, 2003) B2B suite of specifications, which also includes core specifications for reliable and secure messaging based on SOAP, collaboration agreements and profiles, a registry/repository, and core components. It is based upon prior UN/CEFACT work, specifically the meta-model behind the UN/CEFACT Modeling Methodology (UMM). The specification schema supports the specification of business transactions and the choreography of business transactions into business collaborations. These patterns determine the actual exchange of business documents and business signals between the partners to achieve the required electronic commerce transaction.

The transaction part of the model is based on a proven, robust model for long-lived e-commerce business transactions used by previous B2B standards, such as Rosetta Net. There is explicit support for specifying quality-of-service semantics for transactions such as authentication, acknowledgements, nonrepudiation, and time-outs:

- *Organization*: ebXML.org (*http://www.ebxml.org*)
- *Features*: Collaboration- based modeling, workflow, long-running business trans-action model, exception handling, service interface descriptions for each role, agreements. There is no support for internal execution semantics.

BPEL4WS

Business Process Execution Language for Web Services (BPEL4WS) provides a language for the formal specification of business processes and business interaction protocols. By doing so, it extends the Web services interaction model and enables it to support business transactions. BPEL4WS (Wohed, 2002) defines an interoperable integration model that should facilitate the expansion of automated process integration in both the intracorporate and the business-to-business spaces.

BPEL4WS represents a convergence of the ideas in the Microsoft's XLANG (XLANG) and IBM's WSFL (WSFL) specifications. Both XLANG and WSFL are superseded by the BPEL4WS specification.

- *Organization*: BEA, IBM, Microsoft, SAP AG, et al. (*http://ifr.sap.com/bpel4ws/*).
- *Features*: Collaboration-based modeling, workflow, long-running business transaction model, exception handling, service interface descriptions, and agreements.

BPML

Business process modeling language (BPML) is a meta-language for the modeling of business processes. BPML provides an abstracted execution model for collaborative and transactional business processes based on the concept of a transactional finite-state machine.

BPMI.org and ebXML (ebXML, 2001, 2003) are addressing complementary aspects of e-business process management according to BPMI (Figure 3). While ebXML provides a standard way to describe the public interface of e-business processes, BPMI.org provides a standard way to describe their "Private Implementation."

- *Organization*: BPMI.org (*http://www.bpmi.org/bpml.esp*)
- *Features:* Collaboration-based modeling, recursive decomposition is supported through nested processes, comprehensive control and data flow support, comprehensive support for both ACID (coordinated) and long-running (extended) transactions, robust exception-handling capabilities, service interfaces described using abstract processes. There is no support for security and reliability semantics. There is no support for nonrepudiation semantics. There is no support for agreements, execution supported through abstract interfaces.

Web Services and Virtual Enterprises

As the new economy put on more pressure, organizations are striving to interconnect with their customers and suppliers electronically by traditional means. Their focus, so far, primarily rested on connecting at the data level, rather than at the business process level.

In late 1998, the new idea of business process management emerged. It has since then slowly but steadily gained momentum, resulting in the birth of business process management systems (BPMS). These systems support the full life cycle of process design, deployment, execution, analysis, and optimization, allowing organizations to make their business processes explicit, documented, and manageable.

Based on the BPMS idea, Microsoft, IBM, and Ariba joined efforts to produce a standard for use in the BPM. In 2000, the Web services concept emerged from this effort and gained popularity. Many people consider Web services as the next step in abstraction beyond object-oriented technology.

Web services tend to become mature technology. In combination with its related technologies, such as universal description, discovery, and integration (UDDI) and simple object access protocol (SOAP), BPMS and Web services allow for the creation of truly virtual enterprises.

Software Agents

Software agent (SA) technologies can be used in dynamic and open environments in which, for example, heterogeneous systems must interact, span organizational boundaries, and operate effectively within rapidly changing circumstances and with dramatically increasing quantities of available information. Virtual enterprises are typical examples of such environments, where improvements on the traditional computing models and paradigms are required. In particular, the need for some degree of *autonomy*, to enable components to respond dynamically to changing circumstances while trying to achieve overarching objectives, is seen as fundamental. While this notion does not intend to suggest an absence of control, some application contexts offer no alternative to *autonomous* software.

As shown in the previous paragraphs, Web services now offer fundamentally new ways of doing business through a set of standardized tools and support a service-oriented view of distinct and independent software components interacting to provide valuable functionality. In the context of such developments, agent technologies have become some of the primary weapons in the arsenal aimed at addressing the emergent problems and managing the complexity of virtual enterprise integration.

Autonomous Agents for Information Exchange Processes

The use of intelligent agents for expertise search and information exchange is a research activity of growing interest. A considerable number of applications find a suitable instrument in this technology, from a simple search based on selected queries to the analysis of written messages in order to create an intelligent catalogue. Intelligent agents may be employed for the purpose of intelligent data exchange among enterprises, in order to find suitable business partners and exploit new business opportunities, collecting all the retrieved data in a repository accessible by all the virtual enterprise members. The data format can be designed according to XML specification, allowing for a flexible definition of communication procedures.

Business Processes and Autonomous Agents

A combination of agent technology and Web services could be possible in the services level. In that level, developing a Web service as an *autonomous* agent presents a set of challenges and offers a lot of possibilities.

Web services are generally stateless, meaning that they do not preserve state across invocations. Consequently, control is kept within the caller service. Preserving state by using cookies will often not be a viable option. WSDL describes the smaller unit of action offered by a service as an *operation*. An operation can be a single asynchronous message, or a request/response pair of messages, with optional fault messages. The operation can be either incoming or outgoing. However, WSDL does not specify the operation concern. It could be on a stateless service, which has no knowledge of previous operations, such as a weather retrieval service. Or it could be an operation on an object; in the usual way operations are used in object-oriented programming systems. In that case, the object will have the ability to use its state variables to keep a record of the consequences of previous operations. In the latter case, we usually think of the object as being subservient to the caller—the caller controls the entire life history of the object.

The object has minimal influence regarding the order in which its operations are invoked and has no independent behavior. Another possibility highlighted in Microsoft's XLANG is the use of software agents:

"The service might represent stateful autonomous agents. In this case the service supports stateful long-running interactions in which each interaction has a beginning, a defined protocol for operation invocation, and an end. This is typically the case in cross-enterprise business processes such as supply chains. A seller may offer a service that begins an interaction by accepting a purchase order via an input message, and then returns an acknowledgement to the buyer if the order can be fulfilled. It may later send further messages to the buyer such as shipping notices and invoices. These input and output operations do not occur in random order. They occur according to a defined sequence, a service process. And the seller's service remembers the state of each such purchase order interaction separately from other similar interactions. This is necessary because a buyer may be carrying on many simultaneous purchase processes with the same seller. Finally, every instance of the service process may have a private life of its own and it may autonomously perform activities in the background without the stimulus of an input operation."

Challenges Developing Service Agents

Many challenges arise in describing realistic business processes of this nature, especially in the loosely coupled environment that must be assumed across business boundaries. Some research projects in the past have proposed a central authority that coordinates the virtual enterprise. This scenario is difficult to develop because of practical reasons. Unlike traditional enterprise workflow architectures, *it is difficult to have a central authority that manages the business process for the collection of participating enterprises.* Instead, each enterprise provides one or more process-capable services that act as autonomous agents, and the coordination among them occurs implicitly as a result of the operations performed rather than through a collective state management system. In XLANG, for example (XLANG is the standard of Microsoft that is now obsolete due to the new standard BPEL4WS), they strictly follow the discipline that the behavior of each autonomous agent is specified independently, and the only interaction between them occurs through message exchanges expressed as WSDL operations. They show how the ports and operations of the participants can be linked to each other to construct an overall business process.

CONCLUSIONS

The challenges in realizing virtuality are many. Software agents and Web services have solved or are solving a lot of issues for virtual enterprises, although it was not their primary intention. Most EAI, B2Bi, and workflow projects have addressed virtual enterprise issues.

Web services, through their ease of integration, flexibility, and support of XML vocabularies, provide a platform to realize virtual enterprises. Because vertical or horizontal application domains are being enriched by agreed-upon XML vocabularies, every application or computer–human interaction can be modelled as a Web service. The

XML transformation and other associated technologies facilitate the system-level integration of services and trading partners.

Moreover, as software agent technology matures and becomes more widespread, problems like service autonomy within a BPM system, or the virtual enterprise partner retrieval process, can be solved easily.

Finally, the recent advances in business process management standards for Web services have made it possible for organizations to define, deploy, and interact with Web services within the context of processes spanning the entire virtual enterprise.

There are, of course, drawbacks. Due to the additional description layer, Web services can be "bulky" or slow, and throughput will suffer. Some of the technologies associated with Web services are still immature; SOAP interoperability is still one of these issues, meaning that implementations from different vendors do not necessarily work together well. However, the plumbing issues at the technical integration level can and will be solved over time. This is also true for higher-level issues, most notably, business transactions, security, reliability, metering of Web services, and message tracking.

Today, technologies form a solid base from which to mount virtual enterprises. It seems that problems like process integration, visibility across the enterprise, and consistent and uniform business models can be addressed efficiently. There is no doubt that virtual enterprises will be born and live for the years to come.

REFERENCES

Ader, M. (2001). *Technologies for the virtual enterprise*. France: Workflow & Groupware Strategies.

Apshankar, K., Chang, H., et al. (2002). *Web services business strategies and architectures*. Chicago: Expert Press.

BIDSAVER Project. Vive Project HTML. Available online *http://www.vive-ig.net/projects/bidsaver/*

BPEL4WS. (n.d.). Business Process Execution Language for Web Services. Available online *http://www-106.ibm.com/developerworks/webservices/library/ws-bpel/*

BPML (n.d.). Business Process Modelling Language. Available online *http://www.bpmi.org/bpml.esp*

BPSS (n.d.). Business Process Specification Schema. Available online *http://www.ebxml.org/specs/ebBPSS.pdf*

CPPA (n.d.). Collaboration Protocol Profile/Agreement. Available online *http://www.oasis-open.org/committees/ebxml-cppa/*

ebXML. (2001). Business Process Specification Schema, Business Process Project Team UN/CEFACT and OASIS.

ebXML. (2003). Business Process Specification Advances within OASIS, UN/CEFACT and OASIS (21 October).

Jenz, E. D. (2001). BPMS and Web Services: An unbeatable team. Available online *www.Webservices.org*

PIP (n.d.). Partner Interface Process. Available online *http://www.service-architecture.com/web-services/articles/pip_directory.html*

Setrag, K. (2002). *Web Services and virtual enterprises*. Chicago: Tect.

Sriganesh, R. P. (2003). *Java Platform for integration—Technologies, best practices and case study*. Sun Tech Days.

UDDI, Universal Description, Discovery, and Integration. Available online *http:// www.oasis-open.org/committees/uddi-spec/*

Wohed, P., Wil, M. P. et al. (2002). *Pattern based analysis of BPEL4WS*. Technical Report FIT-TR-2002-04, Queensland University of Technology.

WSDL (n.d.). Web Services Description Language. Available online *http://www.w3.org/ 2002/ws/desc/*

WSEL (n.d.). Web Services Endpoint Language. Available online *http://www.w3.org/ 2001/04/wsws-proceedings/rod_smith/img13.htm*

WSFL (n.d.). Web Services Flow Language. Available online *http://www.service-architecture.com/web-services/articles/web_services_ endpoint_language_wsel.html*

XLANG (n.d.). Available online *http://www.gotdotnet.com/team/xml_wsspecs/xlang-c/default.htm*

Chapter XVI

Interactive Models for Virtual Enterprises

Håvard D. Jørgensen
Computas, Norway

John Krogstie
SINTEF and NTNU, Norway

ABSTRACT

This chapter presents a novel approach to the development, integration, and operation of virtual enterprises (VEs). The approach is based on the idea of interactive models. An interactive model is a visual model of enterprise aspects that can be viewed, traversed, analyzed, simulated, adapted, and executed by the participants of the VE. The approach has been developed in several research projects, where experiences from industrial case studies are used as a basis for validation and further enhancement. A major result of this work is the model-driven infrastructure that integrates and supports VEs. The main innovative contributions of this infrastructure include concurrent modelling, metamodelling, management and performance of work, integrated support for ad hoc and structured processes, and customizable model- and process-driven integration.

INTRODUCTION

Business environments are becoming increasingly dynamic and knowledge intensive. Cooperation across traditional organizational boundaries is increasing, as outsourcing and electronic business are enabled by the Internet and other information systems. In VEs, each partner company contributes unique and complimentary competence vital for the success of the joint project. When interorganizational cooperation moves beyond the buying and selling of goods and well-defined services, there is thus a need for flexible infrastructures that support not only information exchange but also knowledge creation, evolution, and sharing.

While computerization automates routine procedures, knowledge-based cooperation remains a challenge. Paradoxically, studies conclude, "simple and adaptable technologies enable more complex virtual collaboration" (Qureshi & Zigurs, 2001). Low-level tools like e-mail are used far more frequently than sophisticated coordination systems. VE process management tools are currently regarded as "obtuse and inaccessible to the vast majority of knowledge workers" (Delphi Group, 2001). This chapter aims to demonstrate that information and communication technology (ICT) infrastructures controlled by enterprise models can offer rich, but at the same time simple, and comprehensible support to VEs.

BACKGROUND

A VE is defined as "a customer solution delivery system created by a temporary and ICT enabled integration of core competencies" (Tølle, Bernus, & Vesterager, 2002, p. 1). Infrastructures developed for VEs face three highly intertwined challenges:

- *Heterogeneity*, incommensurable perspectives, software infrastructures, working practices etc., among the partner companies
- *Flexibility*, due to need for learning, change, and exception handling
- *Complexity*, the richness and uncertainties of interdependencies among partners, their activities, resources, skills, and products

Heterogeneity, change, and complexity must be managed at different levels:

- *Knowledge*, the skills needed for problem solving and work performance, the shared language and frames of reference needed for communication, etc.
- *Process*, the planning, coordination, and management of cooperative and interdependent activities and resources
- *Infrastructure*, the information formats, software tools, and interoperability approaches of the participating companies

The resulting problem space is summarized in Table 1. Each level is elaborated upon below. For networks of small and medium-sized enterprises (SMEs), these challenges are amplified, as resources are scarcer and high entry costs are prohibitive.

Process Structure, Diversity, and Evolution

Unstructured creative activities are often most important for the competitiveness of an enterprise. Even in seemingly routine work, exceptions and uncertainties permeate the environment. Workers reflect upon and manage these problems in a sophisticated manner (Wenger, 1998). To some extent, most work can thus be regarded as knowledge intensive. On the other hand, most work processes also have routine parts that can be structured and automated. Many companies have prescribed quality management procedures for administration, audit, approval, etc. Systems must thus integrate support

Table 1. Problem space for VE integration

	Knowledge	Process	Infrastructure
Heterogeneity	*Communication*, establishing a common language across companies and disciplines	*Process diversity*, negotiating different procedures between the partners	*Interoperability* across companies' software architectures
Complexity	*Integrate capabilities*, form effective teams across local cultures	*Work management*, planning and coordinating complex and uncertain interdependencies among several concurrent activities	*Enterprise architectures*, managing systems portfolios; avoiding *featuritis* (unmanageably complex systems)
Flexibility	*Learning*, partners must be able to improve practice based on common experience from the VE	Supporting both structured and ad hoc work (with evolving plans); handling unforeseen *exceptions*	*Customized* and personalized support; *Rapid formation* of VEs, allowing partners to join along the way

for ad hoc and structured work (Haake & Wang, 1997; Jørgensen & Carlsen, 1999). Users must be supported in selecting a suitable degree of plan specificity for the current state of their process, balancing plan complexity with the need for guidance and control.

In software engineering, researchers have defined process classification schemes, e.g., to select appropriate methodologies. Reflecting the wide *diversity of processes*, even within a single industry, up to 15 classification dimensions with 37,400 process types have been proposed (Cockburn, 2003). This number suggests that predefined ways of working cannot be constructed for all variants. Instead, base methodologies must be adapted and combined in the particular circumstances of each VE.

Knowledge, Communication, and Learning

Interorganizational and multidisciplinary cooperation require not only information exchange but also knowledge sharing. Effective teams must form across local cultures. Common frames of reference are established through working together, so support systems must allow the meaning of terms, plans, and artifacts to evolve. In communities of practice, this learning process is called *negotiation of meaning* (Wenger, 1998). Ambiguous models are required because the meaning of formal, well-defined terminologies cannot be negotiated. A VE infrastructure must also support the process of negotiating and reconciling diverging views and interpretations.

Lack of integration into everyday work practice is a reported shortcoming of knowledge management (KM), enterprise modeling, and process improvement (Davenport & Prusak, 1993). KM too often becomes the domain of outside experts that lack a full understanding of the complexities of work and the local language of the work community (Wenger, 1998). Work performers become sources of information to KM activities, not active participants. Standardization and codification, rather than local innovation and organizational and social learning, become the focal points of KM. Failure rates above 50% are common (Lawton, 2001).

The gap between what people say and what they do makes it difficult to use enterprise models and other official accounts of work as input to KM (Argyris & Schön, 1978). It must thus be straightforward to modify enterprise information locally. Still, some knowledge cannot be articulated and will remain tacit. Most descriptions are thus incomplete while they are used, subject to an ongoing elaboration and interpretation. Change and learning demand that the modeling of infrastructures be open. Models are completed only when they are no longer in use and may no longer be elaborated upon to reflect exceptions and changing circumstances.

Infrastructure Integration and Customization

The unique nature of each VE, and the dynamic set of partners, seldom makes it economically viable to integrate information systems through developing new software interfaces. Standardization (Chen & Vernadat, 2003) requires that the domain be static and well understood and is thus seldom appropriate for knowledge work. Consequently, we need a flexible infrastructure that allows shared understanding and semantic interoperability to emerge from the project, rather than being a prerequisite for cooperation.

Such flexibility is seldom offered by the tools currently available for VE integration, like e-business frameworks, workflow management, enterprise resource planning, etc. (Alonso et al., 1999). Consequently, flexibility, exception handling, and learning are important research topics in all these disciplines.

Simple tools invite use. Software that offers a wide range of functionality often becomes overwhelmingly complex and incomprehensible. Consequently, only a small portion of the available services is utilized. This condition is known as *featuritis*. We thus need role- and task-specific user interfaces, emphasizing what is needed in the current context. Interfaces and semantics should also adapt to the local needs of each project. Enterprise models, articulating who performs which tasks, when, and why, are powerful resources for such adaptation.

Systems should also adapt to the skills and preferences of each individual. Where experts should be given freedom to exercise skilled judgment, novices need detailed guidance. Personalization fosters a sense of ownership, motivating active participation. Studies have shown that personal templates and configurations spread informally through the organization, improving processes and disseminating knowledge in an emergent manner (Trigg & Bødker, 1994).

Objectives

This chapter aims to demonstrate that enterprise models can help VE participants handle the problems of heterogeneity, complexity, and flexibility on the knowledge, process, and infrastructure levels. We will, however, contend that VE integration is as much a social problem as a technical one. Current modeling infrastructures emphasize technical integration, and the understanding of VEs as sociotechnical systems must be improved. In particular, we seek to replace the common approach of using formal computer languages to control social interaction with the application of human languages to control and customize computing infrastructures.

INTERACTIVE ENTERPRISE MODELS

From past experience with developing flexible groupware and workflow systems (Carlsen, 1998; Jørgensen, 2001, 2003; Jørgensen & Carlsen, 1999; Natvig & Ohren, 1999), we have defined an *interactive models* approach to flexible information systems (Jørgensen, 2004). Models are normally defined as explicit representations of some portions of reality as perceived by some actor (Wegner & Goldin, 1999). A model is *active* if it directly influences the reality it reflects. *Model activation* involves actors interpreting the model and adjusting their behaviors accordingly. This process can be:

- *Automated*, where a software component interprets the model
- *Manual*, where the model guides the actions of human actors
- *Interactive*, where prescribed aspects of the model are automatically interpreted and ambiguous parts are left to the users to resolve

We define a model to be *interactive* if it is interactively activated. By updating such a model, users can adapt the system to fit their local plans, preferences, and terminology. This concurrent activation and articulation (modeling) is depicted in Figure 1.

Related Work

Goranson et al. (2003) point to nondeterminism, uncertainty, social and cultural dynamics, reflection, and handling of multiple perspectives as the major challenges of enterprise integration modeling. Hewitt (1986) claims that enterprises are best described as *open systems*, where people cope with conflicting, inconsistent, and partial information. He shows the shortcomings of conventional notions of computing in analyzing such systems, and forecasts that future information systems will acquire more of the characteristics and structures of human organization, e.g., concurrency, decentralized control, indeterminacy, interconnectivity, and contextuality.

The interaction framework (Wegner, 1997; Wegner & Goldin, 1999) follows along these lines. Its development was triggered by the realization that machines involving users in their computation can solve a larger class of problems than algorithmic systems computing in isolation. The primary characteristic that differentiates an *interaction machine* from a Turing machine is that it can pose questions to users during its computation. The stimulus–response model of Turing excludes such interactions that could be used to establish shared meaning. Hence, research should not solely be concerned with the development of more powerful automation algorithms. We should also look at ways in which the total system of software and humans can solve problems interactively.

Lillehagen et al. (2002) discuss the extension of enterprise modeling to *active knowledge models* (AKM) with enhanced visualization support. Greenwood et al. (1995) argue that active models can enable systems to meet many business needs that current technologies fail to solve.

Although these researchers have pointed to aspects of interactive models and put forward theoretical frameworks for interactive computing, there is a lack of *engineering research* developing and validating interactive models as a *design* approach. Consequently, there has been little investigation into what the practical challenges of interactive modeling are, and what modeling techniques are useful for meeting these challenges. We have elsewhere adapted a model quality evaluation framework to interaction (Krogstie & Jørgensen, 2002), identifying differences between interactive models and models used during software development. Most notably, the immediate availability of the domain simplifies interactive model interpretation and makes overall agreement about

Figure 1. Interplay of articulation and activation

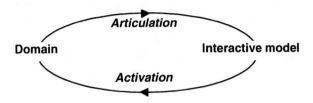

what a model means less crucial. Modeling takes place in the usage context, so the models need not recreate this context, as in a development setting. On the other hand, modeling by end users demands simpler, more user- and domain-oriented languages. The application of system-oriented models such as UML, or even programming languages, for enterprise and process modeling, should thus be questioned.

Simple and User-Oriented Modeling

Our approach relies on the assumption that business users must be actively involved in creating, updating, and interpreting models of their own work, as part of the work. VE participants are the only ones with sufficient knowledge of the joint process. Modeling by end users has met skepticism from the workflow research community (Jørgensen, 2001). On the other hand, studies of user participation in system development, tailoring, knowledge management, and process improvement indicate that our approach is viable (Argyris & Schön, 1978; Wenger, 1998). In workflow management, users also deal creatively with change and exceptions, often by taking the process out of the system and handling it manually (Bowers, Button, & Sharrock, 1995). Systems not designed for user involvement thus present a barrier to capturing local innovation. End user participation remains primarily an organizational problem, involving trust, power, and community building, but simple, user-oriented, and adaptable modeling languages will also help.

The EXTERNAL Interactive Modeling Infrastructure

The EXTERNAL project (Extended Enterprise Resources, Networks and Learning, EU IST, 2000–2002) aimed to support the whole life cycle of a VE, from inception, planning, working, managing, and coordinating, to decommissioning. In the project, interactive models were applied to support three VEs, in business consulting, software development, and research. The EXTERNAL infrastructure integrates five model-driven tools (Figure 2):

- WORKWARE (Jørgensen, 2001; Jørgensen & Carlsen, 1999), an interactive workflow and groupware system, providing worklists, process enactment, awareness notifications, access control, and document management.
- METIS (Lillehagen et al., 2002), a general-purpose, open enterprise modeling tool, used for building and visualizing rich, up-to-date models of the joint enterprise, fostering common understanding among the participants and enabling them to plan their cooperation.

- XCHIPS (Haake & Wang, 1997), a hypermedia tool with synchronous collaboration and process support. It facilitates real-time collaborative modeling sessions and also close collaboration in the context of particular tasks.
- FRAMESOLUTIONS, a framework for building traditional workflow applications.
- SIMVISION (Kuntz, Christiansen, Cohen, Jin, & Levitt, 1998), a process simulation tool that can be used to identify backlogs and potential sources of delay, given the current work plans, personnel allocation, and organization.

Together, the tools offer a comprehensive suite of functionality for creating, maintaining, and utilizing shared models of the VE. XCHIPS provides contextual work support for focused, real-time collaboration, whereas WORKWARE does the same for asynchronous collaboration. The models are managed by a shared repository residing on a Web server. For the representation and interchange of models, an XML DTD is defined. A portal integrates the Web-based user interfaces of WORKWARE and FRAMESOLUTIONS.

SUPPORTING VIRTUAL ENTERPRISES WITH INTERACTIVE MODELS

This section outlines how the interactive models approach and the EXTERNAL infrastructure can meet the challenges of VE integration.

Knowledge Complexity

Enterprise models capture a rich set of relationships between the organizations, people, processes, and resources of the VE. The main constructs of EXTERNAL's extended enterprise modeling language (EEML) (Carlsen, 1998; Jørgensen & Carlsen, 1999) are tasks, decisions, work flow dependencies, roles, and resources (persons, organizations, information, objects, and tools). These process models are carriers of knowledge about *how we do things*. EEML also contains concepts for integrated goal, data, and organizational modeling. The openness of the infrastructure (described below) allows enterprises to extend and specialize in the basic language, to reuse concepts from other modeling domains, etc.

An excerpt of such a model is depicted in Figure 3. It shows the multitude of interdependencies between tasks, tools, and organizational resources in a typical small project. In more elaborate models, other aspects, such as goals, products, information, finances, competence and skills, etc., may also be included. Such complex webs of dependencies between the various aspects of an enterprise would quickly become unmanageable, had it not been for the visualization, navigation, and selection services of METIS. Utilizing this functionality, users may dynamically construct simplified views on the models, tailored for specific roles and tasks.

Knowledge Change

One of the cornerstones of our approach is to integrate learning and knowledge management into everyday work and management practice. This is achieved through

Figure 2. Architecture and components of the EXTERNAL infrastructure

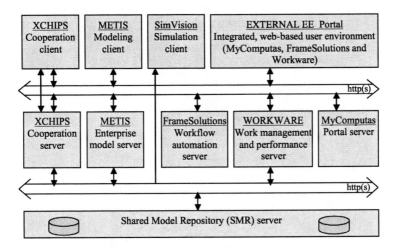

supporting concurrent definition of modeling language (metamodeling), modeling and planning of the work, model-driven management, coordination, and performance of work. There is thus a direct link from knowledge management activities to work performance, as depicted in Figure 4. In some situations, predefined languages and template models may be applied to control and reason about local work practice without much change. In other cases, local exceptions and particularities demand elaboration of the VE model, capturing learning-by-doing. Such emergent models, articulating innovative local experience, may be harvested into templates for reuse in future VEs.

Figure 4 illustrates how the EXTERNAL infrastructure supports concurrent metamodeling, modeling, management, and performance. The work interface (lowest level) includes services for work performance, coordination, and management. The *worktop* is the main component in this interface. Each task has its own worktop. In addition to the services for performing and managing the task, the worktop contains links to all knowledge in the VE models that is relevant for the task. Because the worktop is dynamically generated, and subject to personal preferences, the skill levels of task performers can be taken into account, e.g., to provide more detailed guidelines for people who have not previously worked on such tasks.

For users that enjoy sufficient access rights, the worktop includes services that invoke METIS to redefine the model (or even the metamodel) for the current task. As Figure 4 shows, the metamodel defines the language used in modeling. Similarly, the model defines the content (processes, resources, and tasks) of work management and performance. This feature is crucial for ad hoc, emergent processes, where exceptions and ongoing learning create a need for updating models of the work. The ability to metamodel enables project groups to use their own shared understanding and local vocabulary to model their joint enterprise. Such flexibility has proven to be important for establishing effective teams (Wenger, 1998). Modeling can also be done in the textual forms in WORKWARE, where users may define new tasks, upload new documents, etc.

Figure 3. Example EEML model

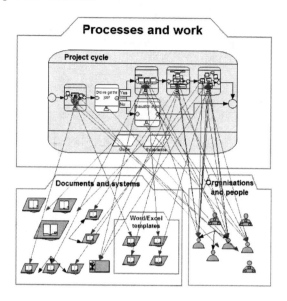

They can even do local metamodeling, e.g., add new properties to a set of objects, or define new classes and templates. Knowledge management tasks are thus thoroughly integrated in the primary work processes.

Knowledge Heterogeneity

Communication is supported by the infrastructure tools and the terminology of the modeling language. By developing models of their joint enterprise, VE participants construct shared understanding of work and management and the language and frames of reference needed for communication. XCHIPS provides real-time collaboration services that may be invoked from the worktop of a task. In addition to a wide range of internal communication and collaboration tools (chat, shared whiteboard, collaborative modeling, etc.), XCHIPS also integrates NetMeeting for videoconferencing and application sharing. These services support focused collaboration among the process participants, using the tools and information associated as resources to the task in the VE model. Real-time communication is particularly important in the early phases of distributed cooperation, in order to quickly clear up misunderstandings, etc. Below, we briefly discuss how the EXTERNAL project applied its own infrastructure to increase cooperation in early project planning.

Process Complexity

VE planning is achieved by the joint construction of an interactive enterprise model by the participants. WORKWARE's work management interface (Jørgensen, 2003) contains an overview of the status of work being processed. A *worklist* consists of tasks to be

Figure 4. EXTERNAL infrastructure user environments

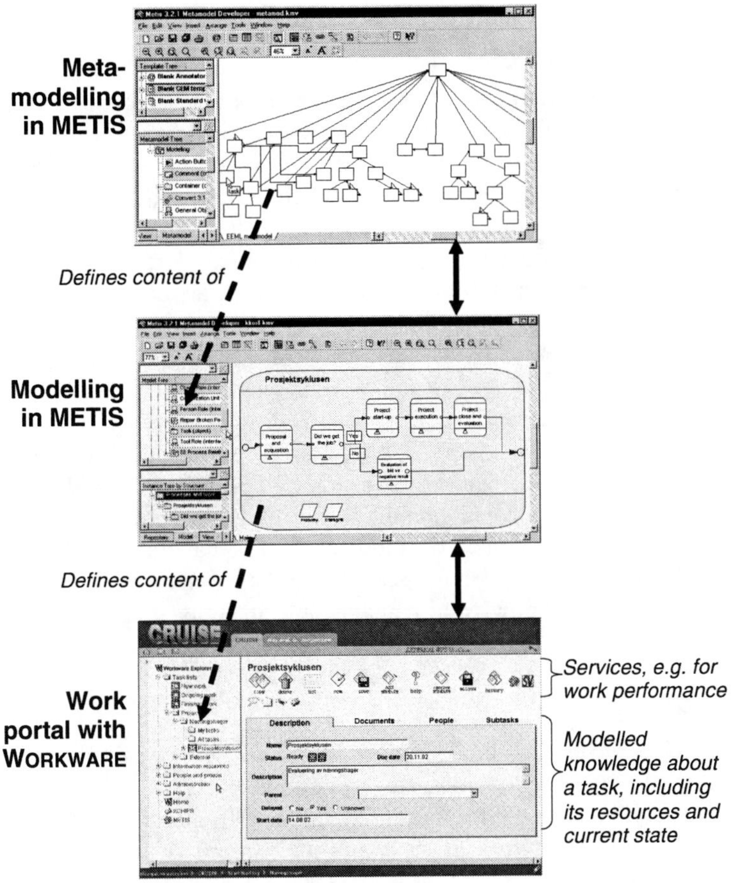

Meta-modelling in METIS

Defines content of

Modelling in METIS

Defines content of

Work portal with WORKWARE

Services, e.g. for work performance

Modelled knowledge about a task, including its resources and current state

performed with priorities, due dates, etc. They can be viewed in a number of ways, e.g., as indented lists and tree structures. Visual models in METIS are also used for work management, as they provide excellent overviews of the current state of the whole project. The different layers of Figure 4 are thus closely integrated.

The status of a task is visualized with colors, both in the visual models and the textual worklists and worktops. There are personalized worklists for each user and shared lists that provide overviews of the current state of related tasks. Users may apply any knowledge represented in the model for defining new worklists, e.g., task status, whether it is delayed, who is responsible for it, what its relations to other tasks are, etc.

SIMVISION performs different kinds of process simulations, analyzing workloads and risk areas for delay. The simulations are based on the process model defined for the VE, extended with properties that specify resource needs, resource availability, skills and competencies, coordination overhead, meetings, etc. Through parameterization, users can simulate several different scenarios based on the same model. Integrated in an infrastructure that also supports model-driven work performance, future extended simulation services can also take the process history into account when analyzing the rest of an ongoing VE.

Process Heterogeneity

Most process support systems target planned processes, where generic models of work are applied to several VE instances. Models are constructed prior to work performance and are not expected to change much during execution. A number of case studies have demonstrated the limitations of this approach. It often leads to models that do not accurately depict the way work is really performed, models that bias management control needs at the expense of straightforward work performance (Orr, 1996). Such models can cause constraining more than facilitating tool support and are poor resources for process improvement. Consequently, our approach also supports emergent processes (Jørgensen & Carlsen, 1999), represented by evolving models, where local changes are allowed, supported, and captured as input to knowledge management (Figure 5).

Reflection is an important aspect of our process integration approach. Through modeling and management, the primary work is articulated, controlled, and coordinated. But modeling and management are themselves work activities, thus models of how we perform the *processes* of modeling, project planning, follow-up, and coordination are defined. These models customize and guide the modelers and managers through their work just like the regular models support those performing the primary work of the VE. In our infrastructure, work and knowledge management are thus supported just like other activities.

Process Flexibility

Flexibility is ensured through *interactive model interpretation*, combining the capabilities of the system to automate predefined parts and the users to handle incompletely specified parts of the model (Jørgensen, 2001; Jørgensen & Carlsen, 1999). The process model is a network of tasks and their interdependencies, with decision objects that control routing and scheduling of tasks (e.g., start and completion). Because emergent processes require evolving, incomplete, process models, the enactment engine is interactive. When a decision is underspecified and cannot be automated, the process participants are asked to manually decide what should happen next. Users may also proactively override the modeled process, by making unscheduled decisions, e.g., to handle unforeseen exceptions. Decision objects allow dynamic, visual rule modeling. This enables EXTERNAL to handle models with varying, user-controllable degrees of specificity, where structure can emerge as the users' understanding of the domain increases, and the process models are elaborated. We thus integrate the support for ad hoc and structured processes.

In order to match the needs of a particular VE, local modifications of models are supported by *instance modeling* (Jørgensen & Carlsen, 1999). This limits the scope of a change to the local situation, removing much of the complexity that has prevented modeling by end users at the class level. It also establishes an immediate connection between the domain and the interactive model, in that the model objects refer directly to individual tasks, persons, documents, etc., in the enterprise. This enables learning and knowledge management anchored in practice, and negotiation of meaning based on concrete facts rather than on abstract points of view.

Figure 5. Concurrent metamodeling, modeling, and work

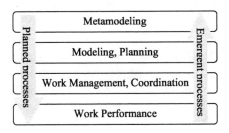

Infrastructure Complexity

Dehli et al. (2003) describe how METIS modeling and visualization services may be applied to manage complex and evolving enterprise ICT architectures. These enterprise architecture models may be integrated with and utilized in models of the VEs that the company participates in.

In the EXTERNAL infrastructure, you can also model and execute the processes of model and infrastructure management. The Web-based portal supports project and model management, utilizing services from the model repository. A WORKWARE component controls access to the repository models and documents, based on the roles that people have in the work process model. This implies that each VE can define its own local access control policies as part of the VE models. When persons are allocated to roles on tasks, they automatically get access to the information related to the tasks, if the general policies allow this. The access controller thus allows the degree of openness to increase as cooperation matures and mutual trust is established among the partners of the VE.

Infrastructure Flexibility

The EXTERNAL infrastructure also executes the work processes for infrastructure engineering and solutions development. Visual models capture dependencies between software services and other enterprise aspects, such as the tasks and roles that apply the services. Software services are, for example, modeled as resources associated with tasks in the VE model, and are made available through the user interface in a customized and personalized manner. The task performers may access desktop tools, organizational information systems, Web services, or automated processes (in FrameSolutions) through this interface.

WORKWARE user environments are generated dynamically based on the definition of processes and tasks in EEML. Forms and components for interacting with different model objects are selected and composed based on user interface policies. These policies are also part of the VE model. Different policies can be defined for different types of objects, for individual objects, as well as for different users. This enables user interface customization and personalization. Currently, new user interface forms and components can be added by programming to a Java API. We also plan to allow users to define new forms through a user interface editor, and support this process of VE solutions provision with modeled engineering work processes. More information about infrastructure customization is available in Jørgensen (2004).

Rapid formation and flexible participation of organizations in the VE are handled by modifying the organization part of the VE model. Such a change automatically updates user registry, access control, and the rest of the infrastructure.

Infrastructure Heterogeneity

The set of services offered through the EXTERNAL infrastructure is extensible and provides support for a range of different functions, disciplines, and perspectives, e.g., management, workers, specialists, quality control, accounting, etc. When such a wider range of practices is gathered around one common model, there is a risk that the model and its language may become too complex and incomprehensible, because each practice wants to include its own esoteric terminology. Our modeling framework handles these problems with user-, role-, and task-specific views, both in the visual model editor and in the work management portal. Through metamodelling, users may add specialized terms and properties to the core language, but this data need only be visible for those who need it. Multiple perspectives may thus coexist in an integrated model, integrated by the common instance model elements that represent concrete entities.

Assessment

In all, interactive models seem to adequately address the challenges that we have identified. Further work is needed both to refine the rudimentary support that the EXTERNAL infrastructure currently offers in some areas, and to explore how the many aspects that need to be represented in a model can be integrated without complicating the infrastructure and thus limiting its practical usability.

USAGE EXPERIENCE

The EXTERNAL project used its own infrastructure for *periodic progress reporting* (Jørgensen, 2001) and *VE project planning*. The first is a routine activity, while the latter demands more creativity. The first implementation of the planning case included the *plan* as well as the *planning process*, but not the operation of the plans once they were completed. Both the plan and the planning process were modeled in METIS. In advance, it was expected that the coordination of plans made by different work package managers would require real-time collaboration. Consequently, XCHIPS was selected as the main activation platform. When two people work on the same object in XCHIPS, they immediately see the effects of each other's actions. The interface also provides real-time awareness of who is currently working.

The resulting plans, however, were not detailed enough to cover all the work. Consequently, the EXTERNAL project also had a Web-based action list located at the project Web server. This solution had a number of limitations:
- It was difficult to change the list, update status information, add new actions, etc.
- The actions lacked context, and were sometimes hard to understand.
- The actions were not explicitly connected to project plans (the process models).
- The actions were not linked to a work area with documents and tools that could be used for performing the work.

- Although the list could be sorted on different attributes and filtered according to predefined criteria, it was not possible to add user-defined criteria.

The action lists were, consequently, not actively used by many of the project participants. For the second version of the planning case, it was thus decided to use WORKWARE for managing actions as tasks, integrating top-down planning with bottom-up, emergent articulation of work. It took just a few hours of work to customize a WORKWARE server for action lists. Worklists were defined that organize actions according to status, delay, who is responsible for performing and following up the work, which work package or team the action relates to, etc. The old, static action lists contained 288 actions after two and a half years of operation, while WORKWARE contained 131 after just two months, even though it was installed during the summer holidays. This increased frequency of use, as well as informal feedback, indicates that the users experienced the second application as a substantial improvement. The result was a more accurate process model.

Other Experiences

In the business consulting company, a general project template was modeled, and then applied in one project (Elvekrok, Lillehagen, & Solheim, 2003). Process modeling consultants from the EXTERNAL project were able to convert an informally described project standard into an interactive, operational VE model. The final EXTERNAL case involved a network of small and medium-sized ICT companies, which tested the system for project management, software subcontracting, and project proposal submission (Elvekrok et al., 2003). While the users in this case were professional software engineers, they lacked extensive process modeling experience. They thus decided to reuse the business consulting model as a starting point for their project. Over the course of the process, this generic template was appropriated, adapted, and extended to fit local practice.

WORKWARE has also been used opportunistically in a handful of research projects. These cases allowed us to explore the tool's customization capabilities. Local metamodelling and customization policies have been applied to adapt interfaces and navigation structures for each project (Jørgensen, 2004). Locally, concepts such as *meeting* and *document categories* have been added to the general language and utilized for organizing worklists and shared workspaces. Generally, it takes just an hour or two before an initial project collaboration infrastructure is established. Users simply have to build a rudimentary process model and define any additional worklists and services that they want to include. As the work progressed, all groups adapted the infrastructure based on usage experience. People have also used EEML to teach enterprise modeling, and evaluated the students' models (Moody, Sindre, Brasethvik, & Sølvberg, 2002). More than 200 students participated, modeling 20 different processes. The unified enterprise modelling (UEML) project ensured interoperability between our language and several others (Zelm, 2003). The continued interest from a user company and a tool vendor, who have been involved in the development of WORKWARE from the start, further testify to the practical relevance of this approach. We are currently exploring the use of interactive process modeling to support customization and process knowledge management in a global certification company (Dalberg, Jensen, & Krogstie, 2003). Here, a harmonized, common process coexists with specialized ones for each country. Another case aims to explore role-play and field experiments as a means for creating templates for the process model repository.

Evaluation Results

An independent researcher, who had not participated in the EXTERNAL project, collected experience from the three cases by questionnaires and semistructured interviews (Elvekrok et al., 2003). Most of the 19 respondents were participants in the EXTERNAL project, so there is a danger for biased feedback. However, increased frequency of use (see above) and improved efficiency of work were measured objectively (Jørgensen, 2004). The *periodic reporting* case achieved better results than the original planning case. The reporting process showed great improvements compared to the first period, when e-mail was the only coordination tool available. Partly, this may be attributed to learning that the participants would anyway experience during the first period. However, the similar process of *summary cost statements*, which was not performed in the EXTERNAL infrastructure, did not achieve the same degree of improvement as the reporting process. Some users thus proposed to model and perform that process in the infrastructure as well. The action list server was later used by the participants in preparing a new project proposal. But there was also negative feedback. One user thought that the logic and language of the system were not intuitive. He was expecting a more document-centric structure with files and folders. In some cases, further simplification and customization is thus needed.

Limitations and Further Work

While the EXTERNAL infrastructure has been implemented and validated by trial use, further development and experimentation is needed. In particular, the organizational benefits related to process knowledge management must be demonstrated in long-term field studies. Methodologies for modeling, infrastructure customization and solution provision, and model-driven project and multiproject management should be developed as operational, interactive process templates. Process reflection thus allows metaprocesses to become ordinary processes, like language reflection treats metamodelling as an aspect of modeling.

A stable, commercially available implementation of the infrastructure is planned. This will open new opportunities for research into the human, social, and organizational aspects of explication, formalization, learning, trust, and community building around interactive models. More model-driven software components should be included, e.g., for resource management, budgets, and accounting. Case studies should explore which kind of model-driven functionality is useful in which context.

FUTURE TRENDS

Continued development of the interactive modeling approach to VE integration, operation, management, and learning, will bring a number of interesting shifts in the way we conceptualize and use computerized information systems:

- Visual modeling taking over parts of the work currently done by programming
- Visual, symbolic, and graph-based communication complementing natural languages
- Open systems, where the automation boundary is flexible, where tasks are distributed between users and software depending on the characteristics of each situation
- Model-driven composition, customization, and personalization of software infrastructures, in part even controlled by users at runtime
- Social computing, understood as bringing the uncertainty, heterogeneity, change, and openness of social systems to computing, rather than seeking to control social environments with the formality, determinacy, and computability of software

The consequences of the interaction perspective for modeling, software engineering, knowledge management, and business process systems, needs more in-depth studies within each discipline. The common approach of bringing the language of computers to human interaction is here replaced with an attempt to make computer languages more human. Our experience indicates that this is needed to meet the fundamental challenges of user participation, domain semantics, exceptions, evolution, and learning.

CONCLUSIONS

Interactive models allow enterprises to control and customize their ICT infrastructures through visual modeling. In an integrated knowledge management framework, concurrent metamodelling, modeling, management, and work performance become interwoven, supporting both planned and emergent work. The EXTERNAL infrastructure has been in use in several case studies, and in part, also in commercial projects. It has been found adequate for building the models of multiple VEs, and for supporting a wide range of tasks.

REFERENCES

Alonso, G., Fiedler, U., Hagen, C., Lazcano, A., Schuldt, H., & Weiler, N. (1999). WISE: Business to business e-commerce. Presented at the *International Workshop on Research Issues on Data Engineering*, Sydney, Australia.

Argyris, C., & Schön, D. (1978). *Organizational learning: A theory of action perspective*. Reading, MA: Addison-Wesley.

Bowers, Button, & Sharrock. (1995). *Workflows from within and without*. Presented at the ECSCW Conference, Stockholm, Sweden.

Carlsen, S. (1998). *Action port model: A mixed paradigm conceptual workflow modeling language*. Presented at the CoopIS Conference, New York.

Chen, D., & Vernadat, F. (2003). Enterprise interoperability: A standards view. In R. Kosanke, J.G. Jochem, & B. Nell (Eds.), *Enterprise inter- and intra-organizational integration*. Boston: Kluwer.

Cockburn, A. (2003). *People and methodologies in software development*. PhD Thesis, University of Oslo.

Dalberg, V., Jensen, S. M., & Krogstie, J. (2003). *Modelling for organisational knowledge creation and sharing*. Presented at NOKOBIT, Norwegian Conference on Organisational Application of IT.

Davenport, T. H., & Prusak, L. (1993). *Working knowledge*. Boston: Harvard Business School Press.

Dehli, E., Smith-Meyer, H., & Lillehagen, F. (2003). Metis LEARN—Leveraging enterprise architecture repository. Presented at the *Concurrent Engineering (CE) Conference*, Madeira, Portugal.

Delphi Group. (2001). BPM 2001—In Process. *The Changing Role of Business Process Management in Today's Economy* (White paper).

Elvekrok, D. R., Lillehagen, F., & Solheim, H. G. (2003). *Use case driven active knowledge models (AKM) in extended enterprises*. Presented at the Concurrent Engineering (CE) Conference, Madeira, Portugal.

Goranson, H. T., Jochem, R., Nell, J. G., Panetto, H., Partridge, C., Ripoll, F. S., et al. (2003). New support technologies for enterprise integration. In R. Kosanke, J.G. Jochem, & B. Nell (Eds.), *Enterprise inter- and intra-organizational integration*. Dordrecht: Kluwer.

Greenwood, R. M., Robertson, I., Snowdon, R. A., & Warboys, B. C. (1995). *Active models in business*. Presented at the Conference on Business Information Technology (CBIT).

Haake, J. M., & Wang, W. (1997). *Flexible support for business processes: Extending cooperative hypermedia with process support*. Presented at the ACM GROUP Conference, Phoenix, Arizona.

Hewitt, C. (1986). Offices are open systems. *ACM Transactions on Office Information Systems, 4*(3), 271–287.

Jørgensen, H. D. (2001). *Interaction as a framework for flexible workflow modelling*. Presented at the ACM GROUP Conference, Boulder, Colorado.

Jørgensen, H. D. (2003). *Model-driven work management services*. Presented at the Concurrent Engineering (CE) Conference, Madeira, Portugal.

Jørgensen, H. D. (2004). *Interactive process models*. PhD Thesis, Electronic edition published at *http://www.ub.ntnu.no/dravh/000262.pdf*, Norwegian University of Science and Technology, Trondheim, Norway.

Jørgensen, H. D., & Carlsen, S. (1999). *Emergent workflow: Integrated planning and performance of process instances*. Presented at the Workflow Management Conference, Münster, Germany.

Krogstie, J., & Jørgensen, H. D. (2002). *Quality of interactive models*. Presented at the ER Workshop on Conceptual Modeling Quality (IWCMQ), Tampere, Finland.

Kuntz, J. C., Christiansen, T. R., Cohen, G. P., Jin, Y., & Levitt, R. E. (1998). The virtual design team: A computational Ssimulation model of project organizations. *Communications of the ACM, 41*(11), 84–92.

Lawton, G. (2001). Knowledge management: Ready for prime time? *IEEE Computer, 34*(2), 12–14.

Lillehagen, F., Dehli, E., Fjeld, L., Krogstie, J., & Jørgensen, H. D. (2002). *Active knowledge models as a basis for an infrastructure for virtual enterprises*.

Presented at the IFIP Conference on Infrastructures for Virtual Enterprises (PRO-VE), Sesimbra, Portugal.

Moody, D. L., Sindre, G., Brasethvik, T., & Sølvberg, A. (2002). *Evaluating the quality of process models: Empirical testing of a quality framework.* Presented at the ER Conference, Springer LNCS 2503.

Natvig, M. K., & Ohren, O. (1999). *Modelling shared information spaces (SIS).* Presented at the ACM GROUP Conference, Phoenix, Arizona.

Orr, J. (1996). *Talking about machines.* Ithaca, NY: Cornell University Press.

Qureshi, S., & Zigurs, I. (2001). Paradoxes and prerogatives in global virtual collaboration. *Communications of the ACM, 44*(12).

Trigg, R. H., & Bødker, S. (1994). *From implementation to design: Tailoring and the emergence of systematization in CSCW.* Presented at the ACM CSCW Conference, Chapel Hill, North Carolina.

Tølle, M., Bernus, P., & Vesterager, J. (2002). *Reference models for virtual enterprises.* Presented at the IFIP Conference on Infrastructures for Virtual Enterprises (PRO-VE), Sesimbra, Portugal.

Wegner, P. (1997). Why interaction is more powerful than algorithms. *Communications of the ACM, 40*(5), 80–91.

Wegner, P., & Goldin, D. (1999). Interaction as a framework for modeling. In P. P. Chen, J. Akoka, H. Kangassalo, & B. Thalheim (Eds.), *Conceptual modeling.* Berlin: Springer LNCS 1565.

Wenger, E. (1998). *Communities of practice: Learning meaning and identity.* London; New York: Cambridge University Press.

Zelm, M. (2003). *Towards user oriented enterprise modelling—Comparison of modelling languages.* Presented at the Concurrent Engineering (CE) Conference, Madeira, Portugal.

Chapter XVII

Machine Learning Techniques for Wrapper Maintenance

Kristina Lerman
University of Southern California, USA

Steven N. Minton
Fetch Technologies Inc., USA

Craig A. Knoblock
Fetch Technologies Inc. & University of Southern California, USA

ABSTRACT

The proliferation of online information has led to an increased use of wrappers for extracting data from Web sources and transforming it to a structured format. The resulting data can then be used to build new enterprise applications. While most of the previous research has focused on quick and efficient generation of wrappers, the development of tools for wrapper maintenance has received less attention. This is an important problem, because Web sources often change in ways that prevent the wrappers from operating correctly. In this chapter, we describe machine learning techniques for verifying that a wrapper is working correctly and repairing it if not. Our approach is to learn structural descriptions of data and use these descriptions to verify that the wrapper is correctly extracting data. The repair algorithm automatically recovers from Web source format changes by identifying data so that a new wrapper may be generated for this source.

INTRODUCTION

Companies have vast repositories of information, which they share among themselves as well as with outside users. Unfortunately, much of this information is presented in a form that can be easily read by humans, not computer applications. Although there are hopes that the extensible markup language (XML) will solve the information extraction problem, it is not yet in widespread use, and even in the best case, it will only address the problem within application domains where the interested parties can agree on the XML schema definitions. Enterprises are instead relying on Web wrappers to extract information from Web sources and convert it to a structured format that can be used by various applications.

Wrappers use extraction rules to identify the data field to be extracted. Semiautomatic creation of extraction rules, or wrapper induction, has been an active area of research in recent years (Knoblock et al., 2001a; Kushmerick, 1997). The most advanced of these wrapper generation systems use machine learning techniques to learn the extraction rules by example. For instance, the wrapper induction tool developed at USC (Knoblock et al., 2001a; Muslea, 1998) and commercialized by Fetch Technologies, allows the user to mark up data to be extracted on several example pages from an online source using a graphical user interface. The system then generates "landmark"-based extraction rules for these data that rely on the page layout. The USC wrapper tool is able to efficiently create extraction rules from a small number of examples; moreover, it can extract data from pages that contain lists, nested structures, and other complicated formatting layouts.

In comparison to wrapper induction, wrapper maintenance has received less attention. This is an important problem, because Web sites frequently change their layout, and even slight changes in the Web page layout can break a wrapper. In this chapter, we discuss our approach to the wrapper maintenance problem, which consists of two parts: wrapper verification and reinduction. A *wrapper verification* system monitors the validity of data returned by the wrapper. If the site changes, the wrapper may extract nothing at all or some data that are not correct. The verification system will detect data inconsistency and notify the operator or automatically launch a wrapper repair process. A *wrapper reinduction* system repairs the extraction rules so that the wrapper works on changed pages.

Figure 1 graphically illustrates the entire life cycle of a wrapper. As shown in the figure, the wrapper induction system takes a set of Web pages labeled with examples of the data to be extracted. The output of the wrapper induction system is a wrapper, consisting of a set of extraction rules that describe how to locate the desired information on a Web page. The wrapper verification system uses the functioning wrapper to collect extracted data. It then learns patterns describing the structure of data. These patterns are used to verify that the wrapper is correctly extracting data at a later date. If a change is detected, the system can automatically repair a wrapper by using this structural information to locate examples of data on the new pages and to rerun the wrapper induction system with these examples. At the core of these wrapper maintenance applications is a machine learning algorithm that learns structural information about common data fields. We will introduce the algorithm, DATAPROG, and describe its application to the wrapper maintenance tasks in detail. Though we focus on Web applications, the learning technique is not Web specific and can be used for data validation in general.

Figure 1. The life cycle of a wrapper

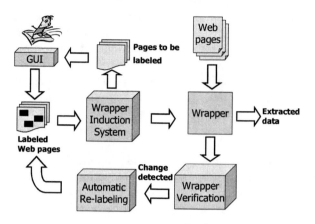

Note that we distinguish two types of extraction rules: landmark-based rules that extract data by exploiting the structure of the Web page, and content-based rules, which we refer to as content patterns or simply patterns that exploit the structure of the field. Our previous work focused on learning landmark rules for information extraction (Muslea et al., 2001). The current work shows that augmenting these rules with content-based patterns provides a foundation for sophisticated wrapper maintenance applications.

LEARNING DATA PATTERNS

The goal of our research is to extract information from semistructured information sources. This typically involves identifying small chunks of highly informative data on formatted pages (as opposed to parsing natural language text). Either by convention or design, these *fields* are usually structured: phone numbers, prices, dates, street addresses, names, schedules, etc. Several examples of street addresses are given in Figure 2. Clearly, these strings are not arbitrary but share some similarities. The objective of our work is to learn the structure of such fields.

Data Representation

In previous work, researchers described the fields extracted from Web pages by a character-level grammar (Goan et al., 1996) or a collection of global features, such as the number of words and the density of numeric characters (Kushmerick, 1999). We employ an intermediate word-level representation that balances the descriptive power and specificity of the character-level representation with the compactness and computational efficiency of the global representation. Words, or more accurately tokens, are strings generated from an alphabet containing different types of characters: alphabetic, numeric, punctuation, etc. We use the token's character types to assign it to one or more syntactic categories: alphabetic, numeric, etc. These categories form a hierarchy depicted in Figure 3, where the arrows point from more general to less general categories.

Figure 2. Examples of a street address field

> 4676 Admiralty Way
> 10924 Pico Boulevard
> 512 Oak Street
> 2431 Main Street
> 5257 Adams Boulevard

Figure 3. Portion of the token-type syntactic hierarchy

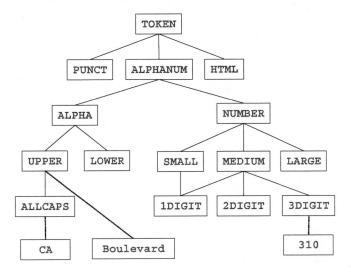

A unique specific token type is created for every string that appears in at least k examples, as determined in a preprocessing step. The hierarchical representation allows for multilevel generalization. Thus, the token "Boulevard" belongs to the general token types ALPHANUM (alphanumeric strings), ALPHA (alphabetic strings), UPPER (capitalized words), as well as to the specific type representing the string "Boulevard." This representation is flexible and may be expanded to include domain-specific information. For example, the numeric type is divided into categories that include range information about the number—LARGE (larger than 1000), MEDIUM (medium numbers, between 10 and 1000), and SMALL (smaller than 10)—and number of digits: one-, two-, and three-digit. Likewise, we may explicitly include knowledge about the type of information being parsed, e.g., some five-digit numbers could be represented as ZIPCODE.

We have found that a sequence of specific and general token types is more useful for describing the content of information than the character-level finite state representations used in previous work (Carrasco & Oncina, 1994; Goan et al., 1996). We do not describe the entire data field, rather, a sequence of tokens describes how a data field begins and ends. This sequence of tokens, a *pattern*, captures the structure of the data field. Using the starting and ending patterns allows us to generalize the structural information for many complex fields, which have a lot of variability. We call the starting and ending patterns, collectively, a *data prototype*. As an example, consider a set of street addresses in Figure 2. All of the examples start with a pattern <NUMBER UPPER> and end with a specific type <Boulevard>, or more generally, <UPPER>. Note that the pattern language does not allow loops or recursion. We believe that recursive expressions are not useful representations of the types of data we are trying to learn, because they are harder to learn and lead to overgeneralization.

Learning from Positive Examples

In Lerman et al. (2003) we introduced an algorithm that learns data prototypes from positive examples of the data field. The algorithm finds statistically significant sequences of tokens. A sequence of token types is significant if it occurs more frequently than would be expected if the tokens were generated randomly and independently of one another. In other words, each such sequence constitutes a pattern that describes many of the positive examples of data and is highly unlikely to have been generated by chance.

The algorithm estimates the baseline probability of a token type's occurrence from the proportion of all types in the examples of the data field that are of that type. Suppose we are learning a description of the set of street addresses in Figure 2 and have already found a significant token sequence—e.g., the pattern consisting of the single token <NUMBER>—and want to determine whether the more specific pattern, <NUMBER UPPER>, is also significant. Knowing the occurrence probability of UPPER, we can estimate how many times UPPER follows NUMBER completely by chance. If we observe a considerably greater number of these sequences, we conclude that the longer pattern is also significant.

We use hypothesis testing (Papoulis, 1990) to decide whether a pattern is significant. The null hypothesis is that observed instances of this pattern were generated by chance, via the random, independent generation of the individual token types. Hypothesis testing decides, at a given confidence level, whether the data supports rejecting the null hypothesis. Suppose n identical sequences have been generated by a random source. The probability that a token type T (whose overall probability of occurrence is p) will be the next type in k of these sequences has a binomial distribution. For a large n, the binomial distribution approaches a normal distribution $P(x,\mu, \sigma)$, with $\mu = np$ and $\sigma^2 = np(1-p)$. The cumulative probability is the probability of observing at least n_1 events:

$$P(k \geq n_1) = \int_{n_1}^{\infty} P(x,\mu,\sigma)dx$$

We use polynomial approximation formulas (Abramowitz & Stegun, 1964) to compute the value of the integral.

The significance level of the test, α, is the probability that the null hypothesis is rejected even though it is true, and it is given by the cumulative probability above. Suppose we set $\alpha = 0.05$. This means that we expect to observe at least n_1 events 5% of the time under the null hypothesis. If the number of observed events is greater, we reject the null hypothesis (at the given significance level), i.e., decide that the observation is significant. Note that the hypothesis we test is derived from observation (data). This constraint reduces the number of degrees of freedom of the test; therefore, we must subtract one from the number of observed events. This also prevents the anomalous case when a single occurrence of a rare event is judged to be significant. Details of the DATAPROG algorithm are described in Lerman et al. (2003).

APPLICATIONS OF PATTERN LEARNING

As we explained in the introduction, wrapper induction systems use information from the layout of Web pages to create data extraction rules and are therefore vulnerable to changes in the layout, which occur frequently when the site is redesigned. In some cases, the wrapper continues to extract, but the data are no longer correct. The output of the wrapper may also change, because the format of the source data has changed, e.g., when "$" is dropped from the price field ("9.95" instead of "$9.95"), or book availability changes from "Ships immediately" to "In Stock: ships immediately." Because other applications, such as Web agents (Ambite et al., 2002; Chalupsly et al., 2001), rely on data extracted by wrappers, wrapper maintenance is an important research problem. We divide the wrapper maintenance problem into two parts, each described separately. *Wrapper verification* automatically detects when a wrapper is not extracting data correctly from a Web source, while *wrapper reinduction* automatically fixes broken wrappers. Both applications learn a description of data, of which patterns learned by DATAPROG are a significant part.

Wrapper Verification

If the data extracted by the wrapper changes significantly, this is an indication that the Web source may have changed its format. Our wrapper verification system uses examples of data extracted by the wrapper in the past that are known to be correct in order to acquire a description of the data. The learned description contains features of two types: patterns learned by DATAPROG and global numeric features, such as the density of tokens of a particular type. The application then checks that this description still applies to the new data extracted by the wrapper. Thus, wrapper verification is a specific instance of the data validation task.

The verification algorithm works in the following way. A set of queries is used to retrieve HTML pages from which the wrapper extracts (correct) training examples. The algorithm then computes the values of a vector of features, k, that describes each field of the training examples. These features include the patterns that describe the common beginnings (or endings) of the field. During the verification phase, the wrapper generates a set of (new) test examples from pages retrieved using the same set of queries and computes the feature vector r associated with each field of the test examples. If the two distributions, k and r, are statistically the same (at some significance level), the wrapper is judged to be extracting correctly; otherwise, it is judged to have failed.

Each field is described by a vector, with an ith component that is the value of the ith feature, such as the number of examples that match pattern j. In addition to patterns, we use the following numeric features to describe the sets of training and test examples: the average number of tuples-per-page, mean number of tokens in the examples, mean token length, and the density of alphabetic, numeric, HTML-tag, and punctuation types. We use the goodness-of-fit method (Papoulis, 1990) to decide whether the two distributions are the same. To use the goodness-of-fit method, we must first compute Pearson's test statistic for the data. The Pearson's test statistic is defined as:

$$q = \sum_{i=1}^{m} \frac{(t_i - e_i)^2}{e_i}$$

where t_i is the observed value of the ith feature in the test data, e_i is the expected value for that feature, and m is the number of features. For the patterns $e_i = nr_i/N$, where r_i is the number of training examples explained by the ith pattern, N is the number of examples in the training set, and n is the number of examples in the test set. For numeric features, e_i is simply the value of that feature for the training set. The test statistic q has a chi-squared distribution with $m - 1$ independent degrees of freedom. If $q < \chi^2(m - 1; \alpha)$, we conclude that at significance level α, the two distributions are the same; otherwise, we conclude that they are different. Values of χ^2 for different values of α and m can be looked up in a statistics table or calculated using an approximation formula.

In order to use the test statistic reliably, it helps to use as many independent features as possible. In the series of verification experiments reported in Lerman and Minton (2000), we used the starting and ending patterns and the average number of tuples-per-page feature when computing the value of q. We found that this method tended to overestimate the test statistic, because the features (starting and ending patterns) were not independent. In the experiments reported here, we use only the starting patterns, but in order to increase the number of features, we added numeric features to the description of data.

Wrapper Verification Results

We monitored 27 wrappers (representing 23 distinct Web sources) over a period of 10 months, from May 1999 to March 2000. The sources and data were diverse, ranging from airport codes, Web search engines, electronic catalogs, books, restaurants, stock quotes, yellow and white pages, and weather. For each wrapper, the results of 15 to 30 queries were stored periodically, every seven to 10 days. Each set of new results (test examples) was compared with the last correct wrapper output (training examples). The verification algorithm used DATAPROG to learn the starting patterns and numeric features for each field of the training examples and made a decision at a high significance level (corresponding to $\alpha = 0.001$) about whether the test set was statistically similar to the training set. If none of the starting patterns matched the test examples or if the data was found to have changed significantly for any data field, we concluded that the wrapper failed to extract correctly from the source; otherwise, if all the data fields returned statistically similar data, we concluded that the wrapper was working correctly. A manual check of the 438 comparisons revealed 37 wrapper changes attributable to changes in the source layout and data format. The verification algorithm correctly discovered 35 of these changes and made 15 mistakes. Of these mistakes, 13 were *false positives*, which means that the verification program decided that the wrapper failed, when in reality, it was working correctly. Only two of the errors were the more important *false negatives*, meaning that the algorithm did not detect a change in the data source. The numbers above result in the following precision, recall, and accuracy values:

$$P = \frac{TruePositives}{TruePositives + FalsePositives} = 0.73$$

$$R = \frac{TruePositives}{TruePositives + FalseNegatives} = 0.95$$

$$A = \frac{TruePositives + TrueNegatives}{positives + negatives} = 0.97$$

Wrapper Reinduction

If the wrapper stops extracting data correctly, the next challenge is to rebuild it automatically (Cohen, 1999). The extraction rules for our wrappers (Muslea et al., 2001), as well as many others (cf. Kushmerick, 1997; Hsu & Dung, 1998), are generated by a machine learning algorithm, which takes as input several pages from a source and labeled examples of data to extract from each page. It is assumed that the user labeled all examples correctly. If we label at least a fe pages for which the wrapper fails by correctly identifying examples of data on them, we can use these examples as input to the induction algorithm, such as STALKER, to generate new extraction rules. Note that we do not need to identify the data on every page—depending on how regular the data layout is, STALKER can learn extraction rules using a small number of correctly labeled pages. Our solution is to bootstrap the wrapper induction process (which learns landmark-based rules) by learning content-based rules. We want to relearn the landmark-based rules, because for the types of sites we use, these rules tend to be much more accurate and efficient than content-based rules.

We employ a method that takes a set of training examples, extracted from the source when the wrapper was known to be working correctly, and a set of pages from the same source, and use a mixture of supervised and unsupervised learning techniques to identify examples of the data field on new pages. We assume that the format of data did not change. Patterns learned by DATAPROG play a significant role in the reinduction task. In addition to patterns, other features, such as the length of the training examples and structural information about pages, are used. In fact, because page structure is used during a critical step of the algorithm, we discuss our approach to learning it in detail in the next paragraph.

Page Template Algorithm

Many Web sources use templates, or page skeletons, to automatically generate pages and fill them with results of a database query. This is evident in the example in Figure 4. The template consists of the heading "RESULTS," followed by the number of results that match the query, the phrase "Click links associated with businesses for more information," then the heading "ALL LISTINGS," followed by the anchors "map," "driving directions," "add to My Directory," and the bolded phrase "Appears in the Category."

Given two or more example pages from the same source, we can induce the template used to generate them. The template finding algorithm looks for all sequences of tokens—both HTML tags and text—that appear exactly once on each page. Templates play an important role in helping to identify correct data examples on pages.

Figure 4. Fragments of two Web pages from the same source displaying restaurant information

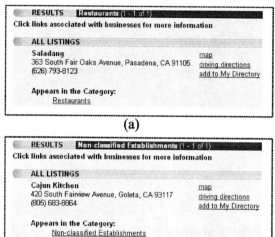

(a)

(b)

Automatic Labeling Algorithm

Figure 5 presents a schematic of the reinduction algorithm, which consists of automatic data labeling and wrapper induction. Because the latter aspect is described in detail in other work (Muslea et al., 2001), we focus the discussion below on the automatic labeling algorithm.

First, DATAPROG learns the starting and ending patterns that describe the set of training examples. These training examples have been collected during wrapper's normal operation, while it was correctly extracting data from the Web source. The patterns are used to identify possible examples of the data field on the new pages. In addition to patterns, we also calculate the mean (and its variance) of the number-of-tokens in the training examples. Each new page is then scanned to identify all text segments that begin with one of the starting patterns and end with one of the ending patterns. Text segments that contain significantly more or fewer tokens than expected based on the old number-of-tokens distribution are eliminated from the set of candidate extracts. The learned patterns are often too general and will match many, possibly hundreds, of text segments on each page. Among these spurious text segments is the correct example of the data field. The rest of the discussion is concerned with identifying the correct examples of data on pages.

We exploit some simple *a priori* assumptions about the structure of Web pages to help us separate interesting extracts from noise. We expect examples of the same data field to appear roughly in the same position and in the same context on each page. For example, Figure 4 shows fragments of two Web pages from the same source displaying restaurant information. On both pages, the relevant information about the restaurant appears after the heading F"ALL LISTINGS" and before the phrase "Appears in the Category:". Thus, we expect the same field, e.g., address, to appear in the *same place*, or slot, within the page template. Moreover, the information we are trying to extract will not usually be part

Figure 5. Outline of the reinduction algorithm

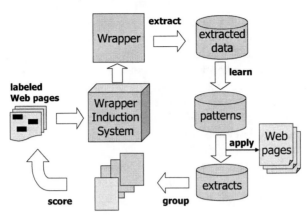

of the page template; therefore, candidate extracts that are part of the page template can be eliminated from consideration. Restaurant address always follows restaurant name (in bold) and precedes the city and zip code, i.e., it appears in the *same context* on every page. A given field is either visible to the user on every page or is inside an HTML tag on every page. In order to use this information to separate extracts, we describe each candidate extract by a feature vector, which includes positional information, defined by the page template and context, and whether it is visible to the user. The context is captured by the adjacent tokens: one token immediately preceding the candidate extract and one token immediately following it. We then split candidate extracts into groups, so that within each group, extracts are described by the same feature vector. Next, we score groups based on their similarity to the training set. The highest scoring group contains correct examples of the data field.

If the scoring algorithm assigns zero to all groups, i.e., there exist no extracts in common with the training examples, a second scoring algorithm is invoked. This scoring method follows the wrapper verification procedure and finds the group that is most similar to the training examples based on the patterns learned from the training examples.

The final step of the wrapper reinduction process is to provide the extracts in the top-ranking group to a wrapper induction algorithm to learn new extraction rules for the changed pages. Note that these examples are required to be correct. If the set of automatically labeled examples includes false positives, the induction system will not learn correct extraction rules for that field. False negatives are not a problem, however. If the reinduction algorithm could not find the correct example of data on a page, that page is simply not used in the wrapper induction stage.

Wrapper Reinduction Results

To evaluate the reinduction algorithm, we used only the 10 that returned a single tuple of results per page. The method of data collection was described previously. Over the period between October 1999 and March 2000, there were eight format changes in these sources. Because this set is much too small for evaluation purposes, we created an artificial test set by considering all 10 data sets collected for each source during this period.

We evaluated the algorithm by using it to extract data from Web pages for which correct output is known. Specifically, we took 10 tuples from a set collected on one date, and used this information to extract data from 10 pages (randomly chosen) collected at a later date, regardless of whether the source had actually changed or not. We reserved the remaining pages collected at a later date for testing the learned rules. STALKER (Muslea et al., 2001) was the wrapper induction algorithm.

The output of the reinduction algorithm is a list of tuples extracted from 10 pages, as well as extraction rules generated by STALKER for these pages. Though in most cases we were not able to extract every field on every page, we can still learn good extraction rules with STALKER as long as a few examples of each field are correctly labeled. We evaluated the reinduction algorithm in two stages: first, we checked how many data fields for each source were identified successfully; second, we checked the quality of the learned STALKER rules by using them to extract data from test pages.

Extracting with Content-Based Rules

We judged a data field to be successfully extracted if the automatic labeling algorithm was able to identify it correctly on at least two of the 10 pages. This is the minimum number of examples STALKER needs to create extraction rules. In practice, such a low success rate only occurred for one field each in two sources. For all other sources, if a field was successfully extracted, it was correctly identified in at least three, and in most cases, almost all, of the pages in the set. A false positive occurred when the reinduction algorithm incorrectly identified some text on a page as a correct example of a data field. In many cases, false positives consisted of partial fields, e.g., "Cloudy" rather than "Mostly Cloudy" (*weather*). A false negative occurred when the algorithm did not identify any examples of a data field.

We ran the reinduction experiment attempting to extract the fields listed in Table 1. The second column of the table lists the fractions of data sets for which the field was successfully extracted. We were able to correctly identify fields 277 times across all data sets, making 61 mistakes, of which 31 were attributed to false positives and 30 to false negatives.

The first column lists the percentage of fields that were correctly extracted by the pattern-based algorithm. We judged the field to be extracted if the algorithm correctly identified at least two examples of it. The *P* and *R* columns list precision and recall on the extraction task using the reinduced wrappers.

There are several reasons the reinduction algorithm failed to operate perfectly. In many cases, the reason was the small training set.[1] We can achieve better learning for the yellow-pages-type sources *Bigbook* and *Smartpages* by using more training examples. In two cases, the errors were attributable to changes in the format of data, which resulted in the failure of patterns to capture the structure of data correctly: e.g., the *airport* source changed airport names from capitalized words to all caps, and in the *Quote* source in which the patterns were not able to identify negative price changes because they were learned for a data set in which most of the stocks had a positive price change. For two sources, the reinduction algorithm could not distinguish between correct examples of the field and other examples of the same data type: for the *Quote* source, in

Table 1. Reinduction results on 10 Web sources

Source/Field	Ex %	P	R	Field	Ex %	P	R
airport							
Code	100	1.0	1.0	Name	90	1.0	1.0
Amazon							
Author	100	97.3	0.92	Title	70	98.8	0.81
Price	100	1.0	0.99	ISBN	100	1.0	0.91
Availabilty	60	1.0	0.86				
Barnes&Noble							
Author	100	0.93	0.96	Title	80	0.96	0.62
Price	90	1.0	0.68	ISBN	100	1.0	0.95
Availability	90	1.0	0.92				
Bigbook							
Name	70	1.0	0.76	Street	90	1.0	0.87
City	70	0.91	0.98	State	100	0.04	0.50
Phone	90	1.0	0.30				
Mapquest							
Time	100	1.0	0.98	Distance 100		1.0	0.98
Quote							
Price change	50	0.38	0.36	Ticker	63	0.93	0.87
Volume 100		1.0	0.88	Price	38	0.46	0.60
Smartpages							
Name	80	1.0	0.82	Street	80	1.0	0.52
City	0	0.68	0.58	State	100	1.0	0.70
Phone	100	0.99	1.0				
Yahoo Quote							
Price change	100	1.0	0.41	Ticker	100	1.0	0.98
Volume 100		1.0	0.99	Price	80	1.0	0.59
Washington Post							
Price	100	1.0	1.0				
Weather							
Temperature	40	0.36	0.82	Outlook 90		0.83	1.0
Average 83		0.90	0.80				

some cases, it extracted opening price or high price for the stock price field, while for the *Yahoo Weather* source, it extracted high or low temperature, rather than the current temperature. This problem was also evident in the *Smartpages* source, where the city name appeared in several places on the page. In these cases, user intervention or meta-analysis of the fields may be necessary to improve results of data extraction.

Extracting with Landmark-Based Rules

The final validation experiment consisted of using the automatically generated wrappers to extract data from test pages. The numeric columns in Table 2 list precision, recall, and accuracy for extracting data from test pages. The performance is very good for most fields, with the notable exception of the *STATE* field of *Bigbook* source. For that field, the pattern <ALLCAPS> was overly general, and a wrong group received the highest score during the scoring step of the reinduction algorithm. The average precision and recall values were $P = 0.90$ and $R = 0.80$.

Table 2. Precision, recall, and accuracy of the learned STALKER rules for the changed sources

Field	P	R	A	Field	P	R	A
Amazon				*Smartpages*			
Author	1.0	1.0	1.0	Name	1.0	0.9	0.9
Title	1.0	0.7	0.7	Street	N/A	0.0	0.0
Price	0.9	0.9	0.9	City	0.0	0.0	0.0
ISBN	1.0	0.9	0.9	State	1.0	0.9	0.9
Avail.	1.0	0.9	0.9	Phone	N/A	0.0	0.0
Barnes&Noble				*Yahoo Quote*			
Author	1.0	0.5	0.5	Price change	1.0	0.2	0.2
Title	1.0	0.8	0.8	Ticker	1.0	0.5	0.5
Price	1.0	1.0	1.0	Volume	1.0	0.7	0.7
ISBN	1.0	1.0	1.0	Price	1.0	0.7	0.7
Avail.	1.0	1.0	1.0				
Quote							
Price change	0.0	0.0	0.0				
Volume	1.0	1.0	1.0				
Ticker	1.0	1.0	1.0				
Price	0.0	N/A	0.0				

Figure 6. Performance of the reinduction algorithm for the fields in the Smartpages *source as the size of the training set is increased*

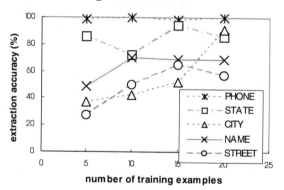

Within the data set we studied, five sources, listed in Table 2, experienced a total of seven changes. In addition to these sources, the *airport* source changed the format of the data it returned, but as it simultaneously changed the presentation of data from a detail page to a list, we could not use this data to learn STALKER rules.

Table 2 shows the performance of the automatically reinduced wrappers for the changed sources. For most fields, precision P, the more important of the performance measures, is close to its maximum value, indicating that there were few false positives. However, small values of recall indicate that not all examples of these fields were extracted. This result can be traced to a limitation of our approach: if the same field appears in a different context, more than one rule is necessary to extract it from a source.

In such cases, we extract only a subset of the examples that share the same context, but ignore the rest of the examples.

We can improve performance for the yellow-pages-type sources *Bigbook* and *Smartpages* by using more training examples. Figure 6 shows that as the number of training examples goes up, the accuracy of most extracted fields goes up too.

PREVIOUS WORK

Kushmerick (1999) addressed the problem of wrapper verification by proposing an algorithm RAPTURE to verify that a wrapper correctly extracts data from a Web page. In that work, each data field was described by a collection of global features, such as word count, average word length, and density of types, i.e., proportion of characters in the training examples that are of an HTML, alphabetic, or numeric type. RAPTURE calculated the mean and variance of each feature's distribution over the training examples. Given a set of queries for which the wrapper output is known, RAPTURE generates a new result for each query and calculates the probability of generating the observed value for every feature. Individual feature probabilities are then combined to produce an overall probability that the wrapper has extracted data correctly. If this probability exceeds a certain threshold, RAPTURE decides that the wrapper is correct; otherwise, that it has failed. Kushmerick found that the HTML density alone can correctly identify almost all of the changes in the sources he monitored. In fact, adding other features in the probability calculation significantly reduced the algorithm's performance. We compared RAPTURE's performance on the verification task to our approach, and found that it missed 17 wrapper changes (false negatives) if it relied solely on the HTML density feature.[2]

There has been relatively little prior work on the wrapper reinduction problem. Cohen (1999) adapted WHIRL, a "soft" logic that incorporates a notion of statistical text similarity, to recognize page structure of a narrow class of pages: those containing simple lists and simple hotlists (defined as anchor–URL pairs). Previously extracted data, combined with page structure recognition heuristics, was used to reconstruct the wrapper once the page structure changed. Cohen conducted wrapper maintenance experiments using original data and corrupted data as examples for WHIRL. However, his procedure for corrupting data was neither realistic nor representative of how data on the Web changes. Although we cannot at present guarantee good performance of our algorithm on the wrapper reinduction for sources containing lists, we handle the realistic data changes in Web sources returning detail pages.

There are many similarities between our approach and that used by the ROADRU-NNER system, developed concurrently with our system and reported recently in Crecenzi et al. (2001a, 2001b). The goal of that system is to automatically extract data from Web sources by exploiting similarities in page structure across multiple pages. ROADRUN-NER works by inducing the grammar of Web pages by comparing several pages containing long lists of data. The grammar is expressed at the HTML tag level, so it is similar to the extraction rules generated by Stalker. The ROADRUNNER system has been shown to successfully extract data from several Web sites. The two significant differences between that work and ours are that they do not have a way of detecting changes to know when the wrapper has to be rebuilt and our reinduction algorithm works on detail pages only, while ROADRUNNER works only on lists. We believe that our data-centric approach is more flexible and will allow us to extract data from more diverse information sources than the ROADRUNNER approach that only looks at page structure.

CONCLUSIONS

Here, we have described the DATAPROG algorithm, which learns structural information about a data field from a set of examples of the field. We use these patterns in two Web wrapper maintenance applications: (a) **verification**—detecting when a wrapper stops extracting data correctly from a Web source, and (b) **reinduction**—identifying new examples of the data field in order to rebuild the wrapper if it stops working. The verification algorithm performed with an accuracy of 97%, much better than results reported in our earlier work (Lerman & Minton, 2000). In the reinduction task, the patterns were used to identify a large number of data fields on Web pages, which were, in turn, used to automatically learn STALKER rules for these Web sources. The new extraction rules were validated by using them to successfully extract data from sets of test pages.

There remains work to be done on wrapper maintenance. Our current algorithms are not sufficient to automatically regenerate STALKER rules for sources that return lists of tuples. However, preliminary results indicate (Lerman et al., 2001) that it is feasible to combine information about the structure of data with *a priori* expectations about the structure of Web pages containing lists to automatically extract data from lists and assign the data to rows and columns. We believe that these techniques will eventually eliminate the need for the user to mark up Web pages and enable us to automatically generate wrappers for Web sources. Another exciting direction for future work is using the DATAPROG algorithm to automatically create wrappers for new sources in some domain given existing wrappers for other sources in the same domain. For example, we can learn the author, title, and price fields for the *Amazon Books* source, and use them to extract the same fields on the *Barnes&Noble Books* source. Preliminary results show that this is indeed feasible. Automatic wrapper generation is an important cornerstone of information-based applications, including Web agents.

ACKNOWLEDGMENTS

We would like to thank Priyanka Pushkarna for carrying out the wrapper verification experiments.

The research reported here was supported in part by the Defense Advanced Research Projects Agency (DARPA) and Air Force Research Laboratory under contract/ agreement numbers F30602-01-C-0197, F30602-00-1-0504, F30602-98-2-0109, in part by the Air Force Office of Scientific Research under grant number F49620-01-1-0053, in part by the Integrated Media Systems Center, a National Science Foundation (NSF) Engineering Research Center, cooperative agreement number EEC-9529152, and in part by the NSF under award number DMI-0090978.

REFERENCES

Abramowitz, M., & Stegun, I. A. (1964). *Handbook of mathematical functions with formulas, graphs and mathematical tables.* Applied Math. Series 55. National Bureau of Standards, Washington, D.C.

Ambite, J. -L., Barish, G., Knoblock, C. A., Muslea, M., Oh, J., & Minton, S. (2002). Getting from here to there: Interactive planning and agent execution for optimizing travel. In *The 14th Innovative Applications of Artificial Intelligence Conference (IAAI-2002)*, Edmonton, Alberta, Canada, (pp. 862–869). Menlo Park, CA: AAAI Press.

Carrasco, R. C., & Oncina, J. (1994). Learning stochastic regular grammars by means of a state merging method. *Lecture Notes in Computer Science, 862*, 139.

Cohen, W. W. (1999). Recognizing structure in Web pages using similarity queries. In *Proceedings of the 16th National Conference on Artificial Intelligence (AAAI-1999)* (pp. 59–66). Menlo Park, CA: AAAI Press.

Crescenzi, V., Mecca, G., & Merialdo, P. (2001a). Automatic Web information extraction in the roadrunner system. In *Proceedings of the International Workshop on Data Semantics in Web Information Systems (DASWIS-2001)*, November 29-30, Yokohama, Japan.

Crescenzi, V., Mecca, G., & Merialdo, P. (2001b). RoadRunner: Towards automatic data extraction from large Web sites. In *Proceedings of the 27th Conference on Very Large Databases (VLDB)*, Rome, Italy, (pp. 109–118).

Goan, T., Benson, N., & Etzioni, O. (1996). A grammar inference algorithm for the World Wide Web. In *Proceedings of AAAI Spring Symposium on Machine Learning in Information Access*, Stanford University, CA. Menlo Park, CA: AAAI Press.

Hsu, C. -N., & Dung, M. -T. (1998). Generating finite-state transducers for semi-structured data extraction from the Web. *Journal of Information Systems, 23*, 521–538.

Knoblock, C. A., Lerman, K., Minton, S., & Muslea, I. (2001a). Accurately and reliably extracting data from the Web: A machine learning approach. *IEEE Data Engineering Bulletin, 23*(4), 33–41.

Knoblock, C. A., Minton, S., Ambite, J. L., Muslea, M., Oh, J., & Frank, M. (2001b). Mixed-initiative multi-source information assistants. In *The 10th International World Wide Web Conference (WWW10)*, Hong Kong, (pp. 697–707).

Kushmerick, N. (1999). Regression testing for wrapper maintenance. In *Proceedings of the 14th National Conference on Artificial Intelligence (AAAI-1999)*. Menlo Park, CA: AAAI Press.

Kushmerick, N., Weld, D. S., & Doorenbos, R. B. (1997). Wrapper induction for information extraction. In *Proceedings of the International Joint Conference on Artificial Intelligence (IJCAI)* (pp. 729–737). Menlo Park, CA: AAAI Press.

Lerman, K., & Minton, S. (2000). Learning the common structure of data. In *Proceedings of the 15th National Conference on Artificial Intelligence (AAAI-2000)*, Austin, TX (pp. 609–614). Menlo Park, CA: AAAI Press.

Lerman, K., Knoblock, C. A., & Minton, S. (2001). Automatic data extraction from lists and tables in Web sources. In *Proceedings of the Workshop on Advances in Text Extraction and Mining (IJCAI-2001)*. Menlo Park, CA: AAAI Press.

Lerman, K., Minton, S., & Knoblock, C. (2003). Wrapper maintenance: A machine learning approach. *Journal of Artificial Intelligence Research, 18*, 149–181.

Muslea, I., Minton, S., & Knoblock, C. (1998). Wrapper induction for semistructured Web-based information sources. In *Proceedings of the Conference on Automated Learning and Discovery (CONALD)*.

Muslea, I., Minton, S., & Knoblock, C. A. (2001). Hierarchical wrapper induction for semistructured information sources. *Journal of Autonomous Agents and Multi-Agent Systems, 4*, 93–114.

Papoulis, A. (1990). *Probability and statistics*. Englewood Cliffs, NJ: Prentice Hall.

ENDNOTES

[1] Limitations in the data collection procedure prevented us from accumulating large data sets for all sources; therefore, in order to keep the methodology uniform across all sources, we decided to use smaller training sets.

[2] Although we use a different statistical test and cannot compare the performance of our algorithm to RAPTURE directly, we doubt that it would outperform our algorithm on our data set if it used all global numeric features. We ran the verification experiment on a subset of the verification data (278 comparisons) using all numeric features, which resulted in $P = 0.92$ and $R = 0.55$. Using the approach described here, on the other hand, led to $P = 0.71$ and $R = 1.00$ for the same data set.

Chapter XVIII

Information Technology Infrastructure and Solutions

Maria Manuela Cunha
Polytechnic Institute of Cávado and Ave, Portugal

Goran D. Putnik
University of Minho, Portugal

Joaquim Silva
Polytechnic Institute of Cávado and Ave, Portugal

ABSTRACT

Agile and virtual enterprise (A/VE) is a leading organisational model characterized by a high flexibility and a fast reconfigurability or adaptability of the networked structure to face the dynamically changing market. A Market of Resources is a tool proposed in the BM_virtual enterprise architecture reference model (BM_VEARM) as an appropriate environment to accomplish the intrinsic requirements of the A/VE model, by supporting the creation, dynamic integration, and operation of A/VEs. The Market of Resources is an electronic and virtual market matching the offer and demand of resources providers, the basic elements that will integrate the A/VE. The existing e-marketplaces support a wide range of features required by the Market of Resources. Given the available software development platforms based on the existing technology and standards that support the e-marketplaces, we discuss in this chapter the feasibility the Market of Resources and its implementation using those software platforms.

INTRODUCTION

Several organisational approaches have emerged during the last decade. Agile manufacturing, concurrent engineering, virtual organizations, extended enterprise, one-product-integrated-manufacturing (OPIM), etc., are examples of emerging organisational models with the main characteristic being interorganizational flexibility, and all of them represent attempts to increase competitiveness and efficiency. Some of these models rely on strong alliances, dynamic partnerships, and permanent alignment with the market, and are strongly supported by information and communication technology, classified in the text as virtual enterprise (VE) models in broad sense.

According to several definitions, virtual enterprises (VEs) are defined as enterprises with integration and reconfiguration capability in useful time (agility), integrated from independent enterprises (resources providers), with the aim of taking profit from a specific market opportunity. After the conclusion of that opportunity, the VE either reconfigures itself or is dissolved and another VE is integrated, due to new market opportunities. Even during the operation phase of the VE, the configuration can change, as the need for readjustment or reconfiguration facing unexpected situations can happen at any time, raising the importance of the reconfigurability dynamics (Cunha & Putnik, 2002).

In the agile/virtual enterprise (A/VE) model, agility means the ability of fast and active adaptation of the integrated resources providers in face of erratic and unpredictable changes in the environment market, implying the substitution of A/VE participants to keep permanent alignment with the market.

During the last few years, several information technologies, tools, and Web-based applications have been developed, with the purpose to enable the electronic business, some of which can be relevant in supporting some of the tasks required by the VE model. We are referring to technologies as Internet, agent-based systems, artificial intelligence, and to (Internet-based) applications as electronic payments, electronic marketplaces, electronic negotiation, electronic contractualization, etc. (Cunha, Putnik, Carvalho, & Ávila, 2002).

Two critical factors against networking and reconfigurability dynamics—the basic characteristics of the A/VE model—can be identified: *transaction costs* and *leakage of firm's knowledge*. To overcome these disabling factors, the authors have proposed a Market of Resources (Cunha, Putnik, & Ávila, 2000) as the environment enabling and supporting management of efficient A/VE (re)configuration, and assuring virtuality, at low transaction costs and reduced risk of knowledge leakage (Putnik, 2000).

In this chapter, we briefly identify the requirements of the A/VE model and introduce a new environment—the Market of Resources—that presents the required functionalities to cope with the A/VE model requirements, and finally, we discuss the features of some commercially available technologies and applications and how could these be used in the implementation of the Market of Resources environment.

REQUIREMENTS OF THE A/VE MODEL

The A/VE model is characterized by a fast reconfigurability dynamics, in order to yield its maximum competitiveness.

The efficient implementation of the A/VE model must assure two main interrelated aspects:

- Reconfigurability dynamics
- Business alignment (aligning the A/VE with the market)

These aspects are necessary in order to be competitive in delivery time, quality, and cost and to yield satisfactory profit margins (Cunha & Putnik, 2004).

In order to assure the above two requirements, it is essential to assure the ability of:

1. flexible and almost instantaneous access to the optimal *resources* to integrate in the enterprise, the negotiation process between them, the selection of the optimal combination, and its integration;
2. design, negotiation, business management, and manufacturing management functions independently from the physical barrier of space; and
3. minimization of the reconfiguration and integration time (Cunha & Putnik, 2004).

The first characteristic implies the existence of a market of independent candidate resources for integrating a VE. This market role has the following characteristics:

1. to provide the environment and technology and the corresponding procedure protocols, i.e., "the open system architecture" for the efficient access to resources, efficient negotiation between them, and efficient integration; and
2. to provide a domain for selection of participant resources in a VE, large enough to assure the best, or near the best (or optimized) options

The second characteristic implies the utilization of the advanced information and communication technologies to the operation of the market of independent resources, i.e., technologies providing technical conditions to efficiently accede to the globally distributed resources providers, efficient negotiation between them and its efficient integration.

The third characteristic is necessary in order to provide flexibility, as high as possible, i.e., reconfigurability as fast as possible.

According to Cunha, Putnik, and Carvalho (2002), these requirements can be translated to a set of functionalities that any environment attempting to support the model, must be able to offer:

- Responsiveness or almost real-time answer, as one instantaneous physical structure (or one instance) of an A/VE may last (on the limit) only for a few days or even hours
- The permanent alignment of the A/VE with the market (business) requirements, which can justify a dynamic process of A/VE performance evaluation and the analysis of reconfiguration opportunities
- The ability to find the right potential partners for A/VE creation/reconfiguration and further efficient negotiation
- Monitoring of the performance of every integrated resource, increased trust, and the highest possible performance of the A/VE

- Reduction of the time-to-contract and risk minimization in a contractual agreement
- Provision of knowledge in A/VE creation and reconfiguration

MARKET OF RESOURCES CONCEPT AND ITS FUNCTIONALITIES

The concept of Market of Resources was introduced by the authors, as an electronic and virtual market, mediating offer and demand of resources to dynamically integrate in an A/VE. Enterprises (resources providers) subscribing to the Market of Resources, make their resources available as potential servers or partners for A/VE integration (Cunha et al., 2000). Brokers act within the Market of Resources as intermediation agents for agility and virtuality. The Market of Resources supports the A/VE model proposed by Putnik (2000) in its BM_VEARM.

In this "virtual" environment, *offer* corresponds to *resources providers* (individuals, enterprises) that make their *resources* (products, components, operations) available, as potential partners for A/VE integration (understanding A/VE integration, or reconfiguration, as including the processes of search or potential partners, selection and negotiation between them, and the integration of the selected in an A/VE), and *demand* corresponds to *client*, the A/VE owner, the entity looking for resources to create/integrate/reconfigure an A/VE to satisfy the *Customer*. *Customer* is the entity giving rise to a business opportunity and is considered outside the Market of Resources.

The service provided by the Market of Resources is supported by:

1. a knowledge base of resources and results of the integration of resources in previous A/VE,
2. a normalized representation of information,
3. intelligent agent and algorithms,
4. a brokerage service, and
5. regulation, i.e., management of negotiation and integration processes.

It is able to offer:

1. knowledge for A/VE selection of resources, negotiation, and its integration;
2. specific functions of A/VE operation management; and
3. contracts and formalizing procedures to assure the accomplishment of commitments, responsibility, trust, and deontological aspects, envisaging that the integrated A/VE accomplishes its objectives of answer ing to a market opportunity (Cunha & Putnik, 2004; Cunha, Putnik, & Gunasekaran, 2002).

The environment supports not only the *integration* process, but, what is most important when the fast and proficient reaction to change is a key element, is also able to effectively support *dynamic integration*, which is the main reason for the concept of Market of Resources as an institution (Cunha, Putnik, & Gunasekaran, 2002).

In order to achieve the highest performances (productivity, costs, response time, quality, etc.) of the A/VE design and operation processes, it is of the highest interest to consider their automation, total or partial (computer aided). A/VEs are integrated by heterogeneous elements (resources) and are based on technologies that provide interoperability, i.e., "open" systems architectures, which is an additional requirement for the operation of the Market of Resources and for A/VE design and operation as well.

As the Market of Resources is intensively based in high-level information technologies (distributed software applications, information systems and databases, telematics applications, and wide-area networks), we are referring to an electronic and virtual market. This market provides information about the candidate resources providers to integrate a VE, about products and about clients or A/VE owners. In the same way, the Market of Resources provides (1) access procedures, (2) remote negotiation and utilization of services, and (3) interaction with existing networks and markets of suppliers and users of information, services, and products.

A more in-depth description of the Market of Resources can be found in a specific chapter of this book, entitled "Market of Resources as a Virtual Enterprise Integration Enabler" (Cunha, Putnik, Gunasekaran, & Ávila, 2004).

TECHNICAL REQUIREMENTS TO SUPPORT THE MARKET OF RESOURCES

Table 1 summarizes the contributions of some technologies and environments to the main VE models in broad sense: VE, extended enterprise, agile enterprise/manufacturing, supply-chain management, A/VE (the BM_VEARM A/VE) and OPIM. It also refers to the importance of reconfigurability dynamics for each model.

The techniques and environments included in Table 1 are able to *contribute* to activities of all the VE models, *but do not to support them*, as the purpose of their development was not the creation of an environment to support the VE models. The Market of Resources is proposed as an ideal environment to support the requirement of fast adaptability of the most dynamic VE model life cycle (BM_VEARM A/VE and OPIM), as validated by the authors and demonstrated (Cunha & Putnik, 2003a, 2003b), while electronic marketplaces were designed to cope only with procurement needs in supply chains and electronic business models that do not require a high reconfigurability dynamics. Functionalities of the Market of Resource are not as indispensable for extended enterprise, agile enterprise/manufacturing, or supply-chain management as they are for the other models included in Table 1.

The technical requirements to support the Market of Resources can be grouped under three heads and are bounded by a reference model (the BM_VEARM) to guide the implementation and operation of the Market of Resources, and to manage the participation of the elements (providers, clients, and brokers) (Cunha, 2003):

*   *An information infrastructure*: The information infrastructure must provide information exchange, security, access, monitoring, recovery and emergency handling, and contingency operations. Technology elements include functional engines (file servers, network servers, distributed database engines, search engines, and security mechanisms), distributed information resources built upon these engines (such as catalogues, distributed databases) and services to access these resources (building on the existing techniques as HTML, file transfer protocol, messaging, collaboration techniques, etc.). It is also essential to have a normalized representation language.

Table 1. Techniques and environments contributing to VE models source: Cunha, Putnik, Carvalho et al. (2002)

	Techniques			Environments		Importance of reconfigurability dynamics
	WWW searches	Electronic auctions	Agent-based brokerage	eMarket places	Market of Resources	
Virtual Enterprise models						
Extended Enterprise	x	x	x	x		medium
Virtual Enterprise	x	x	x		x	high
Agile Enterprise / Manufacturing	x	x	x	x		medium
Supply Chain Management	x	x	x	x		medium
BM_VEARM A/VE	x	x	x		x	high
OPIM	x	x	x		x	high
Ability to support fast reconfigurability				low	high	

- *Appropriate support mechanisms and tools for the supra infrastructure*: An information infrastructure *per se* is not enough; participants require mechanisms and tools to operate within the infrastructure, namely, integrability support, coordination and performance evaluation, electronic negotiation systems, payments, electronic signatures, and other supporting tools. A shared information infrastructure is valuable only if it can support the accomplishment of several dimensions of integrability already referred. Participants (clients and providers) need supporting tools to quantify service levels and to evaluate performance, assess targets, etc., as well as collaborative and information exchange tools. Brokers also need specific management tools (search algorithm, expert systems/ artificial intelligence applications).
- *Coverage of the A/VE extended life cycle*: The traditional VE life cycle includes the phases of creation, operation, and dissolution, where reconfiguration can possibly happen during operation. The A/VE model is characterized by a high reconfigurability dynamics and permanent business alignment. Besides, a life cycle involves a project definition (in our case, an A/VE design phase), which should be an integrating part of it. The extended life cycle concept is directly tied with the *BM_VEARM* and the supporting environment—the Market of Resources. The Market of Resources is part of the extended life cycle.

The coverage of the extended life cycle is mainly assured by the support to the A/ VE needed for reconfigurability dynamics and by the existence of the brokerage function. Technical and procedural support are required to identify potential partners (including a wide variety of mechanisms, such as auctions and bidding), qualifying partners (in terms of technical capability, quality, and background information about results in previous partnerships), and integration in the A/VE (including conformity testing, contract conditions, payment, etc.). The market must also provide coordination and performance evaluation mechanisms, during all the life cycle phases; just to mention two examples:

1.   the substitution of resources due to weak performance is a delicate process as it can implicate indemnities, and
2.   the dissolution of an A/VE, if not properly managed, can generate tremendous costs (e.g., issues concerning corporate intellectual property).

Table 2 presents the core technologies and tools that correspond to the three classes of technical requirements identified above. The table intends merely to be illustrative, not to be seen as an exhaustive list.

Table 2. Technologies for the implementation of the Market of Resources technical requirements (Source: Cunha, 2003)

Technical Requirements		
Information Infrastructure	**Support Mechanisms and Tools**	**Coverage of the A/VE Extended Life Cycle**
- Servers - Distributed database systems - E-marketplaces development platforms - Search engines - Electronic catalogues - Information exchange tools - Communication technologies - Messaging and collaboration techniques - Standards and protocols regarding information exchange, teleoperation, distributed manufacturing, (CORBA, HTTP, STEP, etc.) - Interpreter for a normalised resources representation language or the support of a standard as UDDI/WSDL	- Benchmarking and metrics - Modelling and analysis tools (distributed and virtual simulation) - Integration tools (translation tools) - Electronic negotiation mechanisms - Agent technology - Payments, ordering - Electronic contracting - Algorithms or protocols - Market regulation - Intelligent decision-making systems - Computer-aided tools	- Market organisation - Management procedures - Business models - Performance evaluation - Reconfigurability management - Contract management - Environment management (maintenance, control, coordination, enforcement, etc.)
A/VE Reference Model (BM_VEARM)		

(left margin label: Technologies / Tools)

All the required technologies and techniques to support search and selection of suppliers or of partners to integrate a supply chain already exist, and many valuable applications are already in operation, however, there is missing what we designate an adequate environment to support the need of reconfigurability dynamics required by the A/VE paradigm.

IMPLEMENTATION OF THE MARKET OF RESOURCES WITH THE EXISTING TECHNOLOGY

Information and communication technologies and Internet-based agent technologies are the main technologies for implementation of techniques supporting or contributing to A/VE integration. These techniques and applications include electronic negotiation, electronic marketplaces, and market brokerage services. Other fundamental technologies for A/VE operation are workflow management systems, collaborative design, virtual product, and concurrent engineering.

According to a commonly used definition proposed by Wooldridge (1997), agents are software systems capable of flexible, autonomous action in some environment in order to meet its design objectives. Agents can travel over the Internet, activate and control remote programs, interrogate host Web sites, interact with other agents, and return with information. The agent-based solution proved to be appropriate in Internet-based marketplaces and in the integration of VEs, where agents can search for resources providers, organize auctions and manage bids, manage the transaction, etc.

Agent technology plays an important role in the automation of electronic negotiation, which is defined by Beam and Segev (1997) as the process by which two or more parties multilaterally bargain resources for mutual intended gain, using the tools and techniques of electronic commerce in networked computers.

However, electronic marketplaces seem to be the technology adapted to cover the major aspects of the Market of Resources functionalities. This section explains how the integration of commercially available technology allows the implementation of a Market of Resources, the integrated environment with the desirable characteristics to support the A/VE, allowing reconfigurability dynamics, quality assurance, trust, electronic negotiation, electronic contractualization, optimization in resources utilization, etc.

After the initial boost of new e-marketplaces in 1998, the number of active e-marketplaces decreased in 2001 (Deloitte Consulting and Deloitte & Touche, 2000, 2001), many high-profile B2B e-marketplaces shut down (e.g., Chemdex Petrocosm, Aerospan, BuildNet, Metalsite, etc.). The dot-com stock market crisis demonstrated that the existing e-marketplace models and technology were not mature enough. However, many e-marketplaces thrived in the last two years (Deck, 2002). Right now, the market has stabilized, and several e-marketplaces proved that their time has already arrived (*The Economist*, 2002). Several e-marketplace makers emerged with consolidated business models and technology.

In this section, we include the features provided by six of the most important e-marketplace software platforms, under three perspectives: (1) main software platform features, (2) technologies and standards, and (3) technology partners.

E-Marketplace Software Platform Makers Features

The analysis covers features as automation technologies and integration and infrastructure technologies. Some examples include the implementation of exchanges, auctions, negotiation and payments, project management, contract management, workflow, and marketplace-to-marketplace integration.

From several e-marketplace software platforms, we have selected four leading forerunner vendors and two emerging e-marketplace software platforms from software giants, Microsoft and Oracle, which will be introduced.

Currently, maybe due the recent closing of B2B e-marketplaces, Ariba (*http://www.ariba.com*) and i2 Technologies (*http://www.i2.com*) discontinued their e-market-place standard solutions to focus on specialized e-commerce solutions. Ariba discontinued Ariba Marketplace to focus on Ariba Spend Management. i2 Technologies abandoned the TradeMatrix platforms development to focus on value-chain management. Both companies played a very important role in the development of existing e-marketplace platforms; they manage, at the moment, successful public e-marketplaces (Ariba Commerce Service Network and FreightMatrix, respectively) and offer solutions for building private e-marketplaces. Commerce One (*http://www.commerceone.com*) is a leading e-marketplace maker since the e-marketplace boom and runs CommerceOne.net (*http://www.commerceone.net*). Broadvision (*http://www.broadvision.com*) is turning into one of the most dynamic and prolific e-commerce companies, specialized in the development of business portals.

Two major software companies, Microsoft (*http://www.microsoft.com/commerce*) and Oracle (*http://www.oracle.com/applications*), are engaged in the development of e-commerce solutions, so their importance in the e-commerce arena will increase.

Table 3 describes the features supported by the selected e-marketplace software platform makers. In this analysis, we have also considered features that are not part of the solution but can be easily integrated by the same vendor application packages or close technology/platform partners solutions.

Table 4 lists the main technologies to support the main components and processes of the Market of Resources. Most of the components of the Market of Resources are already supported by the existing e-marketplace software platforms. All the platforms studied provide many tools and technologies for holding up market contents, negotiations, and transactions. But, none of the platforms support agent technologies, user algorithms, and intelligent decision support systems for helping in negotiation processes. They also lack mechanisms for transaction control and coordination, automated business processes, and business services applications security and management.

None of the six platforms suitably supports management, brokerage, and integration processes. Workflow and messaging are fully covered but lack interoperability between different systems. Several solutions include project management and some kind of collaboration, but there is yet no integration of simulation tools and state-of-art collaboration tools. User algorithms needed for efficient brokerage are not possible to use. Data and process integration continue to be a difficult issue, because there are no complete standards for product/services description and no efficient collaboration tools. Oracle is the only solution that supports ebXML specifications. We were not able to identify any tool to support decision support systems, computer-aided systems, artificial intelligence, and other technologies mentioned in Table 4.

Table 3. Most important features supported by e-marketplace software platforms (Source: Cunha, 2003)

Features \ E-Marketplace Platform	Ariba	Broadvision	Commerce One	i2	MS Commerce	Oracle Exchange
Localization (language, currency, date format, etc.)	X	X	X	X	X	X
User and role management	X	X	X	X	X	X
Catalogue/content management	X	X	X	X	X	X
Private exchanges	X	X	X	X	X	X
B2B marketplaces	X	X	X	X		X
Forward auction	X	X	X	X	X	X
Reverse auction	X		X	X	X	X
ATP—Available to promise		X	X	X		X
RFP/Q—Request for proposals/quotation	X	X	X	X		X
Order status tracking	X	X	X	X	X	X
Order fulfillment	X	X	X	X	X	
Order brokering				X		
Multiprotocol order routing	X	X	X	X	X	X
Negotiation mechanisms	X	X	X	X		X
Logistics and delivery support	X	X	X	X	X	X
Consolidated invoicing	X		X	X		X
Security (SSL/HTTPS)	X	X	X	X	X	X
Digital authoring (PKI, X.509)	X	X	X	X	X	X
e-Business analytics (OLAP, KPIs)	X	X	X	X	X	X
Contract management	X	X	X	X		X
Workflow	X	X	X	X	X	X
Project management			X	X		X
Survey and campaign management		X		X	X	X
Messaging	X	X	X	X	X	X
Interactive forum support		X				X
Collaboration planning forecasting and replenishment (CPFR)	X	X	X	X	X	
Complex product configuration			X	X	X	X
High Availability (24/7)	X	X	X	X	X	X
M2M interconnection/integration	X		X	X		X

Table 4. Technologies to support the main components and processes of the Market of Resources (Source: Cunha, 2003)

Market of Resources Components/Processes	Support Technologies and Tools
Market contents: user/buyer profile, catalogues, historic, database of resources	Database management systems Distributed database management systems E-Business development platforms Portals
Negotiation: request for quotes, auction/reverse auction, optimal selection	Intelligent agent technology Electronic negotiation tools Algorithms or protocols Regulation of negotiation Intelligent decision-making systems
Transactions: payment, contractualisation	Electronic payment Digital signature Certification Other security mechanisms
Management: monitoring, performance evaluation, analysis of operation results, decision making	Simulation tools Workflow technology and collaboration techniques Regulation
Brokerage: expert advise, monitoring and coordination	Messaging and conferencing Database management systems Algorithms Management procedures
Integration: file translation, collaboration	Standards for product/services description Collaboration tools Data translation standards and tools Communication protocols
Resources final selection (optimal combination)	Algorithms, heuristics, and computer-aided tools Intelligent decision-making systems Artificial intelligence

This analysis shows that although there is good overall coverage of the Market of Resources components by the existing e-marketplace technology, some important features are not yet supported. The accomplishment of all Market of Resources technological requirements will be done in the future, adapted from the next generation e-marketplace software and from other business areas or specifically developed for this purpose.

Technologies and Standards

Most of the e-marketplace platform features are based on technology or industry standards and rely on their success. Several technologies and standards are the foundation of the e-marketplaces software platforms. The technologies and standards play an important role in the facilities provided for each platform, as well as on the interoperability between different e-marketplaces. Table 5 summarizes e-marketplace software technologies and standards foundation.

The recently launched Microsoft.Net aimed to be a solid alternative to the Java development environment.

XML (eXtensible Markup Language) did not yet deliver all the potential for data interchange, so EDI (Electronic Data Interchange) continues to be an important technology for exchanging information between businesses. Today, many e-marketplace platforms handle EDI-to-XML transactions. The major strength of XML can simultaneously be the major weakness: the ease and flexibility of the creation of new standards can lead to a proliferation of many standards for the same purpose, like cXML (commerce eXtensible Markup Language) and xCBL (XML Common Business Library) formats.

In this study, all the solutions support XML formats, but only Oracle Exchange supports STEP, the Standard for the Exchange of Product Model Data. STEP is a comprehensive ISO standard (ISO 10303) that describes how to represent and exchange digital product information.

Web Services are the most promising technology for business processes integration (webMethods Inc., 2002). The automation of processes, the automatic integration of interenterprise business processes, and the coordination of complex business transactions are determinant to obtain high productivity from technology usage and to create

Table 5. E-marketplace software technologies and standards foundation

Technologies and Standards \ E-Marketplace Maker	Ariba	BroadVision	Commerce One	i2	MS Commerce	Oracle Exchange
Java, JSP, Java Beans, J2EE	X	X	X	X		X
Microsoft.NET		X			X	
XML	X	X	X	X	X	X
cXML	X	X	X	X	X	X
xCBL		X	X	X	X	
CIF (catalog interchange format)	X		X			
EDI	X	X	X	X	X	X
STEP standard format						X
Web services		X	X	X	X	X
BPEL4WS					X	
ebXML						X
RosettaNet			X	X	X	X

dynamic collaboration environments. Several specifications were developed to meet that purpose, like BPEL4WS (Business Process Execution Language for Web services), ebXML, and BPML (Business Process Management Language). BPEL4WS and ebXML are more likely to survive and coexist for the foreseeable future; ebXML will probably dominate a regulated B2B scenario, and BPEL4WS is more compliant with a nonregulated B2B/B2C scenario. RosettaNet is the first integration processes standard implemented worldwide in industry, by more then 400 of the world's leading information technology and electronic components companies.

Besides SSL and PKI, supported by all the software platforms, more high-level security mechanisms for business processes interenterprise integration are required, like SAML (Security Assertion Markup Language) or XKMS (XML Key Management Specification) for Web services security and management.

Technology Partners

All the e-marketplace makers have technology partners to support the implementation of the software platform, covering aspects such as security, application integration, CRM, etc. Microsoft Commerce Server is based on their own technology products, in particular, on the BizTalk Server integration platform. The same happens with Oracle, that has an e-marketplace platform built over its own technology products. But, most of the e-marketplace makers have several partners to support them in specific areas. There are many technology partners that have a very important role in the e-marketplace development framework; some of them are identified in Table 6.

Table 6. E-marketplace software technologies and technology partners and domain

Technology Partner and Technology Domain \ E-Marketplace Maker	Ariba	BroadVision	Commerce One	i2	Oracle Exchange
Actuate: Reporting software platform		X		X	
Bea Systems: Embedded Web logic server	X	X		X	
IBM WebSphere: infrastructure integration software	X	X		X	
SeeBeyond: Real-time infrastructure software		X	X		
Sterling Commerce: Message management software	X		X		X
TIBCO Software: Real-time infrastructure software	X			X	
Verisign: Internet trust services	X	X	X		
Vignette: Complement marketplace and buyer solutions	X				
WebMethods: XML-based solutions	X	X	X	X	

CONCLUSIONS

Technological requirements are no longer the most important barrier for the implementation of new business models and, in particular, of the Market of Resources as an A/VE enabler. It is expected that real standards for reliable messaging, security, and workflow will appear in products by 2005 or 2006.

So, e-marketplace software platform features will soon be achieved, except for those that rely intensively on *de facto* standards, like organisational or legal requirements. Organisational aspects will take several years, maybe decades, to be met. Legal and security issues are also difficult to implement, because they rely on governmental regulation.

Many organizations are involved in the next generation of e-marketplaces and in the whole electronic business; the development of new technology and specifications depends on the efforts of everyone involved. However, the software giants, like Microsoft, IBM, or Oracle, are decisive on the implementation of global industry standards.

REFERENCES

Beam, C., & Segev, A. (1997). *Automated negotiations: A survey of the state of the art* (Technical Report 97-W0-1022). Berkeley, CA: Haas School of Business, University of California–Berkeley.

Cunha, M. M. (2003). *Organisation of a market of resources for agile and virtual enterprises integration.* Doctoral Thesis, University of Minho, Guimarães, Portugal.

Cunha, M. M., & Putnik, G. D. (2002). Discussion on requirements for agile/virtual enterprises reconfigurability dynamics: The example of the automotive industry. In L. M. Camarinha-Matos (Ed.), *Collaborative business ecosystems and virtual enterprises* (pp. 527–534). Dordrecht: Kluwer Academic Publishers.

Cunha, M. M., & Putnik, G. D. (2003a). Market of resources versus e-based traditional virtual enterprise integration—Part I: A cost model definition. In A. Gunasekaran & G. D. Putnik (Eds.), *Proceedings of the First International Conference on Performance Measures, Benchmarking and Best Practices in New Economy* (pp. 664-669). Guimarães, Portugal: University of Minho.

Cunha, M. M., & Putnik, G. D. (2003b). Market of resources versus e-based traditional virtual enterprise integration—Part II: A comparative cost analysis. In A. Gunasekaran & G. D. Putnik (Eds.), *Proceedings of the First International Conference on Performance Measures, Benchmarking and Best Practices in New Economy* (pp. 667-675). Guimarães, Portugal. University of Minho.

Cunha, M. M., & Putnik, G. D. (2004). Trends and solutions in virtual enterprise integration. *Tekhné—Review of Politechnical Studies, 1*(1).

Cunha, M. M., Putnik, G. D., & Ávila, P. (2000). Towards focused markets of resources for agile/virtual enterprise integration. In L. M. Camarinha-Matos, H. Afsarmanesh, & H. Erbe (Eds.), *Advances in networked enterprises: Virtual organisations, balanced automation, and systems integration* (pp. 15–24). Dordrecht: Kluwer Academic Publishers.

Cunha, M. M., Putnik, G. D., & Carvalho, J. D. (2002). Infrastructures to support virtual enterprise integration. In R. Hackney (Ed.), *Proceedings of 12th Annual BIT Conference—Business Information Technology Management: Semantic Futures.* Manchester, UK: The Manchester Metropolitan University (CD-ROM).

Cunha, M. M., Putnik, G.D., & Gunasekaran, A. (2002). Market of resources as an environment for agile/virtual enterprise dynamic integration and for business alignment. In O. Khalil & A. Gunasekaran (Eds.), *Knowledge and information technology management in the 21st century organisations: Human and social perspectives* (pp. 169–190). Hershey, PA: Idea Group Publishing.

Cunha, M. M., Putnik, G. D., Carvalho, J. D., & Ávila, P. (2002). A review on environments supporting virtual enterprise integration. In M. Vladimír, L. M. Camarinha-Matos, & H. Afsarmanesh (Eds.), *Balancing knowledge and technology in product and service life cycle* (pp. 133–140). Dordrecht: Kluwer Academic Publishers.

Cunha, M. M., Putnik, G. D., Gunasekaran, A., & Ávila, P. (2004). Market of resources as a virtual enterprise integration enabler. In G. D. Putnik & M. M. Cunha (Eds.), *Virtual enterprise integration: Technological and organizational perspectives* (this volume). Hershey, PA: Idea Group Publishing.

Deck, S. (2002). Alive and kicking: Are B2B e-marketplaces dead? Not hardly! *Microsoft Executive Circle, 2002.*

Deloitte Consulting and Deloitte & Touche. (2000). *The future of B2B: A new genesis.* Deloitte Consulting and Deloitte & Touche. Retrieved August 20, 2002 online *www.dc.com*

Deloitte Consulting and Deloitte & Touche. (2001). *Collaborative commerce: Going private to get results.* Deloitte Consulting and Deloitte & Touche. Retrieved August 20, 2002 online *www.dc.com*

The Economist. (2002). Profits at Last. December 19.

Putnik, G. D. (2000). BM_Virtual enterprise architecture reference model. In A. Gunasekaran (Ed.), *Agile manufacturing: 21st century manufacturing strategy* (pp. 73–93). Amsterdam; New York: Elsevier.

webMethods Inc. (2002). *Demystifying Web Services.* webMethods Inc. Retrieved January 7, 2003 online *http://www.webmethods.com*

Wooldridge, M. (1997). Agent-based software engineering. *IEE Proc. Software Engineering, 144,* 26–37.

Chapter XIX

Consortium Agreement Template for Virtual Enterprises

José Dinis Carvalho
University of Minho, Portugal

Nuno Afonso Moreira
University of Trás-os-Montes e Alto Douro, Portugal

Luís Carlos Pires
Polytechnic Institute of Bragança, Portugal

ABSTRACT

This chapter addresses the contractual legislation problem as an integration problem within the virtual enterprise context. In order to address the problem in a real legal platform, we create an example of a consortium agreement template based on the existing Portuguese legislation. The legislation is no more than standard procedures and guidelines to address an organization's formalization within the legal system and society. Looking through the existing Portuguese legislation, as an example, we found a way to legally fit virtual enterprises (VEs). Moreover, we propose a consortium agreement template as a preestablished standard agreement to legally support VEs before specific legislation is created. We propose that the enterprises, when joining a market of service providers, would automatically accept this consortium agreement template in order to more rapidly become a partner in a VE as soon as business opportunities arise.

INTRODUCTION

There are some similarities between virtual manufacturing cells and VEs. A manufacturing cell is a collection of machines organized in the same location in order to produce a family of parts; and this concept is normally associated with group technology. Several studies have shown that cellular manufacturing improves production performance (Kadipasaoglu et al., 1999; Shambu et al., 1996; Wemmerlov & Johnson, 1997). One of the main advantages of this type of shop floor configuration is related to the fact that it results in a significant reduction of setup time. On the other hand, dedicating a group of machines to a certain family of parts normally results in unbalanced utilization of resources when changes in demand occur (Kannan & Ghosh, 1996). Rearranging manufacturing cells to follow fluctuation in demand it is not an easy task, because moving machines around takes time and costs money. One solution is to keep the machines in their locations and dynamically assign them to virtual cells, as it better suits the actual needs. These cells do not exist physically, they only exist for scheduling and routing purposes. In this way, we can keep the advantages of reducing setup times without losing the balanced utilization of resources (Kannan, 1998).

Manufacturing cells cannot be looked at only as a group of machines; people are also included in these systems. Some authors argue that the gains that can be obtained by cellular manufacturing are enhanced by the fact that the people involved in the cell develop teamwork with great benefits to the cell performance. Those benefits are not achievable by virtual manufacturing cells (Suri, 1998). This handicap must not be underestimated in VE environments.

To a certain extent, a VE can be looked at as a virtual cell; the main difference is that in one case, the units are machines, and in the other case, the units are enterprises. A VE is a group of enterprises that can rapidly get together to respond to a business opportunity, and normally this cooperation does not last for long. In this way, the benefits that could be obtained by the teamwork will not be achieved. Each VE member does not move to a location next to the other members, because new configurations for VEs are always needed. One of the main lessons from this knowledge is that VEs do not have only advantages and there is a long way to go before they are commonly established.

It is reasonable to assume that a new company specifically designed for a new product will perform better than any existing company (Putnik & Silva, 1995). Existing companies were designed for existing business opportunities, so it is understandable that in the presence of new businesses, new products, and new demand patterns, new companies especially designed for a specific purpose, would perform better. All that makes sense, but we must keep in mind that any new business has its window of opportunity, so the speed in building the enterprise that will efficiently respond to that business opportunity is a crucial issue. Well, how fast can a new company be ready to effectively respond to market needs?

Creating a new traditional company takes a considerable amount of time, and in many cases, it cannot be the answer to the market dynamics. In many cases, the window of opportunity for a particular business is so short that a new traditional company cannot be built in time. In some cases, such as construction of bridges or roads, the problem is solved by assigning the project not to a single company but to a consortium of different companies. This consortium solution could be seen, to a certain extent, as a VE. The VE paradigm has been addressed as the solution to effectively respond to new business opportunities. The right collection of small companies may be, as a whole, the perfect company in responding to a particular business opportunity. Selecting the right set of companies and putting them to work together in the same project cannot also be done overnight. This process also takes time and is far from being easy. There is an interesting paradox around the VE issue: building a VE is a time-consuming task, but it is created to respond rapidly to a new business opportunity. While a traditional company already exists when the business opportunity arises, a VE must be created after the business opportunity is known.

VIRTUAL ENTERPRISES INTEGRATION

Although the idea of creating dynamic networks of enterprises to respond to the needs of agility is already two decades old (Miles & Snow, 1984), the materialization of such concepts has been very slow. There are several difficulties in implementing the VE paradigm. From some points of view, the VE concept makes a lot of theoretical sense, but many practical issues are still difficult to overcome. Some of those practical difficulties are as follows:

- Selection of partners: The big advantage of VEs is the possibility of selecting the best set of partners for a particular business opportunity. The number of partners available to be chosen is crucial to the VE adequacy to the demand. The big question is: where is the information about available service providers or potential partners? Even if it is available, is that information in a standard format?
- Trust: Even if we find information about available service providers, are they able to be trusted? Is it reasonable to share risk and profit with them?
- Teamwork development: As you know, along the years, enterprises build team spirit (also described earlier in this chapter), among its employees, which enhances work performance. This type of atmosphere is difficult to expect in short time relationships between different enterprises.
- Legislation: Is the available legislation appropriate for VEs? This issue will be discussed later.

Many of these and other difficulties occurring either during the formation phase or in the operation phase are related to the integration issue. Integration can be defined as the act of combining or adding parts to make a unified whole or as the act of combining two or more things in order to become more effective (*Cambridge Dictionaries* online). This is a typical dictionary definition and a common popular understanding of integration. The integration issue gained great popularity during the 1980s and early 1990s because of the computer integrated manufacturing (CIM) concept. Under this concept, many authors considered the computer as the main tool for integration. This integration covers not only data integration through a common database for many different processes but also through the integration of different processes (Scheer, 1991).

We believe that the integration problem in VEs cannot be addressed in the way it was addressed in the CIM approach. Common databases may not be suitable, because VE partners come and go in a very dynamic way, and companies do not want to share all their data with other partners (Camarinha & Lima, 2001). On the other hand, as the Internet is used for the communication between partners, the information must be kept away from intruders.

Integration is a crucial issue, and it can be addressed from several different angles, but integration is closely related to the use of standards. The development and acceptance of standards for VEs has a long way to go. We still have difficulties in defining products and services in universal languages. We still have problems with communication protocols between different software (both in technical and management areas). We also have the legislation problem, and from a certain point of view, we can consider legislation as a standard. Without these standards, how can one search for service providers? How can a company communicate with other partner companies? Is the legislation available today suitable to support VEs? Is it possible to legally create a VE in a country like Portugal?

FORMATION OF VIRTUAL ENTERPRISES

Before exploring the formation phase of VEs, it is important to introduce the concept of market of service providers (MSP). The MSP, equivalent to the Market of Resources (Cunha et al., 2000) or the virtual service market (Hoffner et al., 2001), is a place where service providers advertise their services and where customers or brokers can search for services required. In our model (Carvalho et al., 2002), all service providers associated with the Market of Resource providers accept, among others, the following two important conditions: (1) they use a standard language to describe their available services, and (2) they agree on using a standard consortium agreement template when they participate in a VE. This second condition will decrease dramatically the time for legal contract establishment.

According to our VE model, the life cycle of a VE consists of three phases: the VE formation phase, the operation phase, and the dissolution phase. In this work, we are mainly concerned with the formation phase, because it is in this phase that the contract between consortium parties is established. We assume that the formation of a VE can be subdivided into the following five subprocesses activities: business opportunity conception, rough VE project elaboration, partners search and selection, VE project elaboration, and partners relationship formalization. The standard consortium agreement template is important in the partners relationship formalization subprocess.

The trigger for the business opportunity conception and, therefore, for the VE, is the business opportunity idea. The entity that comes out with that idea and wants to start a VE is called here the starter entity (SE). This entity must have the knowledge to develop a first project plan, named the rough VE plan. This plan contains the definition of the main capability requirements that, from the SE point of view, must be fulfilled in order to best reach the business opportunity. This rough VE plan holds the information that is needed to start searching for potential partners with the help of a broker (Carvalho et al., 2001). The broker holds the knowledge and experience in finding appropriate partners in the MSP and also knows the right set of tools needed to perform the searches. From the alternatives presented by the broker, the starter entity selects the one that better suits the requirements for each function or process. This process may take several iterations, because negotiation is needed between the SE and the potential partners. The broker stays in action until the final VE configuration (set of partners assigned to the different processes) is reached. This is called the VE project.

Once the set of partners is established, the administration board must be defined for the VE, which is the entity that holds the responsibility for the business at the highest level. Examples of activities that are performed by the administration board are strategic management, admission of new partners, removal of existing partners, definition of targeted markets, marketing strategies, legal responsibilities, etc. Representatives of each partner or group of partners compose this administration board.

Another important entity in the VE life is the VE manager. This entity, either being a VE partner or an external service supplier, is the entity entitled to manage the VE operation. It includes operational functions covering production, finances, and marketing functions.

At this point in the VE formation, we have the VE partners, the VE project, the VE administration board, and the VE manager. Because all members were selected from the MSP, all of them already accepted the contract agreement template, so it can be established among the partners. According to the contract agreement template, the terminology assigned to each entity is as follows:
- Consortium members: VE partners
- Steering and monitoring committee: VE administration board
- Head of the consortium: VE manager

LEGISLATION ISSUE

The legislation available today for cooperation between companies is not adequate for the needs required by the dynamic networking of enterprises. To a certain extent, the real advantages of VEs are only achieved if companies from different regions of the world get rapidly networked for cooperation to respond to a business opportunity. This type of cooperation, sharing risks and profits, is not reasonably covered by available legislation. The cooperation assumed in this chapter is not a traditional customer–supplier relationship where the custumer's payment by the required service is as far as it goes. The cooperation that is assumed to exist here requires that companies share the risks and the profits in the common business. For these purposes, legal contracts must be rapidly established between partners where the functions, responsibilities, and shares of risks and profits are clearly defined for all partners.

It is clear that many of the traditional points of reference in the legislation, such as nationality, headquarters, legal personality, etc., are not adequate to respond to the concept of VE (Schoubroeck et al., 2001). According to Schoubroeck et al. (2000), the main legal characteristics of VE are as follows:
- The most important is that the VE does not have a legal personality. As a consequence, the VE cannot conclude any legal contract, according to traditional rules it cannot be located in any country, and its members will be jointly and severally liable.
- A VE is perceived, in the market, as a single enterprise, although it has no significant organizational suprastructure (e.g., no head office, no legal personality). Major problems will arise when there is no possibility of identifying the members behind

a VE and, therefore, third parties will face difficulties, as they cannot turn against the VE because of its absence of legal personality.

- It is expected that VEs will work worldwide across country borders, but its members will have to agree upon which national law will govern the VE.
- VEs tend to have an ephemeral character. As VEs will mainly develop to face new business opportunities, members (and perhaps the VE) will come and go very fast.

According to existing legislation, the "joint venture" is probably the best legal alternative to VE (Sorrentino & Santoro, 2001). This legal framework is based on an agreement between two or more enterprises, with the objective of accomplishing a specific project.

We may all agree that the available legislation is not adequate to VE, but we can put out the question: how can we create a VE with the legislation available today? Let us take for instance the Portuguese legislation.

Looking through the Portuguese legislation, we find the first reference to partnerships between enterprises in the year of 1973. The Law No. 4/73 of 4 June defines "complementary groups of enterprises" as the grouping of "individuals, businesses or societies, without prejudice of its legal personality, aiming the improvement of the activity conditions or the income of its economic activities." This first legal reference allowed the generation of groups of enterprises although strongly restricting their objectives, regulating: "the groups of complementary enterprises could not have as main objective neither the profit generation nor profit sharing." Moreover, it obliges the constitutive contract to be reduced into a public deed. These legal constraints strongly restrict the generation of partnerships between enterprises.

Later, the Decree-Law No. 231/81 of 28 July introduced the "Consortium Agreement" (*Contrato de Consórcio*) regulation. In the preface of this law, it is written, "its legal creation gives the legal framework to a form of cooperation between enterprises, which can target several objectives, but requires always simplicity and malleability." Moreover, "the practical purposes of the parties concerned as well as the nature of their established relationships deviate their businesses, very often, from the traditional types, only where an aberrant legal conservantism can insist on confining them." Giving an example, "when several enterprises meet to carry out an important private or public work, it is absurd forcing them in setting up a society, in one of the types of trading company, when they voluntarily deviate from that type of framework." This preface unveils that this legislation intends to create an easier and malleable partnership formula, allowing the participants to reach nontraditional business arrangements, avoiding the generation of a company among them. That is exactly one of the legal characteristics that we pretend for VEs.

In the Decree-Law referred to in the last paragraph, it is assumed that "it is internationally in vogue the expression *Joint Venture* to designate short-lived or lasting partnerships which do not fulfill the requirements for trading companies and, if the expression is, at least in our legal system, unprovided of rigorous juridical content, it exists in reality and should be recognized." This diploma also establishes that the designation of consortium covers a large part of these *joint ventures,* moreover, each consortium member will keep its own activities, although "harmonized with the activities of other members." From this preface, we highlight that the Portuguese legislation defines consortium (*consórcio*) as a special case of *joint venture*, where partner enterprises keep their individuality.

In the referred Decree-Law, a consortium is presented as "an agreement upon which two or more enterprises or individuals, which perform an economic activity put themselves under an obligation to, in a harmonized way, perform a certain activity." In this agreement, the "terms and conditions will be freely established, without the violation of the diploma standards." It also created the head of the consortium (*chefe do consórcio*), designated among the members, who is incumbent on the functions, which are contractually assigned, or, for lack of this assignment, on organizing the "cooperation between the parties in accomplishing the consortium objectives," besides other consortium representation functions before third parties. All consortium members are obliged not to compete with the consortium as well as to supply to all fellow members and to the head of the consortium all the considered relevant information. Other relevant duties are also defined to all consortium members. One last note to the reference that "joint and several liability" is not supposed to exist between consortium members and third parties. When the consortium members assume "joint and several liability" (*Responsabilidade Solidária*), each member assumes the consortium's total responsibility.

This Decree-Law creates the consortium framework, with responsibilities before third parties that are defined in a contract between participant members, enterprises, or individuals. It is established in this contract the way members put themselves under the obligation of reaching certain objectives and establishing the leadership, which represents the consortium before third parties. Not least important is the last note in the preceding paragraph, where we point out that the consortium members are not "joint and severely liable" before third parties, but are only responsible in the conditions defined in the contract. This is a mixed responsibility formula, which protects, on the one hand, consortium members from other members' actions and, on the other hand, protects the third parties in the responsibilities defined in the contract.

This consortium partnership in the building industry, allows enterprise participants to separate their own contributions (Sorrentino & Santoro, 2001). This statement is extremely important when an organizational structure is to be created where each member can clearly identify its contribution. This is also true under the Portuguese legislation.

One of the consortium practical issues is that the consortium does not have its own accounting function, as it is not registered in the finance services. The accounting is kept separately by each consortium partner. This characteristic holds advantages and disadvantages if we compare it with other types of partnerships with joint accounting (e.g., complementary grouping of enterprises—*Agrupamentos Complementares de Empresas*). One advantage is that separate accounting is simple and flexible, allowing for limited liability to each partner. One disadvantage comes from the fact that because the total liability is distributed through many partners, members need to negotiate and put in the contract all unexpected circumstances, bringing complexity and slowing the consortium formation process.

The Portuguese legislation analysis seems reasonably appropriate, however, we cannot forget that a VE is not limited to Portuguese enterprise partners. When we talk about VEs, it is natural to assume that partners could be registered in different countries, and then the legislation from those countries should also be considered. This is also an important issue to address.

PROPOSAL OF A
CONSORTIUM AGREEMENT

The consortium framework defined in the Portuguese legislation was created to allow partnerships between enterprises aiming to carry out joint projects or works. This type of consortium assumes that the group of enterprises involved has well-defined objectives, where tasks assigned to each partner are well defined, with no significant changes along the VE life. According to many authors and according to different VE models, tasks and activities assigned to VE members may change during the project life, according to changes in market demand or changes in the will of partners. It would be desirable for the VE performance and flexibility to have the ability of reconfiguration during its life. Members should be free to leave the partnership, and new members should be able to enter an existing VE in order to better fit the VE needs.

In fact, the Portuguese legislation for consortiums (Decree-law No. 231/81 of 28 July, article 10) anticipates the exclusion of a consortium member. The legislation terms are as follows: "the consortium contract can be solved in regard to some of the contracting party, by written declarations emanated from all the others, occurring just cause." Just cause is understood as "the heavy flaw to consortium member's duties" and "the impossibility, guilty or not, in the accomplishment of obligations fulfillment of certain activity or in realizing certain contribution." These are the juridical principles that can be followed during the consortium life, allowing one or more members from being excluded from the consortium without the need of concluding the consortium.

Going back to the issue of consortium members of different nationalities, we must say that it happens very often in Portugal, especially in large public works, such as motorway's construction, football stadiums, etc. Large consortiums are created including, very often, companies from foreign countries. The consortium is not limited to performing business only in one country, being allowed to have foreigner customers, exactly as traditional companies. Moreover, a foreign consortium member will be under the legislation of its country, namely, in accounting and tax issues, in the same ways as traditional companies. We may say that in the absence of the consortium accounting and tax personality, we can include enterprises from different countries in the same consortium.

The liability of a group of individuals or group of enterprises before third parties can assume the shape of joint liability or joint and several liability. When partners assume joint and several liability, each consortium member assumes to itself the total liability of the entire consortium. On the other hand, when partners assume joint liability, each consortium member only assumes liability assigned to its part of the project. We believe that this last type of liability is more adequate to be implemented in VEs, as the joint and several liability option, among other disadvantages, would make it difficult to exclude a consortium member during the VE life.

The two main consortium organs are the steering and monitoring committee and the head of the consortium. Representatives from each of its consortium members compose the steering and monitoring committee. This organ is responsible for approving the VE project, proposed by the head of the consortium, where project tasks are assigned to each consortium member. This organ is also responsible for approving any proposed changes in the VE project, such as changes in task assignment. As we mentioned earlier, changes in the VE project can be complex if the changes involve the removal or inclusion of VE members. As you may understand, if considerable changes take place in the VE member composition, a new consortium may need to be considered, with a new steering and monitoring committee and maybe a complete new VE strategy.

The head of the consortium is a consortium partner whose core competence is the management of VE-oriented consortiums. This head of the consortium or VE manager is responsible for managing the VE operation covering the three basic functions: marketing, production, and finance (Dilworth, 1992; Heizer & Render, 2000).

The consortium framework foreseen in Portuguese legislation allows for one aspect of virtuality important to VEs ("the VE should appear as one enterprise to the customers"). This aspect of virtuality can be achieved in the following way: the head of the consortium assumes the VE face toward customers; the communication from VE to customers and from customers to VE is performed through this entity; all invoices are sent to customers from the head of the consortium; each VE partner sends the related invoices to the head of the consortium. In this way, partners can be included and excluded from the VE without customer awareness. It is important to point out that the VE manager cannot be seen as an intermediate between customers and the other VE partners (the real service providers) but only a VE partner contributing to the VE with its own technical competencies.

The consortium agreement template (Appendix 1) is an example of what can shape the legal existence of a VE. Assuming a MSP is well established and has appropriate dimensions where every associate (service provider and potential VE partner looking for partnerships) accepts the terms of this template, then, as soon as a partnership (a VE) is reached, this consortium agreement is automatically accepted, and the VE is legally created overnight.

CONCLUSIONS

Even without being foreseen by the Portuguese law, we believe that VEs could have legal existence in Portugal. The Decree-Law No. 231/81 of 28 July introduced the "Consortium Agreement" regulation, which can be used to assure the legal existence of a VE. In order to speed up the formation of a VE, we consider the existence of a MSP, where all potential VE partners are registered as members. To join this MSP, all members should agree upon the use of a predefined consortium agreement template (Appendix 1) that will be used as soon as a VE is created. In this way, once a business opportunity is detected, the SE will search for partners in the MSP, knowing that as soon as all partners are defined, the legal aspects will be rapidly sorted out.

REFERENCES

Camarinha, L. M., & Lima, C. (2001). Cooperation coordination in VEs. *Journal of Intelligent Manufacturing 12*(2), 133–150.

Carvalho, J., Moreira, N., & Pires, L. (2002). *Autonomous production systems in VEs.* Presented at CARs&FOF'2002—18th International Conference on CAD/CAM, Robotics and Factory of the Future, Porto, INESC Porto.

Carvalho, J. D., Pires, L., & Moreira, N. (2001). *Developing a production planning and control system for virtual/distributed enterprises environment.* Presented at the 28th International Conference on Computers and Industrial Engineering, Cocoa Beach, Florida.

Cunha, M. M., Putnik, G. D., & Ávila, P. (2000). Towards focused markets of resources for agile/virtual enterprise integration. In L.M. Camarinha-Matos et al. (Eds.), *Information technology for balanced automation systems in nanufacturing and transportation* (pp. 15–24). Proceedings of the 4th IEEE/IFIP International Conference, Berlin (September 27-29, 2000). Kluwer Academic Publishers.

Dilworth, J. B. (1992). *Operation management—Design, planning, and control for manufacturing and services.* New York: McGraw-Hill.

Heizer, J., & Render, B. (2000). *Operations management.* Englewood Cliffs, NJ: Prentice Hall.

Hoffner, Y., Field, S., Grefen, P., & Ludwig, H. (2001). Contract-driven creation and operation of virtual enterprises. *Computer Networks*, (37), 111–136.

Kadipasaoglu, S. N., Peixoto, J. L., & Khumawala, B. M. (1999). Global manufacturing practices: An empirical evaluation. *Industrial Management & Data Systems, 99*(3), 101–108.

Kannan, V. R. (1998). Analysing the trade-off between efficiency and flexibility in cellular manufacturing systems. *Production Planning and Control, 9*(6), 572–579.

Kannan, V. R., & Ghosh, S. (1996). Cellular manufacturing using virtual cells. *International Journal of Operations & Production Management, 16*(5), 99–112.

Miles, R. E., & Snow, C. C. (1984). Fit, failure and the Hall of Fame. *California Management Review, 26*(3), 10–28.

Putnik, G. D., & Silva, S. C. (1995). One-product-integrated-manufacturing. In L.M. Camarinha-Matos & H. Afsarmanesh (Eds.), *Balanced automation systems: Architectures and design methods.* London; New York: Chapman & Hall.

Scheer, A. W. (1991). *CIM: Towards the factory of the future.* Heidelberg: Springer-Verlag.

Schoubroeck, C. V., Cousy, D. H., Windey, B., & Droshout, D. (2001). A legal taxonomy on virtual enterprises. Available online *http://www.vive-ig.net/projects/alive/procs.html*

Shambu, G., Suresh, N. C., & Pegels, C. C. (1996). Performance evaluation of cellular manufacturing systems: A taxonomy and review of research. *International Journal of Operations & Production Management, 16*(8), 81–103.

Sorrentino, S., & Santoro, R. (2001). Virtual organisation reference life-cycle processes and associated legal issues. CE Project ALIVE Working Group on Advanced Legal Issues in VE. Available online *http://www.vive-ig.net/projects/alive/procs.html*

Suri, R. (1998). *Quick response manufacturing: A companywide approach to reducing lead times.* Portland, OR: Productivity Press.

Wemmerlov, U., & Johnson, D. J. (1997). Cellular manufacturing at 46 user plants: Implementation experiences and performance improvements. *International Journal of Production Research, 35*(1), 29–49.

APPENDIX:
CONSORTIUM AGREEMENT TEMPLATE

Between:

- ...., represented herein by ...., empowered to sign this agreement; and

- ...., represented herein by ...., empowered to sign this agreement; and

- ...., represented herein by ...., empowered to sign this agreement; and

The parties hereby enter into this Consortium Agreement, which is subject to the terms and conditions of the following clauses:

Clause One (Object)
Under this Agreement, the Contracting Parties enter a Joint Liability External Consortium with the object of executing, jointly and concertedly, all material and legal acts necessary to carry out the work and supplies included in the VE Project, and to carry out any other work or supplies that might arise therefrom.

Clause Two (Name and Registered Office)
The Consortium is entitled ...... and has its registered offices at ....

Clause Three (Liability)
1. Before third parties, there shall only be common liability of the Consortium Members when this arises expressly from the contractual document, and it is presumed that whenever this liability exists, it shall be joint.
2. Each one of the Consortium Members shall be fully and exclusively liable for the good and punctual performance of all work in their charge, and for the integral fulfilment of all obligations assumed by the Consortium, regarding the Consortium, in the VE Project.
3. Even in cases of common liability of the Consortium Members, in their internal relationships, each one of the Consortium Members shall be held fully and exclusively liable for all damages that, arising from actions attributable to it, they may suffer, regarding the VE Project and its performance.
4. Subject to the provisions of the previous paragraph, when it is not possible to determine which Consortium Member is to be held liable, the compensation, fines, retentions or any other sanctions or payment of damages that may occur, these shall be distributed between both parties in proportion to their participation.

Clause Four (Administration of the Consortium)
The Administration of the business and interests of the Consortium is the responsibility of:

(a) A decision-making body, which is the Steering and Monitoring Committee (COF);

(b) An executive body, which is the Head of the Consortium.

Clause Five (Steering and Monitoring Committee)

1. The supreme decision-making body of the Consortium is the Steering and Monitoring Committee (COF), which must necessarily comprise a representative of each of the Consortium Members. The Consortium Members shall also designate a reserve representative, who shall substitute the appointed representative when absent or unable to attend. The following are henceforth designated:

1st party:
- Actual Member: ......
- Reserve: ....

2nd party:
- Actual Member:.........
- Reserve: ....

3rd party:
- Actual Member: ......
- Reserve: ....

2. The Steering and Monitoring Committee shall be responsible for the administration of the consortium, as well as the guidance, control, and supervision of the management and executive activities of the Head of the Consortium.

3. The deliberations of the Committee shall be taken by majority of its members.

4. The Committee may be summoned, whenever necessary, by any of its Members or by the Head of the Consortium.

5. The responsibilities of the Steering and Monitoring Committee are:
    (a) To guide and monitor the conduct of the Consortium;
    (b) To deliberate on the VE Project by the Head of the Consortium, including deliberating on the inclusion and exclusion of Consortium Members;
    (c) To deliberate on measures to prevent or correct possible deviations in time-limits, faults or failure to fulfil in the performance of the VE Project tasks, that have been verified or are reasonably foreseeable, by the Consortium Members, at the suggestion of the Head of the Consortium;
    (d) To deliberate on any alteration or amendment to this agreement;
    (e) To deliberate on any alteration to the terms and conditions of the VE Project and on a possible dissolution of the VE;
    (f) To deliberate on each and every issue regarding the joint charges and expenses of the Consortium;
    (g) To pronounce, at the request of any of the Consortium Members or by

imposition of this agreement, on any matters related hereto, to the VE Project or to its performance;

(h)   To seek to resolve any disagreements between Consortium Members;

(i)   To deliberate on the replacement of the Head of the Consortium.

6.   The meetings of the Steering and Monitoring Committee should take place within 10 days from notification thereof.

Clause Six (Head of the Consortium)

1.   The Consortium Member .... is the Head of the Consortium.

2.   The Head of the Consortium is responsible for the operational management of the Consortium and for monitoring and coordinating the implementation of the VE Project including in particular:

(a)   Guaranteeing the general, technical, and administrative management of the Consortium;

(b)   Representing the Consortium before Third parties. Although it may not assume any obligations other than those provided for in the VE Project, or in the Consortium Agreement, without the prior and express consent of   the other Consortium Members given in writing, and it should be accompanied by a representative of these Members whenever their work, rights or obligations are at stake;

(c)   Ensuring the proper and timely performance of the VE Project entered into, as well as of this agreement;

(d)   Defining the VE Project, adapting tasks under the VE Project to the skills of the available potential consortium members in the market of service providers, repeatedly, subjecting the final version to the approval of the COF;

(e)   Monitoring the tasks of the Consortium Members, and promoting the perfect and timely performance of the work carried out by each one of them;

(f)   Proposing measures to prevent or correct possible deviations in time-limits, faults or failure to fulfil in the performance of the VE Project tasks, verified or are reasonably foreseeable, by the Consortium Members;

(g)   Introducing proposals for alterations to the VE Project to the COF, for inclusion or exclusion of consortium members;

(h)   Promoting the defence and realization of the rights and interests of the Consortium and of the Consortium Members;

(i)   Exercising any other powers conferred by the COF.

3.   The Head of the Consortium may delegate its duties to another Consortium member, partially or totally, provided his proposal is authorised by the COF.

Clause Seven (Participation in the Consortium)

1.   The participation of the Consortium Members in the Consortium shall be defined by the VE Project, approved by the COF, which should necessarily contain the proportion of joint liability of each one of the Consortium Members.

2.   The performance of the work shall be distributed between the Consortium Members in accordance with the VE Project, approved by the COF.

Clause Eight (Termination of the Agreement)

1.   The consortium agreement can be terminated, with regard to some of the consortium members, by written declaration issued by of all the others.

2.   Just cause for the purpose of Paragraph 1, besides that provided for in legislation, shall be considered to be the exclusion of the Consortium Member, or Consortium Members, from the VE Project, as approved by the COF.

3.   The termination of the agreement with regard to a Consortium Member should restrict the participation of that Consortium Member in the VE Project, and shall only be materialized after their corresponding values have been taken into account

Clause Nine (Billing and Payment)

1.   The Consortium Members shall bill the Head of the Consortium for the value of their tasks, the bills being sent to the Head of the Consortium.

2.   The Head of the Consortium shall directly bill the Client, in accordance with the VE Project.

3.   Payments shall be made by the Client directly to the Head of the Consortium, which shall pay each of the Consortium Members in proportion to their participation, in accordance with the VE Project.

Clause 10 (Joint Costs)

1.   The costs supported by the Consortium Members and classified as joint costs by the COF shall be allocated thereto in proportion to their participation.

2.   Common costs, which in conjunction shall be distributed under the terms provided for in this Clause, are considered to be the expenses of preparing the proposal, notary fees, charges, taxes or any other expenses inherent to the VE Project and its possible alterations, as well as bank guarantees to the Client and between the Consortium Members with regard to the performance of the work.

Clause 11 (Autonomy)

1.   It is perfectly understood that matters and problems which, although they concern the fulfilment of the VE Project, are of interest only to one of the Consortium Members, without any effect or reflection on the others, on the Consortium as a whole, or on the implementation of the VE Project, and therefore should only be resolved by that Consortium Member are excluded from the decision-making functions of the COF and of the Head of the Consortium.

2.   The provisions of the previous paragraph shall not prejudice, however, the powers of the Head of the Consortium to represent the Consortium and the Consortium Members before the Employer, nor the obligations of the Consortium Bodies to provide all the follow-up dependent thereon, before third parties, for appropriate protection of the legitimate interests of the consortium member in question, in accordance with the guidelines established by the Consortium, where matters and problems are concerned that, by legal implication of this agreement or the VE Project, may only be legitimately dealt with by these Bodies, in their entirety or in part.

Clause 12 (Resources)

Each one of the Consortium Members shall ensure the financial, logistic, and technical resources necessary to their effective participation in the Consortium, in particular for the perfect performance of the VE Project task or tasks that they may accept to perform through this agreement.

Clause 13(Duration of the Consortium)

The Consortium shall terminate when cumulatively:

(a)   All obligations arising from the VE Project have been fulfilled;
(b)   All accounts and possible disputes between the Consortium Members and Third parties have been totally settled and Bonds released;
(c)   All accounts and possible disputes between Consortium Members have been definitively settled.

Clause 14 (Arbitral Agreement)

All divergences, which may arise between the Consortium Members, resulting from the interpretation, application, or performance of this agreement, which cannot be resolved by their representatives in the COF, must be submitted to an attempt at friendly reconciliation, to be conducted between their respective administrations, notwithstanding the normal development of the VE Project.

Clause 15 (Confidentiality)

The Consortium Member that receives from another Member of the Consortium any documents, drawings, or other information regarding this agreement or the VE Project, undertakes to not make any use of those elements other than that arising from those agreements and to consider as strictly confidential all technological data and data of a commercial nature from the other Consortium Member.

Clause 16 (Advertising)

During the term of this agreement and after its termination, all references made to the services that are the subject of this agreement, included in any form of advertising of each Consortium Member, must mention that they have been carried out in Consortium.

Clause Seventeen (Supplementary Legislation)

In all situations not provided for in this Agreement, the provisions of Portuguese Legislation shall be applied, in particular Decree-Law No. 231/81 of 28 July, under the terms of which this Consortium is constituted and will operate.

Section V

Projects and Case Studies

Chapter XX

Virtual Enterprises and the Case of BIDSAVER

Nicolaos Protogeros
University of Macedonia, Greece

ABSTRACT

In recent years, several European projects have been launched aiming to research the new paradigm of virtual enterprise. The projects VIVE, BIDSAVER, and ALIVE are only some of which have run under the auspices of the European Commission Programme for Information Society Technologies (IST). This chapter presents the BIDSAVER project that ran between 1999 and 2002, and aimed at delivering technologies and methodologies that support the creation and operation of virtual enterprises.

INTRODUCTION

According to Hongfei (2003), a virtual enterprise is "a network of several companies, which contribute their core competencies and share resources such as information, knowledge, and even market access in order to exploit fast-changing market opportunities" (Hongfei, 2003, p. 19). The relationship can be long or short term. Thus, virtual enterprises merge geographically dispersed companies so as to develop and commercialize products and, in general, to benefit from business opportunities that would otherwise be outside the technical and production capabilities of each individual participating company.

We briefly refer to research projects related to the theme of virtual enterprises:

- COVE (cooperation infrastructure for virtual enterprises) and electronic business, (COVE project). The project assesses research results and practices in virtual enterprises (VEs) and electronic business, leading to the design of common reference models, infrastructures, etc.

- ICSS (integrated client–server system) used by a virtual enterprise in the building industry (COVE project). It is an Internet-based virtual roundtable which discusses and solve engineering problems in a legal way.
- MASSYVE (multiagent manufacturing scheduling systems in virtual enterprise), (COVE project). It is an application of the multiagent systems paradigm in order to agile scheduling in manufacturing systems.
- DRIVE (drug in virtual enterprise) (DRIVE project). It focuses on the improvement of quality and the reduction of costs in integrated healthcare delivery systems. The project provides a secure infrastructure to support drug processes of an integrated clinical and logistic drug supply chain for end-to-end service delivery.

As far as the BIDSAVER project is concerned, the objective is to develop a methodological, technological, and legal framework to support small and medium-sized enterprises (SMEs) by helping them increase their competitiveness and business potential through the constitution and operation of VEs. The latter are managed on the basis of competitiveness-oriented criteria and by means of adopting a new concept, namely, this of the business integrator.

The general phasing concept for the operational scenario has been derived from the results of the VIVE project (VIVE project, VIVE site); these results have provided the conceptual framework and scheme for the constitution and operation of a "generic" VE.

BIDSAVER concentrates on specific industrial sectors and is aimed at supporting operational issues of specific industrial sectors, based on the sectors addressed in the pilots included in the project. Furthermore, the methodology generalization in BIDSAVER addresses the methods for developing models dedicated to new specific sectors, while it also covers the dynamic aspects and nature of a VE, in terms of supporting the selection of optimized partners' sets through Internet-based search, developed and validated through two pilot showcases: one in the microsatellite area and one in the mechanical engineering area.

In the rest of this chapter, we first start with a general description of the project, followed by a description of the project scenarios and actors. In the third section, an operational scenario is presented, and in the fourth section the operation phases of a VE according to project results. The fifth section copes with integration issues, the sixth with the proposed architecture, while the seventh and eighth sections present the BIDSAVER prototype and the main results. Finally, in the ninth section, conclusions are given that take into account the evolution and the results of the project.

DESCRIPTION OF WORK

BIDSAVER has delivered technologies and methodologies for the creation and operation of VEs among SMEs in different business sectors. The project was organized in the following logical steps:

- Definition of market-based requirements on VEs — this was conducted using a bottom-up approach, starting from the space satellites and the mechanical equipment market sectors, and from two VE types, the value-network-oriented and the supply-chain-based VE

- Definition of the operational concept for VEs and associated methodology, resulting in the definition of the required legal framework and their identification of the conceptual structure of supporting functions and methods
- Development of a reference system prototype according to an incremental methodology, to exploit feedback from pilot operations [An early ICT prototype was released to allow for the pilot operation. The system was composed of a set of commercial solutions for VE operation (project management, active cycle), plus the following three management modules (Figure 1):
- A business breakdown structure (BBS) management module, allowing the management of the evolution of VE through a model (BBS) that accommodates cross mapping of product physical/functional items, tasks, and associated resources/risks/timing, and responsible entities/organizations with associated contractual elements.
- An information capturing agent, responsible for the actual search on the Web of potential partners and for providing updated information on cooperation opportunities.
- The business information integration module, integrating operational functions, that leverage on e-commerce and Internet technology, and on preselected commercial solutions to be configured according to VE requirements.
- Developing and testing the pilot application for the methodology and ICT solution, applied to actual industrial cases:
- A value network pilot focusing on the development of microsatellites
- A supply-chain pilot, to cover a VE for mechanical equipment.

Results from pilot operations were used to upgrade both the methodology and the work environment concept and implementation.

Figure 1. VE information system concept

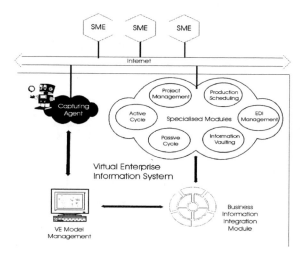

BIDSAVER PROJECT SCENARIO AND ACTORS

The project identified the virtual vertical enterprise paradigm, where a group of SMEs share processes and resources to pursue a well-defined market objective under the coordination effort of the business integrator.

The VE is characterized by an extremely dynamic behavior, where the organizational structure and even the product requirements and specification are rapidly adapting to market needs and best-fit criteria.

In the BIDSAVER scenario, the following actors were engaged and identified:

- The business integrator
- The VE partners
- The VE customer

Overall Requirements and Objectives

When considering the case of a VE, the main requirement is to provide the means to efficiently build and manage it in its dynamic correlation.

For the market sectors addressed, BIDSAVER developed a reference model that we regard as a "Code of Practice" with elements that constitute a guide and support the actors' behavior for the constitution and management of the VE (information and resource sharing, level of commitment, risks and liabilities, operational procedures). This enabled BIDSAVER to promote awareness of the opportunity offered by the VE paradigm among SMEs.

General quantifiable objectives were as follows:

- Reduce product development time and cost by at least 30%.
- Increase SME participation to targeted industrial sector by at least 10%.
- Reduce project management cost by 50%.
- Awareness of the BIDSAVER methodology and solutions to a wide number of SMEs (at least 200 SMEs).

Business Integrator

VIVE project has introduced the concept of a new entity, the "business integrator," in order to support the constitution and operation of VEs (VIVE project, BIDSAVER project). In the frame of the BIDSAVER project, the identified, measurable objectives of the business integrator were summarized as follows:

- To minimize time and effort for constitution of a VE; target effort for the business integrator in the VE constitution has been estimated at two man-months
- To minimize management effort; the current estimate for VE operation management was 10% to 15% of development effort. Target value for BIDSAVER was a reduction of 50%.

During the constitution phase, the availability of a suitable code of practice clearly minimizes the negotiation duration that address partners' participation in the VE.

The BIDSAVER approach for management is based on integrated business models, allowing for an event-driven management. These models cope with evolving product requirements, the work breakdown structure, and VE team organisation. In fact, BIDSAVER supported the possibility of performing a common management action, required in the frame of VE operations, such as:

- To easily replace defaulting partners, through valorization schemes of the work done and the financial impact on the other partners due to the interruption of the work
- To manage team reconfiguration, which can also occur when changes in product requirements imply process modifications, additional skills, capacities, and capabilities to be integrated in the VE

Industrial Partners

The participating industrial partners in the project were able to use the BIDSAVER methodology and tools in order to:

- Acquire the capability of entering business opportunities that could not be entered otherwise
- Increase revenues by adopting the BIDSAVER paradigm in their specific business sectors, and to enter neighboring markets; objectives depended on the individual partner's potentials, and were measured as the number of VEs entered per year

A BIDSAVER qualified industrial partner adapted its process and ICT infrastructure to readily respond to opportunities proposed by the business integrators. BIDSAVER covered the qualification process for candidate partners, to minimize effort and time required to enter the business opportunity.

Finally, through the adoption of the BIDSAVER methodology and tools, the industrial partners were continuously updated on their liability and associated company risk, thus having the possibility to control possible adverse impact by taking adequate management actions.

Customers

The adoption of the BIDSAVER paradigm should induce significant benefits to the intended customer as follows:

- Achieve a substantial reduction of project costs and project duration. Target reduction was estimated at 30% for the market addressed.
- For industrial customers, continuous visibility on VE operations would allow the adoption of a more proactive approach, based on assessment of design margins and changing market requirements. This could also bring the adoption of more evolved and sophisticated supply agreement schemes, in which possible savings originated by the concurrent effort of the VE team and the customer could be shared. This could lead to minimization of the level of the overall venture budget and multiplication of the number of affordable business opportunities.

VE OPERATION PHASES

The target scenario of the project was to address the operations of the generic business integrator for a VE, and provided the methods, mechanisms, and tools to cover the requirements related to:

- The search for partners in relation to a particular business opportunity
- The construction of the management frame for a business opportunity (constitution of the VE)
- The operation of a VE

Search for Partners

The initial phase of the VE life cycle addresses the search for partners; such a search normally requires the capability to:

- Understand specific market characteristics
- Specify the structure of the product, associated development, and production activities
- Specify the requirements for the execution of development and production activities
- Search potential partners over the Internet and evaluate their suitability to enter the VE

Constitution of the VE

The constitution phase of the VE entails the establishment of a cooperative frame and support environment. Major steps of this phase consist of the following:

1. Establishing the actual list of partners and related roles and responsibilities
2. Defining operational procedures and management mechanisms
3. Entering legal agreements for the operation of the VE
4. Upgrading the individual partners' work environments, whenever required for full operation of the VE

Elements developed by BIDSAVER in support of this phase were as follows:

1. The BBS model, specifying the VE in its subdivision of roles and responsibilities, as well as in the aspects of communication lines and information flows
2. The VE model, specific to individual business opportunities, specifying the sequencing of tasks and relationships, to be reflected together with the BBS model into the program management utilities
3. The legal frame, supporting VE's partners to enter binding agreements that reflects individual responsibilities and procedures to manage the dynamic evolution of the VE
4. The business information integration module that is in charge of translating VE models into specific data structures; these data structures are the basis for the communication protocols toward selected commercial tools used for enterprise operation (Project Management, Active Cycle, etc.), see Figure 1.

Figure 2. Model's structure

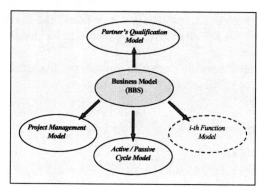

Operation of VE

The operation phase of the VE covers the product development and production phases, and ends with the formal closure of the VE.

Activities that were addressed during this phase include typical industrial operation tasks, such as accounting, material management, design, engineering, production, marketing, and so on.

The main elements supporting this phase were as follows (Figure 2):

- The BBS model, supporting the organizational evolution of the VE (and of the product), to accommodate changes in requirements, partners' identity, and role/ responsibility
- The information capturing agents, supporting the automated collection of operational information of partners for the dynamic management of the enterprise (ongoing and possible work orders), and the continuous verification of best partner combinations, in order to maintain the competitiveness of the enterprise
- The business information integration module, supporting the operational tasks through the interfacing of commercial tools—this module also supports the updating of communication protocols to commercial tools in case of changes in product requirements or organizational or work structure
- The legal framework, regulating the relationships among partners and evolution of the VE, until closure of the cooperation

INTEGRATION ISSUES AND SOLUTIONS

The BIDSAVER project has targeted integration issues based on the key factors discussed next.

Integrated Virtual Model of Process, Product, and Organisation

The integrated model is called the BBS, and it supports the evolution of product, process, and organisation according to the increasing detail in product definition and to the consolidation of partnership structure.

This model specifically supports:

- The management of interfaces at product level and at organizational level
- The concurrent definition of the VE organisation, based on integrated product design, for the establishment of optimized business ventures.

From the ICT point of view, the framework outlined in this project was based on:

- Web technology and solutions
- Knowledge-based product solutions providing innovative supporting tools for the SMEs

Business Information Integration Module

This is a major module in charge of accommodating integrated management of functions needed for VE operation. This module constitutes the "glue" of the VE information system. It is in charge of generating from the BBS module the technological views that constitute the interfaces to selected functional applications (project management and so on), and to manage the interoperability among applications through the establishment of rules that accommodate the VE operational concept. Thus, a rule manager was defined to carry out the required logic and to link with the other modules of the system.

Standardized Cooperative Process and Data Model

The project aims at the standardization of information to be supplied by SMEs willing to enter a VE.

Reference VE Information System

The project has delivered the concept and prototype for a reference environment supporting the business integrators in the constitution and management of VEs.

Adoption of Software Agents for Information Exchange Processes

The use of software agents in expertise search and information exchange is a research activity of growing interest. In the BIDSAVER project, software agents are employed in order to find suitable business partners and exploit new business opportunities. The data format was designed according to XML specifications, allowing a flexible definition of communication procedures.

BIDSAVER Architecture

Generally, the BIDSAVER project consists of three main software components:

- A business breakdown structure management module, allowing the management of evolution of VE, during the constitution and operations phases
- An information capturing agent, performing the actual search of potential partners during the instantiation and providing updated information on cooperation opportunities during VE operation

- The business information integration module, in charge of accommodating integrated management functions needed for VE operation

Business Breakdown Structure Management Module

The "business integrator" (BI) concept is introduced for managing the VE on a basis of competitiveness-oriented criteria and is responsible for the following actions:
- Identifying business opportunities
- Searching for more potential SMEs to enter the VE
- Specifying the required business process, the enterprise integration infrastructure (communication, information sharing means, etc.), the skills, and the capacities needed by the VE to be established
- Supporting suitable SMEs during the operation phase

The BBS provides the BI with the full data structure, integrating three dynamically reconfigurable and strictly interlaced databases:
- Product breakdown structure (bill of materials)
- Work breakdown structure (in which tasks and responsibilities are allocated)
- Organizational breakdown structure

These structures are used to support the VE during the initiation and operation phases. They are initially designed by the business integrator and are maintained for the total life cycle of the VE. A tool is developed to support the initial design and maintenance (update) of the structures with minimal effort. A short description of the structures is provided in order to offer a better understanding of the type of information contained within the generated partner profile patterns used by the ICA.

Product Breakdown Structure (PBS)

This structure provides the framework for specifying the product or service to be developed or produced. It defines the product in terms of hierarchically related elements (tree structure). The PBS is used by the VE as the basis for managing the product and describing its technical characteristics. Also, the PBS should be designed to follow the evolution of the VE cycle and be able to adjust to new needs and requirements. The hierarchical decomposition of the product usually consists of three or four levels, depending entirely on the complexity of the product at hand.

Work Breakdown Structure (WBS)

The main objective of the WBS is to provide the business integrator with a full set of management information relevant to the project activities. It manages all aspects related to the internal processes necessary to accomplish the specific task. WBS is a tree structure and should be represented up to a level where a single responsible partner can be assigned to each activity. Also, the PBS and WBS structures should be closely coupled so that each task and activity refers to a specific subsystem or system of the product. Hence, the WBS is a structure composed of work packages assigned to every element within the PBS structure and activities that have to be performed by each work package.

Organizational Breakdown Structure (OBS)

This structure is composed of organizational entities and the associated human and technical resources that are involved during the VE operation phase. The OBS structures contain information regarding the personnel involved in specific VE activities, links to WBS and PBS elements with access rights and legal agreements among partners participating in the process. The OBS also allows the dynamic evolution of the VE life cycle and is capable of providing information at any given time. Hence, the OBS defines at least the following:

- The responsible entity for all contractual aspects
- The technical entity responsible for the project (work package coordinator)
- The responsible entity for each task

The identification of the responsibilities allocated to each participating party during the operation phase is achieved by the use of OBS.

The information capturing agent's operation depends entirely on information extracted from these three structures and all existent relations set among them. Thus, the concept that the agent is based on differs widely from those that are used by most available search engines.

The extracted information contains "items" that are actually product elements defined within the PBS structure. Each item can be further decomposed into more subitems depending on the initial knowledge of the business integrator on the specific matter. All items may contain an arbitrary number of qualifiers identifying specific characteristics. Qualifiers of three kinds are available: PBS qualifiers indicating product characteristics, WBS qualifiers indicating activities and tasks, and OBS qualifiers containing organizational information.

Information Capturing Agent

BIDSAVER proposed an architecture for resembling software agents that offered autonomy of operation without any assistance from the business integrator.

The agent devoted to capturing information from potential SMEs that belong to a specific market sector, is called ICA (information capturing agent). This agent permits the search in both the design phase of the VE (gathering initial partners to join) and the constitution phase (where the need for a new partner to fulfil a task arises).

The ICA is a software module, part of BIDSAVER that aims to locate on the Internet, potential partners to join a VE. It uses information provided by the business integrator, in the form of three structures: product breakdown, work breakdown, and organizational breakdown structures. The first defines the required products with their characteristics, the second describes the work that must be accomplished by the partners during VE operation, and the last describes the organizational structure inside a company. Based on that information, the agent queries the Internet to retrieve potential partners and passes the result to the business integrator.

At a first stage, the ICA is given the particular breakdown structures, which are then analyzed, and a list of pertinent keywords is extracted. Then the first phase of the search procedure is initiated directing ICA to act as a metasearch engine. It then goes through the replies and discards duplicated and URLs that are useless (it maintains a list of useless sites such as search engine sites). It inserts the rest into the database and initiates the second phase.

In the second phase, the ICA is directed to act as a Web crawler or "Webbot" that drills down all the URLs collected by the previous phase and tries to gather as much information as possible. It locates the keywords searched, their places on the Web pages, the distance from each other, and other useful things.

Finally, in the third phase, all the previous information is processed in the following way. An internal algorithm is used to permit the reconstruction of Web sites. A matching mechanism identifies which site is best suited for the kind of partner for which the system searches. The ranking of the sites that are considered as company profiles is the result of the whole process.

ICA General Architecture

The proposed architecture is an autonomous agent that operates on behalf of the business integrator using partner profiles as input. The agent architecture is implemented on top of the content management and publishing engine named XEOS. XEOS provides a framework to dynamically access repositories and publish information for the business integrator with minimal effort.

The search process is conducted in three separate steps. First, the analysis of the partner profile is performed to generate a valid query to submit to an existing search engine. Next, the search continues with the meta-search process, where the agent submits the generated query to a specific search engine chosen by the business integrator. Finally, the search is completed with the drilldown process, which compares partner profile data against HTML content and collects Web structure information for the recreation of potential partner sites (Figure 3).

Because the search process consists of the three major steps mentioned above, the agent is decomposed into the following three submodules:

- The *analysis module* is responsible for generating appropriate queries from partner profile patterns to be posted to existing search engines, and then retrieves an initial set of results.
- The *search module* utilizes queries generated by the previous module to contact available search engines. It is also capable of comprehending the initial set of results in order to seclude URLs and store them within a central repository. The business integrator can choose the search engine(s) that will be used.
- The *matching module* contacts every URL stored by the previous submodule in order to recreate partner sites and rank them accordingly.

The rest of this chapter will concentrate on the functions of each submodule. The diagram (Figure 3) illustrates the three major subsystems and the sequence in which they operate.

Business Information Integration Module

This module performs integrated management of functions needed for VE operation. This module integrates the parts of the VE information system. In technical terms, this module was developed based on existing products for project management and

Figure 3. ICA architecture based on XEOS

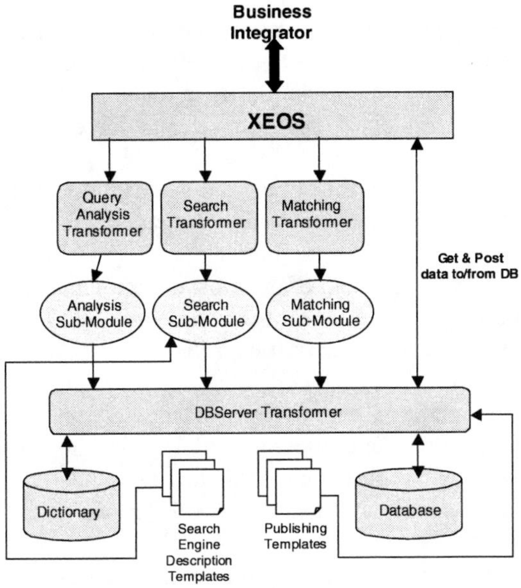

process integration, such as Microsoft? Project? scheduler and of UGS? i-MAN, product life cycle management (PLM), and by integrating those with a newly developed Web-based search engine.

THE PROTOTYPE

BIDSAVER delivers an ICT prototype for the VE information system, leveraging on e-commerce and Internet technology.

The prototype is based on preselected commercial solutions than can be configured according to VE requirements and has been improved by the use of specific software functions necessary for the success of the VE operation.

The chosen software tool was UGS iMAN, which demonstrated to be very useful in supporting the workflow management functions (the missing project management functions have been provided, integrating it with MS Project 2000). The iMAN solution was properly integrated with the ICA module.

BIDSAVER Pilot Projects

BIDSAVER methodology and tools were applied in the integration of two VEs: the first one in the microsatellite sector, and the second one in the mechanical and automobile sector.

The goal of both pilot showcases was to test the ICT infrastructure. This was achieved by adopting a pilot case test plan, the activities of which were derived from the business cases requirements.

The Microsatellite VE

One of the two pilot showcases involved in the BIDSAVER project is the Microsatellite Value Network. In the microsatellite VE in particular, the simulation of a space program Phase B1 scenario has been addressed, with the specific reference to a program for the development of a microsatellite, in the framework of an innovative VE model.

Test activities have been organised accordingly and have been structured in the following main areas:

- Evolution and management of the initial microsatellite VE BBS model
- Identification of the missing actors with respect to the satellite subsystems, performed by the use of the ICA module
- Implementation and management of the most common management processes in the aerospace industry—this included the specification of testing procedures to be adopted during the test case activities, as well as all the information required

In this way, the VE operation potential was adequately tested during the Phase B simulation, by tackling all steps and milestones of a typical design phase in the space context. The target was to guarantee the management of Phase B (quality assurance, configuration management, reviews) under the well-defined constraints and requirements of a space program.

Based on the considerations described above, the plan of the test case activities was derived and the criteria aiming at evaluating the VE performances were identified.

The Microsatellite Value Network pilot case is performed by:

- CE-Consulting—the business integrator
- Teleinformatica e Sistemi (TeS)—acting both as system integrator and partner
- Soditech (SDT)—the partner
- Telespazio (TPZ)—the customer

Tested Scenarios and Achieved Results

The specific Microsatellite Value Network addressed the definition and development of low-cost/low-mass satellites exploitable in a range of scientific and technical applications (telecommunications, earth resources, microgravity, and biology) simply because it satisfies the basic request for a cheap and timely access to space. In examining the current commercial applications and future and possible applications and trends, it appeared that the market will certainly grow with a sustained rate in the next years. Furthermore, the market segment based on microsatellite communications appears to have a large field of applications and consequently a big potential for growth.

The experiment was carried out and organized with the twofold objective of validating the BIDSAVER methodological approach as well as testing and validating the BIDSAVER ICT prototypal infrastructure, by simulating a specific timeframe of Phase B—also known as the design phase.

Furthermore, the following processes have been experimented:

- *Document preparation*: allowing the partners to create and manage a document that will be deployed to the customer in a later stage
- *Change management*: allowing the business integrator to manage upcoming nonconformances of the partners and to evaluate their potential impacts on cost, schedule, or performance

Figure 4. A screen of the microsatellite prototype

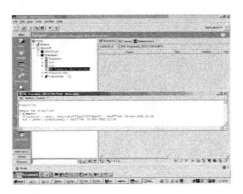

The operation of the Microsatellite Value Network consortium showed that the methodological approach was quite satisfactory, while the ICT prototype did not yet fully satisfy the expectations of the users. This was mainly due to the prototypal essence, which was more focused on functionality and less on software performance and efficiency.

Despite the prototype limitations, the overall achieved results have been considered satisfactory. (See the table of measured results in paragraph 8)

The Mechanical VEs

The second of the two pilot cases involved in the BIDSAVER project was the mechanical supply chain.

The mechanical supply chain pilot case was performed by the following companies (Figure 5):

- COMER—the leader
- INTERMEC and LIVARNA—the partners
- DEMOCENTER—the business integrator

Tested Scenarios and Achieved Results

The Comer Network was strongly interested in the following aspects:
- Support to the information exchange and automatic tracking of communication
- Support to exchange different formats of documents

The experiment has been carried out and organized with the main objective of testing, improving, tuning, and validating the BIDSAVER SW platform.

During the experiment, the mechanical VE members used the new SW platform for managing the cooperative and distributed activities related to the gearbox production (the product of the network chosen for conducting the test case).

The relevant processes defined and experimented with were as follows:

Figure 5. A screen of the mechanical VE prototype

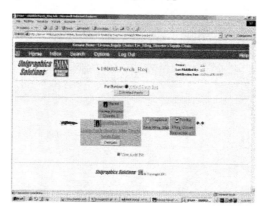

- Purchase requisition: Allows COMER to choose the right supplier for the needed products
- Order communication: Sends an order to the chosen partner
- Exception management: Manages possible problems met by a supplier while executing an order
- Nonconformity communication: Allows COMER to manage the lacks in the quality of the provided products
- General information exchange: Allows the suppliers to send general information and documents
- COMER exception: To manage possible changes requested by COMER in an order execution

Partners were very satisfied with the benefits coming from the data sharing. Thanks to iMAN, the database containing all the processes and information was shared with the other partners of the network, and the information was available to all the authorised people everywhere and at any time.

Furthermore, the introduction of iMAN significantly improved the quality of work of the internal departments of COMER (especially the design department). The new system increased the traceability of information, reducing drastically the waste of time and costs for sending drawings in paper format.

MAIN BIDSAVER RESULTS

The results that were obtained as direct project fallouts can be summarized as follows:
- The validation of the methodology for VEs constitution, setup, and management
- The legal framework, including all the contractual templates, reflecting the BIDSAVER dynamic business model scenario
- An ICT infrastructure prototype and concept demonstrator, based on the integration concept of the BBS, BIIM, and ICA modules, which will be the information system available to the business integrator for dynamical management of the VE

Table 1. Mean measured values of prototype operation

Quantitative Parameter	Final Value
Reduced project overall duration	Up to 20%
Reduced product cost	Up to 17%
Reduced project management effort	Up to 20%
Reduced VE negotiation time	Up to 33%

The Methodology

The methodological framework resulting from the project initiative is composed of the following elements:

- Frame contractual agreement models, suitable for addressing the legal aspects of the cooperation, such as IPR's management, liabilities, and so forth
- Business evaluation metrics
- Business breakdown structure models and crucial management procedures, suitable for organizing any business opportunity exploitable in a VE scenario or by leveraging external resources
- A set of cooperation processes, to formalize and facilitate the progress of the VE operation
- The VE life cycle, prescribing activities' sequence and extent to the business integrator

The Legal Framework

The legal framework covers VE operational issues by structuring the overall VE constitution and management methodology. VE models, and BBS in particular, were used to guide the development of the legal framework that regulates the relationship among partners of a VE, provides the tools to overcome any contractual obstacle, and covers all the issues during the whole VE life cycle. Thus, a general agreement (so-called "master agreement") is created, which can be used as a legal frame for the relationships regulation among the VE partners and for outlining the methodological frames to be used in forming and operating a VE.

The ICT Infrastructure Prototype

The BIDSAVER VEs' operations were supported by an ICT prototypal infrastructure, obtained by the customization of Microsoftâ Projectâ scheduler, UGSâ, i-MANâ product life cycle management (PLM), and the integration of those with a newly developed Web-based search engine.

The infrastructure effectively supports the cooperation among the technological partners and was proven to be adequate for the interoperability level required by the VE's operation typology.

Pilot cases operations highlighted requirements for further enhancement of the ICT infrastructure functionalities.

Broad Dissemination and Use of Intentions for Expected Outputs

In addition to the identification of the project results, potential user categories were also identified:

- More potential business integrators, willing to replicate the approach to different industrial cases, in cooperation to CE consulting
- Regional centres and industrial associations, willing to set up VE service centres— The centres aim to increase SMEs' awareness in the potential associated with the information society technologies, to provide training on the basic methodologies and tools for cooperation and to perform the initial screening for business opportunities' assessment
- SMEs, wanting to adopt the methodology to pursue their own business opportunities
- Large enterprises, interested in adopting the approach as an intermediate means for integrating their suppliers on some basic, cooperation process

The project has disseminated its results through a number of organizations— having declared their interest in acting both as VE catalyst and as service/methodological providers for those SMEs willing to enter the information society. Such organizations have been contacted to disseminate BIDSAVER results within the framework of their awareness and readiness improvement initiatives, for facilitating the adoption of information society technologies for SMEs.

These organizations would act first as a dissemination channel (their reach can easily exceed several thousands of companies, all over Europe), and then as a multiplier of the approach proposed by leveraging regional structural funds for ICT tools and methods implementation at local level.

Finally, according to the companies participating in the pilot cases, the mean saving calculated in different indexes can be shown in the following table:

CONCLUSIONS

BIDSAVER project's overall objective was to show how industrial users could boost their competitiveness in collaboration with Web-based VEs. Also to promote their readiness to enter virtual vertical enterprises and to increase their awareness of the potential associated with the use of tools and methodologies of the information society.

The integration concept of the BIDSAVER project is based on the idea of BBS, that is, the integration of product breakdown structure (bill of materials), work breakdown structure, and organizational breakdown structure.

Finally, in conclusion, the project has contributed to the construction of reference codes of practice, based on the identification of process and information exchange models applicable to the generalized operation of dynamic networked organizations. The codes of practice are addressing legal matters that are specific to the dynamic allocation of responsibilities to partners. It has also contributed with its methodology for VE formation and operation, having its source to the deep understanding of the problems and issues of VE.

By the time that was launched, the technologies for BPM were just emerging (e.g., Web services), and no standard existed in the development of robust mechanisms for business process information exchange. This project, among others, has demonstrated the extremely strong need for integration in the business process level, pushing further the standardization efforts in the BPM level.

BIDSAVER PARTNERS

The following partners participated in this project: CEConsulting—the project leader (*www.ceconsulting.it*), Democenter (*www.democenter.it*), Heletel (*www.heletel.gr*), ELSAG (*www.elsag.it*), Speed (*www.speed.it*), Mazzesci Novelli & Porcari (*www.mazzeschi.it*), Telespazio (*www.telespazio.it*), Teleinformatica e Sistemi (*www.space.it*), Soditech (*www.soditech.com*), Comer Group (*www.comergroup.com*), and Intermec, Livarna Vuzenica (*www.livarna-vuzenica.si*).

REFERENCES

BIDSAVER Project HTML. Available online *http://www.vive-ig.net/projects/bidsaver/*
COVE Project, VE Projects COVE, ICSS, and MASSYVE Project. Available online *http://cic.vtt.fi/projects/voster/projects.html*
DRIVE Project. Available online *http://www.e-mathesis.it/Drive/default.asp*
Hongfei T., (2003) *Grid Computing as an Integrating Force in Virtual Enterprises.* Partial fulfilment of the requirements for the Degree of Master of Engineering in Civil and Environmental Engineering. M.S., Software Technology (2002). Stuttgart University of Applied Sciences.
VIVE. Available online *http://www.vive-ig.net*
VIVE Project. Available online *http://www.cordis.lu/esprit/src/26854c1.htm*
VIVE Project HTML. Available online *http://www.vive-ig.net/projects/*

ENDNOTES

[1]   The phasing approach to space program management was compliant with the standard ECSS-M30A.

Chapter XXI

Implementation Options for Virtual Organizations:
A Peer to Peer (P2P) Approach

Bob Roberts
Kingston University, UK

Adomas Svirskas
Kingston University, UK

Jonathan Ward
Kingston University, UK

ABSTRACT

This chapter explores the challenges of constructing a distributed e-business architecture based on the concept of request-based virtual organization (RBVO). The RBVO is a value network, dynamically formed upon demand to meet identified business opportunities. The work within the framework of the European Union-sponsored LAURA project is presented, as its aim is to facilitate interregional zones of adaptive electronic commerce using, where applicable, the potential of the ebXML architecture. The LAURA realization framework outlined here addressed the structural concepts of an RBVO, based on the typical business requirements of small and medium-sized enterprises (SMEs). The architecture proposed in our work incorporates an innovative approach to discovery and matchmaking of business partners and services that includes usage of peer-to-peer (P2P) technology. The increasing maturity of P2P-based solutions allow, where applicable, for their implementation in the business-to-business (B2B) area. The P2P concept is discussed in comparison to a more traditional client–server approach in this chapter.

INTRODUCTION

IT architectures may determine how organisational structures can evolve in response to flexible and adaptable technologies. However, implementing a virtual organization (VO) model is not a straightforward task in practice for a number of reasons. Innovative organisational models, business scenarios, and underlying technical complexity demand that architects of such systems need to make trade-offs to ensure both the business and technical viability of the solutions. This chapter investigates the use of certain architectures and technologies to implement a highly dynamic type of VO. We first define the concept of request-based virtual organization (RBVO) and its differentiators, which influence architectural requirements of the solution together with the end-user and business requirements. Architectural alternatives are then discussed with a comparison of implementation options for different aspects of partner collaboration.

Three areas of particular importance were singled out for end-to-end business collaboration; discovery and matchmaking of the business partners, secure and reliable business data transmission, and business process specification and enactment. The discovery and matchmaking aspect of the overall B2B problem becomes especially important in the SME e-business context, mainly due to the potential for a great number of collaborative participants, the diversity of their capabilities, and the lack of standardization for product and service description, as well as the absence of mechanisms to harmonize the latter. Traditionally, these problems have been addressed using a B2B marketplace approach (Butler Group, 2000), where an intermediate entity dictates particular marketplace policies, provides infrastructure, and ensures the virtual presence of the participants in the community. The static nature of these virtual formations does not fully address the continuously growing demand to locate products, services, and business partners, regardless of their physical location and affiliation to an intermediary entity. As a result, the whole set of potential business partners is fragmented into "islands," and the potential added value of virtual enterprises is not maximized.

In order to fully reveal the potential of RBVOs as highly dynamic virtual business formations, an innovative approach is taken that is based on natural trading behavior patterns, expressing direct interaction between partners. Recent developments in the peer-to-peer (P2P) computing field allow this pattern to be implemented. This approach results in a more flexible topology for virtual formations and bridges the gap between the isolated islands, thus forming a B2B grid that widens the possibilities for collaboration and increases their availability to business partners. The chapter concludes with a discussion of a practical P2P approach to implementation.

The content of this chapter is partly shaped and influenced by a project sponsored by The European Commission Information Society Technologies (IST) Programme that is part of the Fifth Framework Programme for Research, Technological Development and Demonstration Activities. This project, known as LAURA (2003), aims to create an e-business infrastructure targeted at the business requirements of SMEs in four European countries (Bulgaria, Germany, Greece, and the United Kingdom). It introduces an innovative approach, "any actor to any actor" Internet-based seamless electronic commerce platform in which all request-based business entities can act as a one-channel virtual enterprise.

REQUEST-BASED VIRTUAL ORGANISATIONS IN A BUSINESS CONTEXT

A specific type of VO is the RBVO that is comprised of a cluster of partnering organisations that have replaced their vertical integration into a virtual one through collaborative networks between discrete business partners (Svirskas & Roberts, 2003). Only some of the operations are within a particular organization — operations are now spread between separate organisations, which are linked to the original organization, to produce a new VO.

These characteristics of RBVO mentioned above largely contribute to the agility dimension of a VO. The term "RBVO" may be considered broadly analogous with the concept of the agile enterprise or, to be more precise, the virtual agile enterprise. Meade and Rogers (1997) defined an agile enterprise as an enterprise with processes that are designed specifically to respond effectively to unanticipated change. Preiss (1995) summarized four dimensions of an agile enterprise concerned with cooperating to enhance competitiveness, enhancing customer service, managing change and uncertainty, and leveraging the impact of people and information.

The LAURA project, therefore, innovates in terms of focusing on RBVOs as a specific type of the VO taxonomy and exploits the RBVO concept to facilitate cooperation among SMEs in particular and to enhance the competitiveness dimension of enterprise agility.

DERIVING ARCHITECTURAL REQUIREMENTS

Business and User Requirements

A typical e-business environment consists of two main parts: a business service infrastructure and an e-business software system, which supports this infrastructure. In this section, we will outline the business requirements for such a solution, and following this, we examine the architectural and technical challenges arising as a result of the business requirements.

An RBVO-based e-business solution should address the most common business needs of the participants. Most of the businesses would like to increase their sales and customer base and reach for the new markets as a result of e-business practice adoption. An increase of the supplier base is considered a little less important but still a strong driver. Therefore, the primary business goals of an RBVO-based e-business network are associated with providing the means:

- For potential business partners to advertise their own products and services
- For buyers to advertise purchasing needs so that potential sellers can find them: "Who would supply us with 20 tons of sugar by next Monday?"
- For buyers to search for both the products offered on sale and for the parties interested in collaboration: "Who sells PC main boards, processors and coolers for a bargain price?"

- For sellers to advertise their offerings:
  - Who wants to buy PC main boards bundled with the CPUs, pre-tested and in volumes?"
- To reach across the boundary of the "home domain" when looking for a business partner
- To conduct trusted, secure, and traceable business collaboration sessions with the chosen partners
- For smaller SMEs, to be in touch with a local structure, which could encourage and help to use the potential of e-business

The end-user requirements also cover certain nonbusiness functions, such as user registration, account management, and related activities.

Business Infrastructure Concepts

The LAURA model builds on the life cycle and structural concepts of RBVO and introduces a business context dimension, aligned with the business needs and other requirements of SMEs.

The following concepts distinguish the LAURA conceptual model:

- A LAURA e-commerce (EC) shell (domain) is a set of SMEs belonging to a certain geographical region and registered with the LAURA network via a LAURA support centre. The notion of a domain and the presence of multiple domains in the LAURA network indicate the distributed nature of the architecture.
- A LAURA EC kernel is the focal point of an EC shell. The main component of the kernel is the support centre, which is responsible for provisioning of both commercial and IT (outsourced to the IT provider, if needed) services to the SMEs. The role and added value of EC kernels is to promote and facilitate e-business services among the local SMEs, mainly through the support centres. The support centre hosts the necessary software, which allows SMEs to register with the support centre, manage product catalogues, and conduct their business. The software is accessible by SMEs using a browser interface and, when interregional services are necessary, it also supports communication with other EC kernels on behalf of its EC shell members. In a technical context, the EC kernel, the support centre, or the software behind it is also referred to as a LAURA domain hub.
- The LAURA network is an interdomain collaboration infrastructure that defines a set of rules and provides arrangements for interregional (interdomain) business collaboration between the SMEs. The LAURA effort aims to further enhance the RBVO benefits to SMEs through proactive regional support services. The LAURA support centres aim to shield the SMEs from the technical complexities of e-business interactions, increase trust of the network by screening the SMEs joining it, and facilitate formation of RBVOs by providing SMEs with assistance to identify potential business partners. In this way, the support centres address some of the trust, knowledge, and IT issues that might inhibit the formation of RBVOs.
- The LAURA business collaboration service is the software service in charge of communication between the EC kernels and other participants in the LAURA network.

Figure 1. LAURA conceptual framework (Source: adapted from Svirskas et al., 2003)

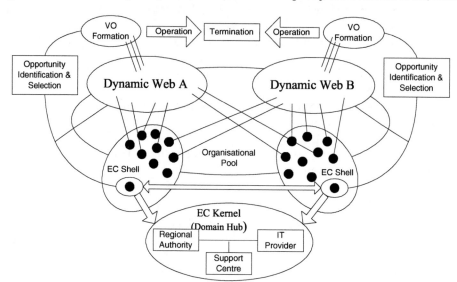

In addition to EC kernels and affiliated hosted SMEs, other Laura network members might be self-connected SMEs, i.e., SMEs capable of installing and running the LAURA business collaboration service connected to their own information infrastructure, such as a back-end ERP system.

The LAURA conceptual model (Figure 1) captures a typical SME involvement scenario, where most SMEs do not have dedicated IT specialists and skills and, therefore, connect to the network via intermediary hubs.

ARCHITECTURAL REQUIREMENTS

As indicated by the business and user requirements, end-to-end collaboration between the business partners is the ultimate goal of the solution. This section explains the implications of end-to-end business collaboration to the architecture of the solution and outlines the main ideas of use case realization. The main tasks, therefore, are to gather and systemize the architectural requirements and to outline realization possibilities of the former.

The gathering of architecture requirements for a particular solution is never an easy task. Eeles (2001) attributed this difficulty to the following aspects of software engineering:

- Greater visibility of domain-specific requirements as opposed to their architectural counterparts: This is true for most systems, from an end-user perspective.

- Less familiarity by the stakeholders with the concept of architectural requirements:

For example, concepts such as "order processing" and "catalogue management" are more familiar for the business audience than "platform support" and "transactional integrity."

- The less mature techniques for systematically gathering architectural requirements compared to those for gathering domain-specific requirements

Eeles (2001) also advocated a systematic approach to the gathering of requirements, referring to the FURPS+ system for classifying requirements, introduced by Grady (1992). While requirements of different categories of FURPS+ taxonomy are architecturally significant, we will concentrate on the functional aspects of the requirements and the "+" of FURPS+. These so-called additional categories represent various constraints, namely, design, implementation, interface, and physical requirements. This approach allows us to concentrate on the specifics of RBVO on one hand and the nature of the proposed business environment on the other hand. The remaining categories group together various nonfunctional architectural requirements, commonly referred to as "ilities," which are further referred to in the comparison of client–server and P2P approaches to implementation. Filman (1998), who discussed achieving "ilities" in his works, also introduces an alternative approach based on four categories of architectural require-ments (functional, aesthetic, systematic, and combinatoric), which broadly matches FURPS+.

Due to the multidomain nature of the LAURA business network community, end-to-end business collaboration between the SMEs is a multistep activity, involving the SMEs and their corresponding support centres, which broker the collaboration. The main issues important for realization of end-to-end business collaboration in this fragmented environment include but are not limited to:

- Discovery of the remaining domains by the support centre (kernel, hub) of a LAURA domain (shell). This activity is responsible for maintenance of a "neighbor domain directory" for a hub. Each entry in this list describes attributes of the hub servicing the domain. There might be several entries per domain if the domain is federated (multikernel). It is necessary to keep the list as accurate as possible by regularly checking availability of the domains (their hubs) and possibly maintain-ing a "ping-time" parameter for a domain to estimate its "proximity."
- Selection of a set of domains for the forwarding of a search request. The service should intelligently choose the domains on behalf of the user, where the search should be performed. The choice should be made based on:
  - Explicit user business preferences (e.g., a wish to do business in a specific geographical region, a specific product or type of service)
  - Explicit user service preferences (e.g., number of business options to choose from, speed, etc.)
  - Indirect user business preferences (e.g., a wish for certain goods of good quality and with fast delivery)
  - Accumulated metadata of business domains, available at the time of choice (e.g., business sector involvement, number of consumers and suppliers per sector, etc.)

- Accumulated historical data about business transactions conducted in the past (business sectors, percentage of completed transactions, amounts, customer retention rate, etc.)
- Explicit business practice related feedback provided by the business partners about mutual business experience (e.g., quality of service, ease of communication, trustworthiness, etc.)
- Efficient propagation of the search requests and delivery of the results to the requestor (e.g., synchronous vs. asynchronous responses)
- Brokerage of business conversations on behalf of the business partners. The interdomain infrastructure should support secure and reliable business collaboration according to the business scenario rules. This is a much more challenging task than support of "local" business collaboration when the business partners virtually "reside" in the same domain. The most important issues here are:
  - Secure and reliable messaging over the Internet
  - Business documents specification, applicable standards
  - Business process decomposition, identification of reusable collaboration scenarios
  - Machine-readable business process definition and their runtime interpretation
  - Atomicity of business transactions
- Security and identity management, which is even more complex in a fragmented multidomain environment: This aspect needs to be addressed properly at the architectural and infrastructure level to ensure that this kind of business network is attractive for security-concerned users.

REALIZATION FRAMEWORK

In the LAURA project, SMEs are provided with services by the support centres (SCs) that, in turn, interact with each other through a P2P network. The proposed framework for the LAURA project is shown in Figure 2. Each SC, labelled as an "l-kernel," provides a point of access for local SMEs. The diagram also shows how it is possible for an SME to be directly integrated into the network, allowing for greater control and flexibility.

The proposed realization scheme captures commonalties of SME B2B e-business; therefore, the conceptual and architectural decisions can be applied to the mentioned class of solutions. This chapter does not discuss in detail all the architectural solutions due to the lack of space; however, the principal decisions and their relationship and contribution to the integration aspects of the RBVO concept discussed earlier are as follows:

- *User interaction*: World WideWeb (WWW) interface and hypertext transfer protocol (HTTP) is used for SME end-user access to the LAURA network, thereby providing a simple and familiar means of interaction with the system. This also allows much of the complexity of the system to be hidden from the user.

Figure 2. The LAURA realization framework

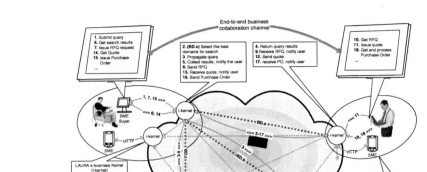

- *Basic functionality*: Open source e-business component framework from *The Open for Business Project* (OFBiz, 2003) is used for the basic functionality, such as catalogue management, user registration, business transaction monitoring, reporting, etc. Roberts et al. (2003) elaborate on OFBiz usage for the LAURA project. The catalogue system is an important element of the discovery stage during the formation of an RBVO. It will need to offer fast and flexible search and catalogue management options, thereby facilitating one of the RBVO goals, i.e., for potential business partners to advertise their own products and services. Each SME will need to advertise not only products, but also services and options for collaboration.

- *Discovery of domains*: Discovery of the remote domains by a domain hub is encapsulated into a generic interface, which allows different discovery techniques. One of these techniques is based on emerging P2P technology and a Java implementation, JXTA (Project JXTA, 2003). Domain hubs use JXTA to exchange their metadata and build lists of remote domains for subsequent product search. In order to support the concept of short-lived ad hoc virtual formations, the system must provide a means for discovery of potential business partners. Providing a selection of different search mechanisms will increase the likelihood of finding a suitable business partner. The interaction between domains extends the reach beyond the boundary of the "home domain" when looking for a business partner.

- *Discovery of products and services*: Domain hubs perform searches of products and partners on behalf of SMEs by propagating the queries to the selected remote domains. The transport chosen for this task and subsequent business conversations is ebXML Messaging (The ebXML Framework, 2003). The ebXML Messaging provides the required secure messaging facilities necessary for conducting

B2B e-commerce. Search queries are selectively forwarded to relevant domain hubs and are performed against the product catalogues as previously discussed.

- *Business collaborations*: Business processes specify the choreography of business transactions in collaborations between the partners, and these are modelled and specified using ebXML BPSS (The ebXML Framework, 2003). Business documents are modelled according to the Open Applications Group Integration Specification (OAGIS; Rowell, 2002; Flebowitz, 2003). Using the ebXML framework, businesses can define and advertise the roles in which they wish to participate, thereby providing the basis for dynamic creation of RBVOs.

SOLUTION ARCHITECTURE

There are many important aspects to consider when constructing a solution architecture, however, we will touch on those most relevant to the nature of the RBVO concept, namely, services available to the participants of such an enterprise and their invocation principles.

One of the possible ways to model an RBVO is to consider it as composed of a collection of interacting *services*; this approach fits the "request on demand" concept, which is pivotal to the RBVO. Brown (2003) argued that exposing functionality as services is the key to flexibility. Each service, therefore, provides access to a well-defined collection of functionality, and the system as a whole is designed and implemented as a set of interactions among these services. This allows other pieces of functionality (perhaps themselves implemented as services) to make use of other services in a natural way, regardless of their physical location. A system evolves through the addition of new services. The resulting service-oriented architecture (Gartner, 2003) defines the services of which the system is composed, describes the interactions that occur among the services to realize certain behavior, and maps the services into one or more implementations in specific technologies (Brown, 2003). This service-oriented architecture (SOA) approach is the latest in a long series of attempts in software engineering that try to foster the reuse of software components (Leymann et al., 2002).

According to Ferguson et al. (2003), SOA differs from object-oriented (OO) and procedural systems in one key aspect, that of binding. Services interact based on what functions they provide and how they deliver them. OO and procedural systems link elements together based on type or name. While component-based development fits between the two mentioned alternatives and gravitates toward the SOA side, the ultimate mission of the components becomes implementation of the services. Components, therefore, can adhere to different standards and depend on different platforms, operating systems, and implementation models. Components are also finer-grained than services and conceptually closer to the implementation domain, as opposed to the services, which tend to abstract application domain and business notions. SOA also assumes that things can and will go wrong in a distributed heterogeneous environment—lost messages, crashing services, malicious invocation attempts, etc., and therefore, assumptions about presence of different errors is made explicit. Leymann et al. (2002) argued that there are also certain differences between the SOA and a "service-based architecture," such as RosettaNet or OBI (Open Buying on the Internet). The latter two examples focus solely on the formats and protocols between services. As such, it represents just one of the pieces of the SOA, lacking the other vital characteristics, such as discovery and binding. The issues of publishing, discovery, and binding are very important for any service-oriented community, and an RBVO community, in particular. The next section discusses a modern P2P approach for service discovery in RBVO communities.

Peer-to-Peer for B2B

Peer-to-peer (P2P) is an emerging technology solution that has been used in a large number of different contexts, a few examples of which are distributed computation, distributed search engines, file sharing, and online collaboration. Such a wide range of very different applications leads to some confusion over what actually constitutes a P2P system. While a P2P system must connect nodes directly for the exchange of information, P2P does not define the protocols used to connect to other nodes, discover resources, and participate in the network. In many cases, P2P systems are a hybrid of P2P and client–server technologies. For example, supernodes and hubs act as servers and answer clients' search requests.

Both client–server and P2P network topologies would be appropriate for the LAURA project, however, they bring different advantages and compromises. The client–server approach to solving this problem is to create a centralized database containing details about products and services offered by each of the SMEs. This server, using specific protocols, then answers all search queries. This client–server architecture has been successfully applied to a large number of similar problems, exemplified by companies such as eBay and Covisint. Bond (2001, p. 4) summarized the client–server situation well with the following comment, "[the use of a central server] attempts to exploit network effects by drawing large numbers of people and large amounts of activity to a single system. But this suffers from decreasing returns as the very success that drives it also results in scalability and reliability problems that reduce the return for each participant." This problem is typical of a client–server topology; however, there are also a number of advantages associated with it. A server can be upgraded to accommodate a greater number of users, which is a tried and tested process. The centralized server also allows for close monitoring and control over the system, from both performance and security perspectives.

Alternatively, the problem could be solved using a distributed P2P network. This approach can be useful in avoiding scalability problems associated with a centralized architecture. Peer-to-peer systems form the fundamental basis of the Internet; IP routing, e-mail, DNS, and NNTP are all well-known examples. Although P2P systems differ considerably in their underlying architecture and design, Hahn et al. (2003) emphasized how participating nodes act as both client and server and thus provide access to shared computing and information resources. They characterize such systems by the absence of central coordination or database, peers are autonomous but have no global view of the system, and peers, and therefore content, are sometimes unavailable. Bond (2001) observed that a P2P network resembles a small business community (virtual organization) and argues that this web of shifting and temporary interconnections is what decentralized P2P systems are good at. In reality, interactions between businesses are essentially P2P in nature, as there is no coordinating central authority; businesses communicate via phone, e-mail, etc., and perform as peers in a P2P network. The proposed topology for the LAURA project is actually hybrid P2P, combining elements of P2P with client–server

Figure 3. The LAURA P2P network topology and a multicountry RBVO

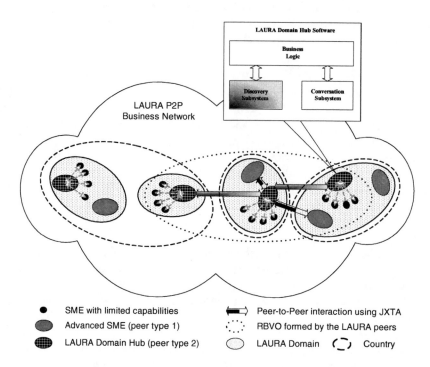

interactions. The conceptual framework is based on the idea of regional service centres (SC) that provide services for SMEs and facilitate interregional transactions. SMEs connect to SCs, which in turn, interact with each other via a P2P network.

Sawhney and Parikh (2001) argued, "that entire industries will soon be organised around the supporting infrastructure of communication networks" (as cited in Benyon-Davis, 2004). The aim of the LAURA project is to provide such a network, based on the business requirements of SMEs and the RBVO concept. The scalability and dynamic relationships found in P2P networks are well suited to the implementation of a RBVO-based business framework. Figure 3 depicts the LAURA network as a P2P formation, where RBVOs are formed as a result of P2P-based discovery process and then more precise partner selection based on the results of product or service search.

COMPARISON OF CLIENT–SERVER AND P2P FOR THE LAURA PROJECT

In order for an application to fulfil its purpose well, it must satisfy both functional and nonfunctional requirements. Functional requirements ensure that the application performs a particular task, whereas nonfunctional requirements ensure the fitness of the application for its purpose. Examples of these nonfunctional requirements include extensibility, maintainability, and reliability, collectively known as "ilities." Manola (1999) argued that such "ilities" have systemic properties, rather than properties of individual system components, and that provision for "ilities" should be an integral part of the design and implementation process. Table 1 assesses the benefits to the LAURA Project achieved through the use of a P2P network topology, particularly with respect to these "ilities."

Table 1. Assessment of client–server vs. P2P for the LAURA project

	Client–Server	P2P
Accountability This ensures that an individual's actions can be uniquely traced and identified.	Due to the central control of the server, accountability is more easily achieved by using client log-in protocols, thereby allowing transactions to be uniquely traced.	In a pure P2P system, accountability is difficult due to the inherent lack of trust between peers. Hybrid P2P topologies can be employed to counter this problem.
Affordability This is the cost of the system, not only in development and installation, but also for maintenance, etc.	This is difficult to estimate, as costs will depend on the particular system. However, servers are always expensive in terms of hardware and resources (e.g., bandwidth).	Hardware costs are shared between participants. P2P can be used to provide reliable services by duplication, while simultaneously reducing costs.
Extensibility This is the ability to modify and augment the product to provide additional functionality.	Modifications to the server software are easily performed; however, changes to client software involve downloading updates, usually from expensive high-bandwidth servers.	The nature of the P2P network can be leveraged to allow distribution of software updates directly between peers, removing the requirement for high-bandwidth servers.
Maintainability This is the ease with which the system can be kept in good working order.	This is closely related to extensibility in terms of software updates, and the same points apply. Hardware is another issue; a central server is more easily repaired.	With P2P, the geographic distribution of peers may hinder maintenance. One advantage is that the cost of the hardware is distributed among participants.
Reliability This is the capability of the system to maintain a desired level of performance under stated conditions, or a stated time period.	This topology can be very reliable if techniques such as data duplication and redundant servers are used. If a server becomes overloaded, then performance quickly degrades.	P2P provides redundancy as services and data can be duplicated over many peers. If one support centre fails, then the problem will only affect a limited number of users.
Scalability This is the ability of the system to continue operation with a desired level of performance when the size of the problem increases.	Scalability is limited by the capacity of the server; however, upgrading a server is a tried and tested process. The server must be augmented as the number of support centres increases.	A well-designed P2P network offers a higher level of scalability. As the number of support centres increases, each brings with it their own resources and thus contributes to the network.
Security This is the extent to which the system can be protected from unwanted intrusion and malicious activities.	Security issues are more easily dealt with as the server acts as a central point of control. Attempted attacks are more easily monitored and repelled as they are confined to a single location.	Each peer in the network is responsible for its own security. This makes individual peers more vulnerable to subversion. Security in P2P is a more complex issue.
Survivability This property of the system is the ability to continue operation under adverse conditions, such as malicious hacker attacks.	The server presents a target for malicious users, meaning that an attack is likely to affect a larger number of users; however, it is possible to closely monitor intrusions.	As there are many peers present, an attack against one of them is not likely to cause widespread damage, however, attacks are not so easily detected and monitored.

A few of the points mentioned in Table 1 require further explanation. The hybrid topology described under "accountability" involves using a central server to store user details. Turcan (2002) maintains that a hybrid P2P model could be a first step toward a fully distributed accountability mechanism in the future. In the LAURA project, the support centres act as semicentralized accountability servers by storing details of all transactions.

The technique for distributing software updates between peers, described under "extensibility," has been successfully applied to the distribution of antivirus definitions by McAfee's MyCIO. By using P2P distribution, the load on central servers is reduced, allowing for faster updates, which is an important advantage in the world of antivirus technology. Security is an essential concern, as care must be taken to ensure that this mechanism is not used to efficiently propagate detrimental code.

The scalability of a P2P network depends to a great extent on the protocol used. The Gnutella network experienced scalability problems due to the manner in which search queries were broadcast across the network, thereby consuming bandwidth (Ritter, 2001). Another concern is that as the network size increases, there are more peers (i.e., support centres in this case) to be searched. P2P systems are highly dynamic, with connections between nodes being opened and closed continuously. This means that the same search request performed at different times will be answered by a different set of nodes, and consequently, the results returned will be different. This can be a problem when a consistent view of the data is required. In a business context, it follows that a buyer will not see details of all prospective sellers but only a subset of them. However, it can be argued that this is analogous to the real-world situation in which a buyer cannot possibly seek advice from every potential seller. The LAURA project tackles this issue through the use of plugable search strategies. Initially, there will be a simple search function allowing a quick "best-fit" response. However, this will also be augmented with other search strategies (e.g., slow, but precise), allowing the user to select the best option for their requirements.

Due to the dynamic way in which peers discover and connect to each other, P2P networks are prone to fragmentation. This means that there could be two networks of P2P users operating on the same protocols that have no connections between them. This would obviously be a problem in the case of the LAURA project, as it would isolate different business regions from each other. It should be also noted that the network topology has no relationship to geographic location, meaning that two support centres in the same country could be unaware of each other. Malicious users targeting peers with high connectivity can increase the fragmentation of the network, thereby reducing its performance. Once again, the susceptibility of the network to fragmentation will depend on the specific protocols used.

PROJECT JXTA

It can be seen from the previous comparison of client–server and P2P topologies that the advantages of using P2P will depend heavily on the protocols used. In the context of this project, Project JXTA (JXTA, 2003) provides a framework that would allow developers to concentrate on providing high-level, business-oriented functionality, rather than implementing the underlying infrastructure. Project JXTA also has an advantage of being open-source and supported by an active community.

Project JXTA provides a simple and generic framework for P2P networking. It provides a base P2P infrastructure over which other P2P applications can be built. The JXTA protocols document describes six XML-based protocols that standardize the methods used by peers to discover each other and interact to form peer groups. JXTA technology has been designed to be independent of programming language, system platform, and networking platform and is accessible to a wide range of devices. Project JXTA uses a virtual network overlay on top of Internet and non-IP networks, allowing traversal of firewalls and NATs using a range of transport methods.

JXTA uses a number of protocols to ensure that a peer can join the network and discover other peers. For any P2P network, the first issue is that the new peer must know how to contact at least one other peer. All resources (e.g., peer, peer-group, pipe, service) within a JXTA network are represented by advertisements containing information about a resource formatted as an XML document following a defined standard. A peer-group is an aggregation of peers with common interests. JXTA does not specify how peer-groups should be created, leaving this to the application developer. Certain well-known peers within the JXTA network maintain large caches of advertisement indices in order to support the peer-group; these are known as rendezvous peers.

The JXTA technology is particularly applicable from the RBVO point of view and especially with regard to the multidomain nature of our proposed solution. The JXTA virtual network allows flexible mapping between the physical resources and the logical entities required for a multidomain e-business network such as LAURA, while the slogan "JXTA Technology: Creating Connected Communities" (JXTA, 2004) captures the essence of the match to the RBVO concept.

CONCLUSIONS

Clusters of SMEs operating as a RBVO can be enabled by a pragmatic choice of architectures and frameworks to support SME B2B transactions. However, there are practical considerations that need to be made in terms of the relationship between the conceptual models of virtual organisations and their implementations. A distributed e-business architecture solution suitable for SMEs has been designed in the framework of the LAURA project. The project aims to bring together the best practices and standards of e-business with local business knowledge and feedback from the field in order to create an efficient and trusted e-business environment for SMEs. The chapter also positions the architectural options of SME-oriented e-business solutions in the context of the choices made by the LAURA project team. The LAURA architecture has been designed to provide the technological foundation underlying the concept of RBVOs. Ease of discovery and dynamic formation of business relationships are key features of the RBVO, and these are supported by the implementation decisions, namely, the selection of an open-source e-business framework as the functional foundation and the ebXML framework as the collaboration vehicle, where appropriate.

These issues have been considered here at a reasonably high level, and the consideration of the problems in more detail requires further discussion which is outside the scope of this chapter. A few examples of areas requiring further architectural and design decisions include:

- A way in which services and peer capabilities are unambiguously described by the system: The description of services is a central issue to the discovery process.
- The domain selection algorithms that specify the scope and the target domains where the search for the partners and products is made: This is a complex issue, touching on many areas of the solution. For example, it may be beneficial to use historical data from previous transactions to route search requests for similar items.
- A subservice for gathering and structuring historical data about business transactions in order to support the selection of the domains—data model, policies, etc.
- A query protocol is needed to search for products and partners in multiple domains and to provide the combined results to the users in both synchronous and asynchronous ways.
- An algorithm for peer communication in order to keep the information about the other peers accurate and up to date: This is necessary to ensure efficient communication between the peers.

Discovery of the remote domains by a domain hub is encapsulated in a generic interface, which allows different discovery techniques, based on emerging P2P technology and its Java implementation. An implementation based on a P2P approach provides a means of aligning the structure of the IT architecture to the flexible and loosely federated structure of an RBVO. Implementation of P2P topology is more complex than a client–server approach, and it needs to be considered whether P2P offers a significant advantage to warrant this additional complexity. However, many of the disadvantages of P2P outlined above can be overcome if well-designed protocols are properly implemented. Furthermore, the nature of the P2P network allows for special strategies that are not possible using a client–server topology. One such strategy is the routing of search queries based on their content, for example, by sending queries to nodes that have previously responded to similar queries. In consideration of long-term sustainability, P2P potentially offers a more scalable and flexible topology. A P2P network protocol can also be designed to be more resilient to attack and hardware failure. This is a very important factor, as it directly influences the reliability of the solution. To conclude, P2P offers certain advantages, although they come at a price. Whether this price is worth paying will greatly depend on the protocols used and the specifics of the implementation.

REFERENCES

Benyon-Davis, P. (2004). *E-business*. New York: Palgrave Macmillan.

Bond, J. (2001). *Business uses of peer-to-peer (P2P) technologies*. A Netmarkets Europe White Paper. Retrieved December 2003 online *http://www.netmarketseurope.com/insider/papers/PB2B.pdf*

Brown, A., Johnston, S., & Kelly, K. (2003, April). *Using service-oriented architecture and component-based development to build Web Service applications*. A Rational Software Whitepaper from IBM. Retrieved March 2004 online *http://*

www3.software.ibm.com/ibmdl/pub/software/rational/web/ whitepapers/2003/ TP032.pdf

Butler Group. (2000). *E-supply chain: Modelling the supply chain in the new market economies, Volume 1: Concept report.* UK: Butler Direct Limited.

Eeles, P. (2001, November). Capturing architectural requirements. *The Rational Edge.* Retrieved March 2004 online *http://www-106.ibm.com/developerworks/rational/library/content/RationalEdge/nov01/CapturingArchitectural RequirementsNov01.pdf*

Ferguson, D. F., Storey, T., Lovering, B., & Shewchuk, J. (2003). Secure, reliable, transacted Web Services. Retrieved November 2003 online *http://www-106.ibm.com/developerworks/webservices/library/ws-securtrans/*

Filman, R. E. (1998, January). Achieving ilities. Workshop on Compositional Software Architectures, Monterey, California. Retrieved November 2003 online *http:// www.objs.com/workshops/ws9801/papers/paper046.doc*

Flebowitz, M. (2002). OAGIS 8.0: Practical Integration meets XML Schema. *XML Journal, 3*(9). Retrieved November 2003 online *http://www.openapplications.org/news/articles/XMLJ-Sept02-OAGIS8PracticalIntegrationMeetsXMLSchema.pdf*

Gartner. (2003). The Gartner Glossary of Information Technology Acronyms and Terms. Retrieved November 2003 online *http://www4.gartner.com/6_help/glossary/Gartner_IT_Glossary.pdf*

Grady, R. (1992). *Practical software metrics for project management and process improvement.* Englewood Cliffs, NJ: Prentice Hall.

Hahn, A., Benger, A., & Kern, E. (2003). Peer to peer networking for concurrent engineering. In Jardim-Goncalves et al. (Eds.), *CE: Vision for the future generation in research and applications* (pp. 1105–1111). Swets & Zeitlinger: The Netherlands.

JXTA. (2003). Project JXTA. Retrieved November 2003 online *http://www.jxta.org/*

JXTA2. (2004). JXTA technology: Creating connected communities. Retrieved February 2004 online *http://www.jxta.org/project/www/docs/JXTA-Exec-Brief.pdf*

LAURA Project. (2003). Retrieved December 2003 online *http://www.lauraproject.net*

Leymann, F., Roller, D., & Schmidt, M. T. (2002). Web services and business process management. *IBM Systems Journal, 41*(2), 199.

Manola, F. (1999). Providing Systemic Properties (Ilities) and Quality of Service in Component-Based Systems—Draft. Retrieved November 2003 online *http:// www.objs.com/aits/9901-iquos.html*

Meade, L. M., & Rogers, K. J. (1997). A method for analyzing agility alternatives for business processes. In G.L. Curry, B. Bidanda & S. Jagdale (Eds.), *Proceedings of the Sixth Industrial Engineering Research Conference* (pp. 960–965), Miami Beach, FL. Institute of Industrial Engineers, Norcross, GA.

MyCIO. (2003). Retrieved November 2003 online *http://www.mycio.com*

OFBiz. (2003). The Open For Business Project. Retrieved November 2003 online *http://www.ofbiz.org*

Preiss, K. (1995). *Models of the agile competitive environment.* Bethlehem, PA: Agility Forum.

Project JXTA. (2003). Retrieved November 2003 online *http://www.jxta.org*

Ritter, J. (2001). Why Gnutella can't scale. No, really. Retrieved November 2003 online *http://www.darkridge.com/~jpr5/doc/gnutella.html*

Roberts, B., Svirskas, A., Yancheva, S., Ignatiadis, I. (2003). *Service Oriented Architecture, Open Source Software and ebXML as the Foundation for the Virtual Organisations of SME's*. Presented at the CollECTeR (LatAm) Conference. Santiago, Chile.

Rowell, M. (2002). OAGIS: A canonical business language. *XML Journal, 3*(9).

Sawhney, M., & Parikh, D. (2001). Where value lies in a networked world. *Harvard Business Review, 79*(1), 79–86.

Svirskas, A., & Roberts, B. (2003). *Towards business quality of service in virtual organisations through service level agreements and ebXML*. Presented at the 10th ISPE International Conference on Concurrent Engineering: Research and Applications. Madeira, Portugal.

The ebXML Framework. (2003). Retrieved November 2003 online *http://www.ebxml.org*

Turcan, E., & Graham, R. L. (2002). Getting the Most from Accountability in P2P. Retrieved December 2003 online *http://csdl.computer.org/comp/proceedings/p2p/ 2001/ 1503/00/15030095.pdf*

Chapter XXII

Collaborative Industrial Automation:
Toward the Integration of a Dynamic Reconfigurable Shop Floor into a Virtual Factory

Armando Walter Colombo
Schneider Electric P&T HUB, Germany

Ronald Schoop
Schneider Electric P&T HUB, Germany

ABSTRACT

This chapter summarizes our latest results concerning the development and the industrial application of the emerging "collaborative industrial automation" technology and its powerful meaning for facilitating the integration of a dynamic reconfigurable shop floor into a virtual factory. It argues, in this respect, that having a conglomerate of distributed, autonomous, intelligent, fault-tolerant, and reconfigurable production units, which operate as a set of cooperating entities, is one promising platform to achieve both local and global manufacturing objectives. Furthermore, the authors hope that understanding the underlying scientific and technological background through the development and industrial application of the collaborative automation paradigm will not only inform the academic, research, and industrial world of an emerging control and automation paradigm, but also assist in the understanding of a new vision of the manufacturing system of the 21st century [a mix of collaborative units, i.e., people, software systems, processes, and equipment (hardware), integrated into a virtual factory].

PRODUCTION SYSTEMS

New Structures, New Markets, New R&D Challenges

The recent production technologies reflect a worldwide trend toward batches of small and medium size, and part/product families of increasing variety. The importance of products' intangible elements has increased considerably, e.g., software, built-in service capabilities, online maintainability, etc. Customers have more individualistic desires and participate in the design and production processes (Camarinha et al., 1999; Kief, 1992; Kusiak, 1986; Tzafestas, 1997).

The tendency shown in Figure 1 often comes in conflict with the demand for high productivity, i.e., on production-time/time-to-market minimization, on simultaneous improvement of machine utilization, and on flexibility of the whole production environment when it is integrated in a global network of related enterprises (virtual enterprise) (Neubert et al., 2001).

The process of globalization forced traditional manufacturing systems development and operation to evolve to inherently multidisciplinary tasks. Manufacturing paradigms such as mass customization generated rapid changes in the economic, technical, and organizational manufacturing environments. Under this new vision, a complicated mix of people, software systems, processes, and equipment (hardware) constitutes the manufacturing system of the 21st century (N.N., 1998, 2000, 2002; Neugebauer et al., 1999). The research and development (R&D) activities linked to the management and control of such complex systems are, as a consequence, a multidisciplinary task grounded in knowledge of manufacturing strategies, planning, and operations, and in the integration of mechatronics, communication, information, and control functions across the entire supply-chain (intra- and interenterprise levels) (Zurawski, 2004).

From CIM/PWS to Heter-Archical Automation

New revolutionary manufacturing concepts and emerging technologies, which take advantage of the newest mechatronics, information and communication technologies and paradigms, and address many of the fundamental problems described above, are being researched and developed since the last decade of the 20th century. The computer-integrated manufacturing (CIM) and the plant-wide systems (PWS) concepts have been promoted as solutions that can somehow deal with all of the above-addressed challenges, e.g., more flexibility in product spectrum and processes, agility of the production system, more responsiveness and integration of hardware and software components (Rathwell, 2001; Williams et al., 1998; *http://www.pera.net/*). Nevertheless, this centralized and sequential manufacturing planning, scheduling, and control mechanism is increasingly being found insufficiently flexible and agile to respond to changing production styles and highly dynamic variations in the product requirements. Moreover, its construction always risks the requirements of huge investment, long lead times, and generation of rigid systems due to large size and centralization. Such a centralized hierarchical organization leads normally to situations where the whole system is shut down by single failures at one point in the CIM hierarchy (Pimentel, 1990; Rembold et al.,

Figure 1. Trends in manufacturing

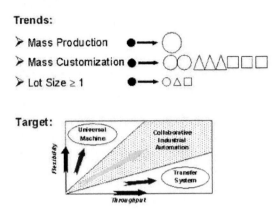

Figure 2. Trend in manufacturing automation

CIM-Architecture ➡ Heter-archical (Modified-CIM) ➡ Dynamic Heter-archical Architecture

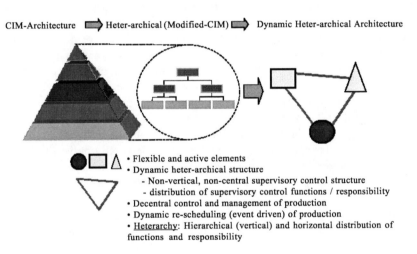

• Flexible and active elements
• Dynamic heter-archical structure
  - Non-vertical, non-central supervisory control structure
  - distribution of supervisory control functions / responsibility
• Decentral control and management of production
• Dynamic re-scheduling (event driven) of production
• Heterarchy: Hierarchical (vertical) and horizontal distribution of functions and responsibility

1993). For this reason, before the CIM idea made its way into practice, its original approach changed from the mainly centralized model to a decentralized one.

One promising architecture, in this respect, is to have a conglomerate of distributed, autonomous, intelligent, fault-tolerant, reusable production units that operate as a set of cooperating entities. Each entity is capable of dynamically interacting with the others to achieve both local and global manufacturing objectives, from the physical/machine control level on the shop floor to the higher levels of factory management systems and global networked enterprises (Colombo et al., 2001). Due to the tremendous amount of interaction between the different components and the variety of performed functions, the control of such production systems is currently based on a hierarchical and distributed structure, i.e., heter-archical structure, as shown in Figure 2.

COLLABORATIVE MANUFACTURING MANAGEMENT (CMM) PARADIGM

Global competition and downward pressure on prices have led manufacturers to recognize their position within a value network or value chain. They have begun to optimize processes for overall enterprise-wide effectiveness rather than individual plant efficiency; and many are moving from isolated business processes to distributed, synchronized business process management (BPM). This means a collaborative enterprise that focuses on business processes to operate and optimize the business from a global perspective (Mick et al., 2003).

In (Gorbach et al., 2002), collaborative manufacturing management (CMM) is defined as the practice of managing key business and manufacturing processes in the context of a global value network. CMM leverages new technologies to build robust relationships with trading partners within a value chain. It knits together internal manufacturing and business processes, and connects them seamlessly and in synchrony with external business processes of strategic partners with the focus on building an effective and agile value chain. CMM builds upon a collaborative infrastructure, BPM services, and real-time strategic business management tools. It connects critical applications, production systems, and enterprise information, to maximize the responsiveness, flexibility, and profitability of the manufacturing enterprise, in conjunction with its value network partners (Gorbach et al., 2002, p. 4).

Recognizing that today's manufacturer needs to operate on information in real-time, CMM provides a holistic approach to manufacturing that is equally well-suited to global multinational companies and small, local operations, as well as to process, discrete, or hybrid production models (Gorbach et al., 2002, p. 4). This approach allows

".. that manufacturers visualize the relationships among plant and enterprise applications, markets, value chains, and manufacturing nodes in order to understand the context for planning and implementing collaborative manufacturing systems." (Gorbach et al., 2002, p. 5)

The central concept of CMM is built around three intersecting domains (see Figure 3): enterprise, value chain, and life cycle.

Up to this concept, a collaborative manufacturing network consists of spheres or manufacturing nodes connected by material, information, and process flows. Above the central plane or disc in a node are business functions. Below it are production functions, where collaborative processes can be formalized in both the business and automation functions, driven by the need for visibility to information throughout the enterprise (Colombo, 2003; Mick et al., 2003).

To meet the emerging business requirements from its customers, Schneider Electric is applying a collaborative model to shape a next generation of automation products and

Figure 3. ARC's CMM model: How a collaborative enterprise manages business and production processes in the context of a global value network (VE)?

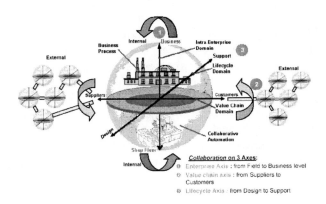

services that increase customer responsiveness and productivity and will combine it with other elements to deliver collaborative automation.

At the automation level, ranging from production management to manufacturing devices, the adoption of a collaborative model takes on a different slant. Certainly, there is a need for information to flow quickly and accurately in both directions in the enterprise domain—between business and automation systems. It is equally as important for operations to work closely with business planning, supplier management, and customer service groups to raise the level of excellence of the entire business.

Intelligent Collaborative Production Automation

In the context of today's markets, many industrial companies are looking for a flexible, network-shaped, but sometimes temporally restricted, virtual cooperation of decentral and distributed production competencies (Bussmann, 2003; Lastra, 2004; Leitao, 2004). This decentralization originates within a single company (spread over several different production sites) or through the association of several different companies within a single supply chain (virtual enterprise). Collaborative automation approaches are required for such scenarios, i.e., a shared but remote supervision is necessary. Autonomous automation units with local supervision functionality installed in each production site interact or cooperate, providing a global (network-wide) super-vision (control, monitoring, diagnosis, HMI, maintenance).

A software agent approach seems well suited in relation to the control and supervision of each mechatronics component in an intelligent manufacturing system. Agent-based software systems are becoming a key control software technology for smart manufacturing control systems. A multiagent-based software platform can offer distrib-uted intelligent control functions with communication, cooperation and synchronization capabilities, and also provide for the behavior specifications of the mechatronics components and the production specifications to be fulfilled by the manufacturing system (Jenning et al., 1998; Parunak et al., 1998; Shen et al., 1999; Schoop et al., 2001).

The result of the integration of emerging technologies and paradigms like smart agent-based control technology, Holonic control systems, and mechatronics is recognized as collaborative industrial automation systems (see Figure 4).

A production system managed and controlled by a collaborative automation system possesses the ability to attain efficiency and versatility by producing a wide range of different product families and different types of a product with a minimal effort in changing the involved manufacturing environment, as it is dynamically reconfigurable. This new generation of production systems is also referenced as intelligent production systems (IPS), with constituent resources that have to be capable of addressing both the knowledge processing about manufacturing process and equipment, and material processing requirements, simultaneously.

The characteristics addressed above, together with the dynamic reconfigurability capacity, are exactly the main requirement for virtual enterprises (VE), when the collaborative units are the different manufacturing environments of a global network of related enterprises.

HETER-ARCHICAL COLLABORATIVE PRODUCTION AUTOMATION AND CONTROL ARCHITECTURES

It is worth noticing that an intelligent production system would be of little use without suitable embedded control software and reliable control architecture. On one hand, it is this system that has to organize the production and to schedule and synchronize the resource utilization. Moreover, the production system's reliability and

Figure 4. Schneider electric proposal: collaborative automation

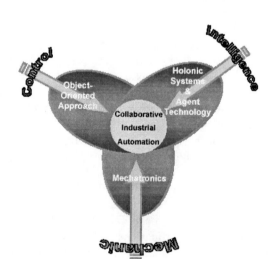

degree of flexibility will not only be conditioned by the reliability and flexibility of its mechatronics components (workstations, storage, handling and transport systems, etc.) but will also depend fundamentally on the reliability and flexibility of the embedded control system (Colombo, 2001).

This trend is accompanied by the fact that modular design of machines and process, combined with aggressive penetration of IT technologies, has pushed the automation architectures from a concentrated treatment to collaboration control, requiring new services over Ethernet TCP/IP to synchronize distributed applications, new engineering tools, and distributed Web HMI.

Let us offer two answers to these requirements:

1. The first is the Transparent Ready™ architecture (Gelin et al., 2003). It is a collaborative platform serving information systems, power and control (see Figure 5):

- Based on open standards: Ethernet TCP/IP and Web services
- Enables visibility through the enterprise and value chain
- Optimized solutions are available for all applications:
    - *Transparent Factory™*: industrial automation processes in industry and infrastructures
    - *Transparent Building™*: building and energy management
    - *Transparent Energy™*: electrical network management

The platform offers a value-added functionality to serve:
- Horizontal collaboration at the control level
- Vertical collaboration to serve enterprise businesses, suppliers, and customers
- Seamless connection between IT and plant floor
- Remote access to processes/machines/equipment
- Cost savings
- Flexibility, scalability, reliability

Figure 5. Transparent Ready ™: open collaborative control over ethernet

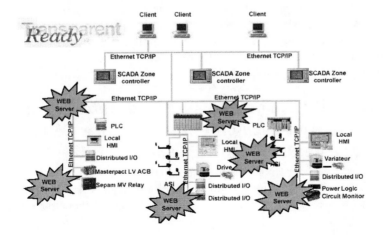

It is a global application, consisting of several applications deployed into different control units. Interconnections of the control units is ensured by Mod-bus TCP, the Ethernet TCP/IP application layer for messaging between devices and for data automatic refresh in Web browsers. High-performance data sharing for PLC synchronization over the Ethernet, is now available thanks to Global Data services, automatic and powerful multicast exchanges, improving determinism.

2.   The second one is the Factory Broker™ solution (see Figure 6 and Zurawski, 2004):

FactoryBroker™ is a heterogeneous agent-orientated collaborative control system that has been developed and implemented by Schneider Electric GmbH, in cooperation with DaimlerChrysler AG, Research and Technology, Berlin, Germany. FactoryBroker™ has been developed as an automation tool to support the implementation, at industrial level, of the collaborative manufacturing automation system paradigm. It is particularly relevant in an industrial process control system to control widely distributed, heterogeneous (i.e., different hardware manufacturers) devices in environments that are prone to disruptions and where stiff real-time constraints must be met to achieve safe system operation. The system embodies the idea of the agile manufacturing paradigm, where "reprogrammable, reconfigurable, continuously changeable production systems, are integrated into an information intensive manufacturing system, making the lot size of an order irrelevant"(Colombo, Neubert & Schoop, 2001, p. 493). The "collaborative smart (agent-based) control components" of FactoryBroker™ are basically formed on a functional modularization of a shop floor. It is complemented by all the essential attributes that are necessary in a holarchy (Colombo, Neubert & Schoop, 2001, p. 493): cooperation, autonomy, intelligence, and transparency.

Remark: The same integration mechanism that characterizes the Factory Broker™ solution can be applied to provide dynamic reconfiguration of a manufacturing system over different companies. And this forms the supply chain/VE.

In despite of these solutions, it is worth noticing that several emerging concepts that advocate intelligent, distributed, and collaborative production structures have been reported in the literature: bionic, fractal, holonic manufacturing, and virtual enterprise, are examples of the newest concepts. Including the e-marketplace and e-factory as submodels, a new paradigm related to the integration of factory automation with information technology has been recently reported in the scientific community: "The Holonic Enterprise as a Collaborative Information Ecosystem" (Ulieru et al., 2001).

Interoperability Among Agent-Based Automation Systems: An Approach on Implementing a Collaborative Intraenterprise Platform with *FactoryBroker™*

There is a set of forces governing the collaborative work of a constellation of intelligent distributed production resources, which are mainly related to optimization of resources and rapid (re-)configuration of schedules to accommodate new orders in a timely manner.

Figure 6. The Factory Broker™: Collaborative control architecture

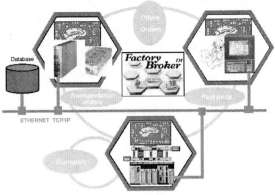

Typical driving forces at this level are, from production specifications:
- Online ordering and negotiation
- Online and flexible production (re)-configuration, fault detection, and recovery
- Online and dynamic (re)-scheduling of orders

And from an infrastructure perspective, they are:
- Registration of collaborative units in the system
- Resources for finding information (including other agent-based collaborative units from another multiagent-based platform)
- Message routing, security management, error handling

All of these capabilities can only be implemented if a reliable and safe communication and the corresponding "interoperability" of both platforms is guaranteed, both in their functional and technical aspects.

The practical experiences of the authors show that two production sections of a collaborative/VE, each controlled by its own multiagent-based control system (such as a collaborative manufacturing cell and a flexible transport system composed of AGVs; see Ritter et al., 1999) can be seen as two collaborative sections within the intraenterprise level (see Neubert et al., 2001).

The main functional specifications of the integration of the two implemented collaborative platforms, using the agent communication language (ACL) released by the Foundation for Intelligent Physical Agents (FIPA) as a communication tool (FIPA, 1997; *http://www.fipa.org/docs/wps/f-wp-00009/f-wp-00009.html*), have been summarized in Neubert et al. (2001). The functional communication between the multiagent-based platforms is based on the speech-act theory, and the technical communication is based on a socket technology. Each host, the workpiece agent of *FactoryBroker™* as well as the agentified mobile robot system, all implement and set up a socket-server and a socket-client. The workpiece agent receives all the messages from the robot system on its socket-server and sends all the messages to the robot system via the socket-client. The mobile robot system performs the same function. Once established, the socket connection continues to exist until the computer is shut down or the connection is broken. (The socket communication is done using the port of a communication channel).

Note: In the socket layer, each FIPA–ACL message is enhanced with a message length descriptor. To specify the communication interface, a document-type definition "DTD-file" is used to describe the grammar of the XML content included in each FIPA–ACL message.

ENGINEERING METHODOLOGY TO DEVELOP COLLABORATIVE INDUSTRIAL AUTOMATION SYSTEMS

The migration from today's factory control strategies to "flexible and collaborative automation systems" and "virtual factories" is the most difficult task on the track to a successful industrial implementation of this new key enabling technology.

It makes no difference whether a plant has to be planned or an existing one has to be upgraded (retrofitted) to a flexible production system, because in both cases, the traditional methods to organize the production processes and to program the process sequences are no longer applicable. This means that the reconfigurability of a VE is a critical issue that generates big challenges around a central question, as shown in Figure 7:

- How can we aggregate machines, especially the new generation of intelligent machinery and systems, manual workplaces and material found on a shop floor at the intraenterprise level, or in different companies within the context of VE, to production units, which are optimal to take over the role of autonomous and collaborative automation units?

Two basic processes are necessary to achieve this new structure in a way that is practicable in industry: break up the typical hierarchical management and control philosophy, and develop structured methods in order to recombine the elements suitable for an agile, efficient, and intelligent management and control of flexible production sites.

Figure 7. Engineering methodology of Schneider for the configuration of collaborative production automation systems

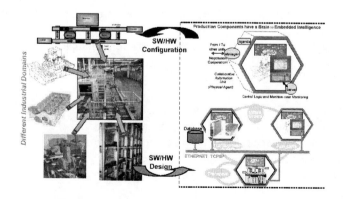

And both processes have to consider the shop floor integrated with the upper levels of an intelligent factory within the enterprise organisation, and within the context of VE, i.e., interenterprise (or networked) organisation.

One of the strengths of the engineering methodology is the identification, characterization, and selection of a representative set of manufacturing scenarios from real industrial applications. Making use of these scenarios, an advanced and efficient application reference path of the innovative collaborative automation technology in the different involved production areas has been developed (Colombo et al., 2004).

The methodology is based on providing knowledge and initial tools for successful, safe, and efficient migration of flexible and collaborative automation techniques in a variety of production scenarios. Applying the reference path addressed above, a production plant engineer and a production system developer and an enterprise architect are able to:

- Identify collaborative production automation units
- Describe production system architectures for the application of flexible and collaborative automation systems
- Coordinate and apply structural methods for modelling flexible and collaborative automation systems in the addressed production systems
- Deliver individual models, requirements, and operation modes of selected application scenarios
- Validate, simulate, and test the models in a joint engineering platform
- Support the configuration of the collaborative production scenarios

Strategic and Technological Significances of the Engineering Methodology

There are necessary further definitions and standardization of interfaces for distributed and collaborative smart control components and intelligent automation platforms, which have to influence and to effectively support the R&D community.

The approach allows Schneider Electric to combine internal development on its preferred architectures and products with external activities [e.g., IEEE, FIPA, IEC standardization 61499 (IEC, 1999), etc.] in this area and to gain know-how and information from customers and competition.

The engineering and control environment support the implementation of an intelligent distributed architecture with real-time "shop-floor" distributed control and dynamic scheduling functions. Moreover, knowledge of the design, behavior, and benefits of collaborative production control systems have been gained, and also the integration aspects of the new technology in a variety of customer production scenarios have been evaluated.

The encapsulation of hard- and software in collaborative production environments that results from the application of the methodology has made, among others, the following characteristics of a VE at shop-floor level a reality:

- Automatic reconfiguration of processes by simply plugging new devices into the shop floor, i.e., new smart components in the system
- Updating production-equipment or system components step by step: New modules could be capable of simulating old production equipment or smart compo-

nents; or the rest of the system could be able to adjust to the new possibilities the new module introduces

- Easy maintenance and, therefore, better-maintained equipment: Intelligent (smart) modules know their internal state and recognize error states

Foreseen New Developments

- Networked embedded intelligence at the real-time production control and rescheduling levels should be extended, allowing for a completely new range of intelligent automation products. This will enormously affect *the manufacturing workforces within a* highly dynamic and agile economic, technical and organizational manufacturing environment *and more particularly the* market of intelligent production controllers in this century.
- Concerning a view for longer-term prospects of scientific and technological developments opened by this approach, it can be stated that it establishes a very sound basis for:
  - Collaborative control systems and smart (agent-based) production controllers, as key enabling technologies (KET) for the integration of mechatronics, information, control, and communication, in flexible and collaborative manufacturing environments, and in virtual factory environments within the VE (see Figure 8).

This way, by using the addressed engineering methodology together with the collaborative solutions, i.e., Factory Broker™ and Transparent Ready™, it is easy to design and build flexible distributed controls, the corresponding coordination mechanisms, and the communication protocols for collaborative manufacturing environments, when they are integrated into an intelligent factory within an enterprise or a VE organization.

Catalogue of Methods and Models for Structuring Collaborative Automation Systems at the Shop-Floor Level of an Enterprise

In Colombo et al. (2002) and Leitao et al. (2003) an approach was presented, i.e., method and principles to model and formally validate agent-based control systems for flexible production systems using high-level Petri nets. The proposed approach allows for a first identification of functional intelligent units [hardware/software (HW/SW) intelligent devices in a networked production automation environment] through the life cycle on the different levels, from device throughout equipment to the complete production system (see Figure 9).

Extending those results allows for the conception, definition, and formal specification of a "encapsulation process" in industrial production systems, when mechatronics, control, and intelligence are considered integrated in an automation unit. Due to its inherent capacities for autonomous behavior and particularly for cooperating and working together with other units, such a kind of capsule is called "collaborative automation unit."

Figure 8. Integration of the Collaborative Shop floor into the intra-and/or inter enterprise architecture

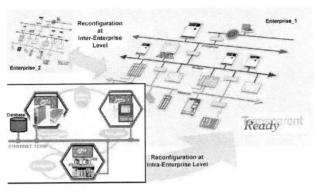

As presented before, the high-level Petri net-based approach facilitates the integration of the four aspects, i.e., mechatronics, communication, control, and intelligence/knowledge. Moreover, all addressed aspects are developed and implemented in a unified manner.

The models of the collaborative units can be considered as basic capsules (modules).

Based on the fact that we are working with networked production automation sites (within an enterprise or in a networked set of enterprises), let us now propose a development path for the modules. It allows basically the manipulation of three kinds of knowledge about collaborative production units: architectural, functional, and compositional. That is:

1. Functional architecture (about the modules as mechatronic components with control and intelligence capabilities, as depicted in Figure 4)
2. Functions to be performed (about how the modules behave and interact)
3. Connectivity between modules (about how the modules are integrated, which mechanisms, technology, standards, etc., are being used for this purpose?)

Remark: With these modules can be constructed and formally specified an entire model of a networked automation system.

Departing from the main concept of collaborative industrial automation, as depicted in Figure 4, the following are the elements or components of the catalogue:

Mechatronic Units
- Modularization: identification of capsules or modules with different degrees of granularity (machine, machine-part, sensor/actuator, periphery, etc.)
- Simplification: break into reusable units, i.e., HW/components => high-level Petri net models of components

Figure 9. Formal approach for the identification of collaborative automation units

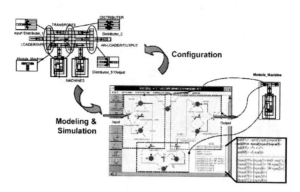

- Categorization: hardware components will be represented by standard high-level-Petri net components; a catalogue of models for different production scenarios is generated
- Standardization: Standardization of component models

Smart (Agent-Based) Control Units
- Predesigned component: Each high-level Petri net model of hardware components acts as a skeleton of the corresponding smart (agent-based) control units
- Implements main functions: control, monitoring, diagnosis, decision-making processes, "predictive and corrective" maintenance; the quantity and quality of the information contained in the structure of the high-level Petri net model of the smart (agent-based) controller strongly supports the above-named supervisory control function; the results of the formal analysis of the models complete the set of information parameters used to supervise the collaborative automation unit
- Catalogization: Control software components will be represented by standard high-level-Petri net components; a catalogue of models for different control components in different production automation scenarios is offered

It follows one of the main results: with only one approach and with the stepwise improvement of the HL-PN model of the hardware (mechatronics) components, the control specifications of a collaborative unit are automatically generated. This means that there are not two catalogues (one for mechatronics and other one for control). The catalogue, as depicted in Figure 10, is only one. The models of the collaborative units found there can be used with different degrees of granularity, according to the necessity of the users.

Formal validation of the models (HW/control/intelligence): The catalogue of models contents the results of the formal validation of specifications (structural and behavioral) when HW/SW (control and intelligence) are completely integrated in each model.

Formal specification of complete collaborative automation scenarios: Based on the outcome of the approach addressed above, it follows the provision of rules for the modelling of collaborative automation systems and the provision of evaluation parameters for each application.

- Catalogization: Taking into account both competence and cooperation and relationships between collaborative units, constraints and rules for the composition of HL-PN-based models of the collaborative units are the results. As an example, rules for respecting sequential and parallel mutual exclusion relationships, shared-resources functions, etc., are generated.

The results of the integration of agent-based models of production components is recognized as a coordination model. The set of rules that are in the catalogue allows us to improve the structure and behavior of the coordination model for being used as formal specification of a complete collaborative automation scenario. This leads to automatic system adaptation and reconfiguration.

In automatic system adaptation and reconfiguration, the coordination model is able to take decisions at system level, supporting one of the main functionalities of a collaborative automation system, that is collaboration/cooperation [for example, introduction of new hardware (new models of the catalogue), break-down of components and replacement, new production specifications for new products, new decisions and new factors for taking decisions, etc.].

CONCLUSIONS

This chapter briefly summarizes our latest results concerning the industrial application of the emerging "collaborative industrial automation technology" and its powerful meaning for facilitating the integration of a dynamic reconfigurable shop floor into a virtual factory.

It is well-known by technology developers and users that the migration from today's factory control strategies to "flexible and collaborative automation systems" is the most difficult task on the track to a successful industrial implementation of this new

Figure 10. Catologization of collaborative automation components

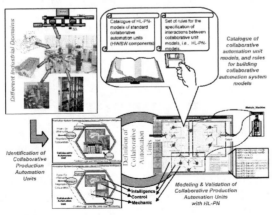

key enabling technology. It makes no difference whether a plant has to be planned or an existing one has to be upgraded (retrofitted) to a dynamic reconfigurable and flexible production system, because in both cases, the traditional methods to organize the production processes and to program the process sequences are no longer applicable.

The key question to be answered is, therefore, how do we aggregate intelligent production components, especially the new generation of intelligent machinery and systems, manual workplaces, and material found on a shop floor to production units that are optimal to take over the role of autonomous and collaborative automation units?

Two basic processes are necessary to achieve this new structure in a way that is practicable in industry: break up the typical hierarchical management and control philosophy, and develop structured methods in order to recombine the elements suitable for an agile, efficient, and intelligent management and control of flexible production, when considering the shop floor integrated into a virtual factory.

As a result of different industrial automation roadmaps (N.N, 2002; Neugebauer et al., 1999; Schoop et al., 2002), and taking into consideration the experience reported by the authors and other developers/producers of automation systems, a set of challenges and solutions for collaborative automation systems was presented.

The authors, working for a world-leader producer of smart production control systems, envision a technology bifurcation, similar to that generated by the PLC in the 1970s, that will happen in the next 5–10 years in the field of intelligent controllers and real-time middleware technologies, derived from FactoryBroker™-like solutions (Colombo et al., 2001). We have the vision of flexible and collaborative automation units, i.e., smart controllers, embedded in a huge spectrum of intelligent hardware (possible manufacturing hardware may be fixed machinery like robots, conveyor belts, or mobile autonomous vehicles), and applied in different industrial production scenarios (see Bussmann, 2003; Lastra, 2004; Leitao, 2004, for recent developments in the manufacturing and assembly areas).

Moreover, the methods and tools proposed for the identification, specification, and implementation of collaborative units on the shop floor at the intraenterprise level will be extended, without complications, to the interenterprise level of a global network of related enterprises, i.e., VE.

ACKNOWLEDGMENTS

The authors would like to thank the European Commission and the partners of the Innovative Production Machines and Systems (I*PROMS; http://www.iproms.org/) Network of Excellence for their support.

REFERENCES

Bussmann, S. (2003). *An agent-oriented design methodology for production control.* Dissertation, University of Southampton. Heidelberg: Springer-Verlag.

Camarinha-Matos, L. M., & Afsarmanesh, H. (1999). Infrastructures for virtual enterprises: A summary of achievements. In L.M. Camarinha-Matos & H. Afsarmanesh (Eds.), *Proceedings of IFIP International Conference on Infrastructures for Virtual Enterprises (PRO-VE'99)* (pp. 483-490). Dordrecht: Kluwer.

Colombo, A. W. (2001). *Integration of high-level Petri net-based formal methods for the supervision of flexible production systems.* Lecture/Tutorial per Internet—Field: Embedded Systems & Factory Automation—on February 20, 2001, 4:00 p.m. GMT, at the 1st Online Symposium for Electronics Engineers. TechOnLine, USA. (*www.osee.net*).

Colombo, A. W. (2003). *Collaborative manufacturing—An industrial experience.* The 1st Presented at Schneider's International Conference & Fair: Initi@tive: Automation & Control 2003. Brussels, Belgium, December 1–5.

Colombo, A. W., & Lastra, J. L. M. (2004). *An approach to develop flexible and collaborative factory automation systems (FLEXCA).* Presented at the Fourth CIRP International Seminar on ICME, Sorrento, Italy.

Colombo, A. W., Neubert, R., & Schoop, R. (2001). A solution to holonic control systems. In E. Dekneuvel & R. Zurawasky (Eds.), *Proceedings of the Eighth IEEE International Conference on Emerging Technologies and Factory Automation (ETFA '01)* (pp. 489-498). Institute of Electrical and Electornics Engineers, Inc. Sophia/Nice, France.

Colombo, A.W., Neubert, R., & Süssmann, B. (2002). A colored Petri net-based approach towards a formal specification of agent-controlled production systems. In *Proceedings of the 2002 IEEE International Conference on Systems, Man and Cybernetics (SMC'02),* (pp. CD-code TA1C5). Information Technology Support Systems, Hammamet, Tunisia.

FIPA (Foundation for Intelligent Physical Agents). (1997). FIPA 97 Specification Part 2: Agent Communication Language.

Gelín, P., & Colombo, A. W. (2003). *Open collaborative control over ethernet.* Presented at the Third International Symposium on Open Control Systems 2003 (Towards Modular Self-Organizing Re-Configurable Automation Systems). Helsinki, Finland, September 9–10.

Gorbach, G., & Nick, R. (2002). Collaborative manufacturing management strategies. ARC Advisory Group. E. Bassett & A. Chatha (Eds.).

IEC. (1999). IEC CDV 61499-1, Function Blocks for Industrial-Process Measurement and Control Systems Part 1—Architecture.

Jennings, N. R., & Wooldridge, M. J. (1998). Applications of intelligent agents. In *Agent technology: Foundations, applications, and markets* (pp. 3–28). Heidelberg: Springer.

Kief, H. (1992). *FFS-Handbuch '92/93. Einführung in Flexible Fertigungssysteme* (in German). Jans Verlag München Wien.

Koestler, A. (1967). *The ghost in the machine.* London: Arcan Books.

Kusiak, A. (1986). *Flexible manufacturing systems: Methods and studies.* Amsterdam; New York: Elsevier.

Lastra, J. L. M. (2004). *Reference mechatronic architecture for actor-based assembly systems.* Dissertation, Technical University of Tampere, Finland.

Leitao, P. (2004). *An agile and adaptive holonic architecture for manufacturing control.* Dissertation, University of Porto, Portugal.

Leitao, P., & Colombo, A. W. (2003). An approach for the formal specification of holonic control systems. In V. Marik, D. McFarlane, & P. Valckenaers (Eds.), *LNAI, volume 2744, Holonic and Multi-Agent Systems for Manufacturing* (pp. 59–70). Heidelberg: Springer-Verlag.

Mick, R., & Polsonetti, C. (2003). *Collaborative automation: The platform for operational excellence.* ARC Advisory Group. ARC White Paper. E. Bassett (Ed.).

Neubert, R., Colombo, A. W., & Schoop, R. (2001). An approach to integrate a multiagent-based production controller into a holonic enterprise platform. In *Proceedings of the IEEE International Conference on Information Technology in Mechatronics (ITM'01)*, Istanbul, Turkey.

Neugebauer, J., & Hoepf, M. (1999). The role of automation and control in the information society. Rep. of the Fraunhofer Institut for Production and Automation (IPA), European Commission, DGIS. Fraunhofer IRB Verlag.

N.N. (1998). Visionary manufacturing challenges for 2020. Committee on Visionary Manufacturing Challenges, Commission on Engineering and Technical Systems, National Research Council, National Academy Press, Washington, D.C.

N.N. (2000). Integrated Manufacturing Technology Initiative, Integrated Manufacturing Technology Road Mapping (IMTR) Initiative, NIST, DOE, NSF, and DARPA—Executive Summary.

N.N. (2002), Minutes of the *IMS Workshop on Standardization Issues for Manufacturing*—European Commission, Intelligent Manufacturing System Program. Brussels, 27 February.

Parunak, V. D., Baker, A., & Clark, S. (1998). The AARIA Agent Architecture: From Manufacturing Requirements to Agent-Based System Design. Working Notes of the Agent-Based Manufacturing Workshop, Minneapolis, MN.

Pimentel, J. (1990). *Communication networks for manufacturing.* Englewood Cliffs, NJ: Prentice Hall.

Rathwell, G. (2001). Design of Plant Control and Information Systems within an Enterprise Architecture. PERA-Standard documentation.

Rembold, U., & Nnaji, B. O. (1993). *Computer integrated manufacturing and engineering.* Reading, MA: Addison-Wesley.

Ritter, A., Neugebauer, J., Schraft, R. D., & Westkämper, E. (1999). Holonic task generation for mobile robots. In *Proceedings of the 30th International Symposium on Robotics* (pp. 553–560), Tokyo, Japan, .

Schoop, R., Neubert, R., & Colombo, A. W. (2001). A multiagent-based distributed control platform for industrial flexible production systems. In *Proceedings of the IEEE IECON2001*, Denver, CO.

Schoop, R., Colombo, A. W., Süssmann, B., & Neubert, R. (2002). Industrial experiences, trends and future requirements on agent-based intelligent automation. In *Proceedings of the IEEE IECON2002*, Sevilla, Spain.

Shen, W., & Norrie, D. (1999). Agent-based systems for intelligent manufacturing: A state-of-the-art survey. *International Journal on Knowledge and Information Systems, 1*(2), 129–156.

Tzafestas, S. (1997). Modern manufacturing systems: An information technology perspective. In *Advanced manufacturing series—Computer-assisted management and control of manufacturing systems* (pp. 1–56). Heidelberg: Springer Verlag.

Ulieru, M., Walker, S., & Brennan, R. (2001). Holonic enterprise as a collaborative information ecosystem. In *Proceedings of the Workshop: Holons, Autonomous and Cooperative Agents for the Industry*, Montreal, Canada (AA 2001).

Williams, T., & Li, H. (1998). *PERA and GERAM—Enterprise Reference Architectures in Enterprise Integration. Information Infrastructure Systems for Manufacturing II, IFIP*. Dordrecht: Kluwer Academic Publishers.

Zurawski, R. (2004). *The Industrial Information Technology Handbook*. Boca Raton, FL: CRC Press.

Appendix

ABBREVIATIONS AND ACRONYMS

- ACID, atomic, consistent, isolated, and durable
- AKM, active knowledge models
- ARB, agent resource broker
- B2Bi, business-to-business integration
- BBS, business breakdown structure
- BCKOA, business-centric knowledge-oriented architecture
- BCL, business contract language
- BM_VEARM, BM_virtual enterprise architecture reference model
- BPEL, business process execution language for Web services
- BPMS, business process management system
- BPSS, business process specification schema
- CDS, cooperative distributed system
- CE, Chaordic enterprise
- CE, concurrent engineering
- CFP, call-for-proposals
- CIM, computer integrated manufacturing
- CIR-agent, coordinated, intelligent, rational agent
- CMM, collaborative manufacturing management
- CNP, contract net protocol
- CORBA, common object request broker architecture
- COVE, cooperation infrastructure for virtual enterprises
- CSCW, computer-supported collaborative work
- CST, Chaordic system thinking
- DRIVE, drug in virtual enterprise

- DRM, digital rights management
- EAI, enterprise application integration
- EDI, electronic data interchange
- EEML, extended enterprise modeling language
- ERP, enterprise resource planning
- EXTERNAL project (Extended Enterprise Resources, Networks and Learning)
- FMS, flexible manufacturing systems
- HTML, hypertext markup language
- HTTP, hypertext transfer protocol
- IMS, intelligent manufacturing system
- ICSS, integrated client–server system
- ICT, information and communication technology
- IMM, information management model
- IOR, interoperable object references
- IPS, intelligent production system
- ISD, Integrated Situation Dictionary
- IST, Information Society Technologies
- IT, information technology
- J2EE, Java2 Enterprise Edition
- JIT, just-in-time
- KM, knowledge management
- MASSYVE, multiagent manufacturing scheduling systems in virtual enterprise
- MME, matchmaking engine
- MR, Market of Resources
- NVE, normalised virtual enterprise
- ODP, open distributed processing
- OEM, original equipment manufacturer
- OKP, one-of-a-kind-production
- OPIM, one-product integrated manufacturing
- P2P, peer-to-peer
- P3P, platform for privacy preferences
- PET, privacy-enhancing technology
- PIP, partner interchange process
- PISA, privacy incorporate software agent
- PLM, product life-cycle manager
- QoS, quality of service
- RBVO, request based virtual organisation
- RDF, resource description framework
- SA, software agent
- SAM, situational analysis model
- SLA, service-level agreement
- SME, small and medium-sized enterprise
- SOA, service-oriented architecture
- SOAP, simple object access protocol
- SR, situation room
- SRA, situation room analysis
- SRM, situation room model

- TQM, total quality management
- UDDI, universal description, discovery, and integration
- UEML, Unified Enterprise Modelling Language
- UML, unified modeling language
- VBE, virtual breeding environment
- VE, virtual enterprise
- VEI, virtual enterprise integration
- VHE, virtual healthcare enterprise
- VO, virtual organization
- W3C, World Wide Web Consortium
- WSDL, Web services description language
- WSME, Web Services Matchmaking Engine

COMPANY/SOFTWARE/PROGRAM NAMES

- Dell™
- eBay®
- Virgin®
- Yahoo!®

Specific Spellings/Term Usage

E

ecoconservative
ecoconsistent

H

healthcare

I

*internet*worked

L

life cycle (n)
life-cycle (adj)
lifelong
life span

M

Market of Resources
metadata

R

> runtime

T

> tele-learning
> time-out
> trade-off

W

> work flow
> worklist

About the Authors

Goran D. Putnik received his Dipl Eng, MSci, and DrSci from Belgrade University, both MSci and DrSci in the domain of intelligent manufacturing systems. His current position is associate professor, Department of Production and Systems Engineering, University of Minho, Portugal. He teaches the subjects of CAD/CAPP, CAM, FMS, and virtual enterprises in undergraduate studies, and CAD/CAPP/CAM systems, concurrent engineering, enterprise organization, IMS and design theory in postgraduate studies. He is also deputy director of the Centre for Production Systems Engineering (CESP) (before, he served as director of the Centre for four years), director of the master and postgraduate course on CIM, and is responsible for the Laboratory for Virtual Enterprises (LABVE), Department of Production and Systems Engineering, University of Minho. His scientific and engineering interests are production systems and enterprises design and control theory and implementations: CIM, CAD/CAPP/CAM systems, intelligent production systems and enterprises, machine learning as a design theory model, design engineering, information systems management, formal theory of production systems and enterprises, and distributed, agile, and virtual enterprises. He is supervising a number of PhD projects as well.

Maria Manuela Cunha is currently assistant professor in the School of Management, Polytechnic Institute of Cávado and Ave, Portugal. She holds a Dipl Eng in the field of systems and informatics engineering, an MSci in the field of information society and a DrSci in the field of virtual enterprises, all from the University of Minho. She is the director of the Department of Informatics and teaches subjects related to information technologies and systems to undergraduate and postgraduate students. She supervises several PhD projects in the domain of virtual enterprises. Her scientific and engineering interests are electronic business, agile and virtual enterprises, and information systems.

* * *

Paulo Ávila received his EngLic from the University of Coimbra in the domain of mechanical engineering, his MSc from the University of Minho, Portugal, in the domain of computer integrated manufacturing, and his PhD from the University of Minho in the area of resources selection for agile and virtual enterprises. His current position is assistant professor in the Department of Mechanical Engineering, at the High Engineering Institute of Porto, Portugal, covering the subjects of production system organization and management, computer integrated manufacturing (CIM), and total quality management. He is a quality consulter and his interests besides that are manufacturing systems and enterprise design and management theory and implementation.

Henrique Lopes Cardoso graduated in computing and management and received his master's degree in artificial intelligence from the University of Porto (1999). He is an assistant lecturer at the Technology School Department of Computing of the Polytechnic Institute of Bragança, and a PhD student at the Faculty of Engineering of the University of Porto, Portugal. His research interests include distributed AI, normative multiagent systems, virtual enterprises, and adaptive learning agents.

José Dinis Carvalho received his first degree in production engineering from Universidade do Minho, Portugal (1989), an MSc from Loughborough University, UK (1992), and a PhD from the University of Nottingham, UK (1997). He is currently an associate professor at Minho University in the Production and Systems Department. His main research interests are in the fields of virtual enterprises in production planning and control models, and in production organization paradigms. He is also involved in new teaching methodologies including project-led education, e-learning, and distant collaborative learning.

Armando Walter Colombo received the Doctor-Degree in Engineering with a scientific work on manufacturing automation from the University of Erlangen-Nuremberg, Germany (1998). In 1992, he was a visiting researcher at the Electrical and Computer Engineering Department, University of Zaragoza, Spain. From 1995 to 1998, he was a research assistant at the Institute for Manufacturing Automation and Production Systems, University of Erlangen-Nürnberg, Germany, and from 1999 to 2000 was an adjunct professor in the Group of Robotic Systems and CIM, Faculty of Technical Sciences, New University of Lisbon, Portugal. In 2001, he joined Schneider Automation GmbH, and is currently working as manager of advanced projects in the P&T HUB Department, Schneider Electric, France, Germany, and EU. His research interests are in the fields of intelligent supervisory control theory, factory automation, simulation-based modeling, analysis and supervision of production systems, and agent-based automation technology. Dr. Colombo has participated in many international projects and has more than 70 publications in journals, books, and conference proceedings. He is a member of the IEEE Industrial Electronics Society, the IEEE Robotics and Automation Society, the IEEE Systems, Man, and Cybernetics Society, and the Gesellschaft für Informatik e.V. Dr. Colombo is listed in *Who's Who in the World*, *Who's Who in Sciences and Engineering*, and in *Outstanding People of the XX Century*.

Sonja Ellmann, born in 1978, graduated in economics from the Universität of Bremen, Germany (2003). She has a Master of Arts in global political economy and finance from

New School University, New York. She worked as a freelance consultant for Volkswagen Coaching GmbH in 2004 before returning to university and joining a PhD program at the Institute of Project Management and Innovation, IPMI. Currently, she works part-time at university and has a PhD contract with Siemens AG, Erlangen.

Jens Eschenbaecher, born in 1968, graduated in business management (1996). He began his career at CSC Ploenzke AG in Kiedrich in the Corporate Controlling Department. In 1998, he joined a PhD program at the Universität of Bremen, Germany, about global supply-chain management and was employed at BIBA since then. In 2004, he became head of the Department of Collaborative Business in Enterprise Networks. He was involved in diverse ESPRIT and IST research projects such as AIT-Implant, ENAPS, BRIDGES, and EXPIDE, dealing with virtual organizations and innovation management. Currently, he is sub-project leader of the ECOLEAD project (*www.ecolead.org*). For his PhD thesis, he is developing an innovation management methodology for enterprise networks and implementing this methodology into a prototypical Web-based environment supporting distributed innovation processes.

Simon Field is technology director of Matching Systems (UK), a company he founded in early 2003 to bring innovative matching technology to market. He was previously manager of the e-Business Solutions Group at IBM's Zurich Research Laboratory, where he led a number of research projects with a focus on service matchmaking and cross-organizational business processes.

Erastos Filos was born in Athens, Greece. After obtaining his MSc in physics from Hamburg University, he worked as a research scientist in high-energy physics and later did his PhD in physical chemistry at Constance University. He then became project manager at Perkin Elmer Corp., and leader of the Electronics Design Team at Bosch-Telecom in Heidelberg. In 1993, he moved to Brussels to take up a position at the European Commission (Belgium) as scientific officer in the areas concurrent engineering and virtual enterprise. His contribution was instrumental in defining the IST Work Programme area Smart Organizations.

Susumu Fujii is a professor of computer and systems engineering at Kobe University, Kobe, Japan. He received a BS in mechanical engineering and MS in precision engineering from Kyoto University and PhD in mechanical engineering from the University of Wisconsin, Madison. His research interests include modeling and analysis of computer-integrated manufacturing systems, production planning and scheduling, and manufacturing system simulation. He is a member of various academic societies, such as JSPE, JSME, ORSJ, ISCIE, SICE, INFORMS, and others.

Hamada Ghenniwa is the director of the software engineering program at the Department of Electrical and Computer Engineering, University of Western Ontario, Canada. He received the BSc in computer engineering (1984) from Al-fateh University, and an MASc and PhD in systems design engineering (1991 and 1996, respectively) from the University of Waterloo. His main research expertise includes computational intelligence with a specific focus on intelligent agent technology, coordination theory, as well as its application to cooperative distributed systems. Application areas include enterprise integration, electronic business, manufacturing, intelligent mobile robotics, collaborative engineering, and pervasive and grid computing. Dr. Ghenniwa is the head of Cooperative Distributed Systems Engineering Group. He is currently leading several research and industrial projects concerned with integration in distributed information systems, e-business, and multiagent systems for manufacturing and mobile robotics. He has authored and coauthored more than 100 papers in world-class journals and conference proceedings as well as several technical and industrial project reports.

Ted Goranson has been in the enterprise integration (and predecessor) field for 35 years, coming from MIT. During this time, he headed many of the U.S. government research programs leading to basic technologies and strategies that advanced and now litter the civil infrastructure. Now, as director of the Advanced Enterprise Research Office, he addresses the next generation of infrastructure for the radical vision of advanced, agile virtual enterprises.

Angappa Gunasekaran is a professor of management in the Charlton College of Business at the University of Massachusetts (North Dartmouth, USA). Previously, he has held academic positions in Canada, India, Finland, Australia and the UK. He has a BE and ME from the University of Madras and a PhD from the Indian Institute of Technology. He teaches and conducts research in operations management and information systems. He serves on the editorial board of 20 journals and edits a journal. He has published about 160 articles in journals, 60 articles in conference proceedings and two edited books. In addition, he has organized several conferences in the emerging areas of operations management and information systems. He has extensive editorial experience that includes the guest editor of many high profile journals. He has received outstanding paper and excellence in teaching awards. His current areas of research include supply chain management, enterprise resource planning, e-commerce, and benchmarking.

Yigal Hoffner is a member of the e-Business Solutions Group at IBM's Zurich Research Laboratory, Switzerland. He works on the dynamic establishment and enactment of business relationships between organizations. His main expertise lies in the field of distributed computing, and he is also interested in negotiations, matchmaking, and policy issues. From 1998 to 2000, he was technical leader of the CrossFlow ESPRIT project, which dealt with cross-organizational workflow management. Before joining IBM in 1996, he worked on the development of distributed system architecture at the Advanced Networked Systems Architecture (ANSA) projected in Cambridge, UK. He holds a BSc in computer science and cybernetics and a PhD in computer science.

Håvard D. Jørgensen has held a position as research scientist at SINTEF ICT (Norway), which is part of Scandinavia's largest research institute. He received a master's degree in information systems engineering from the University of Trondheim in 1993. After several years in industry, he joined SINTEF in 1996. His main areas of interest are flexible workflow systems, groupware, and knowledge management. In 2004, he earned a PhD from the Norwegian University of Science and Technology, for a thesis titled "Interactive Process Models."

Toshiya Kaihara is an associate professor of the Graduate School of Science and Technology at Kobe University, Japan. He received a BE and ME degree in precision engineering from Kyoto University and a PhD in mechanical engineering from Imperial College, University of London. His research interests include theory and implement of social scientific multiagent, and intelligent management on manufacturing and distribution systems. He is a member of IFIP, IEEE, ORSJ, JSME, and many others.

Craig A. Knoblock is a senior project leader at the USC Information Sciences Institute, research associate professor in computer science at the University of Southern California, and a chief scientist at Fetch Technologies Inc. In 2004 he was elected a fellow of the American Association for Artificial Intelligence. Professor Knoblock heads a research group that is developing intelligent techniques to enable rapid and efficient information integration. The focus of the research is on the technologies required for constructing distributed, integrated applications from online sources, including wrapping and modeling sources, record linkage, data integration, and plan execution.

Adamantios Koumpis heads the Research Programmes Division of ALTEC S.A. (Greece), which he founded in 1996 (then an independent division of Unisoft S.A.). His research interests include quantitative decision-making techniques and Info Society economics. He successfully led many commercial and research projects in Greece in the areas of e-commerce, public sector and business enterprise reorganization and information logistics, concerning linking of data/information repositories with knowledge management and business engineering models.

John Krogstie is currently senior researcher at SINTEF ICT, Norway. He earlier worked nine years for Accenture within development and deployment of methodology, knowledge management, and process improvement. He has a PhD and MSc in information systems from NTNU, the Norwegian University of Science and Technology, where he also currently holds a position as adjunct professor. His main research areas are modeling of enterprise information systems, knowledge management, and computer-supported cooperative work.

Kristina Lerman is a project leader at the USC Information Sciences Institute and a research assistant professor in computer science at the University of Southern California (USA). She received her PhD in physics from University of California at Santa Barbara in 1995. After a brief sojourn in the high-tech industry, she returned to academia, this time as a computer scientist. She has been at the USC Information Sciences Institute since 1998. Her research interests include modeling and analysis of complex distributed systems, and machine learning for information extraction.

Abdulmutalib Masaud-Wahaishi is a senior research assistant in the Cooperative Distributed Systems Engineering Group, a PhD candidate and a teaching assistant in the Department of Electrical and Computer Engineering at the University of Western Ontario, Canada. Mr. Masaud received a BSc in computer engineering from the University of Al-Fateh (1986) and an MEngSc in software engineering at Western University, Department of Electric and Computer Engineering, London, Canada (2003). His main research areas include agent technology and multi agent systems, cooperative distributed systems, enterprise integration, privacy based brokering, knowledge-based systems, and resource discovery.

Rinaldo C. Michelini is the leader of the Industrial Robot Design Research Group, PMAR Lab, at the School of Engineering of the Università di Genova, Italy. Member of IFIP W.G. 5.3 and 5.5, fellow of ASME, senior member of SCS, member of the Russian Academy of Engineering, etc. Michelini's main interests are in expert automation and life cycle design of artifacts. Michelini's current research areas include intelligent manufacturing, instrumental robotics, industrial diagnostics, integrated ecodesign, reverse logistics, and similar topics, exploring the concurrence of information and materials flows for the effective development, exploitation, and dismissal of products-services.

Steven N. Minton is CTO and co-founder of Fetch Technologies Inc. (USA). He received his PhD in computer science from Carnegie Mellon (1988). He subsequently worked as a principal investigator at NASA's Ames Research Center, and later as a project leader and faculty member at the University of Southern California. In 1998, he was elected to be a fellow of the American Association for Artificial Intelligence for his contributions in machine learning, planning, and constraint satisfaction. Dr. Minton founded the *Journal of Artificial Intelligence Research* (JAIR) and served as its first executive editor. He has also served as an editor of the journal *Machine Learning*.

Nuno Afonso Moreira is an auxiliary professor at the University of Trás-os-Montes e Alto Douro (Portugal) in the Engineering Department. He received his first degree in mechanical engineering from Faculdade de Engenharia da Universidade do Porto, Portugal (1992), an MSc from Universidade do Minho, Portugal (1999), and a PhD from Universidade de Trás-os-Montes e Alto Douro, Portugal (2004). His main research interests are in the field of virtual enterprises and in operation management. He is also interested in new energy production and utilization processes, namely, in the use of new energy processes of wood gasification for the production of energy, with respect to its technical and economical vantages.

Eugénio Oliveira is a full professor at the University of Porto, Portugal. He earned his PhD at the new University Lisbon in 1984. He is coordinator of NIADR (Distributed Artificial Intelligence Group) at the Faculty of Engineering and co-director of LIACC (Artificial Intelligence and Computer Science Laboratory) at the University of Porto. He is director of both the master's course on informatics engineering and of the master's course in artificial intelligence and computer science at the University of Porto. He is also a member of the SIG on agent-mediated electronic commerce included in the AGENTLink European Network of Excellence. He is coordinating research projects involving learning in multiagent environments, emotion-based agent architectures, and agent-based frameworks for Virtual Organizations.

Luís Carlos Pires was born in 1970 in Bragança, a small village in the northeast of Portugal. He graduated in 1995 in electronics engineering/industrial control, Instituto Superior de Engenharia do Porto, Portugal. In 1999, he received an MSc in CIM from Universidade do Minho, Portugal, and in 2004 a PhD in production and systems engineering by the same university. From 1996 until today, he has been an assistant professor in the Ciências Básicas Department of ESAB, Instituto Politechnic Institute of Bragança, Portugal, teaching informatics and statistics. His main research interests focus on the study of supporting architectures to virtual enterprise life cycle and its associated functionality.

Nicolaos Protogeros is a lecturer in electronic commerce at the University of Macedonia, Thessaloniki, Greece. He holds a PhD in information technology from National Polytechnic Institute, France, a DEA on image processing from the University of Paul Sabatier, Toulouse, France, and a BS in mathematics from the Aristotle University of Thessaloniki. He has worked in the information technology sector for many years specializing in electronic commerce applications. He has been the project leader for many research and development projects in the area of Web-based technologies, software agents and virtual enterprises. He has published articles on electronic commerce, information technologies, and network management.

Roberto P. Razzoli is a researcher in the Industrial Robot Design Research Group of the PMAR Lab, School of Engineering, Università di Genova, Italy. His research activities mainly address the general aspects of concurrent engineering, safety assurance, and total quality. Specific developments are forwarded to CAD environments for the reliable design of mechanical parts and the digital prototyping for the life cycle testing of items to comply with environmental compatibility and technological sustainability frames.

Bob Roberts, Reader, is leader of the e-business group in the Centre for Applied Research in Information Systems (CARIS) and also course director for the MSc course in e-commerce in the School of Computing and Information Systems at Kingston University, UK. His research and teaching activities are concerned with the implementation of e-commerce systems to support business-to-business (B2B) collaborative relationships as well as the sociopolitical and relational aspects of interorganizational systems and virtual organizations. Recent funded research and consultancy activities cover a range of e-business projects in the telecoms, health, construction, and electronic sectors.

Ana Paula Rocha graduated in electrical engineering and computation, and received her PhD in distributed artificial intelligence from the University of Porto (Portugal) in 2002. She is a professor with the Electrical Engineering and Computation Department of the Faculty of Engineering, University of Porto. She is a researcher at the Artificial Intelligence and Computer Science Laboratory of the University of Porto, and a member of AgentLink Network of Excellence and the respective SIG on electronic commerce. Her research interests include distributed artificial intelligence, virtual enterprises, negotiation, and learning agents.

Ronald Schoop is vice-president of the HUB Department, Schneider Electric Industrial Automation, France and Germany. He studied electrotechnology at the Humboldt University, Berlin. In 1985, he attained a doctorate. Subsequently, he was active as project manager for the development of photocopying controllers, as well as upper assistant at the Institute for Automation Berlin. In 1991, he joined Schneider Automation GmbH (former AEG Modicon) and was active in the U.S. and Germany in the areas of distributed control systems, programming tools, and agent technology.

Weiming Shen is a senior research scientist at the National Research Council Canada's Integrated Manufacturing Technologies Institute. He received his bachelor's (1983) and master's (1986) degrees from Northern Jiaotong University, China, and his PhD (1996) from the University of Technology of Compiègne, France. He has been working on intelligent agents and their applications to concurrent engineering design, intelligent manufacturing, and virtual enterprises for about 12 years. He has published one book and about 170 papers in scientific journals and international conferences/workshops, and co-edited nine conference/workshop proceedings in the related areas. He is a senior member of IEEE, and a member of AAAI, ACM, and ASME. He is also an adjunct professor at the University of Western Ontario, Canada.

Joaquim Silva is currently an assistant professor in the School of Management at the Polytechnic Institute of Cávado and Ave, Portugal. He holds a Dipl Eng in the field of systems and informatics engineering and an MSci in the field of virtual enterprises, both from the University of Minho. He teaches in the domain of software engineering and enterprise information systems, and his scientific interests are information and communication technologies, virtual enterprises, and systems interoperability.

Rui Sousa received in 1989 his diploma in electrical engineering — branch of telecommunications and electronics — from the Faculty of Science and Technology of the University of Coimbra. From 1990 to 1993, he was assistant lecturer at the Polytechnic Institute of Leiria–School of Management and Technology. In 1996, he received his MSc on systems and automation — branch of industrial automation — from the University of Coimbra. From 1996 to July 2003, he was assistant lecturer at the Production and Systems Engineering Department of the University of Minho, Portugal. In July 2003, he completed his PhD project titled "Contribution to a Formal Theory for Manufacturing Systems," being promoted to Auxiliary Professor.

Adomas Svirskas, as a senior researcher at the e-commerce research group in CARIS, is responsible for tying together business and technical aspects of modern e-business to find innovative solutions to a number of challenging research and commercial problems. His research interests have focused on the use of modern software architectures and middleware solutions to satisfy growing demands of modern businesses. Adomas' 15 years of IT experience in both academia (Lithuania, the U.S., and the UK) and the leading software companies in Europe and the U.S. (Trilogy, SAP, Kiala) cover a range of projects in the automotive, banking, telecom, logistics and Internet business sectors. The major EU-funded research project he is currently involved in, LAURA, investigates the application of ebXML to support adaptive zones for Interregional Electronic Commerce based on the concept of Request-Based Virtual Organizations (RBVOs) and sector-specific Service-Level Agreements (SLAs). Adomas received his MSc in computer science from Vilnius University in Lithuania and is currently working toward his PhD related to his recent research.

Jonathan Ward, as a researcher at the e-commerce research group in CARIS, is responsible for carrying out a number of research activities related to different projects. He graduated from Kingston University, UK. His interests span various aspects of business process modeling.

Index